VLADIMIR
NABOKOV

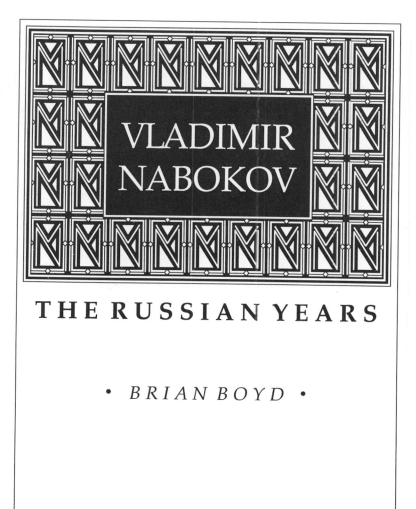

VLADIMIR NABOKOV

THE RUSSIAN YEARS

· *BRIAN BOYD* ·

PRINCETON UNIVERSITY PRESS, PRINCETON, NEW JERSEY

Published by Princeton University Press, 41 William Street,
Princeton, New Jersey 08540
In the United Kingdom: Princeton University Press, Oxford
All Rights Reserved

Library of Congress Cataloging-in-Publication Data

Boyd, Brian.
Vladimir Nabokov: the Russian years / Brian Boyd.
p. cm.
ISBN 0-691-06794-5 (alk. paper)
1. Nabokov, Vladimir Vladimirovich, 1899–1977—Biography.
2. Authors, Russian—20th century—Biography.
3. Authors, American—20th century—Biography.   I. Title

PG3476.N3Z59   1990   813'.54—dc20
[B]   90-8040   CIP

This book has been composed in Linotron Palatino

The following sections of this book have appeared elsewhere in
slightly different form: chapter 2 (*Canadian-American Slavic Studies*),
chapter 7 (*Shenandoah*), chapter 11 (*Russian Literature Triquarterly*),
chapter 13 (Vladimir Nabokov, *Gesammelte Werke: Marginalien*
[Rowohlt, 1989]), and chapter 14 (*Modern Fiction Studies*).

Princeton University Press books are printed on acid-free paper
and meet the guidelines for permanence and durability of
the Committee on Production Guidelines for Book Longevity
of the Council on Library Resources

Printed in the United States of America by
Princeton University Press,
Princeton, New Jersey

1 3 5 7 9 10 8 6 4 2

T O

B R O N W E N

•

INTERVIEWER:
What surprises you in life?

NABOKOV:
*. . . the marvel of consciousness—that sudden window
swinging open on a sunlit landscape amidst
the night of non-being.*

· C O N T E N T S ·

THE RUSSIAN YEARS, 1899–1940

List of Illustrations
xi

Note on Dates
xiii

Introduction
3

PART I: RUSSIA

• *LODY* •

1 Liberal Strains: The Pattern of the Past
15

2 A World Awakening: St. Petersburg, 1899–1904
37

3 First Revolution and First Duma: St. Petersburg, 1904–1906
54

4 Butterflies: St. Petersburg, 1906–1910
68

5 School: St. Petersburg, 1911–1914
86

6 Lover and Poet: Petrograd, 1914–1917
110

7 Foretaste of Exile: Crimea, 1917–1919
136

PART II: EUROPE

• *SIRIN* •

8 Becoming Sirin: Cambridge, 1919–1922
163

9 Regrouping: Berlin, 1922–1923
196

10 Enter the Muse: Berlin, 1923–1925
212

11 Scenes from Emigré Life: Berlin, 1925–1926
241

12 Ideas Away: Berlin, 1927–1929
270

13 Nabokov the Writer
292

14 *The Defense (Zashchita Luzhina)*
321

15 Negative and Positive: Berlin, 1929–1930
341

16 Bright Desk, Dark World: Berlin, 1930–1932
362

17 Distant Prospects: Berlin, 1932–1934
382

18 Translation and Transformation: Berlin, 1934–1937
408

19 On the Move: France, 1937
432

20 *The Gift (Dar)*
447

21 Destitute: France, 1938–1939
479

22 Searching for an Exit: France, 1939–1940
503

ACKNOWLEDGMENTS
525

ABBREVIATIONS
529

NOTES
533

INDEX
583

(Between pages 160 and 161)

Dmitri Nikolaevich Nabokov

Maria Ferdinandovna Nabokov

Ivan Vasilievich Rukavishnikov

Olga Nikolaevna Rukavishnikov

Banquet, Vyra, perhaps on the occasion of Nabokov's parents' engagement, 1897

Nabokov's parents, cycling

Vyra, the Nabokov family summer house near St. Petersburg

Rozhdestveno, the summer home of Nabokov's uncle Vasily Rukavishnikov, inherited by Vladimir in 1916

Plan for renovations to the Nabokov winter home, 47 Morskaya (now Hertzen) Street, St. Petersburg, 1901

47 Morskaya after renovations

Vladimir, summer 1901

Vladimir with father, 1906

Vladimir and Sergey with Cécile Miauton ("Mademoiselle O"), 1907

Vladimir with his mother and his uncle Vasily ("Uncle Ruka"), 1907

Vladimir with butterfly book, 1907

The Nabokov family, reunited after V. D. Nabokov's release from prison, 1908

Sergey and Vladimir at Batovo, 1909

Vladimir, 1916

Stikhi, 1916: Nabokov's first book, inspired by Valentina Shulgin ("Tamara") and published in his penultimate year of school

Valentina (Lyussya) Shulgin

Nabokov's cousin and best friend of his boyhood, Baron Yuri Rausch von Traubenberg

Eva Lubrzynska, Nabokov's romantic partner, 1917–1920

The five Nabokov children, Yalta, 1918

(Between pages 446 and 447)

Nabokov at Cambridge, 1920

Nabokov sharing a punt with his Cambridge roommate, Mikhail Kalashnikov, 1920 or 1921

Nabokov in Switzerland, 1921

Nabokov with his fiancée Svetlana Siewert and her sister Tatiana, 1921 or 1922

V. D. Nabokov at his desk in the *Rul'* office

Nabokov at the Siewert home near Berlin, 1922

Nabokov as a farm laborer in the south of France, 1923

Véra Nabokov, mid-1920s

Vladimir Nabokov, 1926

Nabokov clowning with his pupil Alexander Sak, Constance, 1925

Vladimir and Véra Nabokov with friends, Binz, 1927

Yuli Aykhenvald

Nabokov writing *The Defense*, Le Boulou, 1929

Nabokov hunting butterflies, Le Boulou, 1929

Elena Nabokov, 1931

Ilya Fondaminsky

Nabokov as goalkeeper with his team, Berlin, 1932

Kamera obskura, 1933

Camera Obscura, 1936, Nabokov's first novel to appear in English

Nabokov's revisions to Winifred Roy's *Camera Obscura* translation as he turns it into *Laughter in the Dark*

Manuscript page of *Priglashenie na kazn' (Invitation to a Beheading)*, 1934

Berlin celebration for Nobel laureate Ivan Bunin, 1933

Nabokov, Berlin, summer 1934

Nabokov with Véra and son Dmitri, Berlin, summer 1935

Nabokov with Dmitri, Berlin sandpit, 1936

Nabokov at writing desk, 1936

Vladislav Khodasevich

Nabokov with editorial board of *Mesures*, Paris, 1937

Irina Guadanini

Nabokov and family on the beach, Cannes, 1937

Nabokov with Dmitri, Pension Les Hespérides, Menton, 1938

Nabokov, 1938

Véra Nabokov, 1939

Until their arrival
in London in May 1919, the Nabokov family
adhered to the old Russian calendar. Throughout Part I,
therefore, dates usually appear in both Old Style (Julian) and
New Style (Gregorian) forms. In the nineteenth-century
calendar, Russian dates were twelve days behind
Western ones, and in the twentieth century
(until Lenin scrapped the Old
Style calendar in 1918)
thirteen days
behind

·

VLADIMIR
NABOKOV

I

VLADIMIR NABOKOV* (1899–1977), uprooted by both the Russian Revolution and World War II, could hardly ignore the cataclysms of modern history that so skewed his life. Yet no one has kept more adamantly to his own course—or more determinedly apart from his epoch. His father, imprisoned and deprived of his court title for opposition to the tsar, was a minister without portfolio in the first Provisional Government after the February 1917 revolution, but during that tumultuous year Nabokov himself continued to write love poetry as if nothing were happening around him. After one poem, written on the night Bolshevik troops stormed the Winter Palace, he even notes: "As I was writing, fierce rifle fire and the foul crackle of a machine gun could be heard from the street."[1]

He was born into an old noble family and stupendous wealth. At seventeen he inherited the most splendid of the family manors, begun at the end of the eighteenth century for Prince Bezborodko, Catherine the Great's foreign policy director. But the revolution and emigration soon forced him to support himself by his writing—for a fragmented and destitute émigré audience of less than a million readers. By the late 1930s Nabokov and his wife were living in poverty. Without the generous help of relief organizations and admirers like Rachmaninov they would hardly have survived and would certainly not have been able to flee Hitler for the United States. In America life was easier but still modest until the success of *Lolita* turned Nabokov again, at sixty, into a wealthy man. After retiring from Cornell University, he headed for Europe and settled in Switzerland. There, in a luxury hotel, waited on by a retinue of liveried attendants in lieu of the fifty family servants of his childhood, he could carry on with his writing undisturbed, as if history's convulsions had altered nothing.

Each act of Nabokov's personal drama was played out in a setting unforeseeably different from the one before. First, a small corner of imperial Russia: the most glamorous parts of St. Petersburg lit by the flamboyant sunset of prerevolutionary culture; and two hours' ride away a manor, a fir forest, and a river, the lifelong focus of his passionate nostalgia. Then the Russian emigration, its "material indi-

---

* Pronounced Vluh-DEEM-ear Nuh-BOK-off. The second syllable of the surname sounds very like the British pronunciation of "*awk*ward," a little less like its American counterpart.

gence and intellectual luxury,"[2] its claustrophobia and infighting, its inevitable dispersal. For another twenty years, Nabokov's America, where he and his family shifted winter after winter from the home of one professor on sabbatical to another, only to become totally nomadic in summer, moving from motel to motel in search of butterfly haunts and inspiration for *Lolita* and its companions. Finally Europe again, and a decade and a half surveying Lake Geneva's waterfowl from an eyrie in the Montreux Palace Hotel.

The supporting cast too changes with each new backdrop. On a St. Petersburg street corner, a boy stops as his father chats with old Tolstoy; in Paris a lean Russian writer reads his work in French before Joyce and the Hungarian soccer team. Less suggestive to the English-speaking reader but more substantial are Nabokov's relations in his years of European exile with friends and foes among the writers of the emigration: robust Lukash, gentle Aykhenvald, the acid and exacting Khodasevich, slippery Adamovich, envy-choked Bunin. In the United States Nabokov's closest friend would be Edmund Wilson, until that relationship degenerated into a rancorous transatlantic feud. Also appearing (in alphabetic order): Morris Bishop, Robert Frost, Jorge Guillén, James Laughlin, Harry Levin, Mary McCarthy, John Crowe Ransom, May Sarton, Allen Tate, E. B. White, and Katharine White. In the final act, Nabokov withdraws from publicity into the shelter of his family and sees only a few old friends, publishers, fellow celebrities taking advantage of Switzerland, critics, and persistent fans. Here the most explosive stories would concern Nabokov's rifts with Wilson and then with his own biographer, Andrew Field.

But Nabokov was always a loner, and an account of his life should concentrate on the riddle of his personality and the way it shapes his art. Three traits stand out. First, his unequaled self-assurance: who else would dare begin a nonfiction work "I think like a genius"?[3] Second, his intense, almost ruthlessly concentrated feelings toward others. Although he allowed few people to become his friends, he loved his father and mother, his wife and son, with extraordinarily fierce devotion. Third, his unrelenting individualism. He refused to allow his tastes or strong opinions to be tempered by his times, and he detested groups, generalizations, conventions, anything but the particular and independent.

He had a fascination for human perversity, for the insane, the cruel, the sexually deviant. But although he was himself decidedly singular, he was also quite "normal": lucidly sane, outraged by cruelty, committed to faithful love after a youth of energetic sexual adventure. Part of my task is to explain why Nabokov could create characters as bizarre as Humbert, Kinbote, or Hermann and allow us to see out from within their minds. Imagination cannot thrive in a vacuum: he knowingly extrapolated from his own personality.

Because Nabokov valued the liberating force of consciousness he felt he had to understand how people could be imprisoned in madness, in obsession, or in the everyday "solitary confinement of their souls."[4] Here his interest in psychology shades into his philosophical interest in consciousness, the overriding concern of all his art. Although Nabokov insisted on the critical use of reason, he had no faith in expository argument and scorned discursive fiction, leading many readers to assume he is all style and no content. In fact he was deeply serious as a thinker—an epistemologist, metaphysician, moral philosopher, and aesthetician. I will trace the development of his philosophical views, sketch their final shape, and suggest how they influenced his art.

To do that I must explain his deceptive strategies as a writer. For reading Nabokov is like sitting in a room with a view onto a somehow misleading landscape that seems to wink in the sun and invite us out. Some readers fear they are only being lured to trip on the threshold. Actually Nabokov wants the good reader to step through and enjoy the detailed reality of the outside world. But the good *re*reader who ventures far enough finds another door concealed in what had seemed that solid landscape outside, a door into a new world beyond.

Another part of the challenge has been to tease out the harmony in Nabokov's life—and the harmony between his life and art—without suppressing the inconsistencies. How could someone so devoted to his art, and to the artfulness of art, be such a dedicated naturalist and so obsessive a lepidopterist? How could someone with such a passion for literature, painting, and the abstraction and patterning of chess find music no more than "an arbitrary succession of more or less irritating sounds"?[5] Nabokov admired military courage and was a zealous foe of the Bolsheviks and Hitler. How could he envisage volunteering for the Russian civil war and World War II only if the combat zones took him near a girlfriend or new butterflies? How could he believe so unshakably in democracy and *never* vote? Nabokov declared he knew nothing of social class[6] and could remember twenty years later not only the cleaning lady of the laboratory where he once worked but even her domestic troubles. How then could he appear so snobbish to so many? Such apparent contradictions *can* be resolved.

Nabokov had a keen interest in fate, and in his own destiny every major setback appears almost to have been arranged to provide full scope to his talents. He had an idyllic childhood and youth, but already in his teens filled his poetry with the pain of loss, the anguish of being severed from past happiness, the consolation of memory. Then came the Revolution and intensified those emotions beyond anything he could ever have foreseen. As a young man he meditated and wrote endlessly about death and the possibility of a beyond—and then, when he was twenty-three, his father was killed by the bullet of a rightist assassin. When Hitler invaded France Nabokov had to flee to America. At the age of forty he had to abandon Russian—after having slowly perfected his craft to make Russian prose in certain ways richer than it had ever been—and to start anew in English. That transition was agony, but without it he would never have written *Lolita* and in all probability would have remained almost unknown beyond the Russian emigration for at least another generation. During his long years in America before fame did at last arrive, Nabokov tried repeatedly to have his Russian novels translated into English, but to no avail. Suddenly, after *Lolita*, publishers wanted all the Russian works—just when Dmitri Nabokov was old enough to act as his father's translator. Now there was enough interest in his whole oeuvre for Nabokov to write a spirited foreword to each new translation, now too he had the leisure to supervise in detail the French translations of his works. Without the Revolution, his father's murder, the impact of Hitler, and the delay in his international recognition, Nabokov's writing would have neither its poignant flavor of loss nor the polish and finality it has in the three languages he loved best.

II

Although Nabokov was often hailed as the finest stylist of his time, many readers have found themselves perturbed by the deliberateness of his language. To them, his phrasing calls attention to itself too much to express genuine emotion or even to *say* anything. This puts Nabokov in good company, since it was exactly the reaction Shakespeare provoked in Tolstoy. Surely no old man on a heath in a storm would ever cry out:

> Blow, winds, and crack your cheeks! rage, blow!
> You cataracts and hurricanoes, spout
> Till you have drench'd our steeples, drown'd the cocks!
> You sulph'rous and thought-executing fires,
> Vaunt-couriers to oak-cleaving thunderbolts,
> Singe my white head! and thou, all-shaking thunder,
> Strike flat the thick rotundity o' th' world!

From his premises, Tolstoy is quite correct. Shakespeare's lines testify to an impressive verbal mastery, but they do not represent any plausible human speech. There is not one reader in a thousand, though, who does not feel that if Tolstoy had just turned his stiff neck a fraction he could have espied in Shakespeare all the life and truth he could have wished. A considered style may not convey what naturally comes first to mind or mouth, but for that very reason it can express so much more.

At the end of the first chapter of *Speak, Memory*, Nabokov describes how the villagers living on the fringes of the family estate where he spent his childhood often subjected his father to a spontaneous Russian rite of gratitude. After V. D. Nabokov* had settled some dispute or granted some request, five or six men would toss him high in the air and catch him in their arms. Young Vladimir at lunch inside would see only his father aloft and not the men below:

> Thrice, to the mighty heave-ho of his invisible tossers, he would fly up in this fashion, and the second time he would go higher than the first and then there he would be, on his last and loftiest flight, reclining, as if for good, against the cobalt blue of the summer noon, like one of those paradisiac personages who comfortably soar, with such a wealth of folds in their garments, on the vaulted ceiling of a church while below, one by one, the wax tapers in mortal hands light up to make a swarm of minute flames in the mist of incense, and the priest chants of eternal repose, and funeral lilies conceal the face of whoever lies there, among the swimming lights, in the open coffin.[7]

Some will enjoy that sentence enough to trust its author. Others might suppose it a tour de force too accomplished to be aiming at any response but meek acclamation. To those with an open mind I would like to suggest that the first reaction may be right.

Despite the generalized nature of the church scene that materializes beneath the sky's blue vault, Nabokov in fact anticipates here (as the good reader may intuit at once, as any reader of *Speak, Memory* should gradually recognize) a precise moment later in his own life, the day he looks down at his father lying in an open coffin. Though that first image of a man soaring against the sky seems to start careening away from its occasion, there is nothing haphazard or indulgent in the way the sentence drops down from the figure poised as if forever in the air to the dead man on his bier. For even as Nabokov envisages the funeral, he also half-affirms his father's immortality: "like one of those paradisiac personages who comfortably soar. . . ." But style cannot charm the facts away: the body still lies there motionless in the

---

* Vladimir Dmitrievich Nabokov (Vladimir, son of Dmitri). He will be referred to throughout as V. D. Nabokov, while his son, the writer Vladimir Vladimirovich Nabokov (Vladimir, son of Vladimir), will be either "Nabokov" or occasionally "Vladimir."

church, the candle flames swim because of the tears in young Nabokov's eyes.

Nabokov ends the chapter this way to add his own tribute to that of
the villagers—the oldest of whom, incidentally, still revered the memory of Nabokov's father after more than sixty years of Soviet rule.
V. D. Nabokov died a hero's death, bravely defending his chief ideological opponent within his own liberal Constitutional Democratic
party from two right-wing thugs and being shot in the scuffle. Nabokov's verbal glide from the villagers' gratitude to his father's last
rites foreshadows the fact that in the very manner of his death his
father justified the high esteem in which he was always held.

Again and again throughout *Speak, Memory* Nabokov returns
obliquely to his father's death as if it were a wound he cannot leave
alone but can hardly bear to touch. For Nabokov the love of those
closest to the heart—a parent, a spouse, a child—distends the soul to
dwarf all other feeling. The narrowly focused love that marked his life
also shapes his fiction, whether positively (Fyodor and Zina, Krug
and his son, John and Sybil Shade) or negatively, in the desolation of
love's absence (Smurov or Kinbote) or the horror of its sham sur-
rogates (Albinus and Margot, Humbert and Lolita). Because love matters so much to Nabokov, so too does loss (Krug and his wife or son,
Fyodor and his father). But he had learned from his parents to bear
distress with dignity, and when he depicts his father high in the midday air he alludes to his private grief with the restraint taught him as
a child. The formality and apparent distance in no way diminish the
emotion: he simply feels that even a sense of loss sharp enough to last
a lifetime must be met with courage and self-control.

Some conclude that since his stylistic originality announces itself with
such force, Nabokov therefore can have only style to offer. I find another explanation more convincing: his style stands out so boldly because he has rethought the art of writing deeply enough to express all
his originality of mind.

In the sentence under scrutiny two opposite aspects of Nabokov's
style reveal two counterpoised tendencies in his thought.

On the one hand he admits to an "innate passion for independence."[8] He reveres the particularity of things, all that can break away
from generalization and the blur of habit; he values the freedom of
the moment, the possibility of the freakily unexpected that derails the
iron mechanism of cause and effect; he celebrates the capacity of the
mind to move about within the present. All these impulses make his
style a perpetual declaration of independence: in this case, he chooses

to stress the unconstrained mobility of the mind as his sentence loops off from summer sky to church ceiling—and refuses to return.

On the other hand Nabokov prizes pattern and design, things united in new combinations rather than highlighted by isolation. He is entranced and puzzled by the chance harmonies of the moment, the complex artistry of mimicry in the natural world, the designs of time or fate, the patterns lurking within memory. When he lets a new scene materialize under the flimsy awning of a simile he seems to have yielded to mere momentary whim. But before the sentence ends we discover that it was always under control, and as we read on in *Speak, Memory* we can make out that that image of church and funeral forms part of a pattern at the core of the book: again and again Nabokov foreshadows his father's death, reticently but ineluctably, as if he had no choice but to reconstitute the insidious designs of fate.

Independence and pattern function like the complementary twin hemispheres of Nabokov's mind. He searches out pattern in the music of a phrase or the spell of an anagram, in the shapes of time or the weave of the universe. He pursues independence in everything from his own sense of self to his philosophy of history, from his politics or aesthetics to his way of looking at a face or a tree.

As Nabokov well knew, the manifest artistry of the sentence on his father—or of his style in general—carries its own metaphysical implications. Consciousness at full stretch can pass beyond its impromptu range; here it can also transcend time, by compressing together a past occasion and what was then the future, by freezing the moment to leave someone suspended in that cobalt sky. Through the force of his art Nabokov answers the question with which he began the first chapter of *Speak, Memory*, the question he confesses has always bewildered and harassed him: what lies outside the prison of human time, our entrapment within the present, and our subjection to death? Typically he chooses to display rather than efface the power of a mind working *un*spontaneously and so able to create an image or a thought out of the ordinary. The energy mortal consciousness can have when it vaults over the barrier of the moment suggests more than anything else its kinship with some form of consciousness lurking beyond human limits.

In the last chapter of *Speak, Memory* Nabokov writes:

> Whenever I start thinking of my love for a person, I am in the habit of immediately drawing radii from my love—from my heart, from the tender nucleus of a personal matter—to monstrously remote points of the

universe. . . . I have to have all space and all time participate in my emotion, in my mortal love, so that the edge of its mortality is taken off, thus helping me to fight the utter degradation, ridicule, and horror of having developed an infinity of sensation and thought within a finite existence.[9]

This states the problem Nabokov addresses throughout his art: what can we make of the breach between the limitless capacity of consciousness and its absurd limitation? To answer this, he has searched relentlessly for some consciousness beyond the boundaries of the human.

This interest in the beyond stems not from any denigration or repudiation of the here and now. Quite the contrary. Nabokov had two great gifts as a writer and a man: literary genius and a genius for personal happiness. The hero of *The Gift*—whose giftedness is twofold in just this way—actually anticipates in a rush of gratitude and joy that he will compile "a practical handbook: *How to Be Happy*." But even sunny genius knows another side to experience, for to the degree that the world makes happiness possible it also primes us for the ache of loss. The key to Nabokov is that he loved and enjoyed so much in life that it was extraordinarily painful for him to envisage losing all he held precious, a country, a language, a love, this instant, that sound.

Nabokov extols the freedom we have within the moment, the richness of our perceptions and emotions and thought. Nevertheless we are each imprisoned within ourselves, trapped in the present, doomed to die. It seems brutal and senseless that we must store up such wealth of recollection—and even agonies like bereavement in time become a kind of wealth, a measure of having lived—when we know that it will all be snatched away by death. But *perhaps* at its very best consciousness itself hints at a way out. In art or science, in memory, in the exercise of imagination and attention and kindness the mind seems almost able to peer past the prison bars of selfhood and time.

Nabokov's sentence tosses his father so high he almost condenses into pigment and then dries out at once on a ceiling fresco. Such sudden, disturbing transitions from life to art occur often in Nabokov. Why? A fashionable conundrum? Art for art's sake?

No: Nabokov believed in art for *life's* sake. Cast your eyes around a crowded room: a meeting, a party, a classroom. No artist could create people so individual—in appearance, manner, character, history—or render so flawlessly all the nuances of their interaction. But that does not make art second-rate, a poor imitation of life: on the contrary, Nabokov says, art has awakened us to qualities like detail, integrity, harmony, that we can now recognize as part of the inherent artistry of life. See the world this way, and everything—a crumpled leaf, the smoke above an ashtray—becomes miraculous, a token of the inexhaustible creativity of the world.

Often when Nabokov jolts us from life to art he also tilts us from life to death. In the sentence about his father, or at the end of half a dozen novels, he opens the trapdoor of terra firma, he reminds us not to accept stolidly "the marvel of consciousness—that sudden window swinging open on a sunlit landscape amidst the night of non-being."[10] In life we can never escape being who we are and what we are, but in art we peer inside other souls, we return at will to the past, we look from outside on an invented world. Nabokov deliberately exploits all these special conditions of the work of art. In life the present moment has the very stamp of "reality," but once the moment recedes we can never recall it in its fullness: it becomes almost as if it had never been. But works of art are available for endless reinspection, and Nabokov ensures that in *his* books the past we reexamine will continue to disclose complexities simply not visible at first. He tries to change our relation to time, and that, he suggests, might be one of our freedoms, our new doors to "reality," if we ever escape the limitations of human consciousness.

In the world of art, pain remains unreal, and just as good as pleasure: the greater Lear's agony, the more our world is enriched. Perhaps beyond the human, that might be true of mortal hopes and fears, so that what ultimately matters might not be what we feel but the answering pity or delight our feelings arouse in whoever watches over us. Perhaps: but within this world we can never know, and Nabokov returns from metaphysical speculation to insist that in this life we have no choice but to act as if another's pain is as real as our own. Just as he chooses what sets art apart from life to define by contrast the conditions of being human, so he contrasts our moral immunity from the sorrows of art's invented worlds with the tangled world of "real, or at least responsible, life."[11]

When characters like Humbert, Hermann, Axel Rex, or Van and Ada Veen claim that they are special, that they are artists, that they inhabit a different plane of being from those around them, they exaggerate a real condition of human life. Each of us exists in a sense on a different plane from everyone else: you are all outside my consciousness, the place where I *am*, as I am outside yours. But human consciousness also gives us the imagination to feel how immediate another's pain can be. Nabokov's artist-heroes dare to claim a special dispensation from ordinary morals only because they fail to imagine that others are also special, at least to themselves. Nabokov gives these "artists" all the imaginative scope they want to record their dubious pasts, but he condemns their strategies as mere cover-ups for their failure of imagination: in *this* world, in *this* life, there are no exemptions to be granted from responsibility. And if even those of gifted imagination do not imagine well enough, what of the rest of us?

Nothing could be more quintessentially Nabokovian than the sudden focal shifts in his sentence about his father, as it rises up from a real memory to hover an instant in the world of art or eternity, among those painted paradisiac personages, before returning to this world, where Nabokov grieves for the man who taught him the moral "principles passed down from father to son, from generation to generation."[12] He needs to know more than this world holds, but he never shirks the fact that this may be the only world any of us can know.

And yet, and yet . . . Nabokov tilts the plane of literature—and of life. Reading him we no longer simply observe the drama of character against character, we become ourselves protagonists in a larger arena: the reader confronting the author, the mind confronting its world. In his best works Nabokov makes us recognize that his worlds are not ready-made, that they are being created before our eyes, that the more we participate in their creation—observing their details, connecting up their parts, trying to solve all the problems they pose or feign not to pose—the more "real" these worlds become, and at the same time the more their reality seems only a step toward something realer still. As discoveries multiply, the pulse of excitement quickens, the sense of wonder deepens, until we stand on the threshold of new truth.

And that, says Nabokov, is how things are. If only we refuse to take our world for granted, we can detect something artful lurking at the heart of life, inviting us deeper into the world, allowing us to penetrate further and further into the mystery of its creation, perhaps even promising us a new relation to everything we know.

PART I

RUSSIA

· *LODY* ·

I probably had the happiest
childhood imaginable.

—Nabokov interview,
1972

Liberal Strains: The Pattern of the Past

. . . that spirit of enlightened liberalism, without which civilization is no more

than the plaything of an idiot.

—Nabokov speech, 1935

I

NABOKOV cared passionately for family, but not for social position. He was prouder that his father belonged to "the great class-
less intelligentsia of Russia"[1] than that he derived from old-estab-
lished stock which over the last century and a half had produced soldiers and statesmen of increasing distinction. But he also enjoyed not
behaving as expected, and in writing of his origins he rejected equally
any regard for social class and any show of social humility.

Since his father loathed snobbishness and frowned upon all talk of
family forebears, Nabokov left St. Petersburg in 1917 with little sense
of his ancestral past.[2] When a year later in the semi-exile of Yalta his
cousin and best friend Baron Yuri Rausch von Traubenberg naively
boasted of a family line reaching back to the twelfth century, Nabokov
laughed the subject away: "What about the Nabokovs? Former court
lackeys?"[3]

By the time he was permanently cut off from his Russian past and
especially after he sensed the urge to write his autobiography, Nabokov began to wish he had been less cavalier about his heritage.[4] In
Berlin in the late 1920s or early 1930s his father's cousin Vladimir Golubtsov impressed upon him his conviction that the family was
founded by a fourteenth-century prince—a detail Nabokov appropriated twenty years later in *Conclusive Evidence*'s light-hearted survey of
colorful forebears: "Among my ancestors there have been: the first
caveman who painted a mammoth; Nabok, a medieval Russified Tatar
prince. . . ."[5] After *Lolita* shot Nabokov to world fame in the later
1950s a Russian genealogist in Paris began to trace the Nabokov family
tree with the help of the writer's cousin Sergey Nabokov, himself a
keen amateur genealogist.[6] Hearing about some of his cousin's finds,
Nabokov asked for and received fresh tidbits from the past. Too little

a genealogist to want to sift evidence for himself, he welcomed what others turned up.

Nabokov looked at his origins not through the lorgnette of the snob but with the curiosity of an artist and a scientist alert to the freakish fact, the hidden pattern, the evolutionary tussle between persistence and permutation. Of one ancestor, the eighteenth-century composer Heinrich Graun, he remarked: "one night, having to sing in an opera written by Schurmann, chapel-master of Brunswick, he got so disgusted with some airs in it that he replaced them by others of his own composition. Here I feel the shock of gleeful kinship."[7] But that impudent assurance seems to have been the only link, for Nabokov had no love at all for music. He was not unaware though that a melodic Graun gene had slipped past him to his son, the basso Dmitri Nabokov, and across to his cousin—and Graun look-alike—Nicolas Nabokov.[8] What he learned by following such twists and interlacements in his own ancestry as he transformed *Conclusive Evidence* into *Speak, Memory* in the mid-1960s Nabokov immediately put to use as he reinvented and amplified all the continuities and crossovers of a normal lineage—features, mannerisms, even personality and moral tone—for *Ada*'s tangled family tree.

Nabokov family legend has it that their line began with a fourteenth-century Tatar prince, Nabok Murza—perhaps authentic, perhaps no more genuine than the East Indian potentate, gem of an old genealogy, who turns out to be a cloth merchant from Flanders. It is perfectly normal for an aristocratic family to have memories old enough to be less than certain.

Since Russified Tatars were predominant among new landowners in the fifteenth century, it could add weight to the Nabok Murza legend that the first recorded Nabokovs, Filat, Avdokim, and Vlass, sons of Luka Nabokov, were accused in a document of 1494 of having usurped part of their neighbor's land.[9] Whether or not they descend from Nabok Murza and whether or not they are related to the Nabokovs whom we know remains unresolvable, for the continuously traceable lineage of the modern Nabokov family begins only wispily in midseventeenth century. By the eighteenth century the Nabokovs clearly belong to the middling *dvoryanstvo* (nobility). Etymologically something like "court class," the term *dvoryanstvo* extends far wider than the English "nobility," ranging all the way from the most poverty-ridden of the lower gentry to the titled aristocracy. Titled or not, the *dvoryanstvo* had traditionally been permitted to own land in return for military service to the tsar. Even as bureaucratic careers proliferated during the eighteenth century, it remained customary to begin

one's service in the military, often a path to prominence. So it proved for the Nabokovs. Alexander Nabokov (1749–1807), a full general, was the first Nabokov of any recorded significance and founder of the unbroken line of growth that leads to Vladimir Nabokov. Obviously the family was already looked on with favor at court: Alexander's oldest son, Ivan, was an imperial page at the age of three.

His youngest son, Nikolay (1795–1873), was the great-grandfather of the writer. In 1959 Vladimir Nabokov would experience an eerie shiver of delight when he was informed that this ancestor had been an explorer. Two years earlier he had begun to outline *Pale Fire*, which in this inchoate form was to open with a palace intrigue on Ultima Thule that with covert assistance from Nova Zembla would slide toward revolution.[10] Now his cousin Sergey passed on to him his recent discovery that their great-grandfather had apparently participated in a cartographic expedition to Russia's arctic islands of Nova Zembla, for a river there bore his name. Nabokov was flabbergasted: "When I think that my son Dmitri is an alpinist (and has climbed an unclimbed peak in British Columbia) and that I myself have discovered and named a number of butterflies (and a few—an Alaskan rarity, a Utah moth etc. have been named after me), the Nabokov River in Nova Zembla acquires an almost mystical significance."[11] Always reluctant to mention unfinished work, he did not add that another Nova Zembla was already being mapped out in his own mind.

Alas, his cousin's deduction was wrong, although Nabokov never learned of the mistake. Nikolay Nabokov was no intrepid explorer, and his name graces that remote river only because his friend Count Lütke chose to commemorate his Naval Corps colleague in the course of his 1821–1824 expeditions in the region.[12] In fact the military career of Nikolay Nabokov was bland and brief. Although he began service in the navy, he soon transferred to an army regiment and in 1823 retired altogether to the quiet life of a country gentleman in the province of Pskov, a hundred fifty miles southwest of St. Petersburg.[13]

II

In *Ada* Van Veen remarks how much more appropriate it would have been had mad Aqua and not her tawdry sister Marina been his mother. In Nabokov's own ancestry it would have been far more apt had his great-grandfather been not drab Nikolay Nabokov but Nikolay's colorful brother Ivan. For with General Ivan Nabokov (1787–1852) begins a pattern that evolves through time toward Vladimir

Nabokov: a pattern linking Russian literature with the struggle for individual liberty and against the ultimate encroachment on individuality that the death penalty implies.

Shortly after Napoleon's expulsion from Russia, Ivan Nabokov, a hero of the Napoleonic campaigns, married the sister of the Decembrist* Ivan Pushchin, Pushkin's best friend. His younger brother Nikolay would also marry the sister of a Decembrist, and although many of Russia's leading households could boast of Decembrist connections, these marriages suggest that the marked liberalism later Nabokovs displayed was a family tradition that stretched back a century.

Vladimir Nabokov treasured the thought that his great-granduncle's kinship with Pushchin brought him into contact with Pushkin. Pushkin, Russia's first great writer, was not himself a Decembrist although he was a friend of many among them. But he was from the first an irrepressible individualist with a hatred of the arbitrariness of tsarist power. He would become talismanic for Nabokov by virtue of what Nabokov called Pushkin's "craving for perfect spiritual liberty."[14] At the peak of his career and his creativity, Nabokov would devote far more time than he had ever given any of his novels to his translation of Pushkin's masterpiece, *Eugene Onegin*, and to his massive commentary on it, a project conceived from the first as a resolute defense of the particular and the individual.

At the center of old St. Petersburg the Neva River stretched out so wide that in winter a century ago horse-drawn sleighs would hurtle around a full-size racetrack, encircled by bleachers and grandstand, set up *across* its frozen waters. At any time of year if one looked or looks over that broad expanse one could and still can see the thin golden spire of the Peter and Paul Cathedral rising high above the squat walls of the old capital's fortress. Right beside the cathedral lies Ivan Nabokov's grave. Its position marks the second contact of the Nabokov name with literature. For the general had just been appointed commander of the Peter and Paul Fortress when Fyodor Dostoevsky was brought into its notorious jail, reserved exclusively for political prisoners.

---

* After the death of Tsar Alexander I, a group of aristocratic officers attempted in December 1825 to install his liberal brother Konstantin on the throne in the hope that he might bestow on Russia a more enlightened constitution. Konstantin, who had already refused the throne, supported the designated heir, his younger brother Nicholas, who as Tsar Nicholas I suppressed the rebellion, executed its leaders, and imprisoned or exiled others. The "Decembrists," as the rebel officers were soon called, would be hailed as precursors by all those who later opposed tsarist autocracy.

At the end of the 1840s, the first decade of Russian civic radicalism, young Dostoevsky was arrested along with other members of a St. Petersburg radical circle, the Petrashevtsy. General Nabokov, who presided over the commission investigating the case, showed the Petrashevtsy considerable kindness, even fatherly compassion, in his role as commandant.[15] When it was discovered that another of the prisoners, Andrey Dostoevsky, the novelist's younger brother, had been mistakenly arrested in place of their older brother Mikhail, the rest of the commission were content to keep him in his bleak cell until the trial, but General Nabokov protested and installed him in his own quarters.[16] And according to Vladimir Nabokov, the general lent Fyodor Dostoevsky, already famous as a writer, books from his own library.[17]

His solicitude was hardly in keeping with the regime he served. Tsar Nicholas I, the man who executed or exiled the Decembrists, devised for Dostoevsky and his fellows an infamous mock-execution. Told they had been sentenced to death, the prisoners were taken to a firing-ground, put into hooded death shirts, and formed into groups of three, Dostoevsky in the second row; the first trio were called out and tied to their posts, the guns loaded and aimed, and only then—when one of the three facing the firing squad had already been rendered permanently insane—was Nicholas's cruel joke over: with stagy timing, a messenger dashed in to read out that the real sentence was exile. Nicholas I was consistent, at least. Although he decorated Ivan Nabokov for his role in the inquiry into the Petrashevtsy, he also reproved the general sternly for his leniency in sending one of the prisoners to hospital merely because the man would have died at once had he been taken straight to a Siberian mine.[18]

III

The reactionary mood that led to the arrest of the Petrashevtsy in 1849 ended soon after the death of Nicholas I in 1855, as Russia's losses in the Crimean War led to widespread cries for thorough modernization. At the beginning of the 1860s, Nicholas's son Alexander II instituted the short-lived era of the Great Reforms in response to both popular sentiment and the advice of his liberal brother Grand Duke Konstantin. One of Konstantin's close associates was the second of Nikolay and Anna Nabokov's thirteen children, Dmitri Nabokov (1826–1904)—the grandfather of the writer—who would become minister of justice under both Alexander II and his son.

The long-overdue emancipation of the serfs in 1861 must rank as the most important event in nineteenth-century Russia, but its half-heartedness would generate discontent that persisted until the country erupted in revolution. By far the most satisfactory and farsighted of the Great Reforms was the judicial reform of 1864. In the first half of the nineteenth century, Russia's legal system had been a reproach even to a country notoriously backward. A striking instance of Russia's compulsive rhythm of delay and haste, the 1864 reform brought the country's judicial system level at a single bound with that of France and Germany by setting up open courts, trial by jury, an adversary process, and judges whose independence from governmental pressure was assured by their being irremovable. In a typical endeavor to correct the misapprehensions even highly educated Westerners often have about prerevolutionary Russia, Vladimir Nabokov would point out to Edmund Wilson that for all the continued ineptitude and barbarity of the tsars, "The Russian *sud* [legal system] after the Alexander reforms was a magnificent institution, not only on paper."[19]

When the impetus for change stalled in the mid-1860s, the radicals whose hopes had risen over the previous decade turned toward violence. After an assassination attempt on the tsar in 1866, the gestures of reform froze, and reaction stood waiting in the wings. Another wave of terrorist shootings and bombings in the late 1870s and early 1880s would reach its crest with the assassination of Alexander II in March 1881. Throughout this period the government tried to ignore its new legal system or twist it into a tool for the suppression of terrorism. It failed. Count Pahlen, Dmitri Nabokov's predecessor as minister of justice, fell from power when the jury refused to deliver the guilty verdict he had ordered the judge to secure in the 1878 trial of Vera Zasulich for shooting St. Petersburg's governor-general.

After Pahlen's dismissal, official hostility toward trial by jury and the independence of judges intensified sharply. Those who had had judicial training and were assumed to have greater allegiance to "foreign" ideals of justice than to service to the tsar were suspect, and in fact Dmitri Nabokov was probably picked for office in May 1878, *despite* his judicial training, only because he was so unassertive. The boldly liberal minister of war, Dmitri Milyutin, characterized him as a "bureaucrat to the marrow of the bone"; a conservative called him "featureless."[20] But although he remained dry, undynamic, and lackluster as a minister, Nabokov was committed to an independent judiciary, and steadfastly opposed attempts to overturn the 1864 reforms and to make justice once again a mere weapon in the tsarist arsenal.

By late 1880 some elements of the government were ready to shift from reliance on police repression to a program of moderate reform that might reduce liberal frustration. In mid-February 1881 Alexander II approved a reform proposal which even Lenin later conceded might have become a step toward a constitution. He had a governmental communiqué drafted, announcing that he was about to call an advisory legislative council—a first step toward a parliament—in order "to perfect the imperial reform program."[21] The author of the communiqué remains unknown, but it may have been Dmitri Nabokov, for on the afternoon of February 28, 1881, Alexander II is said to have sent him a note asking him to bring "the new law" after vespers.[22]

The next morning Alexander handed on the draft communiqué to one of his ministers for comment. That afternoon on a St. Petersburg street he fell victim to a third assassination attempt, yet another bomb. Dmitri Nabokov, at home at the Ministry of Justice, dashed to the tsar's deathbed in the Winter Palace. The future Alexander III later handed him as a memento the buttons he had torn from his father's blood-spattered shirt.[23]

With the detachment of time, Dmitri Nabokov's famous grandson would have only this comment to make on Alexander II's death: "Russia has always been a curiously unpleasant country despite her great literature. Unfortunately Russians today have completely lost their ability to kill tyrants."[24]*

Throughout Alexander III's reign (1881–1894) the forces of reaction were securely in command. Dmitri Nabokov's major achievement as a statesman was to resist the concerted pressure to overhaul or even overturn the 1864 judicial reform, especially its most important innovations, trial by jury and the irremovability of judges. He instituted only minor calibrations in order to defuse reactionary criticism while leaving the principles of jury trial and an independent judiciary intact. The reactionaries, "feeling that an adroit hand had taken their best weapon, accused Nabokov of cunning and contrivance."[25]

Conservative attacks on the minister of justice stepped up considerably in 1884. In late October 1885 Alexander III's influential and ultraconservative adviser Konstantin Pobedonostsev drew up a memorandum arguing that the judiciary should once again be made subordinate to the administration: judges should be removable, courts in closed sessions when necessary, jury trials phased out. Within a week, Alexander III politely ordered Nabokov to resign, to the rejoicing of the "servile reaction," and he was replaced by a Pobedonostsev protégé.[26]

---

* Stalin was in power at the time Nabokov made the remark.

The first Nabokov statesman died when Vladimir Nabokov was only five, but his career suggests that much passed on through his son to his grandson. Minister of justice at a time of ferocious reaction, he was the only one among those at the center of power to argue adamantly for fair proceedings against even suspected terrorists. His stance outraged the centrists of the day, let alone the conservatives, but won the approval of people like Lev Deich, an early Russian Marxist exiled in 1884, who described him as "one of the most broadminded men of that period."[27] His attitude marks an enduring family tradition. In a memoir of his father, Vladimir Nabokov's son, also Dmitri, writes:

> I recall his pang of pity upon seeing the grisly newsreels at the time of John Kennedy's assassination—not only for the dead president, but also for a still innocent (inasmuch as only suspected) Oswald, shown bruised and black-eyed: "If they have worked over (*zamoochili*) this poor little guy (*chelovechka*) needlessly . . . ," he said. . . . I wonder how many people had such a first reaction.[28]

In one particular instance, Dmitri Nikolaevich Nabokov's leniency toward radicals at odds with his own ideas curiously echoes his uncle's treatment of Dostoevsky. Fifteen years after Dostoevsky's imprisonment in the Peter and Paul Fortress, another writer of major historical importance, Nikolay Chernyshevsky, the founder of socialist realism, was also subjected to a symbolic mock-execution before being sentenced to exile. After six years in a Siberian prison he was transferred to the even bleaker and more remote Yakutsk area; another twelve years passed before a petition in his sons' names came before Minister of Justice Dmitri Nabokov, who made the report on which Alexander III acted in allowing Chernyshevsky to transfer to Astrakhan.

Chernyshevsky was one of the leaders of the second phase of Russian radicalism, sparked off by the prospect of reform at the end of the 1850s and the beginning of the 1860s. If Vladimir Nabokov regarded Pushkin as the embodiment of Russian literature's desire for spiritual liberty, he saw Chernyshevsky as Pushkin's antithesis, intent on reducing free art, paradoxically, to the status of compelled propaganda in the cause of freedom.

In Nabokov's last and longest Russian novel, *The Gift*, the hero's development as a writer is measured by his progress toward Pushkin. One of the most unexpected stages of this progress is his monograph-length biography of Chernyshevsky, on which Nabokov lavished more energy than on any other literary research before his work on *Eugene Onegin*. In this inset biography Nabokov combines both utter contempt for the tsarist government's harassment, imprisonment, and exile of Chernyshevsky and poignant sympathy for the man's plight with an excoriating criticism of Chernyshevsky's ideas. He knew what he was about. An appalling writer and a muddled thinker, Chernyshevsky's dogmatic demands that literature serve a utilitarian social role soon turned an ideal of political liberation into a plan of intellectual enslavement that stifled the development of Russian verse for three decades and prepared the way for Soviet control of the arts. Lenin's favorite writer, Chernyshevsky had a greater influence on the architect of the October Revolution than Karl Marx. "Chernyshevsky and his disciples," writes Simon Karlinsky, "are the people who supplied the revolutionary style, the ethics, and the aesthetics of both Russian Marxism and Russian anarchism. It is because of the ideas Chernyshevsky formulated in the 1860s that today's Communist societies are puritanical in sexual matters and simplistically utilitarian in their approach to the arts."[29]

Nabokov of course was far from the first to oppose the arguments and the exhortations of radical thought. Dostoevsky rejected Chernyshevskyan materialism, Chekhov ridiculed Chernyshevsky's blindness to life, and in the 1890s the entire Russian symbolist movement proclaimed the independence of art: its right to explore metaphysical possibilities materialism flatly denies, and its allegiance to the primacy of the individual.

The tension between the rights of the individual and the claims of the group has been central to Russian literature and life over the last two centuries. The subordination of the individual to the larger unit—the peasant commune of old Russia or the socialist commune of the new, the Orthodox or the Marxist church, the feudal and autocratic state of the tsars or of the Party—has long been peculiarly characteristic of Russia. But it has not been the only choice. Mildly liberal though he was, Dmitri Nabokov represented another possibility, defending the rights of individual terrorists and revolutionaries against the might of the state, even if these radicals in opposing state power themselves advanced ideas that allowed little room for individual rights.

In his youth Dmitri Nabokov left Petersburg's Imperial School of Jurisprudence a confirmed Westernizer, convinced that ideals of truth and justice fostered in Western Europe were more than local standards of excellence. With Russia's executive and legislative power still completely autocratic, the idea of the state acting for the individual could hardly flourish among government officials except in the "tsar-knows-best" paternalism of conservative thought. The most that could be realized, after an independent judiciary was established in 1864, was that the third branch of government would allow the individual some chance to deflect the crushing power of the state. Although that possibility of relief was often under serious threat, Dmitri Nabokov as minister of justice uninspiredly but doggedly upheld the judicial system as defender of those harried by undue pressure from above. V. D. Nabokov had greater verve and a much more agile mind than his father, but his own political struggles logically develop the scope of his father's juristic liberalism. He in turn was an unquestioned model for his son. Vladimir Nabokov's attitudes take on quite a different color from his grandfather's, but they owe their shape to the family mold.

IV

Our first glimpse of Dmitri Nabokov's private life stands in sharp contrast to his sedate public image. He was the lover of the beautiful, passionate Baroness Nina von Korff, wife of a Russian general. So that they could travel abroad together, the baroness arranged for her lover to marry her eldest daughter Maria, who as his fiancée would provide a respectable cover for his accompanying mother and daughters to Paris. There in the spring of 1859 Baroness Korff refused to pay for two expensive ballgowns she had had made for her eldest daughters, because, she said, their necklines were too low. (Vladimir Nabokov in his version of the story wryly comments at this point, without revealing more, that she was "far less austere in her private morals than it would appear from her attitude toward low necklines.") When a bailiff was sent, Dmitri Nabokov vowed adamantly to throw him out the window, and was threatened with two months' prison.[30]

Although seventeen-year-old Maria disliked acting as chaperone for her mother and her mother's lover, her wedding with the gaunt thirty-three-year-old Dmitri Nabokov took place in September 1859. After the marriage, Baroness Korff and young Nabokov lived in different cities: their affair had run its course.[31]

The marriage of stolid, industrious Dmitri Nabokov and his beautiful, fan-fluttering young wife persisted without love. Maria Nabokov enjoyed her situation chiefly for the social position it promised; her husband, though untitled, was a rising official in a family already close to the throne. She got what she wanted: her daughters all became ladies in waiting to the tsaritsa, her sons gentlemen of the chamber to the tsar. But little credit was due to her. Tactless and insensitive, she proved if anything a liability to her husband's career.

Although she was a hostess in the grand style, her receptions were said to resemble trips to the dentist, short but agonizing. She managed style enough, at least, to keep her husband in debt even while he enjoyed a ministerial salary. On his resignation Dmitri Nabokov was offered by Alexander III the title of count or 50,000 rubles in addition to a generous annual pension.[32] He took the money.

Maria Nabokov, the only grandparent Vladimir Nabokov knew beyond his infancy, always seemed to him "a period piece rather than a live person."[33] Even her admiring daughters describe her as spending most of her life on a chaise longue, keeping herself occupied with embroidery. One person who saw her reasonably often had the impression she was short in stature, but she could not be sure: she had never seen her standing up. After the revolution Maria Nabokov insisted to the White Army officer arranging evacuation that she would not budge unless the chaise longue came too. She meant it: she left Russia in a freight car filled with army officers—and her precious couch.[34] But Maria Nabokov was not simply an inert ornament. She was informal, direct, and even playful with her servants. She was hardy as well as languid. Insistent that the house should be minimally heated in winter, she not only teased the servants that *she* was not brought up to sleep on a stove, Russian peasant style, but she would keep her bed all year round next to an open window. One morning, as Nabokov relates, she was found sleeping serenely under a layer of sparkling snow that had settled on her in the course of a nightlong blizzard.[35]

The parents may have had a chilly marriage, but their nine children remembered their family life as a happy one, divided between long summer days at Batovo, Maria Nabokov's estate on the banks of the Oredezh,* and long winter months in fashionable quarters of the capital, some forty miles to the north.[36]

Vladimir Dmitrievich Nabokov, the family's sixth child and his mother's favorite son,[37] was born at Tsarskoe Selo (now Pushkin) in 1870. Until the age of thirteen he was educated at home, first by French and English governesses, then by Russian and German tutors. From 1876 to 1878, exceptionally, home was Batovo all year round: a special treat, a chance to peek behind the scenes and between the seasons, to watch the servants hew man-sized blocks of ice out of the river where he had bathed last summer and haul them off to be stacked in the cellars as coolers for the summer to come.[38]

---

* D. N. Nabokov, the second son of a third son in a family where eleven children survived into adulthood, inherited no land of his own. Although Alexander II granted him a Cistercian abbey in Poland, he appears never to have lived there.

From 1878, when the family moved into a vast apartment in the Ministry of Justice, home was once more St. Petersburg. Worn down by his office, Dmitri Nabokov became tired, scratchy, and barely accessible to his children.[39] Though he had sent his two oldest boys to the Imperial School of Jurisprudence, at this time simply a training ground for the elite, he deemed a university education apt for his third and brightest son. Since to enter university one had to have attended a "classical" *gymnasium* (high school), he sent the boy to St. Petersburg's leading gymnasium, the Third.[40]

Driven by an overwhelming desire to excel, V. D. Nabokov graduated with a gold medal even though he despised the school's principles. For the current gymnasium system with its deadening emphasis on Latin and Greek grammar had been set up by the reactionary Count Dmitri Tolstoy as part of a plan to make available the education the Russian people so desperately needed if the country was to compete with the West, without fostering any of the critical spirit or interest in modern thought that might threaten autocracy.[41] V. D. Nabokov recalls his Latin teacher (and within this curriculum his principal instructor) as "a halfwitted despot" who "drummed in along with his wretched Latin a deep hatred and disgust of the subject, drying up our minds, killing in us any interest in classical antiquity, which turned into a source of continual suffering and daily fear." He felt that he emerged unharmed only because before, during, and after his gymnasium years he "searched and found other sources for the satisfaction of my thirst for education."[42]

Politically V. D. Nabokov was far more liberal than his siblings, some of whom were of a decidedly conservative disposition evidently derived from Maria Nabokov rather than their father. In this respect, curiously, the gymnasium may have been catalytic. One witness remarked that the whole school system that Dmitri Tolstoy had designed to stifle thought, and therefore sedition, in fact rooted in the minds of the young a hatred of the whole official order of things.[43] V. D. Nabokov's younger schoolmate, Peter Struve, for instance, though in later life more conservative than Nabokov himself, went on in his early twenties to lead the revolutionary Social Democratic movement. V. D. Nabokov's younger brother Konstantin, the family's only other liberal, was also the only other gymnasium student.

After finishing the gymnasium at the young age of sixteen, V. D. Nabokov entered the law faculty of St. Petersburg University in autumn 1887. In the harsh atmosphere that choked even his father's passive liberalism, higher education had become increasingly stifled. Universities were regarded as dens of sedition, a heavy state supervisory apparatus controlled the professoriate and ensured that student organizations and clubs, outlawed in 1884, were not resurrected. Uniforms were reinstituted so that outside agitators could be picked out in student disturbances. Summing up his student days many years later, V. D. Nabokov recalled that a bureaucratic spirit depressed everyone, a whole range of subjects had been withdrawn, lecture halls often remained empty.[44] Student disturbances, protesting mildly against these conditions, erupted regularly every year.

One wave of protests broke in March 1890, after the minister of education denounced as illegal a student petition demanding academic freedom and university autonomy.[45] During a demonstration on March 19, V. D. Nabokov was arrested, along with other student protesters. Though the arrests took place at one o'clock, processing did not begin until evening. Suddenly the town governor arrived to release the ex-minister of justice's son. Told his father was expecting him for dinner, V. D. Nabokov asked if those arrested with him would also be allowed home. "No." "In that case I will stay to dine with my colleagues." After midnight, the students were taken across the river to Kresty prison. Four days later they were released—so soon, one of the arrestees felt certain, only because Nabokov had chosen to remain with them.[46]

V. D. Nabokov's university years saw a hardening of official anti-Semitism. In 1889 for instance the new minister of justice, N. A. Manasein, issued a report that the bar was overflowing with Jews who were forcing Christians out of the profession, and in November of that year admission to the bar of non-Christians became subject to authorization by the minister.[47] By contrast Dmitri Nabokov in his term as minister had strongly and successfully opposed an anti-Semitic measure introduced in 1881 by the then minister of the interior. That family strain would lead V. D. Nabokov eventually to become the most outspoken defender of Jewish rights among all Russian gentiles trained in the law. His son in turn would marry a Russian Jew, would denounce anti-Semitism in his own works, and would escape Hitler with his wife and son only with the help of Russian Jewish émigrés still grateful for his father's sterling defense of their people.

V. D. Nabokov graduated in January 1892 with a first-class degree in criminal law.[48] After military service, he entered the Chancellery, the citadel of the gilded youth in the civil service, where "stately footmen moved silently about in embroidered liveries and white hose, serving tea and coffee."[49] He soon opted for an academic rather than a civil service career, and had his first scholarly article published when he was still twenty-five.[50] As part of his grooming for an academic post in criminal law he was sent to Germany, where he studied at Leipzig and especially at Halle.[51] He was in Halle when a letter reached him from Tagantsev, doyen of Russian criminologists, who considered Nabokov his natural successor as a teacher and scholar and now invited him to teach criminal law at the Imperial School of Jurisprudence.[52] A brilliant future seemed to lie ahead. But after eight years (1896–1904) of lecturing in criminal law and criminal process, his teaching career at the School of Jurisprudence would end abruptly in his dismissal for political opposition.

V

Even in his 1896 inaugural lecture at the School of Jurisprudence[53] V. D. Nabokov made no secret of his allegiance to the progressive potential inherent in the law. Since this commitment anticipates some of Vladimir Nabokov's own political attitudes, it is worth examining what the law meant for Nabokov *père*.

Even for Russia's academic jurists the law was not academic. But more than others V. D. Nabokov insisted on the political import of legal practice. He openly stressed the extraordinary egalitarian implications of instituting trial by jury in 1864, only three years after the freeing of the serfs. In any role in the new courts "yesterday's slave stood from the very beginning on absolutely the same level as a prominent landowner." Trial by jury in particular was "a categorical and striking expression of trust" in the ex-serf's "civic competence, in his ability to sort out all the complex and difficult issues" surrounding a crime.[54]

The rights of the individual before the law, V. D. Nabokov insisted, were not abstract theoretical propositions but "the fruit of long political struggle to guarantee political freedom against the power of the whole, whatever it may be called."[55] As a criminologist he opposed the generalizing force of sociology,[56] emphasizing that the idea of *individual* responsibility was itself a liberating concept to set against the timeless injustice of wholesale reprisals or the "preventive" punishment of those seen to be dangerous or merely different. Homosexuals, ex-convicts, vagrants, Jews, the politically suspect—he defended them all against the oppression of the law.

For Vladimir Nabokov the value of his father's dedicated defense of individual rights against state pressure was confirmed by his own enforced acquaintance with Bolshevism and Nazism. He too denounced intolerance and rejected the sociological generalization in favor of the unpredictability of the individual. And in return for accepting individual freedom he was prepared to stress individual responsibility as an ethical reality and a psychological fact. His liars like Smurov or Kinbote, his bullies like Humbert or Van, his killers like Axel Rex or Hermann are all studies in human viciousness and the endless capacity people have to underplay their responsibility by perceiving it as some sort of necessary satisfaction or perverted triumph.

The ideals of personal freedom V. D. Nabokov championed derived from Western Europe rather than Russia. Although he opposed slavish imitation of the West,[57] he was as strongly pro-Western and anti-Slavophile as his son would learn to be. He saw the law's highest standards as a heritage of justice and democracy developed in Western Europe but universally valid. A leading figure in the International Union of Criminologists, he was nevertheless a patriot as much as an Internationalist: his principal energies were always directed to possibilities that could be realized in Russia. In the same way Vladimir Nabokov emphasized the internationalism and permanence of the best standards—there is a closer kinship between Horace and Pushkin, he thought, than between Pushkin and a compatriot or a contemporary—but as a writer and translator he devoted himself passionately to Russian literature in a way he would never do even for his beloved Shakespeare or Flaubert. Both V. D. Nabokov and his son, it should be noted, restricted their internationalism to Western Europe and its cultural dominions: they were emphatically not comparativists or lovers of oriental or primitive cultures.

VI

V. D. Nabokov's determination to stress the political consequences of the law reflects the fact that the "intelligentsia" to which he belonged by choice did not have the academic, elitist orientation it does in the West.[58] Since it arose toward midcentury the Russian intelligentsia had had a tradition of independent thinking in the service of social change. After the assassination of Alexander II led only to reaction rather than revolution, the opposition lay benumbed throughout the 1880s and the impulse to reform confined itself to a policy of "small deeds." But famine in 1891 reawakened a sense of urgency, and from that year on the volume and variety of dissent steadily swelled.

Although V. D. Nabokov allied himself wholeheartedly to the intelligentsia, he was not in the least cut off from the high society mode of his family. He still lived with his parents on the bank of the Neva, a few houses down from the French embassy, still attended costume balls, the opera, even the court. In 1895, like his brothers, he was made a gentleman of the Imperial Chamber. In the country, too, the high life continued: grand picnics, croquet parties, stiff tennis rallies on Kareninian courts. There he met Elena Ivanovna Rukavishnikov (1876–1939), daughter of the owner of two neighboring estates a mile and a half down the Oredezh. In St. Petersburg too she lived the same distance down the Neva embankment from the Nabokovs—perhaps a symmetry designed by fate to indicate it had something in store.

Vladimir Nabokov, who pointed to the soldiers and squires in his paternal grandfather's family and the crusading knights in his paternal grandmother's line, insisted that the Rukavishnikov name of his mother's family descended from *"rukavitsa* in the old sense of a warrior's gauntlet"—though the "nikov" ending in fact suggests mitten-maker or gauntlet-maker.[59] Whatever their family origins, the Rukavishnikovs, who seem to have belonged to the lesser nobility of Kazan province since the eighteenth century,[60] made their fortune as the owners of mines in the neighboring province of Perm, on the Siberian flank of the ore-rich Urals. Their family is quite unrelated to the equally wealthy Rukavishnikov dynasty of Moscow merchants—although in *Conclusive Evidence*, where his notions of the family background were still vague, Nabokov grandly envisaged the founder of the family fortunes as "a bearded, fabulously rich Siberian merchant."[61]

Of the first certain Rukavishnikov ancestor, Elena Rukavishnikov's grandfather Vasily, little is known except that he came from a line of Old Believers—who like Puritans in England and Jews throughout Europe often prospered in business because other routes for advancement were blocked off. Prosper his mines certainly did: his oldest son is reliably reputed to have been one of the largest landowners in Russia, with estates totaling 843,000 desyatins (2.27 million acres), about half the size of Connecticut.[62]

His other known son, Ivan Rukavishnikov (1841–1901), "a country gentleman of the old school,"[63] was also worth millions. In the various versions of his autobiography Vladimir Nabokov conjures up his grandfather as a brutal, feudal spirit reminiscent of the wild ill-temper in Aksakov's famous family saga: "In old photographs he was a fine-looking man with the chain of a justice of the peace," but in real life he kept his daughter in fear and was so severe and pitiless toward his sensitive, delicate son Vasily that his rages almost threatened the boy's life.[64]

Such a man would seem to be quite out of keeping with the elegant, highly cultured St. Petersburg of the Nabokovs. It is a surprise to discover in Ivan Rukavishnikov a fervent theatergoer and an intimate of the capital's leading actors.[65] His address also suggests how little out of place he was at the center of the smart capital. Just as the gold spire of the Peter and Paul Cathedral focuses the vista across the Neva, so the Admiralty spire, on which the Nevsky and other main avenues converge, serves as the architectural and visual nub of the main, southern, bank of the Neva. The spire shoots up from the middle of the Admiralty, a low structure a quarter-mile long shaped like a sans-serif Ξ without its central prong. The Rukavishnikov house stood midway between the two wings, right along the shadow of the missing prong, on a line between the gold spire and the granite-clad embankment of the Neva.

There Ivan Rukavishnikov had gathered a host of murky paintings, a few old masters among middens of dross.[66] He also set up a private *gymnasium* for his gifted son Vladimir, the darling of the family, and the younger Vasily, the stammering, neurotic butt of his wrath.[67] Not finding a school to his liking, he had "created an academy of his own by hiring a dozen of the finest professors available and assembling a score of boys for several terms of free education" at his home, even paying poor parents in order to assemble "the best-looking boys among the best scholars."[68]

Whatever doubts there may be about Ivan Rukavishnikov's level of cultural development, he certainly married into a family with an impeccably modern outlook and a distinguished academic background. His wife, born Olga Kozlov (1845–1901), was the daughter of the first president of the Russian Imperial Academy of Medicine. Nabokov liked to think that some of his maternal great-grandfather's papers, like "On the Development of the Idea of Disease" or "On the Coarctation of the Jugular Foramen in the Insane and the Suicidal," served as a prototype of both his lepidopterological papers and his literary gallery of pathological types.[69] One of Nikolay Kozlov's daughters, Praskovia, became a doctor and the author of works on psychiatry, anthropology, and social welfare.[70] Olga herself was deeply interested in natural science and after marrying Ivan Rukavishnikov had a room at their manor, Vyra, converted into a chemical laboratory. She also hired a famous university professor of zoology, Shimkevich, to give private lessons to her daughter Elena.[71]

Apart from the money they lavished on their children's education, Ivan and Olga Rukavishnikov also went in for the philanthropy so fashionable among Russia's liberal gentry at that time. Though they both sat on a number of charitable boards in St. Petersburg,[72] their main energies were directed toward the villages near their estate. In the 1880s Ivan Rukavishnikov bought the magnificent turn-of-the-century manor of Rozhdestveno, overlooking the Oredezh immediately upstream from Vyra. In the small village of Rozhdestveno, which lay between his two manor houses, he built over the next few years three schools, a two-story hospital for eighty patients, a free library, and a private theater where the villagers could see performances by actors like Varlamov and Davydov, among the greatest of their day.[73]

Elena was the last of eight Rukavishnikov children, of whom only one other, Vasily, survived into adulthood. She was a gentle, shy, highly cultured and intelligent woman, and to her son her nervous delicacy made her more complex than his unrufflable father. The two neighboring families had obviously been in close contact for many years—V. D. Nabokov's eldest brother Dmitri is also said to have proposed to Elena[74]—but little is known of the courtship of Elena and V. D. Nabokov except that they first met on a fishing party: he, powerfully built, strikingly handsome, mustachioed, with a steely look in his eye, and she, trim-waisted, her hair swept up and back over a cardboard roll above her temple, her down-slanted eyes and the mobile fleshy pout of her long top lip adding a wistful, almost tearful, look to her beauty.

V. D. Nabokov proposed to Elena Rukavishnikov during a bike ride on the road sloping up through the Vyra estate toward the village of Gryazno, where they later planted a linden to mark the spot.[75] They were married on November 14, 1897, and traveled to Florence for their honeymoon.[76] Twenty-five years of splendidly happy marriage lay ahead.

VII

The Nabokov family had stayed close to the center of court life in the 1880s and 1890s. After being dismissed as Alexander III's minister of justice, Dmitri Nabokov still remained in the State Council, and upon Nicholas II's accession he was awarded the St. Andrew Cross, the equivalent of the Order of the Garter, and was assigned a prominent place in the coronation ceremony itself.[77] His children "belonged to the upper aristocracy by birth, by education and by connections,"[78] and by the mid-1890s his most talented son, V. D. Nabokov, was already destined for a dazzling career. Nevertheless this determined young man put all his prospects at risk by moving wholeheartedly into the liberal opposition that aimed to turn the country, against the tsar's wishes, into a constitutional monarchy.

Vladimir Nabokov was proud to call his father "a robust and cheerful rebel"[79] and cherished all that he saw of his father's political activity from the time he became aware of it. In the 1950s, while at Cornell and writing his autobiography, he hoped to travel to the Library of Congress to research a chapter on his father's career, but lacked money and time.[80] When an old family scrapbook turned up in 1961, he incorporated new details about V. D. Nabokov into a revised version of *Speak, Memory*, but he still had the impression that his father's active commitment to opposition politics began only about 1904.[81] In fact V. D. Nabokov made his first move in 1898, before his first son was born.

One of V. D. Nabokov's closest associates, Iosif Hessen, recalls the difficulty of deciding who should be responsible for the criminal law section of the new liberal-left review *Pravo* ("Law," "Right[s]") that he and others were establishing in 1898. Two other prospective contributors had already turned down the offer, and only then did the editorial staff decide to invite V. D. Nabokov,

> about whom we felt apprehensive. . . . In general we all came from one class, one social level. But Nabokov, the son of a Minister, a gentleman of the tsar's chamber, married to the millionairess E.I. Rukavishnikov, living in a mansion on the Morskaya, . . . seemed to us someone from another planet.[82]

To understand the intimidation one has to take into account V. D. Nabokov's imperturbable high style. In October 1905 Russia was in unprecedented turmoil as a general strike advanced rapidly over the country, the fuse that would detonate the first Russian revolution. As chaos loomed, V. D. Nabokov had to travel to Moscow for the congress that would lead to the birth of the Constitutional Democratic (CD) party. He was his usual calm and confident self, and his routine was uninterrupted: "as always, his valet appeared beforehand at the station to make his compartment cozy: a picture of his wife on a little table, an alarm clock, a woven basket with fruit from Eliseev's,* soda water and so on, a dressing gown resplendent on its hanger."[83]

This was the elegant, seigneurially assured figure who in 1898 surprised the staff of *Pravo* by his eagerness to join their ranks. Far from casting a *mondain* chill over the relaxed friendliness of the editorial crew, as they had feared, he proved an excellent comrade who helped knit the team together and an unusually conscientious worker ready to sign up for the journal's weightiest and most dangerous articles.[84]

V. D. Nabokov joined *Pravo* and his opposition course at the time his wife was pregnant with their son Vladimir. A year after his son's birth, he published his first attack on the death penalty,[85] thereby developing a theme from his father's career and anticipating a theme from his son's.

---

* A famous and expensive food emporium on Nevsky Prospect.

Although as minister of justice in a decade of severe reaction, Dmitri Nabokov had not been able even to *suggest* eliminating executions, he had at least been able to minimize their barbarity. Convinced that public hangings, far from serving as a deterrent, had become a mere spectacle "satisfying only the crude and idle curiosity of the crowd," he had instituted a major change in the conduct of executions: after 1881, they were carried out within prison walls before a small group of officials and public witnesses.[86]

When Russia's first-ever parliament, the First Duma, was convened in 1906, the ex-minister of justice's son rapidly proved himself one of its most forceful speakers, and was chosen to introduce a bill outlawing capital punishment.[87] Even in exile, almost two decades later, V. D. Nabokov remained a passionate foe of the death penalty. By a peculiarly "Nabokovian" coincidence, he took his last stand against capital punishment in an article received by a Manchester newspaper on the very day that the paper reported that he had been shot and killed. Conceding that we could argue forever about the practical efficacy of capital punishment as a deterrent, he had appealed instead to the irrefutable *moral* case made against it by those "great analysts of the human heart," Hugo, Dickens, Turgenev, and Dostoevsky.[88]

Another great novelist also spoke out against the death penalty. One day when he was only ten years old, Vladimir Nabokov was walking in St. Petersburg when his father stopped to chat with a little white-bearded old man. "That was Tolstoy," his father told him as they moved on.[89] We do not know what the two men had to say to each other, but three years earlier V. D. Nabokov's eloquence and parliamentary skill had ensured that the Duma passed unanimously the bill abolishing the death penalty, only for Nicholas II to dissolve the Duma before the bill received the State Council's approval. Over the next four years more than two thousand were executed—and Tolstoy, in his eighties, was provoked into publishing his protest, "I cannot keep silent."

Vladimir Nabokov too was obsessed throughout his work with the moment of death, the role of fate in death, the idea of execution. Already a poet in exile at the time his father was shot by monarchist extremists, Nabokov switched to drama the next year with a play called *Death*. His next play, *The Granddad*, carries on the theme: a man already placed before the guillotine flees from the scaffold in the confusion created by a sudden fire. In the fall of 1934 Nabokov was still living in Berlin, a year after Hitler had come to power, when he suddenly broke off *The Gift* and in a fit of inspiration wrote the antitotalitarian *Invitation to a Beheading*.[90] In the course of his research into the life of Nikolay Chernyshevsky for chapter 4 of *The Gift*, he had found out that Chernyshevsky, another enemy of capital punishment—as he notes with approval—had in his time made "deadly fun" of the poet Zhukovski's plan to make executions tastefully discreet and piously uplifting, almost a sacred rite. Now he would open *Invitation to a Beheading* as the hero is informed he has been sentenced to death—informed *in a whisper*, according to outlandish regulations that echo both Zhukovski's grotesque proposal and the sham sentence pronounced on Dostoevsky and Chernyshevsky.

Throughout the novel Cincinnatus waits in his cell to be beheaded for the "crime" of thinking thoughts too opaque to be instantly visible to others. Nabokov here condemns both the normal pressure of the group upon the individual mind and its ultimate expression in the death penalty. Just as his father developed his grandfather's implicit inclinations into more explicit and far-reaching arguments, so he in turn develops his father's ideas to the point where the contrast between individual and group becomes not only ethical, a question of human rights, but also epistemological and metaphysical, a matter of seeing and being. Through the character of Cincinnatus he suggests that only by rejecting the commonplace and the ready-made, only by passing beyond the easy general notion to discover the complex surprise of the particular, only by animating one's own world through one's own individual imagination can one come alive oneself and share in the creativity at the heart of life.

As *Invitation to a Beheading* closes, Cincinnatus is brought to the scaffold before a gaping crowd, kneels down before the block, even sees the shadow of the axeman's swing—and then, as the blow falls, asks himself why he is there. Though presumably decapitated, he gets up, looks around, sees the cheap world where such an affront to human individuality can occur disintegrate like a collapsing stage set, and strides toward a world of genuine value: "amidst the dust, and the falling things, and the flapping scenery, Cincinnatus made his way in that direction where, to judge by the voices, stood beings akin to him."[91] Asked in 1960 by the California Committee Against Capital Punishment to support their cause, Nabokov replied that although he agreed wholeheartedly with their objectives and wished them well, there would be no point in his writing an article for them: he had already done all he could "by writing a whole book on the subject."[92]

As the pattern of protest against cell and scaffold running through his ancestry should make clear, Vladimir Nabokov cannot be understood except against the background of his family, his country, his national literature. Yet he was right to assert his untrammeled independence:

there *was* something about him that kept him apart from his time and place. For while his father and grandfather struggled for legal freedoms, against undue arrest, harsh imprisonment, and the savagery of execution, while writers from Pushkin and Chernyshevsky to Dostoevsky and the aging Tolstoy made their protests for freedom or against the death penalty, Nabokov's own imagination turned away from the issues of his times to the issues of eternity. He fought for freedom too, but his struggle was not so much a social as a metaphysical one: an incessant effort to find a way out of the goodly prison of consciousness, a lifelong campaign to repeal the death sentence nature has imposed on us all.

CHAPTER 2

A World Awakening St. Petersburg, 1899–1904

I was born in 1899—an event I always recall with delight.
—Nabokov letter to Gleb Struve, 1931

What should be really stressed is the fact that Sebastian was brought up in an

atmosphere of intellectual refinement, blending the spiritual grace of

a Russian household with the very best treasures of

European culture.

—*The Real Life of Sebastian Knight*

I

ST. PETERSBURG. Dawn, April 23, 1899.* A day ago the ice began breaking up on the Neva, but at this early hour—already the sun rises at 4:30—the air temperature has dropped again well below freezing. No traffic clip-clops along the embankment, only the growl and boom of the ice can be heard. Heading southward from the Neva through Senate Square, one skirts the statue of Peter the Great on his rearing steed, the symbol of a tyrant's will and of the city itself ever since Pushkin penned his *Bronze Horseman*. Up ahead lies Morskaya Street, the most elegant in the city. Turn east and one would walk past St. Isaac's Cathedral silhouetted against the dawn, past Fabergé's showrooms and through the archway into Palace Square. But on this day, at this hour, history's witness should turn to the right, around the German embassy on the corner, and head westward. Past one house, Prince Lieven's, soon to become the Italian embassy, where six atlantes hold up the doorway and reveal only five armpits (one hairy) among them. Past the next, Princess Gagarin's, and then stop, at number 47 Morskaya Street, a two-story building in Florentine palazzo

---

* Actually April 10, Old Style, which corresponded to April 22 in the West. But since with the new century Old Style dates fell an extra day behind the Western calendar, Nabokov's first and subsequent birthdays took place on April 10/23. When he left Russia, April 23—Shakespeare's birthday too—therefore became his date of birth. See *Speak, Memory*, 13–14.

style. At street level its first, easternmost, windows are still dark, but immediately above, the lights are already on. There, in what is normally her dressing room, lies Elena Nabokov, who has just given birth to her first healthy child, Vladimir.[1]*

From one end of Russia to the other, from the most august societies of the capital to the humblest of village schoolrooms, the country is preparing to celebrate a writer's birth: in May, it will be one hundred years since the birth of Pushkin, the poet who for generation after generation of Russians has been a living presence, the center and symbol of their literature to a degree unmatched by Cervantes in Spain, Goethe in Germany, Shakespeare in England.

These centenary plans already in motion at Nabokov's birth marked that the greatness of Russian culture was less than a hundred years old. But not many years earlier the country had had reason to fear it had already lost its artistic energy. For a whole generation Russia had given birth to no new writers of genius; by the late 1880s, it seemed a long time since the crisp dawn of Pushkin's verse, or even the high noon of Tolstoy's scorching clarity. Then, with the onset of the 1890s, the culture of imperial Russia broke into an opulent sunset that lasted until the revolution. From early in the decade Chekhov was quietly transforming fiction and drama by discarding age-old contrivances of plot. By 1899 the nineteen-year-old Blok was already writing poetry whose new rhythms would intoxicate and inspire a generation. Then, as writers rebelled more and more against the restrictive aesthetics of Chernyshevsky and his comrades, an astonishing range of styles and schools began to jostle for attention. Within a few years, in the decade after the 1905 revolution, Russian literature and art would be enjoying a freedom and a pluralism unimaginable in decades past or to come.

Nabokov once noted that he began as a writer at the age of three.[2] Born in a country where only one in four could read and write, he would himself be perfectly placed to benefit from Russia's literary renaissance. His mother devoured and recited fondly and transcribed in her angular hand her favorite works by the new poets, just as she would later copy and recopy poems and plays by her son. His father's breadth of culture distinguished him from other members of the liberal opposition, itself of a cultural level rare in Western politics; while still young, he joined the Literary Fund, of which he would become president;[3] his up-to-date library would have ten thousand books for his son to rummage through; he published critiques of Dickens, Flaubert, Tolstoy, and his favorite Russian poets.

---

* Elena Nabokov had been delivered of a stillborn boy the year before.

Other arts than literature burgeoned in late nineteenth-century Russia. In the 1880s emerged landscape artists of the first rank, like Levitan and Kuindzhi. More versatile and more penetrating were Serov and especially Vrubel, whose moody genius fractured space into demonic shards of indigo and violet. In 1898, the year V. D. Nabokov's *Pravo* was established in St. Petersburg, Diaghilev and Benois set up in the same city the brilliant and influential journal *Mir Iskusstva* (*The World of Art*). Attempting to make the highest art part of people's lives, *Mir Iskusstva* could not escape the contradictions of its time. Its sophistication could lapse into decorativeness, escapism, and subservience to mere wealth, but at its best it simultaneously awakened a pride in Russian traditions and introduced to the country the latest in Western art. Above all it promoted new talents like the painters Benois, Somov, Bakst, and Dobuzhinsky.

Nabokov has remarked that he was really born a landscape painter.[4] As a boy he cherished the stylized snowscapes of the *Mir Iskusstva* artists, and at one stage of his youth it was expected that he would follow their métier rather than the one he eventually chose.[5] Again his family could give him ideal access to all that St. Petersburg offered. Bakst, the finest portraitist among the *Mir Iskusstva* artists, was commissioned to do a pastel study of Elena Nabokov; Benois, the most learned and articulate, became the regular art critic for the liberal daily newspaper *Rech'*, which V. D. Nabokov edited; works by both Bakst and Benois and their even more gifted confrère Somov shared the walls of 47 Morskaya with old masters and Russian paintings of an earlier epoch; Chagall's teacher, Dobuzhinsky, more purely a draughtsman than the other three, was hired as drawing master for young Vladimir.

The performing arts too would rise to a peak in the decade after Nabokov's birth: the incomparable bass of Chaliapin, the dancing of Nijinsky and Pavlova. The finest European artists visited St. Petersburg—Eleanora Duse usually spent six weeks there each year—but Russia had its own lines to develop. In 1898, Stanislavsky and Nemirovich-Danchenko founded the Moscow Art Theater, which brought to Russian drama a new purity and dedication, and bold new standards of realism. The opposite trend would develop with equal zest over the next two decades under Meyerhold, who stressed the theatricality of the theater, and in the productions of Diaghilev, where, with artists like Bakst, Benois, and Dobuzhinsky designing costumes and sets, every aspect of performance became sumptuous art.

Here too Nabokov's position was ideal. A theater afficionado since youth, his father later wrote memoirs of theatrical St. Petersburg in the 1880s and 1890s and of the first exhilarating St. Petersburg performance of the Moscow Art Theater;[6] as a young parent he continued to frequent the theater and opera regularly, often with his children in tow. Both V. D. Nabokov and his wife loved music; their house was one of the first where Chaliapin sang, and Koussevitsky gave private concerts there.[7] After the February 1917 revolution, V. D. Nabokov would be appointed to a two-man commission to reorganize the state theaters;[8] in exile, he would officially welcome the Moscow Art Theater to Berlin.[9]

Despite his parents' zeal, Vladimir Nabokov remained deaf to these sections of St. Petersburg's cultural ensemble. He cared for the theater's potential but thought even the greatest of plays shackled by convention, he disliked music, and he could remember only his boredom and discomfort when, as a "curly-headed boy in a velvet box," he had to sit through the "cloying banalities" of yet another Chaikovsky opera.[10]* Even in early childhood he was not the passive product of environment: he simply took what he wanted. But it is no small part of his singular good fortune that he was born and grew up in the center of a culture whose recent past rivaled the best that France, England, and Germany had produced over a much longer period, in a city more alert to Western Europe than Europe had ever been to Russia.

II

Nabokov was a Peterburzhets through and through. He never once visited Moscow, and looked on its inhabitants rather as a civilized Roman might have regarded Etruscans (as he would write in the Russian version of his autobiography: "talking with Muscovites and other Russian provincials . . .").[11] Peter the Great's "window to the west," St. Petersburg was one of the two most striking exemplars of Russia's ability to catch up with European culture after lagging far behind. In the early 1900s the city was so emphatically European that even its shop signs appeared in German, French, or English as well as Russian.

Russia's capital also bore witness to the oppressive weight of the Romanov tradition, and the tsars' love of their own magnificence: Catherine the Great's bronze horseman commemorating Peter, Nicholas I's triumphal column in honor of Alexander I. But for Nabokov

---

* By contrast his cousin Nicolas Nabokov, the composer, later attended Berlin's best concerts with V. D. Nabokov—who would sit there with musical score in hand—and remembered his uncle's sharp critical analyses after the performances as a vital part of his musical education.

the St. Petersburg of the tsars was much more the St. Petersburg of Pushkin, "Russia's most essential and most European poet."[12] Even more than the city itself, Pushkin epitomizes Russia's power to sprint abreast or ahead of Europe. His high Europeanism sparked off the greatness of Russian culture, he dared to express a nation's longing for freedom, and in the process he redefined its capital. In one celebrated poem Pushkin cocks a snook at the Alexander column—and soars above it, dwarfing, as Nabokov puts it, that enormous monument "that obsessed, rather than adorned, the moonflooded Palace Square, and went up and up, trying in vain to reach the subbase of Pushkin's 'Exegi monumentum.' "[13]

In "The Monument" Pushkin predicts that Russia will always value him as a champion of freedom. Certainly Nabokov cherished him that way. How apt, then, that in the week of his birth newspapers could explain the excitement of the coming celebrations by their power to focus the nation's revived urge for freedom. In his contribution to the centenary, Sergey Muromtsev, soon to be elected president of the radical First Duma, characterized Pushkin's verse as "the poetic expression of the worth of human individuality, striving toward free self-definition in spite of the fetters put on it by . . . the state."[14] That sums up the spirit not only of Pushkin, but of Russia's welling hopes in 1899, of V. D. Nabokov's opposition liberalism, and of his son's lifelong principles.

III

By the end of the nineteenth century the hare running with Europe's steady tortoise was becoming increasingly schizoid: Russia's will insisted on uninterrupted slumber while its mind and sinews strained to leap ahead. The tension between the old and the new could not help being reflected even in the life of an unusual child.

Young "Volodya" of course had a wet nurse, who complained that her charge—a future insomniac—was always up, smiling and looking around with his bright eyes.[15] But it was his mother who did all she could to encourage her son's exceptional alertness to the new world of light and color that he awakened to more each day. She would bring out for him

> a mass of jewelry for my bedtime amusement. I was very small then, and those flashing tiaras and chokers and rings seemed to me hardly inferior in mystery and enchantment to the illumination in the city during imperial fetes, when, in the padded stillness of a frosty night, giant mono-

grams, crowns, and other armorial designs, made of colored electric bulbs—sapphire, emerald, ruby—glowed with a kind of charmed constraint above snow-lined cornices on housefronts along residential streets.[16]

But while loyal subjects would illuminate the facades of their homes to honor birthdays in the imperial family, many citizens felt that they had good cause to reject "loyalty" on the tsar's terms: V. D. Nabokov for one refused to decorate his house in that way.[17] Others persisted in glorifying the past. A hallmark of Nicholas II's reign and typical of his cult of Russia's feudal traditions were the historic costume balls at the Winter Palace, designed to celebrate the splendors of yore. In 1903 V. D. Nabokov's youngest sister proudly attended one of the grandest and last of these balls, attired in a boyarinya costume designed by Diaghilev and richly studded with gems by Fabergé.[18]

For Nabokov the riches of consciousness have always been infinitely more important than material wealth or social power—and he always mocked the "hilarious atavistic respect for precious minerals."[19] Out of this scorn is spun one of the hidden threads that sew together the quires of his autobiography: the leitmotif of jewels. A few of the Nabokov jewels were taken into exile, and provided the family with enough money to settle briefly in London: thus far, Nabokov acknowledges, his family fits the romantic stereotype of exiled aristocracy. But in *Speak, Memory* he explicitly denounces those White Russians who bemoan lost property, and contrasts that tangible wealth with the other things he smuggled out of Russia—his language, his literary heritage, his memories, his artistic gift—that were his real riches in exile.

IV

In late spring 1899 the newborn Nabokov narrowly escaped being christened Victor by a bungling archpresbyter in a ceremony at 47 Morskaya.[20] Within a few weeks he, his parents, and their entourage had installed themselves for the summer in the family estate of Vyra, some fifty miles to the south by train and carriage. The regular beat that Nabokov's childhood followed unless war or revolution intervened was already under way: winters and early spring in St. Petersburg, summer at Vyra, and, to avoid the capital's misty dampness at that time of year, autumn on the coasts of southern Europe.

The boy was brought up on a mixture of coddling and starched-collar stiffness. The size of the family homes, where the children lived near their nurses and governesses on a different floor from their parents, and the formality of conduct natural in the Nabokovs' time and social sphere meant there was a good deal more distance between parents and children than we are accustomed to. But to a contemporary Vladimir seemed to be doted on by both his parents:

> V. D. Nabokov loved to speak of his children, particularly his first-born, whom he and especially his wife and her parents literally idolized. In his study a large photograph caught one's eyes: over a child's cradle, under a magnificent coverlet decorated with expensive lace, lay the future Sirin*—father, mother and grandfather Rukavishnikov inclined lovingly, staring at the child with rapture in their eyes.[21]

The adoration of young Vladimir did not alter when a second child, Sergey, was born in St. Petersburg in March 1900. One of the peculiarities of Nabokov's upbringing in fact was that despite his mother's sensitivity and his father's sense of justice the two parents so plainly spoiled him—as he himself[†] and his siblings realized—to the emotional neglect of the other children (well tended, of course, by governesses and tutors). Born to a favored position within society, Nabokov was also destined from the start to be very much the favorite even in his own home.

Although his frank sense of his own importance may owe much to parental overfondness, Nabokov was somehow spared the lack of purpose of the spoiled child. Perhaps his need to keep the respect of his father, a man of exacting standards sometimes bitingly expressed, sufficed for discipline.[22]

During the summer of 1901 Elena Nabokov saw both her parents die. Always of a nervous disposition, she seems to have been deeply troubled, physically and emotionally, by her parents' ailing health during the time she was pregnant with Sergey—so much so that her brother-in-law later conjectured Sergey's difficulties (his terrible stutter, his shyness, his early hatred of his mother) may have stemmed from this time of anxiety.[23] Soon after her parents' death, Elena Nabokov was ordered to the south of France. There she took her two sons to stay in Pau (Basses Pyrénées), at Perpigna, the chateau of her brother Vasily. All Nabokov remembers of that trip is a shining wet roof.[24]

V. D. Nabokov could not leave St. Petersburg, where he was still teaching at the School of Jurisprudence. His one unmarried sister,

---

* In 1921 Nabokov would adopt the pseudonym Vladimir Sirin for his Russian writings.

† "Spoiled in the excellent extreme," he sums it up in the Russian version of his autobiography.

Nadezhda, who came to keep him company, records that her brother still led the high society life familiar to us from Tolstoy: every morning, riding in the nearby manège on his own horses; in the evening the theater, with champagne and oysters afterward.[25]

Presumably it was back in St. Petersburg in 1902 that young Vladimir and Sergey's first English governess replaced their Russian nurse: Miss Rachel Home, plump and simple, who would feed the boys Huntley and Palmer biscuits just before they went to sleep (dentists were to be a nightmare for Nabokov).[26]

A third child, Olga, was born on January 5, 1903.* But the Nabokov boys and girls would be brought up the old way, completely separately, and attention remained on young Vladimir. Elena Nabokov tried to foster her son's sense of surprise at life. The jewels she loaned him as playthings mark how attuned she was to his almost innate love of color and light—mixed, in this very synesthetic child, with the treats of taste and touch:

> The recollection of my crib, with its lateral nets of fluffy cotton cords, brings back, too, the pleasure of handling a certain beautiful, delightfully solid, garnet-dark crystal egg left over from some unremembered Easter; I used to chew a corner of the bedsheet until it was thoroughly soaked and then wrap the egg in it tightly, so as to admire and re-lick the warm, ruddy glitter of the snugly enveloped facets that came seeping through with a miraculous completeness of glow and color.[27]

In constructing *Speak, Memory* Nabokov links this "garnet-dark crystal egg" with his mother's jewels and with stained glass, prisms, spectra, rainbows, all of which fuse in his first attempts at poetry: through this theme of jewels and rainbows he at once pays homage to the treasures of the visual world and links them to his own artistic gift.

Nabokov always thought that from its earliest phases his happy childhood played an exceptionally large part in shaping him into the artist he would become. In *Speak, Memory* he interweaves motifs like jewels and matters like consciousness in ways he meant to be puzzles, puzzles almost as perplexing and entrancing as the past itself. Only by disentangling these camouflaged threads and unraveling these unstated riddles can we discover the clews to Nabokov's own sense of his childhood.

Another of *Speak, Memory*'s motifs is the role garden paths, park walks, and forest trails have played in Nabokov's life.[28] His first self-conscious memory dates back to August 1903, in the new park of the

* In *Ada* Nabokov would bestow his high-strung sister's birthday on Van and Ada's fragile half sister Lucette, though a fortunate real-life coincidence allowed him to give Lucette, his favorite character in the novel, his wife's birthday too.

family estate at Vyra, on "the avenue of oaklings which seems to have been the main artery of my infancy."[29] The occasion may have been his mother's birthday. He was walking between his parents, and after asking his mother's age, he realized fully for the first time "that I was I and that my parents were my parents. . . . At that instant, I became acutely aware that the twenty-seven-year-old being, in soft white and pink, holding my left hand, was my mother, and that the thirty-three-year-old being, in hard white and gold, holding my right hand, was my father."[30] Nabokov recalls the shock of wonder and liberation at the discovery of time and the dawn of full self-consciousness, "a second baptism" much more mysterious and promising than the Russian orthodox dunking he had undergone years earlier.[31] Throughout *Speak, Memory* that emphasis on the magic of consciousness persists.

Vyra was one of the three manors around which Nabokov's childhood summers revolved. Although he actually spent more of his Russian life in the family's St. Petersburg house, Vyra was always "home." Summer was his happiest season, the time of year that subtended the largest arc in his memory and had the greatest role in shaping him. Since his father had spent his childhood summers at nearby Batovo and his mother hers at Vyra, their excited recollections added a shimmering fourth dimension to a walk through the parks: "as if come home after years of travel," they would point out to Vladimir "the fond landmarks of events enfolded in an impalpable but somehow ever-present past."[32]

Nabokov's almost pathological ability to conjure up the past and bring it to life was something that he felt both inherited (from the Rukavishnikov *and* the Nabokov sides of the family) and learned—even before he had much of a past to call up.[33] Elena Nabokov in particular encouraged her son to hoard any gift of the moment whose value would inflate with the years:

> "*Vot zapomni* [now remember]," she would say in conspiratorial tones as she drew my attention to this or that loved thing in Vyra— . . . the palette of maple leaves on brown sand, a small bird's cuneate footprints on new snow. . . . Thus, in a way, I inherited an exquisite simulacrum—the beauty of intangible property, unreal estate—and this proved a splendid training for the endurance of later losses.[34]

Nabokov was a devoted disciple. Vyra and its surrounds, he later wrote, "are the places I love more than any on earth."[35] If Russian civilization meant only St. Petersburg to him, Russian landscape meant only the forests of fir and beech and the bogs and meadows characteristic of the region around Vyra. The steppes were as little part of Nabokov's Russia as the pampas would be.

Today where Vyra stood there is nothing but a scraggly clump of trees. Taken over as a staff headquarters by the German army in 1942, it was burned to the ground when they left in 1944, and the bricks of its foundations were taken by the villagers to make chimneys for their stoves. Once a cast-iron staircase divided the house, leading up to the parquet landing beneath a lightwell. Not even that remains now. Built by Ivan Rukavishnikov's father, Vyra was a large, chunky, unpretentious two-story home embellished with the fretted woodwork of the region. Upper-floor balconies looked out onto lime branches, ground-floor verandas decorated with colored glass surveyed immaculate ornamental gardens and the dark firs of the old park beyond. Right behind the house the park sloped abruptly down to a mill. Across the millrace, where the flat expanse of the Oredezh merges with a shallow, reedy bank, the big village of Rozhdestveno stretches along the Petersburg-Luga highway.

The village had been shaped for a generation by the wealth of the Rukavishnikovs. As well as building schools and a hospital there, Ivan Rukavishnikov had also invested in the area's past by buying the stately neoclassical manor of Rozhdestveno, four facades of pillars and pediments in white-painted timber rather than plaster or stone. Though the paint has flaked and the laths have sprung, the manor still dominates the southern end of the village from the oak-and-linden-covered bank of the Gryazno river, which flows into the Oredezh at the foot of the manor hill. When he died in 1904, Ivan Rukavishnikov's new manor passed to his son, Nabokov's uncle Vasily. Vasily instructed his servants to keep the rooms fragrant with flowers but himself lived mostly in southern France or Italy. By the 1900s, therefore, the leading figure in the village was V. D. Nabokov, whose wife had inherited Vyra, just across the river from the village and downstream from the manor of Rozhdestveno, but invisible behind the firs and beeches leading from water's edge up a short steep bank.

Several twists up the dark, glassy Oredezh, past bare red cliffs and gentler wooded slopes, lie the estate and village of Batovo. The early home of V. D. Nabokov and in the early 1900s still his mother's residence, Batovo was much less opulent and well-tailored than Vyra or the showy Rozhdestveno, though it could boast a more distinguished past.* It was here young Vladimir would meet his numerous aunts, uncles, and cousins, before returning by calash, charabanc, or automobile across the Pont des Vaches, along a muddy and rutty road winding through field and forest above the river, and then turning

---

* It was once the home of the Decembrist poet Kondraty Ryleev, whose verse, a century earlier, had celebrated the Oredezh. The site of the no-longer-extant Batovo manor bears a plaque in his honor.

north into the well-kept road through the Vyra estate, past hayfields and a colonnade of thick birches, past the new park on the left, with its avenue of oaklings, and the firs of the old park in stately mourning on the right. Beyond the old park, across the trim garden, stood home, gleaming in its coat of pale green painted afresh every spring.

Back at Vyra, Vladimir could run over the brick-colored sand of the garden to play on a mountainous-seeming artificial hill, all of eight feet tall, flanking the house,[36] or with the help of a servant move a divan just out from a wall in the drawing room to construct a cave with bolsters and cushions:

> I then had the fantastic pleasure of creeping through that pitch-dark tunnel, where I lingered a little to listen to the singing in my ears—that lonesome vibration so familiar to small boys in dusty hiding places—and then, in a burst of delicious panic, on rapidly thudding hands and knees I would reach the tunnel's far end, push its cushion away and be welcomed by a mesh of sunshine on the parquet under the canework of a Viennese chair. . . .[37]

This infant game, with its contrast between the panic of darkness and a radiant reality beyond, prefigures the sudden shifts from disorientation to discovery that become a hallmark of Nabokov's work. That fits one aim of *Speak, Memory*: "to prove," as Nabokov wrote, "that [my] childhood contained, on a much reduced scale, the main components of [my] creative maturity."[38]

At this time, though not for long, Vladimir actually spoke English better than Russian.[39] In the more-than-fashionably Anglophile family in which he was reared, he could be excused for thinking as a small boy that the garden of Eden was a British colony.[40] English

> was the language of my first magazines: *Little Folks, Chatterbox* and those immensely appetising small books with pages more broad than long whose glossy illustrations depicted squirrels preparing leaf-wrapped honey for a despotic owl—one of the squirrels, my representative in 1904, made bold fun of the brutal bird—or the adventures of an early racing car with a fish profile.[41]

Asked by an interviewer what were the first stories he remembered in Russian, he replied: "English fairy tales (see *Speak, Memory*)."[42] In the morning, Miss Sheldon—"Viktoria Arturovna" as she would be addressed in the Russian manner—would read him *Little Lord Fauntleroy*.[43]* No wonder he responded much better to his mother. In the evening, after Sergey had been put to bed, she would sit in the draw-

* Miss Sheldon is the "Miss Clayton" in *Speak, Memory*.

ing room at Vyra with Vladimir (already undressed by Miss Sheldon) and read him in English some full-blooded tale more likely to play on his fancy: the Tristan legend, for instance, or a chance story that would stay with him for life.

Above his bed at Vyra hung a framed aquarelle with

> a dusky path winding through one of those eerily dense European beechwoods, where the only undergrowth is bindweed and the only sound one's thumping heart. In an English fairy tale my mother had once read to me, a small boy stepped out of his bed into a picture and rode his hobbyhorse along a painted path between silent trees. While I knelt on my pillow . . . half sitting on my calves and rapidly going through my prayer, I imagined the motion of climbing into the picture above my bed and plunging into that enchanted beechwood.[44]

That involution—the little boy's consciousness of the parallel between himself and the boy in the story—and that eerie plunge into the mysterious picture, contribute to Nabokov's art again and again. In *Glory*, Martin has this very picture above his bed, and when he leaves European exile to return illegally to Russia, presumably to die, his reckless but triumphant crossing at the end of the book seems to reenact the boy's stepping into the picture. In the first chapter of *Speak, Memory*, Nabokov walks between his parents in their avenue of oaklings, and at the end of the chapter his father soars into death and up into a painted church ceiling; at the end of the last chapter, Nabokov's son walks between his parents in a public park in St. Nazaire and toward the transatlantic liner that will take them to America and freedom, and we leave him still unable to make out, directly ahead, the ship's splendid funnel, "showing from behind the clothesline as something in a scrambled picture—Find What the Sailor Has Hidden—that the finder cannot unsee once it has been seen."[45] And at the end of *Ada*, Van and Ada die *into* their own book, and somehow simultaneously *into* an illustrated edition, from Ada's nursery, of the *Babes in the Wood*.

V

In September 1903 the family traveled to Paris for an operation on three-year-old Sergey.[46] From there they moved on to the Riviera, taking the Mediterranean train de luxe. Nabokov's childhood sense of the enchantment of long train journeys never left him: "I recall kneeling on my (flattish) pillow at the window of a sleeping car . . . and seeing with an inexplicable pang, a handful of fabulous lights that beckoned to me from a distant hillside, and then slipped into a pocket of black velvet: diamonds that I later gave away to my characters to alleviate the burden of my wealth."[47] They stopped in Nice, where the irascibly senile Dmitri Nabokov took some comfort from young Vladimir's mother, the only person whose presence he could bear: "He kept mistaking the attendant who rolled him along the Promenade des Anglais for Count Loris-Melikov.* . . . Dimly I recall running up to his chair to show him a pretty pebble, which he slowly examined and then slowly put into his mouth."[48]

In Nice the three-year-old Sergey and the difficult, willful Vladimir eleven months older, were looked after by their third English governess, "Miss Norcott." Nabokov recalls one bright morning with the mistral making the windowpanes rattle

> and the amazing pain caused by a drop of hot sealing wax on my finger. Using a candle-flame . . . I had been engaged in transforming dripping sticks of the stuff into gluey, marvelously smelling, scarlet and blue and bronze-colored blobs. The next moment I was bellowing on the floor, and my mother had hurried to the rescue, and somewhere nearby my grandfather in a wheelchair was thumping the resounding flags with his cane.[49]

Nabokov's mother would recall that Vladimir was in fact rather a crybaby as a young child.[50] Nabokov chooses the scene not to record that fact but only to trace his development as an artist. The fusion of the different colors becomes a variation on the rainbow theme, and typifies a child's creative desire to transform the given: "there is in every child the essentially human urge to reshape the earth, to act upon . . . environment (unless he is a born Marxist or a corpse and meekly waits for the environment to fashion *him*)."[51]

Vladimir returned to St. Petersburg in time for Christmas 1903 and a bracelet from his pretty cousin Onya (Sophia Nabokov). In Russia, Christmas was a modest affair, much less dominant in the church year or a child's imagination than Easter: a few trifles from Peto's, the toy shop, would be left for the governess to put in stockings, English fashion, on the children's beds; a very un-Russian plum pudding would be bought at Drew's English shop on the Nevsky;[52] and the Christmas tree, the perfectly Russian "yolka" (fir tree) would just reach the pale green clouds of the high painted ceiling in the Green Room, prettiest of the drawing rooms on the ground floor.[53†]

By now 47 Morskaya—which, like Vyra, belonged to Elena Nabokov rather than to her husband—had been transformed into the most

---

* In the last years of Alexander II's life, while Dmitri Nabokov was minister of justice, Loris-Melikov was the most influential of the tsar's advisers.

† This painted ceiling reappears in glorified form in *Ada*, where Demon's Manhattan home has a Boucher plafond.

stylish building in the street. In 1901 a third story had been added, along with a dash of art nouveau: a facade of pink granite, a gilt-and-purple mosaic above the third-floor windows, a coronet of ornate railings on the roof. Down at ground level a carriageway cutting into the left extreme of the house's facade led into a small courtyard and a glimpse of snow on the stacks of birch logs cut for the house's Dutch stoves. Back at the street front, a single step took one up from pavement to front door. From the warm entrance hall, where logs crackled in a fireplace behind a hefty grating,[54] the grand staircase angled upward, the stairs for the concierge and his family downward at right. A right turn before the stairs ushered visitors into an almost oppressively distinguished hall in dark paneling and elaborate wood inlay over ceiling and walls. To the right, facing the street, was the dining room, then the Green Room, and at the end the large library which could easily hold all V. D. Nabokov's books and still leave him space to box or fence almost every morning with his instructor, a rubbery Frenchman, Monsieur Loustalot. On the floor above, V. D. Nabokov's study perched over the carriage entrance, and then followed, still on the street side, the music room, Elena Nabokov's study, the master bedroom, and Elena Nabokov's dressing room (later to be the bedroom of Kirill, youngest in the family). Looking down on the street from the top floor were, from west to east, the bedrooms of the girls and governesses, then those of Sergey and Vladimir.[55]

One February day in 1904 Vladimir was brought down to his father's study to meet General Kuropatkin, the minister of war, who that very day, less than two weeks after Japan's attack on Russian destroyers at Port Arthur, had been appointed commander-in-chief of the Manchurian army.[56] Things would never be the same again in Russia after this disastrous war, but from a child's point of view little seemed to change. On a winter's day, with snow wisping off the cornices, Vladimir would be swathed in black-knit snow pants over his stockings and shorts before Miss Norcott took him to toboggan on a hillock in front of St. Isaac's, or for a walk through the nearby Alexandrovsky gardens, past fluffy white mounds that marked flower beds in summer, or to the Nevsky, where the huge model of a brown-paneled sleeping-car evoked the romance of autumn voyages. Or the slow evolution of spring: before the city thawed, the Catkin week fair, with its stalls and sideshows on Konnogvardeisky (Horse Guards) Boulevard, its bright lacquered wooden toys;* weeks later, servants

---

* Nabokov's favorites were the Russian *matreshki*, hollow wooden peasant-women dolls, each a fraction smaller than the last, which fit one inside the other. The enthusiasm remained: one critic even takes these dolls with their selves within selves, realities within realities, as an image of Nabokov's fiction (Sergey Davydov, *Teksty-Matreshki Vladimira Nabokova* [*Vladimir Nabokov's "Matreshka Texts,"* Munich: Otto Sagner, 1982]).

sweeping dead snow from the shallow roofs, hidden in St. Petersburg as if roofing iron were as intimate as crinoline or whalebone; later still, workmen would prize up the octagonal pinewood paving blocks and trim new ones as the city spring-cleans its streets, and barges creak once more on the Neva or the Moika canal just the other side of the Morskaya.

Ordinarily, this would be the time for departure to Vyra. But in early summer 1904, the family instead took the Nord Express to Paris, before traveling on to Beaulieu. There, staying at the Hotel Bristol, the five-year-old Nabokov fell in love for almost the first time, succumbing to the charms of a dark-eyed Rumanian girl with what seemed to him the strange-sounding surname of Ghika.[57] From Beaulieu a train took the family on to Abbazia, via the St. Gotthard tunnel—chugging in during a thunderstorm, bursting out into light and a rainbow across a crag—and Milan.

In Abbazia, they stayed with V. D. Nabokov's sister Natalia de Peterson (her husband was Russian consul in nearby Fiume, now Rijeka, Yugoslavia) in a rented villa with its own crenellated tower. At that time Abbazia (now Opatija) was a fashionable resort for the aristocracy of the Austrian Empire. But for Vladimir it was a long way from home, from Vyra, which he had not seen since September 1903:

aged five, mooning in my cot after lunch, I used to turn over on my stomach and carefully, lovingly, hopelessly, in an artistically detailed fashion difficult to reconcile with the ridiculously small number of seasons that had gone to form the inexplicably nostalgic image of "home" . . . I would draw with my forefinger on my pillow the carriage road sweeping up to our Vyra house, the stone steps on the right, the carved back of a bench on the left. . . .[58]

Exile forms still another of the leitmotifs in Speak, Memory: Nabokov insisted, as part of his general plan to show how all the markings of his adult form could be seen through the chrysalis of childhood, that he "went through all the sorrows and delights of nostalgia long before the revolution had removed the scenery of his young years."[59]

He pictures himself, too, on the beach at Abbazia. Wearing Onya's bracelet and clambering frogwise

over wet black rocks at the seaside while Miss Norcott, a languid and melancholy governess, who thinks I am following her, strolls away along the curved beach with Sergey. . . . As I crawl over those rocks, I keep repeating, in a kind of zestful, copious, and deeply gratifying incantation, the English word "childhood," which . . . becomes stranger and stranger as it gets mixed up in my small, overstocked, hectic mind, with Robin Hood and Little Red Riding Hood, and the brown hoods of old hunchbacked fairies. There are dimples in the rocks, full of tepid water, and my magic muttering accompanies certain spells I am weaving over the tiny sapphire pools.[60]

In that scene Nabokov shows his writerly imagination already in action, excited by words, lost in solitary reverie: "I think I was born like that," he has said, "a precocious genius, a *Wunderkind*."[61] Even at this stage of childhood, curiously, women are woven into his dreamy fancy: Onya, his pretty coeval; or the lovely, black-haired, aquamarine-eyed Miss Norcott, with whom he was a little in love and whose sudden dismissal (she was found to be lesbian) left him inconsolable; or on other occasions, his mother, always such an eager accomplice in his artistic development.

The war had its effect even here. On a visit to Fiume, "at a waterside café, my father happened to notice, just as we were being served, two Japanese officers at a table near us, and we immediately left—not without my hastily snatching a whole *bombe* of lemon sherbet, which I carried away secreted in my aching mouth."[62] Despite his general apoliticism, Nabokov would later catch up his father's example as he assiduously boycotted anti-Semites, communists, fascists, and Nazi collaborators.

Later in the year the family moved back northward, but only as far as Wiesbaden, where they put up at the Hotel Oranien. A new English governess, myopic Miss Hunt, came to stay, but the boys soon put an end to her. Running through crackling brown leaves, Vladimir led his brother to the jetty from which a Rhine steamer was about to depart. By squeezing among the tourists and lying to some American ladies, the boys managed to evade capture until they were whisked back at a stop downstream. So much for Miss Hunt.[63] In general, though, Vladimir had little to do with his timid, easily dominated brother. Much more congenial a companion for the boisterous child was his cousin Yuri Rausch von Traubenberg (Yurik), eighteen months older, whom he met for the first time in Wiesbaden around Christmas.

> I remember him coming out of a souvenir shop and running toward me with a breloque, an inch-long little pistol of silver, which he was anxious to show me—and suddenly sprawling on the sidewalk but not crying when he picked himself up, unmindful of a bleeding knee and still clutching his minuscule weapon.[64]

It made a lasting first impression on Vladimir that Yurik "hurt himself badly but did not shed a single tear."[65] Throughout the remainder of his boyhood, Vladimir would emulate his lanky, steel-nerved cousin, vying with him as soldier, cowboy, knight, and young *galant*. Inspired by Yurik, in direct homage to the Russian troops traveling out to the Far East on rails hurriedly laid over the ice of Lake Baikal, and naturally oblivious to the discontent the war was causing at home, a chilled but determined Vladimir tried to run toy trains over the frozen puddles in the grounds of the Hotel Oranien.[66]

In St. Petersburg a different struggle was brewing.

First Revolution and First Duma: St. Petersburg, 1904–1906

It is just possible that I shall do after all a special chapter on my father—
if I manage to get to Washington where the material I require
exists. Pullman plus a couple of nights at a good hotel
adds up to a sum I do not possess at present.

—Nabokov letter to Katharine White, 1949

I

THOUGH the rest of the family did not return to St. Petersburg until early 1905, after the first Russian revolution had been under way for months, V. D. Nabokov had hurried back at the beginning of autumn 1904. According to Iosif Hessen, Nabokov had taken his family to Abbazia earlier that year to avoid the disapproval his politics stirred up among relations and friends. When the Machiavellian and much-hated minister of the interior Count von Plehve was assassinated in July 1904 and Prince Svyatopolk-Mirsky appointed to replace him in September, Russia could sense a chance for change. Hessen wrote to Nabokov that he belonged not in an Italian resort but in St. Petersburg, where a leading role awaited him. Nabokov came at once, with his wife's blessing.[1] Over the next two years politics kept him often apart from his family, but his absence and his activities would only increase his heroic stature in the eyes of his son.

V. D. Nabokov had not been idle over the past few years. He was still teaching at the School of Jurisprudence. His legal writings, in which he tried to humanize the struggle with crime, had established him as one of the leading Russian criminologists of his time.[2] His study of sexual crime was the best thing on the subject in Russian: the father of the man who conceived Lolita and Kinbote strongly supported increased protection for the underage and criticized continued punishment for homosexual acts between consenting adults.[3]

But it was in politics that he made his real mark. Since 1899 Russian political discontent had become increasingly organized and vocal. In

1902 liberals active in the zemstvo (local council) movement joined with the radical intelligentsia to found the illegal and highly influential newspaper *Osvobozhdenie* (*Liberation*), published in Stuttgart by Peter Struve, who later recalled V. D. Nabokov as a close ally and contributor from the start.[4]

When forty-five Jews were killed, hundreds wounded, and more than a thousand houses and shops destroyed in a pogrom in the city of Kishinyov in April 1903, V. D. Nabokov responded in *Pravo* with "The Bloodbath of Kishinyov."[5] This unrhetorical, coolly analytical article, considered one of the most dazzling productions of Russian public debate under censorship, set the whole capital buzzing.[6] Nabokov not only asserted the immediate responsibility of the police for not restraining the pogrom until it had died down but also issued a general indictment of the intellectual poverty of anti-Semitism, an attitude fostered by a regime that treated Jews as pariahs and allowed pogromists to feel confident they could escape conviction. What particularly impressed Nabokov's allies with less to lose than he was that although he knew this article marked a decisive step away from his social sphere and career prospects, he made the move without the least hesitation.[7]

II

After von Plehve's assassination, few mourned the man who as minister of the interior had insinuated the police into every aspect of Russian life. His much more broad-minded successor, Svyatopolk-Mirsky, allowed the press greater freedom, just when the newly formed (and also illegal) Union of Liberation had decided to challenge autocracy through a public opinion campaign on a massive scale. As setback followed setback in the war with Japan, and as the possibility of protest dawned, many elements of Russian society discovered how impatient they were at having been so long denied their right to be heard. By giving voice to their frustration and hope, the intelligentsia fueled the mood that made the country blaze into revolution.

Surprisingly the opulent Nabokov home became the site of one major ideological bonfire. On November 6–9/19–22, 1904, the first-ever national congress of zemstvos was held in St. Petersburg. Though nearly prevailed upon to prohibit the congress altogether, Svyatopolk-Mirsky allowed it to continue provided it took place in private homes. The hopes for this great congress, "the most important public assembly held in imperial Russia up to that time,"[8] stirred a festive mood across the nation:

Delegates departing for the congress were accompanied to railway stations by crowds of well-wishers. On their arrival in St. Petersburg they found that even though the meetings were held in private residences that had not been publicly advertised . . . , the cab drivers unerringly knew where to take them; and if they did not, friendly policemen in uniform or plain clothes offered them directions. Each day, a flood of congratulatory telegrams poured in. Addressed simply "Zemstvo Congress, St. Petersburg," they were delivered by the postal authorities to the correct destination. These telegrams exhorted the delegates to speak on behalf of the entire nation, not just the zemstva, and openly to advocate a constitution.[9]

Within the context of tsarist Russia, the congress's resolutions, which publicly called for a constitution, a legislative assembly, and guaranteed civil rights, were nothing short of revolutionary and, "in effect, launched the 1905 Revolution."[10] At V. D. Nabokov's invitation, the final sessions of the congress took place in his home at 47 Morskaya—presumably in the large music room on the second floor—and it was here that the congress's resolutions were signed. After the signing one of the delegates "exclaimed that future generations would commemorate their deed with a marble plaque" on the house.[11]*

Russia's political temper became more heated during the so-called banquet campaign of November–December 1904. In a whole series of public banquets given lavish attention in the newspapers, speaker after speaker demanded thoroughgoing reforms. In *Speak, Memory*, writing of an *official* banquet earlier in 1904, Vladimir Nabokov reports that his father "refused to drink the Tsar's health."[12] By the end of the year, when *Pravo* was openly demanding an end to the war and the reorganization of the state system, V. D. Nabokov's opposition had become much sharper than that. Count Sergey Witte, president of the council of ministers and virtual prime minister, offered V. D. Nabokov a post, only to hear him declare that he refused to serve the present regime in any capacity whatsoever.[13]

Late in 1904 the Union of Liberation had encouraged Father Gapon, a shadowy priest-cum-trade-unionist-cum-police-agent, to politicize the rapidly expanding trade union movement in St. Petersburg. At the beginning of January 1905, a strike at the Putilov works caught like wildfire. By January 7/20, there was almost a general strike in the capital, with over a hundred thousand refusing to work. On Sunday, January 9/22, Gapon led along the Nevsky and up to the Winter Palace a peaceful demonstration of perhaps two hundred thousand, carrying

* There are other reasons now for commemorating that house, and still no plaque. But it may come soon; since spring 1989 there have been official excursions to Nabokovian sites: 47 Hertzen Street (the former Morskaya), Vyra, Batovo, Rozhdestveno.

icons and portraits of the tsar, bearing a petition emphasizing their loyalty but at the same time requesting sweeping changes. When the demonstrators would not disperse, troops opened fire. More than a hundred were killed, almost a thousand wounded. Only a quarter of a mile from the Nabokov home, mounted gendarmes opened fire on one branch of the procession, killing children who had fled to hide in the trees of Mariinskaya Square.[14]

A member since 1903 of the St. Petersburg Duma (City Council), V. D. Nabokov denounced the tragedy of Bloody Sunday at a Duma session three days after the event, and proposed that 25,000 rubles be allotted to the families of those killed. With press censorship unprecedentedly severe in the weeks after the tragedy, only one newspaper carried a report of his proposal, and even that was excised from the published minutes of the Duma.[15] But reaction was swift. Within a week, he was deprived of his post at the School of Jurisprudence and of his court title.[16] He had no regrets whatever about being excluded from *such* a court, and is "said to have coolly advertised in the papers his court uniform for sale."[17]

III

Still in Abbazia, Elena Nabokov worried about each day's news from Russia, while her children simply missed their father. Nabokov could not recall exactly when his mother brought them back to St. Petersburg early in 1905, but the return trip, after this long absence, was the first to make his lungs fill with rapture when he smelled the birch smoke of Russia's trains.[18] That winter, he was already a "writer": "I have been involved in writing since I was very little: I recall vividly that at five in St. Petersburg . . . I used to tell myself, in bed or at play, all sorts of stories, usually heroic adventures. There would be a whole procession of images trooping around me and through me."[19]

In that year of political turmoil, V. D. Nabokov had to forgo the summer retreat to Vyra, except for short visits. On one of these he noticed that Vladimir and Sergey, supervised by English governesses, could read in English but not in Russian. This was taking westernization too far. He arranged for his sons to be taught for a few hours each day by the village schoolmaster, whose young pupil later recalled with zest "my delightful teacher":

Vasiliy Martïnovich Zhernosekov had a fuzzy brown beard, a balding head, and china-blue eyes, one of which bore a fascinating excrescence on the upper lid. The first day he came he brought a boxful of tremendously appetizing blocks with a different letter painted on each side;

these cubes he would manipulate as if they were infinitely precious things, which for that matter they were (besides forming splendid tunnels for toy trains). He revered my father who had recently rebuilt and modernized the village school.[20]

Zhernosekov was a Socialist Revolutionary, member of a young party whose fortunes took wing in that revolutionary year. Young Vladimir was enthralled: "he would gesture vehemently on our country rambles and speak of humanity and freedom and the badness of warfare and the sad (but interesting, I thought) necessity of blowing up tyrants"[21]—something Nabokov would later try in his own way in works like Bend Sinister or "Tyrants Destroyed." In Lenin's Russia, incidentally, Zhernosekov, like countless other noncommunist radicals, would be arrested and sentenced to hard labor.[22]

While Vladimir was building a tower one day from Zhernosekov's alphabet blocks, he casually remarked to his mother that the colors were all wrong. She asked why, and discovered that he associated colors with spoken sounds. Since she did too—though her colors were different—she encouraged rather than suppressed his synesthesia.[23] In retrospect Nabokov prized that sympathy. Many children, he felt, have an imaginative vitality that they lose as adults, and he was proud and grateful that his mother retained her unique response to the world and fostered his.[24] Perhaps too it is no coincidence that the crossing of the conventional borders of the senses was a cherished aim of the symbolists, whose poetry Elena Nabokov read with delight: for her, Vladimir's crisp association of "steely x, thundercloud z, and huckleberry k" may have seemed a preparatory pastel sketch of the future artist as a young boy.[25]

IV

In the wider world, Russia's defeat in the war with Japan and the rise of pressure for reform among zemstvo nobles, professionals, intelligentsia, peasants, and workers soon brought revolution on apace. By May 1905 the countryside was "ablaze with riots"; by the end of the year Russia had suffered more strikes than in the whole of its previous history.[26] Opposition to the regime organized itself on as many fronts as possible.

That autumn and winter the family remained at Vyra as the nation—and especially its capital—plunged into turmoil. Although V. D. Nabokov had to work in St. Petersburg, he knew that his popularity among the peasants in his own village would ensure the safety of his family. In general, relations with the local peasants were most harmonious: "like every selfless liberal landowner," Vladimir Nabokov comments, "my father did a great deal of good within the limits of fatal inequality."[27] Like his father and father-in-law, V. D. Nabokov treated his workers with respect, paid them well, slipped them a little extra if they wished to buy a cow or a horse, and paid for doctor's visits. After the Bolshevik revolution, when it became *de rigueur* to decry one's former masters, V. D. Nabokov's servants knew they had no cause to do so, and after sixty years of Soviet rule could still think their lot had been better before the revolution.[28]

In October 1905 a general strike broke out, prohibiting all St. Petersburg's liberal intelligentsia except V. D. Nabokov and his friend Iosif Hessen from reaching the conference in Moscow that would establish the Constitutional Democratic (CD) party, officially the Party of the People's Freedom. Just as the conference was closing, Nicholas II promulgated his Manifesto of October 17. With his troops still in the Far East, he had realized he could not set up a dictatorship to quell the unrest, and his only recourse was to make the distasteful concession of creating a genuine legislative duma.

Although the Manifesto provoked jubilation in the streets, the politically educated could see that it guaranteed very little. In *Pravo* V. D. Nabokov declared its provisions unsatisfactory, and insisted that there must be "universal suffrage, freedom, and a constitution drawn up by a constituent assembly."[29] Tempers rose sharply in the so-called days of freedom ushered in by the Manifesto. Violence was commonplace from both the left and especially the right.

Unable to placate the country, the government made concessions. Preliminary censorship of books and periodicals was abolished, so that although certain legal restrictions remained (editors could be arrested, newspapers closed down) Russia began to enjoy the freest, most antigovernment press in Europe. Within a few years even the Bolshevik newspaper *Pravda* would be legally on sale. Presumably the young Vladimir Nabokov never bought a copy, but as a youth he thrived on and as an adult he cherished in retrospect the freedom of the Russian press, where any idea or any literary experiment could find a way into print.

In December 1905, in another apparent concession, the government widened the franchise for the new Duma, allowing more representation only for the peasantry—whom they supposed loyal conservatives—and not for the small but obviously radical urban proletariat. Partly because they feared that a nearly representative Duma might mean calm, and so might jeopardize continued revolution, the Social Democrats and Socialist Revolutionaries decided to boycott the Duma.

The Constitutional Democrats on the other hand eagerly prepared for the elections, hoping to transform the rather weak powers of the Duma into something like the constituent assembly they had wanted.

By mid-January 1906 the government had reestablished a degree of control. Troops were back from the east, liberals were split by the October concessions, workers were exhausted by strikes, and moderates of all ranks were reacting to the excesses of extremists. Though the habit of disorder persisted, mass discontent no longer unified the country, and localized disruptions could be met with force.

V

It was into this slightly calmer Russia that Cécile Miauton—the "Mademoiselle" or "Mlle O" of Nabokov's autobiography—arrived from Switzerland to take up the post of French governess in the Nabokov family, still wintering at Vyra. This was the only time the family spent the winter there, and for Vladimir "everything was new and delightful—the Russian felt boots, and the snowmen, and the gigantic blue icicles hanging from the roof of the red barn, and the smell of frost and tar, and the roar of the stoves in the manor rooms."[30] Alarmed by the events of that year, and doubly anxious because of her pregnancy, Elena Nabokov was in St. Petersburg when Mademoiselle arrived. Things began badly between the new governess and the two boys in her charge:

> We had just returned from our first afternoon walk with Mademoiselle and I was seething with frustration and hatred. With a little prompting, I had meek Sergey share some of my anger. To keep up with an unfamiliar tongue (all we knew in the way of French were a few household phrases), and on top of it to be crossed in all our fond habits, was more than one could bear. The *bonne promenade* she had promised us had turned out to be a tedious stroll near the house where the snow had been cleared and sprinkled with sand. She had us wear things we never used to wear, even on the frostiest day—horrible gaiters and hoods that hampered our every movement. She had restrained us when I induced Sergey to explore the creamy, smooth swellings of snow that had been flower beds in summer.[31]

Vladimir prompted his brother to "a wicked plan": leaving Mademoiselle puffing on the doorstep when they returned, they dashed inside as if to hide within the house, and made a break for freedom through a door on the other side. Sunset came quickly, but they still trudged on through the snow. Sergey was cold and tired but Vladimir urged him on, then set him astride the Great Dane walking happily with them. They had gone two miles, and the trees were becoming giants in the moonlight, before a servant carrying a lantern loomed out of the dark to take them back to the frantic Mademoiselle.

This doomed flight only chances to coincide with Russia's thwarted foray toward freedom that year, but it again reveals the man in the boy: even as an adult Nabokov retained the natural conservatism of a child, the clinging to what one happens to have known ("old Miss Robinson I couldn't stand, but *anything* was better than an unknown Frenchwoman"),[32] at the same time as he felt a strong impulse to break loose. After the initial shock of Mademoiselle's arrival, of course, young Vladimir soon found himself perfectly at home in French: by the summer of 1905 he had at his disposal all three of the languages he would later wield with such skill.

VI

In March 1906 there were two new starts for V. D. Nabokov: a fourth child, Elena, born March 18/31, and his election—as one of the most popular CD candidates in St. Petersburg[33]—to the country's first elected legislature. The CDs performed well throughout the country, winning over a third of all seats, while their near allies to the left, the Trudoviki (Labor) party, won almost a third.

At this point, as Russia's first parliament, dominated by the CDs, is about to open, we should pause to consider what the party stood for. V. D. Nabokov was to lead the Constitutional Democrats within the First Duma; he edited and published their official newspaper;[34] and after being barred from future dumas, he would play a leading role in their unofficial newspaper *Rech'* (*Speech*) and would help guide party policy until his death. Vladimir Nabokov revered his father throughout his life and derived his moral standards from him. Although he never cared for the short-term squabbles of politics, he remained confident that the permanent principles his father fought for could not be wrong.

In another context the CDs would have been simply moderate liberals, but in tsarist Russia their confidence that they were backed by both moral right and public opinion and their determination to establish a new system of government despite the wishes of those who held power made them radical reformers.[35] They wanted the rule of law to replace autocratic whim: the basic freedoms of person, opinion, expression, and assembly; equality before the law, in place of legal discriminations according to class, religion, and nationality; a legislative body elected by direct, secret, universal, and equal elections, and ministerial responsibility to the legislature. They did not insist on deciding between a constitutional monarchy or a republic: since the former seemed more feasible to introduce, they favored it as a matter of strategy. Vladimir Nabokov would be the same: "I am ready to accept any regime—Socialistic, Royalistic, Janitorial—provided mind and body are free."[36] But the CDs' demands for unbreachable guarantees of freedom made them seem little different from revolutionaries to a tsar who was resolved to pass on intact to his son the autocracy he had inherited. Unlike the real revolutionaries, in fact, the CDs preferred the force of public opinion to violence. Here lay the insuperable obstacle to their success: popular sentiment alone could not persuade a government ready in the last resort to rely on the firepower of its troops.

The primary aim of the CDs was to establish individual freedoms and a representative legislature where debate among the various interests within the country could take place. The precise economic order mattered less. But they were not laissez-faire liberals. They were not a "bourgeois" party—numerically the Russian bourgeoisie was in any case still minute—but a "professors' party." Without any real social basis of support, they had only the moral force of ideas on their side. Eighty percent of the population were still peasants, living in or desperately close to poverty. The CDs were ready to relieve their situation by the enforced alienation of landowners' holdings (with fair compensation) and its redistribution to peasants already working the land. As one of the party's professors put it, the CDs demanded "from the landowners and capitalists large and serious sacrifices on behalf of the deprived mass, without being at all troubled by the grumbling and anger provoked by such demands within the privileged strata of the population."[37] Although V. D. Nabokov was inspired much more by the constitutionalist than the social program of his party, he loyally advanced within the Duma even the CD social program. Since as his son notes he "thoroughly appreciated all the pleasures of great wealth,"[38] his readiness to promote the policy of the enforced alienation of land must be seen as another instance of the selflessness of the Russian intelligentsia.[39]

The CD policy was close to peasant goals, for the great majority of peasants were not socialists but sought more land per individual household. But it was the Socialist Revolutionaries who captured the imagination of the peasants from 1905 until Lenin abolished the Constituent Assembly in 1918 because of its SR majority. They appealed to the peasants by urging the appropriation of *all* landowners' land, without compensation; that this would then have been reapportioned on a communal rather than an individual basis passed largely unnoticed. Despite the SRs' advocacy of terrorist assassination, the CDs remained close to this democratic side of the socialist intelligentsia. In his years of exile Vladimir Nabokov too would come to know and befriend some of the prominent Socialist Revolutionary leaders (Vladimir Zenzinov, Ilya Fondaminsky, Vadim Rudnev) who published his fiction, and would listen with great enjoyment to their tales of the conspiratorial past.

In contrast to the SRs and especially the Marxist Social Democrats (SDS), the CDs stressed the nonclass nature of their party.[40] They rejected equally the tsar's conviction that he had a God-given duty to determine the interests of all and the Bolsheviks' calculating exacerbation and glorification of class struggle as a means toward a theoretical classlessness in the future. They accepted that since there were different classes, and since differences in individual capacity and interests and occupations made social difference inevitable, it was their chief task to remove inequalities before law among classes and to set up a system of government that would allow the interests of different groups to be arbitrated by reasoned debate among elected representatives. Vladimir Nabokov's reluctance to admit the existence of social class (he conceded that, alas, class *consciousness* certainly exists)[41] is a dogmatic distortion of his father's emphasis on the nonclass nature of the CD party and its policies, an extension of his father's firm theoretical insistence on the individual, a reflection of the conduct of his father and men like him, so clearly at odds with what might be supposed the narrow interests of their "class."

VII

The short-lived First Duma was the time of the CDs' greatest power: partly because the SDs and SRs boycotted the election, and realized their mistake before the Second Duma; partly because the government miscalculated, and allowed the peasants a large share of voting power on the assumption they would be too devoted to tsar and church not to vote conservative (the government also realized its error quickly and restricted the franchise greatly for later dumas); partly because the reaction to the turbulence of 1905 had not yet led to the consolidation of the right.

V. D. Nabokov's finest days as a politician were in the First Duma. As another leading CD, Maxim Vinaver, observed, it was the happiest time of Nabokov's life; all his innate talents had awaited this moment; his spirit unfurled itself to the full. An open political arena, Vinaver pointed out, was essential to him. Nabokov could not limit himself to the dry paperwork of the old-style bureaucrat, but neither could his logic, clarity, elegance, and restraint of manner flourish in a revolutionary atmosphere where matters were decided by temperament, a coarse gesture, or force. He needed an auditorium, but a cultured auditorium capable of appreciating shapely thought, biting irony, verbal accuracy—and this is exactly what he found in the First Duma. His individual, precisely aimed, beautiful Russian, his gentlemanly irony, his crystalline and masterly formulation of ideas made him one of the leading orators in the Duma.[42]

Although he could analyze the complexities of political intrigue very clearly, V. D. Nabokov disliked the machinations of power and preferred an ordered and open debate on matters of principle. The distinguished British historian of Russia, Bernard Pares, happened to be in Russia at this time, and attended the Duma sessions assiduously. "In the House itself," he reported, "the actual leadership in debate fell on a young Cadet of marked ability and great parliamentary promise, Vladimir Nabokov."[43]* On the floor of the Tauride Palace Nabokov's buoyant self-assurance was immediately evident—so much so, some thought, that it seemed like haughtiness or snobbishness. In an assembly where rural representatives often appeared in peasant attire, Nabokov was unabashed by his wealth. His suits were of the finest cut, his impeccable ties, changed every day, were rated one of the sights of the Duma.[44] He felt no more self-conscious about his material wealth than he thought peasant representatives should feel about their own dress or speech.

Equally visible and more significant was Nabokov's calm busyness as a parliamentary manager. Pares found it "often more interesting to watch him than to follow the debates."[45] Nabokov was chosen to guide the keynote Address to the Throne, with which the CD party took the initiative and tried to arrogate to the Duma the powers of a constituent assembly. While the SRs and SDs had to reject the unsafe and barely democratic conditions of the October Manifesto and the moderate Octobrists were content to work within its terms, the CDs tried to do both at once: to work with the Manifesto, in the sense of accepting a Duma very limited in its franchise and powers, and to insist at the same time that the Duma as at present constituted was wholly unsatisfactory and needed to be supplanted. For the very reason that the Duma *was* unsatisfactory and almost powerless, alas, the attempt to use it to set up a more democratic constitution was doomed. But the attempt was a brave one, and Pares found Na-

---

* "Cadet" was a common nickname formed from the initial letters of Constitutional Democrat.

bokov's performance particularly impressive. Despite the breadth and boldness of the Address to the Throne, the entire document was passed unanimously by the Duma, in no small measure through Nabokov's tact and energy on the floor of the house as he reconciled parties divided by fundamental differences.

On May 13/26 the tired, haughty, and disdainful chief minister, Ivan Goremykin, announced to the Duma that the administration rejected the program signaled in the Address to the Throne. As Goremykin concluded, Nabokov leaped up to speak. "In his elegant light-grey suit, with his head held high, his even, convincing voice detailed his charges against the government."[46] "We do not have the beginnings of a constitutional ministry, we have the same old bureaucratic words. . . . The Chairman of the Council of Ministers invites the Duma to constructive work, but at the same time . . . categorically refuses to support the most lawful demands of the people."[47] He ended with a phrase that would long resound in Russian politics: "Let the executive power submit to the legislative!"

Deafening applause greeted his closing words. Nabokov's example inspired speech after speech denouncing the government in more and more intemperate terms, and a vote of no confidence in the ministry was passed. One noted Russian jurist even comments that by setting the tone for this session, Nabokov was "obliquely responsible for the dissolution of the Duma"[48] nearly two months later. Elena Nabokov, who was looking on from the public gallery, "always remembered that speech with pride."[49] Count Fredericks, minister of court, on the other hand, stared at Nabokov from the ministerial bench as if struck dumb. Could this impudent tribune of the people really be the Gentleman of the Tsar's Chamber of a few years earlier?[50]

VIII

Here began a virtual stalemate that lasted for the rest of the Duma's term. While the government showed its open contempt for popular representation, the representatives themselves worked with great diligence in committee, drafting farsighted and far-reaching constitutional laws of the kind that Goremykin had categorically rejected. Nabokov did not often speak in the less fruitful later sessions of the full Duma, except to lead an attack on further pogroms and to introduce the bill outlawing capital punishment—the only bill actually to be passed by the Duma.[51]

As the stalemate persisted, negotiations took place for a CD or partly CD cabinet that might replace the tsar's present ministers and win the confidence of the Duma. V. D. Nabokov was named—at the age of thirty-five—as a possible minister of justice within the shadow CD cabinet. Paul Milyukov, who was conducting the CD side of the negotiations, held out few hopes: court circles, he thought, would be more likely to accede to the CD agrarian policies they found so abhorrent than to accept Nabokov as minister of justice. The plans came to nothing.[52]

On July 9/22, 1906, at 6:00 A.M., V. D. Nabokov awoke to the news that the Duma was dissolved.[53] Delegates who had not heard arrived for the morning sessions to find the gates of the Tauride Palace locked and guarded by machine guns.

Two factors in the CD strategy had proved utterly unacceptable to the government: the demand for a responsible ministry, voiced so memorably by Nabokov, and the insistence on the enforced alienation of land, advocated especially by the party's agrarian spokesman, Gerzenshtein. The CDs had hoped that the government would not dare to contravene a program supported by the whole Duma and therefore presumably by the whole country it represented. As V. D. Nabokov realized in retrospect, the tsar did not feel himself weak enough to be obliged to capitulate—partly because the CD party apparatus had paid little attention to rousing and focusing public opinion across the country.[54] Recognizing that the Duma would not retreat, the government simply dissolved it entirely.

CD delegates gathered the next day in Vyborg in Finland, where the local police would allow them more freedom than in the capital. Assuming that the government would not call another Duma and feeling an urgent need to make some response, the CDs issued the Vyborg resolution, which called for the country to resist the government by refusing to pay taxes or to submit to military conscription. The most revolutionary gesture the CDs ever made, it was no more than "the radicalism of impotence," and was soon regretted.[55] But at the time it was much more difficult to judge Russia's reaction than it would be in retrospect: there had been almost a thousand peasant disturbances in June alone, and in the same month even the tsar's own crack Preobrazhensky Guards had witnessed a rebellion within their ranks. Like many others, V. D. Nabokov opposed the resolution, but when police seemed about to break up the meeting everyone present signed out of party loyalty, since *some* CD reaction had to be made public.[56] For that decision Nabokov and all the other CDs elected to the First Duma were on July 16 stripped of their political rights. Not until the February revolution of 1917 would Nabokov be able once more to play an active role in his country's politics.

Through the force of his eloquence and his clarity of mind V. D. Nabokov had reached a position of great eminence while still in his mid-thirties, only to be obliged to relinquish politics and enter the world of journalism. Just as in *Ada*, Aqua's fate in one generation foreshadows Lucette's in the next, just as Demon's behavior foreshadows Van's, so V. D. Nabokov's fate prefigures his son's: Vladimir Nabokov too would win distinction in his thirties—in émigré literary circles—and find his future barred when Hitler's arrival shattered Russian émigré culture. Like his father, Nabokov would continue to serve *his* cause, literature, while being forced to begin anew in a different mode, a different language.

In July 1906, with the Duma apparently dead, V. D. Nabokov was aghast at the collapse of liberal hopes. "The work of the last two years seems to be destroyed," he wrote to his brother Konstantin, "and we have to begin again. We all feel stunned by a heavy blow and are still unable to recover from it."[57] Late in July the CD agrarian spokesman Gerzenshtein was assassinated. In August, Nabokov and his wife suddenly left Russia for the Netherlands, passing first through Brussels, where his brother Konstantin was stationed. Elena Nabokov had been even more on edge than usual in the weeks following the dissolution of the Duma, and had not been told the reason for quitting Russia: the reactionary "Black Hundreds" had worked out a plan to exterminate the most influential leaders of the left. Gerzenshtein, according to Konstantin Nabokov, "was the first of six deputies on the list, and my brother the second. His friends who had been informed of this discovery exhorted him to leave Russia for a short time."[58] Although in the years after 1922 Vladimir Nabokov probed the past to trace the ploys of fate that had seemed to anticipate his father's assassination, he appears never to have learned that in 1906 his father was next in line to be shot.

Butterflies: St. Petersburg, 1906–1910

They chose me, not I them.

—Nabokov interview, 1963 (on being asked why he chose

butterflies to study)

I

IN 1906 NABOKOV discovered butterflies. One cloudless summer day, on the honeysuckle drooping over a branch facing the main entrance at Vyra, he spied with delight a brightly patterned swallow-tail—which Ustin, the family's town-house janitor, then trapped for him in the boy's cap. (Ustin, a police stooge, had insisted on coming to Vyra that summer, supposing that V. D. Nabokov would hold clandestine meetings there.) Kept overnight in a wardrobe, the butterfly escaped. The next attempt was better: a deep-plush, sticky-footed hawkmoth that his mother dispatched with ether and taught him how to spread.[1]

What started as a passion and a spell, Nabokov explains, was also a family tradition: "There was a magic room in our country house with my father's collection—the old faded butterflies of his childhood, but precious to me beyond words."[2] Like his three brothers, V. D. Nabokov had caught the butterfly "bug" from one of their German tutors, and though he no longer devoted time to the chase, his son could remember his normally imperturbable father

> that summer afternoon . . . when he had burst into my room, grabbed my net, shot down the veranda steps—and presently was strolling back holding between finger and thumb the rare and magnificent female of the Russian Poplar Admirable that he had seen basking on an aspen leaf from the balcony of his study.[3]

In *The Gift*, the hero's father is a loving portrait of V. D. Nabokov that astounded Elena Nabokov by its accuracy and penetration.[4] Nabokov makes his hero's admiration for his father and his desire to commemorate him central to the book—and makes the father a distinguished professional lepidopterist.

V. D. Nabokov may have chased butterflies keenly as a youth, but even as a young mother Elena Nabokov still roamed the Vyra country-side day after summer day in pursuit of her own prized prey: Russian boletic mushrooms. In his autobiography Nabokov deliberately links her passion for collecting with his own—which, with these antece-dents on both sides of the family, developed very quickly. Within a month of that first butterfly, he had captured samples of twenty other common species and had already begun to see his world with a preci-sion and enjoyment that made others' imprecision incomprehensible. As an adult looking back on his "instructive walks" the previous year with the village schoolteacher Zhernosekov, he imagines with won-der a typical answer to his own question: "Oh, just a small bird—no special name."[5]

II

This year Vladimir was no longer taught by English governesses or Zhernosekov but by Mlle Miauton. "Mademoiselle O," his portrait of his French governess, was the first part he would write of his auto-biography. Now chapter 5 of *Speak, Memory*, it exemplifies his life-long gift for detecting another's uniqueness without preconceptions or formulas.

Vast, Buddha-like, isolated by her ignorance of Russian, perpetu-ally imagining herself subject to insult, Mlle Miauton would fill her charges' afternoons by reading out endlessly from stock favorites of French literature, beginning with Corneille and Hugo.[6] What amazed her oldest pupil was the disparity between her unmoving bulk and the graceful mobility and purity of her voice: despite the limitations of her culture, her French was seductive. But even as a young boy Vla-dimir had no patience with her sighs of sentimental sympathy over a character or her laboring a moral as she read. Twenty years later, in *The Defense*, he would give Luzhin both his governess and his irrita-tion. In *Ada*, another forty years later still, the much-derided Mlle La-rivière, Van and Ada's French governess, has Mlle Miauton's moiré parasol, her bosom, her liking for Coppée's verse.

While Mademoiselle's voice streamed on unstoppably, Vladimir would look out through the colored panes of Vyra's veranda or at the sun breaking "into geometrical gems after passing through rhom-boids and squares of stained glass": again the memoirist blends the jewel-spectrum–stained glass motif with the motif of literature.[7] But although as a boy he had to learn by heart "chunks of Racine and other pseudo-classical ravings," he felt that his real sense of literature, even French literature, came not from Mlle Miauton's readings but from his father's books.[8] In distant retrospect, like his character Luzhin, he would treasure the special savor of those afternoons. At the time, he merely stared through the colored glass of the veranda waiting for the lesson to finish.

Rowdy and adventurous, he spent little time with his mentors, unlike diffident Sergey, who adored Mademoiselle and often fell victim to his brother's energy. Looking back after Sergey had died a courageous death in a German concentration camp, Vladimir racked himself with thoughts of insufficient fraternal affection, a long story of unconcern, casual taunts, habitual dismissal: "there was not even any friendship between us, and . . . it is with a strange feeling that I realise I could describe my whole youth in detail without recalling him once."[9]

III

Nabokov's parents returned from their haven in Brussels and The Hague when they judged the emotions stirred up by the First Duma had had time to calm down. Not that Russia was tranquil in the wake of the 1905 revolution. Under Premier Stolypin, firing squads, revolvers, and bombs still continued their work of destruction. The leaders of the CD party, anxious for reform without violence, staged a conference to plan for the Second Duma. Within the conference V. D. Nabokov had a key role to play, although he himself was barred, like all who had signed the Vyborg Manifesto, from the new Duma itself. Denied direct participation in parliamentary politics, he did all he could to support the party in other ways, continuing to publish its weekly bulletin until it was quashed by the censor in 1908, and acting as one of the editors of *Rech'*, an unofficial CD organ and from its inception in 1906 the capital's foremost liberal daily.

When the Nabokov family left Vyra for St. Petersburg in the fall of 1906, they settled not in their own home but in a rented house at 38 Sergievskaya Street, near the Tauride Palace. The killing of the children in Mariinskaya Square on Bloody Sunday had had such an effect on Elena Nabokov's nerves—she even composed a story about the event—that she refused to return to 47 Morskaya until the fall of 1908.[10] Nabokov would later give the Sergievskaya Street house and its architectural ornaments to Luzhin's aunt in *The Defense*, the woman who teaches the boy to play chess.[11]

Influenza with a high temperature early in December 1906 developed into a severe bout of pneumonia early in 1907 and brought young Vladimir close to death. "Life seems to have stopped in this house; it is entirely concentrated at that child's bedside,"[12] his uncle heard in Brussels. For some time Nabokov had had a prodigious capacity for mathematical computation, but after having to cope in his delirium with "huge numbers swelling relentlessly in [his] aching brain," he suddenly lost the gift. His mother, always sensitive to his needs, surrounded the boy's bed with butterflies and butterfly books. "and the longing to describe a new species completely replaced that of discovering a new prime number." During a fever after another childhood illness, the boy experienced a rush of clairvoyance: in bed, he saw his mother taking a sleigh to the Nevsky and watched her enter a store to buy a pencil that was then wrapped and taken out to the sleigh by her footman. He could not understand why she did not carry something as small as a pencil herself—until she stepped out of his vision and through his bedroom door, bearing a four-foot-long Faber display pencil she thought he might have coveted.[13]

In later life Nabokov always sought to test the nature and boundaries of consciousness. These early illnesses offer a partial explanation: the mysterious loss of his gift for numbers; his delirium and his clairvoyance; and especially the sense of having "brushed through death" that he was later to give to some of his favorite characters (Fyodor, John Shade, Lucette). Hopeful that the void of nonexistence before birth might yield clues about the void after death, he would try as an adult to reach back to his first emergence into consciousness in early infancy.[14] His nebulousness during the slow convalescence from his pneumonia seemed to replay the whole process, but with the observer now awake.[15] Partly as a result of his brush with death and his eerie moment of clairvoyance, Nabokov would always suspect that although consciousness might appear to be cut off in death, it could well in fact simply undergo a metamorphosis we cannot see.

This hypothesis, which he preferred to keep tentative, probably owed something to his lepidoptera. In his twenties, echoing Dante, he wrote in a poem: "We are the caterpillars of angels"; in his sixties he joked to an interviewer about his future plans: "I also intend to collect butterflies in Peru or Iran before I pupate."[16] Insect metamorphosis for Nabokov was not an answer to the riddle of death, not an argument, a model, or even a metaphor to be taken seriously. To a Russian Orthodox archbishop who suggested to Nabokov that his interest in butterflies might be linked with the highest state of the soul, he replied provocatively that a butterfly is not at all a half-angelic being and "will even sit on corpses."[17]

But on the other hand metamorphosis *is* a strong reminder that nature is full of surprises. In an early story, "Christmas," a boy keen on butterflies dies in a delirium in wintry St. Petersburg and is buried at his country estate. Before returning to town, his father sifts through his son's possessions in the unheated manor house, and brings a box-ful of mementos back to the heated annex where he will sleep one more night. Sinking for hours into deep despondency, he resolves on suicide rather than a life "humiliatingly pointless, sterile, devoid of miracles." At that moment a loud snap resounds in a biscuit tin he has brought in from his son's room. The cocoon of a tropical moth his son had bought bursts open, warmed by the roaring stove nearby, and a great *Attacus* moth emerges: "its wings—still feeble, still moist—kept growing and unfolding, and now they were developed to the limit set for them by God. . . ."[18]

That last word might suggest another source for Nabokov's interest in a beyond. In fact, once past the stage of children's prayers he always remained completely aloof from "Christianism," as he called it, utterly indifferent "to organized mysticism, to religion, to the church—any church."[19] Because his mother was of Old Believer stock, she had what Nabokov considered a "healthy distaste for the ritual of the Greek Catholic Church and for its priests," but equally important for the boy's development was her intense and pure religiousness: "equal faith in the existence of another world and in the impossibility of comprehending it in terms of earthly life."[20] V. D. Nabokov was more conventional, and would take his children fairly often, especially in Lent, not to the vast St. Isaac's Cathedral nearby but to the very select Church of the Twelve Apostles in Pochtamtsky (Post Office) Lane, almost behind their house.[21] Curiously enough this chapel occupied two elegant halls in a building designed by the celebrated Quarengi for Catherine the Great's favorite, Prince Bezborodko, for whom the Rozhdestveno manor that Nabokov would inherit at sixteen was also built. Despite the gilt-and-marble splendor of the setting, Vladimir told his father on the way back from a service, sometime before he was ten, that he found it boring. "You don't have to come then."[22] Not for him the traumas of a Stephen Dedalus.

IV

Electric tramlines were being laid down everywhere in St. Petersburg in the spring of 1907, and city streets were a mess. But from this year on it would in any case be even sweeter than before to escape town and head back to Vyra, which now held out the prospect of butterfly hunts all summer long. Every morning if the weather was fine enough for the insects to emerge, Vladimir would spend four or five hours in pursuit. Tenser and greedier than usual, gloomy and exultant with concentration, he would also find that for the duration of the chase he was no longer the strictly right-handed person he was in everyday life—as if the jolt to his head when butterflies ousted numbers had also realigned the hemispheres of his brain.[23] One overcast day, foraging in a lumber room, he discovered among engraved and marbled old tomes whole armfuls of more or less recent books on lepidoptera, priceless finds that he took down to devour at leisure in the corner study where he spread his own butterflies.

On his way back from the morning's chase, Vladimir would often see his uncle Vasily's carriage speeding over from Rozhdestveno. Usually there would be a crowd for lunch; afterward, the grownups would move out onto the veranda or into the drawing room. Vasily, however, sporting a violet carnation, would stay behind in the sunny dining room, and sit young Vladimir on his knee, fondling him "with crooning sounds and fancy endearments, and I felt embarrassed for my uncle by the presence of the servants and relieved when my father called him from the veranda: 'Basile, on vous attend.' "[24] Humbert's first feignedly nonchalant fumbles with Lolita, a painter's penchant for little Ada's bottom, the adult Nabokov's disapproval of homosexuals and his solicitude for childhood innocence may all have their origins here.

Although Uncle Vasily looked rather like Proust and suffered from "a Proustian excoriation of the senses," although he set to music his own French verse and had at least one story published in Russian, his nephew summed him up quite fairly as a man whose colorful neurosis should have gone with genius but did not. He was only a society dilettante—and no less interesting for that:[25]

> His flaws and quirks annoyed my full-blooded and rectilinear father, who was very angry, for instance, when he found that in some foreign gambling-den, where the young G., an inexperienced but wealthy friend of Uncle Vasily's, was beaten by a cardsharp, Vasily, a master at sleight-of-hand, sat to play with the cardsharp and very calmly swindled him to recover his friend's losses.[26]

Fifty years later Nabokov drew on this for Ada, where he has Van Veen cheat at cards to recoup what friends have lost to a flashy rogue

V

After early summer at Vyra, the Nabokov family set off in August 1907 for the south of France, their first trip there since 1904, and took an apartment at Biarritz for the duration of the St. Petersburg autumn. On the beach this time Vladimir fell in love with a Serbian girl called Zina—who obviously heard much of his other passion, for she offered him a dead hummingbird moth found by her cat. Eager to discover for himself all the unfamiliar species the new location offered, Vladimir spent hours out with his green muslin net, catching much more fetching prey—like Cleopatra, a positively tropical-looking charmer with lemon-and-orange wings.[27]

Butterflies would become a trademark for Nabokov throughout his writing career. On the title page of one of his early verse albums appears an india-ink drawing of a specimen mounted above the identification label "Vl. Sirin. Poems. 1923." In America relaxed letters to friends would be graced with a butterfly below the signature; books inscribed to family or friends might harbor gaudy multicolored hybrids. After the success of *Lolita*, Nabokov and photographers cooperated to make him—in *Time*, *Life*, *Vogue*—the world's best-known lepidopterist, poised with his net on a mountain slope, or perched in his study over a tray or a page full of butterflies. As if even in 1907 they were already conspiring to set the pose of future fame, his parents brought to Vyra the distinguished photographer Karl Bulla—a year later he would visit Yasnaya Polyana to take one of the most memorable images of Tolstoy—to record their son's passion: Vladimir with butterfly book, Vladimir and mother with book (wrong angle: butterflies not visible), Vladimir with Uncle Vasily (insects conspicuously reemerged).[28]

At this point it might be worth dismissing two misconceptions about the lure of lepidoptera. Butterflies never appealed to Nabokov because of their "beauty" ("All butterflies are beautiful and ugly at the same time—like human beings")[29] unless it was for the beauty of the chase. To a layman, the group Nabokov specialized in during the 1940s consists of rather drab little insects. And to those sentimentalists who opine, over their steak, over their claret from a vineyard drenched in insecticide, that collecting butterflies is a cruel pursuit— and perhaps therefore somehow typical of Nabokov—it should be pointed out that he hated to kill butterflies unnecessarily, and detested cruelty to any creature (man, cat, bird, bull) whose self-consciousness had evolved beyond invertebrate level. *"Beauty plus pity,"* he once wrote, *"—that is the closest we can get to a definition of art."*[30] His own pity for helpless animals was passed on from both parents. When a few years later he idly shot a sparrow, one furious outburst from his father was enough to make him realize what he had done. Here at Biarritz he saw Elena Nabokov, normally the gentlest of creatures, attack with her umbrella a boy tormenting a dog.[31]

In his infancy Nabokov would be dressed each morning by the current governess. Now he was older, he had a personal valet: first one Ivan, then another, then a Christopher who played the balalaika.[32] As his sisters grew older, Mlle Miauton now became exclusively *their* governess, while he and Sergey spent their afternoons in the charge of live-in Russian tutors, usually needy graduate students at the university of St. Petersburg. The first, Ordyntsev ("Ordo" in *Speak, Memory*), had arrived in 1907.[33] He was the son of a Greek Catholic, and the first in a series, as Nabokov noticed in retrospect, that seemed chosen to display all the variety of the Russian Empire: Orthodox, Jew, Roman Catholic, Protestant; Great Russian, Ukrainian, Lett, Pole; democrats, usually, but even, in 1915, for one short season—he would be the last of the tutors—a degenerate aristocrat who Nabokov decided was a madman and a scoundrel and who developed into a war profiteer.[34]

Ordynstev had accompanied his charges to Biarritz, but when the family traveled back to St. Petersburg on the Nord-Express in October, he was no longer one of their party: he had made the mistake of kneeling down before the dumbfounded Elena Nabokov with protestations of love. His successor, Pedenko, a Ukrainian, impressed the young Nabokov by showing him a few conjuring tricks. That same winter there followed a nameless Lett, who would punish his charge for misdemeanors by "suggesting that he and I put on boxing gloves for a bit of sparring. He would then punch me in the face with stinging accuracy." The boy was taught other skills. The coach of the reigning French tennis champion instructed him in tennis. In a less strenuous mode, his mother painted countless aquarelles for him, as she had since he was an infant, but although he remained emotionally indebted to her melting hues, his own experiments only made the paper warp and curl. In 1907 or 1908 his mother's former drawing master, old-fashioned Mr. Cummings, was hired for the boy: "a master of the sunset," he too left a trace in the boy who would render in words so many details of so many sunsets.[35]

VI

Like his mother, his father also watched keenly over the growth of young Vladimir's mind. But in 1908 V. D. Nabokov's politics would once again bar him from seeing his children. In December 1907 he and the other CDs in the First Duma had to stand belated trial for signing the Vyborg Manifesto, while as publisher of the party newspaper, he himself had to face an additional charge. In the reactionary mood then prevailing, a verdict of guilty was certain; barely able to veil his contempt for a court whose judges had to obey the bloody will of Nicholas II and his premier, he corrected proofs while he sat in the courtroom. Before the sentence was handed down, the accused were allowed to speak in their own defense. According to witnesses, V. D. Nabokov's speech was the most memorable because the most honest: if someone at Vyborg had been able to think of a better way of defending popular representation, he admitted, they would gladly have taken it.[36]

The sentence was three months' solitary confinement. After an unsuccessful appeal, he entered St. Petersburg's Kresty prison on May 14/27, 1908. A tall man, he could just stretch up far enough on tiptoe to see from his cell window the cupola of the Tauride Palace, home of the Duma. But he allowed himself little time for daydreaming. Following a rigorous schedule, he read Dostoevsky, Nietzsche, Knut Hamsun, Anatole France, Zola, Hugo, Wilde, and many others. In his double capacity as prisoner and professional criminologist he wrote while still in jail an extended series of articles, published in *Pravo* immediately following his release, arguing the futility of Russian penal practices. He stressed in particular the inability of incarceration to take individual differences into account: a sentence of three months' solitary might be pure torment for one man, while for another the same sentence, despite all its unpleasantness, could provide a chance to catch up on projects otherwise sure to be postponed.* He himself besides his other reading and writing also read the Bible in its entirety and taught himself Italian before broaching Dante and three books by D'Annunzio.[37] That capacity for work and a natural optimism would help his son, too, through oppressive times. While the self-imposed sentence of exile would induce sterility or voluble self-pity in many a Russian émigré writer, Vladimir Nabokov would compose with unstoppable, almost maddening energy and inventiveness as he sat in the cramped quarters of his rented Berlin rooms.

Although V. D. Nabokov was no doubt soothing his wife when he wrote her, "our three months in prison will earn us more laurels than thorns," his circumstances in prison were certainly not severe.[38] A new building, Kresty was vermin-free: he wrote that he only once saw a cockroach, and even that had obviously strayed from its path and looked quite lost. He had his own linen, he was allowed his collapsible rubber tub, there was ample hot water. But at first he could see his wife only every two weeks and even then a cage kept them from touching. He wrote her secret notes, usually on toilet paper, which would be smuggled out through a bribed guard. After receiving a butterfly from Vladimir in a note from his wife he wrote back: "Tell him that all I see in the prison yard are Brimstones and Cabbage Whites."[39] In another note he refers to his son as "Lody,"[40] an anglicized version of the regular diminutive "Volodya" and evidence of generations of Russian Anglophilia (think of Tolstoy's Dolly or Kitty, or of Nabokov's

---

* In *Transparent Things* Hugh Person, imprisoned for killing his wife, will positively scheme to be awarded the "celestial" comfort of solitary confinement.

own "Aunt Baby") that epitomizes in four letters the writer's Russian childhood.

When V. D. Nabokov was released from prison in August, his wife met him in St. Petersburg. Together they took the train back to Siverskaya, the stop nearest Vyra. Between the railway station and the manor house, peasants from three of the neighboring villages feted him in Rozhdestveno, with a ceremonial welcome home under arches of fir needles and bluebottles. His children had gone to wait for him in the village, and as Vladimir saw his parents drive up, he ran along the road to meet his father, crying with excitement. The peasants from grandmother Maria Nabokov's village of Batovo, though, were not there to greet him: she insisted on showing her disapproval of her son's politics by threatening her peasants with economic reprisals for the "revolutionary" act of demonstrating in his favor.[41]

VII

A week later Vladimir's parents set off together for Italy, leaving the children behind. The day before, the family had posed for a photograph by the archery target in the garden, Vladimir scowling with hatred of his stiff collar and Stresa.[42] Still, summer offered him compensations. As a collector, he did not yet venture beyond the woods and meadows between Vyra and Batovo, but twice that year he thought he had caught the first specimens of new species, only to find his ambitious dreams dashed by the experts to whom he had written. Even on the cold autumnal nights before his parents' return he could sugar for moths by painting tree trunks with a sticky-sweet brew. By the end of the year, despite needing a dictionary for almost every word, he had at the age of nine "gained absolute control over the European lepidoptera" in Hofmann's *Die Großschmetterlinge Europas*.[43]

In St. Petersburg that winter, as the winter before, Vladimir and Sergey had a part-time tutor for English, Mr. Burness. Since their tutor would do little more than set a dictation and, at the boys' request, repeat a bawdy limerick, Vladimir thought the man knew no more. In fact, as he later discovered, this reluctant pedagogue was a celebrated scholarly translator of Russian romantic poetry. After Burness's lessons ended, the Nabokov boys had no real occasion to speak English for another ten years, until they arrived in England in 1919.[44]

Summer's return always prefaced new pleasures. To the familiar delights of boating and bathing, tennis and croquet, archery and horseback riding, the summer of 1909 added the spills and speed of cycling. For this year Vladimir spent learning not to wobble off into the rhododendrons when he mounted his new "Dux," a sturdy machine equipped with a small siren rather than a handbell but without the license plate he would need in town. What could be more exhilarating than to defy gravity as he pedaled along the highway with his knickerbockered father beside him, nodding to peasants as they passed?[45]

Summer also meant grand family gatherings. From his earliest childhood, Vladimir had enjoyed the company of his numerous cousins: "with most of my boy cousins I was friendly at one time or another, . . . with most of the girls I was openly or secretly in love."[46] In this large and anniversary-conscious family there was a steady succession of summer fetes (Old Style dates): "namesday, two Elenas, May 21; namesday, three Sergeys, June 5; birthday, my father's, July 8; namesday, Olga, July 11; namesday, two Vladimirs, July 15; birthday, mother's, August 17."[47] Everyone would come—Uncle Vasily from Rozhdestveno, the Nabokovs, the Lyarskys and the Rausches from Batovo, the Sayn-Wittgensteins and the Pykhachevs from their nearby estates—for grand outdoor banquets on tables laid out in the alley of the old park by the garden. Less imposing but more amusing were the family picnics that offered an extra thrill if he could slip a butterfly net onto the charabanc unseen.

Even at his country estate, let alone in St. Petersburg, "a singular air of luminous brittleness" surrounded the young Nabokov.[48] But he also felt his childhood defined by a sense of utter completeness and security, epitomized in summer at Vyra, the altar of his nostalgia, the green backdrop of his Russian novels. *Mary*, *The Defense*, and *The Gift* take Vyra and its surrounds almost intact into fiction, and *Ada*, although it passes everything through the prism of Antiterran fantasy, focuses on the same spot at the same time of year. Once butterflies were associated with the estate, Vyra's power over Nabokov's imagination became even more irresistible. Just as Humbert's pursuit of nymphets was an attempt to relive his idyll with dead Annabel Leigh, so Nabokov's lepping trips in adulthood would be in part the only possible continuation of a broken past: his later searches for lost time succeeded most when he stood among alpine butterflies and trees reminiscent of the flora and fauna and flavor of his remote Russian north.

A party of twelve, including tutor, maid, governess, nurse, valet, and dachshund, the family in autumn 1909 again traveled to Biarritz, where they rented a villa for two months. Making castles down on the gleaming wet sand, Vladimir found himself beside nine-year-old

Claude Deprès, the "Colette" of *Speak, Memory* and the story "First Love." "Je suis Parisienne, et vous—are you English?" she asked, and the ten-year-old boy's first real romance had begun. Since his tutor, Boris Okolokulak ("Max" or "Linderovski" in *Speak, Memory)* had an interest in Claude's pretty Irish governess, surveillance could not have been less restrictive, and young love flourished. The climax was to be an elopement: goal, Andalusia, or perhaps America; funds, one *louis d'or*; luggage, one folding butterfly net in a brown paper bag. Vladimir and Claude got as far as the cinema by the Casino, where Okolokulak found them holding hands in the dark.[49]

En route back from Paris (and one last glimpse of Claude under a cold blue sky, by a fountain choked with dead leaves), young Vladimir succumbed as always to the romance of train travel. Already an insomniac, he found he could induce sleep best by imagining himself as the engine driver. He would picture the passengers under his care, the waiters and cooks and guards, as he stood "goggled and begrimmed" in the swaying cab, and peered ahead into the rushing night. Or in the daytime, as they clattered through some German town, he would attempt to envisage the train as if through the eyes of this or that passerby, stirred as he himself would be to see "the long, romantic, auburn cars" lumber out of the shade of a row of houses and, windows ablaze, catch the glory of the sinking sun.

So far, he was like any imaginative child. But he made a point of exercising his imagination, putting himself in the place of other people, trying to follow the contours of their thoughts and sensations. The more he began to realize how singular his imagination was, the more deliberately he would try to enter the singularity of other people and other things. All his life his tendency to prize highly his own individuality would be matched by his efforts to step outside himself and especially *into* the self of some disregarded person or thing. What began as the curiosity of the child persisted as conscious training for the sympathetic imagination and became Nabokov's characteristic way of looking at his world. And this theme of the imaginative exercise would later become prominent in his stories of the growth of a writer's mind.[50]

Back in St. Petersburg at the end of 1909, his own mind exercised itself through books. His early reading, he later commented, was that of any lively trilingual boy: an unforgettably illustrated, gaudily bound set of Jules Verne; enough English fiction—Conan Doyle, Kipling, Conrad, Chesterton, Oscar Wilde—to make up for the few chances to speak the language; in Russian, *Anna Karenin* and *Eugene Onegin*. When for the first time he reached the point where a disgruntled Oregin insults Lenski by disparaging the young poet's fiancée, he felt so upset he "mentally had Onegin next morning ride over to Lenski's to apologize—with the suave frankness that made the proud man's charm."[51] Lighter reading tended to be English: *Chums* ("Look out for the next instalment of this rattling yarn"), the *Boy's Own Paper*, and *Punch*. Even here Nabokov already knew what he wanted: in Palmer Cox's "Brownies" in *St. Nicholas Magazine*, his favorite, naturally, was "the fop (the individualist) in tophat and tails, with a monocle."[52] By late 1909, he was starting to move beyond such fare, and now had tacit access to his father's library. There in a modest nook his father's private librarian, Lyudmila Grinberg, a shy old woman in a pince-nez, maintained the card index from which a catalogue of the library was published in 1904, with a supplement in 1911. Presumably Vladimir waited till she had gone before tracking down the bits of Rousseau's *Confessions* that Mlle Miauton skipped in confusion.[53]

In 1910 a new tutor arrived: Filip Zelenski, the "Lensky" of *Speak, Memory*. The boys' best and longest-lasting teacher, he would remain until 1914. Every new tutor's arrival caused a scene. In this case, Vladimir was so struck by the contrast between Zelenski's slender front and thick rear that he could not resist a drawing. Zelenski snatched out of his hands the "repulsive caricature" and stormed out to the Vyra veranda—confirming as he walked the accuracy of the sketch. "There is your degenerate son's latest effort," he cried, thrusting it before Elena Nabokov. The boys soon made their peace with him when they discovered he was an excellent teacher and in need of their defense against the anti-Semitic scorn of reactionary aunts. On hearing their jibes, Nabokov reports, "I would be dreadfully rude to them and then burst into hot tears in the seclusion of a water closet." But loyalty did not prevent him from admitting to himself then and later that he never particularly liked Zelenski. All the same, he found him fascinating to observe and analyze. In this gauche pedant, he gradually discovered, "there lived a dreamer, an adventurer, an entrepreneur, and a naive idealist of the old-fashioned kind." High-principled Zelenski disapproved of the Nabokovs' footmen in their sky-blue livery, and considered French, which he did not know, "an aristocratic convention of no use in a liberal's home."[54]

VIII

Young Vladimir learned another curriculum from his cousin and best friend, Yuri Rausch. Because Yuri's parents were divorced, his mother sometimes left him at Batovo for the summer. Spindly, fearless, and almost two years older than Vladimir, Yuri would set the pace for their rivalry in derring-do or love. Courting risk by shooting at each other spring pistols loaded with sharpened sticks, they would reenact scenes from Mayne Reid's wild West stories or fight mock duels beneath the huge lindens and birches of the *grande allée* at Batovo.* Many years later Nabokov looked back on Yuri's death in a reckless cavalry charge in the Civil War and commented that "he never really awoke from the bellicose and romantic daydream in which he was so absorbed during the previous summers, but in which I took a much more casual part. I had lots of things beside mustangs and painted feathers, he had nothing but his heroic youth."[55]

Tired out by their wild West antics, they would stretch out on the grass to discuss girls: "After having made me sign an oath of secrecy with blood, Yuri told me about the married lady in Warsaw with whom at twelve or thirteen he was secretly in love and whom a couple of years later he made love to." With nothing more than memories of children's balls or girls on French beaches, Vladimir had a hard time to match his friend's true confessions. But already he found the boyish was beginning to shade into the manly, and Louise Poindexter, Mayne Reid's heroine in *The Headless Horseman*, could serve as a focus for his fantasies: "her twin breasts sinking and swelling in quick, spasmodic breathing, her twin breasts, let me reread, sinking and swelling. . . ."[56]

What Nabokov does not record in *Speak, Memory* is that in this fusion of the heroic and the romantic his muse was born. This year, he translated *The Headless Horseman* from the English—not, as one might expect, into Russian prose, but into French verse, in its classical garb the alexandrine.[57]

IX

In other respects too Nabokov was maturing rapidly. By 1910 his butterfly passion had fully taken wing. In July, he ventured beyond the familiar Vyra-Batovo terrain to a peat bog his mother and her brothers had called "America" because of its mystery and remoteness. Here a different kind of huntsman could find all sorts of Turgenevian and Tolstoyan game, but for the young Nabokov, a slender boy in a straw hat, there lurked wonderful species of northern, almost arctic, butterflies. By now, too, he had a fair degree of scientific sophistication. Like

* In the 1950s Nabokov would try to prove in his *Eugene Onegin* commentary that Pushkin had fought a real duel on this very avenue (*Eugene Onegin*, 2.433).

his Ada Veen, he reared interesting caterpillars very assiduously and successfully; he had "dreamed his way through" Seitz's multivolume *Die Großschmetterlinge der Erde*; he read English and Russian entomological periodicals and took notes in English on the butterflies he collected, employing terms gleaned from *The Entomologist*—where ten years later his first lepidopterological paper would appear. Already he understood the upheavals in taxonomy and the need to reject the old amateur system of butterfly classification, already he had a lively interest in evolution and mimicry.[58]

Perhaps without butterflies Nabokov's life would have meandered in a different direction, or perhaps he would have found another course through the same fertile plain. At any rate the channels along which his mind ran were gouged out more deeply by his love of lepidoptera—and that would help fix the contours of his mature epistemology, his metaphysics, even his politics.

Contrary to popular belief, Nabokov accepted the world as real, so real that there is always more and more to know—about the scales of a butterfly wing, about a line of Pushkin. Even as a boy he was irate that Hofmann, author of the best guidebook to European butterflies, failed to include rarities not because they were unknown or unobtainable but in order not to burden the amateur devoting summer leisure time to the pleasures of nature.[59] Even then, Nabokov rejected the idea of barriers to curiosity.

But if more can always be discovered, the world can hardly be accepted as a mere given, as what everyone "knows" is "reality." Too much depends on the way each of us looks at the things around us. While young Nabokov's cousins see a wooded slope as a place for cops and robbers, he himself prizes it as the lair of a bark-colored moth. Exotic foreign place-names conjure up in his mind not a bullrun or a monastery on a hillside, but a local species of fritillary.[60] Or as he would later phrase the matter in his lectures, a farmer sees a patch of countryside in terms of his daily round, a city man knows it only as the way to a nice eatery in the next town, a botanist looks at it in terms of grasses and flowers and ferns, "and of course we could bring in a number of other beings: a blind man with a dog, a hunter with a dog, a dog with his man, a painter cruising in quest of a sunset, a girl out of gas—."[61]

While the world certainly exists, so-called objective reality is only a purée of averages and lowest common denominators. Nabokov always prized the particular, both for the sake of the thing (that insect is not just "some bug" but a Yucca moth) and for the sake of the individual who perceives it. As a boy he first sampled the joys of precise knowledge when he stalked butterflies through guidebooks or groves;

in his sixties and seventies such pleasures had only become more addictive, and he would point out to visitors or readers the names and habits of the birds dotting the placid and hazy waters of Lake Geneva like flyspots on a steamy bathroom mirror. Actual discovery promised an even fiercer thrill: a boy's dream of finding near St. Petersburg a strayed Asiatic or Mediterranean butterfly, or a new species entirely; or the dream's revised realization when in America in the 1940s and 1950s he discovered new species, new organic structures, new mysteries in the evolution of wing markings.

For Nabokov epistemology grades imperceptibly into metaphysics. He had a crisp sense of the concreteness of the world but he saw too that the succession of deeper and deeper levels of specificity only emphasizes the mystery of things. At rare moments when the world seems startlingly present it can also seem to recede simultaneously into an infinite unknown, as ecstasy prepares to pounce:

> the highest enjoyment of timelessness . . . is when I stand among rare butterflies and their food plants. This is ecstasy, and behind the ecstasy is something else, which is hard to explain. It is like a momentary vacuum into which rushes all that I love. A sense of oneness with sun and stone. A thrill of gratitude to whom it may concern—to the contrapuntal genius of human fate or to tender ghosts humoring a lucky mortal.[62]

The possibility of discovering endlessly more and more about butterflies, or for that matter any aspect of the world, convinced Nabokov that perhaps nature—or whatever lurked behind it—might almost have hidden its secrets for human detection. While even ubiquitous matter deceives by the complexity beneath its apparent simplicity, nature seems at its most artful of all in mimicry. How can we explain in terms of the struggle for life a protective device like "the imitation of oozing poison by bubblelike macules on a wing (complete with pseudo-refraction)" which has been "carried to a point of mimetic subtlety, exuberance, and luxury far in excess of a predator's power of appreciation"?[63] From the first, Nabokov's fascination for mimicry, that "silent, subtle, wonderfully sly conspiracy between 'nature' and [man]," led him to ponder the artistry of nature: is there some conscious design in the universe beyond what we can see?[64]

Nabokov's development as a writer might be described as his exploration of more and more powerful ways of imparting to his fiction the delights he found in entomology: the pleasure of the particular, the shock of discovery, the intuition of mystery and playfully deceptive design. Having learned through his butterflies that the world is much less to be taken for granted, much realer *and* much more mysterious than it seems, he made his worlds to match.

Lepidoptery also confirmed Nabokov's distaste for the generalization and the pressure of the group. Nabokov's passion for lepidoptera, based itself on an alertness to the particular, became powerful enough to make *him* decidedly particular: it is hardly "normal" to feel steeped in bliss because you are up to midthigh in the mud and chill of a bog. He always appreciated his parents' perfect sympathy for his need to be alone with his butterflies, no matter how odd and "unhealthy" that pursuit might look to his cousins or aunts or schoolteachers. Because he enjoyed so intensely such an eccentric and consuming passion he had his own special motives for adopting his father's political principles and advocating the freedom, in his own version of Pushkin's words,

> To give account to none, to be one's own
> vassal and lord, to please oneself alone,
> to bend neither one's neck, nor inner schemes,
> nor conscience to obtain some thing that seems
> power but is a flunkey's coat. . . .[65]

X

In the early autumn of 1910 the Nabokovs traveled to Germany. At Bad Kissingen Vladimir was about to join his father and the venerable Sergey Muromtsev, the former president of the First Duma, for a long walk, when Muromtsev "turned his marble head to me, a vulnerable boy of eleven, and said with his famous solemnity: 'Come with us by all means, but do not chase butterflies, child. It spoils the rhythm of the walk.' "[66] At the next stop, Berlin, Vladimir and Sergey had to remain three months to have their teeth fixed and set in braces by a celebrated American dentist. Sergey's top teeth protruded, Vladimir's were growing higgledy-piggledy, with an extra one in the middle of his palate, as if he were a young shark.[67] Their parents left them in Zelenski's charge while they themselves visited Munich and Paris before returning to St. Petersburg.

Vladimir did not appreciate at all the "democratic" impulse that inspired Zelenski to move their quarters from the luxurious Adlon Hotel to the lifeless lane where they took a vast, somberly rococo apartment in the gloomy Pension Moderne. Since Zelenski did not know what to do with the boys, especially when it became too cold for tennis, they began to frequent a roller-skating rink in the Kurfürstendamm. Vladimir soon noticed among the regular visitors a group of young American ladies, one of whom he singled out for adoration:

"For obvious reasons"—in honor of Louise Poindexter and her twin breasts—"I decided her name was Louise." The boys also managed to prevail on Zelenski to take them to the Wintergarten—and there on stage, all stockings and flounces, were "Louise" and her friends, mere dancing girls. Vladimir "knew at once that it was all over, that I had lost her, that I would never forgive her for singing so loudly, for smiling so redly, for disguising herself in that ridiculous way so unlike the charm of either 'proud Creoles' or 'questionable señoritas.' "[68]

Still, that disappointment was just part of growing up. This skinny eleven-year-old was after all an ordinary adolescent, and when his parents returned to Berlin to check on the boys, he had to ask his father about erections. "That, my boy, is just another of nature's absurd combinations, like shame and blushes, or grief and red eyes."[69] But at the same time Vladimir's activities in Berlin show the unique adult waiting to emerge: visits to Gruber's famous butterfly shop every other day for the specimens he had ordered of newly discovered species; reading *War and Peace* for the first time on a Turkish sofa in that flat "giving on a dark, damp back garden with larches and gnomes that have remained in that book, like an old postcard, forever"; imagining in bedtime reveries "what it would be like to become an exile who longed for a remote, sad, and . . . unquenchable Russia."[70]

School: St. Petersburg, 1911–1914

the adjustment of the child to group life . . .

—*Lolita*

I

VLADIMIR and Sergey returned to St. Petersburg in December
1910.[1] Like all children of the well-to-do, they had received their
formal education for years at home, among governesses and tutors.
Now it was time for school.

In January 1911 V. D. Nabokov enrolled his sons, almost twelve and
eleven, at Tenishev School, a private school set up in 1900 by a mil-
lion-ruble grant from Prince Vyacheslav Tenishev. From its inception
it was one of the best Russian secondary institutions of its time. Emphatically liberal, democratic, and nondiscriminatory in terms of
rank, race, and creed, Tenishev was the result of a happy combination
of wealthy input and liberal inclination that was neatly summed up in
its splendid hall, the best-appointed auditorium in St. Petersburg outside the city's four main theaters. Designed as a forum for public debate, Tenishev Hall had housed the CD party conference that had
planned for the First Duma. Here too the Literary Fund, "that citadel
of radicalism," held all its sessions, over which V. D. Nabokov presided. With associations like these, he could have no choice for his
sons but Tenishev.[2]

School ran from 9 A.M. to 3 P.M., six days a week, from mid-Septem-
ber to late May, with a two-week Christmas vacation between semesters and a one-week Easter break. "Since snow and frost lasted from
October well into April," Nabokov notes, "no wonder the mean of my
school memories is definitely hiemal." Apart from three years of separate preparatory classes, schooling lasted sixteen semesters, in eight
numbered classes, more or less equivalent in America to the last six
years of school and the first two years of college. Nabokov began in
the second year, at the start of the third "semester" (American eighth
grade, British form two).[3]

After hurriedly preparing the extra homework he had not mentioned to his tutor the night before, he would have a brisk bath, dress—there was no school uniform—gulp down his cocoa and step out to either the gray Benz (first chauffeur) or the black Wolseley (second chauffeur) that would take him down the Nevsky and across the Fontanka Canal to 33–35 Mokhovaya Street, a compact four-story building in purplish-gray stone. Once inside, in the semi-darkness of the crowded cloakroom, he would doff his arctics, his short fur coat and his ear-flapped shapka, and rush up the stone steps into his own classroom. There he and twenty-one other boys sat at their hinged desks two by two, looking swarthy and sickish like everything else in the room under the humming lilac light struggling against the winter dark.[4]

Take out your books, boys. History, geography, geometry, algebra, physics, chemistry, Russian, French, German, and Scripture. As a *realnoe* ("modern") school, Tenishev opted for the scientific and practical (including, in later years, economics and law) rather than Greek and Latin. Since only modern languages were available, the Russian, French, and English Nabokov already knew so well were never to be challenged by the lure of the classics. English was not taught, and German, which he did begin to learn, was swept from the curriculum in the patriotic wave that in 1914 changed St. Petersburg's name to Petrograd. For Nabokov, French lessons even in the advance stream were unbearably slow, and strangely enough his trilingualism found an outlet only in his Russian classes, where the French or English phrases that came naturally to him found their way into his essays—and gave rise to the charge of "showing off."[5]

Not fitting in—at least in the eyes of the teachers—was in fact Nabokov's great problem at school. Whereas for Pushkin the fellowship of school life was a welcome reprieve from an inhospitable family, for Nabokov it was decidedly the reverse, an unwanted severance from a home that he loved and that had always provided him with both education *and* independence.

Starting school, he passed from the position of unqualified favorite to simply one among many. All children prefer the familiar; in Nabokov, that tendency was abnormally pronounced. Never reluctant to hide his distastes, he refused to touch "the filthy wet towels and the communal pink soap" in the washroom and disdained the well-fingered bread and the alien tea that the school provided at lunch, along with meat-and-cabbage piroshki and cold kissel.[6]

Above all he despised and resisted the pressure to conform. He refused to concede to egalitarianism: why should he take the new and "democratic" electric tram to school, if his father arranged every morning for him to be driven by car? One teacher suggested to him that

> the least I could do was to have the automobile stop two or three blocks away, so that my schoolmates might be spared the sight of a liveried chauffeur doffing his cap. It was as if the school were allowing me to carry about a dead rat by the tail with the understanding that I would not dangle it under people's noses.[7]

In future years his sisters, by contrast, would beg the chauffeur to stop behind *their* school so as not to be seen by other girls. Nabokov's choice should not be misunderstood. It was not a parade of wealth but a refusal to suppress differences. He was appalled to meet an old classmate in Germany who seemed to remember a single fact about the schooldays they had shared: that they were the only ones in their form with cars—"as if this linked us firmly together forever." Nabokov defied all the school's attempts to stir up his civic spirit and refused to join any extracurricular groups, unions, associations, or societies. He records that he did not give his school one grain of his soul and hoarded all his energy for home pleasures—*his* games, *his* enthusiasms and whims, *his* butterflies, *his* favorite tasks.[8]

Throughout Nabokov's writings schools cast an oppressive shadow. In *Bend Sinister* a nightmarish tunnel leads into the school where as a boy the philosopher Krug first meets Paduk, the classmate who later becomes the country's thuggish dictator, eager to reduce all to the lowest common denominator. Every morning of the school year Vladimir Nabokov too, in order to reach the pupils' entrance in the yard of Tenishev school, would have to pass through a coachway—"objectively" short, but to a reluctant schoolboy, and even in the memory of the adult Nabokov, quite certainly a tunnel.[9]

But school was no nightmare. Nabokov found as much here to feed his appetite for happiness as almost anywhere life thrust him. For his published memoirs he chose to depict his schooldays in terms of his contempt for enforced communality, but in private he could recollect life at Tenishev with energy and warmth.

He has described at length the glamour and forlornness of his goalkeeping at Cambridge, but it was his autumn and spring soccer in the schoolyard at Tenishev that haunted his memory most. The bell for long recess, a hiatus of silence, a stampede down the stairs, a quick change of shoes in the cloakroom, and out with the regulation rubber ball. The sudden thunder as feet run over iron covers on the ground and rush toward one of the two makeshift goals (the tunnel mouth at one end of the yard, the door into the school at the other) over which

Nabokov invariably stood guard. The burning slap of the ball in his hand, the black trace it left on his forehead. The ponderous reaction of authority:

> One of the more socially-minded teachers, who had a dim idea of foreign games, though thoroughly approving their group and social significance, harried me once with the question why, when I played football, did I (as passionately keen on goalkeeping as another might be on the rigors of monastic life) stand always somewhere "in the background" rather than running with the other "children."[10]

A bright pupil who found his studies no strain, Nabokov looked at his textbooks not for the material the class was required to learn but for the small type, the out-of-the-way facts, the fuel that could stoke the special fires of his fancy.[11] He was a chirping cicada, not an industrious ant, a playful otter, not an eager beaver. Curious, energetic, an excellent sportsman, he could take even to something like woodwork with gusto: "jack-planing and lacquering, making all kinds of nice things, from footstools to miniature helicopters, in an odor of fresh curly wood and heady turpentine." Decades later he could still recall with enthusiasm the smell of glue and paint, the appetizing feeling of a smoothly gliding plane, the rustling of emery paper on wood, and those little helicopters, "which for some reason we called 'flies,' rushing up to the ceiling—and to this day I can feel between my palms the twist of the shaft and then—vhrrr!"[12] Still, it was a huge relief when the last class of the day was over and the chauffeur came to drive him back as he had come, past Cirizelli's circus and Peto's toy shop to his own world again.

II

In Peto's, the best toy shop in town, his parents would buy him complicated jigsaw puzzles designed for adults—an English fad—or a do-it-yourself magic kit, a great box containing double-bottomed hat, spangled wand, trick card pack, and conjuror's manual—which, at eleven, he studied with fascination. He had no special aptitude for prestidigitation. Standing before the mirror, his face grim and pale, he would try to make a coin disappear or change denomination, but neither the legerdemain nor the patter came off.[13] Still, there was something magical in the way he looked at magicians.

Children's balls, dress-up affairs, speckled the winter season: Sergey as Pierrot, Vladimir as toreador, in cummerbund of sky-blue silk made by the house seamstress. One Easter evening, at the last such ball of the year, Vladimir watched Mister Merlin's preparations through a crack in the door, and saw him half-open a *secrétaire* to slip in, calmly and openly, a paper flower, in a familiar way that contrasted atrociously with the enchantment of his art—even though Vladimir knew himself the deceptions of the conjuror's craft. The boy mentioned the rose's hiding-place to one of his cousins. At the critical moment, she pointed to the desk: "My cousin saw where you put it." Nabokov remembered the anguished expression that convulsed the poor magician—yet when the drawer was opened, the flower was not there, but under his cousin's chair.[14]

Another indelible scene took place at Cinizelli's. An English magician, well known in London but a newcomer to St. Petersburg,

> was about to perform a certain trick with a lighted lamp that apparently was going to disappear. The point of his performance was that he at first indulged in a fake display of his trick, that is he let the audience see, *as if* through his own clumsiness, which was wonderfully imitated, . . . the way he was concealing the lamp. The next stage was to be the surprise of the audience at the lamp *not* being where he seemed so clumsily to have concealed it. No sooner had the public noticed his awkward fumbling than it started booing—and so loud was the uproar that the act had to be interrupted. I was very sorry for the conjuror, but on the other hand such a subtle trick was entirely misplaced in a show mainly consisting of dancing horses, rednosed clowns and sad-eyed lions.[15]

Nabokov always saw life as deceptive and magical, operating with more mastery than it seems to show, and truth as a subtle conjuror who feigns to let slip more than was meant but in fact keeps much more, unsuspected, in reserve. As a writer he would gradually perfect techniques to match: the shuffling of conventions, the palming of sympathies, the uncanny transformations of words into worlds.

III

At school, Vladimir tacked a course between what he wanted to study and what he had to.[16] He and Sergey still had tutors at home, too, until 1915, but the most important part of his education during these years came neither from school nor from tutors but from his own reading.

V. D. Nabokov's culture and curiosity provided an excellent model. As a criminologist he read widely in psychology, and when Vladimir was twelve or thirteen had him read his favorite, William James.[17] James's respect for the mystery and many-sidedness of the mind, his critical sense, his eclectic summary of recent clinical findings, and his search for an evolutionary explanation of the mind may have helped shield Nabokov against the archaic mythmaking and witchcraft of Freud. Nabokov kept his admiration of William James for life—and never grew to like the novels of William's brother Henry.

V. D. Nabokov knew intimately the literatures of Russia, England, France, and Germany, and had taught his son at an early age the thrill of a great poem. His particular favorites were Pushkin, Shakespeare, and Flaubert, and by the age of fourteen or fifteen Vladimir, still able to enjoy the *Scarlet Pimpernel* or the *Boy's Own Paper*, had also "read or re-read all Tolstoy in Russian, all Shakespeare in English, and all Flaubert in French." And that was not all: "Between the ages of ten and fifteen in St. Petersburg, I must have read more fiction and poetry—English, Russian and French—than in any other five-year period of my life. I relished especially the works of Wells, Poe, Browning, Keats, Flaubert, Verlaine, Rimbaud, Chekhov, Tolstoy, and Alexander Blok."[18]

In town Vladimir found the books he wanted by browsing on the shelves of his father's library or in the black boxes of its card catalogue. On rainy days in the country he could range through grandfather Rukavishnikov's library at Vyra, or follow the extra shelves that spilled into an inner gallery where the iron staircase stood.[19]

Of course his taste had not yet formed. He first read *Crime and Punishment* at twelve and thought it "a wonderfully powerful and exciting book."[20] That is not the Nabokov we know. But at about this time he also read H. G. Wells's *The Passionate Friends*. Asked at the age of seventy-seven to name a neglected masterpiece, he chose this book—which he had not read for more than six decades—and cited one detail. At a moment of deep distress the hero, just to do *something*, points out the white covers on the furniture, and explains casually to someone else: "Because of the flies."[21] The poetry of the unsaid, the drama of the unsayable. What Nabokov did not recall is that this is the *only* intensely artistic detail in a book weighed down by sociological speculation of a kind that as an experienced reader he could not stomach. Even as an adolescent, he read with acute appreciation; apparently he had not yet learned to focus the hawklike critical eyes that would allow him such gleeful parodic swoops on "dead things shamming life . . . continuing to be accepted by lazy minds serenely unaware of the fraud."[22] Remember too as we read over his shoulder that as an adult Nabokov always denied that he was ever influenced by any writer.

Among the prose writers Nabokov read in these years, the most important to him were Gogol, Flaubert, Tolstoy, and Chekhov. Gogol he enjoyed for the exuberant caricature that reduces human vulgarity to two dimensions but manages to suggest a fourth dimension gaping below the unlatched trapdoors of its style. But Gogol works beyond his limits, losing control as often as he feigns to lose it, and Nabokov knew he was a dangerous model, impossible to emulate. He valued in Flaubert, the Flaubert of *Madame Bovary* and the letters, the dedication to art and to the truth of art, the self-consciousness about his creative task, the poetic handling not only of prose but of storytelling itself.

Nabokov was in some ways especially close to Tolstoy. The visual clarity and the sensory imagination of both writers are strikingly akin, and both probe oblique and fleeting movements of the mind with the same supple touch. Tolstoy's determination to seek the truth in his own terms always appealed to Nabokov, although his intermittent conviction that he had actually *arrived* at Truth may have done more than anything else to warn the young Nabokov that fixed belief only befouls the genuine truth of flexible art. In other ways, too, they could not be further apart: the massive pride and massive dissatisfaction with himself that drove Tolstoy on, the untroubled self-assurance of Nabokov; Tolstoy's deep distrust of art, Nabokov's equally deep sense of the artfulness of the world; Tolstoy's craving for a life free of the burden of consciousness, Nabokov's vigilant reluctance to relinquish consciousness.

Chekhov's conception of art was much closer to Nabokov's: an art that rejected false closures and deterministic structures, that avoided generalities and sought pity in particulars. This would be the only artistic program Nabokov could almost be said to share with another writer, although in Chekhov these aims remain quietly implied where in Nabokov they often emerge as an image, a reflection, a sparkling parody.

But in Russian literature the first two decades of the century were above all an age of poetry. "Never was poetry so popular," Nabokov later wrote, "not even in Pushkin's days. I am a product of that period, I was bred in that atmosphere."[23] In a lecture he summed up the period:

> Every corner of Russia teemed with poets. . . . Any poet who rented a concert hall and gave a reading of his verse could be assured of a numerous audience. One group of poets elected Igor Severyanin, a mellow-voiced mediocrity, Prince of Poets. The futurist poet Hlebnikov countered by proclaiming himself President of the Terrestrial Globe.[24]

Nabokov's father was unsympathetic to the new verse and his library of no use, but his mother was an ardent fellow enthusiast, and from a certain table at Volf's bookstore on the Nevsky, where the white paperbacks of recent poetry multiplied like mushrooms, Vladimir built up his own collection of symbolist, acmeist, futurist poets that he stored next to the butterfly books in his bedroom upstairs. By fifteen he had "read and digested practically *all* of the contemporary poets."[25]

The poetic revival in Russia began at the end of the nineteenth century with the new literary mood that called itself Symbolism. A reaction against the positivism and civic-mindedness that had dominated Russian criticism since the 1860s, Symbolism had three main emphases: first, the individual as prior to society; second, the independent value of art (art not as a means of addressing the social issues of its time and place in a necessarily "realistic" manner, but art as a series of unique cultural traditions that pose a challenge of innovation on their own special terms); and, third, the role of the artist in indicating a higher reality beyond the sensual world. Nabokov was in sympathy with all three. In fact in *The Gift*, his major contribution to Russian literature, his thoroughgoing attempt to revalue the Russian literary tradition by an attack on Chernyshevsky continues the rejection of utilitarian materialism with which Symbolism began.

As a youth Nabokov devoured Symbolist verse rapturously. In retrospect he dismissed almost all except Blok, but still acknowledged that the work of Balmont, Bryusov, Bely, Annensky, and Vyacheslav Ivanov, whatever their limitations, "introduced into Russian verse breaks and substitutions and mongrel meters that are far more syncopic than anything even Tyutchev had dreamed of," let alone Pushkin.[26] Believing strongly in the evolution of literature, Nabokov enjoyed the degree to which both poetry and prose had extended the resources of literary language beyond what had been available in Pushkin's day: the increasing richness and subtlety of mental associations, the greater acuteness and diversity of the senses and the emotions, the readiness to seek other architectures than logic, proportion. classical meter.[27] But neither the mistily sepulchral atmosphere of some Symbolist verse, nor a verbal constriction in which phrases seemed to be squeezed from a dropper, could appeal to him for long.

Nabokov thought Alexander Blok the greatest Russian poet of his time. Blok was much more romantic, fluid, intoxicating than his fellow Symbolists. "The youth of people of my generation," Nabokov has written, "was spent among his poems." Blok was "one of those poets that get into one's system—and everything else seems unblokish and flat. I, as most Russians, went through that stage." What attracted Russian ears was Blok's incomparable music, where thought and sound fuse as in a dream: and as Nabokov noted, no one could imitate that magic, let alone explain it. Less elusive, and closer to Nabokov's own mode of writing, is Blok's pervasive combination of mystery and a stylization that can become almost theatrical. Closest of all perhaps is Blok's "spiritual urge towards something divinely real and hopelessly unattainable which is concealed somewhere in the colors and sounds of the world."[28] Even here there are signal differences. Blok celebrates a Bohemianism of the soul, and reels unsteadily in the streets: he always seems to have just lunged for and missed the skirt-hem of the higher Reality. Nabokov on the other hand, like a clown on a tightrope, makes us dizzy but always keeps his balance even as he reminds us of the abyss below.

The one other poet of the time whose work Nabokov cherished since early youth and continued to value was Ivan Bunin. Generally rated much more highly for his prose (which Nabokov did not care for), Bunin has been called the only significant poet of the Symbolist era who was not a Symbolist—though for Nabokov such labels do not matter at all. As a poet, Bunin can lapse into the merely descriptive and has been dismissed as cold, a realist in verse. But at his best he evokes situations and charges them with feeling in a manner reminiscent of Fet, the last of the great nineteenth-century poets to advance the technique of Russian verse. The poetry of Bunin and especially Fet anticipates Nabokov's poetry more nearly than anything else he was exposed to in his youth. Nabokov notes that Bunin's blood and nerves, like Tolstoy's, seemed somehow like his—"but that is a far cry from literary influence."[29]

By the beginning of the 1910s the Symbolist wave had created its own countersurge, Acmeism. Although the best work of Gumilyov, Akhmatova, and Mandelstam still lay ahead, Gumilyov—a sort of crisper Kipling and one of the favorite poets of Nabokov's youth—was in 1913 already promulgating the Acmeist program.[30] To the murk and visionary glimmers of much of Symbolism he opposed the *craft* of poetry; a master of the rhymed line, he had a concern for technique that appealed to a poet like Nabokov who both in Russian and in English would try to revitalize rhyme. Impatient with the poetic symbol, alive to "this resounding and colorful world,"[31] Gumilyov proposed that Acmeism should be "always aware of the unknown without corrupting its image with likely or unlikely guesses."[32] The most successful of Nabokov's early poems are those in which he heeds this advice. And to some extent the whole development of his later career can be seen as constituting, like Acmeism but along a different track, a reaction to Symbolism: to let things be themselves, stand for nothing else, and nevertheless to allow the very texture of this sharp-edged world to hint at mysteries beyond.

Futurism, Russian modernism's third poetic wave, peaked in the years 1911–1914 and churned into a comic froth of sects: ego-futurism, cubo-futurism, Centrifuge, the Mezzanine of Poetry. To Nabokov it remained a kind of "literary provincialism."[33] Although he had an ear for the radical decomposition and recomposition of language evident in Khlebnikov or Mayakovsky (who at moments can be "bolshie" in the English slang sense: exuberantly disruptive), in his own work such devices were never more than a pause or an overtone in a fluid cadence of thought. The futurists jostled to outflank each other at the extreme, like the poet* who in 1916 anticipated John Cage's most famous piece of music by decades when he wrote a poem with no words. In *The Real Life of Sebastian Knight* Nabokov would concoct a mock futurist, Alexis Pan, "the inventor of the 'submental grunt' " whose output "seems now so nugatory, so false, so old-fashioned (super-modern things have a queer knack of dating faster than others)."[34] The futurists' radical experimentation influenced Nabokov only by helping to immunize him against the urge to experiment for its own sake.

Whenever young Vladimir mentioned some minor poet of the day, his father would retort by triumphantly reciting a torrent of Pushkin iambics.[35] Looking back in *The Gift* at his relationship to his father and his youthful poetic heroes, Nabokov writes:

> But when today I tote up what has remained of this new poetry I see that very little has survived, and what has is precisely a natural continuation of Pushkin, while the motley husk, the wretched sham, the masks of mediocrity and the stilts of talent—everything that my love once forgave or saw in a special light (and that seemed to my father to be the true face of innovation—"the mug of modernism" as he expressed it) is now so old-fashioned, so forgotten as even Karamzin's verses are not forgotten.
> . . . His mistake was not that he ran down all "modern poetry" indiscriminately, but that he refused to detect in it the long, life-giving ray of his favorite poet.[36]

For despite their prosodic innovations, Russia's poets at the beginning of this century, unlike modernists in England or Germany, were romantic or neoromantic, and none more so than Blok. That romanticism—in an uncritical and unfastidious form—would permeate Nabokov's early verse.

IV

The ferment of Russia's poetry affected even the very young. For Russians of Nabokov's generation, a "terrifying facility" for lyrical verse

---

* Vasilisk Gnedov.

was as much a part of adolescence as acne. When a year or so earlier cousin Yuri showed him a poem he had written, the ten-year-old Vladimir wrote another in reply. His cousin thought it looked suspiciously good, and challenged him. Yuri was right: Vladimir's "first poem" was plagiarized, and the two fought a mock duel to settle the matter. Since then Nabokov had been writing verse of his own in English, Russian, and French.[37]*

There were other more normal signs of adolescence. Yuri did not visit Vyra in the summer of 1911, and Vladimir had to cope by himself with his unfurling sexuality. On wet evenings V. D. Nabokov would read out *Great Expectations*, in English of course, to the assembled children,† but in moments of furtive solitude his son would crouch at the foot of a bookshelf to look up in Brockhaus's eighty-two–volume encyclopedia enticing terms like "prostitution" gleaned from school or Chekhov. In sunnier weather the morning's butterfly chase and the afternoon's sports still did not rid him of the physical restlessness that propelled him in the evening light along the country roads on his old Enfield bicycle or his new Swift. This summer he would ride every night at twilight past the isba of the family's head coachman, where Polenka, the coachman's twelve-year-old daughter, would be standing leaning against the jamb. She would survey his approach with a mysterious smile whose welcome disappeared as he drew nearer. He never spoke to her, but it was her image that "was the first to have the poignant power, by merely *not* letting her smile fade, of burning a hole in my sleep and jolting me into clammy consciousness, whenever I dreamed of her."[38]

That summer, on June 4/17, Kirill, the fifth and last of the family, was born, and Vladimir acted as godfather at the christening. In August Elena Nabokov took her children to stay with her sister-in-law Elizaveta Sayn-Wittgenstein at the Sayn-Wittgenstein's second estate, Kamenka, near Popelyukha, in the province of Podolsk, southwest Russia—the only occasion before the revolution, it seems, that Nabokov spent time in Russia other than in St. Petersburg or around Vyra, and a rare chance for him to catch butterflies from a different Russian fauna.[39]

Back in St. Petersburg the gray round of schooldays did not calm altogether the kind of feelings Polenka had stirred. Fleetingly Na-

* He also filled school textbooks with inept stories about kisses, crocodiles, and colorful Pinkerton detectives (letter to Sergey Potresov, September 28, 1921, Bakhmeteff Archive, Columbia).

† V. D. Nabokov was hardly the typical paterfamilias: within a few months he would publish a study of "Charles Dickens as Criminologist" as a vehicle for attacking capital punishment.

bokov refers in his autobiography to "all the flushed, low-sashed, silky-haired little girls at festive parties." Though none is mentioned by name, some of these little girls surely feature in the Don Juan list he drew up in the 1920s in imitation of Pushkin and with, like Pushkin, a playfully lax definition of his "conquests."[40] Marianna, Zina, Maria, Pelageya, Ekaterina I, Ekaterina II, Olga all appear between Claude Deprès (Biarritz, 1909) and Valentina Shulgin (Vyra-Rozhdestveno, 1915), the two girls selected for *Speak, Memory* and protectively renamed "Colette" and "Tamara."* We will never know who these others were or what they meant to him.

Nabokov's last glimpse of Colette conjures up, for the purposes of the autobiography, an image of a "rainbow spiral in a glass marble"; he first talks to Tamara in a "rainbow-windowed pavilion." These rainbows and this colored glass would serve to link the onset of his poetry and the role women played in awakening his imagination. In *Speak, Memory* Nabokov begins to bring the motifs together by focusing on Zelenski's unhappy stratagem of staging Educational Magic-Lantern Projections at the Nabokov home on alternate Sundays and inviting some of Vladimir's classmates to fill out the audience. Zelenski's aim, Nabokov realized in retrospect, was to help a penniless fellow student hired for the screenings, but at the time only two things preoccupied the twelve-year-old boy. First, the fidgety blonde cousin on his left, who sat so close to him in the dark of the crowded nursery that he could feel her hipbone move against his every time she shifted—"and this aroused in me sensations [Zelenski] never counted on." Second, the tedium and embarrassment hotly suffusing his body as he listened to all seven hundred fifty lines of a Lermontov poem, enlivened, if that is the word, by a mere four colored glass slides, and foresaw the revenge his classmates would exact the next day for their wasted Sunday: a thorough ribbing for his being so sissy as to have a tutor still.[41]

V

There was little chance anyone at school could call him sissy in any ordinary sense, for Nabokov's father had passed on to him his own strict sense of manliness and personal honor. To the outer world, the elegant V. D. Nabokov seemed almost a dandy; to his son, who saw him every morning flushed in the face from fencing or boxing prac-

---

* Presumably the "Polenka" of *Speak, Memory* is also a shield for the Don Juan list's "Pelageya."

tice, he was decidedly robust and full-blooded. In *The Gift* Fyodor speaks for Nabokov when he writes that what he loves most of all about his father is "his live masculinity": "had he caught me out in physical cowardice he would have laid a curse on me."[42] No wonder the theme of courage could become so prominent in Nabokov's writings.

One week in October 1911 that theme became all too prominent in the life of the Nabokovs, father and son. Although barred from electoral office, V. D. Nabokov was still a leading CD and one of Russia's best-known newspaper editors. The reactionary press attacked him so regularly that Elena Nabokov could compile, with studied impartiality, an album of political cartoons relating to her husband.[43] But one assault he could not laugh off.

In the summer of 1911 his newspaper, the liberal *Rech'*, charged a man named Snessarev, a writer on the staff of the ultraconservative *Novoe Vremya*, with taking massive bribes from Westinghouse, the suppliers of St. Petersburg's new electric trams. Snessarev responded with insinuations against the editors of *Rech'*, including the slur that V. D. Nabokov, being poor, had married a rich Moscow merchantess.* This affronted V. D. Nabokov's intensely chivalric standards of honor too gravely to be ignored. Despite having written only two years earlier two dazzling and celebrated articles against dueling as a feudal custom, he now felt compelled to call someone to account.[44] Since Snessarev's reputation made him "nonduelable" (*neduelesposobnyy*) in terms of the Russian code, too plainly a scoundrel to be an agent for clearing one's own honor, V. D. Nabokov asked the editor of *Novoe Vremya*, Mikhail Suvorin, the son of Chekhov's friend Alexey Suvorin, to print a retraction of Snessarev's remark and state that it had been published by editorial oversight. If Suvorin refused to oblige, he would construe this as solidarity with Snessarev's insinuation and would call out Suvorin himself.

V. D. Nabokov asked his brother-in-law and friend, Admiral Nikolay Kolomeytsev, one of the few Russian heroes of the Russo-Japanese War, to deliver to Suvorin the request for a retraction and if need be to call Suvorin out in his name. Suvorin refused the retraction, held himself not responsible for Snessarev's article, and declined a duel. The next day V. D. Nabokov summed up the story on the pages of *Rech'*. Rather than hide the fact that he was contravening the excellent case he had himself made against dueling, he explained to the very audience that had read his arguments that it was now "psychologi-

---

* In fact, when he married, V. D. Nabokov, although not fabulously wealthy, was far from poor, and his wife was neither of Moscow nor of merchant stock.

cally impossible" for him to deal with Snessarev's innuendo, after other routes were blocked, except by a challenge—a brave and touch-ing public admission that his abstract principles could not cope with even his own tangled instincts.

Suvorin replied in *Novoe Vremya*, declaring that he had not been called out at all, since the manner of the challenge violated dueling protocol. V. D. Nabokov however had at hand Suvorin's written reply refusing to answer "your challenge," and published this note in *Rech'*, commenting that obviously there was no point in calling Suvorin out again, since while refusing a retraction he also denied accountability.[45]

Young Vladimir, who never read the newspapers and had detected no change in his father's poise, was quite oblivious to all this, although he *had* noted that his father was having fencing lessons not with his normal French fencing master but with an even more celebrated ex-pert. But on Sunday October 23 *Novoe Vremya*'s regular writer of topi-cal doggerel published an account of the challenge calculated to make V. D. Nabokov look ridiculous. At school next day, Vladimir swooped on a copy of the paper that was provoking sniggers as it passed from hand to hand among his classmates. As he skimmed over the jangling rhymes all he could see was that his father might die—might already be dead—on the dueling ground. The rest of the school day passed in an agony of tension, as he ran over all the shades of his relationship to his father, shades unknown to those who saw only the public man: a pride without reserve or focus ("the best man on earth," Peter thinks in a story made from the incident), a sense that whatever his father did—as editor, criminologist, orator, committee member—they were always in touch, and in the midst of any of these occupations so for-eign to him, his father could give him a sign of belonging to the child-hood world where they were both somehow at one.[46]

Returning home at the end of the day, Vladimir heard his parents and his uncle Nikolay Kolomeytsev in casual talk on the stairs, and he "knew at once that there would be no duel, that the challenge had been met by an apology, that all was all right." Then at last the staunch self-control he had exercised all day exploded in hot tears.

In *Speak, Memory* Nabokov notes that ten more years were to pass before his father was shot, but

> no shadow was cast by that future event upon the bright stairs of our St. Petersburg house; the large, cool hand resting on my head did not qua-ver, and several lines of play in a difficult chess composition were not blended yet on the board.[47]

Here Nabokov treats his father's sudden death as some complex chess problem composed by fate, and in fact one of the main structural features of *Speak, Memory* is a whole series of anticipations of the fatal shooting that creates an eerie sense of foreplanning. As a thinker, Nabokov always stalked inscrutable fate, the incomprehensible gap between the unforeseeability of an event and the light it casts, once happened, back over the past, turning hitherto neutral moments into abortive tries or necessary preparations for an outcome now obvious. As a memoirist and a son, he hints again and again at his father's death but cannot bear to face it directly, and he organizes these hints in terms of both chess and fate as a tribute to the love for chess problems and the fascination with fate that along with so many other interests he and his father shared in life.*

VI

Just as his father boxed and fenced, so Nabokov himself learned boxing and savate, even years before commencing school, so that he need never be cowed or afraid to defend his honor. In the schoolyard these lessons stood him in good stead. Popov, the strong boy of the school, held back year after year, haunted the imaginations of the younger boys who shared his class. Gorilla-like, malodorous, frowning at a world he could not comprehend, he was the only person Nabokov ever remembers fearing—until their first fight. One day Berezin, the geography teacher, unexpectedly informed the entire class that young Nabokov and he were both having boxing lessons from the same coach. At recess Popov grinned: "Come on, show us how you box." When Popov hit him in the stomach, the younger boy responded with a straight left to the nose, drawing blood. Popov proceeded to maul him—but the satisfaction remained. Nabokov even acquired a taste for the sport, thoroughly enjoying his fistfights with the two or three main bullies. Although weaker than they, he could use his superior technique to defend ("out of a spirit of sportive foppishness") someone like his poor classmate Nikolay Shustov, a clumsy boy with a bizarre squint, teased for his explosive stutter. Here was more evidence for a charge of nonconformity: he fought English-style, with his knuckles, instead of using the underside of his fist in the Russian way.[48]

Nabokov confessed to having nightmares about Popov even as an adult, and yet sums him up as a rather kindhearted fellow. After all the fights they had, strangely enough, Popov developed a passionate

---

* Peter Struve, one of the most gifted of Russia's liberal leaders, identified the sensation of fate as the single metaphysical principle that defined V. D. Nabokov's every move (*Obshchee Delo*, April 7, 1922).

admiration for Nabokov as a goalkeeper "and oppressed me with his friendliness more than he had with his belligerence."[49] But Nabokov had friends of his own choosing, two in particular, who reappeared in his adult life in more welcome form.

Savely Kyandzhuntsev at eleven was the class genius. An Armenian, he was in Nabokov's judgment the gentlest boy in the school but also quick with the coarse quip. When the skeleton used for anatomy classes was discovered to be a young girl's, Kyandzhuntsev renounced his masturbator's motto "every man his own woman" and declared himself in love with her. Fat and indolent, he had completely lost his early brilliance by sixteen.[50]

Nabokov's closest friend was a boy called Samuil Rosov,

> a small delicate lad with handsome features and the heart of a lion. I remember the astounded stare of our worst bully who stood like a cliff when R[osov] attacked him with his little fists. He was first in my form, and generously helped everybody with tutorial elucidations, especially in mathematics. He and I discussed Chekhov and poetry and Sionism.[51*]

Nabokov mildly envied Rosov's status as the school's Benjamin: everyone liked him, and Rosov took it all so lightly he seemed not to notice. Sensitive, an idealist, Rosov shared Nabokov's sense of life's mystery and his sharpness of observation. He valued especially Nabokov's gift for looking at people with a smile and seeing them as they are: "Classifications did not exist for you—Kyandzhuntsev, *Armenian*, Rosov, *Jew*, Nellis, *German*. You distinguished people only by their individual characteristics and not by labels of any kind."[52]

Nabokov turned the same acute eye on his teachers. He could be impatient and unforgiving: he remembered for decades, for instance, the teacher who briefly and unsuccessfully taught art history and referred by mistake to the "tenuation" of columns. When a geography teacher attempted to spell "Nile" in Roman letters on the board, Nabokov conspicuously added the missing *e* while the teacher was absent for a moment. His classmates reproached him for humiliating the teacher, but he had picked his target.[†] Berezin, author of popular educational travel books (*China: The Land of the Rising Sun*, etc.) was "a cocksure arrogant person, whom it was a pleasure to tease." Nabokov

---

* More than half the class would usually be Jewish, and Rosov, already a Zionist, would bemoan the fact if the proportion dropped. By virtue of teaching subjects like accounting, commerce, economics, and law in its higher classes, Tenishev School came under the Ministry of Trade and Industry rather than the notoriously illiberal Ministry of Education, and so could more easily avoid the 5 percent maximum placed on Jewish enrollments.

† In any case, "Nil" would be correct in German or French.

abstained on the other hand when the class sized up the weakness of another geography teacher, Maltsev—"a pathetic little man"—and badgered him until he retreated to the window with tears in his eyes and stood there running his finger over the pane like a hurt child. But Nabokov's favorite teacher was the well-known historian Georgy Veber, a little man with a dry manner and a panoramic sweep, always wearing an old-fashioned pince-nez, always stroking his pointed beard: "the best teacher of history that I have ever met in any college or university in the world."[53]

VII

After the school year, summer came with a roar as the Nabokov family rode out to Vyra in their hardy convertible, a red Opel NAG with isinglass windows, that the second chauffeur Pirogov drove at a dashing sixty miles an hour. Indeed, Nabokov would recall, "the very essence of summer freedom—schoolless untownishness—remains connected in my mind with the motor's extravagant roar that the opened muffler would release on the long, lone highway." Although the means of reaching Vyra was modern, the estate itself remained in some ways curiously behind the times: since Elena Nabokov preferred it should keep its touch of old-world charm, it still lacked electricity.[54] No wonder that in the lost paradise of *Ada*'s Ardis and Antiterra electricity has been banned, and a little red runabout shares the road with an old calèche.

Once again, summer meant games, picnics, and nameday feasts, and the lure of butterflies, and the strangely ringing shrieks of peasant girls swimming in the Oredezh. And one day, in pursuit of some Parnassians that had fluttered into a riverside thicket, Vladimir caught a haunting glimpse, just a few feet away, of Polenka and three or four other naked children lolling and gamboling about the rotting wharf of an old bathhouse.[55]

Up to about his fourteenth year, when not reading avidly, catching butterflies, writing verse, or exploring the estate, Vladimir used to spend "most of the day" drawing and painting—painting in evening orange, for example, the crowns of the trees seen through the windows of Vyra's balcony.[56]

Since he was expected to become a painter in due time, lessons still continued back in St. Petersburg.* About 1910, Cummings, his

---

* There he also painted in a different style, daubing butterflies on his door and on the white Dutch tiles of the stove in his room as a sort of territorial marker. He would do the same in the Montreux Palace Hotel half a century later.

mother's old drawing master, had been replaced by Yaremich, whose approach—Nabokov dismisses him as "the well-known 'impression-ist' (a term of the period)"—was highly distasteful to a boy with a mania for precision. Far more suitable was the celebrated Mstislav Dobuzhinsky, a master of the fine line, who did for St. Petersburg what Canaletto did for Venice or Bellotto for Vienna. He gave Na-bokov lessons in the *piano nobile* of 47 Morskaya from about 1912 to 1914: "He made me depict from memory, in the greatest possible de-tail, objects I had certainly seen thousands of times without visualiz-ing them properly: a street lamp, a postbox, the tulip design on the stained glass of our own front door." Nabokov conceded that al-though he had a painter's imagination he lacked the technique to ex-press it, as Dobuzhinsky confirmed: "*you* were the most hopeless pupil I ever had." But Dobuzhinsky's training in visual exactitude and in compositional harmony would serve Nabokov well when he came to write fiction.[57]

Although the theater always meant less to Nabokov than literature or painting, it too fed his imagination. The St. Petersburg stage contin-ued to thrive, and V. D. Nabokov continued to frequent it with zeal. Scornful of much, his son nevertheless welcomed genuine freaks of theatrical fancy. He recalled with particular pleasure Nikolay Evrei-nov's version of Gogol's *Government Inspector* at the Crooked Mirror. fragments of the play as it might appear in five different versions: in a provincial theater, in the silent movies, or as directed by Edward Gordon Craig, Max Reinhardt, or Konstantin Stanislavsky. His favor-ite was the Moscow Art Theater parody: "the idea was that the first act must be on a Sunday morning because otherwise the officers could hardly have been able to gather at the Mayor's house, and if it were a Sunday morning *then* the bells of the neighboring church would be pealing. And if they pealed then they would drown the voices on the stage—which they did. Oh it was very amusing."[58] He did not need to wait for Joyce to see that upending realism and trying out multiple perspectives could be fun.

VIII

From his father Nabokov had other lessons to learn. If at school his liberal-minded teachers failed to instill in him a sense of social respon-sibility, it was because he set such store by his father's sense of *per-sonal* responsibility.

At least to the outer world the assured V. D. Nabokov had a cold, almost haughty air. Those who knew him better knew how sensitive he could be to anyone in a position of vulnerability. The brilliant O. O. Gruzenberg, defending lawyer when V. D. Nabokov was tried for his part in the Vyborg Manifesto, had seen his client's imperturbable coolness during the trial, and his refusal to conceal his contempt for judges merely carrying out the administration's wishes. But in 1913 Gruzenberg saw the other side of the man.

That year, Gruzenberg was chief defense counsel for a Jew named Mendel Beilis, who had been placed on trial for murder—although the evidence pointed quite clearly to a gang of thieves as the culprits—only because the notorious minister of justice Shcheglovitov was determined to inflame anti-Semitic feeling by reviving the old bogey of Jewish ritual murder. The Beilis case, Russia's equivalent of the Dreyfus affair, aroused indignation throughout Russia and around the world. Although *Rech'* was already sending its best journalists and although he was needed in St. Petersburg on editorial, party, and committee business, V. D. Nabokov, as steadfastly opposed to official anti-Semitism as he had ever been, felt compelled to travel to Kiev to attend as a reporter himself.

While defending his client, Gruzenberg discovered how different Nabokov looked now when not his own but someone else's fate was at stake. As they talked together a few days after proceedings had begun, Gruzenberg noticed that Nabokov's face had grown pinched, his wide-open eyes looked at him with such a sense of hurt and anguish that Gruzenberg felt he was not alone, that he had a fellow defendant, a fellow counsel, a fellow sufferer.

> From that day it became a necessity for me, like taking a draught of strong tobacco, to search out his eyes at particularly oppressive moments of the trial. I would see there a look of horror and pain. But as soon as Nabokov became aware of my gaze, he instantly let a curtain drop—and sent out before it his irony, his bored contempt for what was happening, his brotherly encouragement urging me on. In every minute of the intervals before and after each session, Nabokov tried with infinite patience to support and reassure me with valuable observations and reflections. Meanwhile, he became paler and gloomier.[59]*

That tension between cool exterior aplomb and inner warmth would belong to Vladimir Nabokov too. The man many readers thought had projected himself into the imperious Van and Ada Veen

---

* To the relief of all but the most fanatical anti-Semites, Beilis was acquitted, and the government set about harassing those who had helped thwart its aims. The journalist whose investigations the previous year had proved Beilis's innocence and identified the real villains was sentenced to a year's imprisonment for having remained seated while the national anthem was played in a Kiev park. V. D. Nabokov was fined for his reporting.

in fact cared more for their outclassed, overshadowed, frail little sister and victim, Lucette.

But sometimes as a boy he aped his father's hauteur without his father's sensitivity, and he had to be taught a lesson. When he was thirteen, his father caught him leaning back in his chair for his valet to remove his shoe for him. Afterward Nabokov senior warned his son firmly that that must never happen again.[60] It never did. Like Fyodor's father in *The Gift*, V. D. Nabokov had "an even temper, self-control, strong will-power and a vivid sense of humor; but when he became angry his wrath was like a sudden frost"[61] that was marvelously effective in passing on his personal principles. When Vladimir Nabokov's reputation for arrogant aloofness was at its height, in his years of fame at the Montreux Palace Hotel, he was in fact known by all the hotel servants as gentle, joking, generous, anxious never to offend or to demand too much.

Nabokov learned from his father as much by example as by stern precept. Over the 1913 Easter vacation Vladimir, Sergey, their father, and Zelenski traveled out to Vyra to ski. Zhernosekov, the village schoolteacher, invited them after their morning in the snow for what he called a snack lunch—in fact, a lovingly planned meal—in his lodgings in the schoolhouse that V. D. Nabokov had built. Just as they were about to eat, a footman arrived with

> a huge luncheon basket packed with viands and wines that my tactless grandmother (who was wintering at Batovo) had thought necessary to send us, in case the schoolmaster's fare proved insufficient. Before our host had time to feel hurt, my father sent the untouched hamper back. with a brief note that probably puzzled the well-meaning old lady as most of his actions puzzled her.[62]

This year, a stocky, kindly Swiss tutor, Nussbaum, filled in over the summer while Zelenski married and honeymooned in the Caucasus.[63] With the snows long gone and the birches and the racemosa in new-season green, Vyra was once again the happy hunting ground of a butterfly maniac. Nabokov provides the perfect emblem of his obsession in this poignant picture of Nikolay Shustov, the gentle boy with the violent stutter, one of his best friends and favorite playmates at school:

> His father had recently perished in an accident, the family was ruined and the stouthearted lad, not being able to afford the price of a railway ticket, had bicycled . . . [twenty-five] miles to spend a few days with me.
> On the morning following his arrival, I did everything I could to get out of the house for my morning hike without his knowing where I had gone. Breakfastless, with hysterical haste, I gathered my net, pill boxes,

killing jar, and escaped through the window. Once in the forest I was safe; but still I walked on, my calves quaking, my eyes full of scalding tears, the whole of me twitching with shame and self-disgust, as I visualized my poor friend, with his long pale face and black tie, moping in the hot garden—patting the panting dogs for want of something better to do, and trying hard to justify my absence to himself.[64]

When Emma slights Miss Bates at Box Hill, it takes Knightley's strictures to bring home the cruelty of her thoughtlessness, but she bears his reprimand "as no other woman in England would have borne it." Leaving Nikolay Shustov to mope in a strange house, Nabokov had his own internal Knightley,* his awareness of his father's scrupulous concern toward anyone in need of defense, to cause him agonies of self-reproach. Nabokov would remember that moment of shame for the rest of his life: it would take time for him to overcome the thoughtlessness of youth, but revering his father as he did he was readier than any other child in Russia to master his father's moral code.

All the same, he still learned too slowly to prevent more blunders, more pangs of conscience. His brother Sergey had been passionately interested in music since the age of ten. He took lessons, went to concerts with his father, played snatches of opera for hours on end on an upstairs piano. Vladimir would creep up behind the younger boy— actually bigger than him, but awkward, stammering and shy—and "prod him in the ribs—a miserable memory."[65] Then one day he saw a page from Sergey's diary on his brother's desk and as he read discovered Sergey was homosexual. In "stupid wonder," he recalls, he showed it to Zelenski, who promptly showed it to the boys' father. The diary "abruptly provided a retroactive clarification of certain oddities of behavior" on Sergey's part. In fact, Sergey had been withdrawn from Tenishev after two disastrous years—of unhappy romances, as now became clear—and had been sent to the First Gymnasium instead.[66] Perhaps Vladimir's belated self-reproach for that glance at the diary and his unthinking impulse to pass on the information may account in part for his fierce opposition in later years to any infringement of personal privacy.

IX

There were other changes in the household than Sergey's attending a different school. Mlle Miauton left the family to return to Switzerland. She had often theatrically packed her bags in response to

---

* Almost without exception those who paid written tributes to V. D. Nabokov after his death stressed the word *rytsarskiy*, "knightly," in describing his moral character.

imagined affronts, especially from Zelenski, whose incomprehension of French she considered willful. Now, on bad terms with the girls' governesses, she was at last allowed one day to continue her packing.[67]

In the spring of 1914 Zelenski too quit for good. By this stage Vladimir and Sergey had no need for a tutor, but a young man called Nikolay Sakharov (the "Volgin" of *Speak, Memory*), an impoverished student of noble birth, was given the role at the insistence of his optimistic patron, although his tutorial responsibilities never amounted to more than playing tennis with the boys and taking over the summer assignments their schools had set (and which some relative of his wrote for *him*). With little more than bland social graces to recommend him, Sakharov turned out to be not only the worst of the boys' tutors but a scoundrel and a madman. The first time he talked to his oldest charge, he casually informed the young lad that Dickens had written *Uncle Tom's Cabin*. Nabokov pounced with a bet and won a knuckle-duster. Wary thenceforth of broaching literary topics, Sakharov stuck to safer subjects, regaling Nabokov with evil rumors and foul stories—but always without a single gross expression—about people the boy liked.[68]

Out in the country too things had changed. To pay off her debts grandmother Maria Nabokov had been forced to sell off Batovo in the autumn of 1913. Henceforth, Vladimir's summer haunts would have narrower bounds.[69] But in other ways life expanded.

Yuri Rausch visited for a week in June. At sixteen and a half, he could easily impress his fifteen-year-old cousin with the formula $3 \times 4 = 12$ engraved on the inside of his cigarette case "in memory of the three nights he had spent, at last, with Countess G." As they strolled back from the village grocery store chewing on sunflower seeds, the older boy confessed to being "a staunch 'monarchist' (of a romantic rather than political nature)" and deplored Vladimir's "alleged (and perfectly abstract) 'democratism.' " He also recited samples of his fluent album poetry and relayed a compliment a fashionable poet had made about a striking long rhyme in one of his poems. Here at last Vladimir could compete, countering with his best—albeit unusable—find: "*zápoved'* " (commandment) and "*posápïvat'* " (to sniffle).[70]

A month later Vladimir first experienced in "the numb fury of verse-making" something that seemed to transcend boyish emulation.[71] As tension in Europe mounted toward war, Russia suffered a sticky, hot July, memorably recorded in the poetry of Akhmatova and Khodasevich. Taking shelter from a thunderstorm in a pavilion in Vyra's old park, Vladimir emerged after its brief cascade to be greeted by a rainbow and a shiver:

A moment later my first poem began. What touched it off? I think I know. Without any wind blowing, the sheer weight of a raindrop, shining in parasitic luxury on a cordate leaf, caused its tip to dip, and what looked like a globule of quicksilver performed a sudden glissando down the center vein, and then, having shed its bright load, the relieved leaf unbent. Tip, leaf, dip, relief—the instant it all took to happen seemed to me not so much a fraction of time as a fissure in it, a missed heartbeat, which was refunded at once by a patter of rhymes.[72]

He roamed through the park, caught up in a trance of composition. Late that evening he recited the finished poem to his mother—his father had been suddenly called to town in connection with the threat of war—and as he finished, he saw her "smiling ecstatically through the tears that streamed down her face. 'How wonderful, how beautiful,' she said"[73]—a judgment the adult Nabokov would be the first to repudiate.

Despite the masses of circumstantial detail in Nabokov's full account of this "first poem," it is a considerable stylization of the actual event. In his autobiography he presents the poem as a bolt from the blue, sudden and unprecedented, when in fact for five years or so he had been composing verse in three different languages. The poem he evokes was written not in 1914, but in May 1917, hundreds of poems later:

> The rain has flown and burnt up in flight.
> I tread the red sand of a path.
>
> .   .   .   .
>
> Downward a leaf inclines its tip
> and drops from its tip a pearl.[74]

A now-lost poem actually written in July 1914—but in the evening, and about one of those emotionally charged country sunsets, not the early afternoon scene featured in *Speak, Memory*—does in fact seem to have been a milestone for young Vladimir, if not in poetic quality, at least in the new sense of inspiration that made his earlier verse seem no more than a childhood fad. Now poetry had become a passion and a vocation. The next morning he wrote two more poems, and the flood had begun.[75]

Nabokov's choice of the 1917 stanzas to render the 1914 experience can be explained by two facts: both poems were composed at Vyra and reflect that setting, and the 1917 lines, being the earliest he included in his collected poetry, mark the beginning of his poetic canon. As for the pavilion which looms so large in *Speak, Memory*'s account: whether or not he was actually standing within it when inspiration struck for either the 1914 or the 1917 poem, Nabokov has introduced it to anticipate "Tamara," the girl with whom in 1915 he would pass beyond the chasteness of childhood romance. In the account of the poem's genesis, her name appears among others scratched on the pavilion's whitewash; one year later, he would talk to her for the first time at this very spot. Nabokov has stylized the facts to indicate that for him his art and his love for women are indissoluble.*

The setting also handily focuses Speak, Memory's pattern of rainbows and stained glass. The pavilion rises midway in its ravine "like a coagulated rainbow," and when Vladimir emerges from his shelter and its colored-glass lozenges the rainbow that arches down into a distant forest makes "poor relatives of the rhomboidal, colored reflections which the return of the sun had brought forth on the pavilion floor."[76] The colored-glass motif itself hints that his lone gropings in sexuality and prosody went hand in hand. For it was in a strangely sumptuous toilet in the children's wing, through whose stained-glass window (a knight with a square beard and mighty calves) he could see the evening star and hear the nightingales among the poplars behind the house, that he would compose his "youthful verse, dedicated to unembraced beauties, and morosely survey, in a dimly illuminated mirror, the immediate erection of a strange castle in an unknown Spain."[77] The poetry he wrote at that time, he says, "was hardly anything more than a sign of being alive, of passing or having passed, or hoping to pass, through certain intense human emotions"—such as, especially, "the loss of a beloved mistress—Delia, Tamara or Lenore—whom I had never lost, never loved, never met but was all set to meet, love, lose."[78]

---

* For Freud, of course, the artistic urge sublimates the sexual. Nabokov reverses the relationship. As a biologist and a keen reader of Bergson, he felt that in evolutionary terms sex shows nature at its most creative, its most imaginative. "It is not the artistic aptitudes that are secondary sexual characters as some shams and shamans have said,' he writes in Lolita; "it is the other way round: sex is but the ancilla of art" (138).

Lover and Poet: Petrograd, 1914–1917

Martin's avid, unbridled imagination would have been

incompatible with chastity.

—*Glory*

. . . in every book describing the gradual development of a given human

personality one had somehow to mention the war. . . . With the

revolution it was even worse. The general opinion was that

it had influenced the course of every Russian's life:

an author could not have his hero go through

it without getting scorched, and to

dodge it was impossible.

—*The Defense*

I

HIS HEART and mind set on love and verse, young Vladimir Nabokov had neither eyes nor ears for the smoke and rumble of history, until history came close enough to thrust him headlong out of the life he had known.

In Sarajevo on June 28, 1914, a Serbian terrorist shot Austrian archduke Franz Ferdinand. Hungry for Balkan territory, Austria blamed the Serbian government for the assassination and demanded a virtual protectorate over its neighbor. Russia, eager herself to nibble at the Balkans, flared with indignation that another country should reach out so rudely across Europe's tempting table. Throughout July 1914, as St. Petersburg sensed war lurching closer, Nicholas II's ministers looked more and more coldly on Paul Milyukov's editorial warnings in *Rech'* against Russian involvement in a European conflict. V. D. Nabokov was called from Vyra to the capital: *Rech'* was in danger. On July 17/30, the day war was declared, the newspaper was closed down.[1]

But only for three days. A nationalistic fervor quickly swept away the radical mood that had been gathering steadily in Russia since 1910. Workers who had been in the throes of a general strike in July now openly declared their loyalty to the tsar. Patriots, Nabokov's uncle Vasily among them, demonstrated outside the German embassy, three doors from the Nabokov home. Some stormed inside, throwing down papers and furniture to fuel a bonfire below and toppling the ornamental structure that crowned the building's facade; one embassy employee was killed. Though generally CDs and those to their left resisted such crude jingoism and signaled their stance by continuing to call the capital St. Petersburg rather than the official new Petrograd, Milyukov was soon leading a campaign stirring up enthusiasm for the war.[2] A foundation of discontent, crowds easily swayed and roused to violence. a drift toward imperialism by Russia's foremost liberal politician—the combination boded ill for Russia's future.

As an ensign in the reserves V. D. Nabokov was mobilized on July 21/August 3. Outfitted in the gray-caped trenchcoat of the Russian infantry, he headed north to Vyborg with his regiment, while his family returned to St. Petersburg. Like other society ladies, Elena Nabokov devoted herself to the war effort, conscientiously but rather ineptly setting up a private hospital for wounded soldiers, donning the gray-and-white nurse's uniform she detested, lamenting tearfully the ineffectiveness of part-time compassion.[3]

Back at school, a foppish boy with a slim Swiss watch, Vladimir had only poetry on his mind. Not a day passed when he did not write something. One short and "terrible" lyric "about the first of the moonlit gardens, with a motto from *Romeo and Juliet*," was dressed up in a violet paper binding and distributed among a few friends and relatives. To judge from the one line Nabokov remembers (*Nad rododendronom v'yotsya ona*, Over the rhododendron it hovers), lepidoptera emerge already in this early spring of his long publishing career.[4]

II

In May, V. D. Nabokov's regiment was transferred to Gaynash, on the gulf of Riga. Elena Nabokov could endure her husband's absence a little more easily for the company of Evgenia Hofeld, who toward the end of 1914 had replaced Miss Greenwood, last of Olga's and young Elena's English governesses. Evgenia Hofeld would remain with the family in Petrograd, Yalta, Phaleron, London, Berlin, and Prague, becoming Elena Nabokov's closest friend and chief support in the poverty and isolation of exile. Even in this first summer in the household she showed her devotion to the family, waiting for the postman every day at the steep bank near the mill, by the oldest lilacs in the garden, to bring Elena Nabokov her husband's letters as fast as she could.[5]

For Vladimir the summer of 1915 was to be a momentous one, but it began inauspiciously enough. He noticed that the chauffeur had left the family's red convertible throbbing by the garage, part of Vyra's huge stable. Next moment the adventurous youth had driven it into the nearest ditch. He would be fifty and balding before he tried to drive again, with almost equally dismal results.[6]

He also spent part of the early summer in bed with typhus. Recuperating slowly, with a nurse brought from Petrograd in constant attendance, was an airy, dream-slow luxury. As he lay in bed listening to the twitter of birds, the distant bark of dogs, the creak of a pump, he imagined with all the luscious languor of reverie what falling in love might be like. That summer his daydream came true.[7]

He had not yet seen her, but she had already spied him out from her tree of knowledge. Earlier in the summer he had been called upon by a youth of eighteen, Vadim Shulgin, who invited him to join a soccer team being formed in Rozhdestveno, and asked if a Nabokov meadow could be used for a friendly match against a team from Siverski. Vladimir rode over with his tutor Sakharov to the Shulgin dacha in Rozhdestveno to grant permission but turn down the invitation to participate himself. Unknown to him, Vadim's fifteen-year-old sister Valentina was sitting high up in an apple tree looking down at the handsome sixteen-year-old below.[8]

She was Valentina Evgenievna Shulgin on the dotted line, "Tamara" in his autobiography, "Mary" in his first novel, but on his lips she was always "Lyussya."[9] Nabokov has recorded his first love in tender detail: her name that she had scratched or penciled here and there on fences or walls in Vyra or the Rozhdestveno estate, all through the summers of 1914 and 1915, as if fate were scrawling advance notices of her presence; his first glimpse of her in a birch grove, with two less pretty graces, a sister and a friend; a charity concert in a barn, where the opera bass from Petrograd was only an intermittent distraction from the sight of her flashing Tatar eye and dusky cheek, her bare neck, her rich brown hair; his circling closer, on horseback and bicycle, to the dacha he had traced her to.

Then on "August 9, 1915, to be Petrarchally exact, at half-past four of that season's fairest afternoon," when he saw her and her companions enter the rainbow-windowed pavilion in Vyra's old park, he followed them in and talked to her for the first time. As he escorted them back to the village toward evening, he invited them all boating next day. The other girls tactfully made way for Lyussya: she turned up alone, and the romance was launched.[10]

Autumn came early that year. Strolling with her down the alleys cf Vyra's parks, throwing mushroom caps into the stone vases that lined Rozhdestveno's paths, Vladimir drank in her humor, her rippling laughter, her rapid speech, her cheeriness, her jingles, catchwords, puns, her vast store of minor poetry. His own verse had now found its object. Lying on the divan on wet August days, with the stove lit in the next room, he would compose poems swearing eternal fidelity— and after showing them to Lyussya, recite them to his mother, who shook her head tenderly as she copied them out into a special album.[11]

Lyussya was spending the summer in a rented dacha in Rozhde-stveno, between the church and that apple grove, with her mother and six brothers and sisters. The father managed the estate of a wealthy landowner in Poltava and lived apart from his family "We are only petty bourgeois, what would we know," she would declare with a silky laugh, but looking back in time Nabokov rated her sub-tler and better and brighter than himself. When he used to tell her they would marry as soon as he finished school, she would quietly reply that he was either utterly mistaken or deliberately playing the fool.[12]

In secluded spots among the meadows of Vyra and Rozhdestveno, the pair discovered the joys of sex. They did not go unnoticed. Evsey, Uncle Vasily's ribald old gardener, spotted Sakharov lurking in the bushes, telescope in hand, to spy on the young lovers. He sportingly informed Vladimir, who complained to his mother. Indignant at the snooping, she kept her maternal anxiety to herself and showed her son only her support. As August and September wore on, Vladimir would light the carbide lamp on his bicycle night after night. cycle through the rain, across park, bridge and highway to the Rozhde-stveno manor (Uncle Vasily was absent that year) and meet Lyussya on one of its pillared porticoes. His mother's only intervention was to tell the butler to leave fruit out every night on the lighted veranda for her son's return.[13]

III

When in September the family moved back to town, V. D. Nabokov had just been transferred there from the front.[14] Unlike his wife, he had some awkward questions to put to Vladimir after reading poems celebrating the nocturnal sequence from bicycle lantern to pillared porch to rustling dress. "What? You filled that girl?" A short lecture followed on the means by which a prudent gentleman kept women out of trouble.[15]

Now in the Asiatic Section of the General Staff, V. D. Nabokov worked in a building on Karavannaya Street—just around the corner from Tenishev School—which his son should in theory have passed every day. But this winter Vladimir had other priorities than school. Lyussya had returned with her family to their Petrograd flat, among the handsome houses on Sergievskaya Street. Skipping school, sometimes for three days in a row, Vladimir would meet her in the Tauride Gardens at the end of her street. Without Vyra's secret retreats, they found the snowbound era of their love a torture. Chaperoned meetings at her house or his were unthinkable, hotel rooms beyond their daring, walks in the frost were agonizing, and the back rows of cinemas and quiet nooks in museums allowed limited outlets for their "furtive frenzy." In retrospect Nabokov would see their restless quest for refuge as a preview of the plight of exile. The lack of privacy imposed a strain on their relationship that showed in his verse, where he reproached her for not loving as intensely as he did, or for not remembering as he did (a tall task) the moments they had shared. And yet, to judge by one of the many details in *Mary* that seem undiluted autobiography, they would both write piercingly tender letters to each other on the days they did not meet, recalling "the paths through the park, the smell of fallen leaves, as being something unimaginably dear and gone forever."[16]

IV

Nabokov's frequent absences did little to endear him to his teachers. One man in particular found his idle brilliance and his foppish independence particularly galling: Vladimir Gippius, his teacher of Russian literature and now also his headmaster. When in the latter role Gippius rang the Nabokov home to check why the boy was away again, he would only hear the doorman Ustin briskly reply that the master's son had a sore throat. Before setting off to see Lyussya, Vladimir would always keep Ustin well bribed.[17]

Once in the wide hallway where pupils let off steam in the winter Nabokov sent a chair's detached seat—the surrogate discus in a contest with a friend—flying squarely into his teacher's stomach as Gippius turned a corner at the wrong moment. Their relations would always have this jarring side. And yet for all their disagreements, Nabokov recognized Gippius as the kindest and most well-meaning of his teachers, someone who treated the boys as adults, and Gippius in turn noticed the originality beneath the boy's habitual insouciance. He once set an essay on the topic of "Laziness." Nabokov handed in a blank sheet—and was given a good mark.[18]

A fiery little man now in his late thirties, with flaming red hair and angular shoulders, Gippius had made a deep impression on Tenishev's one other celebrated alumnus, the poet Osip Mandelstam, a pupil from 1900 to 1907. Mixed with Gippius's passion for literature, Mandelstam recalls, was an intense passion for literary malice— which, it has been argued, might account for the vitriol in Nabokov's own critical phials. But since Nabokov's opinions about science or politics or psychology are as decided and provocative as his opinions on literature, and since they derive from a virtually innate refusal to accept the way others look at the world or to temper his difference from anybody else, there seems no reason to doubt Nabokov's denial that Gippius influenced him at all. He reacted only with irritation when biographer Andrew Field ascribed to Gippius a formative role in his literary development: "The Tenishev School's inflicting Gippius on me is no reason for your repeating the process."[19]

When Gippius spat out a line of Pushkin to demonstrate the false spondee in iambic verse, his outworn prosodic terms failed to arouse the nascent poet in his class. Not until a year after leaving school, when he discovered Bely's new metrical theories, did prosody excite Nabokov and suggest stimulating new technical challenges. But Gippius was himself a poet, who by 1916 had published four volumes of verse, and to the end of his life Nabokov rated his old teacher a much better poet than his celebrated cousin, Zinaida Gippius: his verse could be murky and grandiose, but it also revealed wonderful flashes of inspiration.[20]

But the real impression Vladimir Gippius made on Nabokov was his attempt to make conscientious citizens of his students. The boy enraged Gippius

by declining to participate in extracurricular group work—debating societies with the solemn election of officers and the reading of reports on historical questions, and, in the higher grades, more ambitious gatherings for the discussion of current political events. The constant pressure upon me to belong to some group or other never broke my resistance but led to a state of tension that was hardly alleviated by everybody harping upon the example set by my father.[21]

Far from being a spur to his son's politics, V. D. Nabokov's political activity may in fact explain the boy's indifference. Vladimir trusted his father absolutely, and from early childhood appears to have thought that what father thinks is right: leave politics to him. At school Nabokov's motives were simple. He happened not to like group activities or politics or, above all, gratuitous additions to the school day. The curious experience of watching teachers he knew to be perfectly well-intentioned hounding him with fanatic stubbornness must have steeled him against later demands to ideological commitment. Had he needed support, he could have turned to Chekhov ("Great artists and writers must take part in politics only in so far as it is necessary to put up a defense against politics. There are enough prosecutors and gendarmes already, without adding to the number") or Pushkin himself, harried, as Nabokov would later summarize it, from the left as much as the right: "discomfort and oppression can be engendered not only by the police regulations of a tyrannical government, but . . . by a group of civic-minded, politically enlightened radical minds."[22]

Gippius was one of those always on the alert for apocalypse. In his public lectures and articles he tried to stir a religious consciousness in the writers of his time, and contrasted the joy of life of the young generation, incomprehensibly inappropriate in these "oppressive days" (this had been in 1913), with their severe and unshakably responsible elders. No wonder he was at odds with someone like Nabokov, so full of irrepressible youthful energy. Once for instance when his friend Savely Kyandzhuntsev bet him he could not leap across the pond in the unheated second-floor gallery connecting the school and Tenishev Hall, Nabokov settled quickly on a ten-ruble stake, ran, jumped—and crashed through the surface ice to surprise a pallid goldfish. Just at that moment Gippius appeared. Nabokov claimed he had fallen in by accident, but Gippius syllogized that since he was a good skier, he could not have simply lost his footing, and sent him straight home.[23]

If Gippius wanted the young to appreciate the seriousness of the times, he now at least had some justification. After the humiliating military setbacks of early 1915, Russia suspected that the tsar and his ministers were incapable of winning the war. In some shape or other, catastrophe looked inevitable. But Nabokov still ignored the political world, and he would continue to do so, despite Gippius's exhortations, even through the tumultuous events of 1917. He refused to let anything impinge on his freedom to follow his own interests. But that would change when he awoke to the Bolshevik coup and discovered how much the world of politics could intrude on personal freedom. After October 1917, he would still remain largely indifferent to politics, but *one* political issue would move him to take up his pen again and again over the next six decades. As a youth in the Crimea, already half in exile, he would write poem after poem about Russia's lost liberty and the outrages of Bolshevik bloodthirstiness. As a mature émigré writer, he would incorporate within his last two Russian novels impassioned attacks on the ideology and the coerciveness of Soviet power. As an aging American, he would try to make a wider audience comprehend that it was not Stalin who buried Lenin and the supposed liberty he brought, but Lenin who crushed the freedom Russia had already won for itself in February 1917.

V

Once on a visit to the Nabokovs, the children's poet and literary critic Korney Chukovsky brought along his celebrated guest book, the *Chukokkala*, to which most of Russia's prominent writers and artists from Gorky to Evtushenko have contributed. Both father and son added their offerings: Vladimir's, signed "son of the foregoing," was a poem that has never appeared in print (certainly not in a partial facsimile of the *Chukokkala* published in Moscow in 1979). In February and March 1916 Chukovsky, the novelist Aleksey Tolstoy, the children's writer and historical novelist Vasily Nemirovich-Danchenko (all regular newspaper columnists) traveled to Britain with V. D. Nabokov and two other journalists. The British hoped that these representatives of the Russian press might be able to convince their readers at home, in a country suffering unprecedented military losses, that for all her unwarlike reputation Britain too was giving all she could to the cause. Although himself still in uniform, unlike his colleagues, V. D. Nabokov revealed that his war aims were not quite the official ones. He reported Britain's tactful silence about its alliance with a country whose internal polity offended its standards of liberty, and concluded his dispatches with the hope that the two powers' present cooperation would introduce all the sooner into Russia English notions of progress, justice, and freedom.[24]

Back in Petrograd meanwhile Vladimir had acquired from his mother the habit of smoking heavily. When he turned up at all to school, he was permitted as a senior pupil to sit in the student reading room and smoke, often consuming up to sixty short Russian cigarettes a day. Some senior pupils made better use of the school's space, regularly organizing readings by the city's poets. Vladimir, preoccupied with his own verse, attended only once, for Alexander Blok.[25]

His own work was already going public. Tenishev School's mimeographed magazine, *Yunaya Mysl'* (*Young Thought*), published in 1916 his poem "Osen'" ("Autumn"). In the next issue appeared the first published criticism of his work when the future philosopher Sergey Hessen singled out "Osen'" as the only poem meriting special praise in issue number 6. Also in issue number 7 was a translation of Alfred de Musset's "La Nuit de décembre," which Nabokov had written in December 1915 and dedicated to Lyussya Shulgin (he would publish a far better version of the poem more than a decade later). As not only a contributor to *Yunaya Mysl'* number 7 but also one of its coeditors, he seems to have been less wholly aloof from school activities than he later remembered.[26] A poem about peonies was set to music by a medical officer at his mother's field hospital and in 1916 was sung in a large concert in Petrograd by a singer named Vronskaya. Once while Sergey picked out the tune on the piano in the Nabokov's music room, Vladimir sat next door calling Lyussya from the telephone in his mother's study, and tried to filter the melody down to her through the telephone tube. As he continued to write poems for her, always passionate and personal, at times stylized, at times uncomfortably direct, he decided one deserved a wider audience than his school:

> My sense of utter surrender to art started sixty years ago when my father's private librarian typed out for me and posted to the best literary review [*Vestnik Evropy*] my first poem which, though as banal as a blue puddle in March, was immediately accepted. Its printed image caused me much less of a thrill than the preliminary process, the sight of my live lines being sown by the typist in regular rows on the sheets, with a purple duplicate that I kept for years as one does a lock of hair or the belltail of a rattler.[27]

For a sixteen-year-old to be accepted for Russia's most distinguished "thick journal" was an honor, though possibly not quite the commendation it seemed: *Vestnik Evropy*, admired for its political liberalism, was conservative enough in the arts to prefer the conventionally poetesque.

Perhaps it was the excitement of being accepted by *Vestnik Evropy* that encouraged Vladimir to publish his first book, sixty-eight poems written between August 1915 and May 1916, and all so plainly to and for Valentina Shulgin that its author later misremembered that he had signed it "Valentin Nabokov." When V. D. Nabokov proudly told his colleague Iosif Hessen that his son wrote poems, and not bad ones at that, Hessen dismissed them as he had dismissed proud reports of the boy's lepidoptera. On hearing that Vladimir would publish his verse, he protested so strongly that V. D. Nabokov hesitated before answering: "He has his own means. How can I cross his plans?" Vladimir went ahead and had five hundred copies printed at his own expense by the printer who had just handled his father's *Iz Voyuyushchey Anglii* (*From England at War*). The little white booklet, elegantly typeset, bore on its title page simply the engraved words "*Stikhi* (*Poems*) V. V. Na-

bokov." An epigraph from Musset set the volume's tone: "Un souve-
nir heureux est peut être sur terre / Plus vrai que le bonheur." According to Nabokov's later judgment, the book's versification was fair, its
lack of originality complete.[28]

Once time had eliminated the fear that Lyussya's mother would
choose to economize and stay on in town rather than rent the same
Rozhdestveno dacha again, spring became radiant with excitement
and promise for the young lovers: walking together through the slush
and confetti of the Catkin Week Fair; an interschool soccer game one
Sunday, where she saw him make save after save in goal; a copy of
his first book, fresh off the press, to present to the girl who had inspired it.[29]

It may have been this spring that Vladimir took part for a week or so
in a postexamination school excursion to Finland. Two classes traveled by train from Petrograd to Imatra, where the waters of the Finnish lake plateau appear to brim up right to eye level before spilling
down through falls of reddish-gray rock to make their way toward
Russia's Lake Ladoga. Forced marches and steamship rides took the
boys into the heart of the Lake Saimaa complex, with instructive dis-
courses on Finnish life and lore punctuating the expanses of water
and fir. Nabokov thought little of all this group uplift:

> It was a horrible trip, horrible trip. Horrible. I remember it was the first
> time in my more or less conscious life when I spent one day without a
> bath. It was terrible. I felt filthy. Nobody else seemed to mind.

What vexed him even more was that the butterfly net he had
brought proved almost useless at this time of year, this far north. Although the teacher supervising the boys was a naturalist, young Nabokov's specialty disturbed him:

> He should have been rather pleased to have a young boy who knew
> everything about butterflies. He didn't like it. . . . It would have been all
> right if I had been a group collecting butterflies. But one boy who was
> totally immersed in collecting butterflies—that was abnormal.[30]

At last, the end of spring—and then off to Vyra, never so keenly
awaited, never so sweet in coming. Vladimir and Lyussya lost themselves at once in thickets where they swore eternal love. She noticed,
though, an ominous side to her lover's poems: "the banal hollow
note, and glib suggestion that our love was doomed since it could
never recapture the miracle of its initial moments."[31]

In her rare twinges of moodiness, she maintained that their feelings
had chafed under the constraints of the winter. In Speak, Memory Nabokov chose to evoke the enchantment of first love and skimmed

quickly over the tensions of the summer of 1916. But it seems that for all the joy of their reunion the return to summer freedoms was also a disappointment, a failure to relive the rapture of the past—as the longed-for repetition of past ardors so plainly disappoints in *Mary*, in *Lolita*'s second motel odyssey, in *Ada*'s second summer at Ardis. The creator of Humbert Humbert and Van Veen was a jealous lover. He found especially baffling Lyussya's "habit of hiding behind some girl friend to whom she would attribute details of a romantic experience which so obviously surpassed my own. . . . I was tolerably certain she did not see other boys; but her gay negations were calculated rather to fan my jealousy than to dispel it."[32]

One obvious difference from the previous year was that Uncle Vasily was back at Rozhdestveno, and the pillared porches could no longer serve as a safe retreat.[33] Yuri visited for a week, too, now dressed in the uniform of an officer's training school. Vladimir had caught up with his cousin as versifier, and was drawing close as gallant, but now that Yuri was a soldier, he had to prove again he could match him in bravado. A new test of courage kept their comradely rivalry alive. They would adjust the ropes of a garden swing in such a way

> as to have the green swingboard pass just a couple of inches above one's forehead and nose if one lay supine on the sand beneath. One of us would start the fun by standing on the board and swinging with increasing momentum; the other would lie down with the back of his head on a marked spot, and from what seemed an enormous height the swinger's board would swish swiftly above the supine one's face.[34]

As if to confirm the passing of the test, Vladimir exchanged his clothes for Yuri's uniform on a stroll to the village. When three years hence Yuri rode in battle dress to a valiant if foolhardy death at a time when Vladimir was trying to join his regiment, the young Nabokov could not help an eerie shiver at the thought that they had so often exchanged places as the target for this or that test of nerve, and that that butchered body in the bier could so easily have been his.

Nabokov rehearsed parting from Lyussya too often that last summer, after too many trysts, to recall exactly how he and she made their last farewell. Early in the fall, she moved to town in search of a job, a condition her mother had imposed before agreeing to rent the dacha again.[35] On his return to Petrograd, Vladimir sensed that their love was over.

Back in town he also had to face the reactions to the little book he had "had the misfortune to publish." Vladimir Gippius brought a copy to class and had his students delirious with mirth as he fired his sarcasm at Nabokov's most romantic lines. The poems deserved it, but Gippius must have found it particularly soothing to hold up to ridicule the ardent explanation for all Vladimir's absences the previous year. Given a copy of the book by V. D. Nabokov, Korney Chukovsky wrote the young poet a polite letter of praise but enclosed in the envelope, as if by mistake, a rough draft outlining a franker judgment. Zinaida Gippius, a major Symbolist poet and sharp-tongued hostess of the capital's leading literary salon, told V. D. Nabokov at a session of the Literary Fund to tell his son, please, that he would never, never be a writer. A sycophantic journalist, L——, who had reason to be grateful to Nabokov's father,

> wrote an impossibly enthusiastic piece about me, some five hundred lines dripping with fulsome praise; it was intercepted in time by my father, and I remember him and me, while we read it in manuscript, grinding our teeth and groaning—the ritual adopted by our family when faced by something in awful taste or by somebody's *gaffe*. The whole business cured me permanently of all interest in literary fame and was probably the cause of that almost pathological and not always justified indifference to reviews which in later years deprived me of the emotions most authors are said to experience.[36]

VI

In the autumn of 1916 Vladimir's uncle Vasily Rukavishnikov died, alone, at a hospital in St. Maude, near Paris. Somehow no one had taken his angina seriously, and twenty years later at the climax of his first English novel Nabokov paid a curious atonement by having Sebastian Knight die, also alone and also of angina, in a hospital in St. Damier, near Paris. Writing in that new language Nabokov would eventually remake his fortune. Now, at seventeen, he inherited from his uncle the equivalent of several million dollars,* along with the two-thousand-acre estate of Rozhdestveno and its century-old neoclassical manor. Although the homosexual Uncle Vasily had been intensely fond of his handsome nephew, the inheritance of the family property had long been settled, as a matter of family order rather than personal favor, when the first three children were born: Rozhdestveno would go to Vladimir, the St. Petersburg home to Sergey, and Vyra to Olga. V. D. Nabokov was very much against his son inheriting such wealth at such an early age.[37]

* The bookkeeper told him in 1917 that he was worth £2 million.

Vladimir had spent the happiest hours of his happy youth on the porch of Rozhdestveno manor in the early autumn of 1915. Now the manor was his but the girl part of the past. While others were still deriding his rhymed professions of love, he had moved on. For almost the next ten years he threw himself into the amatory experimentation he thought necessary for an elegant *littérateur*. During late 1916 he seems to have had affairs with three women, one, Tatiana Segerfeld, a sister of Yuri Rausch and married to a soldier fighting at the front. With his new fortune the seventeen-year-old could treat them in style to Petrograd's finest restaurants—and no questions asked.[38]

Looking back at this phase of his life, Nabokov saw himself

> as a hundred different young men at once, all pursuing one changeful girl in a series of simultaneous or overlapping love affairs, some delightful, some sordid, that ranged from one-night adventures to protracted involvements and dissimulations, with very meager artistic results.[39]

In retrospect he judged his youth singularly talentless and derivative, poetically and romantically.[40] He fell for the ready-made experience as he did for the ready-made word. By the time he emerged from this phase, he had learned several lessons: a horror of the conventional all the more intense for knowing he had succumbed himself; a revulsion against the artist who claims that in the pursuit of his art he can treat real lives as he chooses; a sense of the difference between combustible eroticism and the imperishable fire of his first love. Lyussya kindled verse no less derivative than the lines some of her successors sparked, but in her case at least Nabokov attained an emotional heat that glowed through another fifty years of prose.

VII

As the winter of 1916 drew on, the reek of disaster thickened over Russia at war. Nicholas and Alexandra were in flight from reality. Rasputin's influence was unchecked at court, supplies had fallen perilously low, a food crisis was spawning new strikes. On November 1/14, 1916, V. D. Nabokov's colleague Paul Milyukov delivered a speech in the Duma calculated to reverberate through the country, rounding off example after example of governmental ineptitude with the question: "Is this stupidity or treason?" When even the moderate leader of the Fourth Duma hinted that the tsaritsa might be colluding with German interests, all Russia knew something had to give way. Workers found fewer and fewer reasons not to strike. In elegant salons it became fashionable to inveigh against the government. Even grand dukes, ministers, and generals were hoping or planning for a palace coup. And still Nicholas temporized, while the government all but ceased to function, and still Milyukov hoped that the decision would be taken to call the liberals to power.[41]

After a second bout of pneumonia (the first had been in 1907) and then measles, Vladimir was advised by his doctor to recuperate at Imatra in Finland, a winter as well as a summer resort. He set off with his mother in mid-January. There he met Eva Lubrzynska, who differed from Valentina Shulgin in every way: five years older than Nabokov, a Polish Jew, a young lady of fashion, cosmopolitan and learned (she had studied chemistry under Marie Curie in Paris). After Nabokov returned to Petrograd about February 19/March 4 (his mother stayed on, convalescing from bronchitis) his relationship with Eva developed into the only "more or less serious" romance to engage him, intermittently, over the next few years. He loved her thoughtfulness, her readiness to talk over the distant days of childhood, even, at first, her disbelief in simple happiness.[42]

On February 23/March 8 V. D. Nabokov picked his wife up from the Finland Station. The city was restless.[43] The February revolution, unexpected and unplanned, was about to begin. The previous day, after an intensifying food crisis, word had spread that the government had reduced the available bread ration. On February 23, women textile workers began a strike in honor of International Women's Day, and recruited through the streets with cries of "Bread, bread." The next day almost two hundred thousand joined the strike and penetrated into the heart of Petrograd, where Cossack troops proved unwilling to curb the demonstrations. By the twenty-fifth Petrograd was once again in the grip of a general strike. Nicholas II, away at the front, ordered it suppressed. On Sunday the twenty-sixth, armed troops guarded the city, but the crowds still returned. Although fusillades were fired here and there into pockets of demonstrators, the first whiff of rebellion could be detected in the army ranks. On February 27 the soldiers, refusing to shoot down their unarmed compatriots, began to mutiny in regiment after regiment. Arsenals were broken into, guns passed around like toys. The revolution was a fact.

V. D. Nabokov had gone to work as usual on the twenty-seventh. By the time he returned home, rifle and machine-gun fire could be heard.[44] Earlier in the day, still unaware of the speed of events in the capital, Nicholas had given the order to dissolve the Duma. In the Tauride Palace a group of Duma leaders formed a temporary committee that would become the basis of the Provisional Government. In another chamber of the palace, meanwhile, leaders of the socialist intelligentsia began to set up a soviet (council) on the model of those that had sprung up in the 1905 revolution and issued a call to workers and insurgent soldiers to elect deputies to this new body. Thousands drifted toward the palace.

With almost no reliably loyal troops remaining, the government resigned. On the morning of the twenty-eighth V. D. Nabokov kept indoors: officers were having their epaulets torn off or were actually facing attack, and there was heavy firing on the Morskaya and, a hundred yards down the street, on Mariinskaya Square. The fiercest battle of the revolution was fought in the Hotel Astoria, on the other side of the square and visible from the bay window in Elena Nabokov's study. Insurgent soldiers had demanded to have handed over to them the officers staying within the hotel, known also during the war as the Hotel Militaire. A machine gun replied by firing into the crowd below. The insurgents returned fire and stormed the building, and the hotel's entrance doors soon revolved in a pool of blood. Although women, children, and foreign military attachés were unharmed, Russian officers were brought down to the square and a number shot. (Small wonder V. D. Nabokov was never able to idealize the "bloodless" February days.) Refugees from the hotel began to turn up at 47 Morskaya: first V. D. Nabokov's sister Nina and her husband Admiral Kolomeytsev, then a family with small children brought along by some English officers the Nabokovs knew, then another family of distantly related Nabokovs. They were all somehow accommodated, and everyone sat tight that day and the next.[45]

By March 2/15 it was safe for officers to venture out. V. D. Nabokov set off to see what was happening at the Tauride Palace. Red flags were flying, a well-dressed man came up to shake his hand and thank him, strangely—and despite the recent political quiescence forced on V. D. Nabokov by his military office—"for all that you have done." He added vehemently: "Only do not leave us any Romanovs, we have no use for them." En route to the Duma, V. D. Nabokov was filled with elation: "It seemed to me that something great and sacred had occurred, that the people had cast off their chains, that despotism had collapsed." At the Duma Milyukov and others he knew seemed too deathly tired to carry on rational conversation, and he returned home.[46]

The temporary committee of the Duma had been pressuring Nicholas to abdicate—not to carry the revolution forward, but to stop it advancing further. That day Nicholas II abdicated in his own name and his son's, and in favor of his brother Grand Duke Mikhail. Although the next day (March 3/16) Milyukov urged Mikhail to become tsar and provide a constitutional anchor against the rising swell of anarchy, Mikhail refused the throne.

Only at this point did V. D. Nabokov enter the events of 1917. He was called in with Baron Nolde, another CD lawyer, to draft Mikhail's abdication manifesto. V. D. Nabokov in particular recognized the need for the manifesto to provide legitimacy for the Provisional Government. After all, this new body had been set up by a handful of members of the dissolved Fourth Duma (whose highly restricted franchise had in any case made it unrepresentative and little admired) and had survived even this far only by the complicity of the Petrograd Soviet, which commanded the real allegiance of the workers and insurgent soldiers. The act of abdication, penned in V. D. Nabokov's hand and signed by Mikhail that day, marked the end of the Romanov dynasty.

Claiming that the Provisional Government had come into being at the initiative of the State Duma, the abdication manifesto distorted the facts in a desperate attempt to foster the illusion of legitimacy. Assigning the Provisional Government "full power" until a new constitution was established by a duly elected Constituent Assembly, it was on the one hand revolutionary (neither Mikhail nor Nicholas had that "full power" to assign) and on the other a doomed attempt to curb extremist ardor.[47] The Petrograd garrison, fearing that any check on revolution might mean counterrevolution and reprisals for their mutiny, were easy prey to revolutionary demagogy and would allow the Provisional Government, through the Soviet, only the most conditional support.

Adamant that in war conditions the revolution would lead to disaster unless the monarchy survived, Milyukov resigned from the Provisional Government immediately Mikhail decided to renounce the throne. That evening V. D. Nabokov and other CD colleagues persuaded him to stay.[48] That turned out to be a mistake. In the euphoria that followed the revolution the nation at first enthusiastically supported the Provisional Government, but Milyukov's known monarchism and his stubborn rejection of any coalition with the left or any compromise on war aims cost the Provisional Government its chances of continued allegiance.

The majority of the first Provisional Government belonged to the CDs, Russia's leading nonsocialist party. Excluded from the government because of a "tactical need to mollify the Soviet by concessions to the left," V. D. Nabokov was offered the post—meaningless to him—of governor of Finland. He suggested instead that he be created head of chancellery in the Provisional Government, a sort of executive secretary to the cabinet.[49] The appointment was made, and on March 4/17 he was retired from his military commission. Trotsky later labeled him a minister without portfolio, but although this is clearly what Nabokov hoped the chancellery post might amount to, Alexander Kerensky prevented him from playing any political role. The only socialist and the only member of the Petrograd Soviet in the government, the theatrical Kerensky made it clear that if Nabokov participated in discussion and thereby strengthened (as Kerensky saw it) the CD element within the Provisional Government, he would stage another public tantrum.[50]

A war with millions dead, food and supplies on a downward spiral, a people expecting, now that revolution had come, either the immediate transformation of their lives or an outlet for all their accumulated hatred and envy—these were the circumstances the Provisional Government had to master, and without constitutional authority, a secure basis of power or popular support, or strong, unified leadership. (Prince Lvov, the nominal head of the government, was ineffectual, Milyukov and Kerensky, leaders of the liberal and socialist camps, temperamentally and ideologically opposed.) Nevertheless most members of the Provisional Government apart from Milyukov were revolutionary liberals at heart,[51] and within two months they had introduced freedom of conscience, the press, worship, and assembly; outlawed all religious, class, and ethnic discrimination; separated church and state; overhauled the military code; passed a political amnesty, abolished capital punishment and exile, instituted trial by jury for all offenses, and created an independent judiciary; introduced an eight-hour day, industrial arbitration, and rural self-government. At the same time the Provisional Government set up commissions to draft more complex reforms: V. D. Nabokov was a leading figure in the Juridical Council and the commission to review the criminal code. When Lenin returned from Swiss exile in April, he declared Russia "the freest country in the world"—and this in the midst of full-scale hostilities.[52] The Provisional Government's idealistic libertarianism made it impossible for them to refuse Lenin reentry, even though he had been shipped back from Zurich by the Germans, or to arrest him, even though he accelerated, as the Germans had hoped, Bolshevik agitation at the front urging desertion.

While the Provisional Government introduced basic freedoms with almost foolhardy idealism and rapidity, it also sought to defer major social reforms and the upheavals they would cause until after hostilities ceased or at least a Constituent Assembly was elected. But now that revolution had come, the peasants expected more land immediately, and their abstract new freedoms failed to earn the Provisional Government the gratitude and loyalty it had expected. At the front, peasant soldiers, the vast majority, deserted in huge numbers for fear of missing out on land reapportionment back at home. In the villages, peasants began to expropriate land by violence, and arson and lynch-ing grew rife. But no matter how urgent the pressure for land, the CDs adjudged that only the Constituent Assembly could decide on a new basis for property ownership in Russia in a nonclass spirit where *all* social interests could be heard.

To the impatient masses the CD's "nonclass" position seemed a com-mitment to social stability and a defense of bourgeois interests. That underestimated the idealism of the center and left CDs. Still, there was an abyss between popular hunger for the expected spoils of revolution and the social values of the CDs, at least early in 1917, if V. D. Nabokov can serve as a standard. One part of *his* reaction to revolution was to seek social rights he had been deprived of for his earlier opposition to the tsarist system: in March 1917, he petitioned to be reinstated into the Assembly of Noblemen in St. Petersburg Province.[53]

Before the revolution many sections of Russian society had come to blame the tsar and his government for the country's military defeats and appalling losses. Milyukov in particular, now minister of foreign affairs in the Provisional Government, saw the revolution as chiefly a protest against the poor conduct of the war and an opportunity to pursue war aims with more heart. Afflicted by war fever, he was con-vinced Russia could and should acquire the Dardanelles—would be morally wrong *not* to—when the victors divided up the spoils. Driving with Milyukov one day in March or April, V. D. Nabokov told him he was convinced that one of the basic causes of the revolution was war-weariness. Milyukov disagreed emphatically.

By April V. D. Nabokov was responsive to the arguments of the leading left-wing CD, Nikolay Nekrasov, that the party should allow socialists more say in the government, react more themselves to left-wing popular sentiment, and reexamine what opponents called the party's "classical imperialism." Milyukov on the other hand remained intransigent. When the Petrograd Soviet succeeded in pressuring the Provisional Government to commit itself to renouncing "domination over other nations" or "seizure of their national possessions," he sent a secret note to Russia's allies that the country was still aiming at a decisive victory. As soon as this was leaked to the press, on April 24/May 3, Petrograd erupted in turbulent demonstrations demanding Milyukov's resignation. The Provisional Government had come to its first crisis. Refusing to countenance further pressure from the Petro-grad Soviet, Milyukov stormed out of the Provisional Government, hoping to take the other CDs with him. On the contrary, they all re-mained. Despite his sensible criticism of Milyukov's obstinate poli-cies, curiously, Nabokov remained so much under his colleague's per-sonal spell that he regarded Milyukov's departure as a tragedy and continued his own role with little zest.[54]

VIII

One of Vladimir Nabokov's best critics observes that his family connections gave Nabokov "a ringside seat for observing the Russian
Revolution."[55] True, but he didn't show up for the big fight.

During the revolution one Tenishev boy, Friedman by name, a CD,
sagacious and shaggy-locked, clambered up onto a platform of boxes
in a public square in the city and began to deliver a fiery speech. After
his first words he was knocked down. That degree of involvement
was exceptional, but so was the apoliticism of his famous classmate.
At seventy Nabokov wrote:

> I remember, not without satisfaction, how fiercely and frequently, dur-
> ing my last year of high school in Russia (which was also the first year of
> the revolution), most of my teachers and some of my schoolmates ac-
> cused me of being a "foreigner" because I refused to join in political
> declarations and demonstrations.

Again, Vladimir Gippius was the most vehement. To rouse the boy's
political consciousness he assigned him as an after-school punishment an essay on the Decembrist revolt of 1825, the inspiration for the
revolution of 1905 as both were for February 1917. After reading the
essay Gippius told him in the low voice of suppressed rage: "You're
no Tenishev boy."[56]

The pressure had only one effect: to make Nabokov even more determined to preserve his independence. His recollection of classroom
assignments on Russian literature—on Gogol in particular, studied in
the final year—show that he was exposed even then to the social slant
he would later attack as a critic and a teacher. His position was the
same then as forty years afterward: literature appeals to the imagination, to the mind's eye.

> I recall not without pleasure that in my high school days I received
> a 2 [out of 5] or as it was called at Tenishev "highly unsatisfactory"
> for an essay [on Gogol]. . . . When we were assigned *Dead Souls* the
> note of social and moral bookkeeping was expected to sound within us.
> The bookkeeping consisted of the fact that Gogol's novel was divided
> up under the handiest headings—Plyushkin was a miser, Manilov a
> dreamer, Sobakevich clumsy and so on. It all added up, finally, to
> Gogol's merciless indictment of the miserliness, dreaminess and clumsi-
> ness of Russian landowners. Literature turned out to be interesting only
> in so far as writers depicted types, and of course we had to show whether
> the types were negative or positive. The unknown genius inventing our
> essay topics would sometimes give us an even profounder question,

what did the author want to show, say, in portraying General Betrishchev—and it was when I answered that the author wanted to show us
General Betrishchev's crimson dressing gown that I received the "2."[57]

Even then Nabokov sensed that what mattered in life were not the
public generalizations but the individual details no logic could ever
predict, for these are the terms in which our lives are lived. No one,
for instance, could anticipate a recollection as real as this:

> When we were a bit older, in the upper classes [Nabokov wrote to Rosov
> in the late 1930s] . . . you and I loved to visit the recreation hall for the
> "pre-school" class (who would chirp all together, somehow, like birds,
> rush around, catch us at times by the sleeve—a multisonorous shrill little
> hubbub, through which sailed a hoary downed head—what was his
> name, that teacher of the little ones, a little old man himself?—you see,
> I forget names too—Nikolay Platonych! and with a certain strange sur-
> prise, an excited-glum nuance I have often experienced in life since—
> forgive the brackets, but I have to fit an awful lot in) you said: "Were we
> too really like that so little time ago?"[58]

In May 1917 Nabokov had appendicitis and was operated on at
the Kaufman clinic, the best private hospital in Petrograd. While
under ether on the operating table he saw himself vividly

> in a sailor suit mounting a freshly emerged Emperor moth under the
> guidance of a Chinese lady who I knew was my mother. It was all there,
> brilliantly reproduced in my dream, while my own vitals were being ex-
> posed: the soaking, ice-cold absorbent cotton pressed to the insect's le-
> murian head; the subsiding spasms of its body; the satisfying crackle
> produced by the pin penetrating the hard crust of its thorax; the careful
> insertion of the point of the pin in the cork-bottomed groove of the
> spreading board. . . .

After this experience he decided he would never let anyone anes-
thetize him again. He dreaded the loss of consciousness as the foulest
of his most fearful nightmares.[59]

IX

Through their last summer in northern Russia the family stayed as
usual at Vyra, although V. D. Nabokov's political duties kept him in
town. Vladimir had had another poem printed in a venerable "thick
journal," in the March–April issue of *Russkaya Mysl'* (*Russian Thought*).
Over the late spring and summer he wrote the poems that would constitute his next book of verse, including in May "Dozhd' proletel"

("The rain has flown"), the first poem to merit inclusion in his 1970 volume of collected verse.[60] He would take the train in to Petrograd— Rosov recalled strolling through the city with him during the "white nights"—where presumably his chief goal was Eva Lubrzynska. And once, returning to Vyra, Vladimir saw Lyussya Shulgin on the train. Standing together in the vestibule of the rocking carriage he listened, "in a state of intense embarrassment, of crushing regret," to her talk of the office where she worked. She got off the train at an early stop, "and the further away she went"—at least in *Mary*, where the incident otherwise corresponds detail for detail with the remembered event—"the clearer it became to him that he could never forget her."[61] He never saw Lyussya again.

In Petrograd V. D. Nabokov continued to work on the Juridical Council and on revising criminal law. In May he campaigned on behalf of the CD party for elections to the Petrograd Duma. How little he was suited to the revolutionary demagogy that triumphed that year can be seen in his later admission: "When I had to take part in meetings, or whip up enthusiasm for the party, I often felt an oppressive awkwardness. I felt I was perpetrating an act of mental violence on my audience, who should choose themselves which party to follow."[62] He was easily elected himself, but as in local duma elections throughout the country CDs came a decided second to moderate socialists.

Late in June, Milyukov persuaded the CD Central Committee to shock the socialists in the coalition government by resigning. They might then realize, he hoped, that they had to reassert central authority in order to counter rising anarchy in the country, desertion and disaster at the front, and the splintering of the Russian empire. V. D. Nabokov and others opposed the tactic, but their minority was overruled, and on July 3/16 he and the other remaining CDs resigned from the Provisional Government.[63]

Lenin had from the first advocated the overthrow of the Provisional Government, but he was away resting in Finland as rank-and-file Bolshevik soldiers turned their comrades' fears of being sent to the front into the basis for a hasty armed rebellion. On July 3–4/16–17 triggerhappy demonstrators roamed the capital, engaging in pointless clashes in which four hundred were killed. In February the whole city had supported the angry crowds, but this time Petrograd proved indifferent or even hostile, and the indecisive revolt was called off. At the height of the rising V. D. Nabokov walked home from the editorial office of *Rech'* with Iosif Hessen. Trucks laden with rifle-wielding soldiers and sailors rushed past along the Nevsky, while their comrades, also armed, tramped in crowds along the pavement, calling one another to battle and shooting in all directions. When Hessen suggested they should take cover in the public library, Nabokov answered coolly that the bullet destined for him had yet to be cast.[64]

By mid-July Kerensky had been named prime minister. He still remained committed to the war. Those appalled by the collapse of the June offensive and the attempted Bolshevik seizure of power demanded that discipline be strengthened among the troops, and on July 12/25 the death penalty was restored at the front. As he tried to assemble a cabinet, Kerensky invited V. D. Nabokov—whose political leanings he had learned to assess more accurately—to be minister of justice. With his usual ability to persuade others to a position more rigid than they wished, Milyukov convinced Nabokov and two other left-wing CDs to lay down firm conditions before accepting the posts they had been offered: freedom from accountability to the Petrograd Soviet, and the deferment of major social reorganization (such as the transfer of land to the peasants) until the Constituent Assembly met. Kerensky could not afford CDs on these terms, and on July 23/ August 5 he formed a new coalition cabinet dominated by moderate socialists.[65]

X

While the Provisional Government struggled for air, Vladimir Nabokov remained with his family in Vyra, composing verse after verse—still, according to one poem, writing *her* name (Lyussya's? Eva's?) in the sand. The scene favors Lyussya, the statistics Eva: when he totted up his poems the following February, he noted that between June 1916, when he and Lyussya had only three or four months left, and July 1917, when he had known Eva for six, 31 of his 172 poems that year were written to Lyussya, 39 to Eva.[66] The poems had all been set down on separate sheets, but on August 1/14 he began a thin notebook, the first of a continuous run of manuscript albums of verse stretching from 1917 to 1923, growing by a poem almost every other day.

Stormy autumn had set in before the family headed back to town. Searchlights crossed like giant swords over Petrograd. Vladimir was deeper in his poetry than ever. He selected a dozen poems composed at Vyra between May and August to be published together with the work of another Tenishev schoolmate, Andrey Balashov. This second collection of his verse, *Dva puti* (*Two Paths*), was not printed until 1918, when he was already in the Crimea. Only one copy now seems to survive, making it the rarest of all Nabokov's books.

Before finishing his first notebook, he also had someone, probably his father's librarian, type up over a hundred poems he had written between September 1916 and August 1917. These were sewn together to be bound as an album, though any cover it might have had, as well as its first pages and perhaps its last, have now all been lost, and damp and mold have eaten their way through some of the sheets that remain.[67] As soon as his first notebook was filled up, in late September, Vladimir began a new album, dedicated to Eva Lubrzynska.[68] Before the album was finished, another revolution had struck.

XI

After the muddled fiasco of the Kornilov rebellion late in August, the capital's mood swung further to the left. With Milyukov absent from Petrograd, CD leaders like V. D. Nabokov were now ready to provide a bulwark against the swelling wave of Bolshevism by rapprochement with socialists and an end to the war. In September Kerensky attempted to regain the last shreds of prestige he had lost in the Kornilov affair by declaring Russia a republic and establishing a Council of the Russian Republic, or Pre-Parliament, to which yet another Provisional Government, the fourth, would be responsible. This Pre-Parliament did not meet until October 7/20—V. D. Nabokov was on its four-man presidium—and showed little sense of urgency, despite a complete breakdown of authority (banditry, pillaging, riots, arson) and obvious Bolshevik preparations for a seizure of power. Four or five days before the coup V. D. Nabokov asked Kerensky if he considered a Bolshevik rising possible.

"I would be ready to offer prayers for such an uprising to take place," he replied.

"And are you sure that you will be able to cope with it?"

"I have more troops than I need. They will be crushed once and for all."[69]

When the coup came, on the night of October 24–25/November 6–7, Kerensky's defenses proved an illusion. In February the whole city had been convulsed by popular unrest, but now theaters and restaurants still rang with laughter and well-heeled people thronged well-lit streets. Meanwhile, almost unnoticed, without a shot being fired, Bolshevik forces occupied the city's strategic points: railway stations, State Bank, telephone exchange.

There was a widespread eagerness to replace the moribund Provisional Government; multiparty democracy operating through the soviets, the councils of workers' and soldiers' deputies, was a popular principle; most assumed that the Bolsheviks were taking power in the name of the Petrograd Soviet and would learn Lenin's true intentions only over the next few months. Sharing these common attitudes, the Petrograd garrison failed to support the government and by their mere neutrality handed the Bolsheviks power. At 10 A.M. on the morning of October 25, two officers called on V. D. Nabokov, asking for a car to rescue Kerensky and drive him to head loyal troops marching on Luga, but the Nabokovs' old low-powered Benz landaulet, a city runabout, was no help at all.[70] By 11 A.M. Kerensky had found a car at the U.S. embassy and left at once.

During the afternoon of the twenty-fifth V. D. Nabokov and other members of the Council of the Republic were called to the Winter Palace, where the ministers of the Provisional Government were already assembled to conduct an ordinary session under military protection. Nabokov was the only one to respond to the appeal. When after two hours it became clear the ministers were merely adopting a wait-and-see attitude, he left the palace and returned home, half a mile away. The Bolsheviks closed the palace exits twenty minutes later and the storming of the Winter Palace (not the heroic affair of Soviet iconography) was about to begin: V. D. Nabokov had narrowly escaped imprisonment in the Peter and Paul Fortress along with the Provisional Government. Isolated skirmishing around the city set the scene for a night of sporadic firing. At 47 Morskaya, young Vladimir Nabokov continued composing poetry as usual. After the night's ninety lines he noted: "As I was writing, fierce rifle fire and the foul crackle of a machine gun could be heard from the street."[71]

The next day groups of Kronstadt sailors roamed the streets, brandishing the revolutionary bayonet at the bourgeois scum—to adopt the jargon of the times. Perhaps it was this morning that Vladimir was pounding away as usual at the punching ball in his father's library without thinking of the danger in its machine-gun-like ra-ta-ta, when some heavily armed street fighters came in through the window and had to be convinced by the butler that the young man was not a Cossack sergeant waiting in ambush.[72]

Through this troubled autumn Nabokov was still attending Tenishev School. It would have been his last term there even had the Bolsheviks not seized power, but presumably because of the coup, when it was already apparent that the family could not safely remain, he took his school-leaving exams a month before the formal time. He finished school with a four in physics, a five minus in Scripture, and a five, the top mark, in everything else.[73]

Before the Bolshevik takeover, the election for the Constituent Assembly had been set for November 12/25. This election, the first and last truly free election in Russia, marks more clearly than anything else the disparity between the idealism of the liberals and the democratic socialists—between V. D. Nabokov and all he stood for, and all his son admired in his politics—and the cynical manipulativeness that came with Lenin's fanatical drive for power.

One of Lenin's charges against the Provisional Government had been its delay in calling these elections. There had indeed been inefficiency in preparing for them, but for good motives. Since the elections were to decide the basis of Russian political and social organization for the next century, those arranging them had tried to ensure that they would be scrupulously fair and free from disruption, in a country where most were politically illiterate and vast numbers were fighting at the front. The Commission for Drafting the Electoral Law for the Constituent Assembly was frustratingly unwieldy, as large as a parliament—but only because of an idealistic attempt to represent a great many different groups. And it was delayed in first meeting not by a bourgeois Provisional Government dragging its heels to delay popular elections, but because the Petrograd Soviet of Workers' and Soldiers' Deputies was so late in nominating its representatives.[74]

After the coup V. D. Nabokov, who had been president of the Editing Commission of the conference, expected the Bolsheviks to start a campaign against the Constituent Assembly. "They proved to be more cunning," he later commented, "and during the course of the first month after the coup they made a great spectacle of their aspiration to convene it."[75] The closure of the Constituent Assembly by armed Bolshevik sailors, on the first day it met, lay two months ahead, but in November it seemed a vital countermeasure to the coup that elections still be held if at all possible. Nominated himself for the Constituent Assembly, and destined to play a major part in ensuring the elections took place, V. D. Nabokov had to stay in Petrograd.

For his family it was different. Many expected the Bolsheviks to last only a matter of weeks, and since the Bolsheviks themselves were unsure of their power they were forced to be circumspect. But while systematic terror had yet to begin, the dangers of revolutionary hatred were already obvious. Countess Sofia Panin, a leading CD, offered the Nabokovs quarters on her estate, Gaspra, in the Crimea, an area which still remained free. Vladimir and Sergey, it was decided, should leave first—the reason being, Nabokov recalled, to avoid being conscripted into the new "Red" army.[76]

On November 2/15, his last day in Petrograd, Vladimir wrote his last poem in northern Russia, dedicated to his mother and mourning the fact that she might never wander among the birches of her beloved Vyra again. At the Nikolaevski station, V. D. Nabokov saw his sons off, filling the moments of waiting by writing busily at the station buffet—an editorial for *Rech'* or an emergency proclamation, another desperate volley in an increasingly hopeless battle. After making a sign of the cross over his sons, he added casually that he might never see them again, turned round, and strode off into the steam and fog.[77]

The boys traveled first class on the Simferopol sleeper. Vladimir had with him the little manuscript albums of his verse, recent and current, and a pile of his white booklets of Symbolist poets. The heat was still humming on the train, and a hawkmoth pupa he had kept in a box for seven years hatched in the unaccustomed warmth.[78] Soon after Moscow

> all comfort came to an end. At several points of our slow dreary progression, the train, including our sleeping car, was invaded by more or less Bolshevized soldiers who were returning to their homes from the front (one called them either "deserters" or "Red Heroes," depending upon one's political views). My brother and I thought it rather fun to lock ourselves up in our compartment and thwart every attempt to disturb us. Several soldiers traveling on the roof of the car added to the sport by trying to use, not unsuccessfully, the ventilator of our room as a toilet. My brother, who was a first-rate actor, managed to simulate all the symptoms of a bad case of typhus, and this helped us out when the door finally gave way.[79]

Early on the third day of the journey, somewhere near Kharkov. Vladimir stepped over the snoring men in the corridor to get out for a breather. Wearing spats and a derby he strolled in the morning mist, carrying a cane that had belonged to his uncle Vasily, with a coral globe in a gold coronet for its knob. Nabokov writes:

> Had I been one of the tragic bums who lurked in the mist of that station platform where a brittle young fop was pacing back and forth, I would not have withstood the temptation to destroy him. As I was about to board the train, it gave a jerk and started to move; my foot slipped and my cane was sent flying under the wheels. I had no special affection for the thing (in fact, I carelessly lost it a few years later) but I was being watched, and the fire of adolescent *amour propre* prompted me to do what I cannot imagine my present self ever doing. I waited for one, two, three, four cars to pass (Russian trains were notoriously slow in gaining momentum) and when, at last, the rails were revealed, I picked up my cane from between them and raced after the nightmarishly receding bumpers. A sturdy proletarian arm conformed to the rules of sentimental fiction (rather than those of Marxism) by helping me to swarm up.[80]

By November 5/18, Vladimir and Sergey had reached the Crimea.

Foretaste of Exile: Crimea, 1917–1919

Suddenly I felt all the pangs of exile. There had been the case of Pushkin,

of course—Pushkin who had wandered in banishment here,

among those naturalized cypresses and laurels.

—Speak, Memory

I

THE ROAD from Simferopol to Yalta angles up gently through poplars toward the low mountains at the beveled southeastern edge of the Crimean rhombus. Once it cuts through the ranges to the coast, it turns right to wind along the steep southern slopes and becomes a chalk-white thoroughfare lined by cypresses and low walls of white stone. Above, scrubby peaks rise abruptly. Below, lush gardens and parks climb up from the shore to take in the view. On the morning of November 18, 1917, Vladimir and Sergey rode this way, past painted Tatar carts and through crowded Tatar villages, to the estate of Gaspra, five miles beyond Yalta.

In 1901–1902, at Countess Panin's invitation, the ailing Tolstoy had stayed almost a year at Gaspra, a storybook castlet with two towers like chess rooks flanking its crenellated brow. On the terrace beneath, Chekhov and Gorky had often come to sit there with him. Now, since 1915, it had been the countess's stepfather who occupied the manor: Ivan Petrunkevich, first the 1917 leader and then the grand old man of Russian liberalism, a founder of the CD party, a key figure in the First Duma, a treasurer of *Rech'*. A prominent CD herself, Countess Panin had offered her colleague V. D. Nabokov and his family shelter on her grounds, in humbler quarters near the road at the top of the property, a white guest house with a tin and tile roof.

Vladimir was annoyed to reach such a "fascinating" region as the Crimea—entomologically fascinating, of course, he meant—long after the collecting season was over.[1] Like most people, including many of the Bolsheviks themselves, he did not expect the new holders of power to last more than a few weeks or maybe months. But in fact he would never return to the collection he had left in Vyra, he would remain in the Crimea from the first of 1918's butterflies to the last, and even their offspring had already emerged in early 1919 before the Communists' tightening grasp on the country forced him into irrevocable exile.

The move to the Crimea was the first of Nabokov's enforced replantations from the cherished world of his childhood. After a few days in Gaspra he could already introduce the first cypresses into his verse, and a few days later describe magnolias past their seasonal best, but nothing could replace the fir forests of home.[2] But with Nabokov's usual good luck every obstacle in his destiny proved an opportunity and a fulfillment. Despite the massive disruptions of his life, he continued in directions already charted out. He and Sergey had been expected to attend Oxford or Cambridge when they finished school. The Bolshevik coup timed itself so that Vladimir could just squeeze in his matriculation exams, and when a second Communist incursion drove the Nabokovs on from the Crimea, the family headed for England, and Vladimir and Sergey straight for Cambridge and Oxford, respectively. Since 1911 Vladimir had dreamed of filling the gap between school and university by a lepidopterological foray into Central Asia, perhaps with the great naturalist Grigory Grum-Grzhimaylo (who features as one of Konstantin Godunov-Cherdyntsev's fellow explorers in *The Gift*), and after inheriting his uncle's fortune, he had seriously intended to carry out the trip in 1918.[3] Now in the Crimea he found himself flung into a land reminiscent of Asia Minor:

> The whole place seemed completely foreign; the smells were not Russian, the sounds were not Russian, the donkey braying every evening just as the muezzin started to chant from the village minaret (a slim blue tower silhouetted against a peach-colored sky) was positively Baghdadian.[4]

Next spring this new lepidopterological zone would offer up its treasures—and provide Vladimir with the material for his first scientific publication.[5] More importantly for his art, the complete break with his past already signaled in his flight to the Crimea would confirm his great theme, the absurdity of our inability to return to our past.

Sometime late in 1917, perhaps in the Crimean villa he shared with his brother, Vladimir began to compose his first chess problems, a hobby that would become his second extraliterary passion, an overflow valve for surplus creative energy, a training ground in artistic strategy.[6] Nabokov was never quite as good as might have been expected as a conversationalist, a chess player, even a player of Russian scrabble. To position a phrase, a chess piece, or an anagram with the elegance, economy, and duplicity, let alone multiplicity, that he required, he needed time—or a morsel of eternity. In devising chess problems Nabokov discovered the intensity of cerebration he knew from composing poems, a concentration of mental rays sufficient to burn a hole through time itself. As he explains so brilliantly in *Speak, Memory*, he would come to see the relationship between author and reader as analogous to the relationship between chess problemist and solver.[7] In composing chess problems or poems the absence of an immediate partner was a liberation, not a loss. Rather than both parties being subjected to time, as in a conversation or a game of chess, both could make an effort of the imagination that seemed like a knight's move beyond time. At eighteen, of course, Nabokov could construct neither problems nor poems to meet that standard. But without the sort of mind that saw such creative challenge in composing chess problems, and perhaps without the training they supplied, he could never have written those mature masterpieces in which the carefully planned alignment of parts tumbles the lock on time.

At Gaspra, the Nabokov boys were not alone for long. Throughout 1917 there had been a flood of aristocrats and intellectuals from the capitals to Russia's riviera. Anna Yan-Ruban, a concert singer and niece of Petrunkevich, and her husband Vladimir Pohl, a pianist and composer, had been living on the Gaspra estate since early in the year. Other members of the Nabokov clan were already in nearby Yalta. V. D. Nabokov's elder brother Sergey and his family (the Sergeevichi), whom Vladimir knew fairly well, had been in the area since 1915. The children of V. D. Nabokov's eldest brother Dmitri (the Dmitrievichi) with their mother (Lydia, née Falz-Fein) and her second husband (Nicholas von Peucker) were at first strangers to the Vladimirovichi, and found Vladimir haughty and standoffish until they began to see more of him in the spring of 1918. And only a few days after the boys' arrival in Gaspra their mother and sisters joined them, bringing nothing of the family fortune but a few jewels hidden in the talcum powder.[8]

II

In Petrograd V. D. Nabokov participated with rapidly evaporating hopes in various organizations opposing the Bolshevik coup: the CD Party Central Committee, the Petrograd City Duma, the newly formed and essentially socialist Committee for the Salvation of the Fatherland and the Revolution. As acting chairman of the Electoral

Commission of the All-Russian Constituent Assembly, he issued a proclamation to the people of Russia on November 9/22:

> The attempt to seize power has disorganised communications, created anarchy and terror, and interrupted the business of the Commission. Nevertheless, it is necessary to hold the elections wherever there is the slightest possibility of doing so. The gravest responsibility towards the country will be incurred by all who dare to make an attempt to corrupt the elections to the Constituent Assembly, on which the whole country is fixing its hopes.[9]

The Bolsheviks responded by closing down newspapers that published the proclamation. The offices of *Rech'* were smashed. Despite all the upheaval, elections took place on the scheduled dates, November 12–14/25–27, and with the Bolsheviks unable to rig the results, the Socialist Revolutionaries secured a powerful majority.[10] Over three-quarters of the vote was against the Bolsheviks.

On November 23/December 6, during a morning session of the Electoral Commission, Bolshevik soldiers arrived with a document signed by Lenin ordering the arrest of the "CD" commission. V. D. Nabokov was imprisoned for five days with more than a dozen others in a narrow, cramped little room at Smolny. On the afternoon of the fifth day, a disheveled sailor informed them they were free. Even after the ordeal of arrest, V. D. Nabokov did not lose his habitual calm, and hurried from the prison to a charity show at the Mariinsky Theater on behalf of the Literary Fund, of which he was still president. The next morning, the day the Constituent Assembly was to meet, he turned up at the Tauride Palace for a session of the Electoral Commission, and learned that Countess Panin, Shingarev, Kokoshkin, and another leading CD had been arrested a few hours earlier. Although a commandant ordered it to disperse and armed soldiers lined the room, the commission continued its session, expecting every moment to be ejected by force. In fact they were allowed to complete the meeting, and agreed to a rendezvous the next day.[11]

V. D. Nabokov left the house about 10 A.M. on the twenty-ninth, and on the way read a decree ordering the arrest and trial of all leading CDs, "the party of the people's enemies."* That day, strongly advised by his friends, he decided to leave for the Crimea. He was lucky enough to obtain a first-class sleeper berth on the train leaving for Simferopol the same evening. Rather than return home and risk another arrest he telephoned his valet to bring him a knapsack at a secluded corner. Thus equipped, he left that night.[12]

---

* A play on the party's official name, the Party of the People's Freedom.

On December 3/16, V. D. Nabokov reached Gaspra. With his father's reports from the capital to fire his indignation, Vladimir wrote that day a poem now placed second in his collected verse: "To Liberty":

> your bloodstained elbow covering your eyes,
> once more deceived, you once again depart,
> and the old night, alas, remains behind.[13]

III

Three main political currents swirled around the Crimea late in 1917: the Socialist Revolutionary influence dominant in the countryside and in the local zemstvos; the nationalism of the Tatars, one-third of the population, who during the power vacuum of 1917 had set up their own parliament to administer Tatar affairs; and the anarchism of the sailors and soldiers in the port cities, especially Sebastopol, headquarters of the Black Sea fleet. While most of the unruly sailors at Sebastopol felt themselves full of revolutionary spirit, they had little inclination to Bolshevism until heavily armed Baltic sailors were dispatched from Petrograd late in the year. A takeover of the Sebastopol Soviet in December gave the Bolsheviks power in the city and set in motion the first of the region's massacres (more than a hundred officers killed).[14] Elsewhere the Crimea was calm, with Tatar military detachments holding the area around Simferopol.

For a month the calm persisted. Nabokov reports that a few days after his father's arrival the two of them were helping a last old servant carry a heavy couch from Gaspra's manor to the guest house: "*Vot tak* (thus)," V. D. Nabokov remarked pleasantly to his son, "you will help to carry my coffin to the grave."[15] Now that V. D. Nabokov was shut out from his political activity, he had more time for his family than ever before. They strolled day or night through the park and ornamental gardens of Gaspra, with its trees from every climate, Himalayan cedars, cypresses, palms, and oaks. Or longer walks in the December sun: east to Yalta, and the stinging dust of its quay; west to Alupka, past knobbly Ai Petri, tallest of the local mountains; along the beaches of neighboring estates even richer than Gaspra.[16] When at the beginning of December Vladimir began a new album of poems, he named it *Tsvetnye kameshki* (*Colored Pebbles*)—perhaps because the stones and weathered glass of the new shoreline reminded him of early childhood and Biarritz.

On January 8/21 the Nabokovs heard two grim pieces of news: armed Bolshevik sailors in Petrograd had dispersed the Constituent Assembly at its opening session, and Kokoshkin and Shingarev, never released since their arrest at Countess Panin's Petrograd house, had been murdered. Once again V. D. Nabokov could reflect how narrowly he had escaped a premature death.

Perhaps not for long. The next day Yalta was attacked by Bolshevik forces, and a minesweeper bombarded the town. Since telephone lines were cut off, V. D. Nabokov could not call his brother. He noted in his diary: "Worries, fears. Infinitely oppressive mood. . . . In evening chess with Volodya." The bombardment and shooting continued for several days, and it was not until January 15/28 that he found out Sergey Nabokov's home had been hit and his family had had to move in with the Peuckers.[17] Yalta was looted. Scores of officers were arrested and taken to the pier, some to be beaten, some to be shot, and all to be thrown into the harbor with weights attached to their legs.

V. D. Nabokov's political past made him vulnerable to arrest. "In that region of lung specialists," his son notes, his father "adopted the mimetic disguise of a doctor without changing his name." After the fall of Simferopol the first Crimean government was established, notoriously harsh even by the standards of these bloody years. Atrocities in other towns outstripped the horrors of Yalta. Armed searches were widespread, sometimes six a day, with the death penalty for anyone caught with firearms. Food had been short in the Yalta area for a month, and money worries too began to weigh heavily on V. D. Nabokov. His children's governess Evgenia Hofeld had advised him before the revolution to transfer funds abroad. "During the war I cannot take gold out of Russia," he had replied. Now racked by his sense of helplessness, he distracted himself by playing chess every evening with Vladimir. "He has begun to play not at all badly."[18]

Nature at least seemed to smile. On January 28/February 10 the first yellow crocuses appeared, and by the next day spring seemed to have arrived. That day Vladimir wrote his first "play," "Vesnoy" ("In Spring"), "a lyrical something in one act." There are four characters: two young lovers, a chess player, and a stranger. Obsessed with his game with the stranger and only vexed by the spring budding around him, the chess player seeks a way to safeguard against all possible losses, and believes he has found the strategy. Meanwhile the youth (in fact the chess player as a young man) and the girl respond in such harmony to the birds and flowers and stars around them that their love promises a radiant future. At this point, the chess player confidently asks his opponent to resign, but instead the unnamed foe—fate itself, no less—at once declares mate: bringing the lovers together, although apparently the fulfillment of the chess player's strategy, in fact guarantees the anguish of future loss. Though only sixty-one hexameter lines long, the playlet seems a sudden revelation of the Nabokov to come: chess, fate, the focal shifts between two realities, time as inevitable loss. Before Vladimir read the play out to his delighted parents three days later, a storm had already given the lie to spring's false promise, dumping snow thickly over the hills.[19]

Perhaps inspired by his "Vesnoy," Vladimir reread all his poems since June 1916, selecting those he would like to publish. After 100 were rejected in this "severe" scrutiny, 224 remained, all to be included in a volume entitled *Open Windows*.[20] It never eventuated, and sixty years later only a single poem from all this number would make it into his 1979 volume of collected verse.

On the evening of February 13/26 Vladimir and Sergey were playing poker with their mother, a keen card player, as their father and Evgenia Hofeld sat reading. Suddenly in burst "a brigand-like figure, all swathed in leather and fur": Osip Dorzenik, V. D. Nabokov's Polish valet, bringing them three offerings: money (perhaps from Eva Lubrzynska's family, who did send them some that year); good news about Vyra and 47 Morskaya; and a pile of mail. Among the letters was one from Lyussya Shulgin, now living in a hamlet in the Ukraine. Amazed, Vladimir carried it out with him into the night. As he mounted a steep bridle path beside Tatar picket fences and a chalky stream bed, he looked up at the thin sliver of moon, and felt with a rush all the ache of exile.[21]

Soon whenever the wind died down the bright Crimean spring offered him compensations for his remoteness. Within a week he caught his first Crimean butterfly, and by late March he was making regular forays up the stony mountain trails in the glare of the sun or under the intermittent shade of olive and mulberry trees. On a path above the Black Sea, among shrubs in waxy bloom, a bowlegged Bolshevik sentry with a ring in one ear attempted to arrest him for signaling—with his net, supposedly—to a British warship. After an embarrassing encounter with the military authorities, he finally convinced them that his occupation was harmless, and the next day the soldiers brought him a large if not very valuable collection of butterflies.[22]

There had been other brushes with Bolsheviks. Out walking one afternoon V. D. Nabokov and his sons had had an unpleasant encounter with a drunken Red Guard—perhaps the basis for a much-heightened scene in *Glory*. A commissar had come a month earlier to nationalize Gaspra, along with other estates; for the Nabokovs this meant merely paying rent for their guest house to the local Soviet

administration. Once the house was searched, but although the Nabokovs had firearms, the occasion passed without incident. Osip
"knew how to talk to" the Bolshevik scrutineers.[23]

As the German army advanced, newspapers and mail were completely disrupted in Yalta for three weeks on end and rumor became
the only source of news. Out on mountain trails gunfighting could be
heard, and entry into Yalta was forbidden. On April 9/22 V. D. Nabokov noted in his diary "something murky has happened. Rumors
very various." The next day as reports of looting and shooting became
louder it was decided to set up a night watch over the estates. To
judge by his poetry Vladimir had already found exaltation in the Crimean night: moonlight reflecting off the magnolia leaves, or casting
shadows over alleys that cypresses guarded like sentinels, or leaving
its wake over the lilac waters of the bay. Now as he patrolled the
house with his father or brother or Osip, the heightened vigilance and
the surprise of a pre-auroral twilight etched the scene still more
deeply in his mind.[24]

IV

As it became obvious the Germans were about to arrive, warehouses
and shops in Yalta went on strike against the Bolsheviks, and the Nabokovs were caught short of provisions—rice, potatoes, sugar.[25] On
April 17/30 the German troops marched into Yalta without having to
fire a single shot. They came in neat files, their cannons and their
gray-green helmets and jackboots polished and improbable to Russians used to an army where everything from footwear to foot soldiers
was broken down or missing. After the messy and muddled excesses
of Bolshevik rule in the Crimea, the Germans were welcomed as liber-
ators and their orderliness greeted with relief.

V. D. Nabokov immediately sat down to write *The Provisional Government*, his frank, acutely observed memoir of 1917, objective enough
to have been praised for its veracity and mined for its information by
politicians as different in temperament and thinking as Trotsky, Kerensky, and Milyukov. In Yalta he met with other local CDs and Tatars
to discuss the attitude to adopt toward the German occupiers. No one
could agree.[26]

All year this or that combination of Nabokovs explored the gardens
and parks and the shores and crags between Yalta and Alupka. On
more strenuous outings father and son often walked with their neighbor Vladimir Pohl, a small frail bald-headed man in his early forties
who had become a health faddist, Nabokov notes, "after a severe bout

with tuberculosis. In consequence of various forms of physical training, some of them vaguely Oriental, he had developed a giant's stamina, and my father and I had difficulty in keeping up with him along
the steep trails of the Crimean mountains."[27]

One source reports V. D. Nabokov complaining to Pohl that he
could do nothing with Volodya: "He is capable, he writes good
poems, but he just spends his time running after butterflies and catching them. Can you not influence him to try even for a while to tear
himself away from butterflies and write verse?"[28] Despite the direct
speech—after more than sixty years—this third-hand story seems
more likely to reflect Pohl's incomprehension of lepidoptera than
V. D. Nabokov's attitude to his son. He had himself been a keen lepidopterist, he had many strings to his bow (statesman, jurist, journalist, devotee and promoter of all the arts), he encouraged Vladimir
in activities as diverse as chess problem composition and boxing.
And Vladimir never showed any sign of being less than a prolific
versifier—least of all when the butterfly chase had him pulsing with
excitement.

In mid-May news from Petrograd reached Gaspra about Vyra and
the taking of 47 Morskaya by the Red Guard Staff. A week later Vladimir began to write his first longish poem, "Svetloy Osen'yu" ("In
Radiant Autumn"). In the way it looks back at Vyra and first love
through the prism of exile the poem anticipates much of Nabokov's
art. He depicts himself in the Crimean spring dreaming of his northern home in spring, summer, autumn. To prepare the mood for what
follows, he introduces the idea of "colored hearing," describing here
not only the colors evoked for him by particular letters, as he later sets
them out in *Speak, Memory*, but also the conjuring up of letters or
sounds by the hue of something seen. He then broaches his major
scene: two lovers revisiting once a year, on the first day of autumn, a
locale that is plainly Uncle Vasily's manor. They spend the night together and peer out at the world next morning through the colored
glass on a window flanking the balcony. As he proudly noted at the
time, Nabokov wrote this poem of thirty-eight octets in two days, May
19 and 21/June 1 and 3—and it shows. What he did not point out was
that on the second of those days he was also catching butterflies on
the summit of Ai Petri and on the grassy plateau of the Yayla, and that
in the evening he read the poem out to his parents. His father noted
in his diary: "Developing very well."[29]

The next day Vladimir found himself with an excruciating toothache that was still causing pain two weeks later, after two visits to the
dentist.[30] His aching teeth would be as much of a motif in his life as his
colored glass.

As social life began to revive in the Yalta area, Anna Yan-Ruban was invited to give a charity concert for Russian artists in the area in a private home at nearby Simeiz. Needing to find Russian words to suit some of the Schubert and Schumann lieder based on Heine texts, she turned to her neighbor's son. Though his German was poor, Vladimir acquitted himself so well that at the concert both the singer and the translator received ovations, and the next day in Yalta people were ringing up to obtain the words.[31] His version of "Ich grolle nicht" was particularly successful.

On June 8/21, V. D. Nabokov set off for Kiev and Petrograd. He was unable to get further than Kiev. At a major CD conference there, Paul Milyukov, until now tenaciously anti-German, doggedly supported the Germans—who even at this point in 1918 he was convinced would win the war. Such a CD position cost the party its credibility in the Ukraine when the Germans retreated later in the year. By the time V. D. Nabokov returned to Gaspra on July 22/August 4, fortunately, the Crimean CDs had already decided to follow a different course: passive noncooperation with the German occupation.

Most inhabitants of the Crimea merely welcomed German occupation as a relief from responsibility, a holiday from history, a respite from Russia's long crisis.[32] For once, Vladimir was ready to join in a prevailing mood.

Not that he abandoned his private side. He found the butterfly *acaciae* Fabricius plentiful in the cemetery of a Tatar village by the coast. He made several excursions toward the center of the peninsula. On June 30/July 13, for instance, he climbed up a mountain trail on Ai Petri and encountered

> a strange cavalier, clad in a Circassian costume, with a tense, perspiring face painted a fantastic yellow. He kept furiously tugging at his horse, which, without heeding him, proceeded down the steep path at a curiously purposeful walk. . . . I recognized the unfortunate rider as Mozzhuhin,* whom [Lyussya] and I had so often admired on the screen. The film *Haji Murad* (after Tolstoy's tale of that gallant, rough-riding mountain chief) was being rehearsed on the mountain pastures of the range. "Stop that brute . . . ," he said through his teeth as he saw me, but at the same moment, with a mighty sound of crunching and crashing stones, two authentic Tatars came running down to the rescue.[33]

On Vladimir climbed with his net, catching representatives of three species, the last at the very summit, but missing his real target, *Hip-*

* Ivan Mozzhuhin would remain a movie star in exile in French and German movies of the 1920s and 1930s.

polyte euxinus, a Satyrid only recently described by Kuznetsov.[34] It continued to elude him—until he allowed his proxies to catch it in *The Gift*.

In his first novel, *Mary*, and again in *Speak, Memory*, Nabokov compares the letters he and Lyussya exchanged amid the chaos of a civil war to butterflies flying over unpropitious territory. He had answered her first letter at once, but did not receive her reply until July, when he sent her another letter with "Svetloy Osen'yu"—"a poem about Vyra that only you will understand." Weeks later she had still not received the letter. At such a break in the correspondence she would reproach him for neglect, as if mail should be unruffled by the civil war raging around her—"when in fact I did nothing but write to her and think of her during those months. . . ."[35] Almost a decade later he would incorporate five of her charmingly vibrant letters directly into his first novel, *Mary*.*

That summer Yalta resounded with White Army officers—including cousin Yuri, who had arrived early in May—happy to dispel thoughts of the inevitable return to battle. Cafés and theaters flourished, parties popped and fizzed through the night. Nabokov joined in the heady gaiety and in fact planned to enlist as a volunteer himself—not of course before the butterfly season was over, and not for the glory of the cause, but to reach Lyussya in her Ukrainian hamlet.[36]

When Nabokov recorded that he did nothing but write to her and think of her that summer, he added: "—despite my many betrayals." Sexually this seems to have been rather a torrid season for him. He and Sergey enjoyed the carefree hospitality of the Tokmakov family at their nearby coastal estate, Oleiz. Their large, ridiculous villa, full of strange galleries, passages, and stairways, echoed with the giggles and guffaws of countless guests:[37]

> brown-limbed braceleted young beauties, a well-known painter called Sorin,† actors, a male ballet dancer, merry White Army officers. . . . what with beach parties, blanket parties, bonfires, a moon-spangled sea and a fair supply of Crimean Muscat Lunel, a lot of amorous fun went on.[38]

---

* In his autobiography, Nabokov writes of these letters: "Happy is the novelist who manages to preserve an actual love letter that he received when he was young within a work of fiction, embedded in it like a clean bullet in flabby flesh and quite secure there, among spurious lives. I wish I had kept the whole of our correspondence that way." The first sentence leads one to suspect that Nabokov has *not* preserved Lyussya's letters in his fiction, but the next sentence allows a careful reader to see that he has preserved *some* of the letters. The original version of that second sentence was much less reticent: "Twenty-five years ago, I gave Tamara's letters that security and can now reread them at leisure" (MS, Vladimir Nabokov Archives).

† Savely Sorin, later famous as a portraitist in the emigration.

Or as Nabokov put it in the earlier version of his autobiography: "those wine parties on the shores of a phosphorescent sea, under the stars of hot summer nights, with hot-limbed, indolent, lightly clad young girls had definitely, alas, their Dobsonian side."[39]

One of his girlfriends was Lidia Tokmakov herself, a girl his own age. With her he developed a playful, teasing manner. Feeling that the "frivolous, decadent and somehow unreal background" of his summer replayed the mood of Pushkin's visit to the Crimea a hundred years earlier, he amused and annoyed her

> by commenting upon [my] own movements or words in the reminiscent, slightly mincing manner [she] might be supposed to develop many years later when writing her memoirs (in the style of memoirs connected with Pushkin): "Nabokov liked cherries, especially ripe ones," or "He had a way of slitting his eyes when looking at the low sun," or "I remember one night, as we were reclining on a turfy bank—"[40]

The image of Pushkin is worth lingering over. Nabokov was generally hostile to literary biography. Pushkin was the one exception:

> a singular case of a man's outer life fusing so organically with his inner one, that the story of his actual existence seems a masterpiece of his own pen, now lyrical, now sarcastic, now tragic, while his writings seem to be in their turn the footnotes to his life. . . . And as if this were still not enough, life played up to him, involving him in struggles which would disclose in the most vivid way the essential features of his nature and placing at regular intervals along the road of his life sheer cliffs for him to inscribe his name with his pen or his dagger.

Although Pushkin never left Russian territory he was repeatedly subjected to internal exile, first of all in the south of Russia; Nabokov calls him "a most brilliant example of permanent exile." And just as Pushkin was aware of having a predecessor in Ovid, exiled to these same parts, so Nabokov on reaching the Crimea had at once plunged himself into Pushkin's orientalia.[41]

As poet, libertine, exile, Nabokov could feel himself close to Pushkin. No doubt he enjoyed reliving Pushkin's pangs, but his own sense of exile—felt with no less strength than in later years, he has said—was no pose, no mere literary reflex: its full force did not come until that first letter from Lyussya.[42] In fact his abrupt break from his past was also the first case of life playing up to him. Even before leaving northern Russia, he had indulged in the wistfulness of exile; even before parting from Lyussya, he had savored the bitterness of loss. Time for Nabokov always shuts us out of our own past, and the game he played with Lidia Tokmakov not only imitated Pushkin's biographers but in welling up from his own, newly literal, sense of exile from his past it marked the evolving harmony—Nabokovian even more than Pushkinian—between the design of his art and the unplanned shocks of his life: the unpredictable future of the revolution, the inaccessible past of Vyra, the poetic harmony of an individual's life in time.

A more specific tribute to Pushkin came later in the summer. On a lepidopterological expedition in late summer Nabokov visited Chufutkale and Bakhchisaray, the ancient residence of the Tatar khans in central Crimea whose fountain provides the title for two famous Pushkin poems. There, as he stood in the cool hall of the khans' garden palace, with swallows darting in and out, he watched the little fountain trickling from a rusty pipe into dimples of marble, and thought nothing had changed since Pushkin visited a century ago. The idea led to his own poem "The Fountain of Bakhchisaray (in memory of Pushkin)," published in September in the CD newspaper *Yaltinskiy Golos*. A week earlier in the same newspaper there had appeared the first of hundreds of his poems to be published in newspapers over the next sixteen years: "Yaltinskiy Mol" ("Yalta Pier"). Written in early July, this poem draws on the horrified reports of German divers sent down to retrieve the bodies of those dumped off the pier. They were met by the sight of decomposing bodies standing upright on the harbor floor, moving with the swell as if they were talking to one another. In the poem Nabokov dreams that he is under the water and seized by the dead, who inform him they are judging their murderers: "—and no justification can we find."[43]

Perhaps it was in the carnival gaiety that tried to blot out such memories that Nabokov participated in a performance of Arthur Schnitzler's three-act *Liebelei*, translated into Russian as *Zabava* (*Fun*). He played Fritz Lobheimer, dragoon and college student, involved with a married woman. Her husband finds Fritz's love letters to his wife and flings them back in Fritz's face. But before our hero dies in a duel he has time for an extra backstage affair and another bracing flirtation. Though the performance took place in a little village theater, Nabokov recalled with shaky confidence: "I may have been paid. I was certainly paid."[44]

V. D. Nabokov had returned from Kiev on July 22/August 4.* Through his years on the Literary Fund he knew Maximilian Voloshin

---

* Presumably it was during this trip to Kiev that V. D. Nabokov, participating in a clandestine, multiparty meeting "that had to be hastily dissolved because it was learnt that the Cheka [secret police] had got wind of it, risked his life staying behind in order to warn an obscure Menshevik (whom he hardly knew and of whose party he disapproved) who, it was apprehended, might come later and be trapped" (Nabokov to Edmund Wilson, *Nabokov-Wilson Letters*, 33). Nabokov cited the incident to Wilson, without naming his father, to exemplify the selflessness of the Russian intelligentsia.

(1877–1932), the most important writer living in the Crimea, at Kokte-
bel, near Theodosia, a hundred miles to the northeast. A cosmopolitan and highly erudite poet, art critic, and painter, Voloshin kept a
boardinghouse there for poets and artists. But it was in Yalta that he
met Vladimir Nabokov. The younger man later recollected sitting with
Voloshin in a Tatar café, one cold and windy night—this must have
been an unseasonable August eve—with breakers sending spume
over the parapet, and the bushy-haired Voloshin declaiming to the
incoming waves to illustrate one of his recent metrical experiments
in a poem called "Rodina" ("Native Land"): a line of iambic tetrame-
ter with the first, second, and fourth feet all unstressed ("I neosu-
shchestvlénnaya," "And unrealized").[45]

Nabokov regarded Voloshin as an excellent poet, and critics agree
that his most remarkable work was being written at this time, in verse
where he proclaimed, often in highly biblical language, Russia's expi-
ation of its sins in the suffering the revolution caused. Nabokov always remained grateful that Voloshin sat with him and instructed him
so good-naturedly in the art of poetry.[46] But though Nabokov's next
major poetic effort, the nine-poem cycle "Angels," clearly shows
traces of Voloshin in its religious imagery and its cyclic structure, the
older poet's real influence on the younger was to introduce him to
Bely's radical methods of metrical analysis.

Andrey Bely, poet, novelist, critic, was a brilliant and unbalanced
soul whose masterpiece *Petersburg* Nabokov later hailed as one of the
four greatest novels of the twentieth century, along with *Ulysses*,
Kafka's *Metamorphosis*, and *A la recherche du temps perdu*. Voloshin
drew Nabokov's attention to *Symbolism*, a series of essays published in
1910 in which Bely analyzes the relationship between rhythm and
meter and reveals the rippled counterpoint in Russian verse under the
surface of the iambic norm. Nabokov read the treatise entranced.
Twenty-five years later he still regarded it as "probably the greatest
work on verse in any language"; forty years later he made it the basis
for his comparison of Russian and English prosody in his *Eugene
Onegin*.[47]

V

Vladimir could master Bely on his own, but for Sergey, Olga, and
Elena it was time to start school again. For that reason the family
shifted close to Yalta in late September, to the tsars' former residence
at Livadia, a mile and a half from the edge of town. There, they lodged
just outside the palace's sumptuous gardens in the old choristers'

chapel, a two-story house with seven bedrooms on the second floor that looked down on the blazing white palace itself, elegantly spare and light, for all its arched colonnades and pilasters. With bedrooms stacked each side of a central corridor, their new home felt like a hotel—good training for later years.[48]

Nabokov had no friends nearby, and many of those with whom he laughed away the summer had left the Crimea. As the weather cooled, he turned to study. He created his own first-year university program, so that he could "enter a second-year course straight away (it happens sometimes)," as he confided to a woman friend who had left the Crimea. He took Latin lessons from a teacher in Yalta, and drew up his own idiosyncratic reading list from the Yalta library: entomology, duels, naturalist-explorers, Nietzsche. But he could be thorough as well as curious, with the help of "the Imperial Library in our Livadia house,"

> which had accumulated (through a saintly bald little librarian) entire sets of old historical and literary journals as well as thousands of modern poets such as Bryusov and Bely. It is in Livadia, in 1918 that I completed my studies of Russian poetry and fiction.[49]

His judgment was becoming firmer: he reread *Crime and Punishment*, for instance, and now "thought it long-winded, terribly sentimental, and badly written." (A year later he would compose a cheeky but telling poem on Dostoevsky: "Listening to his nightly howl, / God wondered: can it really be / that everything I gave / was so frightful and complicated?") He read voraciously and actively, imposing a rigorous discipline on himself as he applied Bely's system to thousands of lines of Russian verse classics. Two thin notebooks survive, one intended for the iambic hexameter of Vasily Zhukovsky, Pushkin's friend and poetic mentor, one for the hexameters of Pushkin's coeval Evgeny Baratynsky, but including other poets like Mikhaylo Lomonosov, the eighteenth-century founder of modern Russian verse, or the mid-nineteenth-century poet Vladimir Benediktov.[50] On each page hundreds of lines are analyzed in minute and meticulous diagrams—a circle for each expected stress that remains unaccented, lines connecting the circles to disclose triangular or trapezoidal patterns. In some of the diagrams, the circles are colored by pencil according to their position in the strophe: yellow for the first foot, green for the second, and so forth.

Vladimir taught the system to his enthusiastic admirer, his twelve-year-old sister Elena, who helped him compile the tables and color them in. At Livadia he spent much more time with her than he had before, teaching her drawing, quizzing her about butterflies, in which

she showed a lively interest, reading her his poems.[51] She would always remain his favorite sibling.

Rereading all his own poetry, Vladimir was appalled to find that
instead of the elaborate cat's-cradle designs that Bely had found in
analyzing the rhythmic variations of the great poets, his own lines
disclosed plain and gappy patterns, flat and bereft of modulation—

> whereupon for the space of almost a whole year—an evil and sinful
> year—I tried to write with the aim of producing the most complicated
> and rich scud-scheme possible:
>
> > In miserable meditations,
> > And aromatically dark,
> > Full of interconverted patience,
> > Sighs the semidenuded park.

and so on for half-a-dozen strophes.[52]

Nabokov's parody exaggerates the horror and ignores the queer
charm his misguided efforts could have. "Bolshaya Medveditsa"
("The Great Bear"), for instance, written in late September, less than
a month after he encountered the Belyan method, was constructed to
yield a metrical pattern in the shape of the constellation. Despite that
formidable disadvantage it is quite a readable little poem.[53]

Nabokov's zeal for Bely's metrical system needs to be explained.
There is more to it than merely an ambitious young poet's discovery
that his verse lacks the individual suppleness and swing of those who
had already stridden into Russia's hall of poetic fame. Nabokov applied the same energy to his analysis of Zhukovsky's hexameters that
he would later devote to tracing the evolution of butterfly wing markings, where he would count under the microscope the scale-line position of each spot or streak, a precision no one else had ever attempted.[54] He believed that reality hides its secrets, that obscure
details can form patterns of unfathomed meaning. Bely's mode of
analysis naturally appealed to that side of his mind, and suggested
ways of incorporating subliminal design into his own work. These
methods were sterile and misdirected, but in his mature prose Nabokov would search for and find ways to harmonize unobtrusive details into patterns of covert significance.

The foundations of those later techniques may have been laid when
Nabokov encountered Bely's *Petersburg*—and read it four times, enraptured.[55] Exactly when this happened is unclear: a first version of
the novel appeared in book form in 1916, a second in 1922. Bely's
experiments set a bomb under language and logic in a manner very
different from anything Nabokov ever attempted. Bely aimed for the

irrational, by mimicking the collapse of coherence; Nabokov strove to transcend the rational, through presenting a perfectly lucid surface whose limpid smoothness reflects its surroundings so well it hides the sunken city below. Nevertheless the patternings of sound and sense that run through *Petersburg*—secret associations, for instance, in a shape or a rhythm or the sound of a letter—prefigure Nabokov's own phonic patter and cryptic pattern. But where Bely's devices buzz around in an excited swarm, Nabokov's interlock with precision, like that diagram of Ursa Major, or the smooth mechanism of a chess problem.

Speaking of chess problems: Nabokov's interest in them was developing rapidly. A poetic workbook of September–October 1918—the only workbook to survive—bears the title "Stikhi i Skhemy" ("Poems and Schemas"), curiously anticipating his 1970 *Poems and Problems*. The "schemas" here are Belyan prosodic ones, but there are also diagrams for a number of chess problems. A few prose notes and the draft of letters (one to Lyussya Shulgin, one to a girlfriend leaving Yalta for Kharkov, another to a Natalia Dmitrievna) make us wish he had left more such rough material. What seems like an observation on the new quarters at Livadia—"Two scraps of paper stuck to the toilet door. A big red zero on each. Witty use for a desk calendar's red-letter days"—crops up eight years later in his first novel. There is a note on colored hearing, which records the color he associates with each phoneme exactly as it would be several decades later in his memoirs: the letter *l* in 1918 is "dirty white," for instance, and "vermicelli" in *Drugie berega*, "noodle-limp" white in *Speak, Memory*. Another note depicts him looking up at the evening star, his favorite, applying to it simile after simile, finding nothing on his evening walk more beautiful—not the fountains, nor the red roses black in the moonlight, nor the hills in the distance. Suddenly it speaks: "Foolish man! What are you excited about? I'm a world too, not like the one on which you live, but noisy and dark like yours. There is sorrow and coarseness here too—and if you want to know . . . one of my inhabitants—a poet like you—looks on that star you call 'Earth' and whispers to it: 'O pure, O beautiful.' " The idea became a poem and lost its force—to regain it fifty years later in *Ada*'s Antiterra.[56]

The major effort in Nabokov's verse at this time was his "Angel" sequence, nine poems, each devoted to a different order in the celestial hierarchy, written at the request of and dedicated to Vladimir Pohl. Their angelic imagery has been claimed as proof of Nabokov's supposed religious sensibilities, but he himself later denied any inclination toward Christianity in the occasionally biblical scenes and tropes of his next ten years of voluble verse. That the denial was plain fact rather than (as has been suggested) Nabokov's embarrassment at an outgrown youthful fervor is already apparent from the first two of his "Angel" poems. In "Seraphim" some of the angels' tears become stars, and others fall to earth as "live gleams of celestial beauty: . . . the blessed star of fiery love, the heat of inspiration, the dreams of youth." In "Guardian Angel" the angel watches over the sleeping poet, who wakes up in the morning to a life that seems hateful until he sees a first shadow, and beyond it the first rays of dawn: golden feathers from the angel's unseen wings. As Nabokov comments, he was interested not in religion but in developing Byzantine imagery.[57]

An enthusiast for the occult, Pohl had tried to interest his young neighbor in mysticism. Nabokov asked him for books on the subject, which Pohl supplied from Gaspra's large library.[58] Neither mysticism nor Christianity can account for the philosophical flavor of the later Nabokov evident already in the "Angel" sequence and elsewhere in his early poetry. The sequence as a whole generates a very Nabokovian sense of level after level of being, and here already his playfulness—it all seems done for the sheer fun of stocking an imaginary ark to sail the firmament—marks how tentative he wishes to remain about anything beyond the human. Already he implies that *something* seems to lie beyond the visible and tangible, but everything is open, and as an artist he will suggest that openness by multiplying concrete possibilities. That sort of attitude owes nothing to the formal religious conventionality his father observed—taking the younger children to church, reading out at Easter the "Twelve Evangels," according to Russian custom.[59] It owed a good deal more to his mother, whose sensibility Nabokov describes in the person of Martin's mother in *Glory*:

> She firmly believed in a certain power that bore the same resemblance to God as the house of a man one has never seen, his belongings, his greenhouse and beehives, his distant voice, heard by chance in an open field, bear to their owner. It would have embarrassed her to call that power "God," just as there are Peters and Ivans who cannot pronounce "Pete" or "Vanya" without a sensation of falsity, while there are others who, in reporting a long conversation to you, will pronounce their own names or, still worse, nicknames, with gusto twenty times or so. This power had no connection with the Church, and neither absolved nor chastised any sins.[60]

Already Nabokov's attitudes permeated his interest in science, in the mysteries of evolutionary design, in the riddle of life's transformations. In a September 1918 note in his workbook, he reflects:

Contemporary biology shows that the cells of any organism are themselves immortal. What we call "the soul" is completely dependent on matter. Consciousness itself is only lucky chance in one light, the consequence of natural selection in another. Whatever the case, all these materialist arguments are completely unconvincing. Mechnikov* talks only of *possible* immortality. That leaves *us* neither hot nor cold. Until science resolves the question more soundly, *we* are still doomed to annihilation. . . . The existence of eternal life is an invention of human cowardice; its denial, a lie to one's self. Whoever says "There is no soul, no immortality" secretly thinks "but maybe?"[61]

VI

By late September 1918 it had become apparent that the Germans would soon withdraw from the Crimea. The White Army now active in South Russia wanted the Crimea to be directed from General Denikin's headquarters at Ekaterinodar in the Kuban region and treated simply as a landing base for Allied support. But CDs in the Crimea, led by Maxim Vinaver, saw that the imposition of a centralized military rule too concerned with uniting the armed struggle against Communist forces to attend to local needs was a sure recipe for the spread of radical discontent. Instead the Crimean CDs prepared to set up a sort of model regional government, chosen with the support of local zemstvo representatives, combining socialist and nonsocialist leaders, and responsive to local conditions. Solomon Krym, a Crimean CD with a long record of championing local causes, was the popular choice to head a new government. On November 2/15, the day after the German forces withdrew support for their puppet, the unpopular "Tatar" Suleiman Sulkevich, Krym began forming the Crimean Regional Government. V. D. Nabokov was named minister of justice; other members of the cabinet included Vinaver, two other CDs, the Menshevik Bobrovsky, a Socialist Revolutionary, and one nonparty minister.

V. D. Nabokov was now often away in Simferopol, the seat of the new government. William Rosenberg, the historian and frequent critic of the liberal movement in Russia's years of crisis, has this to say of his contribution:

One of the most impressive liberal efforts was Vladimir Nabokov's revitalization of the local judiciary. Just after becoming minister of justice, the former . . . head of chancellery for the Provisional Government

---

* Ilya Mechnikov (1845–1916), Russian physiologist and nobel laureate, devoted much attention to questions of immortality.

formed a special commission to reestablish judicial institutions; he himself personally drafted a comprehensive program for their reconstruction, setting up new courts on every level. The ministry also dispatched
a series of memoranda to administrative agencies, specifically warning
them not to interfere with legal procedures. . . . Even critics were impressed.[62]

The Crimean government began well, but before Communist
forces retook the peninsula in April 1919 the regime had already
begun to collapse from within. Its weakness lay in its relations with
the White Army. The Crimean government could field no forces of its
own: anti-Bolshevik officers had already joined the Whites, and another mobilization of a war-weary populace would be catastrophic
But with civil war raging and Red Terror now official Bolshevik policy
some defense was needed and the White Army was the sole possibility. Denikin and his generals, however, completely distrusted the Crimean government. Standing for a united Russia, they remained unshakably convinced that the Simferopol government favored Tatar
separatism. Finding it difficult to understand that not all socialists
were Bolsheviks, the White Army looked askance at the party composition of the Crimean government, and, even worse, their anti-Semitism made them suspect both Vinaver, a Jew, and Krym, a Karaite
Jew, of betraying Russia. They assumed Simferopol's rejection of a
military dictatorship meant they were soft on internal Bolshevik agitation—almost nonexistent and ineffectual, in fact, until the rough justice of White officers in handling supposed Bolsheviks undermined
local support for the regional government itself. Vladimir Nabokov
reports that as "Minister of Justice ('of minimal justice' as he used to
say wryly)" his father was "in constant friction with trigger-happy
elements in Denikin's army." It was at V. D. Nabokov's personal insistence, Rosenberg notes, that many seized by the Whites were returned to civilian tribunals.[63]

V. D. Nabokov's anger at the barbaric conduct of some of the White
officers may help explain a curious nuance in his *Provisional Government*—and a similar shade in his son. In his history of the revolution
Trotsky quotes V. D. Nabokov's revulsion both against the armed soldiers on the rampage in Petrograd's July 1917 uprising, with "the
same dull, vacant, brutal faces that we all remembered from the February days," and against the soldiers with "senseless, vacant and ma-
levolent faces" who closed down the Council of the Russian Republic.
Trotsky considered such statements self-evident proof of a class hauteur not unlike the social disdain others have since attributed to the
younger Nabokov. (In fact even Gorky feared the thoughtless cruelty
and the destructive instincts of the peasantry, who made up the over-

whelming mass of Russian soldiers.) But Daniil Pasmanik, a CD with V. D. Nabokov in the Crimea, understood him in quite another way. Pasmanik saw Nabokov as a man who not only gave the impression of being finely cultured, but had actually joined the CD party for cultural rather than political reasons, to create a Russia where all could live at a higher cultural level. It was not the social standing of the revolutionary soldiers that aroused V. D. Nabokov's disdain, but the mindless crudity of their behavior—which was for him exactly like the "uncultured" tactics of the tsar's minister of justice in hounding Beilis in 1913, or like the blunt-witted reactionaries among the White officers who now "caused him physical pain by their crude, coarse behavior." Perhaps this background makes it apparent why hostility to *poshlost'*, philistine vulgarity, occupies such a central place in Vladimir Nabokov's mind that it can cover everything from a trite advertisement to the atrocities committed in Lenin's name or Hitler's, or why he observes that in regard to *poshlost'*, place and class make no difference: "Any proletarian from Chicago can be as bourgeois (in the Flaubertian sense) as a duke."[64]

Nabokov seems to have begun the New Year with a resolution to step up his poetic output. His verse notebook for this period contains three poems for New Year's Day: one logged in at 10–11 A.M., one at 4–5 P.M., and one at 9:30–11 P.M. About this time, his 1917 poem "Dozhd' proletel" was set to music by Vladimir Pohl, and a poem about the Last Supper received the same treatment from his young cousin, the composer Nicolas Nabokov.[65] Two weeks into 1919 comes a pleasant surprise: "Dvoe" ("The Two") a 430-line riposte to Blok's most celebrated poem, "Dvenadtsat' " ("The Twelve"). Blok's poem mimics the staccato turbulence of the October Revolution, apparently celebrating the twelve former criminals, now Red Guards, led off behind a figure identified in the last line of the poem as Christ. Often considered Blok's masterpiece, and certainly the most famous poem of the revolution, "Dvenadtsat' " seemed to Nabokov, fifty years afterward, "dreadful, self-consciously couched in a phony 'primitive' tone, with a pink cardboard Jesus Christ glued on at the end."[66]

Less than a year after "Dvenadtsat' " was written, Nabokov's opinion of the poem was already formed. Despite its subtitle "A Contemporary Poem" and its epigraph from "Dvenadtsat'," Nabokov's "Dvoe" begins its reply to Blok so indirectly, with its picture of a young couple in the quiet of their old estate one winter's night, that we might almost misdate the scene to the nineteenth century—especially since Nabokov mimics here the manner of Russian poetry at its peak, the Pushkin of *Eugene Onegin*. With the rapid switches of thought and the brittle mix of urbane sympathy and teasing playful-

ness Pushkin adopts to describe his hero, Nabokov introduces Andrey Karsavin—a chemist and zoologist who has just defended a
weighty dissertation on mimicry:

> The consciousness of the citizen
> was hidden in Andrey's soul
> by the consciousness of being
> and in days of shame was not expressed.
> Sinful, no doubt, but neither you
> nor I, readers, dare
> judge him for that
> and must admit a certain likeness
> to Andrey in ourselves.

Pushkin's unpredictable changes of tone find their echo as Nabokov
shifts to the gentle happiness of married love humming as warmly as
the stove in the room where Andrey and Irina sit together. Andrey
spends the evening in drawing a new butterfly he has caught and
writing its description in Latin. A tender, even ardent love scene and
Irina's recollection of the dream she had when she nodded off briefly
have put Blok right out of mind—when twelve armed peasants suddenly burst into the house and attack its owners. Resisting bravely at
first, the unarmed Andrey realizes quickly he must get his wife away
from these desperate men. Ficking her up, he dashes from the house,
pursued by gunshots, and stumbles into the bitter, refugeless winter
night. The couple trudge on until they collapse in the snowy woods.
Lightly clad, chilled to the core, they accept their death with fear and
courage. Some time later the rioters track them down. One bends over
Irina, removes a ring from her frozen hand, looks at her with an animal sneer, "and"—in a last line as arresting as Blok's—"spat in her
dead face."[67]

A rabble's hatred, Nabokov implies, can usher in no new millen-
nium. To Blok's and the Bolsheviks' appeal to that blind desire to tear
down, that destructive rage which seems the antithesis of all culture,
he responds by declaring himself ready to stand by Pushkin, Russia at
its most cultured and creative and lucid. The poem is a brilliant performance, on the one hand winning genuine sympathy for the quiet
scholar harmlessly pursuing his own interests, on the other slipping
from mood to mood with Pushkinian quickness and ease. Above all it
discloses in Nabokov a storyteller's imagination and a gift for blending parody and passion.

Of course the poem is politically naive, but so was the nineteen-
year-old who wrote it. When in early 1919 Yuri Rausch, after a few
weeks' leave in Yalta, was about to return to the front, Vladimir felt all

the old desire to match his cousin's courage. "Like you, I from my boyhood days have loved joyful danger," he began a poem dedicated to Yuri, and after having wavered for months now decided firmly to join the White Army himself. Before leaving for his regiment, Yuri gave Vladimir his army boots to try on and promised his cousin to do all he could to have his cousin enlisted in the same division.[68]

A week after Yuri regained the front the news came, on February 23/March 8, that he was dead. Spurring his horse ahead of the regiment, he had made a reckless lone charge on an enemy machine-gun nest. One burst of the gun and the whole front of his skull was pushed back. "Thus," records Nabokov, "was quenched his lifelong thirst for intrepid conduct in battle, for that ultimate gallant gallop with drawn pistol or unsheathed sword." His body was brought back to Yalta where he was buried on March 1/14. Vladimir helped carry the coffin. To his old French governess, he wrote simply: "C'était mon meilleur ami." His final epitaph for his cousin he set down in *Speak, Memory*: "all emotions, all thoughts, were governed in Yuri by one gift: a sense of honor equivalent, morally, to absolute pitch."[69]

But as Vladimir came to understand later, the civil war was more complicated than admiration for heroic Whites and contempt for barbaric Reds would allow. Unfortunately for V. D. Nabokov, not all the White Army was like Yuri. Two nasty killings of Jews in Yalta were traced to White officers, but when V. D. Nabokov as minister of justice tried to pursue the matter, the offenders were transferred to the front or the Caucasus, out of his government's jurisdiction. As the military situation became more desperate and White officers' behavior degenerated, similar scenarios were replayed all too often.[70]

VII

The government had no choice: it had to prosecute the excesses of individual officers but still rely on the White Army for its defense. But because of its association with the Whites, the Simferopol government lost the widespread popular support it had commanded four months before. Agitation from the left became increasingly unruly and made the Whites even more suspicious. With few troops to spare and unable to accept the Crimean government's liberal principles, White Army support for the region was limited and begrudging. In desperation Krym and V. D. Nabokov appealed to the French, whose warships had controlled the port of Sebastopol since the departure of the Germans.[71] The troops the French promised never materialized.

On March 16/29, with Bolshevik forces pushing deep into the Pe-
rekop isthmus, Denikin cabled an ultimatum: unless the government
declared martial law and transferred power to the army, troops would
be withdrawn. The government had to agree. But within a week, on
March 21/April 3, the Red Army broke through White defenses and
began to advance quickly through the Crimea proper.

Evacuation was ordered. On March 26/April 8 the Nabokovs left
Livadia—which for Vladimir meant leaving behind his captures of
two hundred–odd species of local butterflies and moths. As the family
drove along the twisting road round the flanks of the Crimean hills,
Elena was sick on one side of the car, Sergey on the other. Sebastopol,
the only way out, swarmed with luggage and people. Many had to
sleep out in public squares. Of course as a cabinet minister V. D. Nabokov had rooms awaiting his family in the Hotel Metropole. Vladimir's was number seven:

> Not quite a bed, not quite a bench.
> Wallpaper: a grim yellow.
> A pair of chairs. A squinty looking-glass.
> We enter—my shadow and I.

Two days in Sebastopol allowed him to explore the famous granite
flagstones of the steps down to the harbor, the guns and sandbags
ranked for the port's defense, the dusty white streets. On March 28/
April 10, the ministers of the Crimean Regional Government and their
families boarded the Greek vessel *Trapezund*, bound for Constantinople. A charred, burnt-out shell, but still a path to safety.[72]

Except that the path was blocked. About five o'clock the next afternoon the French command demanded to know why nothing remained of the government's funds in the State Bank of Sebastopol and
insisted on having all the money handed to them by 11 A.M. the next
day. The Regional Government reported at the stipulated time with a
detailed breakdown of the run on its Sebastopol funds (the cost of the
evacuation, pay for the government's employees—nothing improper
in the least). Still the French would not budge: no money, no passage.
That evening, March 30/April 12, the ministers of the Regional Government and their families were ordered to leave the *Trapezund*, which
had to set sail for Constantinople—as it did in a day or two with the
other two Nabokov families, the Sergeevichi and Dmitrievichi, on
board.[73]

The ministers and their families meanwhile were transferred to another even smaller and "incredibly dirty" Greek vessel moored off-
shore, the *Nadezhda*, carrying a cargo of dried fruit. On March 31/April

13 the final information needed to satisfy the French command was passed on, but neither that day, nor the next, nor the day after was permission given for departure. The seven ministers and their families, thirty-five in all, had to sleep on wooden benches in a single rough cabin. Late on the third afternoon the Bolshevik forces reached the heights around Sebastopol and bombardment commenced. French and Greek forces fought back for four hours before permission was at last given for the *Nadezhda* to leave. Machine guns were firing from the shore as the *Nadezhda* zigzagged out of the harbor and across a glassy bay. Vladimir Nabokov sat on the deck with his father, struggling to concentrate on their chess game, thinking of Lyussya's letters continuing to turn up in Yalta only to find nobody home. Before eleven o'clock on the evening of April 2/15, 1919, he saw the last of Russia.[74]

Upper left: Nabokov's father's father, Dmitri Nikolaevich Nabokov (1826–1904), minister of justice under Alexander II and Alexander III.

Upper right: Nabokov's father's mother, Maria Ferdinandovna Nabokov (1842–1926), née Baroness von Korff, proprietor of the Batovo estate near Vyra.

Lower left: Nabokov's mother's father, Ivan Vasilievich Rukavishnikov (1841–1901), landowner and philanthropist, proprietor of the Vyra and Rozhdestveno estates.

Lower right: Nabokov's mother's mother, Olga Nikolaevna Rukavishnikov (1845–1901), née Kozlov.

A banquet at Vyra, perhaps the engagement party for Elena Rukavishnikov and V. D. Nabokov (*sixth and fifth from right*), 1897. On the left flank of the table Olga Rukavishnikov, Maria Nabokov, and Ivan Rukavishnikov sit side by side. (*Sikorski collection.*)

Elena and V. D. Nabokov. Nabokov's father proposed to Elena Rukavishnikov in 1897 as they wheeled their bicycles up an incline on a road in Vyra. (*Sikorski collection.*)

Vyra, the Nabokov family summer home near St. Petersburg. The photograph dates from the 1920s or 1930s: already the veranda in the middle of the longer wall has gone. (*Sikorski collection.*)

Rozhdestveno, the manor Nabokov inherited in 1916 from his uncle Vasily Ruka-vishnikov. The highway leads at left toward St. Petersburg. On the wet evenings of August 1915 Nabokov would ride over from Vyra, wheel his bicycle up the steps leading at right from the highway, and meet with Valentina (Lyussya) Shulgin on the pillared porticos of the home Vasily Rukavishnikov rarely visited. (*Sikorski collection.*)

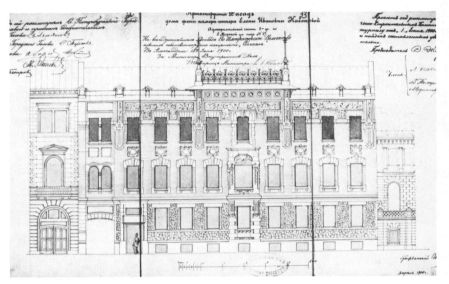

Plan of the renovations made to the Nabokovs' St. Petersburg home at 47 Morskaya (now Hertzen) street in 1901. The former two-story house expanded to three stories to accommodate a growing family and their retinue. (*Central Historical Archive of Leningrad Province.*)

47 Morskaya after the renovations. (*Sikorski collection.*)

Vladimir, summer
1901.

Vladimir, aged seven,
with father, 1906.

Above: Vladimir and his brother Sergey with Cécile Miauton, their French governess (''Mademoiselle O''), 1907. (*Sikorski collection*.)

Upper right: Vladimir with his mother and her brother Vasily Rukavishnikov (''Uncle Ruka''), 1907. (*Sikorski collection*.)

Lower right: Vladimir with butterfly book, 1907. (*Sikorski collection*.) The photographs on this page were taken by the celebrated St. Petersburg photographer, Karl Bulla.

The Nabokov family, reunited after V. D. Nabokov's release from prison, 1908. *From left*, the dachshund Trainy; Nabokov's mother; his sisters Elena and Olga, held by their grandmother Maria Nabokov; his father; Nabokov himself. on the knee of his mother's aunt Praskovia Tarnovski; and his brother Sergey.

Sergey (*left*), aged nine, looking diffident and Vladimir (*right*), smaller but a year older, supremely confident, at their grandmother's estate, Batovo, across the river from Vyra, summer 1909.

Vladimir, 1916.

Title page of Nabo-
kov's first book, *Stikhi*
(*Poems*), which ap-
peared in the sum-
mer of 1916, when he
still had a year and a
half of school to com-
plete. The poems
were inspired by
Lyussya Shulgin
and published with
some of the fortune
Nabokov inherited
from his uncle Vasily.

В. В. НАБОКОВЪ.

СТИХИ.

1916

Valentina (Lyussya) Shulgin. the "Tamara" of *Speak. Memory*, in 1916. (*Izvestia*.)

Baron Yuri Rausch von Traubenberg, Nabokov's cousin and best friend, 1917, in the officer's uniform Nabokov would try on and his cousin would wear as he rode to his death.

Eva Lubrzynska, Nabokov's main romantic partner in St. Petersburg in 1917 and again in Cambridge and London in late 1919 and early 1920. (*Sketch*.)

The five Nabokov children, Yalta, November 1918: Vladimir (b. 1899), Kirill (b. 1910), Olga (b. 1903), Sergey (b. 1900), and Elena (b. 1906).

PART II

EUROPE

• *SIRIN* •

The ghetto of emigration was actually an
environment imbued with a greater concentration of culture and a deeper freedom of thought
than we saw in this or that country around us.
Who would want to leave this inner freedom in
order to enter the outer unfamiliar world?
Personally speaking, I was perfectly
comfortable where I was: at my writer's
desk in a rented room. But then, of course,
I am not a typical émigré. I am a very
non-typical émigré who doubts
that a typical émigré
exists.

—*Nabokov interview,*
1966

Becoming Sirin: Cambridge, 1919–1922

I do not know if anyone will ever go to Cambridge in search

of the imprints which the teat-cleats on my

soccer boots have left.

—*Speak, Memory*

I

ON BOARD the *Nadezhda* the refugees had no more to eat than what they had brought with them: sausages, eggs, bread. Late on their second day out they saw Constantinople loom in the distance and sink in darkness before they arrived. The next morning, April 17, 1919, Nabokov rose early from his hard bench to see dawn on the Bosporus: the ship resting as if in amber, the minarets in the distance. Since Constantinople was already overcrowded with refugees, those on the *Nadezhda* were not given permission to land. After two motionless days the minarets had begun to look like factory chimneys, when at last the ship moved on through the Sea of Marmara.[1]

Two days later the *Nadezhda* sailed into Piraeus, the port of Athens. Although the passengers had already used up all their food and water, the ship had to remain in quarantine two more days in the Gulf of Piraeus, and it was not until Vladimir's twentieth birthday that he and his family disembarked in Greece. The Sergeevichi and Dmitrievichi had also landed here, and all three families moved along the shoreline away from dingy coal freighters and minesweepers and past gleaming yachts to the white hotels of Phaleron, the smart seaside suburb of Athens. For the next few weeks V. D. Nabokov and his family, though desperately short of money, stayed at the Hotel Neon Phaleron—three stars in Nabokov's guidebook—and the other two families at the Actaeon. V. D. Nabokov managed to communicate with the waiters using his classical Greek.[2]

The day they arrived the family took the electric train past sleepy little houses into the city center. To the young poet, the Acropolis seemed "divine," and he promptly wrote a poem about it as he sat on a marble flagstone, amid the pale poppies growing between crumbled remains.[3] In one of the two other poems he composed in honor of the Acropolis, he evokes a curiously romantic scene corroborated by independent witnesses. Some of the young Dmitrievichi and Sergeevichi were visiting the Acropolis by night. Through the moonlight came a rich female voice, singing an aria from *Aida* and then a Russian song: another refugee, the opera singer Marianna Cherkasskaya—as much a star at La Scala as in Russia—was responding in her own way to the place's beauty. As they stood listening, the young Nabokovs saw cousin Vladimir step out of the Parthenon's shadow and cross over to the Erechtheum with a pretty young woman.[4]

Novotvortseva by name,* she was a Russian as "White" as her moonlight-and-marble backdrop. Several years older than Vladimir, and married, she was also something of a poet to unexacting friends. And she was only one of three love affairs Nabokov found time for in his three and a half weeks in Greece. No wonder in retrospect he thought he had spent far longer there.[5]

Apart from the Acropolis he found Greece a disappointment, the people uninspiring, the countryside scorched. One reason for his chagrin was the butterflies. He tried to collect them in Kefisia, half a marathon from Athens, and other places nearby: "braving the constant resentment of intolerant shepherd dogs, I searched in vain for Gruner's Orange-tip, Heldreich's Sulphur, Krueper's White: I was in the wrong part of the country."[6]

II

The exit from Greece was far grander than the entry. On May 18 the Nabokovs sailed for Marseilles on the Cunard steamship *Pannonia*, bound for New York. The decks were clean, the brass polished, the liner had its own picture gallery and a spacious ballroom where Vladimir learned to foxtrot and twostep. Throbbing its way between Africa and "the purple strip of Sicily," then between Corsica and Sardinia, the *Pannonia* reached Marseilles on May 23. From there the Nabokovs took a train straight to Paris, stopping three nights at the Hotel Terminus at St. Lazare. With Evgenia Hofeld, Vladimir tried to sell Elena Nabokov's pearls to Cartier, the Parisian jeweler, but he was "unbelievably dressed" and, suspecting the gems were stolen, the employees held them and called the police. Able to convince the Cartier staff they were who they said they were, they were released before the gendarmes arrived.[7]

---

* By surname, that is. No one seems able to recall her first name.

On May 27 the family crossed from Le Havre to Southampton. When the train reached London's Victoria Station Uncle Konstantin was there to greet them. V. D. Nabokov marched up to his brother, spreading his arms for a Russian embrace. Prim—and homosexual— Konstantin backed off: "*My v Anglii, my v Anglii* [we are in England]." Chargé d'affaires at the Russian embassy in London, Konstantin represented a government abolished a year and a half earlier. With England changing its policy toward Bolshevik and anti-Bolshevik Russia from month to month, but tacking perceptibly toward recognition of the new regime, Konstantin's position resembled that of one of those cartoon characters who run off a cliff and pedal in the air until gravity decides to act.[8]*

V. D. Nabokov had arrived in England hoping to find a post from which he could influence British public opinion into continued opposition to Bolshevik power, a task that would prove impossible. Meanwhile the family rented four rooms at 55 Stanhope Gardens, a smart stucco home in South Kensington near the Natural History Museum. Rent was paid for by the sale of Elena Nabokov's jewels, which would have to cover living expenses throughout the next year in London. Her string of pearls would pay for two years' study for her son at Cambridge.[9]

If V. D. Nabokov had trouble finding the right work, his son had none finding pleasure. Vladimir would not frequent ballrooms for more than a brief stretch of his life, but this summer, fresh from the *Pannonia*, he even foxtrotted with Anna Pavlova. Within a week or two of his arrival he met Eva Lubrzynska again, quite by chance, at a charity ball: a wayward willowy girl, as he describes her, who laughed brightly at their shared past. Soon they were shuffling cheek-to-cheek, and their romance resumed its course. Though still fond of Eva, Nabokov would find her demanding and unsure of what she demanded, unhappy, always torturing herself.[10]

On an erratic court in Kensington Vladimir played tennis with Sergey, the only game they had in common. They also had their education to plan. Together they traveled to Oxford to confer with Gleb Struve (son of Peter Struve, V. D. Nabokov's former colleague in the pre-1905 fight for a liberated Russia) about their choice of universities. Struve—later the first chronicler of the émigré literature now just beginning its existence, and the first to introduce "Sirin" to English readers—was about to enter Balliol, but was already in Oxford to improve his English. As they sat together on the lawn outside Struve's lodgings, the Nabokov lads in their tennis whites, Vladimir recited

* He was relieved of his position in September 1919.

some of his poems, and explained his yen for entomology as well as literature. Struve accordingly advised him to try Cambridge, with its greater scientific reputation, but suggested that Sergey, keenest on French literature, should opt for Oxford.[11]

By late June Nabokov had met another friend from the past: Samuil Rosov, who had just arrived in England and planned to study at the University of London. They played billiards together with another ex-schoolmate: London swarmed with familiar ghosts that summer. Rosov also lent Nabokov his Tenishev diploma. By showing this in Cambridge and explaining he had the same—actually the Cambridge officials, unable to read the Russian script, seemed to think it was his—Nabokov was able to matriculate without having to take the "Previous" Examination.[12*]

Nabokov's poetic output slipped to a poem every three days this summer, and even these are of less interest than much of his Crimean work, except for one poem that reflects the insomnia that racked him all his life: "I suffocate in uninterrupted, unbearable darkness. The marvelous terror of consciousness rocks my soul in emptiness." By early July the family had rented a house at 6 Elm Park Gardens, off the Fulham Road in Chelsea, a wan brick house of four narrow stories arranged exactly the same as its neighbors. Here Vladimir translated a few English poems (Landor and one Seamus O'Sullivan,[†] found in an anthology), translated one of his own poems into English, and composed in September his first, woefully vapid, English verse. The Belyan metrical schemata disappeared from his albums when he left Russia, but in his London notebook there is a chess problem for virtually every poem.[13]

III

On October 1, 1919, "Vladimir Nabokoff"—so he spelled his name until he reached America—was officially admitted to Trinity College, Cambridge. He came as a "pensioner," a student who pays his own way—although he remembers having received some scholarship "awarded more in atonement for political tribulations than in acknowledgement of intellectual merit." He was assigned rooms at R6

* They had the same grade—five, the highest—for everything, except that "Nabokov had a four for Physics and Rosov, not being Greek Orthodox, had no mark at all for Sacred History which earned Nabokov a five minus." Nabokov to Andrew Field, Feburary 20, 1973, Vladimir Nabokov Archives.

† The nom de plume of James Starkey (1879–1958), an Irish poet who rates a mention in Ulysses.

(staircase R, set 6), in the southwest corner of Great Court, the largest and grandest of any of the college courts at either Cambridge or Oxford. At the northwest corner lived Sir J. J. ("Atom") Thomson, discoverer of the electron and the new Master of Trinity. In the northeast corner, diagonally across from Nabokov's rooms, Newton had once lived. And according to tradition it was in the southeast corner of Great Court that Byron kept a bear on a chain in mockery of the rule that no dogs should be kept in college. So we come full circle back to Nabokov—who, when threatened with fines by fat-faced, bowler-hatted college porters for crimes like walking on the grass, was so surprised that people completely tangential to him could allow or forbid him anything that he simply assumed the fines were no more than a time-honored joke.[14]

Experience taught him otherwise. Nabokov's first and most persistent contact with Cambridge officialdom was with Ernest ("Spy") Harrison (1877–1943), his college tutor. Harrison's role was not to teach Nabokov but merely to act *in loco parentis*: to keep an eye on lecture attendance, to grant exeat passes during term, to administer reprimands when undergraduates were fined (for returning after midnight, for failing to wear an academic gown in the evening, for a host of minor misdemeanors). After crossing Great Court to Harrison's rooms the first time, Nabokov established tepid relations between them by tripping over the tea things on the floor of Harrison's dimly lit living room. Over the next three years he would be summoned here "with dismal frequency" for fines he had incurred. Irked by Harrison's constant gloomy smile, Nabokov rated his tutor, a distinguished classicist, "a vile person" and "an extraordinarily stupid man."[15]

At Trinity two undergraduates would share a "set" of rooms. In R6, on the second story (British style), each student had a bedroom overlooking to the west the roofs of New Court and leading out on the other side into the large square living room whose windows gave onto Great Court. Since Harrison thought it "a fine idea to have one 'White Russian' lodge with another," Nabokov shared with Mikhail Kalashnikov, at Cambridge to read history. At first Russia and youthful high spirits united them both, but their differences could not lie dormant for long. Two years younger than Nabokov and intellectually undistinguished, Kalashnikov proved to be a philistine reactionary.[16]

At Cambridge Nabokov never held court like Joyce in Dublin or Samuel Johnson at Oxford. All the Anglophilism of his family was no help: the Englishness of his childhood was something belonging to the nursery, and now as a young man he found a barrier between himself and English undergraduates around him. The whirlwinds of the soul natural to a Russian provoked incomprehension on a well-scrubbed English face; any dropping of the guard—"I'd give my very blood just to see a certain little bog near St. Petersburg again"—was simply bad form. For that reason, Nabokov's closest friends were Russian, and the choice was not wide: Kalashnikov; Eva Lubrzynska's "bright and subtle" brother Mikhail, who had come up to Peterhouse the previous term; Peter Mrosovsky, another first-year student at Trinity, reading chemistry; Count Robert Louis Magawly-Cerati de Calry, also new to Trinity, and Russian only by blood, on his mother's side.[17]

On the other hand Nabokov did not feel overlooked by the English. His keen participation in college and individual sports (soccer, boxing, tennis) and even his very Russianness ensured him attention: "I was made *much* of in Cambridge." In *Speak, Memory* he provides a stylized portrait of a Cambridge contemporary—he calls him "Nesbit"—whom he found it impossible to convince that Bolshevism was no more than "a new form of oppressive tyranny, itself as old as the desert sands." Behind the stylization an individual seems to lurk—a young man who had fought in the trenches, wrote unrhymed verse, became a distinguished scholar. This lanky, pipe-smoking young socialist and his rather decadent friends introduced Nabokov into the argot of the local etiquette: never shaking hands, nodding, or wishing good morning, but greeting an acquaintance, even a professor, with a grin or perhaps a bright interjection; never walking outdoors in hat and overcoat, no matter how cold it was; not following the rules too slavishly. Publicly, Nabokov joined the majority and refused an overcoat; privately, he also squeamishly rejected the tickly woolly underwear that kept his English compeers warm. He caught cold after cold.[18]

Everyone wanted to discuss Russia with him, especially R. A. Butler, the future Tory deputy prime minister, whom Nabokov later identified as the man behind the Nesbit mask and "a frightful bore." In retrospect Nabokov was surprised to remember that in those days he had indeed argued about politics. Six weeks after coming up to Cambridge, on November 28, he even participated in the visitors' debate at Trinity College's Magpie and Stump Debating Society, on the motion "That this House approves of the Allied Policy in Russia." Nabokov, naturally, argued against nonintervention: "Mr. Nabokoff spoke with personal knowledge of Bolshevism, and described it as a loathsome disease. Lenin was mad, the rest scoundrels. He referred to distribution of a piano among several claimants—a reminiscence of Solomon. He advised immediate help from England, support of Denikin and Kolchak, and refusal to deal with Bolsheviks." Nabokov spoke for eighteen minutes and fifty seconds, helped by having learned by heart an English-language article by his father. After reciting what he had memorized he dried up utterly: "and that was my first and last political speech."[19]

After this experience Nabokov not only avoided political debate—although he would continue to attack Bolshevized Russia on paper—he also eschewed in his prose the sort of reasoned marshaling of argument that came so naturally to his father. A lucid thinker who valued highly the right to criticize ("Next to the right to create, . . . the richest gift that liberty of thought and speech can offer"), Nabokov loved to expose logical flaws in others' work, not through the step-by-step of the syllogism but with the sudden cartwheel of a counterexample.[20]* But he rarely resorted to rational exposition in order to advance arguments of his own. Some readers wrongly infer from this that he had no ideas and nothing more to offer than pungent opinions. That is to misunderstand the role of reasoning in human thought.

Throughout his life Nabokov seemed to understand intuitively that however valuable logic may be in exposing falsehood it cannot uncover truth or make an idea impregnable—as Hume had pointed out. to the consternation of two centuries of philosophers, and as the Popperian revolution in epistemology has at last explained. Logic picks out a cautious path from the known toward the unknown, then discovers it has merely circled back on its tracks. Only the freedom to move counter to the next step suggested by the "logic" of common sense—often mere habit, a poverty of the imagination that sees no alternative—can lead us a little way into the unknown and offer a new vantage point on the known. Accordingly, when Nabokov operates in a context where argument might most be expected (in his own critical prose, in the overtly philosophical parts of his fiction) his style becomes defiantly unruly, he stands logic on its head, ruffles its hair, flies in its face, he bounces all around entrenched reason on the pogo-stick of fancy.† But this is to look beyond Cambridge, where Nabokov had studies to attend to.

The day would start with him walking to the Baths in New Court at the end of Trinity Lane, dressed in a beautiful purple dressing gown bought in London and offering little resistance to Cambridge's raw chill. After breakfast in Hall, under a portrait of Henry VIII, "with the porridge as grey and dull as the sky above Great Court," he would grab an armful of books, dash on foot or by tinkling pushbike to one

---

* " 'Reality is Duration,' one voice, Bolotov's, would boom. 'It is not!' the other would cry. 'A soap bubble is as real as a fossil tooth!' " (Pnin, 118).

† "I am triumphantly mixing metaphors," as Nabokov writes at one such point (Lectures on Literature, 373).

of the lecture halls scattered about the town, file in to hear a mummi-fied sage at the lectern and stamp his feet with the rest of the audience to acclaim a joke or a fancy phrase. Lunch would be followed, accord-ing to the season, by tennis, soccer, or boating on the Cam, some strong tea and crumpets in a friend's rooms at midafternoon, and per-haps another lecture or two before dinner in Hall.[21]

What were those lectures about? Nabokov recalled that he began by reading "Zoology. . . . After dissecting fish for one term I told my college tutor (E. Harrison) that it was interfering with my verse-writ-ing and could I please switch to Russian and French." Later he altered the word *zoology* to *ichthyology*, but the only course that might suit that label was Professor Stanley Gardiner's "Life in the Sea," offered only in Nabokov's *second* term.[22] Since tutorial records at that time were considered the personal property of the tutor and were not preserved by the college, there seems no way to smooth out this crumpled page in his dossier.

Certainly Nabokov dissected fish. He disliked their smell, he joked that they then found their way into the college food, he found them boring.[23] In his first two Cambridge terms courses on vertebrate and invertebrate zoology, evolution, and genetics were also available for those reading zoology within the Natural Sciences tripos ("tripos": the examinations for honors in the Cambridge undergraduate de-gree). Under the Cambridge system, he could have taken Part I of the Natural Sciences tripos and then have had the option of taking Part II either in Natural Sciences or in some other tripos such as Modern and Medieval Languages, which would then become his major field for the degree. By the third term of his first year he had at any rate settled on Modern and Medieval Languages, for which two languages were required: in his case, French and Russian. Since Part I of the Modern and Medieval tripos consisted only of translating from French and Russian into English and vice versa and of composing an essay in the two "foreign" languages, he must have seen that it offered him noth-ing new. For that reason, he may have intended from the beginning to complete his degree in the French and Russian literature options within Part II of the Modern and Medieval tripos—this would require the least effort and allow him the most time for his own pursuits—but to take Part I in Natural Sciences as zoological background for serious lepidoptery.

Whatever Nabokov studied formally in his first two terms at Cam-bridge, one kind of involvement in zoology is certain. In his first term at Trinity he wrote his first entomological paper—and his first publica-tion in English—"A Few Notes on Crimean Lepidoptera," published early in his second term.[24] Characteristically it had nothing to do with his classes. Throughout his time in Cambridge, his intellectual development followed its own private course: "Scholastically, I may as well have gone up to the Inst. M.M. of Tirana."* The real life of Vladimir Nabokov in England was "the story of my trying to become a Russian writer."[25] Terrified of squandering the only patrimony he had salvaged from Russia, his language, he was delighted to find a second-hand copy of Dahl's great four-volume Russian dictionary at a bookstall in Cambridge's Market Place† and set about reading at least ten pages every evening, "jotting down such words and expressions as might especially please me."[26]‡

Without knowing he would ever become a major English writer, Nabokov also kept an ear tuned to the language spoken around him: the word "skoramis" (chamber-pot), used by Cambridge dons, entered *Pale Fire* more than forty years later, as did "knackle" (to knock together), overheard in Cambridgeshire. In October 1919 he wrote a couple of English poems, one of them good enough to be published in the *English Review* the next year, though clichéd to our ears ("Like silent ships we two in darkness met . . ."). He also read Rupert Brooke, the darling of nearby King's College; A. E. Housman, whose glum features and drooping-thatch mustache he saw at Trinity's high table almost every night; and Walter de la Mare. For Housman's poetry in particular he continued to have a high regard all his life. In retrospect he noted that the cadences of these fashionable English poets were so much a part of his existence—"running about my room and all over me like tame mice"—that they infiltrated his Russian poetry quite without his awareness.[27]

For all these flirtations with the English language and English verse, it was his devotion to Russian poetry that shaped his life at Cambridge and kept him awake on his bed night after night in a trance of composition, obliviously smoking Turkish cigarettes or glazedly conscious of the shadow a window's crossbar cast on the floor by moonlight. And there was no one there with whom he could share this one thing that mattered. Kalashnikov could barely tolerate someone else reading, let alone a poet gazing into space for a rhyme. More than once he threatened to throw his roommate's books and poems in the fire.[28]

---

* Where many daughters of White Army officers were sent.

† Cambridge bookstalls produced another curio. In London he once dreamed of a green wall and the very next day "was introduced to a person whose name turned out to be Greenwall. I never met him again, nor did that meeting in any way affect the course of my existence, but several years later I picked up a book from a stall and its title was: *Dreams and their Meaning* by A. Greenwall." *The Nabokovian* 20 (1988): 13.

‡ Solzhenitsyn, too, would study Dahl assiduously, and managed to take volume 3 with him—his only book—to his prison camp in Ekibastuz (see Michael Scammell, *Solzhenitsyn: A Biography*, New York: Norton, 1984).

Nabokov's parents were his main outlet, not so much on weekend visits—they were just over an hour away by train—as in a correspondence so steady that a three-day gap could be cause for anxious reproach from either side. Some of the warm letters in both directions have been preserved. Writing to him as Volodyushka, or occasionally "Poops" or "Poopsik,"* his father would draw his attention to a challenging chess problem in the *Morning Post*, mention the death of a French writer, discuss a boxing championship, or reveal the humor, absent in his political writings, that his family recalled so vividly. Vladimir, in return, peppered his parents with poems.

At the end of the Michaelmas term, in mid-December, Nabokov returned to London for Christmas. Still involved with Eva Lubrzynska—though he had been seeing local English girls at Cambridge—he spent a weekend with her and her uncle at the uncle's villa in Margate, Kent, where he took his first ("and penultimate") ride in an airplane, a small cheap contraption. In London V. D. Nabokov was helping to set up an English-language newspaper, *The New Russia*, but with the cost of living high in England and the country reluctant to entangle itself further in Russia, he had begun to recognize that he would have to seek a future elsewhere.[29]

IV

When Vladimir returned to Cambridge in the second week of January 1920, Sergey, who had been unhappy at Oxford, went up with him, to enter Christ's College (he was "allowed" the previous term). With Kalashnikov, Nabokov moved into lodgings at 2 Trinity Lane, a narrow, otherwise houseless gap between the dirty brick back of Great Court and the equally blank flank of Gonville and Caius College. On its eastern outlook 2 Trinity Lane was 38 Trinity Street, a wine and spirits merchant, part of a busy shopping street serving gown more than town: booksellers, bicycle showrooms, and at number 35 the Alma Mater Toilet Club, Hairdressing and Shaving Saloon. Lodging-house keepers had to be approved by the university; Mrs. Alice Newman of 2 Trinity Lane, who offered rooms at 23s., 20s., 12s., and 11s. 6d., as well as a decrepit, ruptured pianola that her lucky undergraduates could play any day except Sunday, no doubt satisfied the requirements amply. But for Nabokov the severance from the brightly colored treats and the fairy-tale luxury that things English had meant for him as a child could not have been more complete. Pear's Soap post-

---

* "Poops": a boy doll; "poopsik," its diminutive: a kewpie doll.

ers had not warned of the cold trudge he still had to make every morning down Trinity Lane to the Baths.[30]

Some time in his first Cambridge year Nabokov introduced Eva Lubrzynska to a Trinity mate, Robert Lutyens, son of the architect Sir Edwin Lutyens and himself something of a poet (he published a book of verse later in the year). By December 1920 Eva would be Mrs. Lutyens, but though he had almost married her himself, Nabokov seems to have felt only relief at her fading from his life. He conducted several love affairs simultaneously among the local beauties, including a shopkeeper's daughter, an Eveline, a Miriam, and "Margaret Fancyname," a Danish war widow.[31]

There were other outlets for his energy. In the boxing trials held at the Corn Exchange in late February he reached the semifinals and then was knocked out by someone from his zoology class, not the son of a rajah, as he remembered, but Paul Leiris, a Sinhalese. The deciding blow permanently damaged the cartilage in his nose, leaving his right nostril S-shaped.[32]

Less inglorious were his soccer games for Trinity College, in which he rated himself "an erratic but rather spectacular goalkeeper." Nabokov—his teammates called him "Nabkov" or, facetiously, "Mac-Nab"—felt that the English code of solid teamwork and "the national dread of showing off" stifled the romance of goalkeeping, the Byronic solitude and independence Italian or Spanish football fans relished in the role. Nevertheless a poignant glamour still pervades his accounts of matches against St. John's or Christ's. On days when the field would be swept by a chill east wind from the fens, his sense of isolation from those around him kept him aglow. While play was concentrated at the other end of the field he would devise lines of verse in a language incomprehensible to his teammates—and sometimes snap out of his trance too late to focus on the rush at his net. Some time this term, it seems, he abandoned his zoology because it stood in the way of his poetry. His soccer stood in the way of getting to the library—but soccer of course remained.[33]

V

In mid-March Vladimir and Sergey returned to London for the Easter vacation. V. D. Nabokov—who had just passed on praise for Vladimir's poetry from Teffi*—was away the whole time at a CD con-

* Pseudonym of Nadezhda Buchinskaya (1875–1952), known as a poet before the revolution and famous in the emigration for her humorous stories and sketches.

ference in Paris and was already planning to start up "a *real* Russian newspaper" in Berlin, where his old colleagues Iosif Hessen and Avgust Kaminka had settled.[34]

In London Uncle Konstantin's wide circle of acquaintances, Russian and English, assured his nephews a busy social life. Lucie Léon, who moved in the same circles, recalled Vladimir in navy blue suit and canary yellow Shetland sweater as "the young *homme du monde*— handsome, romantic in looks, something of a snob and a gay charmer—Sergey was the dandy, an aesthete and a balletomane" who "attended all the Diaghileff premieres wearing a flowing black theater cape and carrying a pommelled cane." Vladimir went roller-skating with Nina Romanov, a grand duchess by birth, and would take her punting in Cambridge. At a charity ball in London he admired a young woman selling balloons. "Oh, that's Marinka," exclaimed Kalashnikov. Nabokov knew her too, it turned out: Marianna Shreiber, whom he had adored at the age of nine in Petersburg, now a ballet dancer in London. They became lovers, and visited one another frequently in London or Cambridge.[35]

Vladimir remained in London for his twenty-first birthday, then went up to Cambridge the same day for the Easter term. By now he had resolved to read only French and Russian for his tripos. He worked hard this term, studying French classics, taking detailed notes in his lectures, not missing any. Nearly all the Russian teaching at Cambridge was done by Alexander Goudy, a Slavic specialist who not only advised on Serbian and Bulgarian but also taught Spanish and modern Greek. In French there were of course far more teachers, none of special renown. In all his formal studies at Cambridge Nabokov's greatest gain was probably the deep love he acquired for the medieval masterpieces he may not otherwise have encountered— *Aucassin and Nicolette* and the work of Chrétien de Troyes—that could share a shelf in his mind with the medieval Russian *Song of Igor's Campaign*, dear to him from schooldays.[36]

When he later recalled his Cambridge years as a time of fierce unhappiness, Nabokov focused on the ache of longing for Russia. That was solid enough: he even gave the name "Nostalgia" to a new verse album begun on the first day of the new term.[37] But what he forgot in his later recollections was the natural exuberance a letter to his mother bears witness to:

> The walls of our little room are repainted white now and that has made it younger, happier.
>   My memory has a temperature of 42° [Celsius]: Cambridge is aflutter with spring, and in one corner of our garden it smells as it smelled in the

evenings in the last ten days of May, on the farthest path of the New Park—remember? Yesterday as the day slid down we ran about the paths and fields like madmen, laughing for no reason, and when I closed my eyes it seemed I was in Vyra. "Vyra"—what a strange word. . . . I came home drunk with memories—with the buzzing of maybugs in my head, with my palms sticky with earth, with a child's dandelion in my button-hole. What joy! What agony, what heart-rending, provoking, inexpress-ible agony. Mother dear, no one except you and I can understand that.

This letter isn't working out, must finish. I am infinitely happy, and so agitated and sad today. . . .[38]

The happiness seemed to dominate: playing tennis on a good clay court with Sergey, with whom he spent more time than he ever had at home; boating on the Cam, under the pink cones of the chestnuts in flower; acting the prankster with Mikhail Kalashnikov and Prince Ni-kita Romanov.[39] Prince Nikita, like Sergey, had entered Christ's Col-lege a term after Vladimir came up to Trinity. Vladimir found him charmingly shy and mischievous—and later made him serve as the original of Vadim in *Glory*:

His rapid, staccato manner of speaking was accompanied by all kinds of hissing, trumpeting, and squeaking sounds like the speech of a child short both of ideas and words but incapable of keeping still. When em-barrassed he would grow even more disjointed and absurd, and would seem like a cross between a shy, tongue-tied adult and a whimsical in-fant. Otherwise, he was a nice, chummy, attractive fellow. . . . a master of foul language. . . . His education was undistinguished, his English very droll and endearing but barely intelligible.[40]

Happy, observant, straightforward, able to act the hooligan or the sensitive, he became the fellow student whose company Nabokov most enjoyed in his first two years at Cambridge. Kalashnikov on the other hand was becoming darker, more bitter and misanthropic. As a threesome, though, they enjoyed their adventures—"and more than one proctor knows our faces. . . . one wild night we broke two of the landlady's chairs and smeared the opposite wall with the cream from some poisonous pastries. We had to pay for that—but not much."[41]

As work eased at the end of term Nabokov struck a rich vein of verse—seven poems in a month that sixty years later he still thought worth including in his collected poetry. One of these, "Lastochki" ("Swallows") he announced to his parents as "an unpublished poem of Aleksandr Sergeevich"—and indeed it soars through Pushkinian air, if not with Pushkinian wings. He also told his father that he was desperately keen to earn a little money in some job over the long vacation, but when he said as much at Cambridge he was given "the most unbelievable propositions—one of which was going to Ceylon as an assistant entomologist."[42]

VI

Earlier in the year, in a less practical mood, he had even dreamed of spending the summer in the United States, but when he ended his first year at Cambridge on June 14, 1920, he simply took the train to London. His father came back a week later from a month in Paris and Berlin, where he had finalized the details of their move. Though food shortages made Berlin life gloomy, and though he found the whole atmosphere of the city alien, V. D. Nabokov felt he had no choice but to resettle his family there.[43]

In London he and Vladimir were talking one day about the difficulties that would face anyone who translated Romain Rolland's *Colas Breugnon*, a novel written in an archaic style with a Rabelaisian verbal gusto that takes every event as a mere pretext "for puns, proverbs and jokes, flourishes and refrains, sayings and charms. It is a Vesuvius of words, an eruption of the old-French lexicon. . . . an uninterrupted game of rhythmic figures, assonances and internal rhymes, chains of alliterations, rows of synonyms." Nabokov made a bet with his father that he would translate it into Russian, preserving rhythm and rhyme. He had no esteem for Rolland as a writer, but was attracted simply by this sheer cliff to climb.[44] Since Rolland had appropriated an antique French for a historical setting more than halfway back from modern times to medieval, and since Nabokov would have to riffle through Dahl for equally venerable Russian equivalents, there could have been no more apt exercise for someone taking the Modern and Medieval tripos in those two languages.

At the beginning of August the Nabokovs, including grandmother Maria, who had been living with them in London since her escape from Russia, moved into a flat at 1 Egerstrasse in Berlin's Grunewald district. Since their landlady was the widow of Rafael Loewenfeld, the translator of Tolstoy and Turgenev, they found a large Russian library at their disposal.[45] A park and a cul-de-sac shielded them from the traffic noise of trams fifty yards away on the Hohenzollerndamm.

Nabokov's cousin Onya (Sophia) Nabokov married in Berlin at the beginning of August. A photograph shows Nabokov sporting sideburns, and looking remote, poised, and dashing behind a row of stiff collars and stuffed shirts in a vast family gathering.[46] But Berlin was only just becoming a main destination for the continuing exodus from Russia. As life became rapidly cheaper in Germany and the last collapse of the White Army in November 1920 sent out a new wave of émigrés, Berlin's Russian population would swell over the next three years to become a thriving city within a city, the center of the emigration and an astoundingly productive hive for Russian publishers.

That evolution was only beginning as Hessen, Kaminka, and V. D. Nabokov negotiated throughout August and September with the mammoth and liberally inclined Ullstein press to set up the first of the Russian publishing firms, Slovo, and a Russian-language daily newspaper. The newspaper's future editors would have liked to call it *Rech'*, but Paul Milyukov, another editor of the old *Rech'*, was involved in and would soon become editor of the Paris *Poslednie Novosti*. In September V. D. Nabokov was still searching for a name. He fancied *Dolg* (*Duty*), brief like *Rech'* and implying a continuing obligation to Russia. Vladimir had a suggestion of his own to make that disclosed *his* attitude to Russia: *Sleza* (*Teardrop*).[47]

VII

On October 4, 1920, Vladimir and Sergey left Berlin for their second year at Cambridge.[48] Two weeks later Vladimir wrote home:

> Mother dear, yesterday I woke up in the middle of the night, and asked someone—I don't know whom—the night, the stars, God: will I really *never return*, is it really all finished, wiped out, destroyed . . . ? In my sleep I saw black, eye-spotted caterpillars on vines of willow herb, then those yellowy-red wooden chairs, with fretwork backs like horses' heads which, remember, stood under the stairway in *our* house (step, step, step and I would stumble, you would laugh . . .)—Mother, we must return, mustn't we, it cannot be that this has all died, turned to dust—such an idea could drive one mad! I would like to describe every little bush, every stalk in our divine park at Vyra—but no one can understand this. . . . How little we valued our paradise . . . —we should have loved it more pointedly, more consciously. . . . People have come into the room, my spirits have suddenly wrinkled up, can't write any more. Not having a corner to oneself is simply torture at times.[49]

Nabokov played a good deal of tennis and soccer, and did almost nothing on the *Colas Breugnon* translation, despite a contract with Slovo. After reading an account of Vladimir's daily routine, his father scolded him: "no danger of mental exhaustion. Not for you at any rate—although 2 hours of mental work a day is a terrible load: . . . *7200* seconds a day!" With the advance for *Colas Breugnon* already paid out, V. D. Nabokov tried to cajole and tease his son into finishing by January 1.[50]

To no avail: he was enjoying himself. On Guy Fawkes Day, he and his friends shrieked into the night, let off rockets, broke streetlamps: "Police were out in hordes. One of them hit me on the back of the head." For some such prank, Nabokov was actually expelled from Trinity, according to one source, until Harrison had the expulsion order lifted. Mikhail Kalashnikov and Nikita Romanov were ideal companions in this mood, equally ready to romp through the town or remember old Russia or a line of Pushkin. A new Russian face at St. John's was that of Lucie Léon's brother, Alex Ponizovski, who ten years later would teach James Joyce some Russian and be very briefly engaged to Joyce's daughter Lucia. Nabokov was fond of Ponizovski, not least for his "streak of quiet eccentricity . . . , such as the time he casually swallowed the contents of a small bottle of ink that happened to be within reach while we sat and talked by the fire."[51]

That autumn H. G. Wells was setting forth in the *Sunday Express* his impressions of the new Russia.[52] After two weeks there* with his son George, who had a smattering of the language, he judged that the country was in its atrocious state only as a result of prolonged war, not because of Bolshevik policies, and argued that however primitive the Marxism of the Bolsheviks, theirs was the only hope of government this side of total collapse and should therefore be supported. His reports were taken for gospel. On November 8, in the rooms of another undergraduate, Nabokov and Kalashnikov met George Wells, who had come up to Trinity that term.

> According to young Wells everything is splendid, and if Ivan Ivanych can't obtain pineapple, it is solely the fault of the blockade. . . . Note that these travellers . . . speak Russian worse than I do Icelandic.
>
> "On the whole, ye know, it's not bad at all. The workmen are really happy. It was most pathetic to see their children—cheerful little chaps— romping in the school-yards." And so on, and so on.

* In the company of Maurice Baring, H. G. Wells had visited Russia once before, in late January and early February 1914. Hosted by the liberal Anglophile element in cultured St. Petersburg, he was invited to dinner at the Nabokovs'. Nabokov recalls one "awful moment" he witnessed, at fourteen, round the family table: "Zinaida Vengerov, his translator, informed Wells, with a toss of her head, 'You know, *my* favorite work of yours is *The Lost World*.' 'She means the war the Martians lost,' said my father quickly" (*Strong Opinions*, 104). That winter Nabokov read avidly the Wells books in his father's library, and the future creator of *Ada*'s Antiterra would never lose his high esteem for Wells as a craftsman of romance.

Kalashnikov and I simply lost our tempers. We went as far as calling all socialists scoundrels. It ended up with Mishka jumping up and shouting out, his huge eyes flashing madly: "Kill the Yids!" Funny and sad. . . .

. . . I told him [Wells]: "But so many have been killed, so many souls crippled, oppressed." . . . And the Fabian's son replied: "And the Cossacks? And the Kishinev pogroms?" Blockhead.[53]

To hear Kishinev used against those who opposed the Bolsheviks must have been especially galling for a young man whose father had attacked the tsarist government in print at the time of the pogrom—and was now criticizing H. G. Wells in the pages of the *New Russia*.

That reminder of V. D. Nabokov's resolute opposition to the persecution of Jews provokes a question: how could his son bear Kalashnikov? As a mature adult Vladimir Nabokov would be admirably strict and uncompromising at any hint of anti-Semitism (and would refuse to see his old roommate), but although by then he would remember having shared quarters with Kalashnikov for only one term and in a state of constant tension, in fact at Cambridge he lived two years with "Mishka" and still chose to spend time with him—no doubt hoping he would not remount his foaming hobby-horse.[54] Nabokov simply ignored it when Kalashnikov tried to foist upon him the notorious forgery *Protocols of the Elders of Zion*, but at Cambridge it was people like George Wells whom he found it impossible to stand. The exploitation of class hatred by the communists seemed more inexcusable than anything else he knew. History would teach him soon enough that racial hatred could be fouler still.

By November his tutor had decided he needed direction, and made him "rot" in Trinity's great Wren Library searching out information from dusty quartos. Nabokov never learned where the main university library was, though, or even whether Trinity College had—as of course it did—its own undergraduate reading room.[55]

On November 18 he wrote to his mother that his big new English poem ("Home") had appeared in the *Trinity Magazine*, and made him feel a hero. He had already published three poems in a Russian émigré periodical early in the year, but it was the newspaper just being born in Berlin that would publish nearly all his early poems, plays, stories, reviews, translations, and even crossword puzzles.

The name *Rul'* (*The Rudder*) had at last been settled upon, largely because in Russian it has the same number of letters as *Rech'* and its masthead could mimic that of its predecessor. More than any other daily newspaper in prerevolutionary Russia, *Rech'* had tried to foster genuine literature on its pages, and *Rul'* gradually followed suit. Its first issue, dated November 16, appeared on Berlin streets at 4 P.M. on the fifteenth, without any literary contributions.[56] On November 27 the drought was broken with a story by Ivan Bunin, the most distinguished of the older émigré writers, and a poem by Nabokov, soon to be recognized as the best of the younger ones. It was signed "Cantab." Under another pseudonym, its author would turn *Rul'* 's literary drought into a flood.

Rul' opened with a lament: the surprise news of the second evacuation of the Crimea, the defeat of General Wrangel, the end of organized resistance to the Bolsheviks. By the time Nabokov returned from Cambridge on December 7, the number of Russians in Berlin had increased markedly, to about one hundred thousand. The audience was growing. In *Rul'* on January 7, 1921, the Russian Christmas issue, there appeared three poems by "Vlad. Sirin," and on the opposite page, by the same author, a story ("Nezhit'," "The Sprite") three years earlier than any Nabokov later recalled.

In the story Nabokov imagines being visited in exile by a *leshiy* (wood-sprite) from the old park at Vyra who has had to flee one wood after another as they are chopped down or filled up as mass graves. All his fellow sprites—wood-sprites, river-nymphs, field-goblins, all the incomprehensible beauty of Russia—have been forced to leave. The story's combination of the elfin and the reproachfully nostalgic cuts a trail Nabokov soon learned not to follow in his attempts to explore an irretrievable past and a world of states not our own.

Nabokov kept the name "Sirin" throughout his career as a Russian writer in Europe. The nom de plume served merely to distinguish him from V. D. Nabokov, whose byline appeared frequently in *Rul'* and elsewhere in the émigré press. Its referent was never secret; the name could appear as Vladimir Sirin, V. V. Sirin, or even, before French or English audiences in the 1930s, as Sirin-Nabokoff or Nabokoff-Sirin.* But of course Nabokov had his reasons for choosing that particular word. In Russian folklore a *sirin* was a fabulous bird of paradise. Two years after choosing the name, he wrote in an English piece signed V. Cantaboff: "I have read somewhere that several centuries ago there was a glorious variety of the pheasant haunting Russian woods: it remained as the 'fire-bird' in national fairy-tales and lent something of its brightness to the intricate roof-decorations of village cottages. This wonder-bird made such an impression on the people's imagination

---

* "Incidentally, circa 1910 there had appeared literary collections under the editorial title of *Sirin* devoted to the so-called 'symbolist' movement, and I remember how tickled I was to discover in 1952 while browsing in the Houghton Library at Harvard that its catalogue listed me as actively publishing Blok, Bely, and Bryusov at the age of ten" (*Strong Opinions*, 161).

that its golden flutter became the very soul of Russian art; mysticism transformed seraphim into long-tailed, ruby eyed birds, with golden claws and unimaginable wings; and no other nation on earth is so much in love with peacockfeathers and weathercocks." The thoroughly English Nabokov might be able to sign himself Cantab. or Cantaboff, but his much longer-lasting pseudonym would reveal both his intense longing for Russia and his more unexpected link to Russia's bright supernatural fancies.[57]

Nabokov left Berlin in the second week of January, hiding the fact that he had translated only one hundred ten pages of *Colas Breugnon*. He now began translating steadily, feeling a scoundrel if he had not completed four new pages by evening—as he told his mother in a letter signed "Dorian Vivalcomb." Throughout the Lent term he was troubled at bedtime by heart palpitations, and gave up the twenty Turkish cigarettes he used to smoke in a normal evening of verse composition for a pipe he would fill three times a day.[58]

Writing home to his parents Nabokov often anticipated the imagery of his later fiction in jokes about his muse. Despite his work load, he would report, he walked out with her on Saturdays. Or when Kalashnikov spent a weekend in London, he invited her round and treated her to tea and strawberry inspiration, a plate of cream dactyls, some fried amphibrachs. There were of course less ethereal (and more ephemeral) women in his life: an Italian girl, and Marianna Shreiber, and three other Russians. Marianna dropped him as soon as she found out about the others.[59]

One day early in February, Nabokov reported, his landlady came in, gloomy and calico-red in the face: " 'Something terrible has happened, sir. . . . Something terrible. . . . I simply don't know how to tell you. . . .'—and I was ready to think that the police had come for me or Mishka had died on the way to his lecture. It turned out though that my football boots had burnt in the stove where they were drying." Two weeks later he and Kalashnikov had a fight with three drunk students who disliked their speaking Russian. Things calmed down and they returned home. At midnight, their opponents climbed up the wall into their living room. Although a fray ensued, Mrs. Newman's lodgers somehow managed to avoid having the authorities called in.[60]

By mid-March when Nabokov returned to Berlin for the Easter vacation he had finished translating Rolland's novel, now Russified as *Nikolka Persik*. Obviously there would not be the least difficulty next term when he had to take his first Cambridge exams, testing his ability to handle Russian and French. While in Berlin the actor Vladimir Gaydarov almost challenged Nabokov to a duel for having a fling with his partner, the actress Olga Gzovskaya, recently of the Moscow Art Theater and soon to be one of the stars of Berlin's film studios. But despite all the complications of his romantic life, Olga Gzovskaya, Nabokov maintained, was not one of them.[61]

VIII

The May term of 1921 opens with a jerky old three-reeler. Reel one: a miners' strike leaves the baths unheated, and Nabokov has to splash and snort every morning in his shaky rubber tub. Reel two: on his first weekend back in Cambridge, his birthday in fact, he and Kalashnikov sample a little English life—tea, lawn bowls—when they cycle out to visit a young Russian lady living among fat parsons and boring gossip. Reel three: the next day in a zoology laboratory he sits down to write a Russian poem with the English title "Biology." Though the poem celebrates the pleasures of dissection and the microscope, Nabokov feels he must explain that this means no betrayal of his muse.[62] Later in life he would not hesitate to extol the passion of science and the precision of poetry as glorious equals.

As examinations approached he took up cigarettes again. The first exams were oral: on April 26, French dictation in the Examination Hall; the following day, Russian dictation and individual questions on Turgenev's *Smoke*; on April 28, the individual part of the French exam, with questions on Voltaire's *Lettres philosophiques*. For the last of these Nabokov arrived before his professors, and sat in the examination room writing a poem, one of his best to date: "Esli veter sud'by radi shutki" ("If the wind of fate, for the fun of it"—if the wind of fate would allow him to meet up with Lyussya Shulgin). Naturally he passed both French and Russian orals with distinction.[63]

Immediately after the oral examinations Nabokov sent his parents his Russian critique of the poetry of Rupert Brooke (who himself twelve years earlier, while composing a poem in Greek for his tripos examination, had sat writing a letter to a friend). Already the article displays the exuberant metaphors of Nabokov's mature critical style, and provides excellent translations of Brooke's verse. Nabokov's emphasis was clear: "No other poet has so often, with such tormented and creative vigilance, looked into the dusk of the beyond." Citing Kipling's dictum that the human heart can love only its native land, and even then only some little corner of it, Nabokov implied that for Brooke Grantchester meant what Vyra had for him. He noted his own cool response to Brooke's Arcadia:

I once passed through Grantchester by bike. Fences, complicated iron gates and barbed wire in the surrounding fields tortured the eyes. A humble humdrumness emanated from the dirty little brick homes. A tomfool wind blew up a pair of drawers hung out to dry between two green stakes over the plant-beds of a pauper's vegetable garden. The faint tenor of a hoarse gramophone wafted up from the river.

What mattered, he knew, was not the "objective" configurations of the scene, but the intensity of the heart's attachment.[64]

As in the previous year, he hit top poetic form in May. Tennis, a little kayaking on the river, everything in flower, even the pressure of examinations—all seemed to help. On May 23 he sat his first two exams in Part I of the tripos, translating into French in the morning. This time he wrote a poem in the examination hall after finishing early, timing the poem "11.42 a.m." And in the afternoon, translation from French. The next morning came the French essay, on a topic in seventeenth-century French literature or history. On the morning of May 27 he had to translate Scott and Dickens into Russian, and went off boating in the afternoon. The following morning he wrote his Russian essay on a nineteenth-century topic and in the afternoon finished Part I of his tripos by translating from Russian. Inevitably he received first-class honors, with distinction in Russian.[65]

IX

Vladimir and Sergey set off for Berlin with Mikhail Kalashnikov on June 13. A week later Kalashnikov took his college roommate out to Lichterfelde, in the southwest of Berlin, to meet his cousins the Siewerts. Nabokov immediately started to court the younger of the two sisters, a vivacious sixteen-year-old beauty named Svetlana: dark slanty Tatar eyes, darkish complexion, dark hair in a velvet ribbon. She found the twenty-two-year-old Nabokov, lean and handsome, sporty and cheerful, witty and ardent, impossible to resist.[66]

He copied out one of his old poems in her album on June 23. Six days later he composed a new one inspired by her eyes and punning on her name. As a third poem testified a week later, he was ready to fall passionately, wholeheartedly, in love again for the first time since he and Lyussya Shulgin had parted, or at least since his heyday with Eva Lubrzynska: "I dreamed of you so often, so long ago, / many years before we met. . . ." The whole poem inadvertently discloses what time would bear out: that Nabokov's love for Svetlana owed more to timing and ripe daydreams than to any profound suitability of character. Yet at first youth, looks, eager predispositions, and lively spirits were more than enough to fan romance to white heat. Nor did it hurt that he could imagine, as he wrote in another poem, "how by Pushkin you would have been loved."[67]

Through that summer Nabokov and Kalashnikov, Svetlana and her twenty-year-old sister Tatiana met as a foursome, playing tennis, clowning around on the Lichterfelde platform before taking the train in to town, sitting on a jetty at Wannsee with canes and boaters at a rakish angle, looking in mock forlornness over the pewter-gray water. In the evening Vladimir would return to the Siewert home and after dinner argue with the family for Chekhov, against Dostoevsky, or listen to Svetlana on the piano, by an open window, near the gentle night breeze.[68]

Shortly after his return to Berlin, Nabokov organized for his father's birthday a little family "magazine" called *Rulik* (*Little Rul'*), with a poem from Olga, one from himself, a few drawings.[69] He also began a verse album for the poems—about Svetlana and whatever else heated his fancy—that poured off him like sweat that summer. Far too many of these poems would appear before the end of the next year in a volume of verse called *Grozd'* (*The Cluster*).

On September 5 the Nabokov family—still including grandmother Maria—moved closer to town, to 67 Sächsische Strasse in Wilmersdorf, a large and expensive fourth-floor flat, overlooking a public tennis court, that was rented to them by a German officer named von Kleist. To afford it they had to sublet two rooms to an unobtrusive Englishman. Nabokov's sisters studied in a Russian high school established by an émigré academic group. His mother sighed for London.[70]

By now the Russian Berlin concentrated around the Wilmersdorf area had become the cultural hub of the whole emigration. V. D. Nabokov was editor of the city's main Russian daily, at the head of one of its two main publishing firms, a participant in cultural and political publications and discussions (a memorial evening for Tolstoy, CD party polemics, and so on), president of most of the major nonmonarchist Russian social organizations and on the committee of almost all the rest. He was, in short, the unofficial head of the emigration's largest enclave. The Nabokov flat had "the full flavor of a wealthy, enlightened St. Petersburg home"; once again the family were at the center of a vibrant Russian culture. In the large living-dining room which doubled as V. D. Nabokov's study they entertained guests like the novelist Aleksey Tolstoy, the politician Paul Milyukov, the director Konstantin Stanislavsky, actresses like Elena Polevitskaya, Olga Gzovskaya, Chekhov's widow Olga Knipper, even the whole Moscow Art Theater. "A constant flow of visitors: writers, scholars, artists, politicians, and journalists," in the words of Nicolas Nabokov, who used to flee the White-Russian atmosphere of his mother's home—"ex-generals, ex-colonels, ex-landowners, ex-counts and barons"—in order to plug in to the intellectual energy of the Nabokov household.[71]

Nicolas Nabokov, the future composer and cultural diplomat, paints a lively portrait of his uncle and aunt: both had "brilliant minds, quick wits, rounded educations, and strong political and cultural convictions."

> Uncle Vladimir had in his bearing, his manner of speech, and his whole appearance something distinctly aristocratic, and, like many liberal Russian gentlemen of his time, he was worldly, ironic, a bit haughty, and cosmopolitan. But when he was *en famille*, he became gay, amusing, and a source of exciting ideas and information.
>
> Aunt Lyolya was quite different. She was nervous and shy, very intelligent, but much more complex and brittle than her husband. It was not easy to win her friendship. . . .
>
> The table talk at the Nabokov's was always gay and lively. We spoke about politics, cultural events, literature, and the arts. When cousins Vladimir and Sergei were around . . . the talk turned into a marathon of questions and answers, accompanied by a certain amount of teasing. The teasing game consisted of asking a victim, usually Babushka [grandmother] or me or cousin Olga, questions we couldn't answer. (Who was the world champion in chess before Lasker? What did Napoleon say when he crowned himself? What caterpillars feed on privet leaves? What did Pushkin write to Gogol after reading what book?) Or else cousin Vladimir would invent a writer or a poet, a king or a general, and ask questions about his nonexistent life. The victims would get upset (especially cousin Olga) and call the teaser names. But these games always stopped short of cruelty. . . .
>
> Volodya always did everything with *une superbe sans égal*, and I was a bit scared of his awesome store of information. If I made a clumsy statement, or gave an inadequate answer to a precise question, or misquoted somebody's verse, he would scoff at me and tease me mercilessly.[72]

As Russians poured in from the east or, lured by Berlin's low costs, from other émigré centers, Russian theater and book production flourished. A sign of the Russian colony's confidence was a new periodical, *Zhar-Ptitsa* (*The Firebird*), a lavishly illustrated full-color monthly devoted to Russian art and literature. The first number appeared in August, with a poem ("Krym," "Crimea") by Sirin. A favorable mention of this "talented" poem in a review of *Zhar-Ptitsa* at the beginning of September—by Mark Tsetlin, who ran the poetry section of *Sovremennye Zapiski*, the emigration's most distinguished literary journal—seems to be the first published evaluation of Nabokov's work.[73]

On August 7, 1921, Aleksandr Blok died in Petrograd. A week later, *Rul'* published a poem by Sirin paying homage to and echoing Blok's lyrics on the Beautiful Lady. In the same issue appeared V. D. Nabokov's reminiscence of Blok's verse, rejecting "The Twelve" and professing himself a devotee of the Beautiful Lady. On September 17 the Union of Russian Journalists and Writers in Berlin arranged a memorial evening for Blok. Among the participants were both V. D. Nabokov, reading a memoir of Blok, and Sirin, reciting his own tribute.[74] Father and son would not have much longer to stand side by side.

X

Vladimir returned for his last year at Cambridge, via Ostende as usual, on October 7. He still occupied the room in Trinity Lane he had shared with Mikhail Kalashnikov, who had been sent down after his flawed English sank him in Part I of the History tripos. Nikita Romanov too had left, and without their companionship Nabokov at first felt despondent. The gap was soon filled by Bobby de Calry. Nabokov found him attentive, kind, invariably charming, and even began to learn Italian from him.[75]

He was working hard, he wrote to Svetlana, reading seventeenth-century French tomes in the Wren Library, but his real interests lay elsewhere: in the new tennis racquet he had bought, in the poems he continued to send his parents. Elena Nabokov lived as usual by his letters, enjoying the complicated bookkeeping his steady output required, copying out new productions, numbering and indexing them all.[76] Meanwhile from the albums of Vladimir's verse on hand in Berlin V. D. Nabokov and his friend Sasha Chorny began to select a volume of Sirin poems to be published by Grani, a new press Chorny was setting in motion.

Sasha Chorny (real name Aleksandr Glikberg, 1880–1932) was Russia's best humorous poet of his generation, "the only unpoetical poet of any worth during the rule of symbolism," and along with Korney Chukovsky, the foremost Russian children's poet of his time.[77] Nabokov appreciated both his humor and the childlike side of his imagination: a little animal in the corner of a poem was a sign of Chorny's presence, he once wrote, as a fluffy toy under an armchair reveals a child's. He valued even more highly the serious poems the revolution had wrung out of Chorny. Most of all he felt a warm gratitude for this meek, indecisive, sad-eyed little man, inclined to retreat into himself, who helped the young Sirin not by overpraise but by concrete advice: a skeptical squiggle beside an obscure line, the correction of a grammatical slip, a suggestion that this or that poem Nabokov had brought to the dim rooms of Chorny's Charlottenburg flat might be sent here or there. As literary editor of *Zhar-Ptitsa* and compiler of two literary miscellanies, *Raduga* (*Rainbow*) and *Grani* (*Facets*), Chorny brought out Sirin poetry, prose, drama. In September 1921 his Grani publishing house was already advertising a volume of *Poems* by Sirin, though neither contents nor title had been chosen and the book would not appear until 1923. Nabokov judged in retrospect that Chorny initiated this project not out of admiration for the young Sirin's verse—his taste was too discriminating for that, Nabokov thought—but simply as an act of kindness to the promising and prolific son of a close friend.[78]

In October 1921 V. D. Nabokov wrote to his son that he had vetoed Chorny's suggestion that just for variety Vladimir should sign a forthcoming poem in *Zhar-Ptitsa* with his real name rather than his nom de plume. The young poet replied with mock zeal: "there may not be many Nabokovs, but there is only one Sirin! Therefore Chorny's fit must be cut short: let him put the signature the whole world knows."[79]

Perhaps it was this that gave Nabokov the idea for a literary prank of his own. In late October and early November he wrote a playlet, "Skital'tsy," and sent it to his parents as a translation of the first act of *The Wanderers*, by the English playwright Vivian Calmbrood, an anagram of his own name. Nabokov chose a safely misty past for this first attempt at drama. At a tavern two brothers meet: one who has roamed the world and longs to see his home again, the other who has remained in his native county but voyaged morally to the opposite pole, to become a brigand and a drunkard. The tavern-keeper's fair daughter, we guess, may save one of them or both, or become the ground for their fatal confrontation. V. D. Nabokov assumed that the translation was genuine, and warned his son that his sheer love of literature might make him waste time translating works of no real interest. Had *The Wanderers* been a genuine English play of the late eighteenth or early nineteenth century, it certainly would not have warranted translation, but as the work of a twenty-two-year-old twentieth-century Russian it is an impressive exercise in literary impersonation.[80]

Sending some new lines to his mother, Nabokov commented: "This little poem will prove to you that my mood is as radiant as ever. If I live to be a hundred, my soul will still go round in short trousers." He entitled the poem "Siriniana," as if it were a profession of faith. So it is:

In solitude there is freedom
and sweetness in blessed imaginings.
A star, a snowflake, a drop of honey
    I enclose in verse.

Dying nightly, I am glad
to rise again at the appointed hour.
The next day is a dewdrop of paradise
    and the day past, a diamond.[81]

XI

One day early in the term the ethereal de Calry had tearfully invited
his friend to spend a week at St. Moritz in December. Eager to ski
again, Nabokov had sought permission from his mother by stressing
that the sight of snow and trees rimmed with frost could be a nostrum
for nostalgia. On those terms, it was impossible to turn him down.
Three days after full term ended on December 5, Nabokov and de
Calry crossed the Swiss border. They went ice-skating at Champéry,
were photographed in riding breeches at the top of the Dents du Midi,
and skied at St. Moritz. Nabokov not only used the skis de Calry
provided, but slept in the same bed, unaware that de Calry was
homosexual.[82]

On the way back they stopped in Lausanne where they called on
Vladimir's former governess, Cécile Miauton. Older and fatter, she
was now almost completely deaf and kept misery at bay only by her
fond memories of Russia—where her earlier misery had been allayed
only by the image of Switzerland. Nabokov squirmed at her sentimental distortions of their common past—a scene that would seep into *The
Real Life of Sebastian Knight*, as alpine Switzerland would be crystallized in *Glory*. The two young men brought her a hearing aid the next
day, assuming it was beyond her means.

> She adjusted the clumsy thing improperly at first, but no sooner had she
> done so than she turned to me with a dazzled look of moist wonder and
> bliss in her eyes. She swore she could hear every word, every murmur
> of mine. She could not for, having my doubts, I had not spoken. If I had,
> I would have told her to thank my friend, who had paid for the in-
> strument.[83]

Nabokov traveled back to Berlin with de Calry, who over the next
month replaced Kalashnikov in foursomes with the Siewert girls.[84]

Early in January a review of Chorny's almanac *Grani* included the
first published criticism to dwell at any length on Nabokov, describing

"the beautiful long poem 'Detstvo' ['Childhood']"—written when he was nineteen—as "a sequence of disciplined and sonorous lines resuscitating memories of early childhood." At the end of the month, V. D. Nabokov had Chorny to dinner at Sächsische Strasse to settle the order of poems in the Sirin volume they planned to send to the printer next day. Vladimir had suggested two titles, *Svetlitsa* (a clean bright room, and intended as "a symbol of light, height, solitude," but chiefly a play on Svetlana's name) or *Tropinki Bozhiya* (*The Tracks of God*). They gave a punning twist to his second suggestion: retaining both the path and its transcendental dust, they altered *gornyy put'* (mountain trail) to *Gorniy put'* (*Empyrean Path*, a trail mounting the highest heavens). V. D. Nabokov teased his son by withholding the title "to avoid the caprices peculiar to young authors."[85]

On January 17, 1922, Nabokov reached Cambridge for the start of the Lent term. He found the college prize he had won for his performance in Part I of the tripos amounted to only £2, which had to be spent in any case "on some of the books listed for that purpose, such as *A Picture Story of Cambridge*." He played football every day, he and de Calry were "always together," and at least briefly during this term he worked on a short novel for Chorny's *Grani*. It never eventuated.[86]

XII

Nabokov arrived back in Berlin on March 18, 1922, for the Easter vacation. *Nikolka Persik* had already been set in type, and Iosif Hessen, as editor of the Slovo publishing house, had made a number of revisions on the margins of the proofs before handing them to V. D. Nabokov to pass on to his son. When he brought the corrected proofs back to Hessen, V. D. Nabokov told him with a smile: "You know, Volodya whispered to me: 'Don't give me away, but I quietly rubbed out all his corrections.' "[87]

While Nabokov's mother had been actively organizing fund raising for famine-stricken Russia, his father was preparing for the arrival of Paul Milyukov, who had been invited to speak in Berlin after his recent return to Paris from a lecture tour in the United States.[88]

Since the defeat of Wrangel in November 1920 Milyukov had been calling for a new tactic for the CD party, a closer alliance with the Socialist Revolutionaries, a rejection of the CDs' nonclass heritage in favor of supporting the peasants. Milyukov and his followers were ready to dream the Socialist Revolutionary dream that the peasants might translate their hostility to Bolshevism into concerted rebellion. V. D. Nabokov led those opposing the new tactic. He pointed out that it was doomed from the outset—the SRs emphatically rejected Milyukov's overtures—and argued that what was needed was not support of one class but a united front of all democratic Russian forces opposed to autocracy whether tsarist or Bolshevist: in other words, the CD party's old ideals. An acrimonious dispute had been waged between Milyukov's *Poslednie Novosti* and Nabokov's *Rul'* throughout the first nine months of 1921, with V. D. Nabokov being subjected to particularly intense vilification. By late 1921 the schism was a fact, with Milyukov having convinced only a small fraction of party followers to side with him.

In spite of their bitter differences of opinion, V. D. Nabokov had written a welcome in *Rul'* when Milyukov became editor of *Poslednie Novosti*. In the same spirit, he had insisted that Milyukov should come to Berlin to share his American impressions, and on the morning of March 28, 1922, he contributed an article to *Rul'*, generously welcoming Milyukov to Berlin and suggesting that changed circumstances in Russia had made the schism a thing of the past. Milyukov did not accept the token of peace.[89]

That night Milyukov spoke at the Philharmonia Hall on the theme of "America and the Restoration of Russia." Almost 1,500 Russians turned up to hear the florid-faced, thick-featured former minister of foreign affairs. After he had finished the first part of his lecture, at about 10 P.M., a dark, short figure advanced and fired several times at Milyukov, crying "For the tsar's family and Russia." Someone threw Milyukov to the ground. Even before most of the audience began to scramble for the exit, V. D. Nabokov had leaped from his seat and as the assassin advanced on Milyukov seized him by the hand and tried to disarm him.

With Avgust Kaminka, V. D. Nabokov knocked the gunman to the floor and kept him pinned there. As Kaminka rushed off to check on Milyukov, a second gunman, a tall, bald young man, jumped on the stage and shot three times at V. D. Nabokov to free his trapped friend. Two bullets found Nabokov's spine, the third passed through his left lung and his heart. He died within moments.

Seven others were wounded before the gunmen were disarmed and arrested. They proved to be extreme rightists who lived and worked together in Munich, center of the Russian monarchists in Germany: Peter Shabelsky-Bork, the first to fire, and Sergey Taboritsky. The assassination attempt (Milyukov escaped unharmed) may have been directed by one Colonel Vinberg, leader of the Russian extreme right in Bavaria, although the evidence was never conclusive enough to bring him to trial. But in any case Shabelsky had for years vowed vengeance on Milyukov, whom he held responsible for the February revolution.

Quite ignorant of Russia's politics and history, as the trial would prove, the assassins did not know who V. D. Nabokov was, but on learning of his leading role in the CD party felt their efforts well repaid.[9C]

In his diary Vladimir Nabokov has recorded in great detail this most tragic day of his life. Apart from its intrinsic poignancy, his account also provides us with our only moment-by-moment record of his thoughts—the clearest peephole, therefore, into his immediate mind—and at the same time prefigures his innovative handling of emotional crisis in his fiction. His memories of that night seem to have offered him a psychological key: acute stress may concentrate the mind, not in the accepted sense of narrowing it on one object, but by intensifying all its centrifugal powers.

> 28 March. I returned home about 9 p.m., after a heavenly day. After dinner I sat in the chair by the divan and opened a little volume of Blok. Mother, half-lying, was setting the cards out for patience. It was quiet at home—the girls were already asleep, Sergey was out. I was reading aloud those tender poems about Italy, about damp, resonant Venice, about Florence, like a smoky iris. "How splendid that is," Mother said, "yes, yes, exactly: a smoky iris." And then the phone rang in the hall. There was nothing unusual in its ring, I was simply annoyed that my reading was interrupted. I went to the phone. Hessen's voice: "Who's that?" "Volodya. Hello, Iosif Vladimirovich." "I am ringing because, . . . I wanted to tell you, to warn you . . ." "Yes, go on." "Something terrible has happened to your father." "What exactly?" "Something terrible. . . . A car is coming for you." "But what exactly has happened?" "A car is coming. Open the door below." "Fine." I hung up, got to my feet. Mother was standing in the door. She asked, eyebrows twitching, "What's happened?" I said: "Nothing special." My voice was cold, almost dry. "*Tell* me." "Nothing special. The fact is, father has been hit by a car. He's hurt his leg." I went through the living room to my bedroom. Mother followed. "No, I implore you, tell me." "Nothing to worry about. They're picking me up straight away." . . . She both believed me and did not. I changed, filled my cigarette case. My thoughts, all my thoughts, clenched their teeth. "My heart will burst," Mother said, "simply burst, if you are hiding anything." "Father hurt his leg, rather seriously, Hessen said. That's all." Mother sobbed, went on her knees before me. "I implore you." I continued to calm her as I could. . . .
>
> Yes, my heart *knew*, the end had come, but what exactly had happened was still a mystery, and in not knowing some hope could still flicker. Somehow neither Mother nor I linked Hessen's words with father's being that evening at Milyukov's lecture or that some sort of scene was

expected there. . . . For some reason I remembered the afternoon: on the train with Svetlana I had traced on the fogged-up carriage window the word "happiness"—and every letter trickled downwards in a bright line, a damp wriggle. Yes, my happiness has run. . . .

—At last a car drove up. Out came Shtein, whom I had never met before, and Yakovlev. I opened the doors. Yakovlev followed me, took me by the hand. "Keep calm. Shots were fired at the meeting. Your father was wounded." "Badly?" "Yes, badly." They stayed below, I went after Mother. Repeated what I had heard, knowing inside that the truth was softened. We went down. . . . Took off. . . .

That night journey I remember as something *outside life*, monstrously slow, like those mathematical puzzles that torment us in feverish half-sleep. I looked at the lights swimming past, at the whitish bands of lighted pavement, at the spiral reflections in the mirrory-black asphalt and it seemed to me that I was cut off from all this in some fateful manner—that the streetlights and the dark shadows of passersby were an accidental mirage, and the sole thing clear and significant and alive was the grief, tenacious, suffocating, compressing my heart. "Father is no more." These four words hammered in my brain and I tried to imagine his face, his movements. The night before he had been so happy, so kind. He laughed, he fought with me when I began to demonstrate a boxing clinch. Then everyone went off to bed, Father began to undress in his room and I did the same in mine next door. We chatted through the open door, talked of Sergey, of his strange, abnormal inclinations. Then Father helped me put my trousers under the press, and drew them out, turning the screws, and said, laughing: "That must hurt them." Dressed in pyjamas I sat on the arm of the leather chair, and Father, squatting, cleaned the shoes he had taken off. We were talking now about the opera *Boris Godunov*. He tried to remember how and when Vanya returns after his father has sent him off. Couldn't recall. At last I went to bed and hearing Father also going off asked him to give me the newspapers, he passed them through the slit of the parted doors—I didn't even see his hands. And I remember, that movement seemed creepy, ghostly—as if the sheets had thrust themselves through. . . .

—And the next morning Father set off for *Rul'* before I woke and I didn't see him again. And now I was rocking in a closed car, the lights were shining—amber lights, screeching trams, and the route was long, long, and the tiny streets flashing by were all unfamiliar. . . .

At last we arrived. Entrance to the Philharmonie. Hessen and Kaminka came across the street to us. They approach. I support mother. "Avgust Isaakievich, Avgust Isaakievich, what has happened, tell me, what's happened?" she asks, seizing him by the sleeves. He spreads out his hands. "Something terrible." He sobs, cannot finish. "So it's all over,

all over?" He says nothing, Hessen too says nothing. Their teeth chatter,
their eyes dart away. —And Mother understood. I thought she would
faint. She threw her head back somehow strangely, set off, looking fixedly before her, slowly opening her arms to something unseen. "So
that's it?" she repeated quietly. She seemed to reason it out with herself.
"How can it be?" and then: "Volodya, do you understand?" We walked
up a long corridor. Through the open side door I saw the hall where *it*
happened flash past. Some chairs were crooked, some overturned. . . .
At last we went into a sort of entrance hall; people were crowded around;
the green uniforms of the police. "I want to see him," Mother repeated
in a monotone. From one door a black-bearded man with a bandaged
hand came out, and somehow helplessly smiling muttered: "You see I
. . . I am wounded too." I asked for a chair, sat Mother down. People
crowded helplessly around. I understood that the police wouldn't allow
us into the room where the body lay. In that room the man whom one of
the madmen shot at kept vigil all night. I momentarily imagined him
standing over the body—a dry, pinkish, gray-haired old man, fearing
nothing, loving nothing. And suddenly Mother, sitting on the chair in
the middle of an entrance hall full of embarrassed strangers, began to sob
aloud and emit a kind of strained groan. I clung to her, pressed my cheek
to her beating, burning temple and whispered one word to her. Then she
began to recite "Our Father . . . ," and when she finished seemed to turn
to stone. I felt there was no reason to stay any longer in that delirious
room.[91]

There the transcript Elena Nabokov made from her son's diary
breaks off.

A first memorial service was held in the city two days later, a second
the following day at the Russian church at Tegel, on the northwest
fringes of Berlin. On April 1 V. D. Nabokov's open coffin was displayed for the last time before his burial that day in the tiny Russian
cemetery of Tegel under a six-foot-high Orthodox cross. The stunned
Russian community responded quickly. Obituaries flowed in from
colleagues, politicians, lawyers, journalists, writers like Bunin, Merezhkovsky, Kuprin. More memorial services were held. A fund was
set up in V. D. Nabokov's name.[92]

XIII

Vladimir responded in his own way, with a poem on his father's
death published in *Rul'* on Easter Day. "Easter": "But if all the brooks
sing anew of miracle, . . . then you are in that song, you are in that

gleam, you are alive." That poem was apparently the last to be written of those collected in *Grozd'*. Perhaps Nabokov assembled the poems himself for one of the new publishers in Russian Berlin's booming book market, before leaving for his last and saddest Cambridge term on April 20. Sergey remained in Berlin to look after his mother, who was still prostrate with grief, until his tripos examinations. Under the circumstances the university waived his residence requirements for the term.[93]

For Vladimir his first springs in exile always reminded him that in Russia it would have been time to set off for Vyra and its lilacs in bloom. Now with the loss of his father added to the loss of his homeland spring was doubly cruel: "At times it's all so oppressive I could go out of my mind—but I have to hide. There are things and feelings no one will ever find out."[94]

There were distractions: chestnuts in flower, the eglantine turning the countryside white, de Calry's company, Peter Mrosovsky bounding into his rooms with a fresh blue copy of *Ulysses* smuggled back from Paris and stomping up and down as he regaled Nabokov with some of the spicier parts of Molly Bloom's monologue. Fortunately, too, examinations loomed close, and Nabokov began cramming fifteen or sixteen hours a day, sometimes, to relieve the monotony, on a boat in the shadow of the willows lining the Cam. Now the almost verbatim lecture notes he had taken over the last two years helped to make up for his indifference to his studies outside class.[95]

His examinations were held in the last week of May, in the Small Hall of the Examination School: first, French Literature, Thought and History, 1688–1870; then Russian History, Life, and Literature before 1700; French Literature, Thought and History, 1495–1688; Russian Literature, Thought and History since 1700; and finally French Literature, Life and History before 1495. Part II of the tripos was far more serious than Part I had been. The last two nights Nabokov was too busy cramming to catch any sleep, and this time there were no poems written in the examination room. Two days before the exams began Nabokov had warned his mother that if he knew he had failed he would come straight to Berlin on June 1 without waiting out the term, but as they progressed he realized he would pass comfortably enough. He particularly welcomed and enjoyed one question on Gogol's *Dead Souls*—describe Plyushkin's garden—which perfectly suited his preference for exact knowledge, precise visualization, detailed recall. He told his mother he was dreaming often of his father, "and before every exam, I looked on his portrait, as if on an icon, and I know that he helped me." Like Sergey, he found on June 17 that he had been awarded a second-class honors for Part II of the tripos and hence for his whole degree. The degree was conferred three days later, and he left for Berlin on June 21.[96]

The Nabokovs' finances had become too insecure for Vladimir to throw away the potential benefits of a good Cambridge degree, but he had done the minimum necessary. Two days after his last exam he wrote to his mother that he could feel the muse returning, could hear her step approaching.[97] She had never been far away. In its variety and bulk his publishing record was remarkable for an undergraduate: an entomological article, two English poems, a critical article and verse translations from the English, the virtuoso translation from French of a difficult novel, a first Russian story, his first descriptive prose, his first verse drama. And above all, his Russian poems: appearing in more than half a dozen periodicals and every week or two in *Rul'*, and two more volumes of verse—his third and fourth— already in press. At Cambridge he had directed all the energy left over from being young, in exile, in love, not into becoming Vladimir Nabokov, B.A., but into becoming Vladimir Sirin.

Regrouping: Berlin, 1922–1923

I met the first of my three or four successive wives

in somewhat odd circumstances. . . .

—*Look at the Harlequins!*

I

WHEN NABOKOV returned to Berlin from Cambridge late in June 1922, he had no special love for Germany and eventually would have good reasons to hate it, but he would remain here, nonetheless, for another fourteen and a half years.

Until his family left for Prague in December 1923, he continued to live with them at 67 Sächsische Strasse. His mother's nerves had always been easily jarred, but she had once been an enthusiast for life and full of joy. Now she was a small, gray-haired woman in black, with a roll-your-own cigarette in one hand, distraught, always needing solace.[1] Vladimir himself, usually unruffled, jocose and radiantly happy, was severely depressed. When he proposed to the seventeen-year-old Svetlana Siewert in Berlin's aquarium, she agreed to marry him—or so she recalled through the haze of years—partly because he seemed so pitifully and uncharacteristically sad. Her parents approved the engagement on condition that the young man settle into a steady job.[2]

Positions in a German bank were found for both Vladimir and Sergey. Sergey lasted a week, Vladimir a mere three hours. He could never be an Eliot or a Wallace Stevens, chained to the office bench in order to be free at his own writing desk. And there seemed to be no urgency about work. After the first gentle puffs of inflation, life in Berlin had become absurdly cheap, only a quarter what it cost in Paris. Over the next few years, as economic conditions altered, Nabokov would support himself more and more by tutoring, passing on to others the French or English, even the tennis or boxing, that he had absorbed as a young Russian from a wealthy and cultured home. But he seems to have begun tutoring in desultory fashion. Noticing his ample free time, Klavdia Siewert invited him in late July with Svetlana, Ta-

tiana, and their younger brother Kirill to a summer resort in Bad Rotherfelde in the Teutoburger Wald for some healthy living, German
style: long walks through the forest, or sipping milk under the maples
and chestnuts to the accompaniment of a Wagner potpourri surging
from the soundshell.[3]

In the summer of 1922 Gamayun, one of Berlin's many new Russian
publishers, commissioned Sirin to translate *Alice in Wonderland* into
Russian.[4] After Gamayun handed him as his advance a U.S. five-
dollar bill—no mean sum by now—he took a tram home, but finding
no change in his pocket, had to proffer the bill. The conductor was so
impressed, he stopped the car to count out the change.[5]

Nabokov found the translation easy work after *Colas Breugnon*. To
make the book a self-sufficient plaything for Russian children he
staged a gleeful raid on the toys and tags of a Russian nursery: the
French mouse that came over with William the Conqueror became
a mouse left when Napoleon retreated, Alice became Anya, trivial
puns became quadrivial. The twenty-three-year-old Nabokov's *Anya
v strane chudes* has been rated the best translation of the book into any
language.[6]

II

Russian Berlin, 1921–1924, was a cultural supernova without equal in
the annals of refugee humanity. A few hundred thousand very temporary settlers in a Berlin already well supplied with its own books
and periodicals published more in three years than most countries
could publish in a decade.

By the middle of 1921 a million Russian refugees had fled the revolution and its aftermath. Some settled in Harbin or Shanghai or
crossed to the United States. Most stayed in Europe, congregating in
Paris, Berlin, and Prague or to a lesser extent in Riga and Sofia. As
prices rose sharply in France late in 1921, émigrés deserted Paris for
Berlin, which by the end of the year had become the unmistakable
center of the emigration. At the same time Germany, still paying for
the war through reparations and the punitive trade policies imposed
by the Western powers, was ready to turn to Russia as a potential
market and a neighbor also in need of friends. With the New Economic Policy (NEP) encouraging an end to economic isolationism,
Gorky managed to persuade Lenin to permit his friend the publisher
Grzhebin to set himself up in Berlin, sending cheaply produced books
back to a Russia where after the chaos of civil war ink and paper were
in as short supply as everything else. Other Soviet enterprises fol-

lowed Grzhebin, while émigré ones backed by German capital now took up the early lead of Slovo. By 1924, an astounding eighty-six Russian publishing firms had been established in Berlin.[7]

The city's chief Russian newspaper, *Rul'*, typifies the special conditions of the time. With the German mark so low that *Rul'* was a bargain everywhere, it was zealously distributed throughout the world by Ullstein, its German backers, for the valuable foreign currency it reaped. Though most émigrés already lived in Germany, *Rul'* was on sale *outside* the country in 369 cities in 34 countries from Manchuria to Argentina. Advertisers invited the wealthy or once-wealthy to buy or sell jewelry or furs, while the advertisements placed by the émigrés themselves, peasants in Harbin or White Army officers in the Balkans, sought to trace missing family and friends. But it was the intellectuals—the artists, writers, and scholars—who made the Russian emigration a mass exodus unique in history. From the end of 1921 to early 1924, they packed themselves tightly into southwest Berlin. In these heady years of émigré life, advertisements from Berlin's Russian publishers would fill five or six full pages of small type—hundreds of titles per page—every week in *Rul'* alone.

For a brief period in 1921–1922 the boundaries between the emigration and Soviet Russia seemed to some rather blurred. As Simon Karlinsky writes: "Russian émigré literature as a phenomenon distinct from Soviet literature had not yet come into existence. The offices of Berlin publishers and the literary cafés frequented by Russians provided a meeting ground for writers who had aligned themselves with the Soviet regime, those who were opposed to it, and . . . those who were still undecided."[8] Not only were émigrés arriving in Berlin from other centers, but the Soviet citizens allowed under NEP conditions to travel more freely abroad also gravitated there. In 1922 and 1923 almost every Russian writer of note, émigré or not, was in Berlin at least briefly: Gorky, Bely, Pasternak, Mayakovsky, Remizov, Pilnyak, Aleksey Tolstoy, Ehrenburg, Khodasevich, Tsvetaeva, Zaitsev, Shklovsky, Aldanov, Adamovich, Georgy Ivanov, and many others.

This was a time for testing old affiliations and forming new ones. Writers jostled one another too much for anyone to remain apart, and bumps and bruises were unavoidable. Some émigrés were ready to accommodate themselves to Soviet Russia, whether for nostalgic, cultural, or cloudily intellectual reasons. Most, Nabokov included, regarded this as close to treachery. Once in 1922 he was dining at a restaurant with two girls, presumably Svetlana and Tatiana Siewert. He reported: "I happened to be sitting back to back with Andrey Bely who was dining with . . . Aleksey Tolstoy, at the table behind me. Both writers were at the time frankly pro-Soviet (and on the point of returning to Russia), and a White Russian, which I still am in that particular sense, would certainly not wish to speak to a *bolsheviza* (fellow traveler).'"[9]

The Soviet government took a lively interest in the bustle of émigré culture. One émigré movement, known as Smena Vekh (Change of Landmarks), found philosophical justifications for a return to Russia and was eagerly encouraged by Moscow, anxious to entice intellectuals back. A daily newspaper, *Nakanune* (*On the Eve*), was established with Soviet funding and soon became a servile party organ. Enticed by the comfortable prospects awaiting him if he returned, the historical novelist Aleksey Tolstoy began to write for *Nakanune* in the spring of 1922. His "defection" from the emigration caused a scandal, and he was excluded from the Union of Russian Writers and Journalists in Berlin. By 1923 lines between opposed political camps were being dug deeper; schisms and regroupings proliferated.

Nabokov later prided himself on being unclubbable: "Considering as I do that the best school for a writer is solitude, I have generally been remote from 'literary life.' "[10] But he too was caught up in the whirlwind of émigré Berlin. At the end of 1921 he had contributed to the first number of the journal *Spolokhi* (*Northern Lights*), founded by a young writer called Aleksandr Drozdov. Although at that stage a committed anti-Bolshevik, Drozdov had kept *Spolokhi* apolitical. When this stance was criticized as spineless, he formed in April 1922 a literary and artistic fraternity, Vereteno (The Spindle), in opposition to Dom Iskusstv (House of Arts), a group of writers with strong ties to their confrères still in Petrograd and Moscow. Vereteno's program proclaimed it could be apolitical *and* anti-Bolshevik *and* for close cooperation with writers in Soviet Russia.[11] Sirin offered four poems for the group's first literary miscellany, *Vereteno*.

On October 22, 1922, Vereteno held its first public meeting at the Café Leon in Nollendorfplatz, a frequent haunt for many of Russian Berlin's hundreds of small organizations and the home of the Union of Russian Writers throughout its existence. Ivan Lukash, Drozdov, Sirin, and Vladimir Korvin-Piotrovsky were among those who read. A schism developed immediately. Sirin, along with others with whom he would be closely allied over the next two years, Lukash, Gleb Struve, Vladimir Amfiteatrov-Kadashev, Sergey Gorny, Vladimir Tatarinov, and Leonid Chatsky,* withdrew publicly from Vereteno in protest against the spirit now pervading the organization: a *Nakanune* writer had been invited to this first session, Aleksey Tolstoy to the next. Their secession was no shying at shadows: by December

---

* Pseudonym of Leonid Strakhovsky.

Drozdov was publishing attacks on the emigration in *Nakanune*, and a year later had returned to Moscow.[12]

In October 1922 one hundred sixty intellectuals and artists were expelled from Russia. Most made their way to Berlin, among them Yuli Aykhenvald, one of the best critics—some thought *the* best critic—of Russian literature in his time,[13] and soon to be the first distinguished champion of Sirin. Some of those expelled, along with writers like Bely, Remizov, and Khodasevich, who had just walked out of the increasingly pro-Soviet Dom Iskusstv, formed a new countergroup, the Klub Pisateley (Writers' Club), whose members like those of Dom Iskusstv were well-established writers.

Meanwhile the mostly young writers who had withdrawn from Vereteno formed their own secret literary circle, at the instigation of Leonid Chatsky. Meeting for the first time on November 8, 1922, at the round table in Gleb Struve's apartment, they chose the intentionally whimsical title of Bratstvo Kruglogo Stola, Brotherhood of the Round Table. Apart from Sirin, the Brotherhood included the poet Vladimir Amfiteatrov-Kadashev, the humorist Sergey Gorny, the novelist and short-story writer Lukash, the poet Sergey Krechetov,* Vladimir Tatarinov, a journalist at *Rul'*, and Nikolay Yakovlev, a teacher of Russian literature. The poet Vladimir Korvin-Piotrovsky seems to have been an occasional member. Among the group's grand and unrealized plans were the publication of a satirical journal and a raid on the *Spolokhi* offices. Soon the meetings became simply gatherings of literary friends who read their works to one another. Chatsky sketched caricatures of other members, recording Sirin as "the Twentieth-Century Pegasus," in two variants, one a giraffe and the other a long-necked sea-horse: tall and thin, Sirin seemed to move only his long neck when he read in public.[14]

Sirin's closest friend among these fellow writers was Ivan Lukash (1892–1940). His plump boyish face, accentuated by his bow tie and button nose, seemed oddly mismatched with his prematurely bald head and the pipe fiercely clasped in his mouth or waved in the air as he paced up and down devising new literary projects. His fiction was solidly three-dimensional but lacked the play of thought. With an eye and an imagination for the concrete and a superabundant stock of adjectives and nouns, he would accumulate too many bright or dusty objects, like an overcrowded antique shop or the set of a fussy historical film. Seven years younger than Lukash, Sirin would soon outstrip his friend's literary achievement, especially after Lukash took to scribbling out a story a week to support his young family. Publicly, Nabokov commemorated him as "a remarkable writer," but to his

---

* Pseudonym of Sergey Sokolov.

mother he summed up Lukash's work: he "writes bad stories in his beautiful language." But Nabokov would never again work so closely with another writer as he would with the feisty Lukash.[15]

III

Nabokov's first four books as Sirin appeared within the space of four months: in November 1922, *Nikolka Persik* (*Colas Breugnon*); in December, *Grozd'* (*The Cluster*); in January 1923, *Gorniy put'* (*The Empyrean Path*); and in March 1923, *Anya v strane chudes* (*Alice in Wonderland*).[16]

While the two translations were well received, the few reviews the verse books attracted conceded Sirin's promise and technical polish but wondered at the poems' lack of freshness and substance. Their criticisms were just: the young Sirin echoes other poets' adjectives, their sense of wonder at life, their flights of rapture or regret so frequently that his lines are more often poetesque than poetry. But perceptive reviewers discerned already some of the first signs of the Nabokov we know: the bold sound play ("V Nazarete, na zare," "In Nazareth, at dawn"), the acute vision (a footprint in sand filling up with gleaming water), the unexpected details (Christ on the cross, remembering the wood-shavings beneath his father's workbench). On the strength of such qualities Aykhenvald, author of the best review, recommended Sirin to Khodasevich as a promising young poet.[17]

In his review, Aykhenvald* prefers *The Empyrean Path* (poems 1918–1921) to *The Cluster* (poems 1921–1922).[18] He was right. In old age Nabokov would choose 32 of the poems from *The Empyrean Path* for his collected verse, more than one-fifth of the 153 poems in the collection, and only 7 from the 37 in *The Cluster*. The slimmer volume looks like the more fastidious selection, but in fact *The Cluster*'s poems were written within ten months (late June 1921–April 1922), with a high proportion dating from just the first two months of that period.[19] Nabokov simply included too much of his poetic output at a time when most of the poems did not rise above the proficiency of a dextrous apprentice. But *The Cluster* does at least mark a decisive move on Nabokov's part toward the discipline—though not the majesty and sweep—of Pushkin: its meters remarkably echo those of *Eugene Onegin*.[20]

For all its frigid aestheticism *The Cluster* began in a rush of passion, in Nabokov's first heady months with Svetlana. Since the engagement, of course, Nabokov had been part of the bustle of literary Berlin

---

* In emigration he published at first under the name "B. Kamenetsky" to protect his family, whom he had been unable to bring with him at the time of his expulsion.

only in the hours he did not spend with Svetlana, either as before at her parents' home in Lichterfelde or now too at Sächsische Strasse.

Later in life Nabokov liked to think that on his way back from Svetlana and Lichterfelde he often shared a streetcar with Kafka: "One could not forget that face, its pallor, the tightness of the skin, those most extraordinary eyes, hypnotic eyes glowing in a cave. Years later when I first saw a photo of Kafka I recognized him immediately. . . . Imagine: I could have spoken to Kafka." But although Nabokov remembered these sightings "on the Berlin–Lichterfelde streetcar" in connection with his return from the Siewerts—and therefore in autumn 1921 or 1922, not 1922 or 1923 as he hazarded—Kafka and his Dora came to Berlin only in September 1923. Nabokov knew that these were only "theoretically possible glimpses of Kafka" that mixed memory and desire. As Véra Nabokov commented: "This 'reminiscence' was born many years later."[21]

A week before Christmas 1922 Nabokov was able to present Svetlana with a fresh copy of The Cluster, one section of which was dedicated to her. But young Nabokov's verse-books and arty translations rolling off the press were not enough for Roman Siewert, a mining engineer, and his wife. The steady job they had stipulated as a condition of the engagement had not turned up, and they dared not trust their seventeen-year-old daughter to this young dreamer and dandy. When Vladimir visited them on January 9, 1923, they announced that the engagement was broken off. He listened in tears to their explanations—her youth, his position—and since Svetlana accepted their arguments and was promptly taken off to Bad Kissingen, there was nothing he could do.[22]

IV

Except write. That day he wrote a poem, "Finis," whose jagged rhythms and broken phrases mix grief with an agonizing self-consciousness in a manner unprecedented in his verse. While Nabokov always repudiated the romantic notion that poetry should spring directly from emotion, he also concurred with Gogol that one must have "a good deal of spiritual depth" to create a masterpiece.[23] The breakup with Svetlana certainly released new energies in him. During the three weeks that remained of January he wrote fifteen poems he later judged worthy of his collected verse, as well as five less successful poems, some translations of Tennyson, Byron, Lamb, and Musset, and his first prose fiction in over two years. Proud self-justification mars the unsuccessful poems, but the best are full of passion ("And all that was, and all that will be") and imagination ("In a Castiliar alley").[24]

In the brief January 1923 story "Slovo" ("The Word"), reminiscence of Poe's symbolic tales, a man wakes in a pearl-and-jasper heaven unable to catch the attention of the angels who troop past.[25] One of them, not quite detached from earth, pauses to listen to the mortal who wants to explain the beauty and suffering of his native land but can only mutter and stumble. The angel nevertheless understands, and divulges to him just one lambent word. This simple solution fills him with ecstasy, courses through his veins, makes him cry it out aloud—and he wakes up to real life with no recollection of the magic word. Like the earlier "The Sprite," "The Word" sets the human and the transcendent too starkly together. Nabokov would soon learn that trying to follow two intersecting planes of existence simultaneously would only lead him to a blind corner. And yet the new story antici-pates something invaluable in the later Nabokov: the all-resolving se-cret the dying man seems about to utter in *The Real Life of Sebastian Knight*; the key to existence Falter hides, perhaps for us to find, in "Ultima Thule"; the treacherous clue "fountain" in Shade's "Pale Fire."

Sometime in 1923, presumably not long after Sirin's second volume of verse appeared in late January, his former Vereteno colleague Aleksandr Drozdov wrote a "vile" (and still untraced) article on Sirin in *Nakanune*, a newspaper whose moral authority had by now slipped so low that it embarrassed even Communists. Nabokov called Droz-dov out to a duel, but received no reply.[26]

But nothing could divert the unpredictable rush of his imagination. Late in February he composed his longest poem to date, "Solnechnyy Son" ("The Sun Dream"), eight hundred fifty lines in the manner of medieval dream-narratives.[27] A white-haired king sends his cham-pion, Yvain, to resolve by personal combat a dispute against the neighboring kingdom and its black-bearded ruler. The first to win ten games of chess will gain the victory. Dreamy Yvain wins, but during the protracted tournament he falls deeper and deeper under the spell of an enchanted city he can hear around the tent that he has pitched on a deserted plain. He returns for his fiancée and persuades her to share his remote abode. For weeks she feigns to hear the sounds he hears, but at last confesses that for her the plain has never broken its silence. When she leaves him, he sinks still deeper in his reverie, hears and even sees the city of strange concords, stretches out his hands in bliss—and is found dead on the grassy plain. Here Nabokov transforms his sense of rejection by Svetlana—the fiancée who cannot hear the divine harmonies apparent to him—into a tale that prefigures

Invitation to a Beheading's isolated visionary, but implies that while a glimpse of another world beyond this one might be a flash of genuine insight, any final conviction within this life of access to another world can only be madness.

In March for the third successive month Nabokov completed a longish work in a new mode: the play *Smert'* (*Death*), a romantic, slightly Faustian closet drama set in Byron's Cambridge, but with Byron a fleeting shadow for no more than a vivid line or two.[28] Gonville, a scientist and don, appears to have lost his wife Stella; his star pupil Edmund, ashamed at his own consuming but unuttered love for Stella, comes to commiserate—and to take his own life, since existence without her has lost its meaning. Before coolly administering him a poison from one of his phials, Gonville warns young Edmund that the momentum of consciousness may persist briefly after death. The stage dims. Act 2, a moment later: Edmund sees the scene around him, Gonville included, as only the feverish inertial impetus of his mortal consciousness running on beyond death. Playing along, Gonville provokes him into disclosing how far his love for Stella was fulfilled. He finds there had been nothing to fear: Edmund had not progressed beyond an unreturned glance of passion. With no need for further pretense, Gonville explains that the potion was harmless. But Edmund refuses to believe that this explanation and the whole scene are anything but a drama his own mind has cleverly cobbled together as a continuation of earthly life. In exasperation Gonville asks "What if I show you that Stella never died?" He calls her up. Edmund, when he hears footsteps ascending, feels as if he were hurtling down an abyss into death. Blackout, curtain. Has act 2 taken place on this side of death, or the other?

Nabokov has tried to devise a plot that both transgresses and remains within the bourne of earthly life: a difficult task, and he fails. More successful than the plot's switches are the meditations of act 1, where the new vigor of Nabokov's verse owes much to the unadorned strength and clarity of Pushkin's verse dramas. Edmund recounts his panic before life's mysteries: "And not only my incomprehension / Terrifies—terrible too is the voice / That whispers, one more effort, /And all I'll understand. . . ."

V

Although Nabokov's sustained creative explosion distracted him from the pain of losing both his father and Svetlana within little more than half a year, he had become extremely run down and nervous, and realized he needed to refresh his mind and spirits. Solomon Krym, head of the Crimean provisional government of 1918–1919, had been an agronomist and viticulturist before the revolution and now in emigration managed a large estate in the south of France owned by the Bezpalov family. Nabokov had the "marvelous" idea of taking seasonal work there as a farmhand that summer.[29]

Perhaps it was while he waited for the fruit picking to begin that Nabokov first worked as an extra in Berlin's burgeoning film industry. One film required a theater audience, and because Nabokov in his old London dinner jacket was the only one in evening dress, the camera lingered on him. "I remember I was standing in a simulated theater in a box and clapping, and something was going on on an imaginary stage": a "real" murder that the audience were supposed to take as part of the performace. Some time later Nabokov chanced to see the movie with Lukash. As his face gleamed and faded, he pointed himself out on the screen, but the sequence was over so quickly Lukash simply scoffed, thinking Nabokov had invented this moment of stardom.[30] Nabokov would soon splice that scene, for the sake of its local color, into his first novel, *Mary*.

Other modes paid less but offered more of a challenge. On April 20 Sirin's first chess problem to be published appeared in *Rul'*, a problem of the type known as retrograde analysis. Before deciding that the key must be a white pawn taking a black one *en passant*, the solver has to deduce from the present position on the board that the last move Black made *must* have been to advance a pawn two spaces to b5.[31] During his émigré years Nabokov spent many nights of creative concentration composing chess problems, and regretted it later only insofar as it meant so much time lost for writing. But it is apt that his first published problem should involve a series of deductions from interlocking details of the past, precisely the kind of analysis so much of his fiction requires.

In his memoirs the editor at *Rul'*, Iosif Hessen, recalled with pleasure Sirin's "very witty chess problems."[32] Later dismissive of his own early work, Nabokov always remained grateful for Hessen's readiness to publish the young Sirin, but implied that Hessen accepted his stuff as an indulgence, almost without perusal:

> He was my first reader. Long before my books began to come out with his publishing firm, he let me, with a fatherly connivance, feed *Rul'* . . . my unripe rhymes. Blue evenings in Berlin, the corner chestnut in flower, lightheadedness, poverty, love, the tangerine tinge of premature shoplights, and an animal aching for the still fresh reek of Russia—all this was put into meter, copied out in longhand and carted off to the editor's office, where myopic I[osif] V[ladimirovich] would bring the

new poem close to his face and after this brief, more or less tactual, act of
cognition . . . he would look at me with half-sarcastic benevolence,
lightly crackling the sheet but saying only "Mm-hmm," and would add
it without haste to the pile of copy.[33]

Hessen had been a friend of Nabokov's father from as far back as
the founding of *Pravo*, and for twenty years had worked closely with
him on *Pravo, Rech'*, and *Rul'*. Nabokov remembered Hessen warmly,
two smiling eyes behind two small round lenses, as part of the world
of frock coats and grave politics he did not understand as a child. Now
as a young man he found he liked this deafish, purblind man even
more than his father had. For his part Hessen was extremely proud
that when the spoiled child he had known twenty years earlier began
to cultivate his talent in the arid soil of exile he could be there to help:
not only as editor of *Rul'*, but also as the head of the Slovo publishing
house and as president, year after year, of the Union of Russian Writers and Journalists in Berlin, which from time to time could offer its
deserving members small subsidies. In the years after V. D. Nabokov's death, none did more than Hessen to ensure that Sirin met
his public. "Editor, publisher, counselor, friend—that is how, refracted in my personal fate, your image gradually clarifies," Nabokov
would toast Hessen in the celebrations for his seventieth birthday.[34]

Rul' was Sirin's way of reaching a worldwide audience. But he
could also have more local exposure. On April 4, 1923, he read his
work at the Schubertsaal in Bülowstrasse as part of a literary evening
on the theme of Russia organized by the Russian Nationalist Students'
Union. Lukash, Gorny, Krechetov, Struve, and Amfiteatrov-Kadashev also took part.[35] On such occasions the tall, slender Sirin with his
"irresistibly attractive fine-featured, intelligent face," would make
more than a few women's hearts beat faster. One such woman was
Roma Klyatchkin, an attractive Jewish blonde with whom Nabokov
had a brief affair about this time, another was Danechka (maiden
name unknown), also Jewish and voluptuous, with whom he had an
even briefer link.[36] A third Jewish woman who had also seen Sirin on
stage was destined to be far more permanent.

VI

On May 8, a couple of days before Nabokov was to leave for the south
of France, he attended one of the charity balls Russian organizations
staged in those years. During the course of the ball, he encountered a
woman in a black mask with a wolf's profile. She had never met him

before, and knew him only through watching over the growth of his
poetic talent, in print and at public readings. She would not lower her
mask, as if she rejected the appeal of her looks and wished him to
respond only to the force of her conversation He followed her out
into the night air. Her name was Véra Evseevna Slonim.*

Three weeks later, already on the farm of Domaine-Beaulieu, Nabokov wrote a poem to commemorate that night. Its epigraph, ap-
propriately, came from Blok's "Incognita":

The Encounter

"enchained by this strange proximity . . . "

The longing, and mystery, and delight. . . .
as if from the swaying blackness
of some slow-motion masquerade
onto the dim bridge you came.

And night flowed, and silent there floated
into its satin streams
that black mask's wolf-like profile
and those tender lips of yours.

And under the chestnuts, along the canal
you passed, luring me askance.
What did my heart discern in you,
how did you move me so?

In your momentary tenderness,
or in the changing contour of your shoulders,
did I experience a dim sketch
of other—irrevocable—encounters"

Perhaps romantic pity
led you to understand
what had set trembling that arrow
now piercing through my verse?

I know nothing. Strangely
the verse vibrates, and in it, an arrow . . .
Perhaps you, still nameless, were
the genuine, the awaited one?

But sorrow not yet quite cried out
perturbed our starry hour.
Into the night returned the double fissure
of your eyes, eyes not yet illumed.

---

* She prefers her first name to be spelled with an acute accent over the "e" so that t
will be pronounced not like "dearer" but more like "fairer."

For long? For ever? Far off
I wander, and strain to hear
the movement of the stars above our encounter
And what if you are to be my fate . . .

The longing, and mystery, and delight,
and like a distant supplication . . .
My heart must travel on.
But if you are to be my fate. . .

Though he had barely had time to meet her before leaving for France, Nabokov already sensed that a future with this woman might be as magical as the way she entered his life. And more than fifty years later, he would still celebrate the day they met.[37]

VII

In mid-May, as Nabokov took the train through Dresden, Strasbourg, Lyon, Nice, thoughts of the past, of Svetlana, weighed down thoughts of the future.[38]

As he had hoped, his months at the Domaine de Beaulieu gave him the chance to bask in the present. The farm lay on flat, burgundy-and-milk-chocolate-colored soil, bordered on one side by a low bush-clad ridge and on the other close to the fruit-market town of Solliès-Pont, fifteen kilometers from Toulon. Nabokov loved the farm day's straightforward routine: rise at six to work in the fields alongside the other laborers, all young Italians, drink cheap wine with them at midday, swim naked in the river skirting the farm, sunbathe, and return to work, stripped to the waist.[39]

When he arrived the cherries were ready:

Picking cherries is quite an art. . . . The first time I worked quite fast and took the ripest cherries and put them inside this basket which was lined with . . . oilcloth. I hung it on a branch. It tumbled down and all the cherries were spoiled. I had to start all over again.[40]

Next came apricots and peaches to pick, fields of young corn to weed, infant apple and pear trees to prune. His favorite task was to irrigate the fields from the circular reservoir pond in the yard, lifting the iron gates to let water glide down the shallow furrows. He and Solomon Krym became good friends. Krym did not mind when from time to time his young compatriot chucked in the farming to catch butterflies or beetles or moths. Once as he sweated in the fields an Englishman, butterfly net in hand, dismounted from his victoria and asked Nabokov to hold the reins while he chased a two-tailed Pasha flying round a fig tree. The swarthy, skinny young farmhand, tousle-headed, in rolled-up denims, startled the old gentleman by asking, using perfect taxonomic Latin, if he had captured this species or that in the area.[41]

In the evenings Nabokov listened to the rubbery croak of frogs and the rich whistle of nightingales. As he steeped himself in the melancholy waning light in the cork grove or among the olive trees, the cypresses, the palms, he yearned to travel further, to leave Europe right behind. He slept with the other laborers in the sandstone-and-tile farmhouse, half stately home, half barracks. Yet although nothing pleased him more than becoming as brown as the other farmhands and passing for one of them, he still had to satisfy his urge to write. He sent off a passionately plaintive letter to Svetlana, as if licensed by the distance that separated them. He wrote poems that distilled the twilight, poems that charted his reviving spirits. But while he could compose lyrics in his head, by mid-June he wanted to sit down to something longer. With nowhere to work undisturbed at night, he contemplated returning to Berlin next month.[42]

A separate room was found for him, and by the end of June he had completed his next verse drama, *Dedushka* (*The Granddad*).[43] His sense of renewal seems to have shaped the play's mood. Set in a French farmhouse in the early nineteenth century, it reflects both his delight in the cycles of growth around him at Domaine de Beaulieu and his generation's fascination with the French Revolution. A passerby seeks shelter from the rain—a former nobleman who has wandered the world for twenty-five years, ever since the smoke and panic of a fortuitous fire saved him from the guillotine's blade. The farmer who welcomes him has also sheltered for the last year a harmless old dodderer, taken over by the family as an honorary "granddad." He proves to be none other than the executioner robbed of his victim twenty-five years earlier. Now, recognizing the chance passerby, "granddad" goes berserk, tries to decapitate him, and dies in the struggle. No fate is inevitable, the play suggests: even imminent death here loses its prey, and not once but twice. Inventive and colorful, blending natural speech and poetic flights in its blank verse, the play nevertheless shows more in its limitations than its achievement. The awkward provisions for forthcoming action, here as in *Death*, reveal by contrast how much the mature Nabokov would advance the art of narrative preparation.

Nine days later Nabokov had drafted another brief verse play, *Polyus* (*The Pole*). Entranced years earlier by the sight of Scott's diary under glass at the British Museum, he now rendered in verse the last hours of Scott and his companions.[44] Well-paced alterations to the actual events keep dialogue flowing naturally and smoothly, even in a snowbound tent where people have sunk near death. Themes first sounded in the play—the challenge of courage, the lure of exploration, the timeless romance still left in modern times—would later return in Nabokov's works in more profitable guise. The play's last lines hint why he was readier to approach documentary here than anywhere else in his imaginative work:

> Captain Scott: People love fairy tales, don't they?
>   You and I here alone, in the snows, far away . . .
>   I think that England . . .

Remember that the first stories Nabokov recalled encountering in childhood were "English fairy tales."[45] Through the bare facts of their deaths, Nabokov suggests, Scott and his men cross over into the realm of legend, story, art, where the pity of their deaths becomes permanent and immortal. In the context of Nabokov's later work, we can see that he imagines all life may perhaps be redeemed by becoming the stuff of art, as it crosses into the timelessness of the past or into death: at the end of *Glory*, for instance, where Martin undertakes a feat of heroism for its own sake and fades into death as if into a picture. But *The Pole* itself fails to set up such reverberations.

While Nabokov was absent from Berlin, a new contributor had appeared several times in *Rul'* as the translator of excerpts from a Bulgarian writer's collection of folk sayings and stories: Véra Slonim. She signed herself simply "V.S."—not to be confused with V. Sirin. On June 24 a new poem by Sirin himself had appeared in *Rul'*: "The Encounter," for one reader at least an unmistakable declaration of passionate interest in her, near-stranger though she was. They exchanged letters. On July 29 a new Sirin poem composed ten days earlier in Toulon was published in *Rul'*, side by side with "V.S." 's translation of Poe's story "Silence": an impeccably literary preamble to courtship, reticent and in public, by mail and newspaper, in verse and in prose.

Late in July Nabokov visited Marseilles, where he haunted and was haunted by a tiny Russian restaurant in the grimiest part of the city. He wrote to Véra Slonim that he frequented the place

> with Russian sailors, and no one knows who I am or where I come from, and I'm surprised myself that I used to wear a tie and thin socks. . . . A sourish freshness and the rumble of portside nights wafts in from the street, and as I watched and listened I thought that I know Ronsard by heart, and the names of tortoise bones, bacteria, the genera of plants. . . . I am very much drawn to Africa and Asia. I was offered the place of a stoker on a boat to Indochina.[46]

He was not to become a Melville or a Conrad, a Jack London or an O'Neill, but even that whiff of the sea was enough to cast up one story with a salty reek, "Port," some six months later.

In the second week of August Nabokov headed back to Berlin, stopping en route in Nice and Paris. He reached home by August 19 and sought out Véra Slonim as soon as she returned to Berlin from her summer vacation.[47]

Enter the Muse: Berlin, 1923–1925

I won't find a better wife. But do I need a wife at all? "Put that lyre away,

I've no room to move . . ." No, I would never hear that

from her—that's the point.

—The Gift

I

THEY SOON discovered that they could have met at several points in their past. Even as a little girl, Véra had walked past the pink granite house at 47 Morskaya and thought its violet mosaic particularly charming. As a young teenager, she belonged with her older sister to the same small dancing group as Nabokov's classmate and close friend Savely Kyandzhunstev and knew a good many Tenishev boys. In the summers of 1916 and 1917 her family rented a dacha on a branch line running out of Siverskaya, the railway station that served Vyra.[1] Then early in 1923, in Berlin, Véra and Vladimir very nearly met in the office of Orbis, a publishing firm Véra's father had set up to translate Russian classics into English for export to the United States. Nabokov recalled climbing the stairs to Evsey Slonim's office with Gleb Struve, discussing how much they should ask for translating Dostoevsky. Although Véra was working in the Orbis office, they did not meet: only as they now probed their past did they recollect that they had seen each other there.[2]

To Nabokov his past near-misses with Véra were almost a sign that fate had persistently contrived to unite them, returning with another plan each time it was thwarted. After the Orbis stratagem, which should have worked, fate appeared to become desperate, and boldly pushed Véra Slonim in Nabokov's way. A similar pattern became the structural basis of *The Gift*, of Sebastian Knight's novel *Success*, of the meeting of Olga and Krug in *Bend Sinister*, and of the opening of *Look at the Harlequins!* This last novel, in which Nabokov travesties all that he held precious, begins:

> I met the first of my three or four successive wives in somewhat odd circumstances, the development of which resembled a clumsy conspir-

acy, with nonsensical details and a main plotter who not only knew
nothing of its real object but insisted on making inept moves that seemed
to preclude the slightest possibility of success. Yet out of these very mis-
takes he unwittingly wove a web, in which a set of reciprocal blunders on
my part caused me to get involved and fulfill the destiny that was the
only aim of the plot.[3]

In private Nabokov affectionately called the book *Look at the Masks!*
in tribute to destiny's last successful move when he met his real-life
"first wife" in her wolf-profile mask.[4]

Véra Slonim, born January 5, 1902 (N.S.), was the second of three
girls, daughters of Evsey Slonim (1865–1928) and his wife, Slava, née
Feigin (1872–1928). Her father studied law in St. Petersburg, completing a brilliant degree, and practiced as a lawyer until a new government regulation restricted Jews in the legal profession. Although not
a practicing Jew, he abandoned the law rather than adopt the degrad-
ing expedient of changing religion, as many Jews who wished to enter
the professions felt compelled to do.[5] He became a timber exporter,
and in his proud daughter's words, he

> was a born pioneer in the truest sense, having taught himself forestry
> and priding himself on never allowing a tree to be felled without having
> one planted in replacement. He also built a real little railway, a kind of
> feeder line, on one of the estates to bring timber close to the bank of
> Zapadnaya Dvina, down which river it was floated to Riga, tied up into
> enormous rafts by skilled peasants. . . . A few years before the revolu-
> tion my father bought up the greater part of a small town in Southern
> Russia which he had planned to develop into a model little city, complete
> with modern canalisation and streetcar transportation, and somehow
> that plan so enchanted me that I was promised I would be allowed to
> take a hand at it when I grew up.[6]

Véra Slonim was a precocious child. Her first vivid recollection
dates from the age of six or seven months. At three she would kneel
on the floor reading the newspaper, and recalls herself at that age
looking up from the paper one day, calling out excitedly to her parents
that a bomb had been thrown at some general. She was brought up by
governesses to speak French and English. She wrote poetry at the age
of ten or eleven, like most of her generation and class. At ten she
attended the Princess Obolensky School in St. Petersburg, and hoped
eventually to study physics at a technical college there. But she was
withdrawn from class because of poor health, though she continued
to take the Obolensky School exams every spring.

As political frustrations and hopes intensified during the war she
began to define herself as a socialist. That changed with the October

Revolution. After the revolution, her family moved to Moscow, then returned to Petrograd, where Véra again attended the Obolensky School and there witnessed the visit of the lame commissar for education depicted in *The Defense*. One night a band of soldiers came looking for her father, who was sleeping elsewhere in anticipation of arrest. The long search settled matters: they had to leave.

Evsey Slonim headed for Kiev, then ruled by Hetman Paul Skoropadsky, leader of the anti-Bolshevik opposition in the Ukraine. The rest of the family tried to reach the home of Véra's maternal uncle in Byelorussia, still in German hands and under German discipline rather than the Bolshevik mixture of anarchy and incipient terror. With forty-three bags and valises they crossed the border by cattle truck. When Byelorussia soon fell to the Bolsheviks, the family tried to rejoin Evsey Slonim. Their train was boarded by Petlyurovtsy, members of a notoriously anti-Semitic Ukrainian separatist militia, henchmen of Simon Petlyura. Sleeping on the family's luggage on the floor of the carriage that night, Véra woke to the sound of one of the Petlyurovtsy insulting and threatening another Jew. Then something strange happened: when Véra said, "He has a right to be here. There's no need to throw him out or threaten him," the Petlyurovets suddenly changed heart. He convinced the others to become the women's protectors, escorting them through fierce skirmishes and the attentions of drunken troops to Odessa, where Evsey Slonim eventually rejoined them. The Slonims survived the bloodbath of Odessa and spent some months in Yalta until shortly before the second fall of the Crimea, in March 1920, when they left on a Canadian ship that Nabokov gratefully commandeered ten years later for Martin in *Glory*. Several months later, and not without more adventures, they were settled in Berlin.[7]

Evsey Slonim, who had lost his fortune in the revolution, was helped back into business by a Dutch friend, Peltenburg, an associate from prerevolutionary days. Through Peltenburg he was able to sell his Russian estates to the German industrialist Stinnes, who was even more ready than others to gamble that Russia would soon be rid of the Bolsheviks. With this money, the Slonims were once again comfortably off. Evsey Slonim used his capital to set up two firms: an import-export business dealing in farm machinery for the Balkans, and Orbis. But by 1924 the inflation wrecked his new enterprises—Orbis failed without having published a single book—and the family was once again without funds.[8]

Véra was to have studied at the Technische Hochschule, Berlin's equivalent to the Massachusetts Institute of Technology, but her father was convinced her health could not take the strain: she had had weak lungs in childhood, and recurrent bouts of severe bronchitis until 1924. In 1922 she began to work in her father's import-export office, handling foreign correspondence. The next year she also worked for Orbis (in the same building) until both firms folded. She moved in a circle of former officers—and herself took riding lessons in the Tiergarten and became a crack shot with a pistol. But although in those first years in Berlin she had taken no part in Berlin's literary life, she had a passionate interest in literature.[9]

Although conscious of having neither a university education nor a writer's gift, Véra Slonim was highly cultured, intelligent, imaginative. Like Nabokov she had a tendency to synesthesia, a delight in easily overlooked trifles, a sense of wonder at the world. She had an inordinately well-developed memory, especially for the things of her childhood and for anything in verse. She would take fifteen minutes to memorize a short lyric and knew by heart not only whole chunks of Pushkin and Zhukovsky's Homer, but virtually every verse line Nabokov would write. Nabokov especially valued in her the best sense of humor of any woman he had ever known.[10]

In other ways she is quite unlike Nabokov. She watches the political world with interest. She admits her disposition to see the negative side of things and people first, where Nabokov for all his ruthless attacks on vulgarity, rough-hewn or veneered, believed in the fundamental goodness of life and judged accordingly. Stiff, resolute, strong-willed, Véra rates people severely, brooking no hint of *poshlost'* or cruelty. Suspicious by nature, she has always made sure she could defend herself or those she loved. In Berlin she carried a gun about with her. V. D. Nabokov's boxing and fencing lessons, his son's boxing and savate, and their duelist's sense of honor were things she understood well. Like V. D. Nabokov, Evsey Slonim had also challenged the editor of *Novoe Vremya* to a duel for a malicious and unfounded slur.

Intensely private, Véra Nabokov never sought the least glory for herself in her husband's success. "The more you leave me out," she told me early in my researches, "the closer to the truth you'll be.' In fact in her dedication to literature and to Vladimir Nabokov she would be his wife, muse, and ideal reader; his secretary, typist, editor, proofreader, translator, and bibliographer; his agent, business manager, legal counsel, and chauffeur; his research assistant, teaching assistant, and professorial understudy. But never, she avers, his model: Nabokov always "had the good taste to keep me out of his books."[11]

Although Elena Nabokov and the rest of the family remained in Berlin, until the end of 1923, Véra never visited 67 Sächsische Strasse. If she rang and one of Vladimir's sisters asked, out of mere curiosity, who was speaking, she would leave her name as Mme Véronique Bertrand, supposedly one of his English-language pupils.[12]

Their meeting-place was on Berlin's evening streets. Nabokov's verse captures the romance they both found in the night, the alertness and curiosity he loved in her mind, the strange blend of strength and delicacy he made out even in her gait:

> I remember in a plush frame
> a daguerrotype dream,
> eyes in a northern grove
> and lips in a thundering port.
>
> But you . . . With erect and slender shadow,
> as if stepping on glass,
> listening to ghostly singing,
> peering intently into the dark
>
> —into the dark, where under an iron maple
> I waited, where, turning the corner,
> transparent ambers with a groan
> flowed into damp mirrors—
>
> soundlessly into that dark you came,
> and all that had long known the chill of boredom
> became a fairy-tale: the dentate maple,
> the geometric lantern. . . .
>
> You. . . . A black dress enters my dream,
> a restrained flame in the eyes,
> quietly on my sleeve there
> rests an elongated palm.
>
> And suddenly, flashing an unexpected
> smile, you point out to me:
> a shady wedge, a deceptive gap
> on the pale and sloping wall.
>
> Yes, it is true: the angular city
> plays with bewitched life
> since you came into the street
> with your glassy gait.
>
> And in this unprecedented world
> of light and shadows we are alone.
> Yesterday beyond the canal we dreamed
> the lights were Venice.
>
> And Hoffmann from a mirrored door
> suddenly emerged and in his cloak passed by,
> and under a bench in the dark public garden
> I found a fan with ribs of bone.

And a strange bronze projection
gleams through distant glass,
and on the wall, sloping, pale—
from where?—a black wing stretches.

Divining, you notice all,
all night's cut-out games,
I start to talk—you answer,
as if rounding off a line of verse.

Mysteriously slipping over vowels,
you whisper, you come to a stop
and on your indistinct face
I catch the shadow of my dream.

While there over the sleepy street,
hiding earthly features,
like a wall strangely lit,
beyond me, stands my life.[13]

II

Just when Berlin had taken on a new magic for two young Russians
the rest of the city was convulsed by inflation. When Nabokov returned to Berlin in August 1923, *Rul'* cost 10,000 marks. By early December, it would be two hundred billion marks an issue, and Berlin
would have a curfew to curb the currency speculators, cocaine deal-
ers, and streetwalkers taking advantage of the giddy conditions. The
Russian publishing industry had begun to totter, and émigrés with no
reason to stay started to leave for Paris or Prague.

Nabokov simply kept on writing. And improving. In September he
wrote "Zvuki" ("Sounds"), a semiautobiographical story recounting
a youth's adulterous affair against a Vyra-like backdrop. In this unpublished story Nabokov hits his true vein for the first time. Evoking
scene and atmosphere superbly, though without his later economy
and speed, he avoids the stagey clashes and reversals of his verse
dramas and creates his story through the mobility of the narrator's
mind. He refuses to stay within the ordinariness of the ordinary: "and
suddenly it became so clear to me, that the world had flourished and
faded for eons, revolved and evolved just in order to link together—
now, at this very minute—to fuse in one vertical chord, this voice . . .
the movement of your shoulderblades, the smell of the pine boards."
The narrator studies each detail of the village teacher's face, sends his
imagination out to "become" first the teacher, and then his mistress,

her cigarette, a paperweight. . . . He feels he has washed in someone else's grief, glistened with someone else's tears. The same sensation has returned at times since then, before a bent tree, a torn glove, a horse's eyes, a radiant feeling that everything around him forms the notes of a single harmony, where nothing is accidental: "The wagtail, the cigarette-holder in my hand, your words, the spot of sun on your dress. It could not be otherwise."[14]

Nabokov called himself a poet in his prose, and so he was, not just in his figures of speech but, like Wordsworth, by virtue of a new sensibility, a new way of looking at the world and the mind. He raises the value of the present moment, its unique configuration of apparently insignificant particulars; he reveals the freedom of the mind as instant succeeds instant. And whereas in the paradise of "The Word," the miraculous city of "The Sun Dream," or the charged situations of his verse dramas he has tried to pass too directly beyond life's limits, here he hints at the mystery of consciousness, both within life and detached from it, perhaps even existing in some other form *beyond* the life we know and yet still pervading this life in some unfathomable way.

Late in September Sirin began to work with Lukash on a pantomime to fit a symphony by the composer V. F. Yakobson. Eventually entitled "Agasfer" ("Ahasuerus"), it depicted Love wandering through many centuries and in many forms, like Ahasuerus, the Wandering Jew of legend. The project took two months to complete, but occupied no great part of Nabokov's imagination. He had little respect for any collaborative work and even less for this ethereal fare.[15]

Some time before October 1923 Nabokov made another kind of contribution to Berlin's lively theater scene. In 1922 the Russian cabaret "Karussel" had opened on the Kurfürstendamm. Twice it printed its own trilingual journal, *Karussel/Carousal/Carrousel*, in German, French, and English, with paintings of sets, scenes, and costumes, and articles and poems evoking the flavor of the Russian cabaret. For the second number Nabokov contributed three different pieces in English over three different names: a poem "The Russian Song" as Vladimir Sirine, and two short essays, "Laughter and Dreams," as Vladimir V. Nabokoff, and "Painted Wood," as V. Cantaboff, the first examples of his use of English prose for an artistic purpose. His poem is banal, his prose already masterly as he meditates on the power of art to find beauty even in the plain or ugly, or as he evokes the toys sold at Catkin Week, "those lacquered curves and patches of rich color which are associated in my mind with the first blue days of a Russian spring" and which he now sees embodied in the cabaret.

By this time he would spend his afternoons crossing Berlin in the city's yellow trams from one language student to the next. Most of his students were Russians, but he also offered his linguistic services to a few Germans. One he recalls in his autobiography: Dietrich, a well-bred, quiet, bespectacled young man, studying for a Ph.D. in the humanities, who requested his help to correct letters he was sending a female cousin in America. Dietrich's passionate hobby was capital punishment. He traveled to witness executions. He commented expertly on decapitations by sword in China, "on the spirit of perfect cooperation between headsman and victim"—and Nabokov filed this away for *The Gift* and *Invitation to a Beheading*. Dietrich complained that "he had once spent a whole night patiently watching a good friend of his who had decided to shoot himself and had agreed to do so, in the roof of the mouth, facing the hobbyist in a good light, but having no ambition or sense of honor, had got hopelessly tight instead."[16] This Nabokov used immediately.

During October he wrote two more stories, much less successful than "Sounds": "Udar kryla" ("A Stroke of the Wing") and "Bogi" ("Gods").[17] Set in Zermatt, "A Stroke of the Wing" draws on Nabokov's visit to Switzerland with Bobby de Calry. It begins well. A man whose wife has committed suicide just after leaving him for another man finds himself, a year later, again near suicide—and here the Dietrich figure hopes to see him in action. But the impulse passes, and he feels almost capable of resurrection as he casts his eye over Isabel, the graceful young skier from the room next door. The plot turns a few more corners when an angel—a bestial, furry specimen who has apparently ravished Isabel—bursts through the window, is wrestled to the ground and stuffed into a cupboard, its wing jammed in the door, before it escapes. The next day, as Isabel soars through the air from a ski-jump, she suddenly convulses in midflight and falls like a stone. Her rib cage has been smashed in midair: the angel's revenge, a blow of its wing.

"Gods" seems wrong from the start. Unlike anything else Nabokov wrote, it is experimental fiction, irksomely so: a series of descriptions and meditations the narrator feigns to find by looking into his mistress's eyes. The wayflights of fancy in "Sounds" here become this story's navigational principle, and the attempt to see everything originally quickly becomes banal. Like "A Stroke of the Wing," "Gods" succeeds in only one respect: it catches Nabokov in the act of searching for a means to render the extraordinary behind the ordinary, the superhuman bursting in on the human.

Another story may also owe something to one of Nabokov's language students, Ivan Konoplin. Konoplin, a member of the Union of

Russian Writers in Berlin, was discovered to be a GPU agent* when he tried to bribe a woman on the staff of *Rul'* for information on the sources of *Rul'* 's frequent reports on the horrors of Soviet life written by Soviet citizens and then smuggled out of the USSR. Sometime in 1923, presumably, Nabokov wrote "Govoryat po-russki" ("Russian Spoken Here"), the curiously flat story of a Russian family running a tobacconist's store in Berlin who capture a Soviet GPU agent and gleefully give up the bathroom of their tiny flat to imprison him there for life, or until Russia becomes free again.[18]

Late in 1923 a newspaper article noted that Sirin was preparing for press a third collection of poems and a collection of stories, as well as writing a five-act verse drama, *Tragediya Gospodina Morna* (*The Tragedy of Mr. Morn*).[19] Neither collection was published, though there were already enough new Sirin poems for a volume of verse far better than *The Empyrean Path* or *The Cluster*. The time was not propitious for new books. Berlin's Russian publishing market had started to crash, and over the coming months hundreds of thousands of books would have to be pulped.[20] Andrey Bely, who had been planning to move to Prague, where the Russian enclave was much more exclusively émigré than Berlin's part-émigré, part-Soviet, mix, surprised everybody by returning instead to Moscow. Khodasevich left for Prague and then Italy. Thousands of others were quitting Berlin.

Among them was Elena Nabokov. A Czech legion that had fought in the Russian civil war with Kolchak's White Russian Army had appropriated White Army funds late in the war, and as a kind of conscience money the Czech government now offered pensions to numerous Russian émigré scholars and writers—Marina Tsvetaeva, for instance—provided they lived in Czechoslovakia. Since even the widows of eminent émigrés qualified, Elena Nabokov in October 1923 moved with her daughter Elena to Prague, where Karel Kramař, the Russophile Czech statesman, had invited her to stay at his villa. Olga followed soon after. Late in December Nabokov and Lukash read "Agasfer" to an invited audience in a Berlin home, while Yakobson played a piano arrangement of his orchestral score. Nabokov then took his brother Kirill, Evgenia Hofeld, the maid Adele, and the dachshund Box to Prague, intending to stay for two weeks while they settled into the small flat Elena Nabokov had found in the Smíchov area of the city, on the west bank of the Vltava. Awaiting them there were three bedrooms for seven people in an apartment bare except for a dozen chairs and seven wooden beds without mattresses. The one

---

* The name of the Soviet secret police changed from Cheka (1917) to GPU (1922), OGPU (1923), NKVD (1934), MGB (1946), and finally KGB (1954).

extravagance, a couch, swarmed with bedbugs that set off to explore the ceiling and dropped on Vladimir and Kirill as they tried to sleep. In the first days after Nabokov arrived they had no money, they had to make do with sandwiches, the rooms were bitterly cold. He had had enough: he would bring his mother back to Berlin as soon as he could.[21]

All the time he was in Prague Nabokov was busy writing *The Tragedy of Mr. Morn*. By day he gazed out at people crossing the Vltava, like musical notes on a page against that background of snow; by night he sat and composed by candlelight, since none of the lamps had arrived from Berlin. One January day he broke off a letter to Véra to attend a party at Kramař's. The conversation was still fresh in his mind when he returned to the flat, to his candlelight perch, to his unfinished page. An elderly woman had asked him:

> Do you go to high school here? I: !!! Woman: Oh, I'm sorry, you have such a young face. So you'll be starting lectures? What faculty? I (with a melancholy smile): I graduated two years ago, in science and literature. Woman (lost): Oh, so you're working. I: For the Muse. Woman (picks up): So, you're a poet. Been writing long? Tell me, have you read Aldanov? Interesting, isn't he? In these difficult times, books are a great help. If you take up Voloshin or Sirin, for instance, your spirits just lift at once. But nowadays books are so expensive. I: Yes, very expensive. And modestly moved off incognito. Amusing conversation? I've set it down word for word.[22]

To his surprise Nabokov was looking forward to Berlin as to an earthly paradise, but by mid-January he realized he would have to stay longer in Prague if he were to finish *Morn*, as he had planned, before returning. A thousand rewordings were needed in the early scenes, his head felt like a bowling alley, he could not sleep before 5 or 6 A.M. When he was seventeen, he wrote to Véra, he notched up an average of two poems a day, each taking twenty minutes. "Of doubtful quality, but I didn't try to write better, assuming that I was creating little miracles, and over miracles I didn't have to think. . . . Now, working seventeen hours a day, I can't write more than thirty lines I won't cross out later."[23]

Since his arrival in Czechoslovakia he had met Marina Tsvetaeva, nine years his elder and already firmly established as a poet. He found her charming. On January 24 they stepped out together for a "lyrical stroll" in the brisk wind on the hills above Prague. Two days later, Nabokov completed *Morn*, his first full-length work, and described himself as feeling like a house just emptied of its grand piano.[24] The next day he returned to Berlin.

III
The Tragedy of Mr. Morn (Tragediya Gospodina Morna)

By far the most significant work Nabokov had yet written in any medium, *The Tragedy of Mr. Morn* still remains in some ways the best of all his plays. Like *Peer Gynt* in relation to Ibsen's later work, *Morn* more than makes up in freewheeling energy for whatever it concedes in structure to the later plays in prose.

Nabokov's four short plays before *Morn* had all been written in the shadow of Pushkin's verse dramas. *The Tragedy of Mr. Morn* unmistakably aims at Shakespeare: in its five acts, its three thousand lines of blank verse, its mongrel names (Dandilio, Edmin, Ganus), and above all in the atmosphere of its plot. Though he sets *Morn* in an undefined future all but coeval with Shakespeare's Venice or Verona or Vienna, VN projects the Russian Revolution onto the cyclorama behind the actors' backs, as it were, so that the play appears fully cognizant of the time elapsed since 1616. Nevertheless *Morn* reopens Shakespearean possibilities that had seemed long since closed: a kingdom won and lost and won again; a ruler incognito; disguise; the private lives of crossed lovers seen against a colorful backdrop of public turmoil sketched with a shimmer of fantasy and a shiver of grim reality.

Since *Morn* remains unpublished, a plot summary seems in order.

Four years before the play's action commences, an unnamed European country long beset by civil strife acquires a new king. Although he rules incognito, he has singlehandedly restored prosperity, order, and culture. He proves to be the man the world knows as Morn, exuberant and sensitive, in love with the vivacious Midia.

Midia's husband, the revolutionary Ganus, was sent four years ago to a labor camp. When the play opens, Ganus has escaped back to the capital. Appreciative of the changes the king has brought about, he no longer believes in revolution, to the chagrin of his former mentor, Tremens, the radicals' mastermind, who remains as enamored as ever of the romance of revolution and the glory of destruction. Tremens's daughter Ella, who has acquiesced in the attentions of Klian, would-be poetaster to the court, finds herself flushing with excitement before an unresponsive Ganus. Ella's characterization is one of the finest things in the play: though Nabokov leaves so much unsaid and has so much other action to keep moving around her, he makes us perceive with absolute clarity why and how her inclinations subtly shift, now from Klian to Ganus, now back again.

When Ganus confronts Morn as his wife's lover, they agree to a duel. Even though Morn's one confidant, Edmin, informs Ganus that

Morn is none other than the king, Ganus will not renounce the right to satisfaction of his honor. They settle on unusual terms: the loser at a cut of cards will shoot himself. The lot falls on the unflinching Morn, who leaves to pay his price.

Despite his courage, Morn at the last moment cannot pull the trigger. He secretly abdicates and elopes with Midia and a loyal Edmin to the country's southern coast. When rumor proclaims the king's death, Tremens foments a successful and bloody revolt. Ganus on the other hand now regards as a saint the man who has restored the country's fortunes and has, as he thinks, sacrificed his life to pay a debt of honor. Ganus himself now becomes a popular hero in opposing the butchery of the revolution.

Beneath the palms of southern beaches Morn sinks into gloom. Without self-respect, he becomes despondent, taciturn, disheveled. The restless Midia leaves him for Edmin, who has loved her mutely all along. From Midia, Ganus learns that Morn had reneged on the duel's terms, and sets out at once to kill him. At the end of act 4, Ganus aims a pistol at Morn's head and fires.

Morn is only wounded. News that the former king is alive and had fled the throne, apparently for a woman's sake, charms the imagination of the populace. Counterrevolution triumphs in the capital, as bloody as the revolution itself had been. Edmin learns of Morn's wound and returns to his master, to find him utterly revived, his old ebullient self, now that he has paid his debt by standing the target for Ganus's fire. Attracted by her former lover's crown, Midia too returns.

On the verge of a triumphal reentry into the capital, and with Midia and faithful Edmin at his side, Morn suddenly realizes the falsehood propping up his life. Admirers near and far assume he fled the capital for love; none but himself knows he simply panicked in the face of death. In love with life again, at the peak of happiness and worldly success, but unable to bear life founded on a lie, he shoots himself.

This summary cannot convey the play's speed, color, or wit, but it may suggest to those who know Nabokov's three later full-length plays that despite its Shakespearean qualities *Morn* already displays the highly idiosyncratic manners of Nabokov's mature dramatic art.

Nabokov's natural mode was a supple, polished prose, the product of a highly observant and reflective mind encountering its world. But superfine senses have no place on the stage, where artificial lights shine into a cardboard Space, nor does branching thought have time to grow when the audience's pulse inescapably regulates Time. As if threatened by silence or a void whenever he cannot scrutinize the world with his own eyes and mind, Nabokov compensates by filling the stage with feverish activity until it reels with people and seethes with words. On the other hand the parody that will become a feature of his prose finds a natural outlet here as he differentiates voice from voice: the vaunting, craven bombast of Klian, the flamboyant spirits of Morn, the florid sagacity of Dandilio. The shifting levels of reality and illusion that will mark Nabokov's fiction, too, clamor for a place on the stage: Tremens's delirium, which seems about to engulf the other characters; Ganus's disguise as an actor playing Othello; the king's incognito; the foreigner who might well be dreaming the whole play. This stranger listens as Dandilio orates, then steps forward:

> FOREIGNER: I often dreamt of your voice
>   in childhood.
> DANDILIO: True, I never remember
>   whose dreams I appear in. But your smile
>   I remember. May I ask you,
>   esteemed traveler, where you
>   have come from?
> FOREIGNER: I have come from
>   the twentieth century, from a northern land
>   called . . .
>   (whispers)
> MIDIA: What? I didn't know that . . .
> DANDILIO: Oh, come on! In children's fairy tales—
>   don't you remember?
>   Apparitions . . . bombs . . . churches . . . golden
>   tsarevitches . . . cloak-clad rebels . . .
>   snowstorms . . .

The foreigner, squinting the other way through the looking glass, notes similarities between the play's capital and his own. This whole transformation of not-quite-Russia into a fantasy kingdom threatened by revolution anticipates Nabokov's unfinished novel *Solus Rex*, his *Bend Sinister*, and especially *Pale Fire*, with its disguised and suicidal monarch.

The Tragedy of Mr. Morn criticizes and refines the devices of Shakespeare and other tragic dramatists. Nabokov opposed the fatalism of tragedy, the inexorability visible from the start, the inescapable logic of cause and effect. He believed passionately that there was too much chance in time, too many accidents in history, too much freedom in life for "inevitability" to be more than an illusion that an absence of imagination conjures up after the fact. He rejected the artificial cleavage of life into comedy and tragedy, and although he admired Shakespeare's instinctive violation of these generic decorums, he wanted

them much more radically confounded. He also studied and criticized
the handling of exposition in drama, and set up against the anxious
overexplicitness of most dramatists the delicacy of preparation and
transition in Flaubert, whom he had begun to reread in January 1924.
He objected to the treatment of character as a cluster of fixed possibilities, and dared to present a character making a complete about-face
and then follow it up with a second or a third. And yet, he thought,
there should be a harmony in each individual's fate discernible
through the freaks of time and the free impulses of personality.

Nabokov's implicit proposals for the overhaul of drama explain the
wild careenings of character and expected outcomes in *Morn*'s plot.
Ganus changes from revolutionary to a royalist who then tries to kill
the king, Edmin from stalwart friend to betrayer and back to friend,
Tremens from superannuate dreamer sunk in moribund delirium to
activist and firebrand, Morn himself from sun-king to beclouded
knave and back again. And his "tragedy" oscillates from tragedy to
comedy throughout, until in his final sunburst of glory one last free
choice brings on the eclipse and blackout of death.

In his other 1923 plays, *Death*, *Granddad*, *The Pole*, Nabokov had
shown people staring death in the face. In *The Tragedy of Mr. Morn*
character after character does the same—Morn himself, Ganus, Tremens, Ella, Dandilio, Klian—sometimes in lines reminiscent of Hamlet's and Claudio's great speeches. And yet this is a tragedy about
happiness.

Nabokov suggests throughout *Morn* that for those who care to look,
life teems with happiness even in the face of death. The absurdly optimistic Dandilio, a gray-haired antiquarian, seems made from the
same mold as Shakespeare's Gonzalo, who sees good prevail only because he shuts his eyes to evil. Dandilio utters his most philosophically blithe speeches as Ella and her newborn infant are being shot in
the next room, just a moment before his own death. But in fact Dandilio has the sharpest eyes in the play.

Like Dandilio, Morn smiles at life, he has an imagination open to
the world, he can wonder at an ant on a rose even when there is a gun
at his head. He views each trifle as a timeless gift from life, a flawless
work of art. Instead of taking the world for granted, we can see it *as if*
each moment and each thing has just been created, as if it were the
handiwork of some artist of reality. Suddenly, the world and its smallest parts seem miraculous.

Morn seems to have made possible his country's good fortune not
by any practical measures of rational politics, but simply by knowing
this twist of thought that taps the generosity of the world. But his
whole carefree state collapses because he has impinged on the happi-

ness of just one other person, Ganus, and has not been prepared to face the consequence of causing him pain. Here Nabokov suggests that while we remain within this world we can never know whether or not the world is somehow a work of art where every part counts and all parts cohere: it is a supposition, a possibility, that liberates the imagination, but it may be no more. Meanwhile we *have* to act as if the pain of other people matters.

If, on the other hand, that supposition were correct, and everything that happens in the here and now were preserved and on display in the infinite gallery of the past, then whatever we can keep hidden during our lifetime cannot cheat death and its release from human time into the endless reappraisal of eternity. Just when he has come to embrace happiness once more, Morn realizes he cannot hide the truth of his life from death.

Morn's tragedy is therefore in a sense a triumph: a triumph of courage in the face of death, a triumphant acceptance of a world conducive to happiness, a noble acceptance of responsibility for another's pain even within such a world.

The one unmitigated tragedy of Nabokov's play is the fate of its text. Never published, the play was thought to be intact when the Nabokovs gave the manuscript to the Library of Congress. Now parts of the last two scenes, perhaps one-tenth of the play's total text, have been found to be missing. Although Nabokov's detailed plans for an earlier conception of the missing fragments survive, the loss of two or three hundred finished lines may prevent his liveliest play from ever being performed.

IV

On January 31, 1924, four days after his return from Prague, Nabokov moved into a spacious, bright room with an excellent desk and "noncreaking cupboards" in the Pension Andersen, 21 Martin-Luther-Strasse, third floor. His landlady was a Spaniard from Chile whose good food and relaxed ways suited him perfectly: he could get up at eleven after a night of composition without having to violate a German sense of propriety.[25]

At the end of 1923 Véra Slonim had typed up Nabokov's "A Stroke of the Wing." Now she typed out the whole *Tragedy of Mr. Morn*, and over the next forty years she would provide the same service for everything Nabokov wrote for publication—including this description of Sebastian Knight's mistress:

And Clare, who had not composed a single line of imaginative prose or poetry in her life, understood so well (and that was her private miracle) every detail of Sebastian's struggle, that the words she typed were to her not so much the conveyors of their natural sense, but the curves and gaps and zigzags showing Sebastian's groping along a certain ideal line of expression. . . .[26]

Nabokov apparently hoped to support himself almost without tutoring for the next few months. One source of income was the Russian correspondent for the *Westminster Gazette* and the *Times*, Vladimir Korostovets, who needed his articles on Soviet and émigré affairs rendered into acceptable English and could pay well. In this case Véra not only typed up the articles but did much of the translating.[27]

Writing for the stage and screen seemed to offer a more attractive livelihood.[28] Over the last year Nabokov's lyric output had begun to dwindle as he switched more to narrative forms, whether in verse, prose, or drama. Although in retrospect prose seems his obvious line of growth, that was by no means self-evident in February 1924. Of Sirin's solo dramatic works, the short verse plays had little prospect of commercial success. *Morn* on the other hand had a pace and exuberance that could have earned it real popularity, had conditions been more propitious for staging it at all. But Sirin was also engaged in collaborative work with Lukash that was aimed directly at the theatrical marketplace.

In the 1920s Berlin was fabled for the vitality and diversity of its theaters and especially its cabarets. The first and by far the most successful of Berlin's Russian cabarets was Yakov Yuzhny's Sinyaya Ptitsa (Bluebird). Founded at the end of 1921, a descendant of Nikita Baliev's famous Letuchaya mysh' (The Bat) in Moscow, it lasted more than ten years, influenced other Berlin cabarets and theaters, toured frequently throughout Europe and in North America. Its program, changed twice a year, could consist of ten sketches (snatches of Russian life and song, exotic fantasies, jokes, grotesques) staged with bold, highly stylized sets and costumes designed by artists like Tchelischew and performed by an experienced and tightly disciplined troupe. In between sketches Yuzhny would provide the continuity, half cozy, half acerbic, in a mixture of Russian and comically mangled German that like the theater's other ingredients appealed equally to Russian and German audiences.[29]

Nabokov and Lukash had written their first pantomime for the Bluebird, "Voda zhivaya" ("The Living Water") at the end of 1923. It began toward the end of January 1924 and ran for more than a month. Nabokov expected $100–$200 for the skit.[30]

He also, very optimistically, asked $1,000 from Yakobson for the "Agasfer" scenario-libretto which he and Lukash had revised at the end of January. Yakobson never paid all he owed. Another composer, Aleksandr Eilukhin, commissioned a piece from Sirin and Lukash: "Kavaler Lunnogo Sveta" ("Cavalier of the Moonlight"), which they wrote in February 1924. The scenario for this ballet-pantomime was simple, a modern dance of death: a moonlit terrace, a princess attended by four prosaic doctors, the cloaked cavalier Death darting through the shadows and at last sweeping the reluctant princess away.[31]

Iosif Hessen had Nabokov to dinner on his return from Prague and promised to assist him in every way. Some of the profits from *Rul'* 's great success in 1922–1923 were being reinvested in *Nash Mir* (*Our World*), an illustrated Sunday supplement that would begin in March 1924. To this Sirin would contribute poems, riddles, crossword puzzles, and probably some of its unsigned anagrams, logographs, metagrams. But with the mark revalued and Germany now expensive, Russian émigrés continued to flock to Paris, large enterprises lost interest in Russian clientele, and *Rul'* both shrank rapidly (less to report, fewer advertisements) and rose steeply in price overseas: in France, it cost three times as much as a local paper. *Rul'* 's well-wishers joked that it had become "the smallest and costliest newspaper in the world," and it would soon have to struggle to survive.[32]

Hessen offered Sirin his house for a private reading of *Morn* before an invited audience including director I. F. Schmidt and his wife, the distinguished actress Elena Polevitskaya, who it was hoped might take a part when the play was produced. For some reason Hessen's plan fell through, and instead Nabokov read *Morn* at the home of a Mme Lakshin on March 8 with Aykhenvald, Aldanov, and other littérateurs present. Sirin tried without result to interest publishers in the play; meanwhile, a public reading was planned.[33]

Readings of one sort or another in fact came thick and fast. As the more established writers left Berlin, the older writers' groups died out and new cultural circles formed, anxious for the services of the few writers who had stayed. Still developing rapidly, Sirin by the spring of 1924 was already foremost among the poets who had remained in Russian Berlin.

One of his readings at least was far from public. Gleb Struve recalled hearing Sirin recite in the flat of his friends Vladimir and Raisa Tatarinov a cycle of quite unprintably licentious poems. Much more respectable was the first public evening of the Friends of Russian Culture on March 25 (a concert, tea, and then literary readings that lasted until 2 A.M., at the Flugverband, Schöneberger Ufer 40), with Sirin as

the star. Six days later at the Café Leon he read *The Tragedy of M*.
Morn at one of the regular sessions of the Literary Club, an organization formed late in 1923 around Yuli Aykhenvald.[34]

Sometime early in 1924 Nabokov wrote "Port" ("The Port"), a story
that does little more than record his sense of displacement as a Russian in Marseilles. Far better was "Blagost' "("Grace") written in
March. An artist waits for his girlfriend on a bleak, windswept Berlin
street, at the foot of the Brandenburg Gate, knowing their relationship
is almost certainly finished and she will not appear. The raw weather
and the disappointment do not matter. Looking at a poor old woman
waiting in vain for customers at her roadside kiosk, he understands
the tenderness of things, the tangible goodness of all that surrounds
him, the pity in every particle of the world—a skirt hem comically
caught in a gust, the iron howl of the wind, the coffee a guard hands
the woman. "I understood that the world is not at all a struggle, not
a sequence of rapacious accidents, but a flickering joy, a benign excitement, an unvalued gift." In this excellent story the sharp detail and
the chilly situation underwrite the flash of lyric insight.[35]

"Mest' " ("Revenge"), also written in the spring of 1924, offers no
advance on Boccaccio: an aged professor of biology, wrongly deduc-
ing his young wife to be unfaithful, scares her to death by placing a
laboratory skeleton in bed beside her.[36] Presumably the story was designed for the screen. Nabokov reported to his mother at this time that
he was involved in writing scenarios : "I write with Lukash, I write
with Chorny, I write with Aleksandrov, I write alone. I visit screen
starlets."[37]

He added that the starlets called him "the English prince" because
of the small crown on the pocket of his Trinity blazer. Noticing the
coronet, people would stop him on the street and ask him if he were
a British *Seeoffizier*. To other émigrés, the good wardrobe he had acquired in Cambridge and had not yet worn out gave him the air of an
English sportsman. And in the best English literary tradition, he had
neglected to pay his tailor's bill before leaving Cambridge—as the tailor reminded him when Nabokov sent a letter about colored hearing
to the editor of an English newspaper.[38]

If any of Nabokov's scenarios was completed, none has been identified, but in April he wrote the story "Kartofel'nyy El'f" ("The Potato
Elf").[39] As in "Vengeance," the action takes place in Britain. A circus
magician brings home his partner, a twenty-year-old dwarf. The magician's wife, eager to repay her husband for his cruelties, makes love
to the dwarf, who mistakenly presumes she loves him. Bitterly disappointed when he learns the truth, he retreats from the world. Years
later the magician's wife tracks him down to tell him she had a son by

him, a normal boy, who has just died. But she cannot bring herself to disclose the fact of the boy's death, and dashes away. The dwarf chases after her to find his son's address, and collapses of a heart attack from the exertion. One of Nabokov's poorer stories, "The Potato Elf" at least reveals his cinematic sense: the crisp division of scenes, the sharp visual contrasts (acrobat and dwarf; the throes of the magician's feigned death, the recomposed features of his instant "recovery").* Introducing the story's English translation fifty years later, Nabokov had forgotten when and why it was written. After dating it 1929, he commented: "Although I never intended the story to suggest a screenplay or to fire a script writer's fancy, its structure and recurrent details do have a cinematic slant."[40] He did not remember that he himself had worked on the scenario "Lyubov' karlika" ("Love of a Dwarf") in July 1924, three months after writing the story and as soon as it caught the public eye in *Russkoe Ekho*.

Late in April Nabokov was still waiting for money from Yakobson and Yuzhny but felt buoyant about the future. When he received 1,000–1,500 marks for his scenario or play, he wrote his mother, he would come at once to Prague and take her off to Ascona, on the Swiss-Italian border, to a literary and artistic Bohemia where one could live for *"one mark a day."* Reality was more modest: he received another 40 marks from Korostovets, 30 marks for a story in *Rul'*.[41]

Readings offered Sirin little money but provided some exposure and a sense of keeping alive the cultural heritage. Berlin's Russian Literary Club on April 20 dutifully commemorated the centenary of Byron's death with an evening at the Flugverband. Aykhenvald and Lvov spoke, Sirin read some poems in English and some he had just translated into Russian, but not even Pushkin's debt to Byron induced the rest of the Russian literary world to turn up. On April 29 Sirin read some of his own poems and his recently revised play "The Pole" at the regular session of the Union of Russian Theater Workers. Another group, the Friends of Russian Culture, had been formed to preserve the cultural traditions most émigrés did not trust Soviet Russia to honor. On May 11 they presented an exhausting program at the Flugverband: a concert of Russian music at 8:30, a poetry reading timed for midnight, with Sirin taking part, and dancing until 4 A.M. For the celebrations on June 8 of the 125th anniversary of Pushkin's birth, Sirin wrote a poem on Pushkin's fatal duel. That same month a Russian Literary-Artistic Circle opened just off the Kurfürstendamm, offering a continuous social and cultural program. On June 18 the circle's first writers' evening included Sirin and Lukash.[42]

* When Sergey Bertenson translated "The Potato Elf" in 1931, movie producer Lewis Milestone liked it so much he wanted to fetch Nabokov to Hollywood to develop other "story lines." See below, p. 376.

Offstage too Lukash and Sirin still worked together. In early June they collaborated on a scenario, and the sanguine Nabokov, with requests for scenarios from three different directors, hoped for one to three thousand dollars apiece. "But I have understood that one must really create for the cinema, and that's not so easy."[43]

Sirin did not even pretend to "create" for the Bluebird sketches. When he called on Lukash, his friend would deposit his baby on a windowsill and pace up and down, puffing on his pipe, while Sirin sat, cigarette in hand, and whatever came into their heads at the moment would serve.[44] Nabokov recalls a number of pieces called "Locomotion":

> One sketch was a little on the *Candid Camera* lines. . . . It was situated on a railway platform. You saw a porter with a red nose trundling his luggage cart containing a very large trunk, very badly closed. At one point the trunk flew open and a skeleton half flopped out of the trunk but he merely pushed it back with his foot and went on his way. Then there was the sketch in which a wildly hirsute man visited a barber. The actor portraying the customer was a small chap, whose real head, concealed inside his collar, was topped by a dummy head, its face partially concealed by thick long whiskers and very long hair. The barber cut and cut, and when the man was finally shaved and shorn, only a tiny head remained, like the knob of a post with very big ears. . . . Another Bluebird "Locomotion" had a Venetian background and presented a blind man going along the bank of a canal, taptapping with his cane. Visible were the edge of the canal and the moon reflected in the water. The blind man got nearer and nearer and at the very last moment, when he was practically at the brink, his foot already raised, he took out a handkerchief, blew his nose, turned and went back, taptapping. . . . These "Locomotions" took about five minutes, there was music and songs explaining and commenting on the action. I wrote the lyrics of the songs, too. I think I saw only one performance. . . . they paid well.[45]

None of the Bluebird sketches survives. More of a loss is the story "Paskhal'nyy dozhd' " ("Easter Rain"), sold in the first half of June for the 1925 Easter number of *Russkoe Ekho*.[46] Not one copy of this issue of an extraordinarily rare newspaper seems to survive. Another story, "Sluchaynost' " ("A Matter of Chance") was rejected by *Rul* ("We don't print anecdotes about cocainists") but taken by the Riga newspaper *Segodnya*, with which Lukash had good contacts.[47] The story concerns an émigré who resorts to drugs to dull both the tedium of being a waiter in the restaurant car of an international express and the pain of having heard nothing for five years of his wife, still apparently in Russia. On the night he commits suicide on the job, his wife herself sits in the train, hours away from rejoining him at the Paris address she found out after her escape from Soviet Russia. Like "Vengeance" and "The Potato Elf," this story focuses on coincidence and the ironies of fate: only a tiresomely Hardyesque chain of accidents prevents husband and wife meeting on the train.

A fourth story on the same theme, written in the second week of June, offers much more: "Katastrofa" ("The Catastrophe"), which Nabokov translated into English as "Details of a Sunset."[48] Like the other three stories, "Details of a Sunset" seems susceptible of cinematographic treatment. Like them, it ends in death: Mark, a hearty young German bourgeois, drinks just enough to lose his footing and get killed by a tram on the very day he would have found out his fiancée had left him for another man. But here the resemblance ends. Not only are fate's ironies subtler and far more plausible here, but the story anticipates the Nabokov to come. Details of background description—a frieze lit up by the dying sun, the spark of light above a tramcar's wire—create a sense of mystery and beauty and space around the waning day, a world much larger than Mark's burg of barbers and beer. The device of the false continuation, already used in "Grace," will become a Nabokov hallmark: here although we are led to infer Mark must have been merely stunned by the tram, we gradually notice that the thoughts still running through his consciousness make sense only if he has died. And for the first time Nabokov fashions the end of a story as a trapdoor dropping us from one plane of being to another. We do not observe a character's death as an inert fact of our solid world, we *experience* the mystifying plunge the dead person makes.

V

When Nabokov returned from Prague in January, he had wanted to take his mother away from her situation there as quickly as possible. His dream of flight with her to Ascona passed like a breeze, and he planned simply to visit her in Prague. By mid-June, he wrote that he was too busy to break off work—another scenario, apparently, perhaps "Love of a Dwarf"—and asked could he fetch her from Prague so she could visit him in Berlin.[49]

Meanwhile one of his movie friends, a "rising star," decided Nabokov could twinkle too. She introduced him to her director. Inventing freely, she explained that Nabokov had had many roles to his credit in the south of Russia. The director "looked me over enthusiastically for two hours and offered me the *leading role* in a new film." Nothing came of it, of course, but all this year Nabokov was exceptionally ready to believe in his own success. Uncle Konstantin had written him enthusiastically about "A Matter of Chance," and had asked to translate it into English. Nabokov told his mother: "My writing career is beginning rather brightly. I have already piled up eight stories—a whole collection."[50]

By July Nabokov and Lukash had begun work on another Bluebird piece, "Kitayskie shirmy" ("The Chinese Screens"), with music again by Eilukhin.[51] Nabokov wrote to his mother in hush-hush terms about another project with Lukash: a secret enterprise called "Ruka" ("The Hand"), for which they already had an office and a typewriter. Though it seems likely to have been a journal—subscribers were being sought throughout the summer—Nabokov envisaged the project as something lucrative enough for him no longer to be obliged to eke out an existence by his writings and translations.[52] Whatever the enterprise was, it was stillborn: Lukash liked proposing schemes simply for their own sake, and Nabokov was a dreamer, not a businessman.

At last, on July 12, Nabokov left for Prague.[53] He found his mother very low and edgy, dreaming of coming to Berlin to visit the Tegel cemetery. Her state sobered his imagination: he planned to find more pupils in Berlin; he was "ready to break rocks" to help her. Apparently it was on this trip that Nabokov told his mother he was engaged to Véra Slonim.

He liked the family's new flat, except that "from 5 a.m. begins a thunderous din of carts, wagons, lorries, so that as one lies half awake the whole house seems to be rolling somewhere, groaning and shuddering": a first sketch for the *pension* in *Mary* that seems to rock and sway and lurch along the rails to the rhythm of the trains passing only a few feet away. Within days Nabokov and his mother left Prague for the country, staying at a good hotel in Dobřichovice whose price forced them to sleep in one room.[54]

He returned to Berlin about July 21 and in three days wrote a new story, "Groza" ("The Thunderstorm"): a young émigré looks out of his room at a storm and sees the prophet Elijah descend from the clouds, lose a wheel from his chariot, slip on a roof as he comes down to find it.[55]* Nabokov was still writing poems, though not as often as fifteen months earlier, and a great many still included God or angels, Peter at the pearly gates, or Christ on or off the cross. Some of these poems have a spiritual flavor, expressing what could be an original

---

* Simon Karlinsky writes: "Pre-Christian Slavs believed that the god of thunder, Perun, rode in his chariot in the sky during thunderstorms. After Christianization this image was passed over to the Old Testament prophet Elijah. This belief survived among peasants. . . . I love this story for its clever use of peasant folklore in its unlikely Berlin setting."

sense of life through a puppet-play of ready-made seraphim that spoils the show. Others seek out the human and individual in the divine: an angel with a splinter in his foot, Peter smelling of fish. In small doses of verse, that can be palatable, but it quickly causes indigestion in a story like "The Thunderstorm." Nabokov was still searching for ways to fit a world beyond into the world of the human, but he had not found his *own* way yet.

"Tell my sisters," he wrote his mother from Berlin, "not a day passes when I do not meet Russians on the street whose heads turn and whisper 'Vladimir Sirin.' . . ." In late July he worked on the "Love of a Dwarf" scenario and finished the "Chinese Screens" sketch, which he sold to the Bluebird for $100. Of that he received only $15, and when his landlady put up his rent to seventy marks a week, he knew he would have to leave.[56]

VI

Around the middle of August Nabokov returned to Czechoslovakia and rejoined his family in Dobřichovice. He wandered among the hills, nodding to familiar butterflies, he relaxed, he basked in thoughts of his future life with Véra, he tried to refuse visits of the Muse.[57]

She came anyway. A few days before returning to Berlin he began a new story, "Natasha," apparently unpublished.[58] A young émigré persuades the girl next door to leave her ailing father for a day's outing. In a pine wood, she tells him she has been visited by the Virgin, he recounts romantic adventures in the remote tropics, they both then confess to each other that their stories are invented, she asks him to continue anyway. On their return, she is surprised to see her father out on the street at a newspaper kiosk, but he is cheerful, he has just forgotten his wallet, there is some surprising news, will she fetch him some money. Entering their flat, she finds her father's waxlike corpse. That previous glimpse was a visitation: life's miracles outdo all our fantasies.

Nabokov returned to Berlin on August 28. At the Pension Andersen the landlady had hidden his coat, assuming he would not pay his final rent. Véra Slonim had had to bail him out, and then found him a pleasant German pension at 9 Trautenaustrasse (drab stucco beneath, pagodalike flourish of tile above) just around the corner from the apartment where she still lived with her parents, at 41 Landhausstrasse. Nabokov realized now that he would have to supplement his literary earnings with more regular work. By the end of September he had as many lessons amassed as he wanted, leaving only one day quite free of teaching.[59]

Nabokov was now rooted in Berlin in a way he had never been before. At first he had lived there because his family, the city's low living costs and its thriving Russian colony made it pointless to look elsewhere. From late 1923, Véra Slonim and the bright prospects of writing for stage and screen had made the city attractive again for the moment. But now that he was settling into a steady income from a sizable teaching load, he was entrusting himself to Berlin until the future chose to spring a new surprise. Though he had no affection for the city, the other natural choices seemed even less promising. Prague, the most active student and academic center in the emigration, simply never appealed to him: "a bleak bridge across a bleak river, rain, the wet gargoyles of some place of worship."[60] Paris was too far from his mother, and too likely to break the vacuum-seal protection around his Russian that a virtually unknown language like German could give him.

As he settled in Berlin he also settled down to prose. At the end of August he informed his mother he was tackling a new play, but nothing came of it. On September 6, he wrote "La Bonne Lorraine," a romantic but wry poem about Joan of Arc, and the first of his poems to deserve in its own right to outlive its century.[61] But the month was devoted to the story "Venetsianka" ("The Venetian Woman"), also still unpublished.[62] A shy, impressionable young Cambridge student appears to walk into a Sebastiano del Piombo painting, to move about in its landscape, and then begins to dry out, to set there like so much pigment; an expert art restorer wipes off the intruding figure, and realizes too late what he has done—but it all proves to have been a trick of the story, and a natural explanation emerges. With colorful characters and well-controlled romantic entanglements, the story reads like Pirandello: clever metaphysical twists, but with none of the nimbus of mysterious meaning the mature Nabokov could imply.

That was his first attempt to use art per se to ruffle the smooth surface of being. His next, the story "Bachmann," written in October, does it much better. In this account of a musician of genius ill at ease outside the harmonies in his head, Nabokov not only anticipates the portrait of Luzhin in his first great novel, *The Defense*, but also reveals his mastery immediately, and for the first time: in the gently comic picture of Bachmann's awkwardness in the world; in the speed and sureness with which he sketches the taverns Bachmann frequents, rivaling Jan Steen in half a dozen lines; in the tension between the entrepreneur Sack, the narrator's cynical source, and the sentimentalist narrator himself, who milks every drop of tenderness he can from the ungainly relationship of Bachmann and Mme Perov. The chords this story strikes keep vibrating: the transcendent power and fulfillment of Bachmann's art, the limitations and helplessness of his life, and the intersection of the two at the brink of inexistence: "I think this was the only happy night in Mme Perov's life. I think that these two, the deranged musician and the dying woman, that night found words the greatest poets never dreamed of."[63]

No line of growth could predict Nabokov's development this year. In November he wrote the story "Drakon" ("The Dragon").[64] Still trying out different modes, still unsure how to circumvent the confines of realism in order to render the mystery and strangeness of things, he adopted an expedient he would never try again. A dragon that has cowered a thousand years in its cave, fearful of the world, emerges into a stretch of modern countryside and ventures meekly into the nearest town. When a tobacco firm plasters advertisements on the dragon's side, its competitors rig up a circus rider as a knight to pierce what they presume to be an inflated rubber model. The horse knows better, and backs off, but the dragon scurries in retreat to its cave, remembering its mother's death from the blow of a lance, and dies. Nabokov's simple fable attacks an attitude of mind—life as a struggle for advantage—that destroys all that is miraculous in the world.

A continuation of "A Stroke of the Wing" which Nabokov sent his mother in mid-December, apparently in published form, has not yet been located.[65] By this time he had completed the first draft of "Rozhdestvo" ("Christmas"), his finest story to date.[66] A father decides to commit suicide after his son's death, rather than face a life "humiliatingly pointless, sterile, devoid of miracles"—when at that very moment an *Attacus* moth his son had cherished, now warmed by the nearby furnace, cracks out of its cocoon and walks up the wall, its wings swelling and breathing. Introducing the English translation, Nabokov commented: "It oddly resembles the type of chess problem called 'selfmate.' " Sleptsov checkmates his own despair: the things he brings back from his son's room to nourish his grief include the cocoon in the biscuit tin that refutes his gloomy conclusion. Characteristically it is Nabokov's exact scientific knowledge that has allowed him to prepare the story's "miracle." The same sure command of nature enables him to describe the winter's day in radiant, specific details that answer Sleptsov's misery even before the moth emerges: for all its pain, the world overflows with joys.

VII

By now Nabokov could give lessons without thinking. Throughout the fall of 1924 he had earned enough from tutoring to leave him the time and freedom to write work that mattered. Now he seems to have planned to visit his mother for Christmas and to be back in Berlin about January 10, when his students resumed. He also intended to move into a new apartment on his return. Neither the trip nor the change of flats came about, perhaps because Véra developed bronchitis.[67]

On January 23, 1925, Nabokov wrote his mother that he was working on a story that would become "part of that long novel that I planned ages ago." The story, "Pis'mo v Rossiyu" ("A Letter that Never Reached Russia") was published six days later.[68*] More than fifty years afterward, Nabokov gave this explanation of the story's composition:

> Sometime in 1924 . . . I had begun a novel tentatively entitled "Happiness" (*Schastie*), some important elements of which were to be reslanted in *Mashen'ka*. . . . Around Christmas 1924, I had two chapters of *Schastie* ready but then, for some forgotten but no doubt excellent reason, I scrapped Chapter One and most of Two.[69]

This seems no more than a reconstruction from the published story's subheading, "From Chapter Two of the novel *Schastie*." While the novel had been conceived much earlier, Nabokov's letters make it plain that "A Letter that Never Reached Russia" was written on its own, not saved from a larger chapter, and was published at once. Nor is there anything to suggest that a Chapter One or another fragment of a Chapter Two were ever written. Presumably Nabokov had the entire plan of the novel in his head, and simply wrote a section out of sequence, as would become his general practice.

Though brief, the story is excellent early Nabokov: a letter from a young émigré writer to the woman he had to leave in Russia in 1917. He has vowed in his previous letter not to mention the past (the few details he does let slip are memories of Lyussya Shulgin) and instead he simply depicts aspects of the Berlin around him. A sample paragraph:

> A car rolls by on pillars of wet light. It is black, with a yellow stripe beneath the windows. It trumpets gruffly into the ear of the night, and its shadow passes under my feet. By now the street is totally deserted— except for an aged great Dane whose claws rap on the sidewalk as it reluctantly takes for a walk a listless, pretty, hatless girl with an opened umbrella. When she passes under the garnet bulb (on her left, above the fire alarm), a single taut, black segment of her umbrella reddens damply.

---

* "Pis'mo iz Rossii" ("A Letter from Russia") was a common heading in the émigré press for the anonymous articles by people unable to leave Russia who managed to smuggle out their reports of Soviet life.

Already Nabokov's imagination is unmistakable: this is no ready-made world. "A car rolls by on pillars of wet light": a metaphor compressed without strain into a single word, and evoking exactly both the headlamps' two slender cones of light, diffused by the drizzle, and the corresponding reflected stripes gleaming on the wet asphalt. Well-chosen details place us within the scene: the great Dane's audible claws that define the night air, the shadow sweeping under feet that become ours as we read. In this perfectly coordinated microcosm, each thing casts its consequence: sound or silence, light or shadow, seeping color or low saturation, movement or stillness. And watching this world is a mind that vivifies everything by daring to see it afresh: the ear of the night, the dog taking the girl for a walk, the sheer painterly pleasure of registering the one segment of the umbrella that reddens.

Here again Nabokov serves up the world according to his secret recipe for happiness: detach the mind from accepting a humdrum succession of moments, and everything becomes magical, a masterpiece of precision and harmony, a gift of absurd generosity. And simultaneously the unique complex of particulars becomes an instant unbearably vulnerable and poignant, fading even now from memory—but surely, surely, preserved in the past? The story ends:

> The centuries will roll by, and schoolboys will yawn over the history of our upheavals; everything will pass, but my happiness, dear, my happiness will remain, in the moist reflection of a streetlamp, in the cautious bend of stone steps that descend into the canal's black waters, in the smiles of a dancing couple, in everything with which God so generously surrounds human loneliness.

By now Nabokov had under perfect control the lyrical pulse that first beat through his fiction in "Sounds." He could express with assurance the world he saw, the way he felt within it, the conclusions he drew from his way of seeing. He still had to reinvent the arts of narrative, of character, of structure, but he was well on the way.

VIII

Though Sirin's real artistic life was solitary, he still worked with others. In mid-February a writers' cooperative named "Arzamas"—after the literary association of poets and critics Pushkin joined as a schoolboy—was set up to publish books. The small circle of members included Aykhenvald, Lukash, and Sirin. A week later the Lukash-Sirin-Eilukhin ballet "Cavalier of the Moonlight" opened in Königsberg to great success.[70] Acting could sometimes provide Nabokov with a change from creative isolation, and perhaps even more change than he needed. On March 12, for instance, he left the city at 7 A.M. for a day's work as a film extra; returned at 5 P.M. with ten dollars in his hand, greasepaint on his brows and klieg-light spots in his eyes; taught until 8 P.M.; then rehearsed a pantomime, "Balagan," under a novice director, Lydia Ryndina, wife of his friend Sergey Krechetov. Performed five days later before the Literary-Artistic Club, the show was utterly panned: as director and theater critic Yuri Ofrosimov complained, it was an outrage that a director ignorant of the rudiments of pantomime should take up the time of people with talents of their own to exercise.[71]

The day before the third anniversary of his father's death, Nabokov wrote to his mother that he would spend the whole day at Tegel cemetery:

> Three years have gone—and every trifle relating to father is still as alive as ever inside me. I am so certain, my love, that we will see him again, in an unexpected but completely natural heaven, in a realm where all is radiance and delight. He will come towards us in our common bright eternity, slightly raising his shoulders as he used to do, and we will kiss the birthmark on his hand without surprise. You must live in expectation of that tender hour, my love, and never give into the temptation of despair. Everything will return. . . [72]

IX

On April 15, 1925, Vladimir Nabokov and Véra Slonim married in the Berlin town hall. Since they wanted as little fuss as possible, they chose two distant acquaintances as the two witnesses the law required. When they left the Rathaus after the ceremony, a fat doorman congratulated them in expectation of a tip. Since Nabokov showed no sign of responding, one of the witnesses "—and he was *echt deutsch*, real German"—tried to hint at the required decorum: "He's congratulated you." Nabokov merely replied, "How nice." "—We just walked out. I didn't have, you see, a *penny* in my pocket! We had to pay a certain sum. We had paid. That was all we had."[73]

That evening, Vladimir dined at the Slonims', and Véra casually reported: "By the way, we got married this morning."[74] They announced the wedding to a wider circle by means of a printed card—in Germany, of two Russians, but written in French, with old- and new-style dates:

Monsieur Vladimir Nabokoff
Mademoiselle Véra Slonim
mariés le 2/15 Avril 1925
Berlin, 13, Luitpoldstrasse[75]

More than a year earlier Nabokov had written to Véra from Prague of a dream in which he was playing the piano, she turning the pages.[76] Véra Nabokov would do much more than that for her husband's art. Sixty years later she would still be transposing his works for other instruments, other tongues.

CHAPTER 11

Scenes from Emigré Life: Berlin, 1925–1926

I

EXILE for the Nabokovs was a succession of rented rooms. Some months before Véra Slorim married, her parents had moved from a large apartment to a smaller one, while Véra herself and her cousin Anna Feigin rented two rooms from a German family on the second floor of 13 Luitpoldstrasse in the Schöneberg area. Since Anna Feigin was leaving for Leipzig at the end of April 1925, the Nabokovs continued living apart for almost two weeks after the wedding until Vladimir could inherit her room.[1] Almost all their married life the Nabokovs slept in separate rooms. Like his character Vadim Vadimych, Nabokov was an insomniac and "a solitary sleeper by principle and inclination," and in his émigré years was often kept up through the night smoking and scribbling at his desk.[2]

Decades later Nabokov recalled composing *Mary* in the spring of 1925. Early in the year he abandoned the initial design for a novel called *Schastie* (*Happiness*), but would retain the title even for the revised draft of a new novel that he finally renamed *Mashen'ka* (*Mary*)[3] But the evidence of the manuscript and of Nabokov's letters to his mother shows that although he may have planned it earlier in the year he did not write *Mary* until the fall. One of the first works to appear after his marriage was on quite another scale: a "puzzle of crossed words." Seven Across: a certain institution (*GPU*). Fourteen Down: what the Bolsheviks will do (*disappear*). Crosswords had no fixed name in Russian then, but Nabokov invented the word "krestoslovitsa," which gradually became a standard émigré Russian term. In the land of the GPU, of course, *krest* ("cross") was an unmentionable word, and *krossvord* prevailed, in the apparent hope that people would not perceive its disgraceful etymology.[4]

Throughout 1925 and until the fall of 1926 Nabokov acted as tutor to two boys from wealthy Russian Jewish families. In the morning he got up at seven, "as regular as a Swiss watch," to be at Alexander Sax's by 7:30 and take this seventeen-year-old lad, intelligent but far too shy to have shone at high school, for lessons in English, gymnastics, tennis, and boxing until about 11 A.M. They built up an excellent rapport, and

Nabokov became "a one-man finishing school for the boy." In the afternoons Nabokov would usually give lessons by the hour in English or French, trekking across the city by bus or tram from pupil to pupil, from girls who made eyes at him to businessmen who tried to make the lesson stretch beyond the time they had paid for. In his European years, he estimated, he had eighty-five regular pupils in all. In the early evening he taught his other tutee, Sergey Kaplan, whose parents often provided him with sumptuous meals.[5]

While he had these two tutees as well as regular pupils, Nabokov had more than enough to live on. The surplus went to his mother, sometimes two hundred marks or more a month. Never one for abstract charity, he later wrote: "I for one felt no compulsion to share anything with strangers. On the other hand, from 1922 to 1939 I helped my mother as much as, and in every way, that I could. Her own life in Prague first with three children, then with a young son, grandson—and dear, devoted but pathetically inefficient Evgenia Hofeld—was a tragedy of mismanagement." In mid-May 1925, Elena Nabokov visited her son and new daughter-in-law in Berlin. Though the visit was a happy one, she still had a bewildered, agitated look, three years after her husband's death.[6]

On June 8 the leading émigré centers celebrated for the first time what would become an annual fixture on Pushkin's birthday:* Russian Culture Day, intended to unite the emigration and express its resolve to preserve a cultural heritage under threat in Soviet Russia. At the Flugverband, Sirin read his contribution, the poem "Izgnan'e" ("Exile"), which conjures up an image of Pushkin as a member of the emigration.[7] In those years Sirin could easily whip up at short notice a birthday verse to satisfy the Russian appetite for anniversaries.

To his friend Gleb Struve he wryly summed up the depleted literary life of Russian Berlin:

> Our Berlin life limps along. [Ivan] Lukash has written a would-be light-historical novel without a trace of lightness or history. Jacques Noir—a nice fellow in everyday life but the most tedious vulgarian in verse—exposes the mores of Berliners, whom he knows by an émigré's complaints against landlords and the sandwiches. Sergey Gorny is the same unbearably monotonous popularizer of his private recollections. V. Sirin still writes the same very regular verse.[8]

In late June and early July Nabokov wrote the story "Draka" ("The Fight").[9] A writer sunbathes and swims in the Grunewald and

---

* Actually a miscalculation, as Khodasevich pointed out at the time: Pushkin was born on May 26, 1799 (O.S.), which was June 6, 1799, in the West.

basks in his own detachment as he describes the life around him in vivid detail: an elderly German with a meaty belly who regularly settles down on the sand nearby; a baby boy waddling with his "soft little beak" between his legs; a fistfight that erupts in a pub between the publican—the elderly German sunbather—and his daughter's lover, over a single unpaid drink. In this study of the interplay between toil and rest, rigidity and flexibility, involvement and detachment, Nabokov anticipates a passage in the last chapter of *Speak, Memory*, where before writing again of the Grunewald he speculates that human consciousness must have evolved not as a weapon in a tense struggle for survival but as a plaything in moments of relaxation. He postulates "a lolling and loafing which allowed first of all the formation of *Homo poeticus*—without which sapiens could not have been evolved. 'Struggle for life' indeed. The curse of battle and toil leads man back to the boar, to the grunting beast's crazy obsession with the search for food."[10] "The Fight" ends: "Or perhaps what matters is not the human pain or joy at all but, rather, the play of shadow and light on a live body, the harmony of trifles assembled on this particular day, at this particular moment, in a unique and inimitable way." The story as a whole seems uneasy: does it back that pronouncement, or does it set out to criticize its narrator's inhuman indulgence in living as if others' pain and joy were merely for his own artistic delectation?

II

When the Nabokovs vacated their Luitpoldstrasse apartment at the end of July, their landlord tried to charge them another month's rent and hid Véra Nabokov's coat as security, even though the taxi was throbbing at the door. Frau Rölke felt the injustice of her husband's demand, and fetched the coat herself.[11] It would not be their last brush with landlords.

On August 1, Vladimir took Véra to Czechoslovakia to meet his family. They spent two weeks in the very small, very Czech dacha at Radočovice (60 Villa Kaura) near Prague, which Elena Nabokov had rented for the summer. The days passed in long walks in the countryside with Box II, the family's venerable dachshund, waddling beside Elena Nabokov or yapping after hares.[12]

For another two weeks Nabokov lay in a black knit swimsuit on the sands of a Baltic beach near Zoppot, acting as escort for Alexander Sak, while Véra stayed with her parents in Berlin. Then, dressed in long shorts to just above the knees and long socks to just below them, with a stout cane in his hand, he set off with Sak on August 27 for a walking tour of the Schwarzwald. Freiburg charmed them with its cathedral and its Cambridge-like air. As they waited in the dusk at the little station of Reiselfingen, flocks of crows flapped heavily over the firs. On August 31 they climbed a trail up Feldberg, and Nabokov felt as if he were nearing the plains of Russia, its sights and sounds— dense fir needles, peat-bog berries—and wrote a poem to commemorate his mood. Past cottages roofed in silvery wooden scales, past cowbells and tinkling streams they walked to St. Blasien and to Wehr. In Säckingen a traveling circus in the town square inspired another poem. On September 4 they took the train to Constance. Véra Nabokov met them there and led them to the Pension Zeiss, where she had rented two rooms with a view over the lake.[13]

III

After eight days in Constance the Nabokovs returned to Berlin and perched in an interim pension. On September 30 they moved into two rooms at 31 Motzstrasse, one of those Berlin streets dotted with the small parks that gave the city such a spacious air. Their rooms were rented from the elderly widow of a major ("she could have been a major herself"), not a pleasant person but impeccably correct as a landlady. While living in Motzstrasse, the Nabokovs frequently dined at the Slonims' apartment, Vladimir often playing chess with his father-in-law. Nabokov was delighted with Evsey Slonim's intelligence and his understanding that for his son-in-law the most important thing in life was to write.[14]

Unable to take his butterfly net on the Schwarzwald tour—he could hardly escort Alexander Sak *and* chase to and fro after prey—Nabokov was compensated back in Berlin one September morning on his way to the Saks'. On a linden trunk near Charlottenburg station he spied an extremely rare moth, the dream of German collectors, and took it at once to the amazed owner of a Motzstrasse butterfly shop, who offered to spread it for him.[15]

Apart from acting as tutor to Alexander Sak and Sergey Kaplan, Nabokov seems to have given a few lectures at an Anglo-French club in Berlin in October. But since his return from the Schwarzwald he had been aching to write. On Frau Lepel's moth-eaten couch, Nabokov recalls, he began to write out his first novel.[16] By mid-October he was well advanced, and told his mother:

> My hero is not a very likeable person, but amongst the others there are very sweet people. I am getting to know them better and better, and it already begins to seem that my Ganin, my Alfyorov, my dancers Kolin

and Gornotsvetov, my old Podtyagin, Klara, a Kiev Jewess, Kunitsyn, Mme Dorn and so on—least but not last—my Mary—are real people, and not my inventions. I know how each one smells, walks, eats, and I understand how God as he created the world found this a pure, thrilling joy. We are translators of God's creation, his little plagiarists and imitators, we dress up what he wrote, as a charmed commentator sometimes gives an extra grace to a line of genius.[17]

By the end of October 1925 he had completed the first draft of his first novel, and spent November revising it.[18]

IV
Mary (Mashen'ka)

When *Mary* appeared in English in 1970 readers enjoyed it for the echoes of Nabokov's first love, the "Tamara" of the recently revised *Speak, Memory* (1966). But to Sirin's first audience the novel was not autobiographical but a portrait of exile, "a novel of émigré life," as the advertisements proclaimed.

Introducing the English version of the novel Nabokov stresses its autobiographical nature and the sheer relief for a young writer of "getting rid of oneself."[19] But although he did feel a pressure to treat his love for Lyussya Shulgin in fiction—it was also to have been the subject of his abandoned novel *Happiness*—his phrase does not mean he spilled his soul all over the page.

Ganin remembers Mary—Lyussya Shulgin in almost every detail—with a passion and precision that make his hitherto sluggish spirit soar. Reanimated by memory, the romance of first love comes radiantly alive. But Nabokov assigns Ganin no more of himself than this single part of his past, and this one autobiographical current flows within a channel he has engineered to his own deliberate design. Later he might recall *Mary* as mere nostalgic indulgence, but back in 1925 he had taken great pains to construct a novel of exile. Ganin's yearning for Mary becomes a personalized image of the émigré dream, the hope of reliving and resuming the happiness of remembered Russia. Not that Mary is in any way a symbol: Nabokov knew he could make her live in the imagination only if he kept true to the irrational particulars of the past.

To the subjective intensity of Ganin's memory he then added a second focus, objective and wide-angled: the cheap Russian pension where Ganin lives in Berlin. In order to make the novel the record of a whole subculture, he devised the pension as a cross section of the emigration, its comedy and pathos: the landlady, a partly Germanized

Russian; Podtyagin, an old poet with no public left to write for, a man who in outliving a Russia he could inhabit feels he has outlived life itself; the homosexual dancers, who fare better because they ply an art unlimited by language, like the arts of Stravinsky, Chagall, Pavlova; Klara, forced to spend all day in the alien world of a German office; Alfyorov, the optimist and would-be entrepreneur, ready to forget the old Russia he regards as dead; and Ganin, listless and without will until galvanized by the image of his homeland.

Nabokov scrupulously observes the facts of émigré life. Set in April 1924, when the rush to leave Berlin peaked, the story shows Ganin planning vaguely to leave for France and beyond, and Podtyagin trying with heartrendingly ill success to assemble all the visas and permits he needs to move to Paris. Nabokov could also invent from the facts of émigré life apt new images of exile, like Russian film extras, shadows whose images flicker on the margin of screen after screen, town after town; or Ganin's pension, so close to the railroad tracks that smoke billows in the windows and vibrations shudder from room to room, as if exile were a railroad, a mere locus of movement, or at best a station where people only kill time between a place they remember coming from and a destination they do not know.

He also relished obscurer details. He has Ganin and Lyudmila make love on the floor of a taxi—a scene Edmund Wilson later objected to: "I don't think you can have had any actual experience of this kind or you would know that it is not done that way." Nabokov replied: "My dear Bunny, it could be done, and in fact was done, in Berlin taxi-cabs, models 1920. I remember having interviewed numerous Russian taxi-drivers, fine White Russians all of them, and they all said yes, that was the correct way. I am afraid I am quite ignorant of the American technique."[20]

Reviewers received Sirin's novel enthusiastically, though a few reacted to his lyrical celebration of a patch of old Russia by judging him slightly old-fashioned. The Sirin who had hymned the landscape of Russia's past often enough in verse seemed ready to till the same soil in prose. What critics could not know was that *Mary* was not Sirin's point of arrival but only a promising point of departure.

For many early reviewers, the novel seemed most striking for its boldness of detail, rapturous or repulsive: the brass knobs of a convalescent's bed in a Russian summer, "each containing a bubble of sunlight," or a ball of haircombings floating in a washbasin. Many years later Nabokov stood up firmly for his young self when his English translator tried to turn into mere "ventilators" the nodules on the roofs of olive-drab railway carriages. In Russian he had written "dark dog-nipples," and that was how they had to stay.[21]

Some reviewers rightly admired the book's inventiveness of structure, the original strategies for its beginning, middle, and end. Exposition has always been one of the storyteller's trickiest arts: how to catch attention and secretly smuggle in necessary information in one smooth movement. Nabokov hit upon a superb solution: the two leading characters get stuck in an elevator, in the dark, and garrulous Alfyorov tries to fill the disconcerting void with his babble.

Then the novel's unexpected middle. Alfyorov, who has just taken the room next door to Ganin's, expects his wife, for years trapped in Soviet Russia, to rejoin him in six days' time and take over Ganin's room. Ganin discovers Alfyorov's wife to be none other than Mary his own first love, the girl with whom in 1915 he had basked in all the radiance of young romance, until a year later they had drifted apart. Then, just when the pull of their past happiness had begun to draw them together again, the smoke of the civil war had finally cut them off from each other's view. Hearing her name again, the inert Ganin is suddenly shocked into life as Mary's advent makes him relive in memory all the bliss of the past with a force that all but blots out the present. Berlin's streets fade as Russia and its remembered forest paths revive. Ganin prepares to leave Berlin with Mary, and on the eve of her arrival plies the overexcited Alfyorov with drink until he collapses. Ganin heads off to the station to meet Mary first and whisk her away.

Better even than the surprise beginning and the surprising reality of Russia revived in memory in the middle of the novel is the surprise ending. Before Ganin reaches the station, he realizes at the last moment that he already has with him all the beauty of his past love, the present has its own claims, and a fresh future lies open ahead. Without waiting for Mary's train, Ganin boards another and makes for France. In a novel called *Mary*, the author dares to leave his hero free enough to choose at last not to meet Mary at the station, not to have her cross the novel's stage at all.

The ending discloses that there is much more to Nabokov than the simple celebrant of Russia's past or his own. He rejoices in the power of consciousness, the strength and passion of Ganin's memory. But he also remains aware of the dangerous blindness of the ego. Dreaming of meeting Mary at the station, Ganin supposes his plan a triumph. He does not recognize it as a triumph of selfishness: his unconcern for Alfyorov, his unquestioned assumption that Mary will leave with him. No wonder the newly married Nabokov had little sympathy for his hero. Only when Ganin changes his mind on the last page of the book does he in fact turn his story toward triumph, when he realizes he has all his past already with him and need not befoul the present.

The Nabokov who had chosen his own new route in life and felt secure enough in his love for Véra to be haunted no longer by his dream of a past love could feel kinship with Ganin only at this final moment of the novel. He has invited us to succumb to the alluring energy of Ganin's emotion—as he will with Humbert or Van Veen—only to point out the danger of the romantic intoxication of the self.

Nabokov describes the spatial world so exactly in *Mary* that he leaves a precise blueprint of the six bedrooms in Ganin's pension in our minds. But to differentiate and order each room in our mental model, he has the landlady number each door with a large digit from her dead husband's desk calendar, the first days of April for the previous year. Time, not space, is Nabokov's real subject: not the Russian Berlin the book renders so well, but the accumulated time of memory that allows Ganin to superimpose the country of his past on the city streets of his present.

Mary is a novel about time: about the reality of the past, even though we can only reach it within the present; about the delusive force of our anticipations of the future (Alfyorov's and Ganin's visions of meeting Mary at the station, Podtyagin's of crossing into France); and about the present, where we are free to act and responsible for the choices we make: free enough for Ganin to decide not to see Mary at all.

It had taken Nabokov a decade of writing well-formed verse to recognize with horror how much he had borrowed without thinking from earlier poets. In *Mary* he mastered at one bound the received art of the novel. He combines clarity and economy, subjective intensity and social range, memorable detail and shapely structure. He finds original solutions for the compositional problem of his novel's beginning, middle, and end, solutions that allow him to treat his special themes of the force and frailty of consciousness and the nature of human time. But it would not be his real manner to play new hands within the old game of fiction. He would learn to change the rules of the game, so that the very idea of an exposition or an ending could be discarded, parodied, inverted, or made to do something no one had ever dreamed of, so that he could re-create this world but somehow reach beyond human time.

Nabokov soon looked back on *Mary* and saw the conventions he had unconsciously accepted. A hermetically sealed community of characters neatly differentiated: a cliché of modern fiction and film. A hero with no character but the memory Nabokov has lent him, a hero whose gifts are to be taken on trust, with no evidence supplied (contrast this with the generous samples Nabokov will supply of Fyodor's prose and verse, Krug's thought, Pnin's scholarship, John Shade's poetry). And above all, a structure so orderly and well signposted it can all be assimilated at once. The pension's rooms numbered one to six; the desk-calendar pages turned steadily day by day from Sunday to Saturday, as if Nabokov dared extend the classical unity of time from a day to a week, but no further; the more absurdly steady disclosure of Ganin's memories of Mary from 1915 to 1919, handily unfolding for the reader's convenience and ignoring the psychology of memory—all this bespeaks a desire for clarity and proportion that Nabokov never abandoned but that he would learn was not enough for him to express all he wished about the mind's encounter with time.

V

For all its limitations, *Mary* was a breakthrough in Nabokov's art, and he seemed to realize it. During October 1925, as he finished the first draft of the novel, and even before he sat down to revise it, he at once drafted another story that even more explicitly contrasted time and space: "Vozvrashchenie Chorba" ("The Return of Chorb").[22]

A young émigré writer marries a charming German girl and honeymoons with her through Germany, Switzerland, and the Riviera, only to see her die when she touches an electric wire on a road near Grasse. Wanting to hoard his grief, Chorb does not inform his in-laws and instead retraces in reverse order every step of the honeymoon, trying to fix and file away each chance trifle they had noticed together. Arriving back in her home town at last late one evening, he stops at the final shrine of the pilgrimage, the cheap hotel they had laughingly tripped off to on their wedding night to escape her parents' fuss. Since Chorb cannot face the solitude of the room he hires a prostitute, not for sexual favors but merely to fill the void next to him in the bed. His wife's parents, meanwhile, who have heard nothing from their daughter for a month, discover that Chorb and presumably their daughter have put up at that same hotel again. They burst into his hotel room, and there the story ends.

Unable to revisit in time all he has shared with his wife, Chorb ties to retrace his past in space. Life has given him much, but it has also inflicted on him the pain of loss and the grotesque humiliation of his desperate attempts to cope. We are handed the most stupendous treasures, Nabokov always believed, but no matter how much we receive we lose it all. We may try to hang on, as Ganin does, in memory, or we may break down, like Chorb, but so long as we are human we are defined by our position in time.

No subject would become more uniquely Nabokov's than the preposterous fact that we cannot retain the real past we have lived through. Like Chorb, many of his characters—Humbert, Kinbote,

Van Veen, Hugh Person—seek to reimpose a vanished past a changed present and become grotesque or cruel in the process. Only within the mind, through memory and imagination, do characters like Ganin, Cincinnatus, Fyodor, Shade, and, again, Van Veen, cope with the pain of loss.

VI

Had he not been married, Nabokov could have written neither *Mary* nor "The Return of Chorb": it needed the confidence of his love for Véra for him to set Lyussya Shulgin behind him in *Mary*, and his dread of any harm befalling her to charge "The Return of Chorb" with such helplessness before the losses time can bring. But his art was maturing at great speed in other directions. In December 1925, as soon as he had revised *Mary*, he wrote the story "Putevoditel' po Berlinu" ("A Guide to Berlin"), and discovered in its deliberately disjointed structure one way to avoid the tidy realism of *Mary*.[23]

The story has no plot. One émigré tells another at their regular pub about things he has noticed during the day: some pipes awaiting implantation in a city street; Berlin trams; the zoo. But this story, apparently so unprepossessing, marks the boldest advance yet in Nabokov's art.

No great artist accepts the world blandly, and least of all Nabokov. His curiosity was alert to everything: a quirk of psychology, a play of light, a tree, a tram. No generalization could account for the stray fact, no category could catch the individual, no explanation for this planet or anything beyond it would satisfy him as more than merely possible. Everything was full of wonder and beauty, everything could be turned around another way to release the surprise of life. After describing the streetcar he took earlier in the day, the narrator of "A Guide to Berlin" comments:

> The horse-drawn tram has vanished, and so will the trolley, and some eccentric Berlin writer in the twenties of the twenty-first century, wishing to portray our time, will go to a museum of technological history and locate a hundred-year-old streetcar, yellow, uncouth, with old-fashioned curved seats, and in a museum of old costumes dig up a black, shiny-buttoned conductor's uniform. Then he will go home and compile a description of Berlin streets in bygone days. Everything, every trifle, will be valuable and meaningful: the conductor's purse, the advertisement over the window, that peculiar jolting motion which our great-grandchildren will perhaps imagine—everything will be ennobled and justified by its age.

I think that here lies the sense of literary creation: to portray ordinary
objects as they will be reflected in the kindly mirrors of future times; to
find in the objects around us the fragrant tenderness that only posterity
will discern and appreciate in the far-off times when every trifle of our
plain everyday life will become exquisite and festive in its own right: the
times when a man who might put on the most ordinary jacket of today
will be dressed up for an elegant masquerade.

With "A Guide to Berlin," Nabokov learns to make even a tramcar
jump the rails of routine. As a young poet he had tried to show that
the world could best be seen by stepping aside, even by stepping right
off: hence God and all those angels in his early verse, so meekly responsive to his call. But used too often the angels' wings soon
drooped like tatty feather-dusters stirring up the unsought implication of religious belief. Now in "A Guide to Berlin" Nabokov finds his
true way, not borrowing the devices of old poets or the panoply of old
creeds but breaking us from our habitual perspective on the world by
flipping end for end the telescope of time.

Or he discloses the magic in every moment by looking as if with the
eyes of art. Not the eyes of a pale periwigged connoisseur or an aesthete of the salons, not the eyes of the young poet he had been, ready
to see "mournful roses" wrapped in rhyme, but those of a man looking from a tram who can make out the beauty in something so ordinary as people at work: a dusty baker-boy on a tricycle, a postman
emptying the mailbox, even a driver unloading sides of beef:

> But perhaps fairest of all are the carcasses, chrome yellow, with pink
> blotches, and arabesques, piled on a truck, and the man in apron and
> leather hood with a long neck flap who heaves each carcass onto his back
> and, hunched over, carries it across the sidewalk into the butcher's red
> shop.

VII

Nabokov seems always to have attended to detail, but in his early
years he would write lyrics of soft-focus poesy even while he may
have projected in his mind a crisp image of a remembered scene. By
1923 he had already learned to transmit to the reader the clarity he
imagined, and nearly three years later when he wrote "A Guide to
Berlin" his command of detail was already approaching that of the
master of his craft: not a thick cement of fact under each step of the
story but a sharp stone here or there to jolt the soul. The mature Nabokov surrounds his details with what he once called "a nimbus of

bright irrelevancy,"[24] a sense that they are inutile, pointless, of no practical advantage, splendid simply because they are there, without human meaning, without human feeling, a foreign song. And yet at the same time his descriptions sparkle with the pleasure of perception and foreground the role of the mind as it apprehends and alters the object it sharpens or softens its focus upon.

Whatever Nabokov's first poems may have lacked, they already showed an intuitive feeling for form. As he turned to fiction he applied the same sense of harmony to the subtle relations between the parts of his world. In "A Guide to Berlin," for instance: "while up the interior slope at the very mouth of the pipe which is nearest to the turn of the tracks, the reflection of a still illumined tram sweeps up like bright-orange heat lightning." He also began to subvert and complicate the classical norms of structure—economy, clarity, harmony— he always adhered to. "A Guide to Berlin" appears to contain half-a-dozen discrete vignettes, whimsically personal observations of Berlin life that signal their own impracticality as a guide to the city's streets. But behind the patchy frame of space, Nabokov allows us to glimpse another structure where the spatial world serves only as the pretext for different possible relations to time, and it was this above all that marked the new course he found for his fiction in the autumn of 1925.

Most prominent of all within this theme is his sense of the absurdity of our inability to return to our past, though we know it to have been just as real as this present moment. It is at this point that Nabokov's mature work splits off from his juvenilia; here is the breach between Sirin the fledgling and the adult bird of paradise. In the early verse his laments for Vyra or a lost love were mere sentimental indulgence or poetic parrotry. In Mary and "The Return of Chorb" and all that followed he reinvents and distances those private feelings to find an artistic shape for his stories, and a chart of the human condition, in the gap between revisitable space or retainable matter and inaccessible time.

Just as the young poet had rendered his world and his feelings in other poets' adjectives and exclamations, so he had tried to suggest something more spacious than this world by rushing to the neighborhood heaven. For all the playfulness and skepticism of his angelic images, their cumulative impact suggested he was not so much stating a problem as offering a solution. He thought he was simply taking up handy tools to rob the grave of its secrets, but it looked as if he were stocking a tomb with propitiatory images.

From the time of Mary, "Chorb," and "A Guide to Berlin," Nabokov marked out a new route to his special goal. Rather than hoarding old icons of the beyond, he subjected the paradoxical conditions of our existence to philosophical analysis. After separating out space, time, and consciousness, he could contrast the absurd limits of the known with an implicit, philosophically possible, return through time, and as he deepened his analysis he would find ways into the unknown much more likely to the rational imagination than had ever been possible on angel wings.

What prompted the sudden advance in Nabokov's art late in 1925? Surprisingly, this inner change in his work may reflect the great outer change in his life: that this was the year of his marriage. At the very end of his career, in *Look at the Harlequins!*, he would deliberately invert the tribute he pays to Véra in *Speak, Memory* in order to pay her an oblique, more private, but still richer tribute. Vadim Vadimych N——, the narrator and central character of *Look at the Harlequins!*, is a Russo-American novelist whose name, career, and oeuvre plainly parallel those of his maker. Nabokov marries him off to three successive wives, all negative images of Véra, before introducing another woman into Vadim's life, a woman known only as "You," as Véra remains only "you" in *Speak, Memory*. Before Vadim Vadimych proposes to her, as before he proposes to the other women he marries, he explains his fears that he may be headed for permanent insanity. In real life he can easily walk in one direction and turn on his heels to return in the opposite direction, but in imagination he cannot. Somehow that seems symptomatic to him of his dangerously quirky mind, his precarious mental balance. Unlike the other women he marries, who make nothing of his confession but nevertheless accept his proposal, "You" resolves his problem. He is perfectly sane, she lectures him, but he has simply confused reversible space with nonreversible time: as he envisages walking down a street, his rich imagination saturates the process with particular events, and what proves impossible for him is not swiveling around in neutral space but doing so in accumulated time.

At this point the book ends, with Vadim about to marry "You," and with long years of unhappy marriages and wasted life suddenly redeemed as a woman plainly intended to evoke Véra Nabokov enters Vadim's life. Since in Nabokov's own life it was in the months immediately following his marriage that he began to resort again and again to the contrast between space and time, and since *Look at the Harlequins!* pays grateful homage to a woman modeled upon Véra for differentiating space and time in a way that satisfies a writer's troubled mind, there seems good reason to conjecture that Véra Nabokov somehow fired her husband's imagination in similar fashion. Did she suggest perhaps that as the mind passes through death it might discover it can make the about turn that life never allows, and walk backwards through the world of the past? Perhaps. We will never know.[25]

VIII

Nabokov had long been waiting for his mother to visit from Prague and looked forward to reading her his novel. During her stay, in December 1925, she took over her son's room while he moved in with Véra. Meanwhile Véra's cousin Anna Feigin had returned from Leipzig. She wanted to learn to type, and after she had mastered the keys, Nabokov let her prepare the printer's copy for *Mary* from the two fair copy notebooks he had penned in longhand.[26]

Just before Christmas the Nabokovs accompanied Sergey Kaplan and another pupil on a skiing holiday to Krummhübel, in the Riesengebirge mountains, dividing Germany (now Poland) from Czechoslovakia, a spot chosen by Kaplan. Though there was no snow until the last day, they enjoyed themselves anyway. The setting inspired Nabokov to a poem in which he imagines soaring from a ski jump all the way back to Russia: the risk and thrill of crossing that closed frontier, he thought, seemed like that of overcoming gravity.[27] Gravity took its mild revenge. When snow fell at last, Véra and Vladimir posed for the camera on their skis, Vladimir tilting nonchalantly, Véra clutching onto her poles as if ready to race off. A moment after the shot was taken, Véra fell on her side—and her husband remembered the scene in *King, Queen, Knave.*[28]*

IX

Back in Berlin on January 3, 1926, Nabokov headed for the Bluebird Theater, whose fifth program had opened on Christmas Day. He found that the skit "The Chinese Screens," which he had written with Lukash, did not work: the words could not be heard.[29]

He also called to see Hessen, Tatarinov, and Landau at *Rul'* 's new premises. With its commercial prospects now dim, *Rul'* seemed to the Ullstein empire a colony no longer worth keeping. Amicably, for 50,000 marks compensation, *Rul'* was granted independence and left its quarters in the vast Ullsteinhaus for three cramped and noisy rooms at 7–8 Zimmerstrasse. For much of the rest of its precarious existence the newspaper would be subsidized by Avgust Kaminka, its business manager, out of his own pocket.[30]

---

* In the revised English version of the novel, the photographer is Mr. Vivian Badlook.

Nabokov knew everyone at *Rul'*. Kaminka had been V. D. Nabokov's closest friend in *Rul'* and its predecessor *Rech'*, and took a protective interest in his old colleague's widow and family. At least once he paid for Elena Nabokov to have a sojourn in Berlin with her son. After Ivan Lukash left for Riga in 1925, Kaminka's youngest son Mikhail had become Nabokov's closest friend, until he too left Germany for France in May 1931.[31] Though coevals and both Tenishev pupils, Nabokov and Mikhail Kaminka had had different tastes in their teens—Mikhail's inclinations were agrarian rather than bookish—and had seen little of each other despite their fathers' friendship. Mikhail had completed an agriculture degree in Berlin by the time they discovered ample common ground in tennis and sheer high spirits.

Nabokov also knew well Mikhail's sister Elena and her husband Nikolay Yakovlev, an occasional contributor to *Rul'*, a learned lover of Russian literature, and head of the Russian high school in Berlin where Olga and Elena Nabokov had studied. Nabokov sometimes read his work to the Kaminkas and the Yakovlevs, but wanted no compliments afterward and no dissection of what he had read. He enjoyed discussions of literature or of etymology with Yakovlev, and would be delighted to receive from his friend a list of names of extinct Russian noble families that he could bestow on this or that character he would invent: Barbashin, Cherdyntsev, Kachurin, Ryovshin, Sineusov would all feature in later novels, plays, stories, and verse.[32]

Nabokov also began to see more of George Hessen, son of his friend and editor Iosif Hessen, at first through tennis and Sunday conversazioni at Avgust Kaminka's. Three years younger than Nabokov, Hessen would become one of the best friends of his adult life. Short, unhandsome, in wire-rimmed glasses, he was a keen sportsman (tennis, boxing), chess player, womanizer. He had studied engineering briefly at Berlin's Technische Hochschule, but disliked it, turned to history, and abandoned that too. Changing course was in fact his specialty. In the late 1920s he wrote film news and reviews for *Rul'* and improved his English in lessons with Véra Nabokov, then in the 1930s began to teach English and to work as a freelance translator, before in the 1940s training as a diamond polisher in New York and becoming a simultaneous interpreter at the United Nations.[33]

Also at *Rul'*—and in fact V. D. Nabokov's successor as editorial writer—was Grigory Landau, a philosopher before he emigrated and a man whose mind Nabokov greatly respected. Another *Rul'* contributor who had had to switch careers was Savely Sherman (pen name A. A. Saveliev), an engineer before the revolution, a White officer in the Crimea, and now a reviewer. Nabokov liked this brilliant, independent-minded man who never quite achieved what people expected of him, but at least wrote some of the most penetrating early criticism of Sirin's work.[34]

Sirin's best-known early reviewer was Yuli Aykhenvald, a critic of distinction in prerevolutionary Russia, valued especially for his often-reprinted three-volume *Silhouettes of Russian Writers*. During the 1910s he had contributed a weekly literary column to *Rech'*, and from his expulsion from Moscow in 1922 until his death he did the same for *Rul'*. A gentle, brave, kindly man, he was a critic admired for his rare gift for sensing, as if from within, the unique contours of a writer's mind. He was famous for mixing impartiality with charity and courage. Unable to comment positively on Aldanov, the most popular author on the very short list of the publishing firm Slovo, headed like *Rul'* by Hessen, he simply kept silent about him. He would treat beginners or weak writers gently if he could detect some pulse of talent, but attacked puffed-up reputations like Gorky's without compromise—although he could also be unresponsive to newer literary modes: to Bryusov, to Tsvetaeva. In the emigration he was untiring in reviews, in his regular literary column, in a plethora of public lectures in German or Russian that could cover any aspect of Russian or Western literature or philosophy. He and Nabokov became good friends.[35]

Two more portraits complete the gallery. Vladimir Tatarinov, a journalist at *Rul'* who often commented on scientific and technological themes also wrote an occasional story. His wife, Raisa, was a much more commanding personality. One of the first women in Russia to train in the law, she had finished her legal education at the Sorbonne in the 1900s. Now she worked at the French embassy in Berlin; as Raisa Tarr, she would later become well known in French literary circles and a good friend of Eugène Ionesco. Widely informed, outgoing, hospitable, she had a gift for uniting people of differing views and tastes within the Russian intelligentsia.[36]

X

Late in 1925 Raisa Tatarinov and Yuli Aykhenvald had founded an informal literary circle that lasted longer and involved Vladimir Sirin more than any other in which he ever took part. Starting modestly, it soon gathered a momentum it kept until 1933, when Hitler's advent sent yet another wave of Russians from Germany. By that time there had been a hundred eighty meetings, one roughly every other week. Members gathered in apartments or small cafés for brief talks on literary, philosophic, political, and scientific themes or readings of new works by poets and writers, followed by tea and discussion.[37] Raisa

Tatarinov and Yuli Aykhenvald had known Sirin and his work well for years and had long sensed he was not just another young versifier. By the time the circle was formed, there was no question that he was Russian Berlin's outstanding literary talent. He gave a good deal to the circle, reading not only his own verse and fiction but also prepared talks on topics like Pushkin, Gogol, Blok; on the horrors of Soviet liter-ature, which he directly attacked, once, and once ironically praised; on Freud, on Conrad; on generalizations and on "people and things."[38]

The topic of his first talk was the most unexpected. After watching a bout between the Basque Lumberman, Paolino Uzcudun, European heavyweight champion 1926–1929, and the local favorite Hans Brei-tensträter, German champion 1920–1924 and 1925–1926, Nabokov gave a talk in December 1925 on the beauty of sport and on the art of boxing in particular. The thrill of our muscles at play, he declared, surely resembles the constant delight the divine juggler of the planets must feel. Coming down to earth he described boxers he had seen, the pleasant sensation of being knocked out on the chin, the bracing vigor in the sinews and the soul even in the crowd watching a good fight: "And this playful feeling may be more important, more pure, than many so-called 'higher pursuits.' "[39]

On January 23, 1926, Sirin read Mary from end to end at a gathering of the circle. The reading lasted three hours, with one break, and it was a triumph. "A new Turgenev has appeared," Aykhenvald ex-claimed, and insisted that Sirin send it to Bunin for publication in Sovremennye Zapiski.* Aykhenvald confessed to cutting out every Sirin piece he saw and by now had amassed "a whole stack" of clippings. Such enthusiasm was enough to make Nabokov feel awkward, but the reading also gave him a less ambivalent extraliterary thrill. In the audience was a Professor Makarov, who had visited the Rozhde-stveno area only five months earlier and at once recognized it in Ganin's memories, even though the fictional village had been re-named Voskresensk. He was able to tell Nabokov that Vyra was now a school, Rozhdestveno manor an orphanage, and that not only was the family vault at Rozhdestveno church maintained in perfect order, but the lamp was still burning.[40]

Nabokov set about finding a publisher for his novel. Meanwhile he translated some songs for Zharov's Don Cossack Choir and dashed off, on February 11 and 12, the skimpy story "Britva" ("The Razor"):

* In fact Mary was published in book form before the next Sovremennye Zapiski ap-peared, and Sirin sent the olive-green volume to Bunin, inscribing it: "I am delighted and terrified to send you my first book. Please do not judge me too harshly" (dedication copy, Beinecke Library, Yale).

an émigré barber recognizes the customer he is shaving as someone who interrogated him in the civil war. As his razor glides along the man's belathered throat he terrifies him with the thought that he is about to exact revenge. The panic is retribution enough, and he lets the customer leave in a stupor of fear and relief.[41]

On February 14 the Union of Russian Writers and Journalists held its annual Press Ball, the high point of the émigré social season and the major source of income for the Writers' Union, which distributed the revenue during the year in the form of grants and subsidies for needy members. This year a special illustrated *Press Ball Gazette* was published, with a copy of Nabokov's poem "Royal' " ("The Grand Piano"), now among the very rarest of collectible Nabokoviana. Ambassadors and members of the German community—publishers, artists, and writers—attended. Before the "Miss Russian Colony 1926" was chosen at the climax of the evening, a contest of wit was held: the best answer to the question "What is contemporary woman?", as judged by a panel of five, including Tatarinov and Sirin.[42]

XI

On February 15 Sirin signed an agreement for *Mary* with Hessen's Slovo publishing house, and by March 21 his first novel was published. As reviews turned up, Nabokov confessed to his mother he was surprised *Mary* pleased people so.[43]

The first reviews appeared on March 31 and April 1, 1926.[44] In *The Gift* the press greets Fyodor's first book with total silence, but on April 1, 1926, the first day of the novel, an unbalanced friend plays him an April Fool's trick, duping him into thinking he has been rapturously reviewed. What Nabokov and Fyodor share, like this April Fool's Day review, often heightens their difference.

Fyodor is a loner who stands apart even from Berlin's émigré life. Nabokov too portrays himself as a loner, but the record of his life in April 1926 shows how little he had in common with his character. On April 1 he writes to his mother that he will spend the evening at the Kaminkas', the next night at the Writers' Union, the next but one at the movies with the Tatarinovs. He has just seen a good production of a play by Ostrovsky, staged by the new Group Theater, founded and directed by Yuri Ofrosimov, a poet, *Rul'* 's theater critic and the chronicler of the émigré theater. Seeing Sirin at the show, Ofrosimov asked him to write a play for his company. A week later, after talking it over with him in detail, Sirin agreed. At the Ostrovsky performance he also met his old drawing master, the painter Mstislav Dobuzhinsky,

in Berlin for an exhibition of his work later in the month. After attending the exhibition, Nabokov wrote a poem in honor of Dobuzhinsky's
drawings and paintings of St. Petersburg scenes. During April he was
one of forty to play against the chess master Nimzowitsch, founder of
the hypermodern school, in a multiple match at the Equitable Café.
Nabokov lost, but lasted from 8:00 to 12:30. (In another round of simultaneous chess—or was it the same game?—he was on the verge of
beating Nimzowitsch when a spectator leaned over his shoulder,
made a foolish move on the board, and Nimzowitsch pounced.) A
week later he played Alékhine, soon to become world champion. On
April 22 Nikolay Kardakov, an entomologist friend, took Nabokov to
the Entomological Institute at Dahlem, then on the outskirts of Berlin.
Nabokov was charmed by the halting but eloquent Russian of a scientist named Moltrecht, "who spoke so wonderfully, so touchingly, so
romantically about butterflies": "I simply loved that old, fat, red-
cheeked scientist," he reported, "watched him with a dead cigar in
his teeth as he casually and dextrously picked through butterflies, car-
tons, glass boxes, and thought that only two months ago he was
catching huge green butterflies on Java. . . . I will go back in a few
days for a little more bliss." Nabokov would swim with Alexander
Sak, give lessons in the afternoon, and then play tennis with Sergey
Kaplan, who belonged to one of the best tennis clubs in Berlin. Because of the standard of his play Nabokov was allowed to become a
member of the club on whose courts he played almost for free. As if all
this variety were not enough, there were the pleasures of writing and
married life, neatly summed up in the one-page manuscript of a story
he began to write on April 26, "Ivan Vernykh": as Véra left the room
and returned, he broke off the story and turned the thing into a playful letter to her.[45]

In May or early June 1926 Nabokov wrote the story "Skazka" ("A
Nursery Tale").[46] The devil, in the guise of a middle-aged madam,
offers meek Erwin the chance to make his fantasy life real. He has one
day in which to select a harem, on only one condition, that the number of girls must be odd. Late on Sunday his eyes have picked out a
dozen temptations, and he has to chase along increasingly deserted
streets after the final prize, who even from behind looks the most
tempting of the lot. At last, at midnight, he catches her eye: she
proves to be the first woman he had chosen that day, and he has lost
the whole game.* Deliberately Hoffmannesque, and with a dash of

---

* "The thing that gives the story its chief charm," Nabokov wrote to Andrew Field
(September 26, 1966), "is that he would have had his harem if he had not added the
nymphet (No. 12) to his list, since the odd number, eleven, would not have been
changed to an even number by the addition of the last, already selected girl (No. 11."

Tolstoy's "How Much Land Does a Man Need?", "A Nursery Tale" derives much of its fun from the comic interpenetration of the human and the inhuman: the devil's boredness with her current avatar, her irritation that people remember only that horns-and-tail costume which in fact she had used only once. The story combines pure fantasy and psychological fact, the fairy-tale form and the everyday truth of male sexual desire. Especially Nabokovian are the subtle signs that tell Erwin that each choice he makes has been duly registered. He sets eyes for instance on a girl with a rose in her jacket lapel and sees in the same glance a billboard advertisement ("a blond-mustached Turk and, in large letters, the word 'Yes!', under which it said in smaller characters: 'I smoke only the Rose of the Orient' "): as if chance were planned in advance, as if each detail of the world formed part of a pattern to which we usually have no key.

XII

While Véra Nabokov spent June and July visiting her mother at St. Blasien and regaining some color herself after a spell of poor health, Vladimir moved into a Russian pension in Nürnberger Strasse. At the Tatarinovs' on June 5 he had to listen to a talk on "the witchdoctor Freud": his first reference to the second of his *bêtes noires*. The first, of course, was Marx and his legacy. In preparation for an attack on Soviet literature ("A few words on the wretchedness of Soviet literature and an attempt to determine its cause") that he would deliver at the next meeting of the Tatarinov circle, he spent the next day reading so intensely in Soviet fiction (Leonov, Seyfulina) that when someone shouted in the yard he wondered where this German voice could have come from. He read—and demolished in his talk—Gladkov, Pilnyak, Vsevolod Ivanov, and Zoshchenko.[47] Later, he came to rate Zoshchenko more highly.

About this time Nabokov was involved in an anti-Bolshevik society, VIR. What the acronym signified has since been forgotten. Organized by Yakovlev and his wife, VIR aimed to combat Bolshevism on an ideological level, on the assumption that other kinds of opposition were best left to those with a more activist bent.[48] To understand the Nabokovs' readiness to join this secret society, one needs to realize how active Soviet agents were even in the emigration's literary circles. One of Nabokov's own pupils had been a GPU agent who infiltrated the Union of Russian Writers in Berlin. Other instances of infiltration abounded in the late 1920s, and espionage stories among the émigrés in the 1930s would be worthy of Hollywood. Nabokov's voluble friend

Ivan Lukash later turned out to have been regularly though unwittingly pumped by the famous cabaret singer Nadezhda Plevitskaya and her husband General Skoblin, unmasked in 1938 as Soviet agents. Marina Tsvetaeva, many in the emigration thought, could not have been ignorant of the fact that her husband, Sergey Efron, himself briefly a writer and publisher of sorts, had murdered for the GPU.[49]*

VIR held a few meetings, but the Nabokovs lost interest because nothing concrete took shape.[50] Possibly it was about this time that Nabokov wrote a story he never published. A young man at first indistinguishable from a peasant makes his way through a Russian village to the old manor-house, and having seen it—for the first time since he lived in it as a child, we are to guess—heads back in quiet triumph for the Polish border he has illegally crossed. An exercise in disguise, the story begins with a peasant flavor alien to all of Nabokov's other works, and was signed with the pseudonym Vasily Shalfeev.[51] The play Nabokov would soon write for Ofrosimov, a very different kind of exercise in disguise, would also harmonize with the aims of the Yakovlevs' shadowy secret society.

On a more public front, Nabokov played the role of Pozdnyshev in a mock trial of the hero of Tolstoy's "Kreutzer Sonata" staged by the Writers' Union in the Schubertsaal on July 13. Tatarinov was one of the judges, Aykhenvald a prosecuting attorney. According to the report Sirin's "final words of the accused" were masterly but threw the court off guard by an inspired reworking of Tolstoy: "Tolstoy's murderer and *raisonneur* became a living, suffering individual, admitting his guilt before the wife he had killed and the possibility of genuine love that he had destroyed. Sirin's Pozdnyshev came to understand after the murder that his hatred for his wife was nothing but the real love he had killed in himself through the false relationship of men to women." This useful training in the sort of self-justification a Humbert Humbert would advance enlivened the debate at the cost of creating two Pozdnyshevs in the box, Tolstoy's and Sirin's.[52]

Nabokov wrote to his mother early in July that he was composing another story. This may have been "Uzhas" ("Terror"), published the following January in *Sovremennye Zapiski*. On July 15 Mark Vishnyak, one of the journal's editors, wrote to Sirin asking for another manuscript of his story "Poryv" ("The Outburst"), which had been accepted for publication years earlier but lost in the papers of another editor, who had committed suicide in January 1925. (According to Véra Nabokov this was a long short story, written before she knew Nabokov.)[53] Had it been published when received, "The Outburst"

---

* Tsvetaeva in fact was probably innocent of her husband's activities until her return to Moscow in 1939.

would have been by far the earliest fiction of a young émigré writer to appear in *Sovremennye Zapiski*. As it was, by mid-1926 the journal had still published no prose by young writers who had begun their careers in the emigration, and despite its high reputation was coming under attack for ignoring the young. But Nabokov had no other copy of "The Outburst" to send, and offered them "Terror" instead.

In "Terror," a story unusually abstract for Nabokov, a young man confesses to a horrifying sense of sudden estrangement from himself, from the woman he loves, then from the whole world, when he looks at things simply as they are, without the meanings human habit attaches. Only the news of his mistress's death saves him from the dread of meaninglessness by engulfing him in ordinary human grief that leaves room for nothing else. "Terror" ends on a chill note: the narrator declares he does not know what will save him when it all happens again.[54]

The story reads like a case study by a man with an analytical mind rather than a storyteller's eye, but its very sobriety and ostensible absence of invention makes it all the more convincing. The only deviations from apparent reportage are quiet illustrative images to explain that sudden sense of distance we can have from things we take for granted: a word repeated to the point of meaninglessness; meeting a person not seen for years, whose face has altered just enough to make the conversation seem an exchange with a stranger in an unconvincing mask; looking in the mirror after deep immersion in work, when one has forgot the habit of self, and being shocked at the apparition staring back; or the sudden sense of mortality in the dark of one's bed, when "one tells oneself that death is still far away, that there will be plenty of time to reason everything out, and yet one knows that one never will do it."* The story hits many of Nabokov's themes dead center—the position of consciousness, the sudden shock awaiting us if we jerk aside from our normal modes of being, the strangeness of everything—and yet is unlike anything else he ever wrote.

At the end of July, a week or so after Véra's return from St. Blasien and Todtmoos, the Nabokovs set off for Binz, another Baltic beach, on the island of Rügen. Once again they were acting as chaperones, this time to three children, Bromberg by name, aged from ten to sixteen and cousins of Anna Feigin. After the children left, the Nabokovs moved on to nearby Misdroy, where Vladimir especially enjoyed the chance to collect moths, "the noblest sport in the world."[55]

On their return to Berlin they stayed briefly in a place where the landlady kept the telephone in a trunk she always locked. Keys and

---

* Translated into German in 1928, "Terror" may as Nabokov thinks have influenced Sartre's *La Nausée* without sharing any "of that novel's fatal defects" (*Tyrants Destroyed*, 112).

locks seemed a peculiarly Berlin grotesquerie (keys to one's room, keys to get out the front door at night: no wonder they play such a part in *The Gift*), but a locked telephone was too much, and the Nabokovs left. They moved into a large room in the apartment of a man with two retarded sons. As they were sitting down one night to the dinner the maid brought to their room, a stranger came in and asked "What are *you* doing here? I pay for this room." "No, we do," the Nabokovs answered. It turned out that the landlord had let it a second time to the Nabokovs, who by now were glad to leave anyway.[56]

When they rented two rooms at 12 Passauer Strasse, they found much more congenial landlords in the von Dallwitzes, he a Baltic German who spoke Russian, she pure German. The Nabokovs remained there two years. From their rooms they could see friends frequenting a Russian restaurant across the street, and a few doors up was a Russian bookstore where Nabokov liked to browse. He later recalled that he never once paid for a book in Berlin, but would read whole tomes little by little in the bookshops.[57]

XIII
The Man from the USSR (Chelovek iz SSSR)

Nabokov spent the autumn writing the play he had promised Ofrosimov for the coming theatrical season.[58] Unlike his early poetic dramas and even *The Tragedy of Mr. Morn*, *The Man from the USSR* was written to be acted. Nabokov was no dramatist by nature, preferring as he did a language that could escape the limiting moment of impromptu speech, but he treated Ofrosimov's invitation to write for the Group Theater not as an enforced compromise with his true manner but as a challenge. He chose dialogue barer and more realistic than Pinter's, quite shorn of imagery and rhetorical effects, and found substitutes for everything that these constraints ruled out in new resources of theatrical construction he had to discover for himself.

Just as *Mary* was advertised to its prospective readers as "a novel of émigré life," so Sirin's first play to be performed was billed as "Scenes from émigré life." Here too Nabokov wanted to sum up the emigration, but tried a different way of reckoning. Where *Mary* keeps to one scene, Ganin's pension, with Russia projected on the cyclorama of memory, each act of *The Man from the USSR* offers a fresh snapshot of émigré life. Act 1: a pseudo-Russian tavern bereft of customers. Act 2: the boardinghouse room of a Russian film actress with enough money to gratify a few bourgeois pretensions. Act 3: the foyer of a hall hired for yet another poorly attended émigré lecture. Act 4: the set, swarming with Russian extras, of a German film about the Russian Revolution. Act 5: a squalid boardinghouse room that the now penniless tavern owner and his wife are forced to leave. This final scene brings to mind the bleakly emptying worlds of the end of *The Three Sisters* and *The Cherry Orchard* and suggests how easily Nabokov could have created from the emigration's enforced stasis a mood of Chekhovian inactivity or a choric yearning for "Moscow." Instead, there is frenetic pace and bustle, and barely time to think of old Russia.

Looked at in retrospect, the plot seems simple, though as it unfolds everything remains riddling until the final few moments. For ten days Alexey Kuznetsov returns to Berlin from the USSR, where he poses as a businessman engaged in trade with the Soviets but in fact masterminds a quixotic anti-Soviet underground. Since taking over this operation he has separated from his wife, to spare her anxiety and make the Soviets suppose him invulnerable to any threat against her safety. Suspecting his motives, and being unshakably in love with him, Olga has played along, feigning indifference to him even to his face, while actually more in love than ever. On his brief return Kuznetsov involves himself in an affair with film actress Marianna Tal, to ensure that he will not weaken his determination to seem unattached to Olga. Simultaneously he tries to ensure that Olga will be protected, supported, and loved, should he be killed, by pairing her off with his solidly decent but not overbright friend Baron Nikolay Taubendorf.

After Olga and Kuznetsov say their farewells before he leaves for the USSR, they meet once more by chance. Having loyally and bravely sustained until the appointed time her appointed role of indifferent ex-wife, and now catching a glimpse of Kuznetsov's concern for her, Olga rebels and throws aside her mask of detachment. As Kuznetsov departs for his train, he acknowledges implicitly that they both now know it is only the heroism of their love and his own dedication to his cause that have set up the camouflage of their estrangement.

One of the key moments in the play occurs when Taubendorf declares his love for Olga. She answers:

> The thing is I have never fallen out of love with my husband.
>
> *Silence*
>
> TAUBENDORF. Yes. Yes, that completely changes everything.
> OLGA. No one knows that. He doesn't know himself.
> TAUBENDORF. Yes, of course.
> OLGA. For me he isn't a leader at all, a hero, as he is for you, but simply— I simply love him, his manner of speaking, walking, raising his eyebrows at something he finds funny. Sometimes I would like to arrange for him to be caught and imprisoned forever, so I could be there in prison with him.
> TAUBENDORF. He'd escape.

OLGA. Now you want to hurt me. Yes, he'd escape. And that's just the trouble.[59]

Language that plain has its own eloquence, but Nabokov's mind works on too many levels for such spareness to be enough. He discovers compensating advantages in the theater: the rhythms of exit and entrance, the sets, the implied space beyond the stage, the implied time between the scenes, the implied people behind the masks.

Urgent and impatient, and with so much to do in so few days in Berlin, Kuznetsov sets the pace for the play. He dashes on stage in search of other characters not yet arrived and speeds away to return for them later in the scene, he rushes off to meetings with people we never see on stage, or stays a moment to arrange with another character appointments that by the time we next see them are already in the past. Implicit in all this speed, of course, is Kuznetsov's hurried exit from Russia, the mass exodus of the emigration itself, and Kuznetsov's final departure from Berlin for Russia and, in all likelihood, his death.

Each new scene creates a strange sense of the space beyond the stage.[60] Act 1 takes place in Oshivensky's basement tavern. High up at the rear of the stage are windows set at pavement level. Two-dimensional legs walk past, but no customer enters. For émigré Russians, Berlin's native inhabitants seem less than real, but it is that world out there that defines the material terms on which émigrés must live. In act 2, Kuznetsov finds Olga embroidering in Marianna's room while her own is being tidied: over the whole scene floats the implication that the natural place for them would be together, in Olga's room next door. Beyond the Oshivenskys' bare room in act 5* looms the prospect of homelessness, unless death offers a refuge, or—and it could be the same thing—the cheap new room at "5 Paradise Street, care of Engel [angel]"; while for Kuznetsov the train waiting to take him back to Russia may well be luring him to his death.

Just as Nabokov updates and localizes the exposition in *Mary* by staging it in a stalled and blacked-out elevator, so here he revitalizes the tradition of the play-within-the-play through his film-within-the-play. This is the first of many occasions when he will incorporate a work within the work as a curved mirror to reflect, invert, concentrate the image of the whole. The film in which Marianna plays the part of the Other Woman and Taubendorf and other Russians serve as extras is a sham in its crude conception of both art and the Russian revolution. Marianna's perception of herself as the one with true grace and the real leading lady as a clumsy seal matches her coarse

---

* In their room a newspaper sheet hangs halfway off the top of the wardrobe, a sign that a suitcase stored there has been removed: Nabokovian detail at its most suggestive.

and mistaken perception of herself in real life as the romantic lead to Kuznetsov.

If the world of the film is one of fraudulent glamour, the émigré world seems seedy and suspect. The doomed Oshivenskys represent the plight of average émigrés at their worst. Both bitterly revile the Bolsheviks and assume Kuznetsov must be a Bolshevik himself. While Mme Oshivensky reveals her anti-Semitism and ignorance of Russian culture, her husband is all contradiction. He feigns to be bitter over principles rather than lost estates, but while life appears more difficult in the emigration than he can imagine it in Russia, he seems half ready to grovel to the Bolsheviks in order to return. But behind this sordid appearance and this poverty, not just of pocket but of soul and mind, there lurks something more, something connected with all the hints of an "elsewhere."

In the last act Marianna visits the penniless Oshivenskys. She has spent too much on clothes to help them, and in any case can think of nothing but her own disappointment: she has just seen the edited version of her movie and discovered herself to be haunchy and horrible while the real female lead moves like a dream. Then Olga enters, the "real-life" female lead whose moral grace cannot help showing up Marianna's grossness. She has just had to say goodbye to Kuznetsov and may never see him again but forgets her own grief to bring the Oshivenskys the little money she has. She comes in on Kuznetsov, who has stopped despite his haste to pick up a parcel for the Oshivenskys' grandson in Russia. Taken aback, drained by the role of estranged ex-wife she has played, Olga mutinies. When Kuznetsov tries to justify himself by explaining the ruthlessness his operation requires and the impossibility of sentiments and attachments, she tells him "Let's talk like human beings." She smiles. "If you didn't love me, you wouldn't care whether I was afraid for you or waiting for you. And, you see, I'll be much less afraid if you leave knowing that I love you." He discloses nothing more than a smile to match hers, but that alone suffices to make his mask transparent.

Nabokov strips disguise and role playing of their theatrical conventionality and at the same time pushes them to new lengths: only in the last lines of the play can we be sure of the hero's personality, his principles, his feelings for his wife. Only because the two have met in a special space beyond what should have been their last farewell— and only because of little acts of kindness amid their own troubles— do we see their courage and their tenderness, the love that glows warmly behind their cold masks, even though they cannot afford soft words or shared hours. And only now do we discover that Kuznetsov will sacrifice everything to keep alive the dream of a free return to Russia.

The play leaves us with a sense that despite all that may seem bleak or dubious in the emigration, in the age, in human life itself, there are things like kindness and courage and love that make apparently sordid circumstances heroic, and connect somehow with an elsewhere beyond the margins of our stage, beyond our last farewells.

XIV

In the fall season of 1926, Sirin took part in several more émigré public readings. For occasions like these, he needed something better than his frayed gray suit or his shiny blue one, but now that he no longer had a regular income from the Saks and Kaplans, the new suit he had to buy meant no money for his mother until he found more pupils.[61]

He worked as a tennis coach, at three dollars an hour. On a sunny Saturday, at least in theory, he could give ten lessons: "I never had it, but it was a kind of possible dream." In order to recruit pupils for boxing lessons, he staged an exhibition bout with George Hessen at one of Iosif Hessen's Sunday salons. As they pounded at each other across the Hessens' living-room floor, George suddenly diverged from the script, landing a blow that made Vladimir's nose gush with blood. Nabokov later thought he may have teased his friend too much during the rehearsal.[62]

Other sources of income occasionally turned up. He was asked to compile a Russian grammar for foreigners—"the first exercise began with the words Madam, ya doktor, vot banan (Madam, I am the doctor. here is a banana)"—but Véra felt he should not lose his time over it, and he passed it on to her. Véra also worked on a German-French dictionary. Once they were asked to translate some letters, until they discovered them to be part of a nasty divorce case and sent them back.[63] Sirin found a more regular source of income in writing reviews for Rul', especially of verse. Beginning in August 1926, he reviewed more than thirty volumes of poetry over the next three years. His reflections on the sorry state of the art appear to have inspired his longest Russian poem.

XV
"A University Poem" ("Universitetskaya Poema")

At the end of 1926 Nabokov wrote "Universitetskaya poema" ("A University Poem"), 882 lines, 63 fourteen-line stanzas.[64] The poem seems a study in detachment: the detachment of émigré life, student life, spinsterly life.

Although only twenty-seven, Violet has already resigned herself to her fate: that men will gently dally with her while at Cambridge, then pass on. Is it something in her that fails to engage with life? Or is it Cambridge itself, where the sound of motorcycles may compete with ancient chimes but the town still remains remote from the world? Or does the fault lie with the life cycle of the undergraduate, cocooned here for three years before breaking out into the adult world?

The narrator is a Russian in England, and for all the enchantment of his surroundings, he neither can nor wishes to break down his own protective reserve or England's reserved response. Spring comes, rather like Violet, "a thoroughly well-brought-up maiden, a thoroughly un-Russian spring." As he floats along the Cam with Violet he muses: "And perhaps not Violet—another, and in another summer, another night, floats along with me. . . . You [the Russian "thou," not the formal "you" always used for Violet] are here, there was no parting, you are here, and have stretched out your hand." Violet's English voice saves him when he nearly reaches out to touch those remembered Russian fingers: "Here's the landing, my dear chap. Careful."

Here Sirin seems to have chosen to treat émigré life a third way: after a novel and a play, a poem; after two representative versions of emigration, a third, atypical, personal, and yet with the aloofness of art rather than the immediacy of life. "A University Poem" also seems a counterargument to the gauche obscurities he had encountered among the young émigré versifiers he had begun to review. He demonstrates here the kind of poetic clarity in which plain literality in an artful stanza can turn a crisp description of a tennis match into better poetry than the grandiloquently rhythmic throes of turbid thought.

"A University Poem" is also a tribute to Pushkin. The poem matches a *Eugene Onegin* canto in length and structure, and its stanzas exactly invert the form Pushkin invented for his masterpiece: line 14 in Pushkin's pattern becomes line 1 in Sirin's; feminine rhyme becomes masculine and vice versa.[65] Sirin shows the young poets he reviewed what could be done with rhyme: the overall pattern, the individual find.

More significantly, Nabokov emulates the special verve of *Eugene Onegin*'s texture, which no one has analyzed as well as he himself was to do thirty years later,[66] the magically light transition from subject to subject, from character to landscape to digression to story to recollection: Cambridge's courts and towers; watching a football game and touching Violet's hand; the old bed-maker and her romance, as a young woman, with a student who is now a professor and has forgotten her entirely; the remembered enchantments of the microscope; the conventions of the cinema, and much, much more.

For all its fragile charm and its brilliant commentary on Pushkin, "A University Poem" seems finally too pallid, too reserved, with too little of Pushkin's music or passion. Though he can be brittle or cold, Pushkin always appears to have gulped life in great draughts. "A University Poem" 's sixty-three-piece set of fine china permits us only to take life in small, sweet, pursed-lip sips. But Ivan Bunin, the grand old man of émigré letters, thought otherwise. When the poem appeared, he wrote Sirin a letter of the warmest praise.[67]

Ideas Away: Berlin, 1927–1929

I

IN THE LAST DECADE and a half of his European emigration, Nabokov's life—or at least the record of his life—takes on a special
texture. Toward the end of his career he would write that the story of
his past resembles not so much a biography as a bibliography.[1] That
would be much truer for his late émigré years than for any earlier or
later phase of his life. In these years he would be writing full time in
a way he never could in America, where other activities—university
teaching, museum research on lepidoptera, summer butterfly expeditions—diversified his life and removed him from the solitude of his
writing desk to the cynosure of the lectern. Even in his last two decades in Europe, when he could once again devote himself full time to
his literary work, he was so busy tidying up his canon—translating
and revising and writing introductions to his own works, supervising
the translations of others, proofreading all the old works suddenly
released in the wake of *Lolita*—that he could not match the prolific
output of his young years, when his works were in any case less complex and his stamina allowed him to write all night.

If Nabokov's novels, stories, and plays come thick and fast in the
years between his marriage and his departure for America, the biographical record becomes singularly patchy—especially for his last ten
years in Berlin—as the bibliographical record fills out. The Berlin émigré community had dwindled drastically, and its once-active press
would soon fall almost silent. For Nabokov's American and Swiss
years there would be swarms of fellow teachers and fellow scientists,
students, publishers, journalists, and critics who knew him at Wellesley, Harvard, or Cornell or visited him in his Montreux retreat, but in
the late 1920s and early 1930s in Berlin there were almost no other
writers as young as Nabokov who would survive the war and could
play the part of memoirists after his death. The frail émigré community of the late 1920s shrank still further when the depression struck
Germany, when Hitler came to power, and when war began to
threaten, until by the late 1930s the subculture in which Nabokov had

lived was completely dispersed. A few years later, the places where the Berlin emigration had made its mark had been bombed into oblivion, and the emigration's best archives, in Prague, had been confiscated during the Soviet advance. When he and his family fled Paris as German tanks rolled closer in May 1940, Nabokov had to leave many of his papers behind in the basement of a Russian-Jewish friend whose apartment would be ransacked and who would lose his own life in a concentration camp. Nabokov's only regular correspondent during most of the 1920s and 1930s had been his mother. Whole batches of his frequent letters to her—by far the best source for his life in those years—would be burned in Prague by his sister Olga after she became alarmed at the risks of harboring the manuscripts of such a notorious émigré.

Even within the Berlin émigré community, Nabokov tended to keep to his desk amid his creative solitude. He had a playful and public side, but his work and his private life came first. Véra Nabokov, the best witness of these years, has an even stronger sense of privacy than he. It would be no accident that the privacy of the soul—or of two souls linked in marriage—would become such a theme in his work

II

For some short stretches of Nabokov's émigré life, therefore, we have to lurch from recorded public events to the record of his published works, while the inner continuity of his life temporarily eludes us. When he does make the news, it can be surprising.

Late in 1926, at the time he was writing "A University Poem," a scandal had broken in Berlin around a Rumanian violinist named Kosta Spiresco, whose wife was found hanged, covered with the marks of a severe beating. Though Spiresco's regular assaults were the cause of her suicide, he escaped punishment. German newspapers commented that no decent restaurant would hire him after this, but a Russian restaurant defied the prediction and a number of blowsy woman began to buzz around the restaurant's new violinist in perverted admiration. Emboldened by the attention and the bouquets he received, Spiresco became more offensive than ever. Nabokov, an individualist in his notion of justice as in everything else, would always dismiss the concept of collective guilt but insist fiercely on personal accountability, and was outraged at Spiresco's escaping retribution. On the night of January 18, 1927, he and his friend Mikhail Kaminka visited the restaurant with their wives, and drew straws to be first to hit the "hirsute, ape-like" Spiresco (Nabokov's description). Nabokov won, slapped him on the cheek and then, according to the newspaper report, "graphically demonstrated upon him the techniques of English boxing." Kaminka pitched in against the rest of the orchestra, who took Spiresco's side. At the police station where the three principals were taken, Spiresco refused to press charges, hinting instead that he would call them out to a duel. He declined however to take the addresses they proffered, and Nabokov and Kaminka waited at home in vain the next two or three days for Spiresco's promised seconds.[2]

The next month shows Nabokov in a more typical light, composing the story "Passazhir" ("The Passenger").[3] A writer conversing with a critic praises the superiority of life's loose ends over art's neat knots, and relates an incident from his experience to prove his point. There, the writer says afterward to the critic: didn't you expect the sleeping stranger to be the murderer? No, replies the critic, I know your methods too well, and they seem too restrictive, since art has the power to render the shapes as well as the shapelessness of life. The perceptive critic was meant to be recognized as a portrait of Nabokov's friend Yuli Aykhenvald: his myopia, his modesty, his verbal and gestural mannerisms, and especially his uncanny sensitivity as a listener.

At the height of his fame in the 1960s and 1970s Nabokov would often underestimate his early work. "The Passenger" offers a striking instance. In the first lines, the writer lights his cigarette and absentmindedly throws the match into the critic's empty wineglass. In the last lines of the story, he refills the glass with wine. Introducing the translation Nabokov notes: "By the end of the story everybody seems to have forgotten about the burnt match in the wineglass—something I would not have allowed to happen today."[4] The old Nabokov simply fails to trust the young Sirin, who already in "Christmas," *Mary*, and "A Nursery Tale" had learned to multiply meaning through subtle internal correlations. By means of the match he hints here that the writer spoils the treat he offers (the wine, the anecdote) by what he discards (the match, the possible resolutions to the anecdote that the critic suggests). "The Passenger" begins with a trifle that the writer throws away, but life—or if you like, a better art—creates its own special shape from the interplay of trifles, makes its own pattern and point from what seems like chance.

Within the remnants of émigré Berlin, Sirin was much in demand. Rehearsals for his play *The Man from the USSR* had begun at the end of 1926 for a projected February opening. Complications arose, but by mid-March he was helping to choose costumes and after an afternoon of giving language lessons would come to watch rehearsals. This first play about émigré life was premiered by the Group Theater, under Ofrosimov's direction, at the Grotrian-Steinweg Saal on April 1, 1927. Author, director, and cast were called out again and again by a full house. Despite this success, the conditions of émigré Berlin allowed only one more performance.[5] Had this been Russian Paris, Sirin's play might have created a sensation, as his next play, *Sobytie* (*The Event*) would do there twelve years hence.

From the theater Nabokov would make his way quickly back to his desk, where in April or May 1927 he penned the story "Zvonok" ("The Doorbell").[6] After seven years roaming the world, a footloose son calls on his mother unannounced, only to imperil her rendezvous with a man to whom she has tried to appear decades younger than she is. Here Nabokov treats a poignant human drama with unsparing directness, as if to prove that the detachment of "The Fight" or "A University Poem" was his narrator's, not his own, and only one of the possible relations of art to life.

Nabokov was still writing verse, though much less often. On May 14 he composed the poem "Bilet" ("The Ticket"): the future ticket for the train that would return him to a Russia made free. Three weeks after its appearance in *Rul'*, it became his only poem to be published in the Soviet Union in his lifetime, when it turned up in *Pravda*—with a doggerel rejoinder from the notorious lackey Demyan Bedny ("Demian the Poor"), now a "proletarian poet" and unofficial poet laureate to the Communist party, but ten years earlier the poetaster Demyan Pridvorov ("Demian of the Court"), who at that time had claimed to be the illegitimate son of royal rhymester Grand Duke Konstantin Konstantinovich.[7]

If Sirin was important enough to repudiate in Moscow, he was worth commandeering in Berlin. To raise more funds the Writers' Union staged a ball on May 27 in addition to its annual winter affair. The drawcard was a two-act comic revue written for the occasion, "Quatsch" (German, "Nonsense"). In act 1, a certain organization decides to put on a charity performance, and the unfortunate organizer has to run simultaneously a stormy ladies' committee meeting and a rehearsal of Nikolay Evreinov's recent hit play *The Main Thing* (first performed in 1921 and soon afterward staged in Rome, New York, and Paris). Evreinov comes in, alarmed by all he has heard and seen, and ironically recommends a variety show in place of the play, a suggestion at once taken up to provide act 2 of the revue. Sirin, Berlin's new Russian playwright, played the role of Evreinov, in flowing locks and clothes of a flamboyant cut. All the energy of the Writers' Union—forty people took part in the revue—did not make the ball a success.[8]

III

In July and August the Nabokovs accompanied two or three boys on their summer vacation, this time to Binz, on the sandy eastern shores of the island of Rügen. There were no rooms in the hotel, but "a flushed fellow in the bar, with a full glass in his hand" offered to share a bed with Véra. Nabokov recalls landing "a hook on the man's jaw, flooding himself and the drunk with the latter's sticky liquor," while one of his charges, a quiet boy belonging to a religious Jewish family, looked on with demure interest. They found rooms instead in a fisherman's home.[9] Nabokov wrote exuberantly to Yuli Aykhenvald, who had sent him a name-day telegram:

> Today I ran about five versts [two and a half miles] along the beach, took off my shorts, turned into a little wood and wandered there completely alone and completely naked, lay on the grass, looked over the butterflies—and felt myself a real Tarzan. A marvelous feeling! It's great here. Vera's sunburn is pinky-brown, mine has a deep orange tint. We lie on the sand for hours, or splash around in the water, or play with a ball. The boys in our charge have turned out to be charming—they laugh at my German.[10]

In 1972, with sixteen novels to his credit, Nabokov could record the by now familiar pattern of his inspiration: two or three days of tingly foreglow, then the sudden flash of a new novel, more or less complete, after which there would follow a long process of mental sorting that could last six months or more, until every detail seemed right. Only then would he begin writing.[11] *King, Queen, Knave* followed that pattern perfectly. On his trip to Binz Nabokov had his first flash—perhaps a result of that sense of being quite unseen by others and quite free of normal constraints only a couple of miles from the thousands of striped booths on the main beach. For his idea was this: husband, wife, and her young lover on the water at a Baltic resort, and a planned murder by drowning that will take place safely out of sight of the crowd—except that the plotter will die and the intended victim escape entirely unawares. He would need another six months before everything was in place.

He and Véra stayed on after the boys left, but were back in Berlin by August 20 and promptly placed an advertisement in *Rul'*: "V. V. Nabokov-Sirin gives lessons in English and in French."[12] Over the next few weeks he wrote "Podlets" (literally "The Scoundrel," translated as "An Affair of Honor"), his longest and best short story to date.[13] Anton Petrovich, a Berlin émigré, returns unexpectedly from a business trip to find a friend conducting an affair with his wife. He challenges him to a duel, but on the fatal morning rushes away, quaking with fear, from the seconds escorting him to the appointed spot. Not daring to return home, dreading to be seen, he holes up in a hotel with only a future of shame ahead.

With grim zest Nabokov deflates the idea of the duel, once a romantic theme in Russian literature and still a surprisingly common fact of European life. (Italy had its special dueling season; the German Reichstag had just tried to stamp out the practice by law.) Everything conspires to humiliate and degrade Anton Petrovich: the tight new glove he at last pulls off and tries to fling at Berg, but instead sends plopping into the washbasin ("Good shot," comments Berg), the margin of fat hanging from the sandwich he greedily devours in the shameful refuge of his hotel room. Antiromantic details like this seem to have proved too much for Russian periodicals: the story remained unpublished until Nabokov's first story collection in 1929.[14]

Where in "A University Poem" Nabokov had countered romantic excess with neoclassical artistic restraint, in "An Affair of Honor" he lets loose his natural instinct for the vividness of life, with a dramatic clarity and psychological complexity worthy of Tolstoy. He follows a mind at a pitch of feeling where every moment becomes heightened, both fantastically dreamlike and uncannily real, like the superslow glide of time as one's car slides out of control toward a truck or a tree. He achieves intensity not by the old-fashioned rhetoric of plucking relentlessly at a single emotional chord, but by showing how the mind shifts from feeling to feeling, jars against the trivial, or confronts the irrelevance of its concerns to the world outside the self. Shame, embarrassment, the dread of not performing under pressure, raw fear, and animal relief have not been rendered better.

By late September Nabokov was thinking over the start of his new novel, but not yet writing. Meanwhile his third novel was about to germinate. Expecting his mother late in the fall, he asked her to bring his chessmen. Since September expatriate Russia had been agog as the émigré Alékhine challenged Capablanca in the longest world chess championship tussle to date. In mid-October Nabokov wrote the poem "Shakhmatnyy kon' " ("The Chess Knight"), a clear precursor of The Defense: an old chess master in a tavern starts to see the world in chess terms, registers a plank floor as light and dark squares and construes two people in the doorway as a black king and a pawn. Trying to escape, he leaps in knight moves across the squares. The laughter of his friends turns to an appalled hush, and away he is taken to an asylum, "captured" by the "black king." Three weeks later Nabokov wrote an enthusiastic review of Znosko-Borovsky's Capablanca and Alékhine, which also seems to prefigure The Defense: Znosko-Borovsky's distinction between chess play "in space" and "in time," his stress on the artfulness of Capablanca's play and on the genius for chess combination in Alékhine's. Two weeks later, Alékhine was world champion.[15*]

Almost always Nabokov's best novels would be those which he had to set aside for some time between the initial impulse and its ultimate realization. In the case of *The Defense*, *The Gift*, *Lolita*, *Pale Fire*, and *Ada*, he would start and finish another novel in the gap between his first idea and actual composition. During that time, apparently unconnected lines of thematic development would suddenly cross in his mind to form surprising new combinations: the growth of a young writer and the life of Chernyshevsky in *The Gift*; the story of a sexual pervert and the motels of Nabokov's butterfly expeditions in *Lolita*; a palace revolution and the poem-commentary-index structure of *Eugene Onegin* for *Pale Fire*; a philosophical treatise on time and a decadent love story in *Ada*. Before he could envisage *The Defense*, the idea of the chess maniac would have to fuse with a quite different story he had not yet even begun to contemplate.

Although novels would soon earn Nabokov more money, *Mary* had so far brought in very little, and he still supplemented his income by writing reviews for *Rul'*. Most were short notices of young poets whom he would arraign for infelicities he itemized tersely. One signal exception was a review of the collected poems of a more established poet, Vladislav Khodasevich, whose boldness of themes and perfection of form he praised to the full. He also worked hard on a long translation with Véra (eight hours one day, ten the next two) and advertised for pupils in a new subject: prosody. Only one pupil turned up, a short, curly-haired eighteen-year-old, Mikhail Gorlin, later a poet and a promising Slavist until he was killed in a German concentration camp. Nabokov taught him two to four times a week, English as well as prosody.[16]

In his later years Nabokov pictured himself as always a loner. Certainly he did not fritter away his time in cafés and bars, but the winter season would involve him in a round of public roles of all shapes and sizes: readings of his verse or prose at meetings of the Writers' Union, in the Tatarinov-Aykhenvald Circle, and in a new group, Na Cherdake (In the Attic) that included Ofrosimov and Gorlin; early in November, duty on a panel to select six women to vie for the title of Miss Russian Colony 1928 at the annual Press Ball; later in the month, in a more serious vein, an article occasioned by Soviet celebrations of the first decade of Bolshevik power (he proposed that the emigration

---

* In June 1928, Nabokov would write a poker-faced review of *An Anthology of Lunar Poets*, supposedly translated from various lunar dialects by "S. Revokatrat," the pseudonym (letters reversed) of chess master S. Tartakover, whom Alékhine later thought— though Nabokov denied it—the original of Luzhin in *The Defense*.

should celebrate ten years of freedom and of contempt for Soviet ideology), and two days later a reading of his verse at a commemoration
of the tenth anniversary of the White Army.[17]

For all his contributions to the public side of literary life, his real
work continued in private. In January 1928, after months of gestation,
he began writing his second novel. The book required some bizarre
research. Nabokov paid his fee to visit a lung specialist to find out how
he might dispose of his heroine. An incorrigible tease, he did nothing
to allay the doctor's suspicions: " 'I have to kill her,' I said to him. He
looked at me in stony silence."[18]

Late in January he told his mother he was completely engrossed in
writing a novel that he would probably call *King, Queen, Knave*. Three
weeks later he had finished three chapters and was pleased with
something "much more complicated and deeper than *Mary*." In another five days he had almost finished the fourth chapter and reported
that he was leading

> a mole-like existence . . . sweating, sweating over my novel until my
> head spins. . . . It's so boring without Russians in the book, I wanted to
> compensate by introducing an entomologist but killed him in time in the
> muse's womb. Boredom, of course, is hardly the right word—in fact it is
> bliss to be in a medium I create and order myself. . . . I am afraid there
> will be quite a few erotic hot-spots in the novel, but what can one do: if
> one describes how a person walks, smiles, eats, then one has to describe
> in the same detail how he acts in matters Cyprian.[19]

While he was writing his second novel, his first unexpectedly
began to pay. There had been talk of a German translation some
months ago. His first reaction had been to think it artistically unwise,
though he added: "But if they pay well. . . ." On March 21 he signed
an agreement for serial rights to *Mary* with one of Ullstein's major
newspapers, *Vossische Zeitung*, a considerable honor and a financial
godsend: more new clothes at last. Prospects looked even better *Vossische Zeitung* was already interested in a German *King, Queen, Knave*,
even though the book still had to be written in Russian.[20]

At the beginning of April Sirin read "A University Poem" before the
Poets' Club. This new group had been founded in February by Mikhail Gorlin, who became the club's secretary. The Poets' Club lasted
from 1928 to 1933, met twice a month, and even published its own
anthologies. Among its members were Evgenia Zalkind, a writer of
short fiction and (as Evgenia Cannac) a future translator of Nabokov's
work into French, the poetess Raisa Blokh, who married Gorlin and
later perished with him in the same concentration camp; and the
club's two acknowledged masters, Sirin and Vladimir Korvin-Piotrovsky, who had not met one another since early 1923, when the Brother-

hood of the Round Table disbanded. Although he knew Korvin-Piotrovsky had now returned to the émigré camp and although he appreciated his steadily developing poetic talent, Sirin at first felt wary talking to a man whom he had not seen since he had joined Drozdov and Aleksey Tolstoy in working for the Communist *Nakanune*. But Korvin-Piotrovsky praised "A University Poem" warmly, and a potential cold war gave way to friendship.[21]

At one point the Poets' Club invited Nina Piotrovsky and Véra Nabokov to join. In order to be accepted, they would have to submit poems of their own. When both women refused, their husbands came to the rescue, Piotrovsky with a serious poem for his wife, Sirin with some humorous verse for Véra dashed off at a session of the club. The Poets' Club smiled at their star poets and gave way.[22]

Evgenia Zalkind has left the only memoir of Sirin in these years. To the club's poetic novices, she recalls, he behaved with friendly condescension, but he was more interesting to catch when friends gathered in a private home. He might arrive late, and explain:

> "I was in a writing vein, and didn't notice how the time was flying." He would have an abstracted, absent look, as if not yet with the other guests, as if still mulling over an unfinished page. . . .
>
> Sometimes he liked to think up games. "Look for two minutes at this picture, then close your eyes and describe all you've retained." Of course he was the only one who could recreate the whole picture from memory, not forgetting the least detail. His memory, especially his visual memory, was exceptional. He even complained at times that it overburdened his consciousness.[23]

By April 4 Nabokov had written three hundred pages of *King, Queen, Knave*, was into his eleventh chapter, and felt in full literary strength. He was delighted that as he read the manuscript to his young pupil Vladimir Kozhevnikov, whom he and Véra saw much of that year, the boy sweated and had palpitations. By mid-May, when the trickle of Sirin reviews resumed in *Rul'*, he appears to have completed the first draft of the novel. By the end of June he had finished his revisions.[24]

IV
King, Queen, Knave (Korol', Dama, Valet)

An abortive murder by drowning: the idea that first came to Nabokov on his trip to Binz the previous year prompted him to devise a novel as different as possible from *Mary*. In 1925 it had been a marked ad-

vance in his art when he shifted from angels and apostles, from drag-
ons and medieval dreams, to observing the here and now. But by
1927, after *Mary*, *The Man from the USSR*, and "A University Poem,"
he had focused more on émigré life than any other serious émigré
writer, and felt he needed relief: "The émigré characters I had collected in [*Mary*] were so transparent to the eye of the era that one
could easily make out the labels behind them. . . . I felt no inclination
to persevere in a technique assignable to the French 'human document' type, with a hermetic community faithfully described by one of
its members—something not unsimilar . . . to the impassioned and
boring ethnopsychics . . . in modern novels."[25]

When Ganin revives his love in memory, *Mary* both commemorates
Nabokov's love for Lyussya Shulgin and affirms unequivocally his belief in the primacy of consciousness and its link to the unshakable
reality of the past. Now adultery and murder freed Nabokov not only
from a specifically émigré milieu but also from the personal, the lyrical, from any temptation to direct statement of his own philosophical
position.

In many of his early poems and stories he had expressed openly
his confidence in the ultimate benignity of things. From the start, his
metaphysics were nothing if not optimistic: as far back as his ideas
are visible, he seems to have suspected that the limits life imposes
on mortal consciousness may be there only to be superseded in death.
But as he matured as a thinker and an artist he realized it would be
more valuable to test his ideas than merely to reiterate them, and
to generate vivid negative images rather than advance positive propositions.

King, Queen, Knave marks the first time Nabokov constructs a story
that appears to invert the values embodied so directly in *Mary*. Ganin
reflected Nabokov's own powerful orientation toward the past. Now
in *King, Queen, Knave* the characters have barely any memories and fix
their gaze toward the future. But throughout the novel Nabokov
shows the poverty of prophecy as chance rewrites even the most carefully planned of scenarios. En route to Berlin Franz eagerly pictures to
himself the bright lights and the prostitutes of Unter den Linden, but
the famous avenue turns out to be only Berlin's marble ceremonial
center, and he takes days to discover that the city's pulsing heart has
moved west. Even worse, hopelessly shortsighted Franz steps on his
glasses as he washes his face on his first night in Berlin, and the next
day passes for him in a bright, giddy blur that no one's vision of the
city could have foreseen.

Another surprise comes for Franz when Martha, the wife of Kurt
Dreyer—his mother's cousin and now his new boss—singles him out

for her first affair. Although begun as a conventional divertissement, it unexpectedly becomes an irresistible passion for Martha and at first for flattered Franz. When the image of a life with Franz, without Dreyer but with Dreyer's money, takes hold of Martha, she mesmerizes Franz into agreeing to murder his uncle. As they discuss scheme after scheme for the murder, Franz turns out to have the gift of imagining with diagrammatic clarity his and Martha's movements and of coordinating them in advance "with those concepts of time, space, and matter which had to be taken into account. In this lucid and flexible pattern only one thing remained always stationary, but this fallacy went unnoticed by Martha. The blind spot was the victim. The victim showed no signs of life before being deprived of it."* Eventually they decide to fake Dreyer's accidental drowning during their summer vacation. At a Baltic resort, they lure him into a dinghy and are about to tip him out when he announces that within a few days he will clinch a $100,000 deal. To cash in, Martha postpones the murder, but too late: out on the bay in the rain she has already caught the pneumonia that kills her two days later.

Nabokov here makes use of Henri Bergson's distinction between a spatial, outer, mechanical perception of the world, and a temporal, inner, creative one. In the spatial schema, everything is predetermined, operating according to Newtonian laws so fixed that in the view of the cosmologist Laplace if one knew the entire state of the universe in infinite detail at any one instant one would be able to work out the future, no matter how remote. In a temporal view of life, on the other hand, one accepts the reality of the past retained in present memory and sees both past and present as fundamentally different from the future, which is undefined, unpredictable, full of genuine novelty. Martha and Franz in their murder plans have reduced Dreyer to rigid spatial terms, to a "purely schematic . . . image . . . very convenient to manipulate," an inert mass that ought to react to whatever forces they apply. That diagrammatic Dreyer seems part of an apparently inexorable future, until to Martha's surprise Dreyer eludes her fixed image of him by announcing that $100,000 deal, and even the weather fatally reminds her that it too has a life of its own.

Even more than Bergson, Nabokov regarded evolution as inherently creative and opposed the Darwinian concept of a struggle for survival, which to him seemed destructive rather than creative, regressive rather than innovative. In *Mary* Ganin briefly thinks of absconding with Mary to leave Alfyorov in the lurch, but on the day

---

* In the 1968 English translation of the novel, Nabokov incorporated hundreds of revisions large and small. In the Russian, the passage quoted ends simply: "The victim never moved, as if he were already wooden and cold."

thinks better of it. He refuses to vie for advantage, and his renunciation of any struggle, along with the creative achievement of his private restoration of his past, seems the best possible triumph. *King, Queen, Knave* on the other hand is dominated by Martha's relentless scheming, first for the mere acquisition of Franz as lover, and then for the murder of her husband. In contrast to her single-minded avidity the imaginative and whimsical Dreyer defies the stereotype of the successful businessman. Out of fanciful curiosity he supports an inventor of "automannequins"—robots designed to move with lifelike suppleness and bend with all the natural flexibility of muscle and skin. Martha's steely determination appears to augur success, but she fails in every way. She leaves Dreyer intact, destroys Franz's love, accidentally kills herself. But Dreyer, never even conscious of his danger, saves himself by announcing the profits due from the automannequins, an invention he has supported through sheer exuberance of mind. The conclusion points to the anti-Darwinian sentiment Nabokov implied as early as the story "The Dragon" and later made explicit: " 'Struggle for life' indeed! The curse of battle and toil leads men back to the boar"; or "a rather anti-Darwinian aphorism: The one who kills is *always* his victim's inferior."[26] Dreyer's impractical creative instinct wins over Martha's ruthless zeal to destroy.

Where in *Mary* Nabokov celebrated directly the power of consciousness, in *King, Queen, Knave* he shows consciousness always ready to decay into something automatic or less than fully human.

The opening chapter brilliantly displays the centrality of consciousness. Franz, Martha, and Dreyer sit in a train compartment almost without talking. Although confined to the same space, with the same landscape gliding by, they disclose their distinct personalities almost entirely by what they notice and the various ways their minds transform everything they see, until each seems part of a different world.

Dreyer's roving curiosity, even as he sits motionless, makes Martha fume that his thoughts will not stay still, as a businessman's should. He does not fit, and she hates being unable to predict or control his wayward mind. Martha is Nabokov's first in-depth attempt to define *poshlost'* (philistine vulgarity), the enemy of consciousness, the denial of individual vitality: a desire to conform to the values of one's group, to see the world as others see it rather than to animate it with one's own perceptions. Martha's irritation at the opacity of Dreyer's thoughts closely anticipates the vexation Martha and all her kind will feel toward the Cincinnatus C. of *Invitation to a Beheading*.

Martha herself covets the accoutrements she supposes appropriate to Dreyer's wealth. She has never felt any emotional warmth in her marriage, only a desire for social success, and she undertakes an affair with Franz merely because it suits the status she seeks. But her discovery that gauche, provincial Franz is so malleable—"young wax" that she can "manipulate and mold"—fires her feelings and complicates her very being in ways she could never have expected.

A traffic accident in which Dreyer could have been killed plants the possibility of his death in Martha's mind, where it soon grows into the necessity of his murder. She works on Franz until he is ready to follow her every move—even literally, as Nabokov synchronizes her teaching him to dance with her instructing him in murder. Like the automannequins, also programmed to perform a few dance routines, Franz has become no more than a compliant robot. Then as Martha and Franz assess their various schemes for murder, they transform Dreyer too into still another kind of subhuman dummy.

Martha does not notice that Franz is more alive than the stiff notion she entertains of him. At first excited by the clandestine love of an experienced, wealthy, beautiful woman, and ready to share her dreams of the comfortable life they could have together once they eliminate Dreyer, Franz feels a physical revulsion against the whole idea and even against Martha herself as soon as she settles on a final script and prepares to have it staged. With no will left of his own, he persists in obeying her commands, but he can cope only by deadening himself to the point of complete automatism: at Dreyer's store he "bowed and turned like a jolly doll"; he continues to exist "only because existing was the proper thing to do." Even sitting on a high window ledge from which he could easily drop down to a death he would welcome, he has too little volition left for suicide. Paradoxically as Franz dies inwardly and becomes more robotlike than ever he also proves himself more alive, more elusive, than Martha's fixed notion of him as her responsive lover—just as Martha in pursuing her goal of a lifeless conformity awakes an unforeseen intensity of passion in herself, becoming more animated than she has ever been, while at the same time turning herself into something subhuman in her rapacity.

Unlike Martha and Franz, Dreyer in a sense represents the creative power of consciousness. But even a mind as flexible and alert as his can reduce others and himself to less than their full measure. Despite his observant nature, his interest "in any object, animated or not, whose distinctive features he had immediately grasped, or thought he had grasped, gloated over, and filed away, would wane with its every subsequent reappearance. The bright perception became the habitual abstraction." After the surprise of discovering in Berlin that Franz, his provincial nephew, is none other than the boy who shared their train compartment, he classifies him as simply an amusing coincidence in human form. Martha he has for years defined as cold and passionless. Although he sees them together again and again, therefore, he never thinks to suspect a thing.

We all have a measure of creative suppleness, Nabokov intimates throughout the book, but without constant attentiveness to the unique, unpredictable particulars of existence it can too easily decay into a rigidity of vision that both deadens our world and diminishes us.[27]

V

For Nabokov the two most severe limitations on human consciousness were the prison of the present—our inability to have immediate access to the real past we have lived through—and the prison of the self—our inability to escape our own minds or enter those of others Both limitations he liked to imagine transcended in death, and both forms of transcendence he saw tentatively prefigured in life: the first in memory, the second in love, and especially faithful married love, where behind the barrier of privacy two people can afford to open themselves to each other in complete intimacy and trust. In *Mary* he does not spell out these implications, but they are there in positive form in Ganin's triumphant re-creation of his past. Even though Ganin comes to realize that any direct return to Mary has become impossible in this life, his successful resurrection of his love and his past sustain him enough for him to venture confidently toward whatever the future holds.

From the year of his marriage, from the time of *Mary* and "The Return of Chorb," Nabokov would define the prison of the present in his fiction through the theme of the impossible return. Whether or not he was inspired to that theme by Véra, one thing seems certain: his marriage itself provided the other of the major themes that would shape his work. In later years he would often bemoan the very meager artistic results of his frenetic love-life in his late teens and early twenties. One inescapable implication is that by contrast his marriage did contribute to his art. For to demarcate not the prison of the present but the prison of the self, he would now focus upon the isolation of the individual within love or marriage, the one place where that isolation might be expected to be overcome. There is a hint of this negative even within the positives of *Mary*, where blithe Alfyorov has no knowledge that Ganin in the next room has such a passion for his wife or such an intimate familiarity with a past *he* can never share. But in *King, Queen, Knave* we witness *only* the negation of the notion of love as an overcoming of the solitude of the soul.

When Martha dies, Dreyer is racked with grief, utterly unaware that behind her recent smiles, usually so rare, so precious, she had been plotting his death. As she dies, the thought of herself and Franz happy alone together lights up her last and most radiant smile of all.[28] But if Dreyer remains horribly deceived in this last tender moment he thinks he shares with her, Martha too dies quite oblivious to her lover's recent disgust and revulsion. She could never have imagined that when at the very end of the novel Franz hears of her death, relief would erupt from him in an explosion of hysterical laughter.

Late in *King, Queen, Knave*, at the Baltic beach where Martha and Franz have planned their murder, they notice a happy couple—Vladimir and Véra Nabokov*—whose harmony stands in such evident contrast to the secret discords between king, queen, and knave. From the time of this novel Nabokov would return again and again, with extraordinary inventiveness and force, to couples whose isolation from one another will only be accentuated by their remoteness from the ideal of fully reciprocal love, a subject that will produce some of his most characteristic and ineradicable images. Tender Mrs. Luzhin knows something terrible is happening to her husband's mind, but for all her desire to protect him, she can have no idea whatever of the bizarre cogitations that agitate him into a state of inescapable panic. Blind Albinus in *Laughter in the Dark* thinks himself installed in cozy seclusion with Margot, and has no notion that day after day her lover Axel Rex inhabits the same house and eats the same meals and even enters the bed Margot tells Albinus *he* is too sick to approach. Poor Charlotte Haze sets her heart on Humbert Humbert, oblivious to the sordid secret that prompts him to share her house and then pretend to share her life.

In other cases, as in "The Return of Chorb," a couple who really have shared their lives are sundered by death: Sineusov in "Ultima Thule," who spends his time composing a helpless letter to his dead wife; Krug in *Bend Sinister*, who feels his mind and his philosophy crumbling in the face of Olga's death; Hugh Person, who in his sleep kills the woman he loves.

And in the rare cases in which Nabokov depicts a marriage like his own, where two people do transcend solitude in the warmth of their

* In the Russian original, the couple are identified only by their language, utterly incomprehensible to German Franz, and by the fact that they mention his name and somehow seem to know all about his predicament. In the revised English version, the man's butterfly net gives the name away.

love, he shuts us out. Fyodor and Zina will enjoy a faithful married love, but we are allowed to see only the barriers that first prevent them from meeting one another at all and then prevent their love developing as freely as it could. Only at the last are these barriers almost removed, and then the novel promptly closes: Fyodor will permit us to see none of their full life together. In *Pale Fire* the Shades have been happily married for forty years, but we glimpse most of their story only through the envious prying and the comic misconstructions of homosexual Kinbote, who assumes John Shade would rather spend his time with him than with Sybil. In *Look at the Harlequins!* Vadim Vadimych discloses the frankest details about his first three unhappy marriages but then drops the curtain immediately on his love for You. Only within the special privacy of a harmonious marriage, Nabokov stresses, can the tender self reach beyond the self enough to share life with another, and to prefigure—as each of these three cases pointedly does—the possible escape, beyond death, from the solitude of the soul.

Although *King, Queen, Knave* anticipates more of Nabokov's mature art than *Mary* could, it remains less than satisfying in itself.

Here certainly Nabokov learns to activate his characters' imaginations with speed and color: the three figures in the railway carriage, each inhabiting such disparate mental worlds; Franz looking at bright blurry Berlin; Martha in her final delirium. He constructs some superbly revelatory and dramatic encounters, especially in the early scenes between Martha and Dreyer at home. But these brilliant flashes of characterization diminish after the first chapters, when plot begins to demand more than psychology can support. Despite his fixed preconceptions about Martha and Franz, despite all the examples time has piled up of spouses who were the last to discover their betrayal, Dreyer's gift for acute observation makes it difficult to accept that when he finds his wife and nephew together *every* night on his return from work he notices nothing amiss. And despite some excellent ironies and some lively scenes they occasion between Dreyer and the inventor, the automannequins limp rather cumbrously and tiresomely across the novel's stage, for all their relevance to the theme of rigid automatism versus the ideal flexibility of consciousness.

In this novel Nabokov has searched for the distance from his human subjects that he felt he needed after the cozy immediacies of *Mary*. Here he tries for the first time to define what being human means by showing people making themselves less than human (the automaton theme) and by hinting at something more than the human (the creative usurpation of the divine, in the attempt to animate these models).

But the automannequins do not provide the compelling solution he will discover in his next novel. Much more successful are his attempts to find new kinds of formal control over the resources of fiction. Here and there he interferes with the smooth spin of events, as if to turn the world upside down or survey it from somewhere else. The strange receding of the scene as a train takes off; a character waking and not knowing whether he has arrived on the right level of reality; a mad landlord who looks at his rump in the mirror and decrees Franz to be a figment of his imagination; a sudden shift to an anonymous crowd where an anonymous figure watching the summer's first swallows turns out to be Dreyer; a transition that takes place before we know our bearings have been shifted—all these show Nabokov trying the handles of doors he will soon open to new kinds of fictional reality.

VI

Nabokov finished *King, Queen, Knave* in June 1928. In July 1928 on the novel's calendar he and Véra put in their brief appearance at the Dreyers' Baltic resort. In real life they spent some weeks that month on the beach at Misdroy, where they were joined by Mikhail and Elizaveta Kaminka and their café-au-lait poodle.[29]

Véra Nabokov's father had died on June 28, and her mother on August 12. To pay off debts incurred by her father's long illness, she needed steady work on her return to Berlin. Raisa Tatarinov found her a job where she worked herself, in the office of the commercial attaché at the French embassy. Véra had to attend a secretarial school to learn German stenography, a skill that would prove useful in the lean years to come.[30]

By September 23 *King, Queen, Knave* was published. More than one reviewer declared that the fear that no new first-rate talent would emerge in the emigration could now be allayed. Several misread the automaton theme as an attack on the lifelessness of contemporary man, an idea some welcomed and others found bleak. As usual Aykhenvald's review was by far the best, admiring the ironies of plot, the touches of psychology and description, but preferring the parts to the whole. Early in November there was even an evening of public debate on the book in Berlin.[31]

Ullstein signed for the German rights to *King, Queen, Knave* on October 24.[32] They would pay 5,000 marks for serialization in *Vossische Zeitung* and provincial newspapers, and 2,500 marks for book rights. This was a coup, three times as much as they had paid for the German *Mary* and vastly more than the minuscule advances Slovo could afford for the Russian first editions: nothing at all for *Mary*, 300 marks for *King, Queen, Knave*.

On November 14 Sirin published a quietly devastating review of *Zvezda nadzvezdnaya* (*Star above All Stars*) by Alexey Remizov, to some a major figure in twentieth-century Russian prose. At a Poets' Club soirée in the home of Evgenia Zalkind, a fat, talentless old painter named Zaretsky read out a rejoinder he had typed up to Sirin's review. He compared Remizov to Pushkin and Sirin to the notorious Bulgarin, the "reptile" journalist in the pay of the secret police and author of scurvy attacks on Pushkin, Gogol, and Lermontov. Sirin asked if this was deliberate, and declared: "If it weren't for your age I would have broken your mug." Zaretsky tried to call him before a literary court of peers, but Sirin "declined to take part in the farce—while offering to fight if called out" to a duel. Zaretsky never availed himself of the offer.[33]

Nabokov took up another literary fight in the first half of December when he wrote "Rozhdestvenskiy rasskaz" ("A Christmas Story"), the last of his stories that he did not later publish in book form or have translated.[34] A Soviet writer of venerable but stolid reputation feels piqued when a critic suggests not to him but to a young peasant writer a story with a Christmas tree for centerpiece and the clash of the old ways and the new for theme. The old writer sits down to prove himself with just such a story. After two false tries, he hits the right opening note: a European city, well-fed people in furs walking by, a huge Christmas tree with expensive fruits, and in front of the shop window, on the icy pavement, a hungry worker, victim of a lockout.

Although unusually tendentious for Nabokov, "A Christmas Story" fortunately has more to it than its dismissal of Novodvortsev's crude concoction. Nabokov limns with uncanny accuracy the petty egoism and self-centered ambition of a writer without talent and contrasts that with what Novodvortsev expects will be read as the noble altruism of his theme. In a subordinate line of the plot Novodvortsev rejects as irrelevant the memory of a Christmas tree reflected in the eyes of a woman he loved, as she reached for a mandarin on the tree, but he fails to realize that the first words of his story spring from that very memory. The pretended transcendence of self in the social struggle, Nabokov's story suggests, is a lie.

On Saturday, December 15, the Nabokovs staged a party in their high-ceilinged bedroom, the larger of their two rooms at 12 Passauer Strasse. Yuli Aykhenvald, standing by the stove—it was a cold night in an exceptionally cold winter—was unusually lively. He recited poetry, he announced that he had been invited to lecture and to be feted in Danzig and Riga, he had heard from Russia that he now had a grandson. The Nabokovs felt their party was a great success. At about 1 A.M., as Aykhenvald "warily went down the short flight of stairs, with his host following with the door keys, he somehow caught the cuff of his overcoat on an ornamental projection between newel and bannister and got stuck in an odd position of semisuspension. He laughed shyly while his host hastened to disentangle him." Nabokov let him out and relocked the door, watching through the glass as Aykhenvald's rounded spine moved off. Half an hour later Aykhenvald stepped down from his tram and began to cross the Kurfürstendamm toward his home. Too late his weak eyes made out a tram coming at full speed from the opposite direction. He was knocked to the ground and never regained consciousness. He died that Monday morning. All his life he had had a superstitious fear of trams.[35]

Tributes arrived from all over the emigration, and the members of the group he had founded with Raisa Tatarinov at once named it the Aykhenvald Circle.

VII

With the Ullstein money for *King, Queen, Knave* Nabokov was able to settle the remainder of the debt Véra had been working to repay and to finance his first butterfly safari since Greece, 1919. Véra's employer was astonished that somebody would quit work at a time of rising unemployment, but the Nabokovs paid little attention to long-term security.[36]

On February 5 they caught the train to Paris, where they stayed two days and took the Struves to dinner. Gleb Struve, once critical of Sirin's early verse, had now become a champion of his work. Sleeping on the night train from Paris to Perpignan, Nabokov succumbed to the excitement of the approaching hunt as someone in his dreams offered him "what looked uncommonly like a sardine, but was really a tropical moth, the mimic—*mirabile dictu*—of a flying fish."[37]

From Perpignan a bus took them on February 8 fourteen winding miles into the Eastern Pyrenees. They stopped at Le Boulou, near the Spanish frontier: the locality was ecologically right, the Etablissement Thermal du Boulou cheap and set in a beautiful park. Huge lizards scurried between olive and cork trees, mimosas were in bloom, gorse and broom and heather flourished in the hard dry air. The guests were a mixed lot: bourgeois suffering from indigestion and bile, French colonials resting from the colonies, a doctor, a Spaniard with a car, a priest who sang opera and one day, sitting under a tree with his Bible, opened it up to show Nabokov the butterfly he had caught for him in its pages.[38] Nabokov would remember them all at the end of *Despair*, where he has Hermann too stop at a Roussillon hotel with a motley international clientele.

Véra Nabokov caught butterflies here for the first time, and learned how her husband killed his catches by placing them in a tumbler with cottonwool at the bottom soaked in carbona. Though thrilled to be on the trail again, Nabokov had to contend with the chill tramontane wind that seemed to blow whenever the sun shone. (The image in *Despair* of the postman turning his back to the wind also came from Le Boulou.) On fine days he would hunt along the road to Maureillas or another road leading to the Spanish frontier. Once among the arbutus and oak brush near the village of Le Perthus he made out the Elephant Steps of Hannibal's highway. Another time he was accompanied a long way by a wolf. In the evening he and Véra would both net moths on the lighted wall of a lean-to shed, and even caught an obliging quartet of rare Pugs that settled on the wall above the writing desk.[39]

At that desk, covered by a checkered tablecloth, with four volumes of Dahl's dictionary stacked against the wall and an inkwell, a packet of Gauloises, and a brimming ashtray to hand, Nabokov was busily writing his next novel, *Zashchita Luzhina* (*The Defense*).

Early in 1924 Nabokov had begun a story about a character called Aleksey Ivanovich Luzhin. The surname derives from Luga, in honor of Nabokov's past (Vyra and Rozhdestveno were on the St. Petersburg–Luga highway), but Luzhin recalls a childhood as unlike Nabokov's as a Russian childhood could be: a Catholic dormitory school in Italy, the terror of God, hell, and the abyss. The story begins when Luzhin catches sight of the pistol with which he will commit suicide, but the manuscript breaks off abruptly: Nabokov had hit on another way of leading this Luzhin to suicide, one that involved no inversion of his own past, and proceeded to write the story "A Matter of Chance."[40] But he kept his first version for future use. Perhaps by the time he traveled to the south of France in 1929, he had already decided to fuse a different kind of reversal of his childhood with the idea of the demented chess genius of his poem "The Chess Knight." At some early stage the novel was to end with Luzhin recalling in a nightmare the black-bearded peasant who fetched him as a child from his attic hideaway. Still in the throes of sleep, trying to resist the man in the black beard, he would unwittingly strangle his wife lying beside him—as Hugh Person strangles *his* wife in his sleep, more than forty years later, in *Transparent Things*.[41] But one day at Le Boulou as Nabokov was out in pursuit of butterflies, a new idea suddenly flashed before him: "I remember with special limpidity a sloping slab of rock, in the ulex- and ilex-clad hills, where the main thematic idea of the book first came to me"[42]—apparently not so much the chess theme he already had in mind as Luzhin's terrified perception that something was making his past eerily repeat itself, and his oppressed attempt to erect a final defense against that ominous repetition, until he can think of only one last move: jumping down five stories to his death. Before the end of February Nabokov was writing fast and well.[43] Decades later in America and in his final years in Europe he would again find lepidoptera a catalyst for inspiration.

Unable to endure the cold wind at Le Boulou any longer, the Nabokovs moved on April 24 to Saurat in the Ariège, a large village fifty miles further west at an altitude of two thousand feet and cradled around by mountains. They had written to a hotel there, but found its hole-in-the-ground toilet too primitive. They soon located other quarters, a floor in the house of a storekeeper, and hired a woman to clean and cook.[44]

Every time Nabokov walked net in hand through Saurat, he would see in his wake if he looked back "the villagers frozen in the various attitudes my passage had caught them in, as if I were Sodom and they Lot's wife." The roads were difficult, streams had to be forded one after another—even a tourist brochure called it "le pays des eaux folles"—and vipers abounded in the fields.[45] But it would take more than that to thwart this lepidopterist.

Still writing *The Defense*, Nabokov published in May an excited review of Bunin's *Selected Poems*, calling him the best Russian poet since Tyutchev died more than fifty years ago, better, even, than Blok.[46] He would not keep to that judgment, but he would always rate Bunin's poetry unusually highly, and disparage the sonorous prose that made Bunin the writer most esteemed by the emigration.

VIII

Although more species were emerging all the time, the Nabokovs returned to Berlin on June 24 with a "wonderful" collection of butterflies.[47] With the residue of the Ullstein money they decided to buy some land. A newly subdivided estate was being advertised at Kolberg on the Wolziger See, an hour to the southeast of Berlin, and with Anna Feigin they bought a section there, among birches and pines, with a small beach and magnificent waterlilies by the shore. Nabokov later remembered the sliver of land as no greater in size than his far-from-grand suite in the Montreux Palace Hotel, but the plan was for them to build on it in two years' time a small house with three or four rooms.[48]

Construction had not begun when the Nabokovs moved to Kolberg in July and had to rent a small shack from the local postman. Their quarters were unpleasant, but they spent most of the day by the lakeside. The solitude was ideal for Nabokov's work. He continued to attack *The Defense*, writing better than he had ever done. For relaxation, he coached Véra at tennis and entertained friends who visited from Berlin: the entomologist Kardakov (Nabokov was still pursuing butterflies), their ex-landlords the von Dallwitzes, the Kaminkas, who put up overnight in the postman's house, and Anna Feigin, who stayed for a week.[49]

Prospects looked good for Sirin. His story "Bachmann" had come out at the end of June in the place of honor in *Vossische Zeitung*. That same month he gave the Slovo publishing house a collection deliberately following Bunin's formula of combining stories and poems: fifteen stories, omitting eight of those he had published, and his best poems from 1924 to 1928. By the beginning of August, proofs of the volume *Vozvrashchenie Chorba* (*The Return of Chorb*) were starting to arrive. He overlooked one of the galleys when he sent them back, and had to borrow the postman's bike to dash to the nearest railway station to send it off.[50]

On August 15 he wrote to his mother:

I am finishing, finishing. . . . In three or four days I'll add the last full stop. After that I won't struggle again for a long time with such monstrously difficult themes, but will write something quiet and smooth-flowing. All the same I'm pleased with my Luzhin, but what a complicated, complicated thing!

He knew that *The Defense* was a breakthrough, and Véra wrote to her mother-in-law: "Russian literature has not seen its like."[51]

Nabokov the Writer

Our sense of Time may be the draft coming from the next dimension.

—manuscript of *Conclusive Evidence*

THE TRUE STORY of Nabokov's art is the story of his finding the formal and fictional inventiveness to express all the problems his philosophy poses. By the end of the 1920s, he had not only rejected the secondhand words and devices of his early poetry, he had also left behind the direct meditations of stories like "Sounds," "Grace," or "A Guide to Berlin," better as philosophy, but still thin, and as art, much too flat. As his talent burgeoned he discovered new structures and strategies that would allow his ideas their full intellectual value *and* a human context that gave them a local habitation and a name.

In *The Defense* for the first time he devised a means to express his ideas to the full. At this point, before looking at his first masterpiece, we need to examine Nabokov's ideas and the way they would condition all that is unique in his art.

I

Life teems with the stuff of happiness, Nabokov felt confident, if only we can learn not to take our world for granted. That primary disposition—remember that his first novel was to have been called *Schastie, Happiness*—shapes all his work, its curiosity, its openness, and above all its sense of grateful wonder. In an early story he tells us that an incidental character "was a pessimist and, like all pessimists, a ridiculously unobservant man."[1] In an early poem the apostles feel revulsion at the worms crawling out of a dog's bloated corpse, but Christ alone marvels at the whiteness of the dead dog's teeth.[2]

To Nabokov common sense could not be more wrong in accepting life as a struggle for advantage, a global monopoly board. One of his characters admits to coping poorly with "what is called the practical side of life (though, between you and me, bookkeeping or bookselling looks singularly unreal in the starlight)."[3] To "common sense" Nabokov opposed "art," in a special sense that has often been misunderstood.[4] He did not believe, like the truck driver who tells you that transport makes the world go round, that because he was an artist, art as a vocation was more important than other human activities. Nor did he see art as a fugitive and cloistered virtue, escaping from a crass world to a connoisseur's cocoon, spun with the exquisite silks of a bygone age. For Nabokov art was the spirit that could see beauty in a butcher's carcasses, a spirit of detachment from the world's bustle, not to abjure the world but to look at it afresh, to savor the priceless inutility and generosity of life.

In his own art he searched out both the independence of one thing from another and the combinations that link disparate things together. He had a natural inclination for independence, for anything isolated and individual, for the freedom of the mind in encountering a world of free particulars. He abhorred generalizations and enforced associations. The exception, the spark of the unexpected, the detonating detail still to be discovered at a new level of specificity could always explode the prison of classifications, determinisms, general rules. He wanted to see the thing in itself, unlimited by categories or averages, to view the moment in its openness, to cherish everything in the mind that is unconstrained, and to search for some more complete liberation of the soul from the cell of personality, the jail block of time.

But while he exalted the free electron, he also celebrated all the possibilities of the molecular bond. He found just as miraculous and inexplicable as the distinctness of things all their recombinations with other things, moments, minds: the long evolution of natural mimicry's complex designs, the subtle harmonies of a single instant. The world overflows with patterns all too easily overlooked, in the geometry of the snowflake or in a scribble left by chance. And in a universe replete with unexpected coherence Nabokov felt closest to the creative surprise of life when he made up his own combinations that realigned and integrated what appeared to belong to disparate orders: words, worlds, sense.

II

The first postulate of Nabokov's philosophy is the primacy of consciousness, "consciousness, which is the only real thing in the world and the greatest mystery of all."[5] In *Mary*, Ganin's memory re-creates his past with Mary so that Berlin fades altogether from sight. Nabokov stresses the directive force of the mind. Ganin's memories do not depend on the accident of tasting a madeleine from the *patisserie Proust*:

like Nabokov's own memories, they are "direct rays deliberately trained, not sparks and spangles."[6]

At the same time Nabokov was no solipsist: he knew that the external world resists the desires, however desperate, of the world within. While he often glories in the power of human consciousness, he also laments the absurdity of its limits: death, solitude, our exclusion even from our own past. Thrilled by all that the mind offers but aghast at all that it shuts out, Nabokov devotes his whole oeuvre to ascertaining our "position in regard to the universe embraced by consciousness"[7] and to analyzing the bizarre discrepancy between the richness of our life, as it accumulates moment by moment, and its becoming inaccessible, so utterly unlike the present around us, as it retreats into the past or as we advance into death.

While searching for the position of consciousness, Nabokov also keeps an eye on evolution. He sees life as inherently creative, evolving into ampler modes of being, each with more freedom and creative scope than its predecessors: from egg to caterpillar to the winged splendor of a butterfly, from the single cell to homo sapiens, from the rain chant to Tolstoy. Here he certainly owes something to Henri Bergson, at the peak of his popularity and influence in the mid-1920s, and the sudden prominence in *Mary*, "The Return of Chorb," and "A Guide to Berlin" of the contrast between space and time strongly suggests Nabokov's recent exposure to Bergson, whom he read avidly in his years of European exile.[8] Nabokov heartily approved Bergson's cutting time off from space in order to emphasize the indeterminism of the world,[9] and he accepted Bergson's stress on time as a richer mode of being than space, although the insistence on the absurd contrast between a possible return in space and an impossible return in time is his own.

How much Nabokov took from Bergson and how much was in him already is difficult to assess. Bergson set space and time at loggerheads in order to counter the mechanistic materialism he attributed to a narrowly spatial or outer view of the world, rather than a time-oriented or inner view. Through his mother and Russian symbolism Nabokov was himself a product of the reaction against nineteenth-century materialism and therefore may have found Bergson's aims already congenial without necessarily endorsing his arguments or conclusions.

Already as a schoolboy Nabokov had reinterpreted the Hegelian dialectic of history as an opening out of the closed circle into a spiral in which the first arc, the thesis, leads into the ampler arc of the antithesis, and that in turn into the synthesis, thesis of a new series.[10] That image of the expanding spiral never ceased to unfurl in his mind.

He applied it to the structure of his own life, to his scientific speculations about the evolution of butterfly wing markings, and above all to
his metaphysics, to his sense of time as a progressive widening out—a
sense that seems to stem from an almost innate yearning for freedom
that precedes his exposure to either Hegel or Bergson:

> every dimension presupposes a medium within which it can act, and if,
> in the spiral unwinding of things, space warps into something akin to
> time, and time, in its turn, warps into something akin to thought, then,
> surely, another dimension follows.[11]

In a previous book, I have explained the structure of Nabokov's
metaphysics as a double spiral in which his twin passions for independence and combination determine his attitude to each of the arcs
of being he defines: space; time; thought, or human consciousness;
and something further beyond.[12]

To map human consciousness, consciousness in the round, Nabokov feels compelled not only to describe Being from within its three
dimensions, but to collapse the world into one or two dimensions or
to expand it to four or five. It is this that imparts the characteristic
wobble to his universe that begins in *King, Queen, Knave*, the uneasy
sensation that the world of one of his books is now too flat, now too
multileveled, with one or two axes more than the three we can manage to keep in mind. And it is this that annoys readers who feel certain
that metaphysics has long been dismissed.

The dismissal of metaphysics is itself a metaphysical issue; its dis-
missers have themselves been dismissed; and metaphysics will not
die until humanity does. As Nabokov poses these problems from the
1920s on, he makes them seem worth facing afresh and injects into
them an urgency only the numb would not feel. His skepticism is
ruthless, his indifference to any religion complete. He refuses to rely
on tradition, he shucks off the intellectually untenable and the emotionally indulgent, and he offers answers not as firm conclusions but
as philosophical possibles that force us to reopen doors we thought
we had reason to shut.

III

In his lifetime Nabokov was often charged with being a trickster with
nothing to say. The "tricks" he made up and mastered over a lifetime
of writing in fact bear witness to an extraordinary imagination striving
to convey all that is original in his sense of the world.

Nabokov states the primacy of consciousness baldly in a sentence of *Bend Sinister* and argues it at length in Fyodor's "Life of Chernyshevsky," but he also signals its cardinal role everywhere in the shape he gives his stories. Even direct confrontation with the so-called objective world confirms the centrality of consciousness, as in that railway compartment in the opening chapter of *King, Queen, Knave*, where each character appears to belong to a different world. Often that difference will grow the hard husk of obsession: Kinbote's Zembla, Hermann's double, Luzhin's chess. Nabokov often engulfs us in the consciousness of a character and lets us out only after we have lost our bearings: external reality appears still to present its impeccable credentials, but we discover with a jolt that we have been trapped in reverie, hallucination, madness, or the last mental spurt of a dying brain. In "Terra Incognita" we cannot tell which is delirium, which is reality, just as we can never taste the objectively real: subjectivity is all we know.

Consciousness not only radiates from the individual, it seems somehow present out in the world. Nothing is more characteristic of Nabokov's imagery than a sense of animation in which even inert things spring to life or exist as if by some conscious intent: a shadow dives forward to listen, a mirror has to "work . . . hard that night" as someone passes and repasses, rain stops and starts again "as if practicing," clouds are poorly sculpted, a director lurks behind the pines. This is not old-style personification, not the ritual of the pathetic fallacy, where a character's mood saturates wind and tree by a kind of seepage as natural to careless poetry as it is to watercolor. Nabokov's images leap a gap of surprise, they are meant to look artificial, unnatural, and yet awaken the possibility of a universe somehow coruscating with consciousness in ways we cannot see. *King, Queen, Knave* opens:

> The huge black clock hand is still at rest but is on the point of making its once-a-minute gesture; that resilient jolt will set a whole world in motion. The clock face will slowly turn away, full of despair, contempt, and boredom, as one by one the iron pillars will start walking past, bearing away the vault of the station like bland atlantes; the platform will begin to move past, carrying off on an unknown journey cigarette butts, used tickets, flecks of sunlight and spittle. . . .[13]

All his animated objects, like this clock face, those pillars, that platform, scattered throughout Nabokov's work engender a cumulative subliminal impression that matter or space may be somehow alive with thought; all his animators "playing a game of worlds"—artists, authors, puppeteers, chess masters, fates, gods, even the jolting hand of a railway clock—stir the suspicion that time could well be less innocent than it seems.

IV

Now to turn to Nabokov's spiral of being and its first arc, Space—which of course we can never know except at its intersection with the present time of consciousness. Nabokov rendered the physical world not by a steady Balzacian amassment of information but through rapid shifts of focus that may mix the exact detail of a Van Eyck with the casually unfilled space of a Hokusai: "I recall one particular sunset. I lent an ember to my bicycle bell," or "She was Lo, plain Lo, in the morning, standing four feet ten in one sock."

Nabokov could impart to his details a sense of the endless specificity of the world. He explicitly extols the curiosity of the scientist and the artist, and their rejection of limits to what is worth knowing. He violates decorum in the precision of his references: ophryon, corpuscles of Krause, or "glossy red strawberries . . . all their achenes proclaiming their affinity with one's own tongue's papillae."[14] He refuses to be satisfied with approximate color when exact shades are available Uncle Vasya's eyes are "gray-green . . . flecked with rust," and in summer he would sport one of his various suits, "dove-gray, mouse-gray or silver-gray."[15] He pays attention to details of an order not expected: the haze over a frying pan, the colors and shapes of shadows.

Details in Nabokov are never inert but are surrounded by a static charge. Things are simply *there*, extraneous to our purposes, and can catch our attention when our mind seemed to be somewhere else just by being so much more fully realized by life than we had bothered to expect. So Humbert mowing the lawn notices "bits of grass optically twittering in the low sun." Or Nabokov intensifies the poignancy and value of a trifle by flicking to another focus: a sudden distance, on the buttons of the tram conductor's uniform in "A Guide to Berlin"; a sudden magnification, in the "long tusks of saliva" as the old father of "Signs and Symbols" removes his painful new dentures.

As a scientist and an artist Nabokov saw the world not only in terms of pinpointed detail but as an array of combinations, patterns, harmonies. The harmonies of chance in this or that patch of space excited the artist in Nabokov from the first: the interlacements of sun and leafy shade on a park footpath; the comic contrast between a black-faced coalman driving his massive truckload of coal and the divinely green lime leaf he holds by the twig in his teeth.[16] And Nabokov the scientist never ceased to wonder at the elaborateness of nature's designs, the regularities at every level from atoms and crystals to clouds and comets. He knew how the forms of life branched out from willowherb to bog orchid, waxwing to grebe, elm to paulownia, cichlid to sea-squirt. He studied the orchestration of ecology:

Freshly emerged . . . Selene Fritillaries. . . . An already rather bedraggled but still powerful Swallowtail. . . . Two violet-tinged Coppers. . . .
All this fascinating life, by whose present blend one could infallibly tell
both the age of the summer (with an accuracy almost to within one day),
the geographical location of the area, and the vegetal composition of the
clearing—all this that was living, genuine and eternally dear to him,
Fyodor perceived in a flash, with one penetrating and experienced
glance.[17]

Most unfathomable and breathtaking of all for Nabokov were the
intricacies of natural mimicry, which seemed to carry design far beyond the necessities of survival, to a degree of minuteness and finish
undetectable to any predator. At this extraordinary level, it seemed as
if nature itself took an inexplicable *artistic* pleasure in the complexity
and perfection of its work and in its apprehension by our intelligent
eyes.

Nature was one rival Nabokov knew he could not outdo at its own
game. Apart from the occasional Zemblan bird or Antiterran plant, he
did not bother to reinvent his own tree of life, though he drew the one
nature provided—the chick-fluff of a mimosa, the small helicopter of
a revolving samara—with a surer skill than almost any artist. But what
Nabokov could do was invent his own world replete with surprising
pattern, on small scale and large, with some of the variety, complexity, and interlacing of hierarchies he had been entranced by in nature
since early childhood. He always favored rhymed verse for the surprises that could be found within natural sense, and mimicry he once
defined as "Nature's rhymes."[18] The sound play, the anagrammatic
recombinations, the motifs, the hide-and-seek patterns so noticeable
at some levels and so elusive at others in Nabokov's mature novels
look at first glance more artificial than anything else in his work. Perhaps, Nabokov could reply, but nature is the first and most fabulous
artificer.

V

Nabokov resolutely cuts the spatial world off from time: by direct as-
sertion and argument, as in *Ada*, or by contrasting, in this form or
that, symmetrical space and the asymmetry of time.

Within the world of time, he preserves freedom by ruling out the
future as "an item of time." He may deny its existence outright, as in
Bend Sinister, *Ada*, *Transparent Things*. He may seem to allow the whole
shape of a work to build up reliable expectations, only to dash them

completely. Despite the title of his first novel, Mary never appears in Ganin's Berlin; the looming event that throws Troshcheikin into panic throughout *The Event* never comes to pass; the Carmen theme in *Lolita* sets up the false expectation that Humbert's victim is Lolita herself. In novels like *Lolita* and *Ada*, sudden breaks in rhythm jar the assumption of steady continuity. False continuations lure us along a possible line of development in *The Gift* or in *Ada* only to disclose that what had seemed a solid step underfoot was the ghostly staircase to unrealized possibility. Or Nabokov upends science fiction, in "Time and Ebb," "Lance," *Ada*, so that the fancy future turns out to be less strange than a past—our present—that we accept as commonplace, and no more and no less than a plain perpetuation of the miracle of human hopes and fears.

Looking backward, Nabokov finds the past alive with patterns to a degree no one before him had even imagined possible. Whether they mean anything is another matter: how much do we simply perceive them, how much create?

The impact of love impels characters in *The Gift*, in Sebastian Knight's *Success*, and in *Bend Sinister* back to the past to explain why they ever met. In each case the couple have all but touched more than once earlier in their lives. Do the repeated approaches before this last successful linkup mark the false tries of a fate that wants to persist in making its match? Or is it only that the lovers' fond curiosity has allowed them to probe a past always crisscrossed with patterns of every kind?

Despite the difficulties of attributing significance to the patterns of the past and despite his own defense of the indeterminism of time, Nabokov searches assiduously for evidence of some kind of fate. Not a fate that works by adamantine decree, but one that will advance one move and devise another should the first one fail: "But precisely in regard to such a contingency, Fate had prepared an alternate continuation. . . ."[19] Obvious coincidences of course happen often enough in life, and Nabokov gives them their due, but he also takes the greatest care not to build plots in which coincidences are chained to one another with the phonily inexorable logic of tragedy.

Some of Nabokov's characters themselves take on the role of fate. Nothing could be more cruel and depraved than those characters— Rex, Clare Quilty—who torment other human beings by playing cat-and-mouse with their lives. On the other hand nothing could be closer to the tenderness Nabokov intuits might lie behind even time's patterns of tragic loss than the care with which Fyodor, Shade, and Nabokov himself probe their own lives and try to impersonate fate in the artistic shape they give to their past.

What enabled Nabokov to explore pattern in time in entirely new ways was the gradual mastery he acquired over the recombination of fictional details. He transmutes a recurrent element sufficiently for the repetition to be overlooked, he casually discloses one piece of partial information and leaves it up to us to connect it with another apparently offhand fact, or he groups together stray details and repeats the random cluster much later in what appears to be a remote context. En route to each of the two major and ostensibly unrelated climaxes of *Lolita*, five years apart, separated by thousands of miles of traveling, and with different destinations ahead, Humbert makes a phone call each time from a gas station in a place called Parkington, a town where no other scenes in the novel take place. An accident, an automatic memorial repetition, or a playful coincidence? Or when other coincidences start to join the pattern, should we try to find a meaning? When even more join up, can we *refuse* to explain the apparent pressure of significance? In *Ada* a motorbike, the phrase "forest ride" and the word "gypsies" occur in close proximity within each of two scenes set years apart, against different backdrops, with different characters, different motorbikes, different "gypsies." In a book swarming with detail and abounding in obvious patterns these details are so slight and their repetition subjected to such transformation that no reader could even notice these matching clusters until a careful re-rereading. Even then they may be overlooked as mere incidental decoration— *until* we discover how they take their place in a larger design that insists on an urgent explanation.

Whatever the patterns Nabokov builds into time, whether they are disarmingly obvious or teasingly obscure, whether or not they look in retrospect like the handiwork of fate, he never allows them prognostic value for the future:

> As with so many phenomena of time, recurrent combinations are perceptible as such only when they cannot affect us any more—when they are imprisoned so to speak in the past, which *is* the past just because it is disinfected.[20]

Disinfected, that is, from the possibility of free human choice within the present.

VI

Consciousness at the moment of choice, stationed at its perpetual guardhouse of the present, serves most novelists for subject. Nabokov happens to have other subjects too, but not to the detriment of this. If he explores dimensions of being narrower and broader than our own, it is in order to survey better the boundaries of human possibility.

He consistently celebrates the magnitude of human consciousness and at the same time bemoans its paltriness compared with other states of being we could imagine. Let us inspect the positive side first.

In Nabokov's style the unique laws of motion that his sentences obey demonstrate the power of the mind as he sees it. He extends the freedom of prose by refusing to let the choice made at one instant predetermine the next. *Transparent Things* opens with a paragraph of one line, apparently spoken by the narrator:

Here's the person I want. Hullo, person! Doesn't hear me.

The next line, the next paragraph, continues, if that is the word:

Perhaps if the future existed, concretely and individually, as something that could be discerned by a better brain, the past would not be so seductive.

At the top of a page in Tolstoy, we know the mood likely at the foot of the page, unless there supervenes one of those radiant sweeps of emotion, like sunlight flooding a sullen field. On a page of *Ulysses*, we can expect in advance the style of the coming paragraph, though we could never anticipate where Joyce will dig up this particular verbal truffle or the next. But even within one sentence or one paragraph of Nabokov's mature prose, we have no clue to what will follow. In *Speak, Memory* a sentence starts with Nabokov's father in midair and without a pause in the rhythm ends fifteen years or an eternity later inside a church. In *Lolita* a sentence introduces and dismisses Humbert's mother, to finish, after strange meanderings, somewhere within our own memories:

My very photogenic mother died in a freak accident (picnic, lightning) when I was three, and, save for a pocket of warmth in the darkest past, nothing of her subsists within the hollows and dells of memory, over which, if you can still stand my style (I am writing under observation), the sun of my infancy had set: surely, you all know those redolent remnants of day suspended, with the midges, about some hedge in bloom or suddenly entered and traversed by the rambler, at the bottom of a hill, in the summer dusk; a furry warmth, golden midges.

Physics tells us that the greater the momentum, the greater the force needed to alter course. Often in the 1930s and in sentence after sentence over the decades that follow, Nabokov's prose breaks this rule, moving at high speed but making transitions of every kind even within the sentence: from passionate involvement to playfulness, scorn, detachment, grotesquerie, beauty; from the here and now to another point in space-time and then perhaps a third; from close to distant, abstract to concrete, first person to third or even second ("Gentlewomen of the jury!" or "in the last nights of a life, which I do not regret, my love"). Van leaves Ardis for the last time after discovering Ada's infidelity, holding back the bitterness of his grief with a patter of preparation:

> Good morning, and good-bye, little bedroom. Van shaved, Van pared his toe-nails, Van dressed with exquisite care: gray socks, silk shirt, gray tie, dark-gray suit newly pressed—shoes, ah yes, shoes, mustn't forget shoes, and without bothering to sort out the rest of his belongings, crammed a score of twenty-dollar gold coins into a chamois purse, distributed handkerchief, checkbook, passport, what else? nothing else, over his rigid person and pinned a note to the pillow asking to have his things packed and forwarded to his father's address. Son killed by avalanche, no hat found, contraceptives donated to Old Guides' Home.

No decorously uniform despair here, but a mind careening from inside to outside, from Ardis in summer to snowy mountaintop, from businesslike briskness to that absurd but somehow satisfying closing sneer.

Nabokov refuses to believe that we are sponges entirely filled with some salty solution at a moment of grief, and, when the mood changes (*squeeze*), now soaking up, to saturation point, the smooth syrup of happiness. Instead he saw consciousness as incredibly complex, mobile, multichanneled, capable of an aside of thought or a stray conviction even at a moment of supreme stress, and always ready to be aware of being aware of itself. His style is psychology at its finest. Early in *Lolita* Humbert works himself up to a stealthy spasm as innocent Lolita in her Sunday best sits on his lap. Even as he concentrates tensely on his furtive pleasure, his mind darts this way and that:

> The implied sun pulsated in the supplied poplars; we were fantastically and divinely alone; I watched her, rosy, gold-dusted, beyond the veil of my controlled delight, unaware of it, alien to it, and the sun was on her lips, and her lips were apparently still forming the words of the Carmen-barmen ditty that no longer reached my consciousness. Everything was now ready. The nerves of pleasure had been laid bare. The corpuscles of Krause were entering the phase of frenzy. The least pressure would suffice to set all paradise loose. I had ceased to be Humbert the Hound, the sad-eyed degenerate cur clasping the boot that would presently kick him away. I was above the tribulations of ridicule, beyond the possibilities of

retribution. In my self-made seraglio, I was a radiant and robust Turk, deliberately, in the full consciousness of his freedom, postponing the moment of actually enjoying the youngest and frailest of his slaves.

All the vents of Humbert's being are open. As he glances out the bright window, he matches the exact harmony of light and flickering shade with the pattern and precision of his prose; his eyes screw to a close-up, focusing on the luminous rim of Lolita's face; he jumbles together the categories of ardent arousal, scientific technicality, poetic rhythm; he holds himself at a mocking distance even as he describes the swell of self-absorption; his mounting excitement fires the remoter reaches of his imagination.

Note that despite Humbert's having an exceptional freedom to redirect his mind, time pulses steadily on. Very occasionally Nabokov may jar the gliding progress natural to his prose, though even then he will keep switching modes and moods. From the index to *Pale Fire*:

Onhava, the beautiful capital of Zembla, *12, 71, 130, 149, 171, 181, 275, 579, 894, 1000*.

Otar, *Count*, heterosexual man of fashion and Zemblan patriot, b. 1915, his bald spot, his two teenage mistresses, Fleur and Fifalda (later Countess Otar), blue-veined daughters of Countess de Fyler, interesting light effects, *71*.

Or as Krug rushes out of the ward where his slaughtered son lies, the English text erupts into a Russian mock-report on the bungled death and offers a retranslation with shaky confidence:

Tut pocherk zhizni stanovitsa kraĭne nerazborchivym [here the long hand of life becomes extremely illegible]. *Ochevidtzy, sredi kotorykh byl i evo vnutrenniĭ sogliadataĭ* [witnesses among whom was his own something or other ("inner spy?" "private detective?" The sense is not at all clear)] *potom govorili* [afterward said] *shto evo prishlos' sviazat'* [that he had to be tied].

These freak effects have their good reasons, comic or nightmarish, in their contexts, but they are not typical. Normally Nabokov maintains an illusion of steady forward momentum but subverts it by constant redirection. He eschews the disjunctures, the fractures in time, the jumps from mind to italicized mind that have become such conventions of modern literature: in this life, after all, we each stay within the one consciousness, and we can never escape the smooth advance of the moment. But between the tick we have heard and the tock we can expect, Nabokov shows us, our minds can make any choice they want.

VII

In a century that saw the rise of minimalist art, Nabokov was a maximalist. He explored human nature at the upper reaches of consciousness. Nothing could be further from his characters than the automata of Beckett, programmed to wait for the oblivion that will end their decay, or the communities of quarter-wits, half-wits, and three-quarter-wits we find in Faulkner.

Thought in Nabokov's work does not know the ordinary bounds. At times he frees his characters from narrative altogether to let them loose in pure cerebration, abstract but intensely personalized and alive: Fyodor's flamboyant critique of Chernyshevsky's metaphysics and epistemology and aesthetics; the mental drafts of philosopher Krug; Shade's highly crafted musings; Van Veen's boisterous treatise "The Texture of Time." More often thought thrives within the story. He makes his central characters, especially his narrators, supremely intelligent and articulate, a tendency that becomes more pronounced as his career advances and he chooses more and more to dramatize effects.

If even someone like Hermann, the chocolate manufacturer who recounts his own story in *Despair*, is endowed with literary genius, it does not mean that Nabokov believed that all people are intelligent or that only the intelligent count: it simply betrays his desire not to abandon the full scope of his own resources, even as he pursues the inventive advantages of handing his characters the pen. Van and Ada's self-satisfaction with their own "super-imperial" gifts places them at the center of their world, but *Ada*—as Nabokov's novel rather than as the Veens' memoir—argues cogently on behalf of people its narrators relegate to the periphery.

Nabokov wants to test thought at its highest and its most diverse. For reasons that will become apparent, this rarely happens in dialogue: to endow a speaking character with the eloquence a writer can achieve at the desk may have been possible in Shakespeare's day or even Henry James's, but no longer. Only in a plausibly brief spurt of insight (Shade to Kinbote) or in a mode of high stylization (Fyodor and Koncheyev, Van and Ada) does Nabokov release the genie of spoken genius. Nor does he try to mimic in words the evanescence of private thought. He might dip into someone's mind ("passport, what else? nothing else, over his rigid person") or briefly parody interior monologue, permit us to follow the caprices of Fyodor's imagination through the filter of reported thought, or place us in the turmoil of Krug's intellect, but he did not commit himself as Joyce, Woolf, or

Faulkner sometimes did to the task of rendering verbally the immediacy of thought. He knew that it was impossible to transcribe the mind into a sequence of words when consciousness operates in "the no-time of human thought,"[21] varies in its levels of verbality, flicks from channel to ill-defined channel, or broadcasts simultaneously from several stations as signals well up and fade.

Nabokov wanted thought individual and dramatized, the product of his invented characters' minds, but also at its maximum, with "all the shutters and lids and doors of the mind . . . open at once at all times of the day,"[22] and with the time to expand each fleeting impulse to its utmost sinuous strength: he had to allow his characters access to all the resources of written language. Humbert on the davenport typifies Nabokov's methods: thought anything but spontaneous, but boiling all around the event with a heat the instant alone could never generate. Making no pretense to *simulate* Humbert's immediate mind, it can *stimulate* the molecules of the reader's mind into motion all the better because Humbert has had the chance, literally, to compose himself.

For Nabokov there was more to consciousness than thought. Emotion too he pushes to its extremes: love refracted through loss (John Shade and daughter, Sineusov and wife, Fyodor and father); tenderness faced with a doom it cannot avert (Mrs. Luzhin and a husband plummeting into madness, Krug with a son butchered by the state, the parents in "Signs and Symbols," with a son condemned by his own insanity to suicide) or the sheer passion of Humbert for Lolita, Van for Ada. The intensity, the lyricism, the romanticism of love in these last two cases has struck some readers as impermissibly old-fashioned. One wonders if they remember *whom* these lovers celebrate (a twelve-year-old stepdaughter, a sister) or whether they have registered all the novelties of characterization that complicate and undercut the figure of the beleaguered and insufficiently requited lover Humbert tries to project. Nothing could be further from an artificially simple emotion artificially inflated to bombastic bursting point. What seems exaggerated to some modern eyes must be the sheer magnitude of feeling, but we have only to look at *Speak, Memory* and Nabokov's own love for Vyra, his parents, his son, for "Colette," "Polenka," "Tamara," and the implicit crown of the series, his wife, to see why love looms so large in his work.

Nabokov, the first entomologist to count under the microscope the scale-rows on a butterfly's wing markings, insisted as an artist too on a new precision of the senses. He applied a scientist's and a psychologist's curiosity and knowledge to perceiver as well as perceived. Not limiting himself to the time-honored five senses of tradition, he attends to proprioception or a minor phenomenon like the *muscae voli-tantes* (the ocular infusoria rolling across our field of vision). He has Van Veen build on the findings of William James; he anticipates in a story's random observation J. J. Gibson's brilliant theories of visual perception; he sets forth in *Speak, Memory* an account of his synesthe-sia that he was delighted to see cited in scholarly studies of the sub-ject. He had a painter's sense of light and a draftsman's or an actor's or a sportsman's sense of movement, gesture, facial feature. He ex-celled in specifying one impression in terms of another or in stimulat-ing the imagination to see an object or feel a sensation. On one page opened at random, Lolita's lipstick-smudged teeth glisten "like wine-tinged ivory," while Humbert refuses to be diverted from his suspi-cion of her infidelity "by the feeling of well-being that my walk had engendered—by the young summer breeze that enveloped the nape of my neck, the giving crunch of the damp gravel, the juicy tidbit I had sucked out at last from a hollow tooth." Nabokov exhorted his stu-dents and his readers to exercise the sensory imagination, to *see* Anna Karenin's neck, to savor in a Bosch canvas not some dreary and doubt-ful symbolic meaning but "the joy of the eye, the feel and the taste of the woman-sized strawberry that you embrace *with* him, or the exqui-site surprise of an unusual orifice."[23]

Some critics charge Nabokov with being too cerebral, others call him too romantic, others again find him too sensual. Precisely. Na-bokov values human thought, feeling, and perception at all their max-ima, and even that is not enough.

VIII

Nabokov's impulse to extend consciousness may be all very well, but we happen to have only what nature and culture and chance endow us with. How does his disposition toward human limits allow him to deal with actual people, with all those far from the fringes of achievement?

There are two answers: his psychology, his ethics.

Nabokov's notorious dismissal of Freud stems not from an antip-athy to psychology but from a love of the subject's possibilities. He had the same curiosity about all aspects of the mind that he had for perception, though this is not the place for a full treatment of his psy-chological views. Following our present theme we can say this much about his sense of character: the passion for independence that drives him to the boundaries of consciousness also sharpens his awareness of human individuality and of the measure and value of our differences. He believes in the unpredictable particulars by which we exist, undeducible from any generalization and yet fitting the mysterious and unique harmony of each self. Lolita is not "the fragile child of a feminine novel" but the girl who sits down to pick up pebbles with her toes and ping them at a can; Ada will always be the girl with a drop of honey at the wick of her mouth, tossing her head, considering, considering the person she is looking at, with a defiant smile that masks some secret, and yet ready to pounce forward in an overflow of eagerness and energy; Luzhin remains the helpless creature who rushes into the room of a woman he barely knows, informs her she will be his wife, bursts into tears as he sits down by the radiator, seizes her by the elbow and kisses "something hard and cold—her wristwatch."

Although our individuality may be irreducible, we do not consist of discrete, unconnected instants or spring from nothing at every moment: some unity through time certainly exists in us all, though no general rule will ever find it out. For Nabokov each of us has "a certain unique pattern of life in which the sorrows and passions of a particular man . . . follow the rules of his own individuality."[24] The components of the pattern may be as incalculable as anything in life before they come together, but they will combine in a way that extends their own special harmony. All the heterogeneous constituents in a character like Kinbote—his paranoia, his homosexuality, his fantasy-ridden nostalgia, his offensive intrusiveness on a neighbor and fierce tetchiness about his own private life, his ping-pong, his boarders, his solitude, his role as a literary critic, half parasite, half usurper, his longing for suicide—all fuse without contradiction into one flawless whole.

Like everything else in Nabokov, his ethics spring from his view of consciousness. He sees consciousness as the space of freedom: as his style proclaims, the mind has an enormous ease of movement and range of choice and room for self-awareness within the moment. And yet consciousness, although it seems to be the agent of liberation, is also, being only human, the site of our confinement. Nabokov devises characters of astonishing mental freedom who are at the same time utterly obsessed. The intensity of their emotion seems to them to raise them to new heights of tenderness and the point of self-transcendence—and right here, in the ardent pursuit of their passion, they become their most blindly selfish and cruel. Even here, though, he points out, they never lose all their openness and mobility of mind: even obsession never confines us to one channel from which we cannot diverge. When Humbert sits under Lolita on the davenport, rubbing away at her innocence, his mind remains as unfettered as ever. A year later he will be her lover, her jailer, her tormentor, more ob-

? sessed than ever but with his mind still fantastically free. By letting us inside a Humbert or a Kinbote or a Van Veen, Nabokov shocks us more than any other author into experiencing in another person the blindness of self.

Perhaps it will be clearer now that when Nabokov makes a great many of his characters artists and hangs the fact of their art in a prominent place he is not simply an aesthete or an egomaniac populating his worlds with little Nabokovs. For him the creatures of imagination on whom his stories focus are those who ought to be at the last ramparts of consciousness, ready to jump the moat to total freedom if anyone can. Instead they prove the moat an impassable abyss, or the prison, for all its illusion of light and air, an inhospitable dungeon. The artist-madmen (Bachmann, Luzhin, Hermann, the boy of "Signs and Symbols," Kinbote) who attempt to escape through some narrow cranny in their world emerge in the most cheerless of mortal cells, haunted and alone. The artist-criminals (Axel Rex, Hermann, Humbert, Van Veen) who try to vault over moral responsibility crash back down. And then there are the many artists and thinkers flawed simply by being mortal, who have to cope with death and loss: Cincinnatus, Fyodor, Sineusov, Sebastian Knight, V., Krug, Humbert, Pnin, Shade, Kinbote, Van and Ada, Hugh Person, Vadim Vadimych. Even those meditative minds like Krug's, Sineusov's, or Van Veen's that come closest to confronting their limits by trying to stare through the dark glass of death see no more than their own reflection. Only those who decide on art's indirection, its plexed rays and reversed images, seem almost to peer through the periscope into something beyond.

IX

At one point John Shade writes four words that could be the motto for all Nabokov's later work: "not text, but texture."[25] In context, the phrase implies that while any direct statement aimed past human consciousness will simply ricochet back off the walls of our ignorance, something in the very weave of a work of art may just be able to offer a clue to what lies beyond. Most readers judge Shade's phrase a pretty one but ignore its sense or find it too remote or dismiss it as the self-advertisement of art. Nabokov meant it. There is some strange shimmer in the gaps between his words to lure readers through until they can see the world of his books as if from the other side, from beyond the limits of consciousness. To find how to accomplish that, Nabokov had to rethink what fiction could do.

As he marks out the arbitrary limits of human consciousness, Nabokov makes us feel the absurdity of accepting without question that there cannot be anything beyond them. He works by direct statement (in *Speak, Memory*), by dramatization (Humbert tells Quilty before shooting him: "The hereafter for all we know may be an eternal state of excruciating insanity"), and especially by imagery that can prick the imagination of those normally indifferent to such matters or too sure of what they think they know. Shade recalls

> a time in my demented youth
> When somehow I suspected that the truth
> About survival after death was known
> To every human being: I alone
> Knew nothing, and a great conspiracy
> Of books and people hid the truth from me.

Or as Fyodor puts it: "the unfortunate image of a 'road' to which the human mind has become accustomed (life as a kind of journey) is a stupid illusion: we are not going anywhere, we are sitting at home. The other world surrounds us always and is not at all at the end of some pilgrimage. In our earthly house, windows are replaced by mirrors; the door, until a given time, is closed; but air comes in through the cracks."

Even imagery like this stays too close to statement to suffice. Nabokov needs something that can slide past the sentinels of sense. To define the limits of consciousness with an immediacy we cannot assent to or reject but can only *experience*, Nabokov modifies the structure of fiction and the texture of prose, jarring us against the bars of our cage or showing how we almost slipped through.

Now it may be more apparent why Nabokov seems suspicious to many a twentieth-century liberal. In an age when the idea of democracy has become muddied with a sense of guilt at anything that exceeds the average, Nabokov fixes on the highly endowed, and declares that for all they have even *they* could have so much more. That does not make him a reactionary, but it does indicate how far he is from the social concerns of his age. He is a freedom fighter, but his fight is philosophical and metaphysical, not social.

X

Anyone who reads Nabokov's interviews of the 1960s and 1970s hears someone who hugely enjoyed being himself: "V.N." was a game he played to the hilt. But let us not forget that in everything he wrote outside his interviews and introductions he became other people. No wonder: he saw personality, like everything else in consciousness, as both prize and prison.

To break free, Nabokov grabs the iron bars of self, measures their thick girth between palm and fingers, and still tries to twist. He reaches for a lever: a momentary judder of language (". . . thought Krug, the circle in Krug, one Krug in another one"), or a structural surprise the length of a book. Early in *The Eye* the narrator kills himself—already this could only be one of Nabokov's worlds—but apparently persists in his Berlin life by the momentum of thought, and becomes obsessed by an elusive new face in the old crowd, one Smurov, who turns out to be himself.

Some of Nabokov's characters hope that in the ecstasy of love they will somehow assimilate or amalgamate with their beloved (Humbert and Annabel or Lolita, Van and Ada); others desperately search out the inaccessible secrets of someone else's being (Fyodor and his father, V. and Sebastian, Kinbote and Shade); still others yearn for the solitude of bereavement to be broken by some sign from beyond (Martin and his father, Fyodor and his father, Sineusov and his wife, Krug and *his* wife). All of them fail.

When certain sensitive characters pretend to enter the minds of other people in their story (Fyodor, or the narrator of "Sounds"), they may keep it up for pages on end until the other person's imagined consciousness takes on a life of its own, and yet it is still no more than a feat of the sympathetic imagination desperate to break free. But in *Transparent Things* the ghosts of dead characters narrate for us, by sidling in and out of his soul, the story of a man they knew while they were still alive. They themselves pulse between individuality and some more fluid pooled identity. In *Invitation to a Beheading*, everyone around the central character seems two-dimensional, operated by clockwork rather than consciousness, and only in death does Cincinnatus appear to head toward beings like himself. Elsewhere in Nabokov characters are mirrored or doubled in one way or another around the plane of death: Hermann and the man he thinks his mirror-image, whom he kills to collect the insurance on his own life; V., who pursues the past of his half-brother Sebastian, finds the trail slippery, blocked, humiliatingly tortuous, and only then realizes that this very looped and knotted line mimics the structure of Sebastian's books, as if in the chase for his dead brother V. has enacted a new Sebastian Knight novel, as if he has become Sebastian; Humbert, who kills his mocking reflection Quilty; John Shade, shot in place of Kinbote, his shadowy image in Zembla's azure mirror, who appropriates

Shade's poem and his very self; Van and Ada, who write *Ada* jointly in their last years and as it were fuse together in the book and in death.

In reality there may be an inflexible barrier between the self inside and the world outside, but Nabokov also knew that language could almost breach it. More freely than any other writer before him, he glides back and forth from third-person to first-person narrative within the same story, swiftly or slowly, abruptly or so smoothly as to escape detection. He may let us accept the illusion impersonal prose gives of an immediate access to the world and other minds, then jerk us back to a narrating self: Fyodor and Humbert, Kinbote and Van Veen, all flicker in the space of a blink between their individual "I" and fiction's impersonal eye. Knowing that in everyday life none of us can cross the line between absence and presence, self and world, Nabokov exploits the special conditions of written language to smudge or sharpen the line at will and does it with such speed and grace that we feel nothing could be simpler than to step over to the other side and back—if only life could allow us the freedom we find here in language.[26]

XI

As with personality, so with time: Nabokov's structures compel us to recognize the fading of the past as an absurd constraint on human consciousness rather than a direct reflection of the way things are.

The fates of his characters indicate again and again the gross discrepancy between our ability to return in space and our inability to return in time. As soon as he can after his wife's death, Hugh Person revisits the places in Switzerland where he met and was routinely humiliated by her. The narrator mockingly asks: "What had you expected of your pilgrimage, Person? A mere mirror rerun of hoary torments? Sympathy from an old stone? Enforced re-creation of irrecoverable trivia?"[27] Memory at least offers us some power over our personal past, and of course Nabokov's characters have their maker's capacity to recall with precision and to fix their recollections in words. All the same, even characters as well endowed as Van and Ada, who have retold their past to each other all their lives, bicker over details. By dint of arduous research Fyodor seems able to re-create an animated eidolon of Chernyshevsky and his nineteenth-century milieu, and with the far better access his memory gives him to his own past he can make a spacious and sumptuous work of art like *The Gift*. But even Fyodor's talents cannot match the pointedly unlifelike power Sebastian Knight permits himself in his novel *Success*, where qua novelist he can pursue ad infinitum any thread of his characters' lives, or the decidedly magical and improbable Silbermann, with his picklock for time's secrets. Still further from human limits are the storytellers of *Transparent Things* who can see through the present to the past of a pencil or a Person, and fold one level of time against another.

Most of the first readers of *Transparent Things* were astonished by the ghosts that seemed suddenly to have obtruded themselves into Nabokov's work. They should not have been. Sentence after sentence in his mature fiction aims by its very shape to imply in its language something beyond human time.

We have already seen that the peculiar texture of Nabokov's prose allows him to render the mobility of the mind—the narrator's, the reader's—within the relentless advance of the moment. In the staccato of Bloom's mind the Joyce of *Ulysses* too creates the sensation of thought in the present moment, but in quite a different way. Encountering Joyce we savor the long deliberation behind each of his lexical choices, with the result that our own pace in reading slows right down. Nabokov on the other hand preserves the sense of openness within the moment so essential to his vision of consciousness: he rethinks at every phrase not only the next word or idiom (here of course he cannot approach Joyce's range), but also the mood, tone, setting, voice, and every other variable and nevertheless retains a fluid melodic line that preserves the sense of briskly advancing time.

But even as he defines the freedom of human consciousness within time he also feels the narrow limits of this freedom: "time, so boundless at first blush," he knew, "was a prison."[28] His sentence structure therefore performs a second feat, the inverse of the first: a persistent attempt to pass beyond the bounds of the moment.

Formed and delivered in a moment, likely to be forgotten soon after, spoken language smacked to Nabokov of the prison of the present. The very nature of written language meant something special to him: an opportunity to revisit the impulse of a past instant from which time has forced us to march on, a sort of access to a more elastic time where one can loop back on an idea and develop it to maximum power and grace. In the 1960s he began to refuse interviews unless questions were submitted well in advance and answers could be fully prepared in writing. That may look like mere personal vanity, but he was simply hyperconscious of the difference between his spoken language ("I speak like a child") and what he could achieve given the rubbery time of revision. No wonder he became proud of the fact that he wore out erasers faster than his pencil lead.

Bedridden, failing rapidly, ninety-seven-year-old Van Veen corrects the galley proofs of *Ada* and adds a last-minute note:

> . . . about the rapture of her identity. The asses who might really think that in the starlight of eternity, *my*, Van Veen's, and *her*, Ada Veen's, conjunction, somewhere in North America, in the nineteenth century represented but one trillionth of a trillionth part of a pinpoint planet's significance can bray *ailleurs, ailleurs, ailleurs* (the English word would not supply the onomatopoeic element; old Veen is kind), because the rapture of her identity, placed under the microscope of reality (which is the only reality), shows a complex system of those subtle bridges which the senses traverse—laughing, embraced, throwing flowers in the air—between membrane and brain, and which always was and is a form of memory, even at the moment of its perception. I am weak. I write badly. I may die tonight. My magic carpet no longer skims over crown canopies and gaping nestlings, and her rarest orchids. Insert.[29]

Even where Nabokov mimics someone nervously aware of time slipping catastrophically away, someone who actually loses his bearings in the rush to beat the impending avalanche of death and who has no chance to correct a word, we can sense the author beyond, making *his* choices in that special space that writing and rewriting afford just outside time, taking advantage of first thoughts, second thoughts, third thoughts to allot his character the illusion of a mind that, despite its panic, still remains wonderfully free to dart this way or that.

Or Nabokov produces a memory retrieved as a small victory over elapsing time:

> I try again to recall the name of Colette's dog—and, triumphantly, along those remote beaches, over the glossy evening sands of the past, where each footprint slowly fills up with sunset water, here it comes, here it comes, echoing and vibrating: Floss, Floss, Floss![30]

Along one continuous line the sentence glides from Nabokov at his desk to "glossy evening sands of the past" made real underfoot by that glimpse of sunset water, so that against all logic it is the 1950s or 1960s Nabokov standing on a 1909 beach, calling out excitedly as a memory bounds panting closer, responsive to its master's call. By its sheer elegance and command the sentence becomes a triumph over time of a higher order than Nabokov's private thrill of recollection, a triumph he has prepared for us to share in as we read. Because the transition is so fluid and the sentence so swift and lucid he teaches us here as so often that even as our minds move rapidly onward within the present they can also leap as far aside as imagination can take us with a deftness and ease and range far greater than we were prepared to think. On the wings of art, we can almost fly the prison isle of the present.

XII

After personality and time comes the third constraint upon conscious-ness that Nabokov defines, unsettles us into noticing, and tries to transcend: the closed circle of mortal knowledge.

Throughout his novels he undermines the comfortable solidity books usually seek. Something out of kilter here or there suggests that the worlds we have immersed ourselves in as if they were real are only two-dimensional compared with a reality beyond. From time to time the texture thins, the stage props show, or a character observes "the thick green grease-paint of the foliage." Parody and illusion strain at the stitches in what cannot be a seamless naturalistic world. One of the dramatis personae runs from audience to stage and back again or steps out from a painting or down from the screen. A book or play written by one of the characters appears to mirror the whole world of the novel, including events that have not yet happened: against all logic, the part contains the whole, the inside surrounds the outside. Or "the world of the book" confuses us by parading at once both its identity with ours and its difference: *Pale Fire*'s Zembla, *Ada*'s Antiterra.

Death especially jangles our nerves. A favorite exercise among teachers of literature is to compare the death scenes in nineteenth-century novels. The deaths that conclude many of Nabokov's novels place us not at the character's bedside, standing behind the shoulders of the grieving family, but drop us down into the gaping grave until a plank in reason breaks. Cincinnatus gets up after being beheaded and walks toward the voices of creatures like himself; Krug, just before he dies, realizes he has been invented by the author of *Bend Sinister*; Ada and Van die into the book or its blurb; the chief narrator of *Transparent Things*, ghost of the novelist R. within the story, welcomes Hugh Person in the novel's last words across the line of death.

Here too Nabokov expresses himself not only through statement, imagery, and the dislocations of structure but also through the ubiq-uitous texture of his prose. He has Krug imagine death as "either the instantaneous gaining of perfect knowledge . . . or absolute nothing-ness."[31] Whatever else human knowledge may be, it is neither instan-taneous nor perfect. We learn only in time and bit by bit. Every new moment generates more information than we can possibly attend to, every year elapsed means that so much even of what we had attended to keenly as it happened has slipped away beyond recovery. We have no certain grounds for knowledge, no direct organ of truth, only imperfect senses and more or less shrewd guesses. Our sample of the universe is absurdly small, our knowledge of anything outside mortal life simply nonexistent.

Throughout his work Nabokov takes all this into account as he refines his implicit logic of artistic discovery. He sets up carefully spaced obstacles to our comprehension, to match the difficulties our minds have in coping with our world, but on the other side of every hurdle he invites us to an exhilarating splashdown into discovery. His particularity and precision, far from working against or scoring off his readers, show him here at his most generous. He allows us to find out through our own curiosity and imagination the excitements and achievements of the mind in confronting its world, and for those ready to persist he even prepares something akin to the unspeakable shock of "death knowledge,"[32] of finding ourselves suddenly in a consciousness beyond the human.

Even early in his career Nabokov avoided conventional exposition. He knew life does not supply information neatly labeled, but discloses it piece by piece to the searching eye and the wakeful mind. In his art he devised his own equivalent. In *Bend Sinister* Krug comes down from the hospital floor where his wife has died. Despite the grief shouting for attention he notices the head nurse: "With her faded blue eyes and long wrinkled upper lip she resembled someone he had known for years but could not recall—funny." Thirty pages later Azureus, the president of Krug's university, steps forward to welcome him,

> his arms open, his faded blue eyes beaming in advance, his long wrinkled upper lip quivering—
> "Yes, of course—how stupid of me," thought Krug, the circle in Krug, one Krug in another one.

The chapter ends there. The nurse's eyes and lip quietly posed a problem to which we expected no solution; Krug's "how stupid of me" poses another in its immediate context, which the lucky reader with a good memory can solve at once and the ordinary reader with no more than curiosity can solve by a moment's scanning the page: the faded blue eyes and the long wrinkled lip will recall some similar combination in the past, and the solution to this second problem will unlock the first. The double puzzle is part tease, part compliment to the reader's energy, and partly the built-in reward of the pleasure of discovery.

Nabokov sets and resolves that problem with the clarity that almost always marks his prose. Not often, but at strategic points in his novels, he also ruffles his usual lucidity to confront us with a passage that conveys little except that sense has suddenly started to slip away. Four professors including Krug have been brought by the toady Dr. Alexander to see Azureus, who for the university's sake needs their signed allegiance to the country's bestial new dictatorship. While Dr. Alexander parks the car, the professors mount the stairs.

> But they did not have to ring or knock or anything for the door on the topmost landing was flung open to greet them by the prodigious Dr. Alexander who was there already, having zoomed perhaps, up some special backstairs, or by means of those nonstop things as when I used to rise from the twinned night of the Keeweenawatin and the horrors of the Laurentian Revolution, through the ghoul-haunted Province of Perm, through Recent, Slightly Recent, Not So Recent, Quite Recent, Most Recent—warm, warm!—up to *my* room number on *my* hotel floor in a remote country, up, up, in one of those express elevators manned by the delicate hands—my own in a negative picture—of dark-skinned men with sinking stomachs and rising hearts, never attaining Paradise, which is not a roof garden; and from the depths of the stag-headed hall old President Azureus came at a quick pace, his arms open, his faded blue eyes beaming in advance, his long wrinkled upper lip quivering—
>
> "Yes, of course—how stupid of me," thought Krug. . . .

In 1949, when the Dutch translator of *Bend Sinister* asked for help, the Nabokovs replied:

> . . . this is a hard passage. It develops simultaneously on several planes. The word "Keeweenawatin" is a telescopic combination of two terms "Keewatin" (name of a schist of the Archaeozoic—the oldest—period) and "Keewanawan" (subdivision of the Proterozoic). Laurentian belongs to the Archaeozoic, Permian to the Paleozoic. Through Early Recent etc.—further partly existent partly invented periods of geological development. In other words—from the dimmest past into the present, through all the phases of the earth's development, as he rides up in the elevator through the numerous floors of an American skyscraper. Some sideline additions: in "ghoul-haunted Province of Perm" there are both a hint at the horrors of Soviet labor camps and a hint at the esoteric world of Edgar Poe's "Ulalume" (brought in by means of similar rhythm— "ghoul-haunted region of Weir," I believe it is). . . . this remote past of the world is actually still here with us, a few floors removed, with its savagery etc. . . . The "I" (*my* room, *my* hotel floor) tragically alone not only in the present world but in one still infinitely larger, with all the past

actually still present. "delicate hands" etc.—the elevators are mostly manned by Negro attendants ("my own in a negative picture"—the Negro's black hands). "Sinking stomachs, rising hearts"—sensations frequently experienced in fast elevators of very tall buildings. Going through all these floors the Negro attendant never reaches paradise, or even a roof garden. And the world, by implication, though having reached from the Archaeozoic to the Present, and from cave dwellings to skyscrapers with roof-gardens, is just as far removed from true Paradise on earth. Incidentally a slight reflexion on the awful position of the Negroes. "The depth of stag-headed hall" etc.—ever so slightly this covers the whole ground covered by the book: Professor Azureus with his flat materialistic world is a kind of Troglodite coming out of his cave. . . . The "long, wrinkled upper lip" adds to the remote indication of his apishness.[33]

The dizziness and difficulty of the passage explicated here are exceptional in Nabokov, a sudden opacity to remind us how little any of us can master of all there is to know. But some imagination and a modicum of curiosity—looking up Keeweenawatin in a good dictionary—are all that are needed to stop the sense plummeting away from us and to provide the incidental surprise of Keewatin/Keewanawan.

Challenges to the understanding, large and small, permeate Nabokov's later fiction at every level. Sometimes they depend on external information, like "Keeweenawatin," although external allusion in Nabokov is in fact much less frequent or troubling than the two characteristics we have already noted in his style: the vertiginous independence of part from part, when a sentence or a paragraph or a chapter springs right away from any expected order of succession, like that sudden elevator ride through time; and the compounded relationship of part and part, like the "faded blue eyes . . . long wrinkled upper lip." The problems Nabokov poses may provide no more than incidental color and a stimulus and reward for curiosity, or they may enrich the world of the book. Krug's remembering *whom* the nurse resembled catches an experience familiar to us all, which Nabokov has ensured we do not merely read about at a distance but reenact it also demonstrates—one of the novel's themes—that even a great mind like Krug's remains subject to the petty limitations of consciousness.

Nabokov's sense of the tussle between the mind and the world prompted him to extraordinary feats of invention in posing and solving and interrelating riddles. As a scientist, he knew that nature gives us some clues and hides others, allows us to pursue wrong trails, offers one false bottom of truth, then another. As an artist, a chess problemist, a one-time conjurer, he found modes to match. He learned to mask or highlight problems or solutions, to distract attention, lull curiosity or send out false alerts or fake clues, or simply keep the mind too busy, in a crowded world and advancing time, to discover a new difficulty or a new resolution. Just as in nature one discovery may precipitate others or upset old orthodoxies, so Nabokov linked solution to solution, so that each answer could trigger or inhibit another: *b* becomes problematic only when *a* has been solved; *c* and *d* suddenly seem clear, though until now we had not even thought them obscure, only after *e* has been answered; *f* and *g* and *v* we recognize in a flash are related to each other and to the old puzzle of *m* and *n*.

Like nature offering a challenge to a scientist's eye, Nabokov lures us to the excitement of discovery, invites us back to tackle new difficulties and uncover new surprises, encourages us as nature does with a sense of plunging to deeper and deeper significance. Solutions to the problems he poses not only enrich the surface of his world, revealing more about an event, an unexpected motive, a complexity of character, but as solutions dislodge other solutions—as they do for the first time in *The Defense*—they can unearth a Rosetta stone of new meaning and lead us to a novel's hidden structure or the moral or metaphysical hieroglyphs on its most secret chamber walls.

Even before he started school, Nabokov had read enough about lepidoptera to be entranced by the wonders of natural mimicry. That discovery may have been the most powerful single boost his imagination ever received. From that time on Nabokov knew that by delving into the particulars of the world the mind could find out in nature a staggering complexity of design within design, a mysterious artfulness within things that seemed to be hidden there for the sake of eventual human discovery. He builds his own worlds the same way, inviting us to probe deeper by layering problem upon problem and welding reward to reward. As we scrape through new strata of meaning, the problems and their solutions start to change in kind, coming at us in an unexpected rush of speed and significance. Suddenly, as in *The Defense*, Nabokov allows us to see something we had never thought to look for: the participation in the novel's world of some force beyond, a pattern in time so clearly visible it discloses its patterner, a creator leaving its creations to be discovered at deeper and deeper levels of understanding.

The narrators of *Transparent Things* recognize the presence of a pencil now before them in the log they can see being cut down in the past, "as we recognized the log in the tree and the tree in the forest and the forest in the world that Jack built." They are the ghosts of characters who have died in the course of Hugh Person's past and are now watching over his present; not conventional spooks, "transparent things," but beings with a new relation to time who can investigate any level they choose of the past as they look at the common stuff of the present, at all these "transparent things, through which the past shines!"

Since on the other hand matter and time and mind are all opaque to us, Nabokov does not let his readers look into one of those conventionally obvious worlds of fiction where the author hurries to let us know everything as soon as it can be told. His style remains lucid in the extreme, but an obscurity placed here or a will-o'-the-wisp gleam there in paragraph after paragraph entices us to explore the book's world for ourselves. Here more than anywhere Nabokov exploits the difference between life and art. In any book we can come back as often as we like—if there is some reason to return. By offering us the excitement, the surprise, the value of discovery Nabokov makes it worth our while to circle back again and again to newly noticed challenges and still-undiscovered rewards. When every detail of one of his complex books becomes so clearly present to our minds that we can see the strangeness of a repeated phrase or the insistence of an emerging pattern—when, in other words, we have ourselves established a new relation to one book's unfolding time—Nabokov lets an opaque world become suddenly translucent and allows us to see through to other worlds beyond.

XIII

Nabokov makes the problems of metaphysics urgent again. He shows how it may well be possible that this world might hide more that we just cannot see, simply because human consciousness wears such blinkers. If there can lurk within the circumscribed world of a novel so much that we cannot notice or do not even have reason to suspect on a first or second encounter, how much more might there be hidden in our own world, where one run through time is all we get.

To those of his readers prepared to keep on looking and wondering at the real world or at his own invented microcosms, Nabokov suggests, at this last level of his work: Might there not be some ultimate artfulness behind things. inviting us to take our world apart and put it together again, to play the creative game of life? Might it not offer us, beyond death, in some new relation to time, the chance to discover at ever deeper levels the particulars and patterns of the world and the creative force that holds it all together? Does there not seem to be something luring us to discover more and more about an infinitely complex world, as if in the thrill of discovery we are granted the closest approach possible to the joy of creation?

In pursuit of ways to express these ideas, Nabokov rethought the possibilities of fiction in profoundly radical ways By the mid-1930s, and even more by the 1950s, he had developed in his fiction an uncanny freedom of part from consecutive part, and at the same time more complex relations of part to part than perhaps any writer before him. In the process he also found how to make his books more and more a contest of discovery between author and reader.

As he mastered the style and structures and strategies he had invented, Nabokov learned to solve the problems he first began to tackle in his own terms and with his own techniques in the mid-1920s. He discarded the angel plumes stolen from sonnet and sacristy, he set aside the direct pronouncements of his early stories, he even passed beyond the barrier he marked out in 1925 between a Space that let us return and a Time that would not. In *Mary* he had established his first themes when he defined consciousness not only by its freedom within the present and its power to recall the past but also by the infrangible line that excludes us from the past except in memory. Against all odds, he learned by the time of *The Defense* how to cross that line, to take us as if into a time where all past is present.

Nabokov never asks us to turn our backs on the world we know, but by the magic of his mature art, he offers us a chance life can never allow. He lets us discover for ourselves how much more valuable this inexhaustible world of ours might look from somewhere beyond human time.

The Defense (Zashchita Luzhina)

I

IN *THE DEFENSE*, his first masterpiece, Nabokov perfected the surface of his art and at the same time discovered how to plumb its
depths.[1]

He aimed here as he had in *King, Queen, Knave* to define our position
between the subhuman and the superhuman, but this time his novel
sheds all the ungainliness of definition to become poetry and drama
and much more. When Franz and Martha and Dreyer appear less than
human, they are also in danger of appearing less than interesting.
Luzhin, on the other hand, unable to face life or other people, seems
both less than human and all the more human for that. If ever we have
felt ill-equipped for our world, we recognize ourselves in him: he
sums up all our vulnerability, all our need for pity. Powerless within
life, he attains through his genius for chess an eerie, unfathomable
might and grace that seem to allow him far beyond the world we
know. He seems "a man of a different dimension": two clumsy dimensions rather than the crowded three of normal human life, and
yet with access to a fourth that transcends our own.

Luzhin's whole being seems bent in the shape of Nabokov's great
question mark: where does human consciousness fit into its universe?
Such a character could be hard to place within a plot, but Nabokov
manages to assign him a fate as poignant as it is formally perfect.

Luzhin's story has three movements. In the first (1910–1912), a boy
who for ten years has only recoiled from life's stings and scratches
discovers his refuge in a gift for chess.

Nothing sustained Nabokov as a writer more than his memories of
a radiantly secure childhood that let him grow up an exceptionally
assured young man. In *Mary* he simply replayed part of his past; in
King, Queen, Knave he avoided it. In *The Defense* he inverted it, as he
would invert so much of his life to create his future heroes: his own
security becomes Luzhin's fear, the parental love he thrived on becomes for Luzhin just another unbearable irritation. Even so, Nabokov gives his character as much as he can of his own past: his dread

of a new French governess, his vexed regret at the journey back from summer manor to wintry city. He also constructs Luzhin out of elements common to any childhood—the bruises and bumps, the clinging to old routines, the threat of a new school, the cruelty of other children—rendered so sharply that they revive our oldest memories and at the same time delineate someone pathologically different from ourselves.

Luzhin construes the whole world as a relentless attack, and wavers between blinkering himself from painful facts and scanning his environment to descry new threats. But all the horrors and humiliations of childhood that he feels so keenly do not turn him into a sentimentalist's youthful martyr. For Luzhin, like any child, learns to erect his own defenses: in his case, retreat, withdrawal, or counterattacks like the tantrums that intimidate his parents and governess, or the pleasure of crushing a beetle beneath a stone "as he tried to repeat the initial, juicy scrunch."

In creating Luzhin, Nabokov uses his eye for psychological quirks common to us all but rarely attended to. He bestows on him an alertness for pattern and a knack for strategic defense: the boy divides up in a special way the number of the cab that takes him to school so he can recall it later, although in fact he will never need to; he slyly steers his walks with his governess as far as possible from the noonday firing of St. Petersburg's cannon. Out of such traits Nabokov manages to construct an exceptional individual and simultaneously to reveal something about any childhood, any mind.

Luzhin's unique features suddenly fuse into a new configuration and his hapless childhood begins to draw to a premature end when at eleven he discovers chess and finds in his mastery of the game an immediate relief from his usual misalignment in life.

Unexpectedly the novel now jumps from 1912, the year of Luzhin's first tournament, to its second movement, summer 1928 and Luzhin's preparations for a new tournament that will decide the challenger for the world championship. Even more surprising, we find him with an attractive and sympathetic woman who not only can decode his inept conversation as courtship, but accepts his advances. Strange, sullen, awkward, almost uninterested in his world, Luzhin remains utterly credible, raising his elbow to defend himself from a wasp, or responding to his future wife's question, how long has he been playing chess?

> He gave no answer and turned away and she felt so embarrassed that she began to reel off a list of all the meteorological indications for yesterday, today and tomorrow. He continued silent and she also fell silent, and then she began to rummage in her handbag, searching agonizingly for a

topic and finding only a broken comb. Suddenly he turned his face to her and said: "Eighteen years, three months and four days."

Her ability to see Luzhin for what he is, her pity, her determination to protect him against life's sharp edges are deeply moving. But tragedy looms when his passion for chess and his love for his fiancée vie for position. In attempting to maintain concentration, the chess side of his mind struggles to crowd out his new craving for tenderness, and the clash ends in his mental collapse during the adjournment of his match against his great rival Turati.

The final movement (winter 1928–1929) begins as Luzhin recovers. For almost twenty years chess has seemed a triumphant retreat from life into a safer realm where he has control. Now as he recovers, his fiancée and his well-meaning doctor convince him that chess itself is the greatest threat life could pose him. Before his mental mist has cleared, they persuade him to erase chess from his consciousness: in its stead they will substitute the caressive love that surrounded him in early childhood.

We enjoy a Luzhin able to taste simple human happiness once again, but his soul remains rolled in a ball. We are torn between two desires: to see him happy with the splendid woman who has married him and to see him return to himself and the triumph of his art. Luzhin's compliant readiness to defend himself by resisting the intrusions of chess leads him straight to disaster, for as his selfhood unfurls, his natural predisposition to detect threats, ponder patterns, and erect defenses convinces him that the patterns of time are repeating his past in order to channel him back to chess. To save himself from this attack on his new life and the new defender he has in his wife, Luzhin feels he must devise an impregnable new counterstrategy like the one he had tried to prepare against Turati. The more desperately he tries to ward off the threat to his happiness, the more relentlessly we sense fate closing in. Unable to shield the warmth of his life from the cold world of chess in any other way, he chooses the unanswerable move of suicide—only to realize that somehow even this last ploy has been twisted into a chess design: as he hurtles down to his death, he sees with horror the flagstones in the courtyard below group themselves into light and dark squares.

Few things in literature are finer than the noble resignation of Luzhin's wife in this closing phase of the novel as she slowly discovers the hopelessness of her attempt to awaken Luzhin to the mundane pleasures of life, or her steadfast courage as she tries to avert the final crash of his mind. Especially heartrending is the theme of the solitude of the self. Although Luzhin's wife notices the impenetrable gloom settling on her husband, he will tell her nothing, convinced as he is that he needs to concentrate on a reply to the secret combination time seems to be preparing against him. She can have no way of knowing his crazy reasoning or of understanding that his suicide was a last pathetic affirmation of allegiance to her, a final tragically loyal attempt to resist being taken away from her and into the flatland of chess.

II

Even before we reach *The Defense*'s rising tragedy, we know we are in the grip of a masterpiece. The novel begins:

> What struck him most was the fact that from Monday on he would be Luzhin. His father—the real Luzhin, the elderly Luzhin, the writer of books—left the nursery with a smile, rubbing his hands (already smeared for the night with transparent cold cream) and with his suede-slippered evening gait padded back to his bedroom. His wife lay in bed. She half raised herself and said: "Well, how did it go?" He removed his gray dressing gown and replied: "We managed. Took it calmly. *Ouf* . . . that's a real weight off my shoulders." "How nice . . . " said his wife, slowly drawing the silk blanket over her. "Thank goodness, thank goodness. . ."

Like a crack tennis serve delivered before we thought we were ready to receive, the first sentence of the book hurtles us at once into young Luzhin's mind. It becomes all the more surprising when the next sentence, rushing back at us to a different part of the court, proves that somehow we must have returned the service: enticed by his father's cold cream and suede-slippered gait, we discover we have left Luzhin behind and stand already in position in his parents bedroom. Somehow, without giving us any quarter, Nabokov shows us we can place ourselves wherever his imagination sends the shots. By paying us the compliment of assuming we can play like champions, he allows us—and this is the secret of his art—to experience the exhilaration of outperforming ourselves.

The rally continues:

> It was indeed a relief. The whole summer—a swift country summer consisting in the main of three smells: lilac, new-mown hay, and dry leaves—the whole summer they had debated the question of when and how to tell him, and they kept putting it off so that it dragged on until the end of August. They had moved around him in apprehensively narrowing circles, but he had only to raise his head and his father would already

be rapping with feigned interest on the barometer dial, where the hand always stood at storm, while his mother would sail away somewhere into the depths of the house, leaving all the doors open and forgetting the long, messy bunch of bluebells on the lid of the piano.

Nabokov can be so confident of the reader because he is so confident of his world. His swift summary of a swift summer—"lilac, new-mown hay, and dry leaves"—lets the lowliest of the senses conjure up duration and depth, a whole season that has anxiously held its breath for this moment. "They had moved around him in apprehensively narrowing circles, but he had only to raise his head"—that one slight gesture switches summary into scene—"and his father would already be rapping with feigned interest on the barometer dial. . . ." The stuck barometer needle, the bluebells in the foreground, the vista into the house: details that create a luminous, Vermeer-like interior within the mind, and recall Kenneth Clark on Vermeer's "flawless sense of interval. Every shape is interesting in itself, and also perfectly related to its neighbors, both in space and on the picture plane."[2] Except that here there is no static canvas but a charged family drama that sends parents recoiling from their child as if from a basilisk—and all in half a sentence.

Still within the same paragraph, Nabokov shifts the scene again:

> The stout French governess who used to read *The Count of Monte Cristo* aloud to him (and interrupt her reading in order to exclaim feelingly "poor, poor Dantès!") proposed to the parents that she herself take the bull by the horns, though this bull inspired mortal fear in her. Poor, poor Dantès did not arouse any sympathy in him, and observing her educational sigh he merely slitted his eyes and rived his drawing paper with an eraser as he tried to portray her protuberant bust as horribly as possible.

Nabokov knows that with the right guidance, the right detail, our minds can move with far more freedom than we think. He builds up Luzhin's world not through a ponderous accumulation of leaden fact but by a limpid mobility of imagination that makes each speck live and all space cohere.

We began abruptly within Luzhin's mind, not knowing why he should be struck most by the fact that from Monday on he will be Luzhin. Who is this young boy, and why does he inspire such terror in his parents and his governess? Like Shakespeare introducing another mysterious and sullen son, Nabokov heightens the curiosity by delay. Instead of answering our question, he extends Luzhin's world another twenty years ahead and then returns again for another extreme close-up on the past:

Many years later, in an unexpected year of lucidity and enchantment, it was with swooning delight that he recalled these hours of reading on the veranda, buoyed up by the sough of the garden. The recollection was saturated with sunshine and the sweet, inky taste of the sticks of licorice, bits of which she used to hack off with blows of her penknife and persuade him to hold under his tongue. And the tacks he had once placed on the wickerwork seat destined, with crisp, crackling sounds, to receive her obese croup were in retrospect equivalent with the sunshine and the sounds of the garden, and the mosquito fastening onto his skinned knee and blissfully raising its rubescent abdomen. A ten-year-old boy knows his knees well, in detail—the itchy swelling that had been scrabbled till it bled, the white traces of fingernails on the suntanned skin, and all those scratches which are the appended signatures of sand grains, pebbles, and sharp twigs.

Unexpectedly Luzhin gazes back on those tiresome afternoons of the past with a sense of swooning delight: unexpected, but a sure psychological touch, for we treasure fondly even the aches of the past—because they no longer have the power to hurt, because they now constitute part of our own unique selves, because they cannot be retrieved. By introducing Luzhin's long backward glance at this point Nabokov also alters the way we assimilate Luzhin's whole past. As a child, Luzhin flinches from life's pinpricks and jagged edges, but although in this scene he recalls a tack on a seat, the crisp crack of a wicker seat, a skinned knee, a mosquito's bothersome bite, here every trifle seems strangely precious, as if the very fact that it has been recollected, against all the odds, makes it somehow hallowed, magically preserved from oblivion. Like air from which every mote of dust and every floating microbe has been removed, the past in *The Defense* stands out with an unforeseen clarity and radiance, preserving in all its sharpness the pain Luzhin felt or the pain he caused, but removing the menace that had once charged every moment. Even before he lets us understand the tension in the Luzhin household, Nabokov opposes present threat and the indestructible security of the past.

Young Luzhin, taught until now by his governess, will have to begin school after this summer vacation. His father, dreading his difficult son's reaction and expecting another tantrum, mentions among other things, and as if in compensation, that he will be called by his surname like a grown-up. At this

the son blushed, began to blink, threw himself supine on his pillow, opening his mouth and rolling his head ("Don't squirm like that," said his father apprehensively, noting his confusion and expecting tears), but did not break into tears and instead buried his face in the pillow, making bursting sounds with his lips into it, and suddenly rising—crumpled, warm, with glistening eyes—he asked rapidly whether at home, too, they would call him Luzhin.

Luzhin's head buried in the pillow, the bursting sounds he makes with his lips, his touchingly childish question—these details that defy his parents' expectations belong to a world irreducible to stock formulas like temper and tears.

On the day the Luzhins drive to the station for the train back to town, they suddenly see their apprehensions justified. Their son turns rigid; the chill in the air seems to emanate from his ominous mood. His mother, noticing the look in his eye as she tries to arrange his cloak, snatches her hand back. At the station, Luzhin's tension bursts its banks. Pretending to stroll casually to the end of the platform, he runs off through the wood and back to the manor to hide for the winter and live on cheese and jam from the pantry. His parents chase him to the manor, a burly peasant retrieves him from the attic, he is bundled off to town. Nothing can halt the threat that time holds in store: come Monday, he will be "Luzhin" and at school.

The surprise of the novel's first line never diminishes, no matter how well we know the book. But our sense of the rightness of that line, as of so much else in the book, continues to expand until the very end. Not once during the course of the novel do we hear the first name that will be ousted by "Luzhin" on his first day at school. Only on the novel's last page, when he has already locked the bathroom door, clambered up to the window, and thrown himself through it to his death, do we find out his name:

> The door was burst in. "Aleksandr Ivanovich, Aleksandr Ivanovich," roared several voices.
>
> But there was no Aleksandr Ivanovich.

And from the first line of the novel to that last line the battle between adult and child in Luzhin, the battle between the rosy past and the thorny future, never ceases for a moment.

III

Ever since Rousseau and Wordsworth, writers have found warm, sunny, dust-free nooks in their fiction for glimpses of their childhood. No one has valued their early years more than Nabokov, and, in the ten-year-old Luzhin who knows his knees well, he revisits his own tenth summer and invites us along. He even has Luzhin look back with as fond a recollective gaze as his own. Drawing on his own "perfect past," he creates a world built for happiness—and then places in it someone whose nature condemns him to grief. As a child Nabokov was "a *Wunderkind*, a precocious genius," inventing stories, feasting on the beauty of the Eden around him. Even before he learns chess, young Luzhin too stands out as different, but for him the whole world resembles some great Rappaccini's garden where every plant spells death: instead of opening him up to life, his special genius closes him off.

Nabokov's double perspective allows him to make Luzhin's childhood both luminous and chillingly unhappy. Then, when Luzhin finds himself thrust suddenly into the adult world, his love for his wife and his love for chess grapple for ascendancy as tragedy gapes below. For most novelists a conflict as deadly as this would suffice, but without ever lessening the force of the drama, Nabokov adds much more.

At the start of the novel's third phase Luzhin's doctor and his fiancée impress upon him the deadly danger of chess. So well do they succeed that before he fully resurfaces he suppresses all consciousness of the game. His recovery seems a new awakening to his world. Strolling in the sanatorium garden, he even asks his fiancée the names of flowers. Since chess, and with it all his recent past, remains off limits, his thoughts revert again and again to childhood:

> His pre-school, pre-chess childhood, which he had never thought about before, dismissing it with a slight shudder so as not to find dormant horrors and humiliating insults there, proved now to be an amazingly safe spot, where he could take pleasant excursions that sometimes brought a piercing pleasure. Luzhin himself was unable to understand whence the excitement—why the image of the fat French governess with the three bone buttons on one side of her skirt, that drew together whenever she lowered her enormous croup into an armchair—why the image that had then so irritated him, now evoked in his breast a feeling of tender constriction.

For the first time, Luzhin has returned to thoughts of his past. More than that: he seems to have landed right in a completely revised version of his childhood where all pain has been edited out. After the match with Turati, chess thoughts crowded his brain until they turned the city around him into a swarm of phantomic images. When a gruff voice at his ear prompted "Go home," the dazed Luzhin, instead of making for his fiancée's apartment, had tried to return through the streets of Berlin to the Russian country home of his childhood. His panicky stumble "homewards" ends in a blackout. When he wakes from his coma, he sees the sanatorium doctor leaning over him, his black, curly beard recalling that of the peasant who retrieved Luzhin from the attic after his childhood flight homeward. As he looks out the window from his hospital bed, the trees beyond evoke within his blurred consciousness the trees around the old manor, and the window seems filled with "the same happy radiance." His doctor and his fiancée swaddle him with concern, the world appears benign, chess remains unknown: he has returned to his childhood, sanitized.

For Nabokov, the bounty of life is ultimately the bounty of the past: what we perceive is "a form of memory, even at the moment of its perception."[3] But time locks us even from our own past, and memory can provide no more than an unsteady glimpse in a rear-vision mirror. Luzhin's genius for chess has already allowed him into a dimension of harmony and control beyond the normal chaos of the human. Now at first blush his virtual return to the past might seem another triumph over human limits, but this childhood paradise will not long be regained. Slowly, it becomes a descent into hell. For Nabokov, only art at its best could point to an eventual exit from time's prison by creating its special worlds where every trifle is guaranteed immunity from oblivion. Standing somehow outside life, art can perhaps prefigure a state of consciousness with unqualified access to the paradise of its past. Luzhin's return *within* life to a talc-soft childhood simply denies the fact of mortal time, robs him of two-thirds of his past, ignores his prickly self, and even suppresses chess, his sketchy surrogate for art.

Life—or time—takes its revenge. With the blessed intractability of human personality, Luzhin's selfhood slowly revives. His natural wariness, his eye for pattern, and his instinct for defense all tell him that something ominous has stirred in his fate and that he should plan a counterattack. Though he cannot detect the nature of the threat, we, looking on from outside, can begin to guess. Constrained against its nature to repeat itself rather than advance, life now replays the past all too well. The innocent reprise of childhood, instituted to protect Luzhin from chess, now begins to follow the original contours of his childhood and so to lead straight back to his first discovery of chess. Luzhin meets a man he had known at school, who vaguely recalls him—though Luzhin denies the recollection—as a newly risen chess star. When a visitor from the Soviet Union mentions the aunt who first showed him the moves of chess, Luzhin at last remembers, and fills with "the keen delight of being a chess player, and pride, and relief, and that physiological sensation of harmony which is so well known to artists." Almost in the same instant he realizes that the combinations of time forming around him have developed one stage further ("country house . . . town . . . school . . . aunt") and in a panic he tries to devise some defense against the pattern closing in on him. Instead he comes across a tiny pocket chessboard his wife had overlooked, and keeps it and his chess thoughts hidden—just as he had been obliged to do when he first discovered chess as a child.

As he strives to fathom the combinations forming around him, Luzhin lapses into the gloom of lone concentration. Unwittingly he now relives not only the end of the first phase of his life, his childhood drift toward chess, but the end of his second phase. As he climbed up the chess ladder and grappled with Turati for the right to dislodge the world champion, he had sought without rest for an impregnable defense against Turati's famous new opening. Then, the pressure of concentration drove Luzhin to collapse. Now, worse still lies ahead.

As Luzhin's oppression deepens, one repetition of his past crowds on another: his chess-free childhood, his flight back to the manor, his discovery of chess, his truancy from school to play the game, his lonely years on the chess circuit under the impresario Valentinov, his search for a defense against Turati, his benumbed flight from the adjourned Turati game back to the murky mirage of the manor. Even the surprise moves that the by now terrified Luzhin makes to break the patterns of repetition succeed only in spawning other repetitions in still denser swarms.

Some leap out from the page, others remain too oblique or too subtly transmuted to be detected at all on a first reading. And in such a profusion of interlocking patterns, nothing much can be seen at first except fate closing in on Luzhin. As we discern more, we can distinguish two warring factions: one that promotes Luzhin's wife and the snug repetition of childhood security she can provide, and another, apparently more powerful, that twists this repetition, with many a fancy flourish, into a repetition of Luzhin's discovery of chess and his resumption of the abandoned match against Turati. When Luzhin at last perceives the point of the attack the fates are mounting against him—that he should leave the haven his wife offers and return to the chill of chess and the tutelage of the callous and calculating Valentinov—the thought of such a future fills him with dread. Against such an attack, he can envisage only one defense: he will drop out of the game, he will end his life. As he plummets to his death, he sees the shadows in the courtyard below

> divide into dark and pale squares, and at the instant when Luzhin unclenched his hand, at the instant when icy air gushed into his mouth, he saw exactly what kind of eternity was obligingly and inexorably spread out before him.

Luzhin cannot escape himself or the need for defense and the alertness to pattern that made it so natural for chess to fill his life.

In the last few months, indeed, all the unique mental powers that lead to his tragedy have been raised to vertiginous new heights. As a boy, he shut out life for the sake of chess. As a man, he has allowed his wife to reopen him a little to his world. At this point he begins to look for combinations and strategies at work not merely on the chessboard but unfolding in life itself around him. This seems close to insanity—except for the fact that he gains a haunting, impermissible insight into the design of time. For the patterns are not mere delusion: situated beyond his world, we can as we reread detect patterns closing in upon Luzhin even before he notices them. But that *he* should be able to detect the patterns of time as they evolve should provoke in us a metaphysical shiver.

The Defense begins as a world that cherishes the particular and the unpredictable: suede slippers and bluebells and scrabbled knees; the strange bursting sound a boy makes into his pillow, his wonder at becoming "Luzhin," his futile flight back to the family manor. Slowly but inexorably this world that so generously grants the particular its due has become replete with pattern, and Luzhin's own bizarre particularity in turn permits him to see this pattern imposed on his world from beyond. Perhaps for all the triumphant independence of the things of this world, Nabokov suggests, some force beyond does put its own stamp on the myriad accidents of our lives.

IV

In *The Defense* Nabokov has learned to put one part of a world together with another, selecting details, controlling angles, shifting foci, proliferating patterns, with a speed, economy, fluidity, and harmony fiction has rarely attained. By his masterly handling of the relationship of part and part he has refined the classical narrative virtues to new standards of perfection.

So much for the surface of his art, itself no mere matter of verbal style; now for the depths. Because in *The Defense* Nabokov also rethinks the relationship between author and reader, he discloses here for the first time that he will be one of the great innovators of fiction. He would later declare that just as the real struggle in a chess problem was not between black and white but between the problem's designer and its hypothetical solver, so the great drama of a novel lay less in the conflict between its characters than in the tussle between its author and its reader. Perhaps the chess analogy came to mind because it is in *The Defense* that he first deliberately poses problems for the reader from the first sentence (why is this boy to be called Luzhin from Monday?) to the last (why are his first name and patronymic withheld until now?).

The real problems Nabokov poses the reader are those set by the patterns he weaves in time. Why do patterns of repetition pervade the last phase of the novel? Do they exist only in Luzhin's head? Does Nabokov expect us merely to marvel at their intricate interlacement, as if they were so much Celtic knotwork? Does he tease us to strain nail and finger to unravel what he means to be inextricable, as some readers suppose? Or does he overcomplicate the design inadvertently, so that it can never be untied?

Patterns that seem intended to pose us problems whose solutions might lurk just over the page or back in what we have just read begin to interlock with other patterns to the point where solutions seem impossible. At this point some readers conclude either that Nabokov has been toying with us or that the sheer pleasure of design has after all been his only objective. But Nabokov the lepidopterist knew the convolutions of nature's designs and that they could with patience be slowly disentangled.

He was also a composer of chess problems. In *The Defense* he learned not only to pile pattern upon pattern but to pose problems as exact as those he could set in a chess diagram. And like his chess problems, he expected his fictional ones to be solved.

After unfolding events in steady sequence for several chapters the narrative suddenly jumps sixteen years in the middle of a paragraph to introduce Luzhin seated in conversation with a woman kept nameless and off camera. Before she becomes visible the scene clouds over and hangs suspended. Nabokov then turns aside for a whole chapter to Luzhin's father—the only time in the novel we leave Luzhin's viewpoint for so long—and his account of the sixteen years the previous chapter so ostentatiously skipped over. Only at the beginning of the third chapter in this sequence do we return to the scene left in midair. The cameras roll again, and we find

> Luzhin still fiddling with the handbag and still addressing his blurry companion whereupon she unblurs, takes it away from him, mentions Luzhin Senior's death, and becomes a distinct part of the design.

After presenting this résumé in the foreword to his English version of the novel, Nabokov proceeds to compare the whole sequence to a chess problem. He expected some solution, but what?

V

Elsewhere I have explained in detail my suggested solutions to *The Defense*'s problems.[4] Let me now summarize them starkly.

One group of patterns insistently associates Luzhin's grandfather with the boy's discovery of chess, another associates Luzhin's father with the woman who so precipitously enters Luzhin's life. The curious fact is that each of these patterns begins shortly after grandfather or father has died.

Long before *The Defense*, Nabokov had treated of the mysteries of a hereafter in poems and stories and the meditations of his private notebooks. His future fiction would explicitly involve characters who die in the course of the story, participating after their death in the lives of others. In tackling the problem of an afterlife and influences from the beyond in *Pale Fire*, he would write that key phrase, "Not text, but texture." I suggest that Nabokov invites us to deduce from the riddling patterns of *The Defense*'s texture what we cannot read in any statement within the novel's text: that Luzhin's dead grandfather has somehow led his grandson to chess, that Luzhin's dead father leads his son to the woman he marries.

Luzhin's grandfather was a violinist and a composer, "albeit a somewhat arid one and susceptible, in his mature years, to the doubtful splendors of virtuosity." On the anniversary of his death the violinist who plays grandfather's music for a memorial concert rhapsodizes during a break that he would rather play chess than resume the music: "Combinations like melodies. You know, I can simply *hear* the moves. . . . The game of the gods. Infinite possibilities." "They are awaiting you, Maestro," someone calls, but already his paean to chess has inspired Luzhin: still entirely ignorant of the game, this boy who has done little but shrink from life now quivers with eagerness to learn. Before long he is a grand master, and at the peak of his career he fights for the right to challenge for the world championship. A strange echo rings out as someone comes to fetch him ("They are awaiting you, Maestro") to the hall where he will play Turati. In this, Luzhin's finest game, musical imagery repeatedly floods across the chessboard, from the "muted violins" of the first quiet moves to the "musical tempest" and the "*agitato*" of its climax. These and other patterns associating Luzhin's chess and his grandfather suggest that after his death his grandfather has detected Luzhin's alertness to threat, his gift for defense, his love for recombinative pattern, and has prompted the boy to take up chess as a vicarious outlet for his own desire for virtuoso combinational play.

Luzhin's father, a writer of uplifting tales for boys, a sentimentalist fond of treacly resolutions, dreams that his son may become an artist or a musical prodigy. On learning the boy's real genius, he realizes that his son in fact remains as baffling to him as ever. He loses the boy to the impresario Valentinov, but just before his death he tries to write a novella, *The Gambit*, that will commemorate—and prettify—his son's chess career. Less than a month after the father's death, the perfect woman suddenly enters Luzhin's life—and it is at this point that the narrative obtrusively shifts back to Luzhin Senior's view of the Valentinov years, his plans for *The Gambit*, his death—before the scene unfreezes, and the woman declares her regret at "not having known your father. . . . He must have been very kind, very earnest and very fond of you." (Luzhin sits silent in reply.) Just as the images of music that sound line after line in Luzhin's game with Turati bear witness to the lurking presence of the old composer, his grandfather, so here a jarring shift in the story line marks the strange intrusion of the old storyteller, Luzhin Senior, into his son's meeting with the woman he will marry.

This woman at first appears to offer Luzhin the adult life that his passion for chess and Valentinov's cool policy of suppressing the boy's development have denied him. But Luzhin cannot cope with both his most difficult tournament *and* this first budding of his social self. After his collapse, he seems to have been guided back to childhood. His fiancée, strolling through the sanatorium garden with Luzhin "in new bedroom slippers made of soft leather," thinks for some reason

> of a book she had read in childhood in which all the difficulties in the life of a schoolboy, who had run away from home together with a dog he had saved, were resolved by a convenient (for the author) fever—not typhus, not scarlet fever, but just "a fever"—and the young stepmother whom he had not loved hitherto so cared for him that he suddenly began to appreciate her and would call her Mamma, and a warm tearlet would roll down her face and everything was fine.

Luzhin's fiancée cannot recall the book's title, but she rightly senses that its sentimentalist tone almost defines the new atmosphere surrounding Luzhin at the sanatorium: in fact, the book is none other than *Tony's Adventures*, by Luzhin Senior. When she and Luzhin are married, a woodcut hangs between their beds, showing "a child prodigy in a nightgown that reached to his heels playing on an enormous piano, while his father, wearing a gray dressing gown and carrying a candle, stood stock-still, with the door ajar"—exactly the image that had been Luzhin Senior's most private and cherished dream for his son. And when Luzhin sinks into his final gloom, the only recourse his wife can devise is to urge him again and again to visit his father's grave.

Unable in life to complete his son's story in the festive hues he would like, Luzhin Senior seems after his death to have selected this compassionate and sensitive woman as the easy resolution to all the difficulties in his son's life: Luzhin may keep his chess, but he should also be allowed to know the pleasure of adult love. But the entry of this woman into his life resolves Luzhin's difficulties no better than his father's fervently awaited discovery of the boy's genius had resolved everything in his past: the tension between Luzhin's love for his fiancée and his chess only brings on his collapse. After the collapse Luzhin Senior seems to decide that if his son cannot function as an adult and a chess champion, then let him be returned to the security he could never be made to feel in childhood. Luzhin had fled deliriously through Berlin to his remembered manor; now he wakes at the sanatorium, where his fiancée and his doctor (whose Assyrian beard reminds Luzhin of the peasant his father sent to fetch him the first time he ran back to the manor) convince him to suppress chess and to accept the snug childlike happiness of the home he will move into after his marriage. Like all Luzhin Senior's plans, the resolution simply ignores all the difficulties of life: Luzhin is not a child, he is not an adult, and he cannot exist without chess.

Other patterns in the novel suggest that after the woman is introduced into Luzhin's life, his grandfather fights back by making Luzhin construe the room where he now spends his evenings with his fiancée and her parents in terms of hostile chess forces ranked against him. But instead of making him reject his fiancée and return to chess, the conflict within Luzhin leads to his blackout. His subsequent restoration to health, home, and a wholesome repetition of his past seems wholly his father's work, but grandfather, the virtuoso, now turns this new move against his opponent, for he makes the repetition of childhood lead into a repetition of Luzhin's initial discovery of chess. Around this basic strategy he unfurls flamboyant flourishes, complications of the repetition theme, as if in scorn of his opponent's naiveté.

Beyond father and grandfather, another more powerful force coordinates their conflict to its own more farsighted ends. Grandfather seeks to develop the chess line in Luzhin's life, father to advance the line of wife and home. Neither wishes him to die. A force beyond them, however, allows their clash to push Luzhin inexorably toward death, his only possible relief. Promoting both Luzhin's chess skills and his new attention to life, this overarching fate establishes a new synthesis from the opposition of grandfather's thesis (Chess, or Art) and father's antithesis (Wife and Home, or Life). In the last phase of Luzhin's life, this designing force harnesses the competing repetitions of Luzhin's past to raise his combinational talent to an uncanny new level where he can detect the patterns of time: a new triumph of his strange mind, but so disturbing in its implications that he feels he has no choice but to take his own poor life.

Perhaps beyond death Luzhin may find still further scope for his genius in detecting the patterns of time, as his father and grandfather already appear to have found richer possibilities for their more meager talents. Examined in more depth, *The Defense*'s patterns seem to intimate that

> Luzhin's death may mean a return "home" to the past, where the fundamental goodness of things will somehow disclose itself on a level beyond life that does not scant the difficulties of life at *this* level. From the blank of death, perhaps, he will awaken to a world where the past becomes both his haven, home, defense, *and* the new domain of his art where he can endlessly explore the pattern of time.
>
> At this level *The Defense* suggests that there may be a design in fate, even in a hierarchy of fates, that allows us the maximum opportunity to become ourselves, even when in mortal perspective our lives might seem stunted, tormented, the sport of the immortals.[5]

The conflict between grandfather's sterile "art" and father's saccharine "life" appears to have been resolved by a mysterious artfulness that lurks somewhere behind life.

VI

In *The Defense* Nabokov has taken great care not to present his metaphysics in overtly positive form. As in *King, Queen, Knave*, but now much more resonantly, he inverts all he treasures in order to put his ideas to the test. Always grateful for the security that surrounded him in his own idyllic childhood, he now inflicts on Luzhin in his boyhood a disposition that makes him flinch at the most innocent objects and events. Finding a respite from our human helplessness in the control art allows, Nabokov bestows genius on Luzhin, but a genius for something less than art, something that offers him a retreat from life but no power whatever to resolve its tensions. Blessed with a marriage that revived the security of his childhood in another guise, serenely happy with a woman who understood every nuance of his art, Nabokov marries Luzhin off to a woman whose very concern to protect him from his art makes her a danger and a threat and condemns him to the solitude of his paranoid ruminations. Predisposed to imagine that one day we may relive our past in a timeless world free from all danger of loss, Nabokov imposes on Luzhin a repetition of his past that at first seems soothing but soon degenerates into a stultifying flight from reality and then into a nightmarish trap. Longing to peer further behind life than life allows, Nabokov endows Luzhin with that very gift until it drives the poor man to his death.

In Luzhin's fate Nabokov allows everything most precious in his own life to turn to bitterness. Yet even here, he suggests, even for someone who has had only the inverse of all his own advantages, there may lurk, at some ultimate level, beyond the conflict of father and grandfather, a force designing life with infinite tenderness, preparing for Luzhin in death a painless recovery of the painful past and an outlet and a fulfillment for his special powers that will recoup all the horrors of his life.

VII

As an artist Nabokov knew how to impart life and a sense of its unique value to every detail, and at the same time to preserve the coherence of all the parts of a world. But for all the accuracy of its indelible details and the harmony of its parts, Luzhin's world cannot be explained solely on its own terms.

Luzhin uneasily suspects time of forming a pattern around him, and the insight drives him mad. Even on a first reading of *The Defense* it disturbs us that Luzhin seems so justified in looking for an explanation behind events, although of course he cannot find it. At the end of our first reading, we suppose that the fates controlling his life are not to be identified, unless perhaps as the novelist himself. Even after several rereadings, the participation in Luzhin's life of his dead grandfather, his dead father, and a force beyond them orchestrating their counterpoint might well seem a preposterous idea. But because we are outside Luzhin's world, Nabokov can alert us to the special way that world coheres. By posing problems like the sudden narrative shift to Luzhin's future wife—her blurred introduction, Luzhin Senior's stepping forward, her delayed reentry, in focus at last—he invites us to detect gradually levels of action and significance the story at first appears not even to hint at.

Our first close look at *The Defense* began with the surprise of that opening sentence that places us within Luzhin before we know where we are. Stranger still, we withdraw to follow his father, and only after scanning the background through his eyes do we return to the scene first glimpsed: Luzhin Senior telling his son he must commence school and begin the next phase of his life. Though hardly ready for his new "grown-up" name, the boy will be "Luzhin"—and only by that name do we know him until his death.

Several chapters later, another scene rushes up before we are ready: Luzhin suddenly sixteen years older, talking to a woman. Once again we leave the scene in midair, follow Luzhin Senior, learn through him of the intervening years, and return to the uncompleted scene. As if to prove that once again it is Luzhin's father who pushes his son, though still half a child, into grown-up life, the woman who bursts into Luzhin's life will never be known to us by any name but "Mrs. Luzhin" (in Russian, simply "Luzhina"). The sudden attack of the novel's first sentence seems more surprising than ever—and more justified.

At the end of *The Defense*'s first chapter, Luzhin runs back to the manor and clambers in through the open drawing-room window.

> Once inside the drawing room, he stopped and listened. A daguerreo-type of his maternal grandfather—black sidewhiskers, violin in hand—stared down at him, but then completely vanished, dissolving in the glass, as soon as he regarded the portrait from one side—a melancholy amusement that he never omitted when he entered the drawing room.

Luzhin's little ritual with the portrait of his grandfather appears at first simply one of Nabokov's superbly unexpected details, so right, so full of its own self-assured life. From the perspective we have reached now, however, it seems a sort of signature to the fact that Luzhin has been lured back to the manor and up to the attic—where a cracked chessboard fails to interest him—by a recently dead grandfather who has not yet learned to prepare his moves.[6]

That window through which Luzhin climbs of course prefigures the last window he will struggle through before he plunges to his death. Some force has designed Luzhin's fate from the first, and the window here signals that someone knows the final outcome, still twenty years off, of Luzhin's impulse to retreat from life. The window also identifies at the very outset the ultimate designer's plan to harness the contrary aims of the grandfather whom Luzhin sees behind his glass rectangle and the father and black-bearded assistant whom Luzhin watches through *another* window, one page later, storming up to his attic retreat. The first chapter ends with details as fine as those with which it begins—and with patterns just as pointed.

Patterns are visible everywhere from the first, but they seem to mean nothing. It is essential to Nabokov's purposes that the profuse chess notes in *The Defense* at first yield no more than the pleasure of their own muted melody and only much later can be heard as an elaborate fugue, a drama of intrigue and counterintrigue, and a philosophical debate between life and art resolved by the artfulness of life. If he can conceive and conceal completely within the novel the astoundingly complex and harmonious spiral of Luzhin's fate. what might the endless clutter of life itself hide?

The patterns of *The Defense* have Bach's melodic beauty and bracing rigor of design, but to this exhilarating combination Nabokov adds more. In our century science has disclosed undreamt-of worlds within worlds within worlds, our cosmos has stretched and our microcosms have shrunk to unfathomable dimensions. If physics can reveal a universe so much more multileveled and elaborate in design than was ever expected, Nabokov seems to ask, why may not our metaphysics do the same?

VIII

In *The Defense* Nabokov has written for the first time a novel that seizes the imagination from the beginning, creates individual and unforgettable characters and subjects them to a destiny that moves us. Luzhin, doomed whatever choice he makes, either condemned to the solitude of his genius or fated to suppress his very self if he seeks ordinary human love, and his wife, whose heroic compassion and self-abnegation prove of no avail—these two are among the warmest and most touching characters in fiction.

By means of their story Nabokov treats us to a study in abnormality, genius and insanity, a domestic tragedy, and a poignant portrayal of the solitude and vulnerability of the self. He examines the child within the adult, the adult within the child, the relationship of individual and family. He analyzes the role of the artist in human life and adds a critique of sentimentalism and sterile virtuosity. He considers memory and our relation to our past, fate and our relation to our future, and the intolerant advance of human time. He charts the strange position of human consciousness and explores the possibility that a hereafter may hold some richer relation to time and the self. He wonders whether the independent particulars of our world may form some design we cannot see, and whether our random life may conceal some almost unimaginable artfulness beyond. Certainly he does all this in such a way as to advance the whole art of fiction, but the misconception that his work is all style and no content can arise only from his ability to integrate so many ideas so seamlessly into the shape of his stories.

Besides, Nabokov values a new world that can spin around our own more than some new headings for an old chart of familiar ideas. What matters in the novel are the details, the gestures, the pulses of feeling that create Luzhin's world: the hungry, blind kiss that he plants on his future wife; the laceless shoes that she abandons under a hotel bed; Luzhin bending warily over a dahlia that, "maybe might bite," and his surprise that it does not smell.

CHAPTER 15

Negative ard Positive: Berlin, 1929–1930

I

IN AUGUST 1929, as *Graf Zeppelin* cut its silent course through the clouds and around the world, Nabokov was enjoying his own shadow-skimmed patch of tranquillity below at Kolberg. He had all but completed a novel far better than anything he had written so far, he had the Ullstein empire keenly interested in his recent work, there seemed to be every chance he would soon be able to support himself by writing alone. He joked to his mother: "High time to kill Luzhin and give his corpse to Ullstein so they can buy it to dissect and trans-late."[1] His confidence was sadly misplaced: the better his work be-came, the more difficult it would be to sell it outside the émigré press. In two years' time instead of beginning to build at Kolberg he and Véra could no longer keep up payments and would have to let the land revert to the vendor.[2] There would be only one compensation: that out-of-town site would serve nicely as the murder scene for *Despair*.

Toward the end of August Véra took the train to Berlin and found two furnished rooms, a parlor and a bedroom, in the "vast and gloomy" apartment of General von Bardeleben and his family.[3] At the beginning of *The Gift* Nabokov describes Fyodor's sensation on mov-ing to a house within the same neighborhood: a section of street that once glided by without any connection to him would now acquire an interior life of its own. The Nabokovs knew the feeling well. After their marriage they had lived at 13 Luitpoldstrasse, then just around the corner in Motzstrasse with Frau von Lepel, then three blocks away in Passauer Strasse with the von Dallwitzes. Now they were back in quiet Luitpoldstrasse, number 27.

As Vladimir Nabokov settled back into the shrinking center of Russian Berlin, Vladimir Sirin began to take his rightful place at the center of Russian émigré literature: in October, the first of three long install-ments of *The Defense* appeared in *Sovremennye Zapiski* (*Contemporary Annals*).[4]

Without question the best journal in the emigration, the Paris-based *Sovremennye Zapiski* continued the long tradition of the Russian "thick journal," in tsarist times a monthly mix of literature and thought with a decidedly antigovernment tone. In the emigration, with far fewer contributors, a much smaller audience, and more limited funds, *Sovremennye Zapiski* could be published only three or four times a year, but usually filled 500 pages or more. Although edited not by writers but by four Socialist Revolutionary politicians, the journal kept itself independent of party politics and maintained a literary standard consistently higher, many thought, than even the best of prerevolutionary journals. *Sovremennye Zapiski* survived from 1920 until Hitler took Paris in 1940. Its rivals were neither so enduring—only one other journal lasted even half as long—nor so distinguished, and since it appeared at such wide intervals and offered so much, readers and reviewers awaited each issue as a major feast within the literary year.

Only one major reproach could be made against the journal. Not professional littérateurs themselves, *Sovremennye Zapiski*'s editors defined their task as serving Russian culture. To them, that meant keeping to the well-tried names: prose writers Ivan Bunin, Dmitri Merezhkovsky, Alexey Remizov, Alexander Kuprin, Ivan Shmelev, Boris Zaitsev, and Mark Aldanov, poets Zinaida Gippius, Vladislav Khodasevich, and Marina Tsvetaeva. By 1926 it had become a frequent complaint that *Sovremennye Zapiski* was not welcoming young writers not established before the emigration. Sirin, preeminent among the younger generation, had had short lyrics published in *Sovremennye Zapiski* in 1921 and 1922, when it was only one among many journals, but only in 1927 did his long "A University Poem" and his story "Terror" appear. From October 1929, that neglect changed utterly: all seven of Sirin's remaining novels (plus an unfinished eighth novel and a couple of stories) would be published in thirty-eight of the forty-one issues still to come, sometimes in chunks more than eighty pages long. In Sirin's wake other young prose writers—Nina Berberova, Gayto Gazdanov—bobbed up and down in the journal.

Before October 1929 Sirin books had been borrowed from Russian libraries and he had been discussed by Russian writers—Khodasevich commented that almost everyone had praised him by word of mouth if not in print[5]—but he had not commanded inescapable attention. Although one critic (in a *hostile* reaction to the first installment of *The Defense*) called Sirin a writer who had quickly won widespread attention for his exceptional mastery of Russian verse and after switching modes had with the same speed earned a position for himself as a "wonderful master of Russian prose," most commentators claimed Sirin had hitherto been neglected—perhaps even deliberately—by the critics.[6] Both the sheer quality of *The Defense* and the fact of its publication in *Sovremennye Zapiski* made it impossible to ignore him any longer.

In a literary conversation in Paris in the autumn of 1929 one of Sovremennye Zapiski's editors, Mark Vishnyak, announced that in the next
issue something wonderful would be published. Nina Berberova, one
of the two most promising prose writers of the younger generation,
felt a rush of excitement. "Who?" "Nabokov," answered Vishnyak.
Berberova's excitement faded: Vishnyak was no critic, and Sirin's
work did not deserve *that* kind of response.

But when the fortieth issue of *Sovremennye Zapiski* appeared, in its
invariable sober, scholarly format and drab cream cover, Berberova
sat down to those first chapters of *The Defense* and read through them
twice. "A tremendous, mature, sophisticated modern writer was before me, a great Russian writer, like a Phoenix, was born from the fire
and ashes of revolution and exile. Our existence from now on acquired a meaning. All my generation were justified. We were saved."[7]

André Levinson, one of the most talented of émigré critics, reported
the same sense of shock. He described a reviewer's mechanically cutting the pages of another tome: "Soudain, vous vous sentez projeté
hors de ce reposant automatisme, agrippé, et les tempes battantes, le
coeur à la fois dilaté et oppressé, vous restez en . . . un délicieux sus-
pens. . . . vous vous sentez, tout à coup, en présence d un grand
livre."[8]

No one could respond calmly. One critic wrote: "How terrible, to
see life as Sirin does! How wonderful, to see life as Bunin does!" Nabokov's reaction to this review was revealing: "I read [Kirill] Zaitsev's
article and had a good laugh—not at Zaitsev, but at the fact that in life
and in my whole mental makeup I am quite indecently optimistic
and buoyant, whereas Bunin, as far as I know, is rather inclined to
dejection and black thoughts—but in Zaitsev's article it comes out the
other way round."[9] Bunin himself, until now the undisputed master
of émigré literature, commented on *The Defense*: "This kid has
snatched a gun and done away with the whole older generation, myself included."[10]

II

Among the few negative voices, by far the most influential was that of
Georgy Adamovich.

When he arrived in the emigration in 1923, Adamovich had two
slight books of verse to his credit. Before the end of the decade he had
become one of the two foremost émigré critics and the literary law-
giver of Russian Paris. In newspapers, journals, illustrated weeklies,
in literary clubs and the cafés of Montparnasse, he struck the tuning

fork of "the Paris note": the despair of the exile, the anguish of the modern soul, too heartfelt to heed form and somehow truer and more sincere as its verse approached the artlessness of a diary. Nabokov disliked much about Adamovich and his influence: the attempt to decree the correct response to "our times," the hostility to formal mastery, the programmatic gloom, the spirit of clubbiness. He disliked the unhealthy atmosphere of Montparnasse, the drugs, the homosexuality, and above all the currying and bestowing of favor that destroyed disinterested literary judgment.*

Adamovich returned the dislike, treating Nabokov's attention to form as equivalent to neglect of content or lack of depth. Since Adamovich wrote little verse and instead probed in print the spiritual dislocations that, he claimed, rendered émigré poetry all but impossible, he felt threatened by someone who wrote with such assurance and brio. He was a foe of Khodasevich, whose verse Nabokov had praised, and a friend of Zinaida Gippius, who in her previous reign as queen of literary St. Petersburg had sharply dismissed the sixteen-year-old Nabokov's verse.[11] Now co-ruler with Adamovich of Russian literary Paris, she was adamantly anti-Sirin. Just as Gertrude Stein "ignored Joyce and did not invite to her place people who spoke of Joyce, so Gippius did not speak of Nabokov and did not listen when others spoke of him"—unless, of course, in derisive tones.[12]

Reviewing the fortieth number of *Sovremennye Zapiski*, Adamovich noted, as many critics had, the non-Russian, Western qualities of Sirin's art. But he went further: *The Defense* so closely imitated current French models—which he did not and could not name—that it would cause far less of an impression in the *Nouvelle Revue française* than it had in *Sovremennye Zapiski*. Events neatly disproved the allegation: Levinson's ecstatic review in *Nouvelles littéraires*, followed within a week by a contract with the French publisher Fayard, even before the novel had been published in full in Russian. Undeterred, Adamovich would continue for years his "cautious, but unswerving 'anti-Sirin line.' "[13]†

---

* Nabokov was not alone in his attacks on Adamovich. The doggedly honest Khodasevich consistently opposed Adamovich's cavalier disregard for the truth, while Marina Tsvetaeva blasted Adamovich in her "A Poet on Criticism" (*Blagonamerennyy*, April 1926), showing him up, in Simon Karlinsky's words, as "inconsistent, irresponsible and superficial" (*Marina Tsvetaeva*, 157). Adamovich for his part frankly admitted, with a guilty smile, to writing flattering reviews of those he wished to befriend: "Literature passes, but relationships remain" (Don Aminado, *Poezd na tret'em puti*, 1954, 307–8).

† In his treatment of Adamovich's critical posture toward Sirin, Gleb Struve writes simply of Adamovich's "sinning against the truth" (*Russkaya literatura v izgnanii*, 279).

III

Late 1929, when *The Defense* began to make its impact, is one of those periods where the record of Nabokov's private life suddenly thins. During September and October he wrote several reviews and worked in the Dahlem museum classifying rare butterflies—"moving and exciting work."[14] In mid-December his first collection of stories, *The Return of Chorb*, was published. By that time he must have been writing his novella *Soglyadatay* (*The Eye*).

The idea for a new novel, complete in all its parts, would come in a flash of surprise. Even so, months would pass while he clarified and adjusted the details of story and structure in his mind without setting a word on paper. In the next phase he would lie on his divan all day, smoking and writing with his knees propped up as a desk, and his four volumes of Dahl's dictionary beside him. He would fill thin blue school exercise books with what began as neat, legible handwriting, "dipping pen in ink and using a new nib every other day . . . crossing out, inserting, striking out again, crumpling the page, rewriting every page three or four times." In those years, Nabokov later explained, he still "generally followed the order of chapters when writing a novel but even so, from the very first, I relied heavily on mental composition, constructing whole paragraphs in my mind as I walked in the streets or sat in my bath, or lay in my bed, although often deleting or rewriting them afterward." When his invented double, Vadim Vadimych of *Look at the Harlequins!*, describes the working methods of *his* émigré years, he partly matches his maker: the text "followed a regular sequence only for a few pages, being then interrupted by some chunky passage that belonged to a later, or earlier, part of the story. After sorting out and repaginating all this, I applied myself to the next stage: the fair copy. It was tidily written with a fountain pen [and in a different ink, Nabokov could comment *in propria persona*] in a fat and sturdy exercise book or ledger. Then an orgy of new corrections would blot out by degrees all the pleasure of specious perfection." Finally Nabokov, unable to type, would dictate the whole book to his wife as she typed it out.[15]

Energy and inspiration could keep him writing for twelve hours at a stretch, often until 4 A.M., and rarely would he be up again before midday. Morally and physically he felt wonderful, he wrote his mother in January 1930.[16] Raw-nerved Smurov and the grim void around him were a radiant invention, not a mood transcribed. By the end of February, he had finished *The Eye*.

IV
The Eye (Soglyadatay)

In *The Eye*, for the first time in his career, Nabokov writes a novel in the first person.[17] Having already drawn on negative versions of his own life and his values in *King, Queen, Knave* and *The Defense*, he now selects a first-person point of view to allow him still closer to an inversion of himself, of his very sense of self.

Always extraordinarily self-assured, Nabokov had good reason after *The Defense* to know the value of his own work, and to know that some of its richest treasure was buried deep enough for readers to take a long time to recover it and to recognize the book at its full worth. Conscious of so much more in the novel than he expected any of its first critics to see, he could be serenely indifferent to the reactions of others. With such an easy confidence in his own singularity and in his own place as a writer, he had no need to be self-obsessed.

Not so the narrator of *The Eye*, a young émigré beaten up by a jealous husband while his two tutees look on, who finds the disgrace too much and shoots himself. Although he tells us he has died, he somehow continues his story, explaining that the hospital ward, his recovery, a new job, new lodgings, new friends are the product of his mental momentum: his powerful imagination has devised a plausible continuation of his mortal existence. Within this new life he finds himself drawn to the émigré family upstairs, especially the attractive young Varvara (nicknamed Vanya). Visiting almost every night, he becomes fascinated by a young man called Smurov, apparently also a new friend of the family, and scrutinizes the impression made on Vanya by this quiet young man who seems to harbor an inner boldness and fire. Others too take note of Smurov: Mukhin, for instance, another friend of Vanya's, who soon recognizes that Smurov's tales of bravado are a lie, or Smurov's new employer, who discovers that his assistant may be some sort of spy.

Increasingly obsessed by the search for the true Smurov, the narrator studies other people's reactions to him, asks them directly for their assessments of him, even searches their rooms or intercepts their mail for evidence. At one point it seems that Vanya loves Smurov and expects to marry him. At the next, this proves an embarrassing mistake: she is already betrothed to Mukhin and devoted to him. Suddenly the narrator loses all interest in Smurov.

When he catches Vanya alone just a week before her marriage to Mukhin the narrator finds he cannot restrain himself. He seizes her wrist, declares his importunate love, and is gently but firmly spurned.

Mukhin, who has returned and listened from the next room, calls him a cad. Humiliated again, the narrator heads straight for his old lodgings to check the bullet-hole in the wall, which "proves" that he *did* kill himself, that everything is unreal, that nothing matters. But the irate husband who had beaten him up months earlier catches him on the street, hails him ("Mr. Smurov!"), and now that he has found out his wife's—ex-wife's—other infidelities, offers him an apology. For readers who had not yet guessed, the secret is out: the narrator *is* Smurov.

Nabokov had merely laughed when Kirill Zaitsev voiced his horror at what he took to be Sirin's bleakly gloomy world. Knowing so well that nothing—certainly not the incomprehending opinions of others—would affect his own buoyancy of spirit, Nabokov felt no need to reply. Things could not be more different for Smurov. He ends his story with a desperate, strident protest:

> And yet I am happy. Yes, happy. I swear, I swear I am happy. I have realized that the only happiness in this world is to observe, to spy, to watch, to scrutinize oneself and others, to be nothing but a big, slightly vitreous, somewhat bloodshot, unblinking eye. I swear that this is happiness. . . . The world, try as it may, cannot insult me. I am invulnerable. And what do I care if she marries another? Every other night I dream of her dresses and things on an endless clothesline of bliss, in a ceaseless wind of possession, and her husband shall never learn what I do to the silks and fleece of the dancing witch. . . . I am happy—yes, happy! What more can I do to prove it, how to proclaim that I am happy? Oh, to shout it so that all of you believe me at last, you cruel, smug people. . . .[18]

Nabokov may have begun his tale by inverting himself, but he did not expect his readers to know or care about that: Smurov and his world would have to suffice in their own terms.

Within the brief scope of *The Eye*, Nabokov manages both concentrated focus and wide range. He compresses the narrative without crushing scenes that need full scope: Smurov's affair with Mathilde, his beating at the hands of her husband, and his suicide attempt are all over within a few pages, but we feel every blow of Kashmarin's cane and every second the two boys stare at their cringing tutor. Compulsively attuned to one character, *The Eye* at the same time sounds a whole diapason of émigré notes (priggish Roman Bogdanovich, a Baltic Russian; Mukhin, engineer and former White officer; Weinstock, Jewish bookseller, eccentric, spiritualist; and aristocratic, unintellectual, sensitive Vanya, to name a few) in order to find how they resonate with Smurov's own.

Nabokov's great technical advance in *The Eye*, his bold handling of point of view, prefigures much of his later art: his almost insanely egocentric narrators; his glides back and forth between first- and third-person narration; his sudden focal shifts that jar one reality against another and force us to resolve their clash. Does the narrator of *The Eye* "really" die? If not, does he think he does? Is his persistence after death a fact, a fixed delusion, a metaphor, a deliberate device? Are narrator and Smurov really one, and if so, is "each" conscious of the "other"?

Smurov has been publicly trounced, he has resorted to suicide, he has bungled even that. To compensate, he imagines himself omnipotent, creating after death the illusion of continued life. That secures him other advantages. He removes himself at once from all the turmoils of the heart: "I . . . found wonderful comfort in the thought that now there was nothing to worry about." Of course he cannot hide it even from himself that at least some echo of his mortal existence *appears* to persist, a craving for food and cigarettes, a need for a job and a home. But he tries to preserve a detachment from this humdrum and nameless physical presence—only the point of view his imagination has adopted, only the socket for his free eye—and at the same time spies as if from outside on himself as Smurov, a new person, a new set of possibilities.

Soglyadatay means a spy, a secret observer. Nabokov could well have called its English translation *I Spy*, but went one better with *The Eye* and its pun on "I." By diverting attention from the "I" that persists and tells his story, Smurov thinks he escapes the relentless eye of others—like those two boys unforgettably, seemingly endlessly, peering down on his humiliation. Although the narrator participates in the life of Vanya and her family, no one seems to notice him. Since all the attention is on Smurov, the sensitive narrating eye watching Smurov and watching others watching Smurov can feel safe from anyone else's gaze.

By setting up Smurov as a stranger, the narrator not only immunizes himself from the attention of others but also offers himself a chance to escape his own identity, to project his whole being onto a more satisfying self. Pretending to pure objectivity, he attempts to surround Smurov with an aura of bravado and enticing mystery, but his style gives it all away: "Smurov kept nodding approvingly as he listened. He was obviously a person who, behind his unpretentiousness and quietness, concealed a fiery spirit. . . . If Vanya was any judge of character, she must have marked this."

His secret love for Vanya and the love she might feel for him—no, not for him, for that fascinating Smurov—look like new escape routes from himself. But as he pursues the possibility of love he shatters his dream of remaining the aloof inventor of this world, safely above the fury and the mire of human veins.

Smurov's fiction that he can elude the humiliations of his mortal state fails utterly. And that leads to the real aim of *The Eye:* to let the terms of his failure define the human condition by contrast with a genuine beyond—which for Nabokov would be quite incompatible with Smurov's tightly tethered selfhood.

Smurov's spying, his self-obsessed attempt at self-detachment, of course begins when he persuades himself he has passed through death, but Nabokov also links it with other dubious attempts to catch hold of immortality: Weinstock's séances, Roman Bogdanovich's diary. The bookseller Weinstock combines two obsessions: a paranoid suspicion of Soviet spies in Berlin, and an enthusiasm for asking questions of the dead. In one of his almost nightly séances the spirit of Azef, the double agent, warns him that Smurov may be dangerous: "He spies, he lures, he betrays."

Smurov *is* a spy, of course, but only on himself, or rather on other people's sense of himself. Roman Bogdanovich, a regular visitor to Vanya's household, writes a diary that he dispatches every week to a friend in Tallinn in order to prevent himself revising it later. A new obsession seizes Smurov: Roman Bogdanovich may prove a modern-day Pepys, "who knew how to immortalize . . . an airy landscape . . . or the oddities of an acquaintance. At the very thought that Smurov's image might be so securely, so lastingly preserved I felt a sacred chill, I grew crazed with desire." Rabidly compulsive, he snatches a letter off Roman Bogdanovich, pretends to drop it in a mailbox, and scurries off into the night to read it. Although he has the unexpected luck to seize a letter partly devoted to analyzing Smurov, Roman Bogdanovich's version of Smurov as homosexual contains nothing remotely recognizable to Smurov himself.

As that desperate grab for immortality fails, so does all Smurov's neurotic self-delusion. And yet Nabokov suggests the very force of Smurov's attempt to escape the conditions of life—the rawness of the self-conscious mind, the pangs of solitude, the nauseating pitch and toss of the emotions—testifies to a soul operating at full intensity, and that is its own reward. Impatience with the limits of life, Nabokov implies, may be one of the surest signs of being fully alive.

V

Even before the depression took hold of Germany in 1930, Russian Berlin continued to empty, and when on February 27 Sirin read the first chapter of *The Eye* in the noisy, crowded, and smoke-filled premises of the Café Schmidt, it was the first Union of Russian Writers evening for months.[19]

At the end of February in the quiet of the Aykhenvald circle he also read a paper called "Torzhestvo dobrodeteli" ("The Triumph of Virtue"). A parodic paragraph in The Eye on Marx's historical determinism seems to have sparked this satire on Soviet literature, which begins by mimicking Soviet jargon and ends by asking "has it been worth mankind's while to spend century after century deepening and refining the art of writing books . . . when it proves so simple to return to long forgotten models, mystery plays, fables?"[20]

In March 1930 a new journal called Chisla (Numbers) appeared in Paris, consciously challenging the supremacy of Sovremennye Zapiski. Edited by the poet Nikolay Otsup but inspired by his friends Adamovich and the poet Georgy Ivanov, the journal's first issue caused a scandal because of one small item: Ivanov's survey of the four latest Sirin books.[21]

Sirin's novels may look new in Russian, Ivanov began, firing off Adamovich's guns without Adamovich's ballistic skill, but almost everyone writes that way in French and German. Then came a random spray of abuse. Sirin is a philistine journalist. He is the self-styled count you see in the movies who turns out to be lowborn, a cook's son, a peasant. In poetry his mentors are Prince Kasatkin-Rostovsky, Rathaus, Dmitri Tsenzor (all nonentities); in prose, his models—until he discovered the Germans and French—were Kamensky and Lazarevsky.* Outraged criticisms of Ivanov's attack resounded in the émigré press for months, and when they were about to die down, Zinaida Gippius came to Ivanov's defense and started up the clamor again.[22]

Nabokov knew what had caused Ivanov's spiteful sputter. Several months earlier the poet Irina Odoevtseva, Ivanov's wife, had sent Nabokov her first novel, with the inscription "Thank you for King, Queen, Knave," making it appear as if he had sent her his latest novel. "Now, on the niveau of Adamovich and Ivanov," Véra Nabokov explains, "this bribe ought to have influenced the review my husband might write of O[doevtseva]'s book. It had the opposite effect, if any." Nabokov replied to the unsolicited gift—a poor novel, in any case—by publishing a dismissively offhand review. Ivanov saw red, and charged. Nabokov "considered a duel but gave in to people who assured him that Ivanov was not duelesposoben."[23]

---

* Anatoly Kamensky was known for his sexually explicit fiction. Boris Lazarevsky, a journalist and friend of Chekhov, wrote some stories on amatory themes. Ivanov names these two minor writers to suggest Nabokov's fiction was semipornographic, a strange insinuation from the man whose Raspad atoma (The Splitting of the Atom, 1938) would be as "pornographic" as Henry Miller.

With *The Defense* now appearing in installments and his first collection of stories inviting an overview of his development, Sirin was the subject of intense critical attention all year long. The experience curiously prefigured what would happen when *Lolita*'s star burst in the late 1950s: after years of keen admiration in a restricted circle, sudden fame, the rediscovery of his earlier works, high praise and extravagant abuse.

Sirin only found the disparities of judgment amusing. Ivanov accused him of imitating the hacks who wrote for an old Russian illustrated weekly and then of copying what everyone was writing in French; Levinson on the other hand, a Russian deeply imbued with French culture, found Sirin's work startlingly new and his style "very individual in spite of its Tolstoyan base." In a Warsaw newspaper one writer found Ivanov's review dazzling, while another called its author a Salieri. One Paris critic declared Sirin unable to create characters in whom we can live, another rated Luzhin on a par with Tolstoy's Natasha or Pierre. Some reviewers found Nabokov non-Russian, others declared that he had suddenly answered the question whether Russian literature, émigré or Soviet, could carry on at the high level of the nineteenth century.[24]

All his life Nabokov had been unconsciously gathering materials for what would be his greatest Russian novel, *The Gift*. In 1930 he had still to conceive of the book, but life began to furnish future material more and more often. In chapter 5 of *The Gift* he would transform the reviews of *The Defense* into the farcical Babel that greets the first of Fyodor's books to make the critics crow, and there too it will be a review by Adamovich (renamed Christopher Mortus, but with his whims and worries intact) that sets off the whole cracked chorus.

VI

When Ivanov's review appeared, Nabokov's thoughts were elsewhere. On March 20 he began writing the story "Pilgram" ("The Aurelian"), and finished it ten days later.[25]

A German who has never even left Berlin, Pilgram has dreamed for fifty years of catching for himself the exotic specimens he sells in his butterfly store. When at last he makes a little money, he decides to spend it all on a butterfly trip to Spain, leaving his wife behind even though he knows she cannot manage the shop. Dragging out his packed suitcase, he has a heart attack. His wife finds him dead, but it does not matter: "Yes, Pilgram had gone far, very far. Most probably he visited Granada and Murcia and Albarracin, and then traveled farther still, to Surinam or Taprobane; and one can hardly doubt that he saw all the glorious bugs he had longed to see—velvety black butter-flies soaring over the jungles, and a tiny moth in Tasmania, and. . . ."

The story is a triumph of perfectly blended themes: the outwardly ordinary person who carries his special secret within; the excitement of discovery; the dream of perfect happiness, unattainable in this life; the terrible exclusiveness our dreams can have; and death, which will cut off all our dreams or perhaps make them come true. Everything seems right: Pilgram, not at all sentimentally conceived, hardened, bitter, selfish, and cruel to his wife, but living for his dream; the sud-den vistas that open around every detail, the glimpses of unexpected life in every direction (the bartender, the eraser a schoolboy buys, the memories stirred by a neighbor's wedding); the beauty of the scenes Pilgram's imagination conjures up. Best of all, perhaps—and one can-not understand Nabokov without grasping such facts—is that for all Pilgram's gloom at his drab street, his shop, his dingy apartment, his uncomprehending wife, the story somehow turns every one of these into a prize as rare and strange as any treasure in his shop or on the jungle slopes of Surinam.

"The Aurelian," too, points toward *The Gift*, to the incomparable beauty of the voyages of exploration that Fyodor's lepidopterist father makes through Central Asia, to Fyodor's special dream of somehow accompanying his father on that last expedition from which the old man never returned.

VII

In later life Nabokov recalled himself as never being a union member, a signer of group letters, a committee man. In fact he had been all three, though as little as he could manage. In *The Gift* Shirin, a fel-low member of the Society of Russian Writers, invites Fyodor to help rectify

> a rather comical (in Fyodor's opinion) and absolutely outrageous (in Shirin's terminology) affair . . . going on with the Union's funds. Every time a member asked for a loan or a grant (the difference between which was about the same as that between a ninety-nine-year lease and life ownership) one had to track down these funds which at the least attempt to catch up with them became amazingly fluid and ethereal, as if they were always situated equidistantly between three points represented by the treasurer and two members of the Committee.[26]

Shirin asks Fyodor to help oust the shady trio by standing for the committee himself. He refuses: "I don't want to play the fool." "Well, if you call your public duty playing the fool . . ." "If I go on the Committee I shall certainly be playing the fool, so I am refusing precisely out of respect for duty."[27] That might have been Nabokov's attitude by 1935, but when in real life his caustic friend the writer Viktor Iretsky (or was it another friend, the writer and artist Iosif Matusevich? Véra Nabokov cannot be quite sure) asked him to stand for the committee of the Union of Russian Writers in precisely the same circumstances, Nabokov at least allowed himself to be elected to the Inspection Committee at the annual general meeting in April 1930, and in 1931 and 1932 he served on the Union Committee itself.[28] The meeting in *The Gift* verges on scarcely credible farce; in fact, Nabokov transcribed it almost from life. There is one main difference: Fyodor walks out of the meeting, but Nabokov stayed—more for material for a future book than for the sake of the union.

Like the fictional Shirin, Iretsky had arranged the prior discussion of strategy at the Berlin Zoo. After his friend's passionate expostulations about the composition of the committee, Sirin drew his attention to the hyenas. As if he had barely realized that one keeps animals in a zoo, Iretsky glanced perfunctorily at the cage: "We Russians know so little about nature"—a wonderfully absurd remark to make to Vladimir Nabokov.[29]

VIII

Already Nabokov had worked out the plan for his next novel. Its hero, Martin Edelweiss, conjures up the idea of Zoorland, a fairy-tale Russia, an ogrish tyranny of enforced equality, and bravely crosses its boundary to death. Sometime in April Nabokov sounded an advance notice of this theme in the poem "Uldaborg (A translation from the Zoorlandian)": in a land where mirth is outlawed, a condemned man boldly laughs as he mounts the scaffold.[30] The imaginary northern land, the moment of execution, laughter as the ultimate defense— these themes would return again and again.

In May Nabokov began writing the new novel, tentatively entitled *Voploshchenie* (the "realization" of a plan, the "embodiment" of a dream) but altered it later to *Zolotoy vek*, "golden age," or *Romanticheskiy vek*, "romantic times."[31] At least since he wrote "On Generalities" in 1926, he had been tired of journalistic lamentations about "our epoch." He had had enough, he declared, "of hearing Western journalists call our era 'materialistic,' 'practical,' 'utilitarian,' " enough of Spengler's trumpeting the decline of the West, and certainly more than enough of the obligatory anguish of the Paris school of Russian poetry. After several novels whose superficial inversions of his own values kept his innate inclination to happiness in firm intellectual check, he could afford in his next novel to stress the glory, the high deeds, to be found in his world, the romance of the distant and daring, "the thrill and the glamour" that his hero "finds in the most ordinary pleasures as well as in the seemingly meaningless adventures of a lonely life."[32]

Before he had written much of the new novel, Nabokov visited Prague. Arriving in the second week of May, he found his mother quite changed, calm and cheerful, revived in spirits by her newfound faith in Christian Science—"so I can only approve," he wrote back to Berlin.[33] Within his work, he would always remain hostile to the conventionality of religion; speaking as a public figure outside the work, he kept his mother's case in mind and took care not to undermine other people's private consolations.[34]

His mother had lovingly laid several volumes of The Entomologist by his bed, his sister Elena was drawing up posters for his public reading. Kirill, almost nineteen, he found handsome and elegant, happy-go-lucky, excellently read, a passionate poet ("he reads [his poems] aloud, I criticize").[35]

Shortly after his arrival, Nabokov read the whole of The Eye to his family. They misunderstood the story, thinking that the hero had really died in the first chapter and that his soul then entered Smurov. Nabokov attended an evening of the literary group Skit Poetov, to which Kirill belonged, and found himself cornered by the poet Daniil Rathaus. "They compare you with me," Rathaus—whose very name had become synonymous with bad poetry—innocently remarked, unaware what Georgy Ivanov had intended by the comparison. Three days later Nabokov wrote back to Véra, refusing the invitation to participate in an enterprise that Mikhail Gorlin was arranging for the young Berlin poets: "I am not young and I am not a poet."[36]

In Prague he inspected the museum's entomological collections with a lepidopterist friend, Nikolay Raevsky. As they talked of tropical butterflies, Raevsky observed that it was just as well Nabokov had no money or he would have died of malaria in New Guinea or the Solomon Islands. Nabokov laughed: "I don't know whether I would have died there, but I certainly would have gone there." Raevsky asked him if he liked Proust: "not just like; I simply adore him. I've read all twelve volumes through twice."[37] He rooted around in the Russian Historical Archive—the superb hoard of émigré material later confiscated by Soviet troops—in search of an article he wanted to find ("It's becoming rather difficult, this chasing after articles about me, isn't it? After all I'm not an actress.") One sunny day he climbed up a nearby hill and looked down at the canvas township of a traveling circus, heard the roar of lions and tigers, saw glittering carousels and fences announcing green tigers, teeth bared, around an intrepid trainer in mustache and sideburns—an image to be met years later in the story "Spring in Fialta." On May 20 he gave a public reading (the beginning of *The Eye*, "The Aurelian," some poems) before a crowded and enthusiastic audience in Ičrasek Hall, the next day read "A University Poem" before a dozen dinner guests, and four days later returned to Berlin.[38]

Although the depression was sending shock waves through the city, Véra Nabokov in her husband's absence had found a job, five hours a day working as secretary (French and German stenography, French and English correspondence and translations) to a firm of lawyers, Weil, Ganz and Dieckmann, who acted as consultants to the French embassy. Nabokov came to fetch her from work some days, noticed this dusty Dickensian cffice, and pumped her about the firm. In *The Gift* he would render it exactly, albeit refracted through a Gogolian prism, as the Traum, Baum and Käsebier for whom Zina works.[39]

Véra and Vladimir both continued to give a few lessons in English— fortunately, for Nabokov's purely literary income was meager. His books brought in very little in their Russian versions, somewhat more in translation. Although *The Defense* was being translated into both French and German, the potentially more lucrative German version ran afoul of the depression.[40] *Rul'*, financially shaky for years, was about to collapse.

Only serialization in *Sovremennye Zapiski*, partly subsidized by the Czech government, offered a reasonable return. Early in the summer of 1930 one of *Sovremennye Zapiski*'s editors, Ilya Fondaminsky, visited Sirin while on business in Berlin. From its inception Fondaminsky had thrown his whole life into *Sovremennye Zapiski*. He became the soul of the journal and its most ardent propagandist. He made it his special business to secure the best émigré writers, and in order to do so paid out unusually generous advances.[41] More than anyone else, he made *Sovremennye Zapiski* the chief cultural record of the emigration.

Nabokov would later call him "a saintly and heroic soul who did more for Russian émigré literature than any other man."[42] Others too saw him as a saint, though joked that as a Jew and a Socialist Revolutionary his chances for canonization were slim. Fifty, ardent, animated, with a pile of wavy hair swept high above his forehead. Fondaminsky charmed the Nabokovs and was charmed by them in return.[43] Nabokov had only just resumed his novel on his return from Prague, and renamed it, finally, *Podvig* (*Glory*), but Fondaminsky was ready to buy it "*na kornyu*, 'in the rooted state' (said of grainfields before they are harvested)." "Vividly do I remember," Nabokov wrote, "the splendid zest with which he slapped his knees before rising from our grim green divan after the deal had been clinched!"[44]

An entomologist Nabokov had met in Prague had tempted him with the idea of a butterfly expedition in summer, a mirage he was easily susceptible to at this time of year.[45] Instead he remained in Berlin, composing *Glory* every day, and every night reading what he had written to Véra.

In September, the Union of Russian Writers marked the return from vacation time to the serious business of the year with a "newspaper-farce in three sections" in the Schubertsaal. Sirin not only took part in the mock news format, but fought a boxing match with his friend George Hessen—a chance to add a detail or two, perhaps, to the fight between Martin and Darwin in *Glory*. By October 23, he had finished the novel's first draft.[46]

IX
Glory (Podvig)

From infancy Martin Edelweiss—Russian, despite his name—has seen life as a romantic adventure. When his mother reads him a fairy tale about "a picture with a path in the woods, right above the bed of a little boy, who, one fine night, just as he was, nightshirt and all, went from his bed into the picture, onto the path that disappeared into the woods," he hopes she will not notice that there is just such a picture above his own bed and remove it so he cannot explore *its* forest path and disappear among *its* painted tree trunks. Everything remote, forbidden, inaccessible, beckons to him: lights like jewels amid the dark countryside that a train clatters through; a cliff face that demands to be scaled; all the risks of love.[47]

Readers of *Speak, Memory* will see that Nabokov has given Martin his own sense of romance, his own picture of a forest path, his own jewel-like lights in the dark. But he has not given him his talent: to the outer world, Martin himself seems unromantic and unremarkable.

In April 1919, with Bolshevik forces poised to retake the Crimea, Martin and his mother flee southward. After an affair with an older married woman in Greece, he spends the summer in Switzerland, where his father's cousin Henry offers his mother and himself shelter and support. In October 1919 he heads for Cambridge, and falls in love with a young émigrée living in London, Sonia Zilanov, mercurial, critical, a tease, a flirt, a challenge promising little hope of success. Soon he has to watch her toy—more seriously than she has ever toyed with him—with his best friend, Darwin, an apparently indolent older student, in fact full of sangfroid and *savoir-vivre*, decorated in the trenches and a highly promising writer. When Darwin proposes, however, Sonia turns him down, and after finishing his degree Martin cannot resist following her when her family moves to Berlin.

Years earlier Sonia had asked him why he did not join the White Army, as her brother-in-law had done. Uninterested in politics or other people's causes, but tempted by the lure of adventure and especially by performing a feat for the sake of a fair young maid, Martin begins to contemplate a lone expedition across Russia's forbidden border. With Sonia, he turns Soviet Russia into a private fantasy, Zoorland, a nightmare of enforced equality beneath a chilling drizzle of decrees. For all the fantasy, his plans take firm shape: he will venture through the woods and across the Russian border for twenty-four hours. He tells no one but Darwin, and slips away from Berlin before his friend can stop him. Nothing more is heard from him. Weeks later, unable to trace him further than Latvia, Darwin returns to Switzerland to break the news to Martin's mother, and there the novel ends.

At first glance *Glory* seems a straightforwardly realistic tale. In private Martin may have an imagination that can derive a thrill even from washing himself in his collapsible tub on the floor of a filthy, cramped toilet compartment in a jolting train, but when he speaks or writes he produces merely "an effect of good sense, of solidity." His mind appears to lack the highly individual hue of Luzhin's or Smurov's. Color comes instead from the exoticism of changing outer environments— St. Petersburg, a Biarritz beach, Yalta, Athens, Switzerland, London, Cambridge, Berlin, a farm in the South of France—and from characters like Alla, Sonia, and Darwin, and a cast far larger than in any previous Nabokov novel.*

Without the lurid tints of a bizarre mind, *Glory* also appears to lack tautness of plot. *Mary* chronicles a week in Ganin's life; *King, Queen, Knave* lasts a year; *The Defense* takes a long shot of Luzhin learning chess in childhood but quickly narrows its focus to the last few months of his life and leads to his death with relentless inexorability. Nabokov began to recoil from the neatness and the implicit determinism of dramatic concentration and in his later works tended to prefer the randomness of a lifetime or more—*The Gift* and *Ada* cover a century apiece—and would replace contours smoothly converging on the vanishing point of death with broken or uncompleted lines of development, the doodles of impulse, the zigzags of chance. *Glory* is the

---

* In April 1971, as he was translating *Glory*, Nabokov told Stephen Parker he was perturbed that the picture he had painted of Cambridge life would no longer seem exotic for the book's new English readers, as it certainly had for the émigré readers he had first had in mind.

first Nabokov novel shaped to match the lack of structure in an individual life. The novel does not even end, it simply fades away—into Corot colors, into one of Chekhov's great grisailles.

By denying himself the seductive shapeliness of dramatic thrust and counterthrust Nabokov repeatedly spurred his imagination to find bolder, fresher ways to satisfy his sense of formal harmony. In *Glory* he discovered it in the transitions, the back-and-forth switches that structure the novel. Some gentle, some stealthy, some positively glaring, these transitions reflect the unique pattern of Martin's mind and impart a quiet restlessness to the narrative, making its rhythms anticipate Martin's own attempt to slip across a forbidden border and back. One sequence must suffice.

In chapter 18, as Sonia and her mother return to London from a visit to Martin in Cambridge, Mrs. Zilanov asks him to give her regards to his mother when he writes. He does not; in fact he has trouble writing letters. He scribbles a few lines when

> Suddenly, in his mind, he saw the mailman walking across the snow; the snow crunched slightly, and blue footprints remained on it. He described it thus: "My letter will be brought by the mailman. It is raining here." He thought it over and crossed out the mailman, leaving only the rain.

Martin has imagination, but he cannot express it in words. For the moment, that seems all, but that unvoiced vision will reverberate when Martin himself has vanished.

Finishing the letter Martin accidentally blots the envelope and turns the mark "into a black cat seen from the back." Now comes the sudden transition: "Mrs. Edelweiss preserved this envelope along with his letters. She would gather them into a batch at the end of each semester and tie them crosswise with a ribbon. Several years later she had occasion to reread them." Here is the first glimpse of a time beyond the end of the novel, when Martin's mother has to face the loss of her son. As she rereads his letters she recalls "with piercing clarity how she used to walk with Henry along the scintillating road between fir trees weighted down by lumps of snow, and suddenly there was the rich tinkling of multiple bells, the postal sleigh, the letter."

Something strange is in the air. Martin's vision of the mailman walking across the snow was evidently mistaken—and yet it will come truer than anyone could have known, for Darwin, having mailed off Martin's postdated postcards, has to cross that same strip of ground in the last scene of the novel to tell Martin's mother her son has disappeared, and on the way he will leave those footprints Martin has somehow seen.

Mrs. Edelweiss's reminiscences of Martin's letters and the vacations he spent with her between each batch then serve as another transition back to Martin's first Christmas homecoming from Cambridge, seen now from his own vantage point. On reaching Switzerland he has "a queer sensation of having returned to Russia," and as he puts on new skis he recalls a snow-covered slope in St. Petersburg and the special skis of his childhood. He pushes off on his skis: "Yes, he found himself back in Russia. Here were the splendid 'rugs' of snow spreading in the Pushkin poem which Archibald Moon recited so sonorously." A recent impression of Cambridge (his Russian lecturer reciting Pushkin) mingles with a present scene that calls up his remote past.

The Swiss scene holds for now, though, and Martin whistles down the slope on his skis "faster and faster. And how many times afterwards, sleeping in his chilly Cambridge room, he dream-sped like that and suddenly, in a stunning explosion of snow, fell and awakened. Everything was as usual. He could hear the clock ticking in the adjacent parlor. A mouse was rolling a lump of sugar on the floor. . . ." Another hurtling transition, with Martin back in his Cambridge bed before his ski-run has finished.

Everything in Martin's imagination propels him across the borders of time and space and builds toward a pattern that will become charged with meaning only at his death.

As he stands on a Cambridge soccer field, keeping goal for Trinity College, Martin crosses again into the Russia of his past and the childhood football reveries that he now enacts, reveries

> in which he used to luxuriate so lengthily, so artfully, when afraid to reach the delicious essence too quickly, he would dwell in detail on the pregame preparations—pulling on the stockings with the colored tops, putting on the black shorts, tying the laces of the robust boots. . . . In childhood years sleep would overtake him just in those opening minutes of the game, for Martin would get so engrossed in the details of the preface that he never got to the main part of the text.

Now, saving a shot at goal by the St. John's captain, he notes a certain peculiarity in his adult life: "the property that his reveries had of crystallizing and mutating into reality, as previously they had mutated into sleep."

Martin's greatest dream of all, his lone foray across the Soviet border, will itself mutate into reality. To others, his deed remains baffling and pointless, but Nabokov has set himself the task of proving that this young man who has led an outwardly bland life and dies an apparently senseless death has the stuff of glory within him. Darwin has seemed the one singled out for greatness in the world's terms: the man of action, a war hero, where Martin has merely escaped Russia's civil war to the safety of Switzerland; a gifted and original writer, where Martin's imagination lacks the power to express itself; the apparently successful lover, where Martin never seems more to Sonia than a sort of overgrown childhood friend. But Darwin settles down to a thoroughly unimpeachable fiancée, to stolid respectability, to the complacent prospect of success as a commentator on political and financial matters. Martin on the other hand remains true to the restless bright imagination of childhood. With his lack of talent, he could seem another Nabokov protagonist drawn as a reversed image of his maker, but it is he and not Darwin who remains true to Fyodor's and Nabokov's behest: "Oh, swear to me to put in dreams your trust, and to believe in fantasy alone, and never let your soul in prison rust. . . ."[48] And it is he whose life will prove an imperishable triumph.

But how? When he leaves Berlin to live out his dream, he simply vanishes entirely from the novel's sight. After his disappearance, Darwin comes to Switzerland, picks his way through a fir forest to tell Martin's mother her son has disappeared, and an hour later returns the same way without our hearing the grim disclosure. Only the picture of the path remains, and a pregnant sense of Martin's absence. That is all.

Although the whole novel and Martin's whole life have seemed a long series of reveries in preparation for his ultimate adventure, we have only the preface, while the main text—the crossing itself into Russia and death—is left right out. But that is precisely the point. The ending marks the irrational fulfillment of Martin's childhood fantasy: he simply fades into the picture, as the nightshirted boy steps into the painted forest on his wall.

Something has slipped the leash of realism. But why? Why does Nabokov have Martin die as it were *into* the pattern of his life? Why does he only imply a remote Russian border behind the Swiss scene we see, a distant death behind the life continuing before us?

Precisely because we do not witness Martin at the border but simply see again the familiar Swiss scene, with him no longer present, he seems to have enacted that childhood dream of the boy who disappears into the picture that has been there all along. His vanishing proves to be the perfect realization of the apparently impossible dream: the very absence of the expected "main part of the text" of his adventure story, of some glimpse of him at the border, itself becomes the fulfillment of his story. By some strange twist of logic everything prior to his disappearance into death now becomes itself in retrospect the unexpected main text, the picture into which he disappears, the dream triumphant. But what could Nabokov intend by this?

Two passages from later works may suggest an answer. Sineusov in "Ultima Thule" asks Falter—whose mind seems to have hurled him into a state of being where all mysteries are resolved—to tell him that "everything—life, patria, April, the sound of a spring . . . is but a muddled preface, and that the main text still lies ahead." "Skip the preface," Falter replies, "and it's in the bag!"[49] Or in *Look at the Harlequins!* Vadim declares that "*this* was the simple solution, that the brook and the boughs and the beauty of the Beyond all began with the initial of Being."[50] What lies beyond death may be the main text to which life is only a preface: because at death one's life may be read backward or forward, in any order at all, so that this timeless version of one's life itself becomes the main text, unreachable in mortal time, that allows the unique design of one's life to show through.

Martin, this apparently levelheaded youth, accepts the world as high adventure, where the near-at-hand does not have to be the taken-for-granted, where the precarious present is threatened or both sides by a past from which we are barred and a future we cannot broach. All his life he slips clandestinely from the near to the remote, from the present into the recollected past or the projected future. He reaches Switzerland before leaving Greece or switches back to the Swiss autumn after his body has landed him in Cambridge. He lives out an adult romance before leaving childhood, or returns to a Russian child's dream as he stands goal on an English football field. He sums up what is heroic even in an imagination of no outwardly special power, and at the end of the novel takes his whole life boldly over into the unknown future and across the closed border to the past, to the death where perhaps all the times of his life coexist and the whole picture is preserved.

Bright Desk, Dark World: Berlin, 1930–1932

I

IN OCTOBER and November 1930, as he was finishing *Glory*, Nabokov published translations of three excerpts from *Hamlet* ("To be or not to be," Gertrude's "There is a willow grows askaunt the brook," Laertes and Hamlet in Ophelia's grave) and prepared to translate the whole play.[1]

Instead, despite more than two full-length novels and one shorter one in less than two years, his imagination kept prompting him to more fiction of his own. A blind man betrayed by his wife and her lover: the image took hold of him suddenly, and late in January 1931 he set down the title for a novel on this theme, *Rayskaya Ptitsa* (*Bird of Paradise*), and began to write.[2] By the end of February he reported to his mother that he had just finished his new novel and "taken it to the beauty parlor, giving it a manicure, massaging its little face—there— taking out the wrinkles. . . . Soon you'll see it in all its beauty."

In the same letter, he criticized some poems by his brother Kirill that had just appeared in *Volya Rossii*, a Prague émigré journal that was for years *Sovremennye Zapiski*'s only near-rival:

> Why "a beast howls," and then "a bird" turns up—what kind of bird?
> . . . why this naive antithesis—there a star, here a factory, roses there,
> electricity here—how are factories worse than roses, might I ask? All this
> is parlor metaphysics and has not the least relation to life, to poetry—to
> real birds and real roses. On the other hand, though, all the poems I have
> to read in *Volya Rossii* . . . are on the same level.[3]

Nabokov's mind, able to look so critically at his brother's poems, seems also to have reconsidered his own current work and decided it needed not just a mudpack but radical corrective surgery. It would be another three months before he completed his new novel, it would emerge with a new name, *Camera Obscura*, and it would have nothing in common with the two surviving pages of *Bird of Paradise* except the idea of the blind man betrayed.

Nabokov consulted an oculist about the terms of his hero's sudden loss of sight,[4] but there was another new theme in the novel that he could look out for by himself: the cinema. About once a fortnight in Berlin he and Véra would go to the movies, usually to the cheap corner theater rather than the expensive first-run cinema palaces around the Gedächtniskirche. Nabokov loved the comedy of Buster Keaton, Harold Lloyd, Chaplin, Laurel and Hardy, and the Marx brothers, and more than thirty years later could reel off scene after scene in sharp-focus detail. He admired a few serious features like Dreyer's *La Passion de Jeanne d'Arc*, René Clair, or the best of German gothic (*The Hands of Orlac*, Murnau's *The Last Laugh*), but most of all he enjoyed the grotesqueness of cinematic cliché. When George Hessen began to write film reviews for *Rul'*, he could sometimes let them in on his complimentary tickets. Hessen's father captures a characteristic image of Nabokov: "For Sirin there seemed no greater pleasure than to single out intentionally an inept American film. The more casually stupid it was, the more he would choke and literally shake with laughter, to the point where on occasion he would have to leave the hall."[5]

It was only fitting that his new novel should become in English *Laughter in the Dark*. In Russian, its cover would be printed to look like a strip of movie film bearing on each frame the title *Kamera obskura*. It was the shortest of all his novels in conception: a mere six months, he later thought, between the image and its transfer to paper.[6] Signs of haste survive even in the final version. And still he had time for other things.

On March 20 he read a paper, "Dostoevsky without Dostoevskyitis," as part of a Union of Russian Writers evening on Dostoevsky at the Gutmansaal—preparation, as it would prove, for *Despair*, the next novel in line.[7] In the past Nabokov had expressed in verse his relation to the Russian tradition, writing poems on Blok, Gumilyov, Pushkin, Tolstoy, and Nekrasov specifically for commemorative evenings like this. Now on such occasions he would subject Pushkin, Dostoevsky, or Blok to prose examination. The switch to prose and a more analytical relation to his tradition prefigure *The Gift*: there he would study Fyodor's evolution from poetry to prose and trace Fyodor's complicated relation to the traditions of Pushkin and Gogol on the one hand and on the other to Russia's century-old demand for literature to become a political purgative or social salve.

Four weeks later, in mid-April, Nabokov wrote a mock sales pitch for the elixir "Freudianism for all" ("Chto vsyakiy dolzhen znat'," "What Everyone Should Know").[8] Another trend was developing in his art: the parodic, either purely literary (Luzhin Senior's stories, the lively Proust parody just completed in *Camera Obscura*) or engaging satirically with current intellectual fashions (Marx, Spengler, Freud). From this point on, parody would be a well-primed weapon in Nabokov's arsenal, a way of criticizing the taken-for-granted, "dead things shamming life, . . . continuing to be accepted by lazy minds serenely unaware of the fraud."[9]

After writing a piece on Sirin for a new French journal, *Le Mois*, Gleb Struve suggested to his friend that he might like to write something on Freud and literature for a Francophone audience. Nabokov said no, he did not see Freud in literature, except for fashionable vulgarians like Stefan Zweig, "and that is not literature."[10] Instead he devoted his first work in French, written in May, to the idea of "the contemporary": the individuality of each person's "epoch," and the magic our age's overlooked trifles will have in the eyes of the future.[11]

In late spring Nabokov read a borrowed copy of Joyce's *Ulysses*. At Cambridge in 1922 he had heard Peter Mrosovsky recite passages of Molly's soliloquy, but apparently he had not read the novel since. "Obscene, but what genius. A little artificial in places, however. Do you like the book?" he asked Struve.[12]

In the fourth week of May, he completed *Camera Obscura*.[13]

II
Camera Obscura (Laughter in the Dark)

When wealthy and respectable art critic Bruno Kretschmar becomes obsessed with cinema usherette Magda Peters, she turns her natural instincts as a courtesan to good effect and forces him to leave his wife and daughter. Robert Horn, a gifted but chillingly cynical artist, Magda's first lover, meets Kretschmar, discovers Magda has become his mistress, and cultivates a friendship with the man. Magda and Horn secretly become lovers again.

Alerted after several months to Magda's infidelity, Kretschmar tries to kill her. When she convinces him she just might be innocent, he drives off with her, though inexperienced at the wheel, still half-crazed by suspicion, and all but suicidal. The car crashes, inevitably, and Kretschmar becomes blind.

After leaving the hospital, Kretschmar comes to terms with his blindness in a secluded Swiss chalet, with Magda as nurse. He does not know that Magda chose the chalet with Horn, who has picked out the best room, or that Horn not only sleeps with Magda every night but helps her to siphon money from Kretschmar's accounts and walks round the chalet naked, impudently sunning himself before Kretschmar's sightless eyes and tormenting Kretschmar with the sound of unaccountable footfalls. When his brother-in-law Max walks in on this perverse *ménage à trois* Kretschmar learns of the ghastly deception.

Armed with a revolver, he tries to corner Magda in a room whose door he has blocked. Unable to see her, he misses his target, she wrestles with the gun, and a second shot resounding through Kretschmar's darkness kills him an instant later.*

Few images in literature can be more horrifying or more gratuitously cruel than that of the blind Kretschmar in his chalet, teased and tormented by Magda and Horn. He suffers no physical pain, there is nothing here to match the plucking out of Gloucester's eyes or the Grand Guignol of *Titus Andronicus*. Horn merely mocks Kretschmar's blindness by parading his naked body before him, or has Magda tell him just for fun the wrong colors for this table or that wall. While Kretschmar presses Magda to his breast, she rolls her eyes at Horn in comic resignation; when he looks at her with special tenderness, she pokes out her tongue at him. They abuse his dignity, his trust, his helplessness, and the very intimacy of love. At first he takes comfort from the delusion that Magda's nursing him vouches for the purity of her feelings, but as his other senses sharpen, that repose gives way to a dread that he and Magda are not alone. With idle glee, Horn watches as Kretschmar's tension mounts until his whole face strains with suspicion at every sound.

The horror of these almost unbearable scenes seems without doubt Nabokov's inspiration for writing *Camera Obscura*. Composed immediately after *Glory*, the novel appears deliberately designed as a contrast to *Glory*'s world. In the earlier book life seems an exalted, romantic, disinterested adventure, in *Camera Obscura* a pit of cowardice, selfishness, and cruelty. Incapable of expressing his imagination in art, Martin finds in life a heroic outlet for the "demanding and magical impulse" within. Horn by contrast has artistic talent but indulges in a foul travesty of art as he turns a living person into one of his cartoon figures, the butt of his ridicule. In *Glory* Martin simply fades away into the landscape of the novel, but his very invisibility marks his living out a childhood dream. In *Camera Obscura* on the other hand blindness mocks Kretschmar's dream of possessing Magda's beauty and leaves him all too vulnerably visible to people he cannot see at all.

A number of themes radiate out from *Camera Obscura*'s infernal conclusion. The scenes at the chalet are the most graphic inversion Nabokov ever makes of his ideal of love as a partial release from the essential isolation of the self. Less immediate but no less important is the contrast between art and what Nabokov considered its antithesis,

* Readers of the English translation will notice that Nabokov later altered the German names of the original to more international forms, from Kretschmar to Albert Albinus, Magda to Margot, Horn to Axel Rex, Anneliese to Elisabeth, Max to Paul. Other changes Nabokov made in his 1937 translation are discussed below, in chapter 19.

poshlost', vulgarity in all its forms, ranging from the harshest cruelty to the insensitivity of sham art, pseudo-refinement, fake sentimentality.

Magda thinks herself an actress, Kretschmar is an art connoisseur, Horn a gifted draftsman. Where Martin pursues a private glory whose mysterious connections with the exaltation of art he himself cannot understand, Magda's cheap imagination merely debases art into the trite dream of stardom, gorgeous furs, swank cars, gaping fans. Seeing Magda, Kretschmar experiences for the first time the artistic urge to hold fast a fleeting image of beauty, just as Martin before his fateful voyage suddenly wishes he could record and preserve the trifles of a world he almost knows he will never see again. But most telling of all is the contrast between Martin and Horn. Martin has an artistic disposition in everything but talent, an inherent purity and nobility of the imagination. He feels a fineness in life that transforms the commonplace into an adventure. Horn on the other hand, for all his artistic gifts, merely enjoys "life made to look silly, as it slid helplessly into caricature."

At the center of the novel lies another kind of contrast—one key to its meaning—between Horn's and his creator's control over Kretschmar's destiny. For Nabokov art requires curiosity, tenderness toward all that is frail in the world, and trust in the fundamental goodness of things. Horn adds to cold curiosity a conscious cruelty and a delight in exploiting credulity: "his itch to make fools of his fellow men amounted almost to genius." Because Kretschmar is blind, Horn can manipulate and mock him as easily as if he were one of his own cartoon characters, and at the same time derive a ghoulish glee from knowing that Kretschmar is a living, suffering human being. Nothing could be less like Nabokov's own aims in controlling Kretschmar's fate: to awaken our compassion for the human helplessness of Kretschmar. In the same way, Nabokov implies, perhaps the artists of mortal fate may permit the imperfection and pain of mortal life for the sake of a tenderness it awakens in some unseen audience beyond. Though in the first half of the novel we see Kretschmar as unsympathetic, a liar, a coward, and a fool who has put his wife through torture, the second half of the novel stirs up our pity as Horn twists and tears at Kretschmar's tenderness and trust.

Early in the novel Kretschmar's wife and his brother-in-law appear merely lumpish and stolid. By the end, they both feel a deep compassion for Kretschmar, despite all the pain he has caused them, and by now these two unglamorous characters seem the only appealing people in the whole book. Nabokov often sides with those spurned by the flashier figures at the center of his novels. Scorned as unimaginative by Kretschmar, who has been scorned in turn by Magda and Horn, Max and Anneliese prove by their tenderness and pity to be further from *poshlost'* and closer to the real values of the imagination than the novel's three perverters of the artistic impulse.

All the images of art—drawing, painting, film—that proliferate in the novel mingle with images of darkness and light, of sight and blindness, whether literal or metaphorical or even suprasensual. These images of seeing and being seen in turn form a force field around Kretschmar's fate to suggest the ultimate kinship of moral and artistic vision.

Accustomed to being seen—she was once an artist's model—Magda looks forward to seeing herself in the movie she has enticed Kretschmar to finance. But on screen she looks inept and graceless, and as she watches she feels "like a soul in Hell to whom the demons are displaying the unsuspected lining of its earthly transgressions." Magda and Horn, similarly, seem delighted with the show they stage for themselves around the unseeing Kretschmar: perhaps, the novel implies, they too might one day have to see their actions in quite another light as death projects them onto a very different screen. Even within life someone else's eyes can completely transform actions performed in the false certainty they can never be witnessed. Sitting naked before Kretschmar, taunting him with a blade of grass as if it were a bothersome fly, Horn turns around to find Max has been watching him, and then runs away, cowering and covering his nakedness with his hand "like Adam after the Fall."

As if he were the moral sense itself, the apparently dim-sighted Max in fact proves uncannily alert to foul play: an illicit phone conversation between Kretschmar and Magda; a glimpse of Magda and Horn whispering together at an ice-hockey game; a sordid wrangle when Magda tries to prevent Kretschmar from seeing his dying daughter; and Horn here tormenting Kretschmar. But if Max sees without spying, Anneliese appears to see even without looking: she acquires an almost telepathic sensitivity to Kretschmar's fate, on the day of the ice-hockey match, on the day Kretschmar crashes his car hundreds of miles away, on the day Max decides to check on Kretschmar in Switzerland.

Beyond Kretschmar's blindness is Max's acute vision, beyond that Anneliese's clairvoyance. Something else may loom further out still. As Kretschmar drives his car around the curve to disaster, a woman gathering herbs looks down from the cliff above. Higher still, a dirigible pilot surveys two villages twelve miles apart. "Perhaps, by rising still higher," the story suggests, one might have been able to see both this Provençal scene and Berlin—where at this very moment Anneliese senses something about to happen. From a high enough point of vantage, all our actions can be seen, as Goethe implied as he pointed his cane at the stars above: "There is my conscience." In the world of Camera Obscura the moral eye seems the highest and surest form of vision, and no one can avoid its gaze.

For all their emotional and moral resonance, the novel's climactic scenes place too much of a burden on the rest of the book. To prepare for his climax, Nabokov must overstrain the plot with too many minor implausibilities of character or causation: Horn becomes a different character between his first appearance and his second; convenient eavesdroppings occur at precisely the right moment, equally convenient deafnesses seem to afflict the characters just when anything else would have given the game away too soon.

Nevertheless there are excellent psychological and structural touches. While his wife is in a maternity hospital Kretschmar dreads that she might die in childbirth, but at the same time feels tempted to avail himself of her absence and pick up a girl. As his daughter dies eight years later, Magda and Horn now take advantage of Kretschmar's absence at her deathbed to act where he had only dithered. Especially skillful is the agonizing scene when Kretschmar discovers his blindness: Nabokov avoids the word "blind" altogether, as if it would substitute a commonplace concept for the shock he wants to render in all the unique novelty it has for Kretschmar.

Nabokov wrote Camera Obscura seeing it as a motion picture.[14] Kretschmar falls in love with an usherette who dreams of becoming a screen star, and from that point its characters choose to make their world one of movieland vulgarity. The plot evolves with cinematic speed, and the trim language ensures that little would be lost on screen. Images of light and dark, vision and blindness, cartoon and cinema and show should encourage an inventive response from a talented director. Only two years into the sound era, Nabokov thought up a climax—Kretschmar's attempt to kill Magda, "seen" entirely through his sightless eyes—that would require a blacked-out screen and the wordless silence of hatred, broken only by the sound of breathing, scuffling, and two gunshots, all amplified like Kretschmar's sense of hearing.

Poorly served by the one movie adaptation so far, Camera Obscura could nevertheless make an excellent film. But there was a literary cost to pay. As a novel, Camera Obscura is too thin in texture and too hasty in structure to satisfy on the level of Nabokov's other works. Geared to the clack of the clapboard, it cannot like the other novels open all the shutters and doors and lids of the mind.

III

After a few warm days early in May 1931, outdoor tables appeared once more in front of Kurfürstendamm cafés, only for the rain, the slush, and the cold to return. But by the end of the month Nabokov was already bathing in the Grunewald sun.[15] An émigré acquaintance recalls meeting him occasionally there. "We both seem to be sun-worshippers," Nabokov remarked—and readers of *The Gift* will remember Fyodor soaking up the sun in the Grunewald day after day through a hot May and June.[16]

At the start of the fourth week in June, Nabokov wrote the story "Obida" (English title "A Bad Day").[17] For an adolescent boy, a festive summer visit to his cousin's estate turns into a nettlefield of humiliations. No doubt Nabokov recalls here the boredom of family outings to his cousin's, the Sayn-Wittgensteins, at Druzhnosel'e near Vyra.[18] A trial attempt to capture the sensations of the past in all their fullness, "A Bad Day" both recalls Bunin's crisp images of Russia's past—Nabokov even dedicated the story to Bunin—and anticipates *The Gift*, *Speak, Memory*, and the games in Ardis Park. The sensitivity that makes Peter so vulnerable also makes the world he watches a cavalcade of wonders. On this particular day he can only feel the pain, but even as it looks through his eyes the story records a magic in the whole scene that, it implies, Peter will himself come to treasure in future years.

Published two weeks later in *Poslednie Novosti*, "A Bad Day" announced a new flood. Once when Berlin had been the center of the emigration and *Rul'* its main newspaper, Sirin poems had showered down steadily on readers. Now only thirty thousand Russians were left in Berlin, and half of these, part German by birth, no longer formed part of the Russian colony.[19] *Rul'* had only three more months to live. But in Paris, the center of France's four-hundred-thousand-strong Russian population, émigré publishing could still thrive. There, *Poslednie Novosti*—the city's main Russian daily, and the emigration's most important newspaper—began to carry one Sirin story after another as well as excerpts from the novels that *Sovremennye Zapiski* was publishing complete and in a continuous stream.

As the two novels and a novella Sirin had written in the last year and a half saw publication, Adamovich, *Poslednie Novosti*'s regular critic, began to change the grounds of his attack: although Sirin might write dazzlingly well, something must be wrong for him to do it so fast. Adamovich and his circle felt convinced that in the current crisis—always urgently current, for such connoisseurs of crisis—the

strength of the sensitive soul was sapped by despair. Someone as prolific as Sirin must therefore be a soulless writing machine. Others took
up his cry.

Sirin had anticipated the attacks. Before *Glory*'s serial publication,
he had told Struve that the book would come out to "the quiet whis-
tle of Sodomovich and other Georgies" (Georgy Adamovich, Georgy
Ivanov).[20] He sent Struve and Fondaminsky a cutting epigram on
Ivanov, and was delighted at its rapid progress through Russian
Paris.[21]

On July 1 he launched another attack on Adamovich and his circle
in a longer poem that invoked the aid of Pushkin, an even deadlier
epigrammist and literary skirmisher. Nominally a translation from the
English poem "The Night Journey" by the invented Vivian Calmbrood—references to young Wordsworth would date the poem about
1800—it describes a carriage ride to London during which Calmbrood
listens in the dark to an unidentified fellow writer's confession that
his lyric muse is turning satiric.[22]

> Into one critic's disgrace
> I fall because
> I find ridiculous his gloom,
> his sensitive favoritism,
> his languor of judgment, his affected style,
> the constant echo of offense,
> and above all—his verse.
> Poor wretch. His bones squeak,
> strumming on his tin lyre;
> he inclines over the grave pit
> his Adamic head.*

Calmbrood hears out the poet, and as dawn lights the carriage he
wonders could this man be who he thinks it is:

> I could hold off no longer. "Tell me,
> what's your name?" He looks
> and answers: "I am Chenston."
> We embraced.

In that last line, Sirin allies himself with Pushkin—who had presented his superb minidrama "The Covetous Knight" as a translation
from the invented Chenston—and against both Adamovich, who had
argued that Pushkin's mastery of form was something no longer adequate to a world grown so much more complicated, and his crony

---

* A pun on Adamovich and "Adamova–golova," idiomatically "skull," literally
"Adamic head."

Ivanov.* Sirin also joins forces with Vladislav Khodasevich, the greatest poet and in the eyes of many the greatest critic in the emigration, singularly devoted to Pushkin's era and art and life, a poet whose verse retained an uncannily Pushkinian clarity and formal grace, but with a highly individual mode of recoiling from the bright world Pushkin welcomed. Not unlike Adamovich in mood, Khodasevich insisted that it took more than a heart full of feelings to make good verse: it needed mastery of the instrument, and in Russian verse no one had greater mastery than Pushkin.

From the mid-1920s Khodasevich and Adamovich were entrenched opponents, feuding bitterly on issue after issue. Sirin and Khodasevich on the other hand had never met, but over the last few years their love of good writing had drawn them together. In their reviews Sirin praised Khodasevich's verse and Khodasevich Sirin's prose, and each of them was outraged that Adamovich (with Ivanov in support) could concoct reasons for downplaying the other's work precisely because of its excellence. Now, with " 'I am Chenston' . . . We embraced," Sirin signaled that he would fight together with Khodasevich under the banner of Pushkin.

But there was also a much more playful side to the poem. Sirin read it in the Poets' Club, prefacing the reading of his "translation" with a few trumped-up biographical details about Calmbrood. Afterward he confessed to the hoax, which had taken everybody in—just as his "translation" from a "Calmbrood" play had foxed his father ten years earlier.[23]

IV

Between September 17 and 26, 1931, Nabokov wrote the story "Zanyatoy Chelovek" ("A Busy Man").[24] At thirty-two, Grafitski, a lonely émigré, suddenly recalls with the immediacy of the original event a youthful dream that he would die at thirty-three. Panic sets in, he dreads even the most unlikely deaths, he lives out the whole year in limbo. Only on his thirty-fourth birthday does the terror lapse.

Partly a black-comic parable on the absurdity of shaping one's life— or one's abstention from life, in this case—according to one's terror of death, the story becomes much more by dint of Nabokov's style. Thought rebounds and rebounds against the walls of its prison cell, hitting one Nabokovian theme after another: fate, solitude, death,

* The poem has already taken a swipe at Ivanov in the person of "Johnson" (the English equivalent of "Ivanov"), a critic trounced with a candlestick for a "marked [as in cards] article": none other than Ivanov's much-deplored *Chisla* attack on Sirin.

consciousness, time. On one typical night Grafitski looks "too long at the firmament and suddenly felt unable to suffer the burden and pressure of human consciousness, that ominous and ludicrous luxury." Relentlessly he searches for signs of his impending death, but recognizes that "The more one heeds coincidences the more often they happen." On the morning after his thirty-fourth birthday, he relaxes at last, and drifts off into a dream. He wakes, and as his memory of the dream fades, he feels he has not thought something through. Then, as if his year-long terror of death has faded utterly from memory, he carries on with life as normal.

Two things strike one at the conclusion of this complex tale. A host of apparent fatidic signs that crowd the end of the story point to Grafitski's having been granted an extension. Ivan Ivanovich Engel, a new fellow tenant in his apartment block, may appear to have been sent as the agent of God or fate, a sort of guardian angel. On the day after his thirty-fourth birthday, safely past the danger zone, Grafitski notices on a table in the hallway a telegram Engel had received the previous day: "extension agreed." But now that Grafitski's panic has left him, this and other signs slip past his notice. Perhaps events around us are signs of fate, Nabokov suggests, perhaps the supernatural is closer than we think, but no matter how desperately we look from within life, we cannot recognize the right clues. That will certainly be the burden of a later story, "The Vane Sisters," which also ends with the central character awake all night, dropping into a dream at dawn, and finding that the dream's yellow visions proffer no more than a sense of something "not understood, not thought through to the end."*

But perhaps the real point of the story can best be summed up by two lines from *Pale Fire*: "we die every day; oblivion thrives / Not on dry thighbones but on blood-ripe lives."[25] Unconsciousness surrounds us every moment; every moment forgotten yields to the sepulchral chill of the past. Obsessed by death lurking ahead in a future he cannot know, the story's hero ignores his present and discards his past, so sentencing each day to the death of oblivion.

V

By late 1931 Berlin was in serious trouble. German unemployment stood at five million. Relief kitchens had sprung up everywhere. Thousands of empty apartments were left behind as people sought

---

* In "A Busy Man," everything was somehow soft and luminous and enigmatic" in the hero's dream; in the narrator's dream in "The Vane Sisters," "Everything seemed blurred, yellow-clouded, yielding nothing tangible."

cheaper accommodation or quit the city altogether. Political hooliganism flourished while the country tried to decide whether to lurch right or left. Fascist students took to the streets, and *Rul'*, hobbling financially all year, had its offices attacked early in October—by communists, it was assumed.[26] By the time "A Busy Man" appeared in *Poslednie Novosti* on October 20, *Rul'* was dead.

Nabokov's imagination was continents away. In late October and early November he wrote the story "Terra Incognita."[27] An explorer-naturalist describes his last feverish hours in a tropical swamp. Through his hallucinations a bedroom keeps trying to show, as if he were bedridden with a high fever in some European city and the jungle were mere delirium. The evidence seems to suggest that must indeed be the case, but the narrator rejects the notion: "I realized that the obtrusive room was fictitious, . . . that reality was here, here beneath that wonderful, frightening tropical sky." Like the Chinese sage Chuang Tzu waking from his dream (is he a man dreaming he was a butterfly or a butterfly dreaming he was a man?) the story makes us feel we can know where our reality stands only by stepping outside it—but we cannot take that step in life.

"Terra Incognita" might have been merely a Borgesian conundrum, had not Nabokov's passion for exploration and for nature made it something more: a drama of courage set in a luxuriantly invented tropical world that only someone himself a naturalist could devise. Both the story's fabulous exoticism and its oscillation between two realities, curtained room and trackless terrain, are advance preparations for the daring expedition that makes up the great second chapter of *The Gift*.

As *Rul'* 's presses stopped, as Russian cafés closed their doors, and Russian concerts and shows played to sparser and sparser audiences, Russian Berlin struggled bravely on.[28] With journalists' outlets now so few, the Press Ball—canceled the previous year because of the grim economic situation—had to be held again in a desperate attempt to raise funds for the neediest writers. A thin weekly tabloid, *Nash Vek* (*Our Age*), edited by a group that included Ofrosimov and Saveliev, tried to fill the gap left by *Rul'*. The Aykhenvald circle, at least, managed to continue, and there in mid-November Nabokov read out parts of *Camera Obscura* to an overflowing auditorium.[29]

Over the following weeks he wrote the story "Usta k ustam" ("Lips to Lips"), completed on December 6.[30] A lonely, widowed, middle-aged businessman who has dabbled gingerly in literature decides to write a novel. On completing the cloyingly romantic thing, he is lured into subsidizing an ailing literary magazine whose editor feigns enchantment with his work. The next issue of the revived magazine publishes an excerpt from his novel—a humiliating three pages. In a theater foyer Ilya Borisovich overhears a conversation that reveals he has been duped and the magazine's editor considers his work a joke. But although at first he rushes away as fast as possible from something "shameful, odious, intolerable," he soon recovers and swallows his pride: "he must forgive everything, otherwise the 'to be continued' will never materialize. And he also told himself that he would be fully recognized after his death."

The deception of the harmless Ilya Borisovich seems the product of a ghoulish imagination. Indeed it was. Unfortunately, it had all happened in real life. A writer called Alexander Burov had let it be known he was planning to found a new review. When after four issues the Paris journal *Chisla* seemed about to collapse, its editor Nikolay Otsup and his friends Adamovich and Ivanov shamelessly flattered Burov, and a fifth issue of *Chisla* shortly appeared, with three pages by Burov in a style of wretchedly impassioned romanticism, and "To be continued" underneath.

Poslednie Novosti accepted Sirin's story on its fictional merits, and set it in type. Only then did someone recognize *Chisla* as the target of its satire. The type was broken up, and the story not published for another twenty-five years.[31]

After Nabokov's story was written, on the other hand, Burov's novella was in fact published in full in successive issues of *Chisla*, and a volume of his stories reviewed there in a breathless paraphrase that could be read as either rapt admiration or a barely suppressed sneer. Only in issue 10 of *Chisla*—the last—did Adamovich write a frank and damning critique of Burov's style. A few months later Burov and Ivanov clashed when they met, and a duel almost ensued (Ivanov called Burov out, Burov refused).[32] Years later Burov himself published a bitter lampoon on the whole affair, where he made it clear he still thought himself the unrecognized heir to Gogol, Tolstoy, and Dostoevsky that his flatterers had led him to believe he really was.[33]

VI

As Russians continued to flow westward from Berlin, other Russians trickled in from the Soviet Union. After a campaign against Evgeny Zamyatin for his novel *We*—the model for *Brave New World* and *1984*—Zamyatin was allowed to emigrate, perhaps because Gorky intervened on his behalf. On reaching Berlin in December 1931, he was able to read émigré writing for the first time, and hailed Sirin as a dazzling talent, the greatest acquisition of émigré literature.[34] Other Soviet writers visited Western Europe over the winter—Aleksey Tolstoy, Mikhail Zoshchenko—and to counter these westward forays by writers with "bourgeois inclinations" the Soviets sent a series of *proletkult* writers to Europe as cultural representatives.[35] Among them was Alexander Tarasov-Rodionov.

In his celebrated novel, *Shokolad* (*Chocolate*, 1922), Tarasov-Rodionov commends the Party's decision to kill a good Communist whom they know to be unjustly accused, in order—and here comes the stirring moral—to impress on the masses that the Revolution can afford to spare no one. (In 1937 Tarasov-Rodionov would himself fall victim to the same principle when he was denounced and died in a camp the next year.) In Berlin in December 1931 he left a note in Lyaskovsky's bookstore, where Sirin often browsed. Out of sportive curiosity, Sirin agreed to a meeting. As they sat together in a Russo-German café, Tarasov-Rodionov invited him back to extol the joys of farm life, Party life, village life. Sirin told him he would be delighted to return, under the condition that he would be "as perfectly free to write whatever I chose as I was abroad. 'Oh yes,' he answered, 'we can guarantee to you the best freedom that exists—freedom in the limits of the Communist Party.' " When a former White officer spoke to them in Russian—he was merely selling shoelaces—Stalin's stooge started in panic, supposing he was being spied upon: "Oh, so that's what you are doing to me."[36]

This scent of Soviet air may have started a Sirin story written in the middle of December, "Vstrecha" ("The Reunion").[37] In his Berlin flat an émigré hosts his brother, away from the Soviet Union on a brief business trip. Never close, with nothing in common in their recent lives, they can only be strainedly polite. At last a single chance memory, a rather tenuous one at that, promises to revive a shared past, but already they have to part again.

Another incident in mid-December may have lain in Nabokov's mind a little longer. A Russian student shot himself on a remote path in the Tiergarten.[38] In *The Gift*, the student Yasha Chernyshevsky shoots himself in Berlin's other famous park, the Grunewald. Perhaps the much more elaborate fictional incident sprang from the bare reported fact of the real event, but then in Berlin suicide had long been called "the émigré crime," and in these last two years more and more among the German populace too were taking their own lives.

VII

At the beginning of 1932 Sirin made his own response to the strain of the times. On the front page of *Poslednie Novosti* on January 2 1932, he made this uncharacteristic solo appeal:

It takes a person idle, cold and with an untenanted heart to turn from another's need or simply not notice it. Fortunately such people are few. It is impossible to imagine that in today's immeasurably difficult, hungry times anyone with a healthy conscience will refuse the utmost aid to the unemployed.

The next day Sirin met someone who might help him out of his own private financial slump. Sergey Bertenson, former Moscow Art Theater director, now working in Hollywood, had translated Nabokov's early story "The Potato Elf" and shown it to producer Lewis Milestone. The Russian-born Milestone was then at his peak, having just directed *All Quiet on the Western Front* (1930) and *The Front Page* (1931). He planned to turn "The Potato Elf" into a scenario—as Nabokov himself seems to have done shortly after writing the story in 1924—and wanted to fetch Nabokov to Hollywood to devise story lines for other scenarios. Bertenson talked over Milestone's proposals with Nabokov, noting in his diary: "He grew very excited at this. He told me that he literally adores the cinema and watches motion pictures with great keenness." Nabokov gave him the manuscript of *Camera Obscura*, but Bertenson judged it too erotic and too negative for Hollywood.[39] Nabokov agreed to send synopses of any of his work that might make a movie. At the end of the year he proposed his next novel, *Despair*, to Bertenson, and again nothing resulted.[40] But more and more frequently Nabokov's thoughts would now turn to a future in England or the United States.

On December 30 he began the story "Lebeda" ("Orache"), completing it on January 14, 1932.[41] Centered again on Peter Shishkov, the hero of "A Bad Day," it suggests Nabokov may have had in mind a large-scale fictional record of his childhood and adolescence, an idea that would take a much more radical form in the first chapter of *The Gift*. Or perhaps the story should be seen as the first germ of *Speak, Memory*, where the whole incident recurs. Here Peter hears at school that his father has called someone out to a duel. Bravely he controls his agony of suspense, and only the next day at school, when he discovers that the duel has already taken place and no one has been harmed, does he burst into uncontrollable tears of relief.

As a schoolboy himself in his first year at Tenishev, at the time of his father's near-duel, Nabokov had tended one of the school's makeshift goals every day that the weather allowed a game of courtyard soccer. Now he briefly began to play again. In November 1931 a Russian Sports Club had been set up in Berlin, its main venture a soccer team in which Nabokov was positioned, of course, at goal. By the end of the month he and the rest of the team were training twice a week on the fields of the Fehrbelliner Platz. On February 14, the team played its first match against a German club. Since they were still two players short, even with two reserves on the field, Nabokov had a busy time of it in goal. Only a few games and a few weeks later the Russian team played a very rough team of German factory workers. After diving for the ball Nabokov was knocked unconscious and had to be carried off the field. As he came round he found a teammate impatiently trying to pry the ball loose from his frozen grip. "After he had broken his ribs," Véra Nabokov recalled, "I put my foot down": and that was the end of soccer.[42]

"All these years the stupidest worry of my life has been a fruitless struggle with poverty," Nabokov later wrote to a friend.[43] Early in 1932, in severe financial straits for some time, the Nabokovs had to move a mile west from the Bardelebens, into a single room in the crowded apartment of the Cohn family, 29 Westfälische Strasse. It was an interim arrangement: a block away in Nestorstrasse was the apartment of Véra's cousin, Anna Feigin, whose co-tenant, a cousin on the other side of the family, would shortly be passing her rooms on to the Nabokovs when she left to get married.[44] Normally April 1 (like October 1) was the great day for shifting house in Berlin,* and never again would there be as many wanting smaller and more affordable rooms as on April 1, 1932.[45] But the Nabokovs had simply not been able to wait.

They had just enough for themselves, but it had become very difficult to send money to Elena Nabokov in Prague. On February 29 Nabokov resorted to a new expedient, raising funds through an invitation-only reading of his works in a private apartment.[46] There he read a chapter of *Camera Obscura*, some poems, and a new piece, "Muzyka" ("Music"), a straightforward but compelling story—possibly written with such an occasion in mind—of a man who at a private concert notices in the audience his ex-wife, whom he still loves.[47] As the pianist plays on, the man relives his past with his wife. Evidently she has seen him too, for she leaves as soon as the first piece on the program ends, and he discovers that the music he had thought a prison confining them together was actually bliss: it allowed him once more to breathe the same air as she did. Though the music appears to unite everyone in the same space and time—and the scene and the performance are brilliantly observed—the man's mind beats with a private passion, quite irrelevant to the music, quite irresistible, and evoked with superb power. As Simon Karlinsky comments:

---

* *The Gift* begins: "One cloudy but luminous day, towards four in the afternoon of April the first. . . . " Nabokov chose that date not only because a character will play an April Fool's prank on Fyodor, but also because Fyodor changes his flat that day. Bold authorial design turns out to be also accurate social observation.

"The story is as virtuosically composed as the piece the pianist is performing."

VIII

As another bout of election fever and another war of posters (Hindenburg! Hitler!) gaudily filled Berlin streets, Nabokov left Véra to the problem of evading their landlady's incessant chatter and took a train for Prague on April 3. Unmoved by the city's beauty, he found it as usual wretched and muddy, he could not stand the crows on grimy old monuments—but all the time he was storing impressions for the beginning of his next novel.[48] He had come of course for his family: his sisters and Kirill had kept a "surprising purity of spirit"; his mother was still in excellent form; and he took great delight in Olga's new son Rostislav, his mother's first grandchild. With his friend Raevsky he inspected a fresh collection of butterflies in the museum, and announced "in summer we are going to Bulgaria. That is decided." At the home of the philosopher Sergey Hessen, another of Iosif Hessen's sons and a Tenishev old boy, he met and liked very much a future friend, Harvard historian Mikhail Karpovich, who at the end of the decade would do perhaps more than anyone else to secure the Nabokovs' entry into America. He reread *Madame Bovary* "for the hundredth time."[49]

Already dissatisfied with *Camera Obscura*, even before its first serial appearance, he confided to Véra the plan for a new novel:

> Imagine this. A person prepares for an automobile examination on the city's geography. The first part will talk of the preparations for this and conversations linked with it, and also, of course, his family and his human surroundings, with a misty detailedness. Then an unnoticed transition to the second. Off he goes, finds himself at the examination, but not at all an automobile one but—how shall I put this—an examination of earthly existence. He has died and they are asking him about the streets and crossroads of his life. All this without a shade of mysticism. In this exam he tells all he remembers of . . . the brightest and most solid parts of his whole life. And those examining him are people long dead, for instance, the coachman who made a toboggan for him in childhood, an old high-school teacher, some distant relatives he had only heard about in life. That's the embryo. I can only put this badly it seems, but it's difficult, for the novel is still at the stage of feelings, not thoughts.[50]

In fact it would never be written. But the attempt to have a character die and somehow continue beyond death would be one Nabokov made again and again.

He tried hard to obtain his own copy of *Ulysses* but could find Joyce only in Czech translation. In any case he knew the book well enough by now to offend a fellow émigré by declaring he preferred Joyce to Dostoevsky.[51] He also tried to obtain a two-day extension for his visa, and ran into trouble. One bureaucrat refused to talk with him in German (which Nabokov at least knew better than Czech) "Because, after all, we are both Slavs"—but then hinted that his fellow Slav would hardly be welcome another two days. "I simply don't give a hoot if they try to jam a log into my little watch's cogs," he wrote to Véra, "I'll stay here until the twentieth, and then let things happen as they will. Might be trouble at the border, but I'll get through." But his worried mother insisted he follow correct channels and after two more trips to the visa office, all the right papers had all the right stamps.[52]

Late on the evening of April 20, Nabokov's train pulled into Berlin's Anhalter Bahnhof. The next day he began writing the story "Khvat" ("A Dashing Fellow"), and finished on May 5.[53] A traveling salesman, an émigré of former gentry stock, picks up a woman on a train, stops off at her home town, accompanies her to her flat. While the woman is out briefly, someone calls to tell her that her father is dying. The impatient traveler does not pass on the message when she returns, but hastens to possess her, manages no more than a premature ejaculation and then, feigning to pop out to buy a cigar while she cooks dinner, returns to the station and carries on to his destination.

An excellent study of a hearty, heartless, self-satisfied vulgarian seen from the inside, the story is told with a lurid vitality to match the colors and forms flicking past the train window and a speed that keeps pace with the clattering train or a male in rut. It follows the unpleasant twists of the hero's mind this way and that: the fraudulent patter of the pickup, a polluted stream of consciousness, a would-be imposing narrative "we" that grates like everything else about the man: "We have a swarthy complexion, a network of purple-red veins, a black mustache, trimly clipped, and hairy nostrils. . . . During the last trip we were unfaithful to Katya three times, and that cost us thirty Reichsmarks." There is little so *dramatic* as this in Nabokov, so completely an entry into another mind. The miracle is that the story makes a squalid mind and manners so colorful—albeit in the repellent hues of a garish tie.

On May 7 Sirin traveled to Dresden for a reading of his own work in the cellar of a Russian church.[54] Back in Berlin over the next month he wrote another story arising from his travels across Germany, "Sovershenstvo" ("Perfection").[55] This time he turns sharply from negative to positive, from outrage at life without a trace of tenderness to a glance ahead to another state where tenderness might be all. Ivanov, an impoverished émigré, ekes out a living as a tutor. Outwardly shy before life, he has learned to compensate for the loneliness of a drab existence by accepting with quiet gratitude the gifts the world distributes free of charge—clouds, the sight of old men on a bench or little girls playing at hopscotch—and especially by imbibing in imagination the excitement of all that he has never seen and will never experience:

> Sometimes, as he looked at a chimneysweep . . . or at an airplane overtaking a cloud, Ivanov daydreamed about the many things that he would never get to know closer, about professions that he would never practice, about a parachute, opening like a colossal corolla. . . . He had a passionate desire to experience everything, to attain and touch everything, to let the dappled voices, the bird calls, filter through his being and to enter for a moment into a passerby's soul as one enters the cool shade of a tree. His mind would be preoccupied with unsolvable problems: How and where do chimneysweeps wash after work? Has anything changed about that forest road in Russia that a moment ago he had recalled so vividly?

One summer he chaperones a young Russian Jewish boy he tutors in Berlin on a vacation at a Baltic beach. When the bored young boy feigns drowning, Ivanov swims out to rescue him, and his weak heart gives way. Somehow he emerges again onto the sand, as if in twilight, and cannot see David. He rehearses explaining the boy's death to his mother, but realizes "there was something amiss about these thoughts, and when he looked around once more and saw himself in the desolate mist all alone with no David beside him, he understood that if David was not with him, David was not dead." With the realization of his own death, things suddenly clear: "The dull mist immediately broke, blossomed with marvelous colors, all kinds of sounds burst forth. . . ." He can see David, alarmed at the result of his prank, he can see the search for his own body,

> and the Baltic Sea sparkled from end to end, and, in the thinned-out forest, across a green country road, there lay, still breathing, freshly cut aspens; and a youth, smeared with soot gradually turned white as he washed under the kitchen tap, and black parakeets flew above the eternal snows of the New Zealand mountains. . . .

Perhaps because he has imagined so vividly the excitements of life outside his own, perhaps simply because he has died, Ivanov now appears to have all life before him, all his longings satisfied, all his questions answered.

In July Nabokov wrote "Vecher na pustyre" ("Evening on a Vacant Lot"),[56] his first poem in his mature verse manner, and halfway between insomnia and somnambulism, like Richard Wilbur's splendid

"Walking to Sleep." Waiting for inspiration on a vacant lot, the poet feels a haunting absence in the air, and contrasts his taut wariness now with the easy rhymes he could knock together in the past, as he waited on the paths of the old park. Now he hears a whistle, a man comes toward him and calls. He can tell it is his father

> I recognize
> your energetic stride. You haven't
> changed much since you died.

At the end of *The Gift*, Fyodor will dream of walking to meet his dead father, and somehow his father's presence seems to shadow and shine through the whole novel. By the time Nabokov wrote "Evening on a Vacant Lot," almost all the materials his life had been unconsciously amassing for *The Gift* were at hand.

Distant Prospects: Berlin, 1932–1934

I

AT THE BEGINNING of June 1932 Hindenburg dissolved the Reichstag and called for elections in late July. When he rescinded the ban on the storm troopers and the SS, Brown Shirts and Black Shirts took to the streets. Murderous clashes erupted between Nazis and Communists. Flags, uniforms, and the blare of music set new low levels for an election campaign. The National Socialists were about to become the largest party in the Reichstag, and it would be only a matter of time before Hindenburg had to appoint Hitler chancellor.

Despite the turmoil in the streets, despite the advent of Hitler, the Nabokovs would remain in Berlin for almost another five years. With European unemployment still at record levels, there was one immediate reason to stay put. When Nabokov met a Russian acquaintance, Alexander Brailow, quitting Germany because of the storm troopers' political assassinations, he confessed he would like to leave too, but could not afford to as long as Véra still had her job as a secretary.[1]

The other reason lasted longer: the Nabokovs' happy base in a charming, spacious flat in an "almost idyllic retreat." Under the dusty lindens of late summer, at the end of August 1932, they moved in with Véra's cousin Anna Feigin, taking two rooms in her four-room flat on the third floor of 22 Nestorstrasse in the Wilmersdorf district of Berlin, and splitting the rent with her. A talented pianist who never had the chance to pursue her studies, Anna Feigin was no intellectual, but Nabokov would value her friendship highly over the fifty years he knew her, and come to think her "a marvellous example of humanity."[2]

A month before moving in to Nestorstrasse on July 31, 1932, Nabokov had begun to write a new novel, *Otchayanie* (*Despair*). By September 10, worn out, he had finished the first draft.[3]

II
Despair (Otchayanie)

Hermann, a Russian of German descent, now a chocolate manufacturer in Berlin, discovers on a business trip to Prague a tramp whose features appear absolutely indistinguishable from his own. Happy in his marriage but restless and dissatisfied with the bland routine of apartment and office, he insures himself heavily, dupes the tramp into exchanging clothes with him, and shoots him. He heads off for France, where his wife, Lydia, is to join him with the insurance booty.[4]

Installed in a village in the Pyrenees, however, he discovers in the newspapers that his plan has fallen flat: Felix's corpse has not been taken for his, and the police are quite bewildered that Hermann could have "hoped to deceive the world simply by dressing up in my clothes an individual who was not in the least like me." To justify the artistry of his crime, unappreciated by a crass public, Hermann at once sets about writing the story of his masterpiece. Only when he has almost finished does he find in a recent newspaper that his car—left as a marker at the scene of the murder, but then stolen—has been retrieved, and an object in it has provided detectives with the victim's name. What possible object, Hermann snorts to himself, since the whole point of all his planning had been to force the world to identify the corpse wrongly, to pass off murderer as victim. To check, he rereads his own story. Suddenly he sees the fatal flaw, the elementary blunder: a walking cane with Felix's name inscribed on it, casually left behind by Felix in Hermann's car. Perhaps the public are right, Hermann winces: perhaps after all he is not a criminal of genius but a madman and a fool. He picks up his manuscript and writes on it the only title now possible: *Despair*. Defeated, he sits and waits for the police to close in, finishing off in his last two days of freedom the manuscript he had begun in celebration of the perfect crime.

A murder novel and a story of doubles, *Despair* refers again and again to "old Dusty," Dostoevsky. The book was originally to have had an epigraph from Dostoevsky, and even its first working title, *Zapiski mistifikatora* (*Notes of a Hoaxer*) would have echoed *Notes from Underground*.[5] But *Despair* appears to lack all the criminal psychology we might expect from the man Nabokov called "that famous writer of Russian thrillers," "our national expert in soul ague." Hermann's motives seem virtually nonexistent. Of course he welcomes the thought of insurance money and a life of leisured ease, but for someone like him these do not add up to anything like a compulsion to murder. As for remorse, he has none. Nabokov rejects Dostoevsky's fascination with the criminal and his trust that the hand that plunges into the mud of shame and humiliation will extract some spiritual pearl.

If there is little apparent motive in any ordinary sense, Hermann advances what for Nabokov was the highest motive of all, the incentive of art. Hermann sees himself as an artist in crime, a creative genius who has turned an accident life presented (his face reflected in

Felix's) into a flawless plan. Insurance money will be gratefully accepted—as a sort of royalty for his completed design—but the sheer perfection of the work has been his goal.

Hermann begins his tale:

> If I were not perfectly sure of my power to write and of my marvelous ability to express ideas with the utmost grace and vividness . . . So, more or less, I had thought of beginning my tale. Further, I should have drawn the reader's attention to the fact that had I lacked that power, that ability, et cetera, not only should I have refrained from describing certain recent events, but there should have been nothing to describe, for, gentle reader, nothing at all would have happened. Silly, perhaps, but at least clear.

His murder plan is only the latest in a long series of exuberant creative exercises: verse and stories composed in his head as a child, an unpublished novel or two, but most of all his "inspired lying": "I lied as a nightingale sings, ecstatically, self-obliviously."

Hermann's buoyant literary confidence makes *Despair*, despite its title, a thing of joy. Self-consciousness and parody are for the first time fully liberated in Nabokov's style, to remain at large for another forty fertile years. Rushing on without revising, Hermann digresses, coaxes the gentle reader, lurches forward, cannot settle down: "My hands tremble. I want to shriek or to smash something with a bang. . . . This mood is hardly suitable for the bland unfolding of a leisurely tale." But as his hysteria subsides, he succumbs to the sheer delight of composition. In this mood he may choose to offer three openings for a chapter, each at first evocative but brilliantly exposed by the play of his critical intelligence as a suspect and facile device. Or, as the book draws to a close, he rapidly sums up, only to confess he has led us into an old-fashioned epilogue concocted from events he has just invented. Hermann cannot resist parading his mastery of literary ploys, his criminal ploys, his own hysterical self.

Self is the key word. Where Hermann sees his crimes as a work of art and himself as the consummate artist, Nabokov exposes both as the negation of all he understands by art. For him art is not an occasion for self-display, but a chance to reach beyond the self, not an indulgent pastime but a moral positive, a means of defining human existence and an intimation of something beyond.

Whether creating or responding to a work of art, the imagination passes as it were beyond the boundaries of the self to enter into other life: another time, another place, another mind. Without that capacity of consciousness, art could not exist—and neither could moral choice.

For without the imaginative sympathy that allows one mind to intuit another, without the ability to imagine another's pain, morality would be meaningless. In his most famous single statement on his own art, Nabokov would declare himself

> neither a reader nor a writer of didactic fiction, and, despite John Ray's assertion, *Lolita* has no moral in tow. For me a work of fiction exists only insofar as it affords me what I shall bluntly call aesthetic bliss, that is a sense of being somehow, somewhere, connected with other states of being where art (curiosity, tenderness, kindness, ecstasy) is the norm.[6]

But he later welcomed the idea that "one day a reappraiser will come and declare that, far from having been a frivolous firebird, I was a rigid moralist, kicking sin, cuffing stupidity, ridiculing the vulgar and cruel—and assigning sovereign power to tenderness, talent, and pride."[7] In the light of that later statement and of his whole philosophy, the definition of "aesthetic bliss" seems more illuminating than the label: "other states of being" means what it says, and Nabokov links the phrase to moral values that stress the transcendence of self. Perhaps beyond death the soul can *stand outside itself* (the literal sense of "ecstasy"), and enter, in a spirit of curiosity and tenderness and kindness, into each disregarded trifle, each bruised and battered mortal heart. A work of fiction can anticipate such a state by eliciting this kind of response within life, as *Lolita* does when it traps us within Humbert's mind but invites us to escape, to imagine Lolita's pain—for the sake of which Nabokov wrote the whole novel.

Hermann's bloated sense of self and his obliviousness to everyone else makes him for Nabokov the antithesis of the artist. His awe at himself is matched only by his disdain for the rest of creation, even for the wife with whom he thinks he shares a cloudless marriage. He considers his "connubial bliss" complete only because Lydia—"a bird-witted but attractive wife who worshiped me"—acts as an enlarging mirror for his own pride. The few characters in the novel outside Hermann—Felix, Lydia, her cousin Ardalion, the lawyer Orlovius—remain sketchy because seen through his eyes. He dismisses them all behind their backs ("numbskull," "brainless") and to their faces ("blockhead," "fool"). Far from trying to enter into Felix's mind, he simply ignores it. Denying Felix a life of his own, he need think nothing of putting him to death.

Hermann's crime parodies as well as negates the attempt of art to transcend the self. Rather than feeling for Felix in any way, Hermann tries to stamp his own face on Felix's, eliminate him, and head off with Felix's purloined identity. But crime, in Nabokov's eyes, always contains the germ of its own imperfection: the insane claims of self at the expense of all else, the impossibility of controlling a future that after all is not willed into being by one's own desire. As Felix steps out of Hermann's car, supposing he will be allowed to drive it once he and Hermann change clothes, Hermann notes that Felix admires the car now "No more with the longing of ogling indigence, but with an owner's quiet satisfaction." What Hermann does not realize until far too late is that in this mood Felix would leave his stick in the car upon getting out, "naturally—for the car temporarily belonged to him." In a world where everything has its own independent life—as Martha Dreyer found out in *King, Queen, Knave*—nothing can be perfectly planned.

Hermann thinks his ploy a stroke of dazzling genius whose mastery a dim-witted world fails to appreciate. He seems not to realize that fiddling an insurance claim is one of the most hackneyed of crimes. Much of the comedy of the novel in fact springs from the gap between Hermann's notion of his genius—his perceptiveness and originality— and the grotesque reality. Dazzled by the brilliance of his scheme, he does not see what everyone else in his world can see: that he and Felix have no special similarity whatsoever. Perhaps most absurd of all is Hermann's unruffled confidence in his marriage and his ignorance of the blatant affair between his wife and her cousin, the painter Ardalion.

Hermann's self-importance appears to blind him completely to Lydia's and Ardalion's sexual shenanigans, their inseparability, their endearments. In fact it merely blinkers him, and he knows below the threshold of direct awareness that if he turned his head he could see. But even to himself he will not face the possibility. How could he hold on to his sense of being so special—and this is his whole world—if he had to admit that Lydia could love someone else as much as or even more than him?

Like a true artist, Hermann stresses that what excites him about his crime is the sheer perfection of its design. What he does not admit even to himself is that he has undertaken the murder in order to rid himself and Lydia of the shadow of Ardalion and to prove himself more of an artist than this rival he refuses to acknowledge.

Here Nabokov poses for the first time the sort of challenge that he would set himself again and again in the future. Whatever else he may be, Hermann is highly articulate and alert as a writer. How then can Nabokov convey a meaning quite the converse of the one Hermann wants to express? Here, as in *Lolita* and *Ada* and elsewhere, Nabokov incorporates covert parallels that form a sort of private code which eludes Hermann's attention but can be deciphered by the alert reader.

Hermann sees a tramp stretched out asleep, as if dead, on a hill above Prague. Obsessed by himself yet full of an unvoiced urge to escape from self and situation, he sees just what he wants to see, a face exactly like his own:

> "Nonsense," I told myself. "Asleep, merely asleep. No reason for me to intrude." But nevertheless I approached, and with the toe of my elegant shoe flicked the cap off his face.
>
> Trumpets, please! Or still better, that tattoo which goes with a breathless acrobatic stunt. Incredible! I doubted the reality of what I saw, doubted my own sanity, felt sick and faint—honestly I was forced to sit down, my knees were shaking so.

Now when Ardalion first appears in the novel he too is asleep and trumpets are once again at hand. Ardalion has prevailed on Hermann and Lydia to drive out with him to his new lakeside lot some hours out of Berlin, but he has overslept.

> Long did I keep toot-tooting, with my eyes fixed on his window. That window slept soundly. Lydia put her hands to her mouth and cried out in a trumpet voice: "Ar-dally-o-o!" In one of the lower windows . . . a curtain was dashed aside furiously and a Bismarck-like worthy in frogged dressing gown glanced out with a real trumpet in his hand.
>
> Leaving Lydia in the car, which by now had stopped throbbing, I went up to arouse Ardalion. I found him asleep.

When in this first scene with Ardalion we arrive at his new lot, Hermann's imagination runs forward again and again to the murder that will take place here later in the year: snow and the bare trees of winter show persistently, hysterically, through the summer scene. As Hermann drives off the road and toward the forest, Ardalion announces, interrupted by the jolts of the car: "We shall soon (bump) get into the wood (bump) and then (bump-bump) the heather will make it easier (bump)." Months later, half an hour before he kills Felix, Hermann drives his victim over the same stretch of ground and listens to Felix's keen chatter: "I'll manage this car without any trouble (bump). Lord, what a ride I'll take (bump). Never fear (bump-bump), I won't do it any harm!" Felix of course leaves behind his telltale cane, which Hermann forgets until the police discovery reminds him about it. But Ardalion on his first visit to the future murder site had brought a bottle of vodka which Lydia confiscated and buried. By the time they left, they had forgotten about it, and like Felix's stick it remains unremembered until the police search of the murder site recalls it to mind.

Once the murder is accomplished, once Lydia receives the insurance money and travels abroad to join Hermann, safe in a new identity, Ardalion will be left forever behind: no one—and that means especially Ardalion—must ever know Hermann has not really died. As the pointed parallels between Felix and Ardalion suggest—sleep and trumpets, bumpy conversation, object left behind at the murder site—it is Ardalion himself Hermann wants to dispose of, it is Ardalion he would have lured to that murder site if only he could have obliterated him as easily as he could a homeless tramp.

Not only does Hermann want to kill Ardalion off in Lydia's mind and her life, he also wants to prove himself to her by outperforming Ardalion as an artist. Curiously, he only repeats in far grosser form Ardalion's own shortcomings. At the site of the future murder, Ardalion tries to draw a portrait of Hermann. It does not succeed, but when Ardalion completes another portrait, Hermann comments: "Look as one might, none could see the ghost of a likeness!" Later, of course, no one will see the likeness of himself that he has tried to create in Felix, and on that same patch of ground: "that masterpiece of mine (finished and signed on the ninth of March in a gloomy wood)."

Far from shaking Ardalion off, Hermann finds himself haunted by his presence even in his Roussillon refuge. In his fantasy epilogue he has Lydia happily declare: "How glad I am . . . that we are forever rid of Ardalion. I used to pity him a good deal, and gave him a lot of my time, but, really, I could never stand the man." In real life Hermann, already aware his murder plan has gone horribly awry, calls at the Pignan Post Office for mail for "Ardalion." (Forced to choose an alias his forgetful wife would not let slip from memory when she wrote to him in hiding, he had had to suggest the name Ardalion.) He finds only one letter, not from Lydia but from Ardalion himself, in whom Lydia, now suspected of complicity in murder, has of course confided. The letter's tone is extraordinary: deliberately, willfully cheap, and at the same time seething with moral indignation at what Hermann has done in embroiling the intimidated and uncomprehending Lydia in his scheme. I may not be much, Ardalion suggests, but look at you. After almost two hundred pages of Hermann's self-glorification, no matter how transparently undeserved, it comes as a shock to encounter the ringing—and perfectly justified—contempt felt for him by Ardalion, a sloven, a cadger, a weak-willed drunkard, who has seemed till now only a slightly sleazy joke. For all that jars in his letter, he displays a compassion for Lydia infinitely beyond Hermann's reach.

Ardalion points out to Hermann that "Those little tricks . . . with life policies, have been known for ages," and that not only was there no resemblance between him and his victim but that "in the whole world there are not and cannot be, two men alike, however well you disguise them." Here he echoes an earlier exchange with Hermann. After Hermann had prated of facial types and resemblances between faces, Ardalion had retorted: "Every face is unique. . . . what the artist perceives is, primarily, the *difference* between things." Too blind to the world outside himself to notice the uniqueness in anyone or anything else, Hermann insists *he* alone counts, he alone has the kind of brilliance needed to devise the perfect crime. And how does the crackpot set out to prove how unique he is? By trying to convince the world that someone else is exactly like him.

For Nabokov the criminal ignores what the true artist knows, the gap between human desire and the frustrating world of fact. The permanence and perfection of a work of art offer our only legitimate, albeit limited, escape from our life imprisonment within an evanescent and imperfect world. But art can function like that only if the artist has a firm grasp on the distinction between art and life. Vaguely dissatisfied with his own existence, Hermann tries to create a masterpiece within life that will allow him to sneak beyond the boundaries of death, killing "himself" but living on in another guise. Like *The Eye*, *Despair* can be seen as a fantasy about surviving after death and "transcending" the self. But for what, in Hermann's case? For a life of bourgeois ease with a wife he has not taken the trouble to know. His goal is as banal as his method, and far from reaching the timeless freedoms of art he ends his tale trapped in one last lair, scribbling out his diary in the relentlessly eroding present, writing of his last moments of freedom *in* these desperate last moments as the police march up to his door.

Nabokov's sheer intelligence crackles in every line of *Despair*, but for all the brio of the book's style something seems sadly lacking in its structure. Hermann allows Nabokov to parody his own sense of art as a step beyond the self and toward a sympathy for others perhaps even richer than life allows. Nabokov has never inverted values he holds dear with more gusto or glee, but Hermann's unwarranted supposition that another face looks like his remains a brittle and meager basis for a whole novel. It never quite convinces, and page after page that would make one tingle with excitement in another context can here only intermittently overcome one's remoteness from a story whose central premise fails to merit the suspension of disbelief.

III

In early October, a couple of weeks after Nabokov finished the first draft of *Despair*, Véra took a two-week vacation. Normally they could not afford an out-of-town holiday, but friends had invited Vladimir's cousin, the composer Nicolas Nabokov, with his wife, Nathalie, and their son, to a little house on their estate in Kolbsheim, near Strasbourg, and the NNs in turn invited the VNs. With the summer well over and the butterfly-collecting season past, Vladimir had to be content to walk and talk in the almost incessant rain.[8] When Véra returned to her job in Berlin, he remained at Kolbsheim, since he was about to travel on to Paris for his first public reading there. He wrote back to his wife:[9]

> I am saving mice, there are lots in the kitchen. The maid catches them, and the first time wanted to kill the one she had caught, but I took it out into the garden and let it go. Since then all the mice are brought to me, with a snort. . . . I've already let three go that way—or perhaps it's all the same mouse.*

He had a story in mind that he hoped to compose before leaving, but for once inspiration would not come. Instead his francophone surroundings suggested another idea: an essay on the special French world of the Russian gentry, with their *Bibliothèque rose* volumes, their governesses, their French verse.[10] And even that idea would have to wait another three years.

IV

In late October Nabokov took his first trip to Paris since the city had become the center of the emigration and Sirin the emigration's foremost young writer. The trip was partly a reading tour, partly an exploratory mission—could he and Véra find some means of living there?—and wholly a public occasion.

He arrived in the late afternoon of October 21, settled in the flat of his cousin Nicolas, 9 rue Jacques Mawas, and by 7:30 was at Fondaminsky's, where he would call every day. Like others, he soon came to think Fondaminsky "simply an angel." As so often, he found others there when he arrived at the Fondaminsky flat. Vladimir Zenzinov, another *Sovremennye Zapiski* editor and an old Socialist Revolutionary terrorist,† an inseparable friend of Fondaminsky and his wife, would become a good friend of Nabokov in his Paris and American years. Alexander Kerensky was also there, near-sighted, gruffly jo-

---

* Curiously Chekhov, with whom Nabokov has many affinities, writes in one of his letters about releasing mice caught in mousetraps (*Letters of Anton Chekhov*, ed. Simon Karlinsky and Michael Henry Heim, p. 226).

† Zenzinov earned an embarrassing fame as the man who allowed the notorious double agent Azef to escape while under his surveillance.

vial, and as theatrical as he had been on center stage in 1917. When compliments passed on *Camera Obscura*, Kerensky shook Sirin's hand, held it for a long pause, peered through his gold lorgnette, and whispered dramatically: "Wonderful!" With Fondaminsky, Sirin then went on to the home of jolly, roundish little Mark Vishnyak, the third *Sovremennye Zapiski* editor. There he also met quiet Vadim Rudnev, the fourth and final editor, and the two literary stalwarts of *Poslednie Novosti*, Igor Demidov and a pudgy-looking Mark Aldanov.[11]

The next day Sirin's tall, lean, sporty figure appeared at the *Poslednie Novosti* offices. He met the talented young poet Antonin Ladinsky, working there as a telephone boy, and set off with Aldanov and Demidov for a nearby café. Novelist and poet Nina Berberova came up to them, her animated eyes flashing, and recounted in detail for Sirin her recent split with Khodasevich, with whom she had lived for the last ten years.[12]

Every day continued in the same manner, with one visit flowing into another, all day long, in cafés, offices, apartments, public halls, cafés again: his brother Sergey, glassy-eyed, somehow tragic; aunts and cousins; friends of his father's, like Paul Milyukov, Alexander Benois, Mme Vinaver, all proud that V. D. Nabokov's pride in young Volodya had been so amply justified; friends from school, from Berlin's émigré heydays, from the first years of his marriage; French writers, translators, editors, publishers; and most of all Russian literary Paris. Anyone he rang knew already he was in town. Paris was full of talk about him, he wrote back to Berlin: "they find me 'English,' 'high-quality.' They say I always travel with a tub, like Martin I suppose. And already my *bons mots* are coming back to me."[13]

He visited Ivan Lukash, unhappy and isolated in Meudon. He tried to avoid the Merezhkovskys, but one night arrived at Fondaminsky's as they were leaving: Zinaida Gippius, red-haired and deaf, and her husband Dmitri Merezhkovsky, shortish and bearded like a prophet. A little chill swept through the room, and neither side uttered a word before each went its separate way. He met Mikhail Osorgin, a journalist and novelist and one of his long-term admirers in Paris, but did not care for him. Boris Zaitsev, surrounded by icons and pictures of patriarchs, he found rather likable and straightforward. He did not meet Remizov, whom Zaitsev warned him he had mortally offended with his review. He dined at the home of playwright Nikolay Evreinov, and detected a "mystical-Freudian-Goyaesque" air mingling with the cooking smells: "Evreinov is a person of a type quite alien to me, but very funny and welcoming and ardent. When he mimics something or someone, he seems wonderfully talented, but when he philosophizes, awfully vulgar. He said, for instance, that all people are divided into 'types' . . . and that Dostoevsky is the greatest writer in the world."[14] He met Alexander Kuprin, whom he liked as a writer, and found him "terribly nice, a little old muzhik with narrow eyes" who could barely speak French at all. He delighted in Mother Maria (Elizaveta Kuzmin-Karavaev), "fat and pinkish," nun and poet. He called on André Levinson, sitting in state in his luxurious apartment, wrapped in a red dressing gown, his eyelids solemnly and benevolently lowering themselves, each of his words flanked by its own respectful pause, his whole attitude to the émigré press like an emperor's disdain for some distant, small, intractable country.[15]

But the people Sirin really became close to in émigré literary circles were Khodasevich, Aldanov, and Fondaminsky.

Late on the afternoon of October 23 he called on Khodasevich, living in poverty in a small, slovenly, sour-smelling apartment on the outskirts of Paris. They had admired each other's work for years but never met. Sirin found the forty-six-year-old poet's emaciated, boyish face rather monkeylike. He sensed something touching in Khodasevich and liked him at once, despite the gloomy backdrop to his existence, his unfunny jokes, his way of clicking out words, and he appreciated all the kindness the older poet showed to him.[16]

In anticipation of Sirin's visit Khodasevich had invited Nina Berberova, along with other young writers, Yuri Terapiano, Vladimir Smolensky, and Vladimir Weidle. In her memoirs Berberova recalled the conversation that day between host and guest of honor as the prototype of Fyodor's imaginary talks with his fellow writer Koncheyev in *The Gift*.[17] Nabokov denied the identification, and undoubtedly he was right. Two days after his second visit to Khodasevich he called at Berberova's, where he met Yuri Felzen, a young prose-writer and Sirin admirer. Although he liked Berberova, he found her conversation tiresome: "the talk was exclusively literary, and I soon began to feel sick of it. I haven't had such conversations since high-school days. 'Do you know this? Do you like this? Have you read this?' In a word, awful."[18]

One of the things Nabokov liked about Khodasevich was the speed with which he caught Nabokov's jokes. Mark Aldanov on the other hand could never tell whether he was joking or not.[19] That was symptomatic of the whole relationship between Nabokov and Aldanov: genuine friendship, but limited by radical differences in temperament. Aldanov, a chemist by training and now a historical novelist by profession, was by nature a literary diplomat and broker. In awe of Sirin's talent, he feared it as something barbed and unruly. Sirin for his part respected the skeptical intelligence and conscientious construction of Aldanov's novels, but knew they lacked any trace of artistic magic. But he would always be grateful for his friend's kind solicitude and advice about the literary marketplace.

Through Aldanov, Sirin met another émigré, a professor at the University of California named Alexander Kaun. Kaun liked Sirin's work and took several books to show to American publishers he knew. Sirin wrote back to Berlin: "If the Americans buy even one novel—well, you know the rest." At the dinner where he met Kaun, a heated argument developed on the theme of the young émigré generation and the modern world: "Zaitsev uttered Christian platitudes, Khodasevich literary platitudes, my dear, holy Fondik [Fondaminsky] very touching things of a social character, and from Vishnyak . . . we had some healthy materialism. . . . I of course vented my little idea about the non-existence of the epoch."[20]

Nabokov also entered French literary circles. He met Denis Roche, who was translating *The Defense* into French, and was pleased by his attention to detail. He found the poet Jules Supervielle "terribly nice and talented," and they quickly became friends. He translated some of Supervielle's verse into Russian, while Supervielle went into raptures over excerpts from the French *Defense*. Nabokov became friends too with the philosopher and dramatist Gabriel Marcel, who already had a keen interest in his work, and dined with Jean Paulhan of the *Nouvelle Revue française*. He visited Grasset and Fayard, his two forthcoming French publishers. He met Doussia Ergaz, about to translate *Camera Obscura*, and found her charming. With her excellent contacts within literary Paris, she soon became his main European literary agent.[21]

In between his professional visits Nabokov had friends and family to see. In 1926 he had met C. Bertrand Thompson, husband of Véra's close friend Lisbet Thompson, and the two men became friends for life. An American in his forties (with, like Pushkin, some African ancestry), Bertrand Thompson had entered university at fifteen and emerged with a law degree at eighteen. Too young to practice, he wrote on legal subjects and studied music, then acquired a social science degree and lectured at Harvard, turning down an assistant professorship there to become a management consultant while writing books on management, sociology, and economics. In his sixties he would study biochemistry and briefly hold a university position in the subject until forced to retire, when he would begin cancer research that lasted until his eighties. He read widely in mysticism of all kinds, Christian, Muslim, Persian, and Hindu; he once set Lermontov to music. Nabokov judged that Thompson "could speak more interestingly and knowledgeably on virtually any subject" than anyone else he ever met. In Paris the Thompsons regaled him more than once with champagne, bottle after bottle of wine, and Bertrand's sparkling, heady conversation.[22]

Nabokov also called several times on Savely Kyandzhuntsev, his Tenishev schoolmate, and was delighted to find not only that he and his mother had not changed at all, but that they "knew to the last line all I have written. . . . I felt as if I'd been at their place on the Liteyny just a few days ago. . . . Sava went to his room, rooted around and returned with a long poem I sent him from St. Petersburg to Kislovodsk, October 25, 1917, first day of the Soviet era."[23] Since Sirin had no tuxedo to wear at his public reading, Kyandzhuntsev promised to have his own altered for the occasion.

He was "simply amazed," in fact, at "the wonderfully disinterested, tender attitude everyone has shown me": fellow littérateurs, friends, family. When Nathalie Nabokov returned from Strasbourg, he moved in, on November 5, with a poor but hospitable cousin, another Baron Rausch von Traubenberg, at 122 Boulevard Murat. He had to sleep in the living room, some nights with another guest sharing the room. What with his daily round of visits and this lack of privacy, he found the story he had been trying to write—for some reason it required rereading Ronsard—impossible to complete, and it seems not to have been resumed even when he returned to the comparative calm of Berlin.[24]

Before the social whirl began to leave him distracted and exhausted, Nabokov had felt that Paris would be an ideal place to write, and prospects looked much better than in Berlin. He wrote to Véra "I think we must come here," and suggested January as a good time to move. He thought that Vasily Maklakov, once his father's CD colleague and now the official representative of Russian émigrés in France, would easily obtain them a visa.[25] Less confident that his literary work alone could support them in Paris, Véra remained reluctant to move.

V

By mid-November the last sidewalk cafés had retreated indoors and smoke from chestnut braziers puffed up from the corners of busy avenues. Badly needing to catch up on sleep before his public reading, Sirin transferred on November 13 to the Fondaminsky's, 1 rue Chernoviz, in Passy, Paris's Russian quarter. This large, elegant apartment—paid for by the good income Fondaminsky's wife received from a tea plantation in Ceylon—had been the Fondaminsky's home since they fled Russia in 1906.* Sirin's change of address was worth it. The first night there he slept thirteen hours, and Fondaminsky was waiting at hand to run a bath for him when he awoke. Amalia Fondaminsky mothered him. She provided him with a special dressing table with his own talc and eau-de-cologne and soap. She typed up the thirty-odd pages of *Despair*—its revision just completed—that he planned to read. She even said nothing when his constant smoking badly affected her lungs.[26]

As he dressed for his reading, Sirin found Kyandzhuntsev's tuxedo jacket too short, leaving exposed both the cuffs of his silk shirt (which Kyandzhuntsev had also lent him) and the belt of his trousers. Amalia Fondaminsky quickly made some elastic armbands, Zenzinov gave him his braces, though his own trousers kept falling down, and when Sirin could at last be pronounced elegant, all three of them took a taxi (the rest had gone ahead) to the Musée Sociale, 5 rue Las Cases.

Sirin's first Paris reading had aroused tremendous excitement in the émigré community, in no small measure because Fondaminsky, as organizer of the reading, had peppered the press with his name. Paris knew firsthand his worth as a writer, and had heard reports from elsewhere of his talents as a reader. The hall was full, with not a ticket left. Old-timers declared they had never seen such a crowd for an émigré writer. Writers of the older and younger generations were there, representatives of the press, and "thousands of women."

The reading was to start at 8:30. From an elegant briefcase he had borrowed from Rudnev, Sirin unhurriedly laid out his papers. Feeling perfectly at home, he began to recite by heart, without haste, the poems that were becoming his standard repertoire: "To the Muse," "Aerial Island," "The Window," "To an Unborn Reader," "First Love," "Little Angel," and "Inspiration, rosy sky." He recited in a declamatory style, more like an actor than a poet, and every poem ended in loud applause. He drank a glass of water and began to read the story "Music." The acoustics were wonderful, the attention perfect. More thundering applause, and then interval.

People thronged around him again. A dreadful woman reeking unbearably of sweat approached him and said something he did not catch: it was Novotvortseva, his mistress in Greece in 1919, who later in the week sent him two scolding letters.[27] Face after face flashed past, friends and strangers, until he was tired smiling.

* Fondaminsky did, however, return to Russia after the February 1917 revolution to play an active role in Russian politics in the brief phase of freedom that ended in October.

After the interval the real enjoyment began when he read the first two chapters of *Despair*, thirty-four pages in all. He was in splendid form, taut and expressive, able to stress just the right word to animate the phrase. The crowd was "a great, kind, sensitive, pulsing beast that grunted and guffawed at the places I needed it, and again obediently fell silent." The reading lasted until 11:30. Afterward, a large group piled into a café, Sirin gave a little speech, congratulations continued to flow. In the early morning hours Sirin and the Fondaminskys returned home, and Fondaminsky counted the money—evidently quite a sum, since even before the reading he had handed Sirin 3,000 francs from advance sales alone. Everyone proclaimed the evening a triumph.[28]

VI

The next day a woman Sirin did not know offered her chateau in the south of France, at Pau, almost beside Perpigna, the chateau of Uncle Vasily Rukavishnikov. He and Véra could live there for three or four months with a servant and a car at their disposal. Delighted, Sirin wrote home: "This automatically decides our move to France." He planned to be in Paris in January—he was expecting the French *Défense* and *Camera Obscura* to be published at that time—and to take the chateau from the beginning of February until June. "Just between us, for your ears only," he wrote to Véra, "I want to be in Pau precisely from February to June because that coincides with our stay in Boulou and Saurat. It's important . . . for me to compare by the day the appearance of this or that butterfly in the eastern and the western Pyrénées."[29] It all sounded too good to be true, and it was. As it turned out, the Nabokovs would spend those months in the Berlin of book-burners, looters, and informers.

In Paris "the whole city" was talking of Sirin's reading. "An epithet beginning with g, then e, then n, has even reached me so I am getting puffed up, like the young Dostoevsky." The social round continued. He began to see more of Sergey. Sergey's homosexuality had always made Vladimir awkward, and the brothers' first meeting in Paris had not been a success. Nevertheless Sergey indicated he wanted to speak seriously to Vladimir and confront their differences, and a week later they lunched near the Luxembourg Gardens with Sergey's partner. "The husband, I must admit, is very pleasant, quiet, not at all the pederast type, attractive face and manner. All the same I felt rather uncomfortable, especially when one of their friends came up, red-lipped and curly." A week after the public reading, Vladimir and Ser-

gey talked together earnestly, calmly, even warmly.³⁰ That warmth—
never present between them until now, even in childhood—would
endure when they met in the future.

At Kolbsheim in October Vladimir and Véra had met Nathalie Nabokov's mother, Princess Shakhovskaya. On her return to Brussels
the princess had mentioned meeting Sirin to her daughter, the writer
Zinaida Shakhovskaya, who invited him to read in Belgium on his
way back from Paris. At last the visa complications were resolved,
and on November 26 Sirin left Paris for Antwerp, where he read that
evening to the Russian Circle, at the Brasserie de la Bourse. In Brussels the next night he read to the Russian Jewish Club at the Maison
des Artistes.³¹ After three exhausting days in Belgium, he was back in
Berlin.

VII

Toward *The Gift*

Nabokov brought with him the revised text of *Despair* for Véra to type
up. Shortly afterward, he recalled Chaplin in *The Gold Rush* turning
into a turkey before Big Jim's ravenous gaze, and suddenly thought a
movie treatment of *Despair* might be possible if there were some technical means to render Hermann's distorted image of Felix. He suggested to Sergey Bertenson that director Lewis Milestone might like to
pursue the idea, but nothing came of it.³²

With *Despair* out of the way, Nabokov was ready to plan for his next
novel, *Dar* (*The Gift*). When completed it would be his ninth Russian
novel, and like Beethoven's Ninth it would be immensely more massive and more formally daring than anything he had previously composed in the genre. The story of a writer's discovering the true measure of his art, it would allow him to put his whole self in the book,
just as Proust and Joyce had put all of themselves into their masterpieces: his love for Véra, his reverence for his father's memory, his
passion for Russian literature and for lepidoptera, his blissful Russian
past and his mottled émigré present. And yet much more than Proust
or Joyce he wanted to distinguish his invented young writer from
himself, even to the point of providing sample after sample of his
character's early efforts that would be quite unlike his own. His first
decision therefore was to make Fyodor splendidly gifted, but without
his own flair for narrative invention: all Fyodor's work would be either
personal recollection or historical reconstruction.

One of Nabokov's deepest wishes was to pay tribute to his extraordinary father, but he also needed to refrain from intruding on his own

privacy. The solution he hit upon was to have Fyodor write an account of *his* father, prominent and courageous just as V. D. Nabokov had been—in fact Nabokov's mother later wrote in astonishment to her son how exactly Godunov captured her husband's every nuance—but famous not as a statesman and journalist but as a lepidopterist and an explorer of Central Asia. Nabokov had himself hoped to undertake a lepidopterological expedition into Central Asia until 1917 changed everybody's plans. By having Fyodor imagine himself accompanying his father on a last trip from which Godunov would never return, he and Fyodor could both fulfill their lepidopterological fantasies, pay homage to a beloved father's bizarre death, and write a new kind of narrative blending high romance and scientific precision. To succeed here of course both Nabokov and his invented writer would have to research thoroughly the literature of discovery left by Russia's great naturalist-explorers, especially Nikolay Przhevalsky, the explorer of Central Asia.

Nabokov felt very strongly that much of what was best in himself came from his father. To sum up this sense of his origins he wanted to have Fyodor emulate his father's courage as an explorer, although in his own special domain, Russian literature. And since Nabokov could express his own current situation best by showing how his young writer's love for Russian literature and his achievement within it more than offset the frustrations of exile, it would be ideal if he could provide Fyodor with a sample work that somehow both demonstrated his literary fearlessness and at the same time linked Russia's traditions and his own émigré status.

Nabokov had just the solution. The centennial of the birth of Nikolay Chernyshevsky had been celebrated with great fanfare by the Soviet Union in 1928. Chernyshevsky was Lenin's favorite imaginative writer, and according to Lenin's own testimony it was Chernyshevsky's novel *What Is to Be Done?* that transformed him into a committed revolutionary. In the Soviet Union Chernyshevsky was hailed as the father of the socialist realism now being proclaimed as the country's official aesthetic. More than that, he was, although barely known outside his own country, a key figure in the nineteenth-century Russian literary tradition. As the émigré critic Vladimir Weidle commented, the characteristic spirit of Russian literature in the second half of the nineteenth century was neither Dostoevsky nor Tolstoy, neither Tyutchev nor Fet, but the socially committed utilitarian literature of the 1860s, "the sixties coarseness of thought and clumsiness of style."[33] Chernyshevsky's ineptly written and barely readable *What Is to Be Done?* had set the tone for literary debate and political agitation from the 1860s to the 1890s. For all its shoddiness as literature, his work was still revered as a monument, not only by the Soviet Union but also by the socialist intelligentsia whose members had been driven into emigration by other heirs to his ideas and who now dominated the émigré press. To topple that monument would take real literary nerve.

In the 1920s biography had enjoyed a revived vogue and regained high literary respectability with the work of Lytton Strachey and André Maurois, or in the emigration with Khodasevich's brilliant *Derzhavin* and his projected life of Pushkin. But for Nabokov the trend had its preposterous side. He was appalled by Maurois's claim that a real life could seem truer if it were novelized than if biographers limited themselves to documented history. If he could have Fyodor compose a biography of Chernyshevsky that would stick scrupulously to ascertainable facts but at the same time explode both the decorums of biography and the shrine built up around Chernyshevsky, he could satisfy half a dozen aims at once. A boldly original literary work in itself, the Chernyshevsky biography would reveal in Fyodor a spirit as daring as his father's and distinguish him utterly from Sirin, whose prose works had all been pure fiction. It would allow Nabokov to pay tribute to the Russian literary tradition and to exorcise its grim shadow of censorship from right and from left; it would provide a chance to expose the philosophical flaws of utilitarian materialism and to advance an alternative metaphysic; its gleeful debunking and its tragic notes would offset the celebratory tones of Fyodor's account of his father and his own lucky life.

The Chernyshevsky biography—eventually to become a hundred-page inset within *The Gift*—would take even more research than Fyodor's evocation of his father's forays into Central Asia. Nabokov knew that both in effort and achievement *The Gift* would dwarf everything he had so far written. He also knew that the whole thing would fail if he could not bring off the Chernyshevsky biography and Godunov's Central Asian expeditions, both unlike anything he had ever tried. Just as he would later tackle John Shade's poem before feeling confident that he could proceed to compose the rest of *Pale Fire*, just as he would write Van Veen's *The Texture of Time* before anything else in *Ada*, so he now set about researching and writing first the biography of Chernyshevsky—it took most of 1933 and 1934—and then Fyodor's father's travels.[34]

At the very moment he was ready to begin his research, he fell ill with neuralgia intercostalis, an excruciating affliction he later described as "a cross between pneumonia and heart trouble with the addition of an iron finger prodding you in the ribs *all* the time. It is a rare illness, as is everything about me."[35] After the first attack another soon followed, and he spent almost the whole winter in bed.[36] Two friends kept him supplied with books. Magda Nachman-Achariya, a friend of Anna Feigin, lugged from the state library volume after volume of Chernyshevsky and the enormous tomes in which Russian explorers—Miklukho-Maklay, Grand-Duke Nikolay Mikhailovich, and especially Nikolay Przhevalsky and Grigory Grum-Grzhimaylo— recount their Central Asian expeditions. George Hessen, in his role of perpetual student, could draw on the university library for Havelock Ellis, Swinburne, and what ever else might distract an avid reader from his pain.[37]

VIII

As Nabokov readied himself for *The Gift*, Adolf Hitler began the changes that would drive Nabokov from Germany before he could finish the novel. Within two months of his appointment as chancellor in January 1933, Hitler had suppressed political opposition, rendered the Reichstag defunct, and quashed civil liberties.

His advent sparked unpredictable reactions. The right wing of the Russian emigration was quick to declare itself. Even Sirin, one speaker commented, although he bears the good Russian name Nabokov, has been denationalized in the company of the Jews in *Sovremennye Zapiski*: "Educated among monkeys, he has become one himself." On the other hand a German couple with whom the Nabokovs were friends—the husband had been a former head of a Berlin military district—made a point of inviting Véra to dinner. At the end of March 1933, Jews were being beaten up, informed on, looted. Véra had to leave her secretarial position when Weil, Ganz and Dieckmann was closed down.[38] The official Nazi boycott of Jewish shops began, with uniformed soldiers stationed at shop doors to daunt prospective purchasers, and Nabokov and another non-Jewish acquaintance walked the streets, deliberately entering all the Jewish shops that still remained open.[39] Or in a lighter mood—and he would later write that the way to have tyrants destroyed was through laughter—he would call up George Hessen and ask disconcerting questions like "When will our communist cell meet?"[40]

Ever since February 1930, when André Levinson's rapturous review of *The Defense* in *Les Nouvelles littéraires* had led at once to a contract for the French translation, Nabokov had been hoping to move to Paris. Now the impetus to leave was far more urgent, and the translation of his best book still unpublished. Even in December 1932, he had still thought he might be in Paris for the book's launching in February. Two months after that date, nothing had happened, and he wrote to Gleb Struve: "My situation is wretched and to be frank has got worse and worse these last few months. The French publication of my novels is dragging on. . . . my oldest dream is to be published in English."[41]

Struve had been reviewing Sirin enthusiastically for almost a decade, had undertaken the first translation into English of his fiction (the story "The Return of Chorb"), and was now lecturer in Slavonic at the University of London, where his second lecture, after one on Bunin, had been devoted to Sirin. Nabokov asked his friend if he could help him arrange the publication of his works in English.[42] Struve tried unsuccessfully to interest British publishers, including the Hogarth Press, but with drawing-room bolshevism widespread in Britain, émigrés were viewed with suspicion.[43] One London liberal magazine even rejected the idea of publishing further Nabokov stories simply because he was a White Russian.

Meanwhile in Berlin things were getting worse. May 1933 brought book burning. As she hurried home in the twilight one day Véra Nabokov witnessed the start of an auto-da-fé, the bonfire laid, the crowd bursting into patriotic song. She did not linger.[44]

Unlike the university, which succumbed to the vogue for book burning, the state library had kept its holdings intact. Now that he had recovered from his neuralgia intercostalis, Nabokov would take the tram himself to the library on Unter den Linden, pass through its grand arches and atrium, and request from the stacks the volumes he needed for Chernyshevsky.

While his research advanced, he also had to work on short-term projects. In May he wrote the story "Admiralteyskaya Igla" ("The Admiralty Spire").[45] Obviously inspired by his encounter with Novotvortseva, this story takes the form of a scornful and outraged letter from an émigré reader to an émigrée authoress. The writer of the letter has found in a new acquisition in his local Russian library a horribly distorted account of his own love affair in 1916 and 1917 with a girl called Katya. He reproves the authoress for hiding behind a male nom de plume, and derides her style. He recalls the lyricism of their early love, and their attempt *then*, when they had no past, to look at all their present as they might from some distant future. He describes the reactionary philistinism of her smart set, the increasing distance that had come between them, her love for another. Only when he has reached their farewell does he drop the pretense that the authoress must know Katya's story at second hand: "after your book, Katya, I am afraid of you. Truly there was no point in rejoicing and suffering as we rejoiced and suffered only to find one's past besmirched in a lady's novel." A critique of the vulgarity equally possible in aristocratic Russia or émigré Europe, a witty study of the gap between male and female, youth and maturity, past passion and present disenchantment, vividly individual recollection and tarnished literary cliché, the story easily bears the multiplicity of themes and perspectives that characterizes Nabokov's mature fiction.

As research for "The Admiralty Spire," Nabokov had read "all" of Virginia Woolf and Katherine Mansfield and felt his critical talons twitch. He thought *Orlando* a "first-class example of *poshlost'*," Mansfield better but still very irritating for her "banal fear of the banal, and a kind of colored sweetness." Presumably diffident about writing for an English literary magazine, he asked *Poslednie Novosti* if they would print something he might write in English. They would not, and with the help of that refusal he restrained himself.[46]

At the beginning of July Nabokov sat "on the piney banks of the Grunewald Lake" writing the story "Korolyok" ("The Leonardo").[47] In an apartment in a Berlin working-class suburb, a new tenant vexes his neighbors, two hearty brothers, by his books, his light burning almost all night, his springy walk that seems to allow him on each rising tread "a chance to perceive something uncommon over the common heads." What does he do? Why can they not find out what makes him different? Frustrated because they cannot force him to enjoy their own beery pleasures, they attack him with fists and a sudden knife thrust. After his death the police discover the romantic recluse Romantovski toiled all night not over a new page of immortal verse but over the design of counterfeit notes.

Nabokov apparently recalled the Russian artist Myasoedov, tried in Berlin the previous October for forgery, but he made the incident wholly his own. A clear response to Hitler's first months in office, the story anticipates *Invitation to a Beheading* not only in its outrage against those who want to crush the mystery and difference in another's soul, but also in its rebellion against realism. The author plays the part of a demiurge or a puppeteer, calling up trees and houses to construct his scene, enlarging the oppressive brothers to gigantic size as their tenement dwindles to the dimensions of a dollhouse. For a writer to attack materialistic minds on their own realistic terms, Nabokov suggests, is a fatal strategic error. Imagination drives the world, and when thick-soled boots try to stamp out the free play of mind, he turns the solid ground under them to a slippery magic carpet. That does not stop a Romantovski's murder, but it does remind us of another power than physical force.

IX

The easiest way to cope with the world of the Nazis of course was to leave it entirely. In the late summer of 1933 Nabokov was excited at the prospect of teaching English language and literature at a small university in Switzerland. Nothing came of his application, and once again a move to France seemed the simplest next step.[48] But first there was work to finish in Germany.

By August Nabokov had read *What Is to Be Done?*, Chernyshevsky's correspondence and other writings, and could see "this amusing gentleman" alive before him.[49] Committed to this long-term project, he and his wife desperately needed another income. When Véra's secretarial job ended, she put her wits to other work: as a guide and interpreter for foreign tourists, especially Americans, as a freelance French stenographer, as an interpreter for private clients and international conferences.[50] The conference paid especially well. When her former chief at the French embassy told her

> to ring up the chancellery of the German Minister who was in charge of the International Congress of Wool Producers and tell them he sent me for the job, I said "they won't engage me, don't forget I am Jewish." But he only laughed and said, "they will. They have been unable to get anyone else." I did as I was told, and was accepted with alacrity, whereupon I said to the German to whom I was talking, "but are you sure you want me? I am Jewish." . . . "Oh," he said, "but it does not make *any* difference to us. We pay no attention to such things. Who told you we did?"[51]

On the other side of the Atlantic, a rumor that Ivan Bunin would get the Nobel Prize stirred an interest in émigré writing. Albert Parry, in an article for the *American Mercury*, singled Sirin out for praise in terms comically wide of the mark: "Sirin is an adroit, unostentatious follower of Dr. Freud."[52] Nabokov's thoughts were quite ready to veer toward America as well as toward France or Britain. Within a year he would have a New York agent, Altagracia de Janelli, trying to place his books in the United States.

Rumor was right for once: in November Ivan Bunin did win the Nobel Prize for literature, the first Russian to do so. The Union of Russian Writers in Berlin planned an evening in his honor on December 30 at the Schubertsaal. Iosif Hessen would introduce the program, Fyodor Stepun talk on his fiction and Sirin on his verse. N. E. Paramonov, a publisher and the owner of several large garages in Berlin, warned Hessen there should be no speeches by "a Yid and a half-Yid" (Hessen and Sirin).[53] Although Hessen had lost a friend and Sirin a father to the bullets of a Russian rightist at a similar assembly, they were determined not to let the hooligan element triumph and carried on with their plans.

Unexpectedly Bunin himself arrived, en route from Stockholm back to France. The first large gathering of the local intelligentsia for a long time, the Bunin evening offered a chance for a roll call of those who still remained in Berlin—not quite as few as many had felt. Sirin spoke in lofty and enthusiastic tone of Bunin's verse, underrated in the era of Symbolism and certain to be remembered when Symbolism and its fellow "schools" were long forgotten.[54]

A few days later he lunched with Bunin in the rear of a bustling Berlin restaurant, where they had to sit beneath a huge Nazi flag. Later in Paris Bunin, a brilliant raconteur, told him that as he left Berlin he had been stopped by the Gestapo, interrogated, searched for smuggled jewels, stripped, and searched again. Nobel Prize or not, he had had to swallow a strong dose of castor oil, squat over an empty bucket until the treatment had its effect, then be searched again, naked, by the Gestapo agent who wiped him.[55]

X

In January 1934 Nabokov's friend Nikolay Yakovlev replied from Riga to his request for the names of extinct lineages of Russian noble families.[56] Among them was Cherdyntsev, which Nabokov bestowed—after modifying it to Godunov-Cherdyntsev—on the central family in his story "Krug" ("The Circle"), written by mid-February.[57]

Innokenty, the radical son of the village schoolmaster, despises on principle the aristocratic Godunov-Cherdyntsevs in their mansion across the river. One day in 1914 he attends a formal fete on the mansion's lawns, and the beautiful young Tanya Godunov invites him to play with her and her friends. He joins them often that summer, but remains on the fringes of their fun, certain he is being laughed at. One night Tanya sends him a note to meet her. Suspecting a practical joke, he comes anyway. She cries, nuzzles him with her lips, tells him her mother is taking her the next day to the Crimea "and—oh, how could he have been so obtuse!" Twenty years later, an émigré now, he meets her, enchanting as ever, with her husband and daughter. Alone in a Paris café afterward, his mind circles and circles around that distant past, around all his ruffled relations with the Godunovs ever since he was a child of three or four.

Told in a sober, weighty style that imparts a grandeur to every detail, the story shows the Godunovs, even through the hostilely narrowed eyes of Innokenty's idealistic prejudice, as a family of rare dignity and charm, quiet courage and unassuming generosity. A wonderful piece in its own right, "The Circle" also astounds anyone who cares for *The Gift*, which itself is an account of his own life by Fyodor Godunov-Cherdyntsev, Tanya's younger brother. In "The Circle" we see the world of Fyodor's childhood from a totally unexpected angle, through the unsympathetic gaze of someone who does not feature at all in *The Gift*. Here, the Godunov-Cherdynstevs, almost despite Innokenty, take on a noble allure Fyodor is too modest to strive for on his own account within *The Gift*.

Most astounding of all is the utter confidence in the solidity of Fyodor's world that every line in the story bespeaks—almost four years before Nabokov had finished writing *The Gift*. Unable to trace its first publication, Véra Nabokov in the 1960s dated it "1939? end 1938?"—in other words, after the completion of *The Gift*.[58] Introducing his translation of the story in 1973, Nabokov himself assumes the story could only have been composed once *The Gift* was all but written: "By the middle of 1936, not long before leaving Berlin forever and finishing *Dar* (*The Gift*) in France, I must have completed at least four fifths of its last chapter when at some point a small satellite separated itself from the main body of the novel and started to revolve around it."[59] Not only had he not finished that last chapter when he wrote "The Circle," it was another three years before he would even start. This story provides the best possible proof of the absolute clarity with which Nabokov envisaged his fictive worlds, long before they had condensed from the incandescent gas of inspiration to the crystal of his prose.

After a visit to Prague, Iosif Hessen reported early in February that Nabokov's mother was unwell, jaundiced, thin. Nabokov felt tormented by his helplessness: "I rack my brains," he wrote, "perhaps some idea will come—never been in such a wretched situation before—we'll get out of it, of course—but when?"[60] He approached Aldanov about the possibility of arranging another reading in Paris, where his first novel to appear in French, *The Defense* (*La Course du fou*) was receiving excellent reviews. Meanwhile, *The Gift* was still growing.[61]

But since it would be years before the novel could be published, he tackled in the meantime other projects with a more immediate return. In March 1934 he wrote "Opoveshchenie" ("Breaking the News").[62] As the story opens, the son of a widow living in Berlin has died in Paris on the previous day. She has not yet been told. Old family friends hear of the accident first, and pass the news on to other friends, but cannot bring themselves to break it to the mother. On her return from shopping, friends gather in her apartment, no one daring to begin shouting the news—even with her hearing aid the woman is very deaf—until tension thickens to the point of suffocation and one old friend at last roars out in an agony of helplessness: "What's there to explain—dead, dead, dead!" Those who have called Nabokov cold and inhuman have not read this story, so full of warm, unexpected, wonderfully accurate human observation, so full of compassion for all the bitter ironies of loneliness and loss.

By early April, Nabokov was writing his third story in three months, "Pamyati L. I. Shigaeva" ("In Memory of L. I. Shigaev").[63] Written in the form of an obituary of a friend, the story recounts the narrator's disappointment in love, his ensuing alcoholism and hallucinations—toadlike little devils that clamber over his writing desk— and his rescue from that state by L. I. Shigaev. He rents a room next door to Shigaev, and describes the man, unremarkable in every way, indifferent to art, literature, nature, and yet irreducibly alive in every unpredictable particular. When Shigaev lands a job in Prague, where he has now died of heart failure, the narrator asks:

> Did it occur to me that I might be seeing him for the last time?
>
> Of course it did. That is exactly what occurred to me: yes, I am seeing you for the last time; this, in fact, is what I always think, about everything, about everyone. My life is a perpetual good-bye to objects and people, that often do not pay the least attention to my bitter, brief, insane salutation.

This compact, modest story again shows Nabokov at his best: its wonderful devils, taxonomized with the care he would give to describing a new butterfly; its gentle proof of the irreplaceable value of an ordinary life, even one visible only from the outside; its haunting and humorous record of the narrator's inner life that no one else would ever have been able to compile for *his* obituary.

As spring came on, Nabokov's spirits rose. Dreams of flight were always cheaper than railway tickets, and he felt ready to travel in the autumn, to Paris, to Majorca.[64] Still, he could write to Khodasevich: "Berlin at the moment is very attractive, thanks to spring, which this year is especially juicy, and I am like a dog going crazy from all sorts of interesting smells." He also confided:

> The novel I'm writing now—after *Despair*—is monstrously difficult. Among other things, my hero is working on a biography of Chernyshevsky, so I had to read all the masses of books written on the gent— and digest all this my own way, so that now I have heartburn. He had less talent than a lot of people, but more courage than many. In his dia-

ries there is a detailed account of how, by what means and where he vomited (he was poverty ridden, slovenly, ate junk in his student years). Every one of his books is of course utterly dead now, but I searched out here and there (especially in his two novels and in the little pieces written in the penal colony) some wonderfully human, pitiable things. He was thoroughly tormented. He called Tolstoy "a vulgarian, decking out his vulgar buttocks with peacock feathers," Tolstoy called him "bedbug-stinking" (both in letters to Turgenev), and his wife . . . was rabidly unfaithful.[65]

XI

There was more than spring to Nabokov's high spirits. His next letter to Khodasevich began: "We have a son, we're calling him Dmitri." Dmitri Vladimirovich Nabokov was born in the early hours of May 10, 1934, at a private clinic near Bayerischer Platz. Although the Nabokovs had continued their normal social life late into Véra's pregnancy, the pregnancy had been kept a secret by Véra's careful dress and posture and silence. Among their closest friends only Anna Feigin and George Hessen were allowed to know. Even to Nabokov's mother it came as a complete surprise.[66]

In *Speak, Memory* Nabokov describes himself returning from the clinic at 5 A.M., with all the shadows in the dawn light on the wrong side of the street.[67] His world *was* reversed, it *had* gained a new focus. Always delighted by children, Nabokov now noted with rapture his son's perfectly formed nails, his silky hair, his way of yawning when Véra yawned.[68] He would remain entranced, a devoted and indulgent father, as Dmitri grew and grew, and over the coming decades the love of parent for child—again in both positive and negative forms, in *Bend Sinister, Conclusive Evidence, Lolita, Pnin, Pale Fire,* and *Look at the Harlequins!*—would become another major theme in his work.

The week of Dmitri's birth brought another new beginning. A literary agent, Otto Klement, had managed to interest the British publisher Hutchinson in *Camera Obscura* and *Despair.*[69] At first apparently no more than a business proposition, these first novels in English heralded a change as important in Nabokov's writing as Dmitri's birth was in his private life. Within a year, the problem of having them translated to meet his standards would set him on the path to writing his fiction in English.

Translation and Transformation: Berlin, 1934–1937

I

EARLY in the summer of 1934, deeply involved in drafting for Fyodor his *Life of Chernyshevsky*, Nabokov suddenly set Fyodor's world aside to broach another novel. He began writing *Priglashenie na kazn'* (*Invitation to a Beheading*) on June 24, and completed its first draft "in one fortnight of wonderful excitement and sustained inspiration."[1]

Normally dates on Nabokov's manuscripts, like those on John Shade's, record the time of first creation, not final completion. The manuscript of *Invitation to a Beheading*, however, has a terminal date of September 15. Apparently the suddenness of the novel's composition made Nabokov hesitate and set it aside, as if for the yeast to rise, before reworking it to the point where he could consider all but the baking over.

Between first draft and first revision he seems to have carried on with writing the Chernyshevsky biography. At the end of July, he wrote to Struve: "My Chernyshevsky is growing, rebelling and I hope will soon die."[2]

That month he also wrote a new story, "Krasavitsa" ("A Russian Beauty").[3] A beautiful Russian girl for whom schoolboys were once ready to shoot themselves turns slowly into a thirty-year-old émigrée, still beautiful, but impoverished, tense, and aware she has passed beyond the age at which anyone will fall in love with her. After the intervention of a matchmaking friend, a widower makes her a formal and unpromising proposal. She accepts—what else can she do?— "and next summer she died in childbirth." The nerves of the story are stretched taut enough to twang. The fortune that had seemed to favor Olga slowly deserts her, leaving her bereft of hope, until an unexpected reprieve from the bareness of a lonely, destitute, joyless existence leads at once to her death. The arrows of all kinds of prosperous fates missed their mark, but death did not.

At the end of July, ablaze with the ideas of *Invitation to a Beheading*, Nabokov replied to a letter from Khodasevich, taking issue with his friend's latest weekly column in the Paris daily *Vozrozhdenie*. Writers should ignore problems of émigré ideology, he declared, and just work away in their own space, like stokers knowing only their own furnaces, whatever might be happening on deck or at sea. They should

> occupy themselves only with their own meaningless, innocent. intoxicating business and justify only in passing all that in reality does not even need justification: the strangeness of such an existence. the discomfort, the solitude . . . and a certain quiet inner gaiety. For that reason I find unbearable any talk—intelligent or not, it's all the same to me—about "the modern era," "*inquiétude*," "religious renaissance," or any sentence at all with the word "postwar." I sense in this "ideology" the same herd instinct, the "all-together-now" of, say, yesterday's or last century's enthusiasm for world's fairs. . . .
>
> I am writing my novel. I do not read the papers.[4]

Early in August Nabokov caught a bad cold in the neck, his muscles became unbearably sore, he could not turn his head, as if he had caught fright from Cincinnatus C.'s imminent beheading. Although a couple of months earlier an agent in London had sold rights to both *Camera Obscura* and *Despair*, his writing remained minimally lucrative, and with Véra unable to work, he was gloomy and depressed. Debts were piling up. His mother needed help he could not possibly afford. And the English translation of *Camera Obscura* that he had just received was atrocious.[5]

He continued revising *Invitation to a Beheading* and by September 15 thought it finished. Since Véra was exhausted looking after Dmitri, he expected the typing to take a whole month. In fact things went even slower. His revision continued intensely throughout November, turning the manuscript into a crazy palimpsest of insets and excisions squiggled in the violet ink that he preferred to blue. By late November he was dictating to Véra at the typewriter day and night, and even in the last week of December he had still not completed final checking of the typescript.[6]

Before *Invitation to a Beheading* was ready to send to *Sovremennye Zapiski*, Anna Feigin had visited Vadim Rudnev—now in practice if not in title almost sole editor of the journal—and explained Sirin's situation, literary and financial. Nabokov had thought that if *Sovremennye Zapiski* could take an excerpt from the Chernyshevsky biography for the next issue it would bring him a little financial relief. Ironically, in the light of later events, Rudnev was eager to publish whatever he could from the still unseen *Life of Chernyshevsky*. But Nabokov changed his mind, wisely realizing that an excerpt would harm the book, and gratefully accepted an advance instead.[7]

After its lightning conception, *Invitation to a Beheading* had suffered unexpected complications in the womb. But 1935 arrived, and at last it was delivered.

II
Invitation to a Beheading (Priglashenie na kazn')

A dystopian fable that sets the individual imagination against a world that denies it, *Invitation to a Beheading* is the second of Nabokov's masterpieces (the others are *The Defense; The Gift; Speak, Memory; Lolita; Pale Fire; Ada*). Its plot could not be simpler. On the first page of the novel, Cincinnatus C. is sentenced to death; for nineteen days, not knowing when he will die, he remains in solitary confinement; on the last page, he is beheaded.[8]

Cincinnatus's crime is to be opaque in a transparent world where everyone around him understands one another at the first word. To them, nothing exists outside common knowledge, and when Cincinnatus looks about him with curiosity and wonder, as if there were something more to things than the names everyday language assigns them, he commits the crime of "gnostical turpitude."*

Unprepared to question their simple but convenient labels, Cincinnatus's fellow citizens remain content with a world much less than real. Cincinnatus is in fact the only genuine creature in his world: everything else is a cheap fabrication, a slapdash sham. The book swarms with unrealities of every kind. A storm is "performed" outside the fortress. A spider in Cincinnatus's cell, fed with flies every day by the jailer, turns out to be made of springs, plush, and elastic. The director visits Cincinnatus's cell, Cincinnatus leaves—the room has somehow become the director's office—walks out of the prison and back into the city, opens the front door of his house and finds himself back in his cell. Worst of all, the people around him are nothing but "specters, werewolves, parodies."

Why does *Invitation to a Beheading* pile up so many fakes, falsities, fantasies, and contradictions? In one of the most brilliant articles ever written about Nabokov, Robert Alter suggests: "If consciousness is the medium through which reality comes into being, the sudden and

---

* The original phrase, *gnoseologicheskaya gnusnost'*, seems repellent to a Russian ear. Words like *gnusavit'*, "to sing through one's nose," *gnusnyy*, "foul, vile," and the substandard swearword *gnus*, "vermin," give the *gn* combination a special hideousness. Marina Tsvetaeva once refused to attend a lecture whose title contained the word *gnoseologia*, because it sounded too disgusting to her. Cf. Robert Hughes, *Triquarterly* 17 (1970): 290.

final obliteration of consciousness . . . is the supreme affirmation by human agents—the executioners—of the principle of irreality."[9]

An exaggerated and phony kindness surrounds Cincinnatus from the moment the death sentence is announced, in the opening lines of the book, *in a whisper*—so that it will seem softer. The prison authorities do all they can to foment friendship between Cincinnatus and the executioner, M'sieur Pierre, who he is led to believe is merely another prisoner. M'sieur Pierre drops in to chat (and confides with grim irony that *his* crime is attempting to help Cincinnatus to escape the prison), passes around photos, tells jokes, performs card tricks, plays chess. Headsman and prison director even feel aggrieved that Cincinnatus does not enjoy their ersatz sociability and fails to melt in gratitude. They expect him to inhale happily what M'sieur Pierre calls "that atmosphere of warm camaraderie" between executioner and executed so "precious to the success of our common undertaking."

For Nabokov that remark parodies *poshlost'* (philistine vulgarity) at its most deadly dangerous, when it appeals to or apes noble, civilizing sentiments, "when the values it mimics are considered, rightly or wrongly, to belong to the very highest level of art, thought or emotion." He likens the attempt to establish a jovial coziness around Cincinnatus before he is put to death to a pail of the "milk of human kindness with a dead rat at the bottom," and Robert Alter justly compares the hearty cheer and the pompous phrases of Rodrig Ivanovich and M'sieur Pierre to the brass bands that played patriotic marches to welcome victims arriving at Hitler's death camps or an uplifting slogan like *Arbeit macht frei* over their gates.[10] Or the prevalent falsehood in support of supposedly lofty motives finds its parallels in Soviet Russia, in literature (Tarasov-Rodionov's *Chocolate*, where the execution of an innocent man is justified by the need to prove the Revolution can override any other value, even justice) or in life (the show trials of the mid-1930s, where Bukharin and other old Bolsheviks became convinced they had to admit to being Trotskyists and foreign spies in order to further the cause to which they had devoted their lives).

It was no accident that Nabokov began *Invitation to a Beheading* while Goebbels as Minister of People's Enlightenment and Propaganda was striving to make all German culture Nazi "culture," or while Stalin's grip on the Union of Soviet Writers and on everything else in the Soviet Union was becoming still tighter. But the optimistic Nabokov did not foresee all the horrors of the next ten years, and his novel is not a narrowly political one. He could keep his invented world lightly comic in a way he could not in the much more grimly political *Bend Sinister*, written one brutal decade later. Set somewhere in the future, after the death of the internal combustion engine (electric wagonets in the shape of swans ply the streets like so much pure *poshlost'* in motion), the action of *Invitation to a Beheading* takes place in a Russian-speaking world with a Central European flora but devoid of specific implication, and in a provincial city whose civic administration, all pomp and no substance, can inspire neither awe nor terror. Citizens need hardly be oppressed because all save Cincinnatus (and a few of his predecessors in previous generations) already accept the transparent truth of the commonplace. No rebel himself, Cincinnatus meekly tries to hide his ineradicable, "criminal" propensity to observe and think and imagine in a way he cannot help.

The novel attacks not so much a political system as a state of mind possible under any regime—though of course exemplified in its worst form in ideological dictatorships, past or present, religious or political, left or right. All human communication must employ words that contain prior assumptions, descriptions that simplify their objects. We can conform to the world of Cincinnatus's fellow citizens and accept everyday language as so perfectly adequate that the very idea of something unknown or uncaught residing in people or things becomes a disturbing notion to be extinguished at once. Or like Cincinnatus himself we can view human words and images as no substitute for an inexhaustible reality.

Sitting in his cell, Cincinnatus tries to express on paper his sense of the untapped fullness of life. For him reality *proves* itself by being always more particular and more complex than we had thought, by remaining inexpressible and irreducible to our glib formulas. Where the mentality of the jailer would like to extirpate whatever cannot be locked up in the prisonhouse of language, it is this evasive extra that for Cincinnatus seems the true measure of things. Frustrated not only by the bars on his cell window but by the prison of his "whole striped world" and the collapsing time that will not allow him to set his thoughts in order, he dreams of a state where reality can be known in all its depth, a fulfillment infinitely beyond the trite self-satisfactions of Rodrig Ivanovich or M'sieur Pierre, a world where all the elusive beauty and harmony in things would fill the air around him:

> Not here! The horrible "here," the dark dungeon, in which a relentlessly howling heart is encarcerated, this "here" holds and constricts me. But . . . *There, tam, là-bas*, the gaze of men glows with inimitable understanding; *there* the freaks that are tortured here walk unmolested; *there* time takes shape according to one's pleasure. . . . *There, there* are the originals of those gardens where we used to roam and hide in this world. . . .

At the end of the novel, Cincinnatus arrives "there" in death. As he mounts the scaffold, his world becomes more and more plainly spurious, until the remote figures in the crowd seem merely daubed on a backdrop. When the ax falls, his mind spurts on, he rises from the block, looks around him at the ripping canvas of his painted world, "and amidst the dust, and the falling things, and the flapping scenery, Cincinnatus made his way in that direction where, to judge by the voices, stood beings akin to him." Only beyond death can a mind so alive find its true scope.

In life Cincinnatus rejects those around him not through haughty pride—he is actually rather mild and frail—but because he simply has no choice. He craves companionship, in fact, but cannot find it among creatures for whom nothing has depth or uniqueness. He longs for a visit from his wife, but then Marthe arrives in his cell, no more than a parody wife, equipped with in-laws and children and current lover, with furniture and utensils and makeshift walls. She is a travesty of intimacy: she cannot understand him, she makes love to any man who even hints at an interest in her, she cannot distinguish one lover from the next.

If the present holds nothing, Cincinnatus tries to hope for something from the future generation: little Emmie, the jailer's daughter (or at times the prison director's), so lithe and graceful, so different from the crippled boy and the obese girl that Marthe has given birth to by other men. A diminutive ballerina who seems to float on air, Emmie reminds Cincinnatus of his own childhood and somehow seems to promise escape. But when he finds himself outside the fortress walls and Emmie pops out from behind a bramble bush she leads him not to freedom but back to Rodrig Ivanovich at supper.

What of the past, then? Cincinnatus has never met his mother, Cecilia C., until she comes to visit. Unprepared for her, he touchily rejects her maternal fuss and dismisses her as "just as much of a parody as everybody and everything else. . . . And why is your raincoat wet when your shoes are dry—see, that's careless. Tell the prop man for me." There is more to her than his disappointment allows, however, and she tells him that his father, too, "was also like you, Cincinnatus." For an instant he can make out in her eyes "that ultimate, all-explaining and from-all-protecting spark that he knew how to discern in himself." But once again she lapses into motherly prattle and the director whisks her away. When Cincinnatus next hears news of her, she has betrayed that one brief hint of kinship: terrified at her bond to a doomed criminal, she has implored Marthe to sign a statement that she, Cecilia C., had had nothing to do with Cincinnatus before his arrest.

Early in the novel when the director informs his sole inmate that another prisoner will soon arrive, Cincinnatus's heart leaps at the thought that he might meet someone like himself. M'sieur Pierre arrives, proffering not just the hand of friendship but ten slimy tentacles, and Cincinnatus realizes at once he is only another elaborate parody. Even a game of chess between them turns into an offensive farce:

"I'm a bachelor myself, but of course I understand. . . . Forward. I shall quickly . . . Good players do not take a long time to think. Forward. I caught just a glimpse of your spouse—a juicy little piece, no two ways about it—what a neck, that's what I like . . . Hey, wait a minute, that was an oversight, allow me to take my move back. Here, this is better. . . ."

Night after night Cincinnatus hears through the wall the sounds of a tunnel inching toward his cell. At last a hole appears in the wall and out tumble, laughing, M'sieur Pierre and the director. Only when at M'sieur Pierre's insistence Cincinnatus takes the tunnel into his fellow prisoner's cell does he (with the reader) find out what he realizes he should have guessed at once: this hearty chum will soon chop off his head.

A unique and complex individual, Cincinnatus feels a loneliness unknown to those around him for whom one friend or lover or even self is interchangeable with another. All the companionship Cincinnatus can hope for is a future reader of the few musings he manages to scribble in his cell: "I would give up if I were laboring for a reader existing today." But at the end of the novel when he stands up after decapitation he makes his way toward those "beings akin to him": death will not be solitude, but his first chance for true companionship.

Invitation to a Beheading is no direct image of life but an uncomfortable—though surprisingly gentle—comic nightmare that aims to sharpen our sense of waking reality. Cincinnatus sits beleaguered and alone in his world, but the book itself assumes, as Cincinnatus cannot, readers who will understand his need to express himself without the frothy formulas of Rodrig Ivanovich or M'sieur Pierre. In a world that others take for granted Cincinnatus shows up, by his refusal to accept it, the counterfeit currency of the commonplace.

Nabokov once commented that *Alice in Wonderland* if read very carefully "will be seen to imply, by humorous juxtaposition, the presence of a quite solid, and rather sentimental, world, behind the semi-detached dream."[11] The special shoddy unreality of *Invitation to a Beheading*'s world does not imply the unreality of our own world but quite the reverse. Our poor notions can turn everything to falsehood, and Nabokov makes the novel a bewildering, bracing experience, a course in the detection and rejection of *poshlost'*—which the book defines as the falsity of the commonplace—that will cause more than a few readers to jump up, ruffling their hair. Reality so outstrips the human mind, he suggests, that it seems to promise there must be some better way to apprehend it all. If throughout our lives we have cared enough to settle for no simplified silhouette of our world, perhaps at death we might, like Cincinnatus, step into some richer reality beyond.

A word on origins. Nabokov denied that he had been influenced by Kafka, and there seems no reason whatever to doubt his disclaimer. He never learned enough German to be able to read a newspaper, let alone a novel. As a boy he scoured German butterfly books with the aid of a dictionary. Upon moving to Berlin he

> was beset by a panicky fear of somehow flawing my precious layer of Russian by learning to speak German fluently. The task of linguistic occlusion was made easier by the fact that I lived in a closed émigré circle of Russian friends and read exclusively Russian newspapers, magazines, and books. My only forays into the local language were the civilities exchanged with my successive landlords or landladies and the routine necessities of shopping: *Ich möchte etwas Schinken.*[12]

Later in life Nabokov would certainly read Kafka, as he read Goethe, in a facing translation. But in 1934 Kafka's name was only beginning to be heard widely outside a German-speaking audience. In 1959 Nabokov commented that émigré reviewers, "who were puzzled but liked [*Invitation to a Beheading*], thought they distinguished in it a 'Kafkaesque' strain."[13] His memory erred: émigré writers did compare the two writers, but only long after the novel's first publication. In reviews of the serial edition (1935–1936) and even the book version (1938) not one of the leading émigré reviewers—well-read men prone to postulating influences—mentioned Kafka's name, presumably because they either had not read him or had no reason to suppose him well known. There was only one exception to this critical silence: at a literary reading in Paris in 1936, Georgy Adamovich asked Sirin if he had read *The Trial*. "No," he answered.[14]

By the 1950s a comparison between *The Trial* and *Invitation to a Beheading* could seem obvious. In fact Nabokov and Kafka have little in common except their originality. In Kafka's broodingly oppressive world the doors of meaning clang shut all the more ominously the louder Joseph K. knocks. In Nabokov's much lighter universe, executioner and prison director shrivel away and Cincinnatus tears a hole in his world to reach his likes beyond. *Invitation to a Beheading*'s topsy-turvy world may owe a little to Lewis Carroll or to the dystopian tradition—Nabokov had recently read Zamyatin's *We*, still unavailable in Russian, in its French translation,[15] and he makes imagination a crime in Cincinnatus's world, as illness had been criminal in *Erewhon*—but the book owes nothing to Kafka. If anything it seems to have relocated Hamlet onto Prospero's island.

Nabokov jokes in his introduction to the English translation that the only author to influence *Invitation to a Beheading* was "the melancholy, extravagant, wise, witty, magical, and altogether delightful Pierre Delalande, whom I invented." But the real joke is that he means almost exactly what he says. He invented Delalande in the course of writing *The Gift*, and his work on that novel is the real source of *Invitation to a Beheading*.

By mid-1934 Nabokov was engrossed in writing Fyodor's *Life of Chernyshevsky*. As he told Khodasevich, he considered Chernyshevsky often risible but sometimes admirable. Bestowing the same reaction on Fyodor, he wrote in chapter 3 of *The Gift*:

> He sincerely admired the way Chernyshevski, an enemy of capital punishment, made deadly fun of the poet Zhukovski's infamously benign and meanly sublime proposal to surround executions with a mystic secrecy (since, in public, he said, the condemned man brazenly puts on a bold face, thus bringing the law into disrepute) so that those attending the hanging would not see but would only hear solemn church hymns from behind a curtain, for an execution should be moving.

In his research on Chernyshevsky Nabokov had already been reminded of the ghoulish farce of the Russian penal system: Chernyshevsky was himself sentenced to death and obliged to undergo a mock execution—the Dostoevskyan torture, now refined into a bizarre ritual—before having his sentence commuted to Siberian exile. Nabokov continued the passage above:

> And while reading this Fyodor recalled his father saying that innate in every man is the feeling of something insuperably abnormal about the death penalty, something like the uncanny reversal of action in a looking glass that makes everyone left-handed: not for nothing is everything reversed for the executioner; the horse-collar is put on upside down when the robber Razin is taken to the scaffold; wine is poured for the headsman not with a natural turn of the wrist but backhandedly; and if, according to the Swabian code, an insulted actor was permitted to seek satisfaction by striking the *shadow* of the offender, in China it was precisely an actor—a shadow—who fulfilled the duties of the executioner, all responsibilities being as it were lifted from the world of men and transformed into the inside-out one of mirrors.[16]

No wonder Nabokov felt he had to break off writing *The Gift* at this point and cross at once into the looking-glass world of *Invitation to a Beheading*.

After writing his *Life of Chernyshevsky*, Fyodor will confide to Zina in the last chapter of *The Gift* that one day he will create a novel out of the story of their meeting—*The Gift* itself, in other words—but that first he must prepare himself by translating an old French sage, Pierre Delalande. Already within this chapter he has quoted several of Delalande's elegant dismissals of death. Nabokov had not yet composed chapter 5 of *The Gift* when he wrote *Invitation to a Beheading*, but for more than a year his mind had already been working from an exact blueprint of all its parts. Delalande was an old friend, a familiar inspiration, by the time Nabokov chose to "borrow" from him for the epigraph to *Invitation to a Beheading*. He knew precisely what he wanted Delalande to stand for, and when he "quoted" him in his epigraph, he once again *meant* what seems no more than a joke: "*Comme un fou se croit Dieu, nous nous croyons mortels.*"

III

By this time, Nabokov was no longer tutoring, and his skimpy income came solely from his writing. The figures for 1934 show:

	Reichsmarks
Royalties for Russian *Kamera obskura*, Petropolis, Berlin	51.20
Honorarium for Russian *Despair* in *Sovremennye Zapiski*	233.50
Honorarium for story "The Circle" in *Poslednie Novosti*	82.53
Honorarium for story "Breaking the News" in *Poslednie Novosti*	43.00
Honorarium for story "A Russian Beauty" in *Poslednie Novosti*	34.19
Honorarium for poem in *Poslednie Novosti*	10.00
Advances for John Long editions of *Camera Obscura* and *Despair* (less agent's percentage)	250.00
Advance for French *Camera Obscura*	100.00
Advance for Swedish *The Defense*	158.42
Advance for Czech *Camera Obscura*	103.63
Honorarium for German translation of story in *Vossische Zeitung*	50.00
Grant from Union of Russian Writers in Paris	40.00
	RM. 1,156.47[17]

By now Nabokov had literary agents in both Europe and America trying to interest publishers in translating or adapting his books. Movie rights or translation rights into Czech or Swedish might bring in valuable extra income, but much more important, both artistically and in the long run commercially, were editions in English or French.

Late in 1934 Nabokov had received Denis Roche's translation of *The Eye* into French. He was pleased with the translation, but made copious small corrections. Early in February 1935, he found from Roche that the printers had printed the book from a proof lacking not only Nabokov's corrections, but even Roche's own. The author "emitted peacock cries," but it was too late.[18] Translations would spell trouble all year long.

By mid-February Nabokov had sent *Poslednie Novosti*—the newspaper was now banned in Germany—a new story, "Tyazholyy dym" ("Torpid Smoke").[19] A young émigré poet lies musing on his couch in the semidark, breaks off to fetch some cigarettes from his father at his sister's request, and returns to his couch, the excited tremor in his soul now crystallized into a line of verse. This brilliantly condensed story owes much to *The Gift*'s study of the process of composition. Everything flows together: colors and shapes and sounds and smells, in the poet's trancelike mind and in the unlit room half-brightened by streetlamps below; ancient memories, recent impressions, immediate observations, future recollections; inside and outside, body and soul, self and other, individual reverie and family tension. The story shifts as it mounts to its climax from past to present and back, from third person to first and back again. But when inspiration hurtles down, we are right in the poet's mind, we feel the pulse of the present in his veins. The verses about to burst forth will soon wither, no doubt, "but no matter: at this moment I trust the ravishing promise of the still beating, still revolving verse, my face is wet with tears, my heart is bursting with happiness, and I know that this happiness is the greatest thing on earth."

On April 6 Iosif Hessen held a Sirin reading in his home. Over a hundred turned up to hear Sirin read poems, a story, and a dazzling excerpt from his recently composed *Life of Chernyshevsky*. At mid-month in reply Sirin spoke at a formal gathering in honor of Iosif Hessen's seventieth birthday, his first and last after-dinner speech. Hessen himself recalls an incident from about this time. He was reading *Glory*, and pronounced aloud a phrase that caught his fancy: "furtively kept shooting raisins, borrowed from the cake." "Yes," Nabokov promptly replied, "that's Vadim firing at Darwin, when Sonia comes to Cambridge." Hessen was amazed, and to test him chose something a hundred pages on. "And where's this from: 'On so-and-so's cheek, just below the eye, was a little stray lash'?" "Of course: Martin notices it on Sonia, when she bends over the phone book." Again he had landed right on target. "How have you remembered these phrases so exactly?" Hessen asked. "Not just 'these phrases.' I could dictate almost all my novels right now from start to finish."[20]

His mother found his latest novel less easy to manage than that. When she proposed a symbolic reading of *Invitation to a Beheading*, Nabokov wrote back: "You shouldn't look for any symbol or allegory. It's extremely logical and real, it is the simplest everyday reality and doesn't need any special explanation." In a more sober vein, he was worried about his brother Kirill, who had abandoned a job in Amsterdam several years earlier and had been doing little since, letting his mother and Evgenia Hofeld slave to keep him fed. Now he had been accepted at Louvain University for the coming academic year. Nabokov insisted to Kirill that in the meantime he should leave his mother's flat and support himself: some heavy physical labor, far from a "sinking to the bottom," as Kirill seemed to view it, would be the best thing for him.[21]

IV

When he had written "Torpid Smoke" in February Nabokov may have been preparing for the many scenes in *The Gift* where Fyodor soars into or lapses out of a fit of creative concentration, especially in chapter 2, where he tries to recount his father's life and travels. It was to this section of the novel that Nabokov appears to have turned in mid-1935, after completing Fyodor's life of Chernyshevsky.

Over the next three years, Nabokov's mastery of English kept distracting him from his greatest Russian novel. In May he wrote to his English publisher in exasperation over the translation of *Camera Obscura*:

> It was loose, shapeless, sloppy, full of blunders and gaps, lacking vigor and spring, and plumped down in such dull, flat English that I could not read it to the end; all of which is rather hard on an author who aims in his work at absolute precision, takes the utmost trouble to obtain it, and then finds the translator calmly undoing every blessed phrase.[22]

The publishers tried to correct the text, but Nabokov thought it hopeless. Unwilling to lose the chance of his first English publication, however, he decided not to stop the book's being published as it was "—if you think it fit for publication in its present condition."[23]

To avoid even worse disappointment with the much more complex style of *Despair*, the Nabokovs briefly tried to find their own translator. Véra called the British embassy and asked if they could suggest a translator "who would be an experienced man of letters with fine style." The voice at the other end joked: "Would you like H. G. Wells?" Unruffled by the sarcasm, Véra replied: "My husband would accept him." By the end of June, her husband had in fact gone one step further, offering to translate the novel himself provided Hutchinson would undertake to correct any imperfections in his English.[24]

At 22 Nestorstrasse the Nabokovs and Anna Feigin had a maid in to cook. A nanny or governess on the other hand was far beyond their means, even had they wanted one. Nabokov good-humoredly played his part in looking after Dmitri, and would show friends how to wring out diapers "with an elegant backhand twist of the wrist" like a tennis stroke. While summer shone, he would take Dmitri by bus to the Grunewald, stretch out a blanket under the trees, and watch the boy hunt for pine cones.[25] There he planned the story "Nabor" ("Recruiting") and, back at Nestorstrasse, had written it out by the end of July.[26]

An old émigré attends a friend's funeral, thinks of all he has lost, his sister, his unfaithful wife, a friend tortured in the civil war—and still, as he sits on a park bench, feels suffused with a rare happiness. But next to him on the bench reading a Russian newspaper is the author of the story, who has merely selected this stranger for a chapter in his novel and invented for him a plausible past. He would like to be able to share his wild creative happiness with the old man seated beside him, but he cannot be sure he has succeeded. In fact as the image of the newspaper-reading "author" comes more into focus, we realize that he too of course is only the real author's dummy. Prefiguring *Pale Fire*'s game of worlds within worlds within worlds, this subtle story suggests that life for all its poignant immediacy may be only the creative fancy of some force beyond, which tries to impart the ecstasy of creation to all that it has willed into being. And beyond that force, might still another force lurk. . .?

The story can also be seen as another of the variations Nabokov composed on themes to be sounded in *The Gift*: in this case, Fyodor's attempt to enter his father's mind as he describes his last expedition, or to look through the eye of a friend deranged by the death of his son.

In late summer Nabokov wrote something quite unexpected: a small autobiographical sketch in English of his associations with England in early childhood, which he would later rework into chapter 4 ("My English Education") of *Speak, Memory*. The sketch would serve as an exercise in English before he translated *Despair*, and by stressing his early links with England it might prepare the way for his acceptance there. The very title of the piece indicates the difficulties before him, despite his background: "It is Me," neither the natural English "It's Me," nor the "It is I" that muddled purists suppose more correct.[27] Unfortunately, nothing survives of this piece except those three words.

As if to reward him for this effort in English, the *New York Times Book Review* featured an article on Sirin. He wrote to his mother: "The *New York Times* says 'our age has been enriched by the appearance of a great writer,' but I have no good trousers and I just don't know what I will wear to Belgium, where the Pen Club has invited me." Summing up his financial situation as "utterly disastrous," he asked Gleb Struve if there were not some way he could teach Russian or French literature in England.[28]

Early in September he wrote the story "Sluchay iz zhizni" ("A Slice of Life").[29] For the only time in his career, Nabokov narrates a complete tale in the feminine first person—and succeeds superbly. A sensitive woman, fated to love the only men available and to be passed over for women less worthy than herself, finds once again she has simply been used: she becomes the inadvertent accomplice of a man who tries to shoot his wife, who has just abandoned him for someone else. Not for the first time, the heroine finds herself embroiled in the moral squalor of other lives and humiliated by her own desperate need for love. Nevertheless she somehow retains her kindness, her dignity, her hope. Behind the "deliberately commonplace, newspaper nuance" Nabokov sought for in the outer events of the story lies his confidence in the imperishable values of the spirit. His heroine's life may be unhappy, even grotesque, and certainly unenviable, but it also enshrines something triumphant.

As soon as the story was finished, he set about translating *Despair*, which his publisher wanted by Christmas: "my first serious attempt . . . to use English for what may be loosely termed an artistic purpose."[30] Autumn was the cruelest season that year: looking after Dmitri "a mixture of hard labor and heaven," the time pressure and the sheer challenge of the translation unsettling to the nerves. "To translate oneself is a frightful business," he wrote to Zinaida Shakhovskaya, "looking over one's insides and trying them on like a glove, and discovering the best dictionary to be not a friend but the enemy camp."[31]

On December 29 at 3 A.M. he finished the translation of *Despair*: "I opened the window, all was dark, not a light anywhere, and for some reason it smelled of spring." A rather grumpy Englishman, obtained through an agency in Berlin, thought the manuscript smelled of something else when Nabokov asked him to check his idioms. Nabokov considered the translation stylistically clumsy, but the Englishman, after finding "a few solecisms in the first chapter, . . . refused to continue, saying he disapproved of the book; I suspect he wondered if it might not have been a true confession."[32]*

V

Nabokov was anxious to return to *The Gift* ("it is three years already since I ordered its bricks"), but first he hoped to rewrite his English reminiscences. He was rather alarmed to learn from Zinaida Shakhovskaya that he was expected to read a new piece in French when he appeared in Brussels at the end of January 1936. Three years earlier he had thought of writing on the special French subculture of the Russian gentry, and now with a piece on his English infancy to prompt him— governesses and English fairy tales and *Chatterbox*—he naturally turned to the poignant figure of his French governess. In two or three days at the end of the first week in January he dashed off "Mademoiselle O." Suspicious of the ease of its composition, he thought it third-rate.[33]

After another bout of dreading that visas would not arrive in time, Nabokov left in mid-January for a reading tour of Brussels, Antwerp, and Paris. In Brussels he stayed with Zinaida Shakhovskaya and her husband, Sviatoslav Malevsky-Malevich, and grew to like them both. There he met Paul Firens and Belgium's leading writer, the novelist Frans Hellens, whose *Oeil-de-Dieu* Nabokov had read enthusiastically several years previously. He hit it off right away with the monocled, aquiline-nosed Hellens, who served as librarian to the Belgian parliament and was married to a Russian.[34]

Nabokov had asked Zinaida Shakhovskaya to look after Kirill ("a nice young man, but . . . childish, lightheaded, dreadfully inexperienced") and was relieved to find him changed for the better. He missed Dmitri already, and wrote wistfully to Véra: "I feel that new words are hatching without me." He reworked "Mademoiselle O," but still feared an audience might find it long and tedious. Instead his Pen Club evening on January 24 was a dazzling success, although the crowd was small. Hellens suggested he offer his sketch to Jean Paulhan for the *Nouvelle Revue française*.[35]

On January 26 Belgium's Russian Jewish Club staged a Sirin evening in Brussels. Before the large audience he read poems, the story "Lips to Lips" (its first public airing), and the last three chapters of *Invitation to a Beheading*, which were received so well he thought he

---

* By a bizarre coincidence, the *New Yorker's* capsule description of Rainer Werner Fassbinder's film version of *Despair* in 1979 inadvertently stated—until the complaints poured in—that the movie was based on Nabokov's "autobiographical" novel.

would repeat them in Paris. The next night he read in Russian again ("The Aurelian") for the Cercle russe of Antwerp, a boring evening not at all redeemed in his eyes by someone else's magic show.[36]

VI

Two days later Sirin arrived in Paris. From the Gare du Nord he headed straight for 130 Avenue de Versailles, where Fondaminsky assigned him a charming bedroom in his spacious new apartment (Amalia Fondaminsky had died the previous year). At 7:30 he was just sitting down to talk to Fondaminsky and Zenzinov when Bunin appeared, half-drunk, talking through his nose, and in spite of Sirin's firm opposition, dragged him off to a restaurant. Nabokov wrote home the next day:

> At first our conversation flagged, mainly I think because of me. I was tired and cross. Everything irritated me: his manner of ordering hazel-grouse, and every intonation, and his bawdy little jokes, and the deliberate servility of the waiter, so that he later complained to Aldanov I was thinking about something else all the time. I haven't been so angry in a long time as over going to dine with him. But toward the end and later, when we went out in the street, sparks of mutuality began to flash here and there, and when we went into the Café de la Paix, where plump Aldanov was waiting for us, it was quite cheery. There I saw Khodasevich for a minute—looking very yellowish. Bunin hates him. . . . Aldanov said that when Bunin and I talked to each other and looked at each other it felt all the time as if two movie cameras were rolling.[37]

Recounting the event in *Speak, Memory*, Nabokov remembers the night's early bitterness and the aftertaste that spoiled his future relations with Bunin, but not the détente in the Café de la Paix. According to this later recollection, which Bunin altogether denied—even the fact of their dining *à deux*—they had become utterly bored with each other by the end of the meal. Bunin, notorious for his sharp tongue, told Nabokov: "You will die in dreadful pain and complete isolation." (On another occasion Bunin had complained that Nabokov was not open enough, or as Nabokov put it, "that I didn't pour my soul over the cutlet.")[38] After they left the restaurant, a farce ensued when Bunin had to drag out of his coat sleeve Nabokov's woolen scarf stuffed into the wrong armhole by the cloakroom attendant.

> The thing came out inch by inch; it was like unwrapping a mummy and we kept slowly revolving around each other in the process, to the ribald

amusement of three sidewalk whores. Then, when the operation was over, we walked on without a word to a street corner where we shook hands and separated. Subsequently we used to meet quite often, but always in the midst of other people. . . . Somehow Bunin and I adopted a bantering and rather depressing mode of conversation, a Russian variety of American "kidding," and this precluded any real commerce between us.[39]

Nabokov had come to Paris for a joint reading with Khodasevich, who was in failing health and almost destitute. In advertising the reading, *Poslednie Novosti* had printed Khodasevich's name in much smaller type than Nabokov's (Khodasevich ran a literary column in the rival Paris daily, *Vozrozhdenie*, and he and Adamovich, his *Poslednie Novosti* counterpart, regularly took aim at each other from their respective newspapers). Nabokov was outraged, and made *Poslednie Novosti* give them both equal billing.[40]

The reading took place on February 8, once again in the rue Las Cases and once again the large hall was filled, extra chairs and all. As the audience continued to crowd in, Khodasevich began. Long respected for his expertise on the poetry of the Derzhavin and Pushkin eras, Khodasevich astounded his audience by recounting his discovery of the hitherto unknown work of Vasily Travnikov, fourteen years older than Pushkin, who even before Pushkin's immediate poetic forebears had begun "the conscious battle against the conventions of literary affectation which was one of the legacies of the eighteenth century" to the nineteenth.[41] The few surviving details of Travnikov's life and the brief samples of his work that Khodasevich could quote excited everyone in the audience who cared for Russian literature. In his performance that night Khodasevich brilliantly demonstrated his affinity with Sirin, master maker of literary masks, for as Sirin knew— and as no one not in the know seems to have guessed—the Travnikov story was a hoax.

Sirin, sucking on lozenges to soothe a bad sore throat, had been sitting beside Bunin, who, dreading a cold, kept on overcoat and hat and muzzled his nose in his collar. In the second half of the show Sirin stepped forward to read three stories: "A Russian Beauty," "Terra Incognita," and "Breaking the News." The evening was so successful a reviewer rated it sufficient in itself to refute those who denied the achievements of émigré literature, and called Sirin the justification of the whole emigration.[42]

After the performance a large group of writers and friends set off for champagne at the Café La Fontaine: Aldanov, Berberova, Bunin, Khodasevich, Sirin, Weidle at one table, Fondaminsky and Zenzinov nearby. When the conversation touched on Tolstoy's *Sebastopol Sketches*,

Sirin confessed he had never read that juvenilia. (Actually Tolstoy wrote them when he was twenty-eight.) Bunin stammered in indignation. Aldanov, who had modeled his art on *War and Peace*, screamed: "You despise us all!" Khodasevich simply laughed and said he did not believe him. At another point of the evening, in another mood, Aldanov in an access of Russian excitement hailed Sirin as the foremost writer of the emigration and urged Bunin to offer his signet ring to him as a token of his superiority. Bunin demurred.[43]

While Sirin was in Paris, Khodasevich invited him to call—the only person he had invited all year, the physically and emotionally shattered poet confided to a friend a few months later. Sirin also called on a man named Dostokiyan, whom he hoped to interest in a project he had for a film, "Hotel Magique" (possibly the forerunner of *The Prismatic Bezel* in *The Real Life of Sebastian Knight*, in which a boardinghouse where a murder has occurred dissolves into a family's country home and back again). He had a meeting arranged ("Not that I want it") with the critic Edmond Jaloux, "totally second-rate and terribly influential." He visited the Kaminkas, the Kyandzhuntsevs, Raisa Tatarinov, he met Kerensky, Teffi, Ladinsky.[44] He saw Lucie Léon Noel, the sister of his Cambridge friend Alex Ponizovski and an acquaintance of his own from London in 1920. Her husband, Paul Léon, offered to introduce Nabokov to his close friend James Joyce, a meeting much more to Nabokov's taste, but issued so many warnings on what should and should not be said that Nabokov told Léon he was busy and there was no real point to a meeting. He wrote to Vera:

> Joyce and Proust met only once, by chance. Proust and he were together in a taxi, the window of which the former closed, whereupon the latter rolled it down, and they nearly quarreled. All in all it was rather tedious, and anyway, in these new things of his [*Work in Progress*], the abstract puns, the verbal masquerade, the shadows of words, the diseases of words . . . in the end wit sinks behind reason, and, while it is setting, the sky is ravishing, but then there is night.[45]

On February 15 Sirin read at a poets' evening along with Adamovich, Berberova, Bunin, Gippius, Khodasevich, Ivanov, Merezhkovsky, Odoevtseva, Smolensky, and Tsvetaeva, a roll call of a standard inconceivable in Berlin since the heady days of 1923. He managed to be rude to Adamovich, he confessed—perhaps when Adamovich suggested Kafka as a model for *Invitation to a Beheading*.[46]

"Mademoiselle O" had been such a success in Brussels that Nabokov was asked back to read it before the Russian Jewish Club there. Since he had no time to obtain a visa, Zenzinov told him of the standard method Socialist Revolutionary terrorists had used to cross secretly from France to Belgium: disembark at Charleroi, walk across the tracks in the subterranean station there and board the underground train direct to Brussels, on which passports were never checked. Sirin left Paris on February 16 and found that the old ruse still worked.[47] He read his story and returned two days later to Paris. On February 25 "Nabokoff-Sirine, le célèbre romancier russe" read "Mademoiselle O" in the elegant salon of Mme Ridel, after being introduced by Gabriel Marcel. The reading was particularly successful, and Jean Paulhan eagerly took the sketch for the new journal *Mesures*.[48]

VII

Arriving back in Berlin on February 29 from an unusually pleasant month in Paris, Nabokov found several letters from agents. When Nina Berberova had recently passed on to him still another agent's name, he had thanked her but added:

> I have more agents than readers, and the business side of my life consists of the complicated distribution of countless, hopeless options. If they herded all these men and women together it would make a huge international hospital—for it's strange, after the first passionate period of telegrams there follows a mysterious silence, which several queries later is explained by "an illness." A little clinic in a pine forest could be made up just of my female translators.[49]

Resettled in Berlin, Nabokov sat down again to *The Gift*.[50] By now he had finished chapter 4, the *Life of Chernyshevsky*, and probably a first version of chapter 2, Fyodor's account of his father's travels in Central Asia. One more part of the novel required special treatment: the delicate poems that make up Fyodor's first book, which we glimpse over his shoulder in chapter 1. These poems constitute the young writer's attempt to probe the deepest recesses of childhood, the mysterious darkness from which the bright light of his consciousness has somehow emerged. In these skillful but slightly brittle poems Nabokov had to concoct verse that could demonstrate both Fyodor's gift and the limitations of his early craft.

In April Nabokov diverged from *The Gift* to write "Vesna v Fial'te" ("Spring in Fialta").[51] An émigré recounts a chance meeting in the seaside resort of Fialta (a blend of the Adriatic's Fiume and the Black Sea's Yalta) with a glamorous woman who has often streaked through his life like a bright but giddy comet. He relives his whole bizarre relationship with her over fifteen years. Since Nina's first generous kiss one night in 1917, before they had even exchanged a word, Vasily

(Victor in the English version) has known her random largesse in amatory matters, but their meetings have been brief, accidental, and all but once unconsummated. Deeply haunted now by all their repeated meetings and partings to the dance of time, Vasily tells her he loves her—and retracts it when he sees her frown. Half an hour later, driving out of Fialta with her husband, Nina is killed when their car crashes into a circus truck.

In *The Gift* fate repeatedly tries to bring together a young man and woman, who will fall in love and marry when at last they discover each other. "Spring in Fialta" seems a deliberate converse: here fate arranges for Nina and Vasily to meet again and again, only to cut off consequences every time. Yet somehow the long history of their tenuous connection, a history consisting almost entirely of gaps thinly divided from one another only by fleeting chance encounters, acquires its own compelling force.

Vasily at one point recalls meeting Nina at a big railway station, in whose life-quickening atmosphere "everything is something trembling on the brink of something else." That phrase could apply to every aspect of the story: to the strange weather in Fialta, where rain and leaden sky seem almost a haze of perspiration; to the force of the present, which always sends Vasily's thoughts promptly back into the past; to Nina, somehow destined to be so unattainable although so thoroughly available, so unretainable although never quite possessed; to the story's unique richness of style, which creates a world extraordinarily dense, substantial, and extensive despite the irrepressible play of Vasily's imagination as he narrates; to the sheer crowded *life* of it all, suddenly snuffed out by Nina's death. Never has Nabokov conveyed better the richness mortality bestows on time's incidentals, never has he imparted a more vividly haunting personal force to time's designs. No wonder "Spring in Fialta" always remained one of his favorite stories.

By now, with Dmitri two years old, romping around on his own two feet and boisterous enough for the family to call him an out-and-out hooligan, Véra was free to work again. Surprisingly—even though Hitler had been in power for three years—she managed to find a position handling the foreign correspondence of an engineering firm, Ruths-Speicher. The job, which she sometimes supplemented with other part-time work, lasted three months, until the engineer, an Austrian Nazi, squeezed out the Jewish owners and Véra too as another Jew.[52]

In May 1936 General Biskupsky, a rightist intriguer long disliked throughout the emigration, succeeded in having himself appointed head of Hitler's department for émigré affairs.[53] As his second-in-command he chose none other than Sergey Taboritsky, V. D. Nabokov's assassin. Nabokov reacted immediately, writing to Mikhail Karpovich, the Harvard historian he had met in Prague in 1932. Explaining his poverty, he declared himself ready to teach Russian literature, with French as a sideline, in any American university, no matter how provincial.[54] But neither politics nor poverty could becloud the Nabokovs' family life. Countering Andrew Field's overemphasis on their poverty—which the Nabokovs on the other hand underemphasized in retrospect, secure in the knowledge that they had survived—Nabokov suggested he write instead:

> Although there was not enough money, perhaps, for automobiles, fur coats, diamonds, and other commonplace trappings of wealth, the Nabokovs had always had enough for clean, comfortable quarters and good food, including as much fresh orange juice as a baby could imbibe.[55]

Which, according to *Speak, Memory*, amounted to the juice of a dozen fresh oranges per day, for between the ages of two and five Dmitri was forbidden milk in any form. Nabokov added: "H. G. Wells has a story *The Food of the Gods*, and Dmitri might be a character in it." The boy grew so rapidly in fact that when in Brussels his father had shown a photograph of his twenty-month-old son, a woman had remarked: "He can't be more than five!"[56]

Poverty meant tighter scrimping for the parents, never for their child. Wealthy friends helped out too, buying Dmitri on his second birthday a four-foot-long, silver-painted Mercedes pedal car, a racing model—forerunner of his future Ferrari and Alfa Romeo racers—that he quickly learned to steer with style along the sidewalks of the Kurfürstendamm. Nabokov himself never learned to drive a car, but he had always loved the poetry of motion—bicycles, trains, imagined flight—and as he strolled out with Dmitri from 9 A.M. to 12:45 every day that the sun shone, he watched with wonder Dmitri's instinctive attraction to the tram depot or a little bridge over the railway track or trucks standing by the sidewalk, and was grateful that the whole quarter throbbed with garages and machines of every kind.[57]

Perhaps it was in the late spring and summer of 1936 that Nabokov expanded his account of a Russian's early associations with England into a small book.[58] He had recently written of both his English education and his French, and "Mademoiselle O" had proven that his portraits of people and things that had meant much to him could matter for others. In Brussels his cousin Sergey, an irrepressibly enthusiastic genealogist, had shown him an engraved portrait of their ancestor the composer Graun—and much other family information. Over the last few years Nabokov had been planning within *The Gift* a full-scale life of one writer's mind (the Chernyshevsky biography), a family portrait richly evocative of Vyra, and a fictional autobiography tracing the development of a writer's self and art. As he composed the poems where Fyodor traces the birth of his consciousness, Nabokov was also watching his son's mind stir. He notes in *Speak, Memory* that although most of his autobiography was not written until 1947–1950, the order of chapters had been established in 1936, at the placing of the cornerstone, "Mademoiselle O."[59] The key to *Speak, Memory's* outer structure would be simple: at the beginning, Nabokov's own waking to consciousness; at the end, the same miracle in his son.

But nothing survives of the 1936 autobiography, apparently three or four chapters and his longest effort yet in original English composition. Here and there in Nabokov's correspondence between 1936 and 1938 occur various tantalizing titles: "It is Me," "Elizabeth," "My English Wife," "English Games in Russia," "Memoirs," "A Russian's Early Associations with England." Some are titles for parts, some presumably for the whole, and some perhaps alternative names for the same thing, but unfortunately there seems no more that can be discovered.

Nabokov's past was about to offer something he had no need to work at. Some years previously the German courts had begun to liquidate entailed property, and one of Nabokov's cousins had called his attention to a notice seeking claimants to the estate of their Graun family forebears. In June 1936 Nabokov inherited his share of the estate, a sum—a thousand reichsmarks—that provided over half of his income in what would otherwise have been a very lean year. He thought of spending a holiday in late fall—summer would be too expensive—in the Belgian countryside. Or perhaps he might move there permanently. But there seemed no urgency. In the end, Véra and Dmitri spent only ten days in Leipzig at the beginning of October, staying with a cousin of Anna Feigin's, while Vladimir remained in Berlin.[60]

VIII

With the most difficult parts of *The Gift* already drafted, Nabokov could now after three and a half years start to write out the novel from beginning to end. On August 23, 1936, he commenced chapter 1, inserting in the frenzy of revisions the neat fair copies of Fyodor's verse. He worked on the novel with such zeal that his writing hand was soon aching.[61]

Meanwhile things were slowly stirring in England. Nabokov had not sent his publishers his translation of *Despair* until early April, and now after a long delay Hutchinson & Co. informed him they had not made any publication plans. Their readers were not enthusiastic, "especially in regard to your translation." The problem was not the translation, Nabokov replied, but the book's originality, or to put it another way (he was more tactful), the problem was that Hutchinson's John Long imprint published cheap popular fiction, a category *Despair* had even less chance of fitting than *Camera Obscura*.[62] When Hutchinson did decide to publish, Nabokov asked Gleb Struve for the name of someone who could check the English of his translation. Struve recommended one of his students, Molly Carpenter-Lee. Nabokov gave her the translation early in the fall, joking that she had to scour the book "in search of the split infinitive."[63]

A month later, as Hutchinson prepared to add *Despair* to the John Long list, Nabokov again complained that in that company his book would resemble "a rhinoceros in a world of hummingbirds." To no avail: Hutchinson continued as planned. Aimed at the wrong audience, *Despair* sank as quickly as *Camera Obscura* had. The advances Nabokov had received for the books were a slender £40 apiece, but in view of their fate he was lucky even to have this much in hand.[64]

IX

In September 1936 General Biskupsky tried to register all Russian émigrés in Germany. Registration was easy to avoid, but the project boded ill, and during the next twelve weeks Nabokov instituted a search for work more or less related to literature, anywhere in the English-speaking world. He wrote to Aldanov's friend Alexander Kaun at the University of California. He asked Mrs. Carpenter-Lee about a Cambridge position Struve had failed to get.[65] Although his letters, sent from a dictatorship, naturally maintain a wary silence about political matters, in other respects they are a revelation. When he applied to the Yale archaeologist and former CD, Mikhail Rostovtzeff, Nabokov wrote:

> My situation has become so difficult I have to search for any kind of work at all. My literary income is minuscule: I could not live on it even by myself, but I have a wife and child, to say nothing of the wretched material state of my mother and in fact the whole family. . . . I cannot count any longer on any kind of supplementary income. In a word . . . my situation is desperate.

He added that he had long dreamed of lecturing in Russian in England or America, and repeated what he had told Karpovich, that he was ready to serve in any provincial college, that he would even teach

French if that would help.[66] To the distinguished Slavist Sir Bernard Pares, an old admirer of V. D. Nabokov, he wrote:

> I never thought that I could arrive at such a stage of financial distress, as I always supposed that as years went translations of my novels would help me to exist. It appears that I was mistaken: my literary earnings are so sparse as to be absolutely insufficient for the making of the most modest living, and the better I write and the greater my fame among connoisseurs, the more difficult it gets to have my works translated. This is what makes me long for some kind of intellectual work which would be enough to support my small family. Any kind of work—a lecturer's job or one connected with some publishing firm (where, perhaps, my perfect knowledge of French may come in handy?),—anything, anywhere—and if not in Great Britain then in the U.S., Canada, India or South Africa. I really feel that I could be of some use in an English-speaking country,—unfortunately, I cannot hope for any sort of occupation here.[67]

Nabokov had been planning another reading tour to France and Belgium and hoping vaguely to link it up with leaving Berlin altogether. Originally scheduled for late December, the tour was postponed from the Paris end only a couple of weeks beforehand. He had by now completed the fair copy of the first chapter of *The Gift*, from which he had planned to read for his Russian audiences. This time too he had prepared well in advance an offering for French listeners: an essay on Pushkin, the centenary of whose death would be commemorated in January 1937. This radiant meditation on the artfulness of life—as Nabokov calls it, "a firework display of festive thoughts on the velvet background of Pushkin"—anticipates the mood of the great chapter 5 of *The Gift*, which also happens to end with a homage to Pushkin.[68] All Goebbels's attempts to Nazify culture could not dent Nabokov's faith in something deeply and genuinely artistic lurking in life, forever immune from the vicious travesty blaring around him.

On January 18, 1937, he left Berlin to read in Russian, French, and English in Brussels, Paris, and London and to seek out a future for his family wherever the three languages he had taken from Russia would allow him a new refuge.[69] Never again would he set foot on German soil.

On the Move: France, 1937

I

NABOKOV arrived in Belgium on January 19 and stayed three days with his friends Zinaida Shakhovskaya and her husband, Sviatoslav Malevsky-Malevich. He saw his brother Kirill, whose blithe insouciance as usual roused his paternal instincts, and exhorted the Malevsky-Maleviches and his cousin Sergey to look after him. On the evening of January 21 Nabokov read his Pushkin essay at the Brussels Palais des Beaux-Arts and the next day set off for Paris and another reading.[1]

He hoped to establish a base for himself and his family in France, or if at all possible England or America, while Véra would follow as soon as they had settled on a destination and she could dispose of all the endless formalities associated with departure from Germany.[2] He had considered moving to Paris as early as 1930, and in many ways France still seemed the natural goal. There were four hundred thousand Russian émigrés in the country, and the main newspapers and journals for the whole emigration were firmly based in Paris. Nabokov had impeccable connections with the émigré community there, and when he arrived in the city, he stayed as before in the apartment of Ilya Fondaminsky, "the nerve center of the Paris emigration."[3]

On the other hand Nabokov could not obtain a French work permit[4]—it would take him more than a year to obtain even a *carte d'identité*—and the chances of supporting his family solely by writing in Russian were nil. Though his French was first-rate, he never felt it as supple or secure as his English. Apart from his memoir "Mademoiselle O" and his Pushkin essay, he had composed nothing in French, whereas he had already translated *Despair* into English, written a series of autobiographical sketches in the language, and had an agent active in New York. Readings and a job search in London were scheduled for February.

On January 24, Khodasevich introduced a Sirin evening at the rue Las Cases, part of a series organized by Fondaminsky. Sirin fans had turned out in large numbers to hear him read two excerpts from his work in progress, *The Gift*—one of them a parody of an émigré literary evening.[5] More than an hour long, the reading was in Aldanov's words "one continuous, uninterrupted flow of the most unexpected formal, stylistic, psychological and artistic *trouvailles*."[6] That sort of talent could be hard for rivals to take. Afterward Sirin was invited to tea by Bunin, whom others have reported flying into a fit of envy at the very name of Nabokov. On this occasion Bunin told him he considered "A University Poem" his best work—and hoped that his comment would offend the younger writer.[7]

The reading was not just a literary event. In the crowd were a woman called Vera Kokoshkin and her thirty-one-year-old daughter, Irina Guadanini. Knowing that Irina was strongly attracted to Sirin, her mother had approached him after his February 1936 reading in Paris, complimented him assiduously, and invited him back for tea. He had accepted and had been amused by Mme Kokoshkin's acting the procuress for her daughter. Now once again she took matters in hand, and invited Nabokov for dinner with Fondaminsky and Zenzinov.[8]

Her plans worked. Irina was an attractive blond with the strikingly regular features of classical statuary, a cultured woman, observant, playfully derisive, with a fine memory for verse. She was soon frequenting cafés and cinemas with Nabokov. By February an affair was under way.[9]

In St. Petersburg Irina's family had belonged to the same circle as Nabokov's.[10] The brother of her stepfather, like Nabokov's father, was a leading CD, arrested by the Bolsheviks at Countess Panin's Petrograd house just before V. D. Nabokov was released from arrest and escaped to Countess Panin's Crimean home. The shooting of Fyodor Kokoshkin and Andrey Shingarev in January 1918, without trial and while they were both patients in a hospital, had sent a chill throughout liberal Russia: this kind of execution was unprecedented in pre-revolutionary Russia and gave liberals and non-Bolshevik radicals their first taste of Lenin's and Trotsky's political style. Even young Vladimir Nabokov had taken note, and a year later had composed a poem to mark the anniversary of their deaths.

In the emigration Irina had been briefly married to a Russian she met in Belgium while he was on leave from work in the Congo. When her mother forbade her on health grounds to return to Africa with her husband, she had remained behind, divorced, and reverted to her maiden name before moving with her mother to settle in Paris. Although after World War II she would work for Radio Liberty and would publish in the 1960s a thin volume of poetry, in the 1930s she had to find what employment she could. An animal lover, she earned a skimpy living as a poodle trimmer.

Ten years earlier Nabokov had introduced himself and his wife into *King, Queen, Knave* as a contrast to the novel's sordid adulterous triangle. In real life, he could sternly disapprove of one cousin's infidelity or think little of another's constant remarrying. He did not take easily to his new situation, and in February the nervous tension the affair caused him brought on a severe attack of psoriasis, whose "indescribable torments" almost drove him to the brink of suicide.[11]

Meanwhile he was writing to Véra daily and imploring her to come as soon as she could so that they could settle in the south of France. Unaware of the affair, Véra insisted they had to travel together to Prague and fulfill their promise to Elena Nabokov, now an old woman with few joys left except the prospect of seeing once more her favorite son and the grandson she had never seen. At a time when he was busily making literary contacts in Paris and London and trying to open an escape route westward, Nabokov was reluctant to cross back and find himself stuck with a bloody-minded Germany blocking the return route to freedom. Rather than allow himself to be dragged "to the wilds of Czechoslovakia, where (psychologically, geographically, in every sense) I shall again be cut off from every possible source and opportunity of making a living," he wrote to Véra, "*I shall simply take the next train to Berlin*, i.e. I shall come to fetch you, which will certainly be neither wise nor cheap."[12]

One day in the second week of February Nabokov had just finished rewriting his Pushkin essay for the *Nouvelle Revue française* when Gabriel Marcel rang. The Hungarian woman writer Jolán Földes, author of the recent French best seller, *La Rue du chat qui pêche*, had fallen ill and had just cabled Marcel that she could not speak at the next lecture, only a few hours away, in the series Marcel was organizing. Could Nabokov take her place? He could.

When Nabokov arrived at the Salle Chopin (February 11, 5 P.M.), the Hungarian consul mistook him for the writer's husband and dashed toward him with condolence on his lips. Then as Nabokov mounted the stage to speak, a whirlpool stirred in the large audience. The whole Hungarian colony had bought tickets and now were leaving after finding out about the change in program. Most of the French contingent also drifted away, and only a few Hungarians stayed on in blissful ignorance. Foreseeing all this, a number of Nabokov's friends had done their best to round up the kind of audience they knew he would like to have: his translator, Denis Roche; his old friend Raisa Tatarinov; Aldanov, Bunin, Kerensky. James Joyce too was there, brought by his friends and Nabokov's, Paul and Lucie Léon. "A source of unforgettable consolation," Nabokov later recalled, "was the sight of Joyce sitting, arms folded and glasses glinting, in the midst of the Hungarian football team."[13]

II

Nine days later Nabokov was in London for a reading organized by the Obshchestvo Severyan, one of the more prominent Russian organizations in England. He had few to read to.[14] The small émigré colony in London had little cohesion, and though local Russians made Nabokov's visit to England affordable and even profitable (he earned money from Russian readings and stayed with Mark and Tatiana Tsetlin in Kensington Park Road), he had really come to gain access to the English academic, publishing, and film worlds. He saw the gifted actor Fritz Kortner, by now an exile from Nazi Germany, who wanted to make a film of *Camera Obscura*. He sought a £45 translation fee from John Long for his English rendering of *Despair*. He lunched near the British Museum with Gleb Struve, now lecturing at the School of Oriental and Slavonic Studies, and heard that academic prospects were bleak.[15]

Still, Struve did what he could. One of his students was the daughter of Katharine Ridley, herself daughter of the former Russian ambassador Count Benckendorff. He managed to arrange a dinner at the Ridleys', inviting Leonard Woolf, Peter Quennell (later to edit a book on Nabokov), and many others in London's literary circles. Among those who did turn up were L. P. Hartley, Desmond MacCarthy, and Baroness Budberg. Nabokov read out a chapter from his embryonic autobiography, *A Russian's Early Association with England*, and although several guests later asked for the manuscript, nothing came of the evening.[16]

With a former Tenishev schoolmate, Savely Grinberg, he traveled up to his old university: "I made the dreadful mistake of going to see Cambridge again not at the glorious end of the Easter term but on a raw February day that reminded me only of my own confused old nostalgia. I was hopelessly trying to find an academic job in England."[17] No one he had known then could help him now. He dined with "Nesbit," as he named one former student acquaintance, "at a little place, which ought to have been full of memories but which, owing to various changes, was not." When Nesbit launched into politics, Nabokov

knew well what to expect—denunciation of Stalinism. In the early twenties Nesbit had mistaken his own ebullient idealism for a romantic and humane something in Lenin's ghastly rule. [Now], in the days of the no less ghastly Stalin, [Nesbit] was mistaking a quantitative increase in his own knowledge for a qualitative change in the Soviet regime. The thunderclap of purges that had affected "old Bolsheviks," the heroes of his youth, had given him a salutary shock, something that in Lenin's day all the groans coming from the Solovki forced labor camp or the Lubyanka dungeon had not been able to do. With horror he pronounced the names of Ezhov and Yagoda—but quite forgot their predecessors, Uritski and Dzerzhinski. . . .

He looked at his watch, and I looked at mine, and we parted, and I wandered around the town in the rain, and then visited the Backs, and for some time peered at the rooks in the black network of the bare elms and at the first crocuses in the mist-beaded turf.[18]

The visit to Cambridge may have been a failure, but Nabokov stored the scenery and the frustration in some creative cell of his mind next to his English autobiography. A year and a half later they fused in *The Real Life of Sebastian Knight* into V's trip to Cambridge on the trail of his brother's past.

One concluding image of that day deserves mention. As the light dwindled to a last yellow streak in the west Nabokov decided to call on his old tutor, Ernest Harrison.

Like a sleepwalker, I mounted the familiar steps and automatically knocked on the half-open door bearing his name. In a voice that was a jot less abrupt, and a trifle more hollow, he bade me come in. "I wonder if you remember me . . ." I started to say, as I crossed the dim room to where he sat near a comfortable fire. "Let me see," he said, slowly turning around his low chair, "I do not quite seem . . ." There was a dismal crunch, a fatal clatter: I had stepped into the tea things that stood at the foot of his wicker chair. "Oh, yes, of course," he said, "I know who you are."[19]

On the last day of the month Nabokov gave one more reading, this time in the Russkiy Dom, the home of Evgeny Sablin, the former Russian chargé d'affaires in London. A mimeographed circular advertising the reading stressed Sirin's poverty and solicited the steep price of half a guinea a seat.[20] This time a larger crowd turned up, and Nabokov returned to Paris at the beginning of March not only with a cold and a sense of stunned exhaustion to show for his pains, but with a few pound notes and with plans (they would remain unrealized) for an English collection of his stories.[21]

III

Nabokov expected to revisit England in April, after *Despair* was published there, but meanwhile obtained a permit for himself and his wife to stay in France. Véra and Dmitri, it had now been decided, would travel to Czechoslovakia and in May rejoin Nabokov in the south of France. By now Véra had liquidated the Nestorstrasse apartment, put their few belongings—papers, books, Dmitri's toys—into storage, and moved with Anna Feigin into a temporary flat while she waited for the Czech visa.[22]

In Paris Nabokov's life was hectic. One day he might lunch *porusski*, with Mark Aldanov, the former CD leader Vasily Maklakov, Alexander Kerensky, the historian George Vernadsky, and Ilya Fondaminsky; another *à la française*, with writers Jean Paulhan, Jules Supervielle, Charles-Albert Cingria, and Henri Michaux; a third time American-style, with Henry Church and Sylvia Beach. Nabokov wrote to Véra that he had sold "The Outrage" ("A Bad Day") for the May issue of *Mesures*.[23] The story never appeared, but one concrete memento survives from mid-April and Nabokov's lunch just outside Paris at the villa of Henry Church, the American writer and millionaire who sponsored *Mesures*. After the meal a virtual meeting of the magazine's editorial board took place around the stone table in the garden outside, an occasion recorded by photographer Gisèle Freund: the Churches, the Paulhans, and among others Joyce's friends Adrienne Monnier and Sylvia Beach (with whom Nabokov got on "swimmingly"). Nabokov himself—misidentified in the photograph as Jacques Audiberti—stands looking down at something white in his right hand. Although blurrily outlined against his dark sweater, it must surely be a butterfly.[24]

Nabokov wrote to Véra: "I've put on weight, got a tan, changed my skin, but am in a constant sense of irritation because I have no place and time to work." Sunbathing certainly eased the psoriasis, as did radiation treatments a kind Russian woman physician, Dr. Elizaveta Kogan-Bernstein, gave him for free.[25] But one cause of both the psoriasis and the shortage of time was still there: Irina Guadanini. Nabokov was never a person who knew how to love lightly, and the situation naturally fanned his feelings and hers: none of the innumerable minor frictions of living together day after day, all the excitement of new love and the fear that it could not last.

Late in April Véra took Dmitri with her to Prague, heaving a sigh of relief as their train crossed beyond the German border. Since the plan was now for Nabokov to join them as soon as the Czech authorities would grant him a visa, there was no point in his journeying back to England. His Nansen passport had expired and could not be extended unless he returned to Berlin.* To add to toothache and the task of

* Emigrés who left Russia as Russian citizens had passports of a country that ceased to exist once the Soviet Union was recognized. In the early 1920s, in place of their old papers, they and other stateless persons were issued temporary "Nansen" passports

revising Denis Roche's French version of the stylistically intricate "Spring in Fialta," there was the torment of obtaining a new Nansen passport from the French authorities.[26] At the préfecture an official calmly informed Nabokov that he had lost the application papers that he had been given. Picking up Nabokov's passport, by now only a tattered sheet of green paper, he pretended he was about to fling it out the window: "What do you need this old piece of scrap paper for?"[27]

At last Nabokov had his new passport and the authorities in Prague sent the authorities in Paris his Czech visa and the authorities in Paris in turn released it to Nabokov. He left Paris immediately, on May 20. Since Véra wanted him to avoid the Germany of Hitler and Tabor-itsky, he took a train via Switzerland and Austria. The trip was ex-hausting but beautiful: Alps, altitude, waterfalls, the smell of snow.[28]

IV

On the morning of May 22 he saw once more the steep slate roofs of old Prague, his son, a thriving three, his wife, and his mother. After a few days there, strolling together through the undulating unkempt-ness of Stromovka Park and catching up on time spent apart, the Na-bokovs moved on to Franzensbad and fango baths for the rheumatism that had afflicted Véra all year. They stopped at the Hotel Egerländer: fields on one side, a park full of pheasants and hares on the other.[29]

In Czechoslovakia Irina Guadanini's image glowed brightly beyond the horizon, while the immediate foreground was darkened by Na-bokov's unease and guilt at the need for deceit. He wrote secretly to Irina, telling her that his life with Véra had been fourteen years of cloudless happiness—throughout his correspondence with his mis-tress, there was never a hint of criticism of his wife—and that they knew each other's faintest shades and that now all this was de-stroyed. Véra had received an anonymous letter from Paris, four pages long, in a Slavic hand but in Roman script, recounting the affair in detail. He had denied it all but found it agony to pretend that things were on their former happy plane. "The inevitable vulgarity of de-ceit," he wrote to Irina. "And suddenly your conscience puts its foot

---

(named after the explorer Fridtjof Nansen, League of Nations High Commissioner for Refugees). These flimsy documents, obtained with difficulty and accepted with great reluctance at frontiers and immigration offices, were supposed to last for one year but often had to suffice until World War II.

down and you see yourself a scoundrel." At the same time he could not stop: he asked her to write poste restante to "V. Korff" in Prague, where his mother had arranged for him to give a reading.[30]

His train broke down en route from Franzensbad and was so late by the time he reached Prague that he barely made it to his own reading. He stayed on in his mother's two-roomed flat, playing cards and talking with her all night long. On June 23, after five days in Prague, he parted from his mother for the final time. He rejoined Véra in Marienbad, where she had gone to meet Anna Feigin, who had at last scrambled safely clear of Germany.[31]

Next week in Marienbad, staying at the Villa Busch, Nabokov wrote the story "Ozero, oblako, bashnya" ("Cloud, Castle, Lake"), a fable-like tale rooted for good reason in a specific time and place: Germany, 1936 or 1937.[32] Simply because he is somehow different, a sensitive Russian émigré who wins an out-of-town excursion as a prize so offends the hearty Germans he finds himself with that on the return journey they beat and torture him.

The story can be read in many ways: as a damning verdict on the German spirit that could opt for Hitler, as a specific critique of the Nazi program of Strength through Joy, as a study in universal philistinism, as a contrast between the desire to be happy in one's own way and the cruelty of imposing one's conception of happiness on others, as a tribute to a world predisposed for happiness and a lament for a world nevertheless condemned by history to so much unhappiness. "Cloud, Castle, Lake" lies half way between *Invitation to a Beheading*— a phrase that the hero even applies to his trip—and the later *Bend Sinister*. In *Bend Sinister* Krug finds relief from the tortures inflicted on his son only in the madness of learning he is merely a character in a novel. In "Cloud, Castle, Lake" an unexpected authorial voice calls the central character "one of my representatives," and at the end,

> After returning to Berlin, he called on me, was much changed, sat down quietly, putting his hands on his knees, told his story; kept on repeating that he must resign his position, begged me to let him go, insisted that he could not continue, that he had not the strength to belong to mankind any longer. Of course, I let him go.[33]

Presumably that means death, the end of that person's story. But through the image of the controlling author Nabokov also implies, here as in *Bend Sinister*, some creative force behind life in sympathy with the hero humiliated by history. This brief story, which always remained one of Nabokov's favorites, would be the first he translated after reaching America.

V

At Marienbad on June 29 the Nabokovs bought a ticket for the Paris international exposition, which entitled them to a 50 percent reduction on the train fare to Paris at the small cost of traveling directly across Germany. The next day they arrived at the Gare de l'Est. Nabokov made his way to Fondaminsky's, Véra and Dmitri stayed with her cousins, the Brombergs. They visited the exposition. Since they had to pass through an entrance flanked on one side by a monumental German pavilion and on the other by a monumental Soviet pavilion, there could only be one judgment: "vulgar and meaningless."[34]

Nabokov called into the Gallimard offices and sold the French rights to *Despair*. For the first time one of his books would be translated into French from the English version rather than the Russian, a pattern to be followed for all subsequent translations from his Russian fiction. The negotiations with Gallimard also provided a screen for seeing Irina Guadanini: four days of snatched meetings, and a last farewell in front of the metro. Nabokov told her they would soon meet again, but she felt it would not happen. She was right.[35]

VI

On July 7 the Nabokovs left for Cannes, a much cheaper and much less crowded city then than now. They found rooms on the edge of the old town at the two-star Hotel des Alpes, rue St. Dizier and rue Georges Clemenceau: a railway bridge on one side, a moment's walk down to the Plage du Midi on the other.[36]

A few days after their arrival in Cannes, Nabokov confessed to Véra he was in love with Irina Guadanini. He told her all. If he felt that way about the woman, Véra answered, he should go to her in Paris at once. He hesitated and said: "Not now." Except for the night his father died, this was the worst evening of his entire life.[37]

Once the shock of the disclosure was over, the Nabokovs set up a new relationship, friendly and solicitous. But though things once again seemed cloudless to the eye and Véra said nothing more, Irina's image was not fading in Nabokov's mind. Cannes, he wrote Irina in secret, was full of her.[38] He basked on the beach. He distracted himself playing tennis with an acquaintance, or tramping in the heat along the red cliffs of the Estérel hills, not so much to catch butterflies as to reread them, as it were, since the local species were all well studied and he had collected in the area himself during his 1923 sojourn at Solliès-Pont. Once he returned toward evening on "a truck with a bad heart," and was asked: "Alors, monsieur, vous faites l'élévage des papillons?"[39] But much of the time, especially in the evenings, he was writing at white heat.

In April he had published in *Sovremennye Zapiski* the first chapter of *The Gift*, which had been ready since the beginning of the year. Now there were four more vast chapters to commit to final draft, each almost a complete novel in length. Copy was due for the next issue of *Sovremennye Zapiski*, but Nabokov saw that he needed time for a substantial reworking of the start of chapter 2. He set the chapter aside and instead prepared a fair copy of the long chapter 4, Fyodor's *Life of Chernyshevsky*, which had been close to final form for over two years. He felt "ridiculously pleased" with the chapter.[40] Since it was such a detachable chunk of text, he hoped *Sovremennye Zapiski* would accept it out of sequence.

Late in July the Nabokovs moved to a two-roomed apartment opposite the hotel, at 81 rue Georges Clemenceau. In the heat they lived an amphibian life, moving from apartment to beach via a tunnel of clay and cement.[41]

At the beginning of August Nabokov sent off the completed chapter 4. At *Sovremennye Zapiski*, Vadim Rudnev was furious at the substitution: how could he offer his readers chapter 4 after chapter 1? How at this late stage could he possibly find other fiction to fill the gap? Nabokov sat down at once to rework the beginning of chapter 2.[42]

He also wrote to Irina, telling her that Véra had found out that their correspondence had not ceased. He reported such storms that he thought he would end in a madhouse.[43] Irina replied saying she could come to Cannes and go off with him somewhere. Nabokov wrote back for her not to come. She left for a holiday with her mother, gloomy about her prospects.[44]

Another bombshell dropped from Paris. Rudnev had now read the Chernyshevsky chapter and refused outright to publish it in *Sovremennye Zapiski*.[45]

In chapter 3 of *The Gift* Nabokov shows the difficulties his hero faces in publishing such a controversially revisionist work as his *Life of Chernyshevsky*. But Fyodor is almost unknown as a writer, whereas Sirin had been hailed within the emigration as the best writer of his generation and for nearly ten years had had every one of his novels serialized in full in *Sovremennye Zapiski*. Although the very name of the journal was a tribute to *Sovremennik* (*The Contemporary*) and *Otechestvennye Zapiski* (*Annals of the Fatherland*), the great organs of the nineteenth-century radical intelligentsia, although it had been set up by a group of Socialist Revolutionaries in whose catechism Chernyshevsky was a god, *Sovremennye Zapiski* had been praised for nearly two decades for its nonpartisan nature, its exemplary tolerance, its fidelity to the principle of utter freedom of thought. Nabokov had never expected the journal to turn him down.

In despair he wrote back to Rudnev:

> By your refusal for reasons of censorship to print the fourth chapter of *The Gift* you make it impossible for me to publish this novel at all with you. Do not be angry, but judge for yourself. How can I give you the second and third chapters (in which there already begin to show the images and evaluations rejected by you and developed in the fourth) and then the concluding chapter (in which among other things there are four complete reviews of the *Life of Chernyshevsky* variously scolding its author for offending against the memory of "a great man of the Sixties" and explaining how sacred his memory remains) when I know that *The Gift* will be not a whole but a hole [*v Dare budet dyra*] with no fourth chapter. . . . I'll tell you straight out, I can accept no compromises or joint efforts and have no intention of striking out or altering a single line. Your turning down the novel hurts all the more because I have always harbored a special feeling for *Sovremennye Zapiski*. The fact that from time to time it has printed both creative work and articles developing views with which the editors plainly could not be in agreement has been a singular phenomenon in the history of our journals and a declaration of freedom of thought . . . that was a telling indictment of the situation of the press in present-day Russia. Why do you talk of "society's reaction" to my piece? Let me say, dear Vadim Viktorovich, that society's reaction to a literary work can only be a consequence of its artistic function, and not an a priori judgment. I do not intend to defend my *Chernyshevsky*—the thing is, in my ultimate view, on a plane where it needs no defense. I merely note for your coeditors that as a fighter for freedom Chernyshevsky is in no way belittled—and not because I have done this consciously (as you know, I am quite indifferent to every political party in the world) but no doubt because there was more justice in one camp and more evil in the other. If [coeditors Mark] Vishnyak and [Nikolay] Avksentiev respected Chernyshevsky not only as a revolutionary but as a thinker and critic (which is the main theme of the thing) then my researches could not fail to convince them. Finally let me draw your attention to the curious situation I have fallen into: I can publish *Chernyshevsky* neither with any Soviet publisher nor any rightist press nor *Poslednie Novosti* . . . nor you. You ask me to find some way out for *Sovremennye Zapiski*: may I point out that my own situation has no exit at all.[46]

Thanks to Rudnev's decision, *The Gift*—in the eyes of many, the greatest Russian novel of the century—was not published entire for another fifteen years. But Rudnev still wanted to take the remaining chapters. Since Nabokov needed the journal's money, he had no choice but to agree, and kept busily revising chapter 2. On Thursday September 2 Rudnev wrote that unless the manuscript arrived by 8 A.M. the next Monday the printer—who had already set the rest of the issue in type—would refuse to have anything to do with the whole issue. On Sunday night Rudnev lay in bed fretting all night, dreading an empty mailbox. Next morning, there was the typescript, and he wrote Nabokov a grateful "Ouf!" of relief.[47]

VII

A day later Irina Guadanini arrived in Cannes. Though Nabokov had asked her not to come, her mother had persuaded her to try.

She arrived by the overnight train, found his address, walked down toward the beach. From the Square Frédéric Mistral she could see their apartment and three swimsuits hung out to dry. A woman's hand removed a man's and a boy's trunks. Irina waited, her heart beating fast. As Nabokov brought Dmitri down to the beach for the morning swim, she rushed up to him, her high heels rapidly clicking. He recoiled in surprise. Although he still loved her, he told her, he felt too much for his wife. He asked her to leave, but she would not, and when he and Dmitri settled on the beach she sat down some distance off. An hour later Véra joined her husband and son. When the family all left for lunch, Irina still remained. Later, Nabokov told Véra about Irina's vigil. It was the last time he and Irina ever met.[48]

At the end of *Eugene Onegin* Tatiana, in love years ago with an unresponsive Onegin, has now married. Still in love with him, she sits reading the letter in which he declares his new love for her. He enters her home, he kneels at her feet, but she renounces him:

> I love you (why dissimulate?);
> but to another I've been given away:
> to him I shall be faithful all my life.

Nabokov's commentary on these lines for once breaks silence on matters of character and conduct:

Tatiana, if anything, is now a much better person than the romanesque adolescent who (in [Chapter] Three) drinks the philter of erotic longings and, in secret, sends a love letter to a young man whom she has seen only once. . . . her newly acquired exquisite simplicity, her mature calm, and her uncompromising constancy are ample compensations, morally speaking, for whatever naïveté she has lost. . . .[49]

When Onegin rises from his knees and stands as if thunderstruck, Pushkin leaves his hero there and calls a sudden halt to his poem. For Nabokov this whole scene was one of the great moments in literature. At the end of *The Gift* he leaves Fyodor and Zina, just committed to a life together, with a paragraph that takes the form of a *Eugene Onegin* stanza: "Good-by, my book! Like mortal eyes, imagined ones must close some day. Onegin from his knees will rise—but his creator strolls away . . ." In the English foreword to *The Gift*—"that great wedding song," Julian Moynahan calls the novel[50]—Nabokov writes: "I wonder how far the imagination of the reader will follow the young lovers after they have been dismissed." What he wanted us to imagine can be inferred from his later comment that Fyodor is "blessed with a faithful love."[51]

By September 1937 Nabokov had already mapped out chapters 3 and 5 of *The Gift*, but he still had to write them in final form. It is extraordinary to think that Nabokov completed this homage to fidelity and its built-in echo of Pushkin's Tatiana almost immediately after he had himself dismissed Irina Guadanini from his life, in the spirit of Tatiana renouncing Onegin.

But there was one crucial difference. When Onegin came upon Tatiana she was tearfully rereading for the hundredth time his letter to her: even though she feels she has to dismiss him, the poem implies, her love will remain. Nabokov by contrast was absolute in his decision. He sent Irina's letters back to her and asked her to return his: they contained so much invention, they were not worth keeping. She kept the old letters and tore up only the new. When another letter followed by registered mail, she refused even to sign for it.[52]

Nabokov resolutely put the past behind him, and he and Véra soon found their old footing. Ahead lay another forty years of serenely happy marriage. To those who saw Vladimir and Véra Nabokov at close range, they seemed like young lovers even in their sixties and seventies.

VIII

Finding the heat of the Côte d'Azur congenial, Nabokov continued to write as he never had before. After chapter 2 of *The Gift* he moved to chapter 3 without a pause.

As he sat on the beach with Dmitri one September day Véra stepped over the sand, waving a telegram: "We're rich, we're rich." An American publisher, Bobbs-Merrill, was ready to buy the American rights to *Camera Obscura* for a $6co advance. By the end of September Nabokov had signed the contract and committed himself to submitting copy next January 1—and at the same time signed a contract with New York agent Altagracia de Jannelli giving her exclusive rights to represent him. He was to receive half of Bobbs-Merrill's $600 over the next three months and the balance on submission.[53] Since he needed the money badly and had months before *Sovremennye Zapiski* required the remaining chapters of *The Gift*, he at once set about rewriting the novel to appeal more to himself and America and Hollywood.

He ignored Winifred Roy's 1935 translation and started afresh. He mulled over a less obscure title: "Blind Man's Buff"? "Colored Ghost"? "The Magic Lantern"? With moth and candle in mind, he noted down "The Clumsy Moth" and "The Blind Moth"—and then hit upon *Laughter in the Dark*.[54] He altered names to make them less German. He revamped the opening, stressing the movieland banality of the story, as if to lure an unimaginative producer. He introduced villain and hero not via the villain's static comic strips but by way of the hero's plan to make old master paintings spring to life as animated cartoons—as if in this case he wished to introduce the novel's cinema theme right from the start and to inspire an imaginative director. He improved the mechanism by which hero meets villain, he redesigned the means by which hero discovers the villainy of villain and heroine. There were some losses in the revision—the "Cheepy" comic strip of the Russian version, and a fine parody of Proust—but far more gains.

IX

By mid-October autumn could be felt in the air, and the Nabokovs left for Menton, where the tufted crags to the north hemmed in a second summer. They took rooms in the pension Les Hespérides, by the Place St. Roch, now right in the center of town, among the eighteenth-and early nineteenth-century additions to the *vieille ville*. For the Nabokovs, life in orange-palmy-blue Menton seemed far, far better than in Cannes. They swam, splashed, or sunbathed on the Plage des Sablettes, or watched Dmitri fossick along other beaches for shards of porcelain, round pink pebbles, sea-smoothed bottleglass. Friends came to visit: Fondaminsky, Nicolas and Nathalie Nabokov and their son Ivan, the Malevsky-Maleviches, Anna Feigin, Nikita Romanov and his wife. The family strolled up to the Val de Gorbio and the Vallon du Borrigo, to the Plateau St. Michel and to Garavan. Curly-locked Dmitri climbed like a mountain goat and implored his parents to cross the Italian border. They did, illegally—bracingly sweet sport after Nansen passports.[55]

Nabokov carried on unflaggingly, working steadily from 7 to 10 A.M., spending two hours on the beach until the noonday cannon, settling down at his desk again from 3 P.M. until 11:30, and then resuming in bed the nightly war against the whine of winter mosquitoes.[56] It must have been a strange feeling for him to write out the last chapters of The Gift, his greatest Russian work and a resounding celebration of Russia's literary heritage, and to know, after Despair and Laughter in the Dark and his English autobiography, that he would soon be forced to abandon Russian altogether in order to become an English writer. But he was not in a mood to quail, or to say farewell to new Russian ideas.

Early in November, after sending off chapter 3, he at once sped off in another direction. During the winter of 1936–1937 Ilya Fondaminsky had supported a new venture in Paris, the Russian Theater. As the theater's second season approached, Fondaminsky encouraged writers to compose for its stage, and with this prompting Nabokov had for some months been mulling over a plan. By mid-November he was writing his first play in over a decade, Sobytie (The Event: see chapter 21). Four weeks later he had finished all three acts, and rehearsals were set up in Paris for a February premiere.[57]

No sooner was The Event completed than Nabokov turned to the last and most brilliant chapter of The Gift, a radiant fusion of all the book's wildly disparate themes. After five years' research and writing—and time "off" for another novel, two translations, a play, eleven stories and a small-scale autobiography—he completed The Gift in January 1938.

Nabokov at Cambridge, 1920.

Nabokov in punt on the Cam with his Cambridge roommate, Mikhail Kalashnikov, 1920 or 1921.

Nabokov as mountaineer on a trip to Switzerland with his Cambridge friend Robert de Calry, December 1921. The cardigan worn under a jacket and unbuttoned up to the waist would become standard Nabokovian attire. The Swiss locale would find its way into *Glory*.

Nabokov with his fiancée Svetlana Siewert and her sister Tatiana, Berlin, 1921 or 1922.

V. D. Nabokov at his desk in the office of *Rul'*, shortly before his death.

Nabokov at the home of his fiancée, Svetlana Siewert, Lichterfelde, near Berlin, summer 1922, shortly after his father's death.

Nabokov as farm laborer on the estate of Domaine Beaulieu, Solliès-Pont, near Toulon, in the spring or summer of 1923.

Véra Nabokov, mid-1920s.

Vladimir Nabokov, 1926.

Nabokov clowning with Alexander Sak, the most regular of his pupils, during a hiking holiday at Constance, 1925.

Vladimir and Véra Nabokov with their charges, the Bromberg children, and friends from Nabokov's Berlin tennis club, Rügen, Pomerania Bay, 1927. The locale inspired the ending of *King, Queen, Knave*.

Yuli Aykhenvald, émigré critic and friend.

Nabokov writing his first masterpiece, *The Defense*, Le Boulou, Pyrénées orientales, February 1929.

Nabokov with butterfly net poised, Le Boulou, spring 1929, on his first butterfly trip with his wife, the first of many joint butterfly expeditions.

Upper left: Nabokov's mother, Elena Nabokov, Prague, 1931.

Upper right: Ilya Fondaminsky, one of the editors and chief financial prop of the leading literary journal within the Russian emigration, the Paris-based *Sovremennye Zapiski*. (*Bakhmeteff Archive, Columbia University*.)

Below: Goalkeeper Nabokov in front of the other members of the Russian Sporting Club soccer team, Berlin, 1932.

Kamera obskura, 1933, Nabokov's only novel designed with the screen in mind.

Camera Obscura, 1936, the first of Nabokov's novels to be translated into English. The poor quality of Winifred Roy's translation prompted Nabokov to undertake translating his next novel, *Despair*, by himself, a major step in his decision to become an English writer.

JOHN LONG'S NEW 7/6 NOVELS

Hotel Exit	ELIOT CRAWSHAY-WILLIAMS
Kelly	DONALD HENDERSON CLARKE
Cartwright was a Cad	T. E. B. CLARKE
The Sussex Cuckoo	BRIAN FLYNN
Gilded Sprays	LORNA WOOD
Don't Do It, Doctor!	NOEL GODFER
Camera Obscura	VLADIMIR NABOKOFF-SIRIN
A New Novel	HELEN ZENNA SMITH
The Prodigal Mother	HELEN HAMILTON GIBBS
Devil's Furrow	LEONORA CARR
Crocodile Tears	BARBARA ROSS FURSE
Beneath the White Lion	B. J. HURREN
To Live Alone	D. MICHAEL KAYE
May Be Tomorrow	CLARE CRAVEN
These Our Desires	JENETTA BOTIBOL
Look on the Fields	CAROLINE ROWE
Forgotten Canon	HOFFMAN BIRNEY
Child of Fire	MARSHAL SOUTH
Flame of Terrible Valley	MARSHAL SOUTH
Wyoming Tragedy	W. B. M. FERGUSON

CAMERA OBSCURA

A fine strikingly original novel
NICOLAI GUBSKY

VLADIMIR NABOKOFF-SIRIN

7/6
NET

JOHN LONG

CAMERA OBSCURA

VLADIMIR NABOKOFF-SIRIN

" *Sirin has risen to the front rank of Russian literature.*"
New York Times

The Staircase was the main feature [keep idol / idol]
of her existence, but it was the idea [not as a symbol]
of ascension [glorious] which to higher things, but a [as]
thing to be kept nicely polished, so that
the her worst dream (after too much potatoes and [renewing a helping of]
cabbage) was a flight of white steps with
the black trace of a boot III then [to the top landing]
then left, then right again and so up She was aged eighteen.
[A poor whim, indeed, and no matter for derision.] [Margot] [her age, eighteen]

HER name was Magda Peters, and she was,
in fact, only eighteen years of age. Her
father was a porter, a disabled soldier, whose hair
was already turning grey; his head jerked un-
ceasingly, and he fell into a violent passion on the
slightest provocation. Her mother was still quite
young, but in weak health—a coarse, cold-
hearted woman, whose hand was constantly
raised to strike. Her head was always tied up in
a handkerchief to keep the dust from her hair
while she was working, but after her great
Saturday clean-up—which was mainly effected
with a vacuum-cleaner ingeniously connected to
the lift—she dressed herself up and sallied forth
to pay visits. She was unpopular with the
tenants on account of her arrogance and her
brusque way of asking any one who came in to
wipe his or her feet on the mat. V
Otto, Magda's brother, was three years older
than she. He worked in a bicycle factory,
despised his father's republicanism, held forth
on politics in the neighbouring tavern and

20

Two pages of the Winifred Roy text, showing Nabokov's manuscript changes
for the revised and retitled novel, *Laughter in the Dark*, 1938, his first American publication.

a kitten's commonest movement is a soft little jump coming in sudden series; hers was a sharp raising of her left elbow to protect her face.

declared, as he banged his fist on the table: "The first thing a man's got to do is to fill his belly!" This was his guiding principle. *and quite a sound one, too.*

As a child Magda went to school, and there she had *her ears boxed, a little less frequently than at home:* an easier time than at home, where she was beaten frequently, often for no reason, so that she had formed the habit of raising her elbow to protect herself. In spite of all, she grew up into a *bright* cheerful, high-spirited girl. When she was eight years old, she joined enthusiastically *with much gusto* in the *screaming, screeching* noisy and excited games of football which the boys of the neighbourhood played in the *in the middle of the street with a rubber ball the size of a fist.* read. At ten years of age she learned to ride *an orange.* her brother's bicycle. With bare arms and flying *flapping* black pigtails she scorched up and down the *pavement* street and then suddenly halted, with one foot resting on the kerb-stone, brooding over something. At twelve she became *graver* rather more sedate. *and there were the days when* At this time she liked nothing better than to stand *gossip in undertones with the coal-man's* at the door, and whisper to the coal-heaver's *exchanging views upon* daughter about the women who visited one of *and discussing passing hats, shoes, furs.* the lodgers or to criticize the clothes and hats of the passers-by. Once she found on the staircase *with a thin pair curled hair adhering to* a shabby handbag containing a piece of soap *it half ... ... which some* and a few indecent post cards. On another *the ... ... photos ... took* occasion a schoolboy kissed her on her bare neck, *very gently.* *who ... ... him up at play* Then one night, she had a fit of hysterics, for which she got a dowsing of cold water followed by a thrashing. *by a sound wallop.*

Heavily reworked draft of the first page of *Priglashenie na kazn'* (*Invitation to a Beheading*), which Nabokov wrote with more speed and less compositional agony than any other novel: he began this page in July 1934 and finished the stage of revision visible here by September. Little wonder he later switched from pen to erasable pencil and from large unruled sheets to ruled index cards. (*Library of Congress*.)

Два поколѣнія русской литературы.
Чествованіе И. А. Бунина в Берлинѣ.

Русская колонія Берлина отмѣтила прiѣзд лауреата Нобелевской премiи по литературѣ, И. А. Бунина публичным чествованіем.

На эстрадѣ знаменитаго русскаго писателя привѣтствует I. В. Гессен, бывшій руководитель кадетской
партіи и редактор газет „Рѣчь" — в Россіи и „Руль" — за рубежом. Аплодируют: справа — поэт Сергѣй
Кречетов, слѣва — талантливѣйшій из молодых зарубежных русских писателей, В. В. Сирин.

Formal Berlin celebration, 1933, for new Nobel laureate, Ivan Bunin, acknowledged as the foremost of the older generation of émigré writers, as "Sirin" was of the younger. Here, *left to right*, Sirin applauds as his friend Iosif Hessen clasps Bunin's hands in congratulation. (*Rubezh*, Harbin.)

Nabokov, Berlin, summer 1934.

Nabokov with Véra and son Dmitri, Berlin, summer 1935.

Left: Nabokov with Dmitri, Berlin sandpit, 1936.

Upper right: Nabokov at writing desk, 22 Nestorstrasse, Berlin, 1936.

Lower right: Vladislav Khodasevich, foremost poet of the emigration, Nabokov's literary ally and friend throughout the 1930s. Longchêne, near Paris, March 1939. (*Nina Berberova collection.*)

Nabokov with editorial board of *Mesures*, an
offshoot of *La Nouvelle Revue Française*, at the
villa of the journal's patron, Henry Church,
Villa d'Avray, April 1937. *Left to right*, Joyce's
friend Sylvia Beach, Nabokov (holding butterfly?), Barbara Church, Adrienne Monnier,
Germaine Paulhan, Henry Church, Henri Michaux, Jean Paulhan *(at rear)*, and Michel
Leiris. Nabokov's involvement with French
literary life was at its peak early in 1937, after
his departure from Germany, but within a
few months *Laughter in the Dark* had been accepted for publication in the United States
and his sights shifted there. (*Gisèle Freund*.)

Irina Guadanini. (*Private collection*.)

Upper left: Nabokov and family on the beach at Cannes, late summer 1937.
Upper right: Nabokov with Dmitri, Pension Les Hespérides, Menton, 1938.
Lower left: Nabokov, 1938.
Lower right: Véra Nabokov, 1939.

The Gift (Dar)

I

IN *ULYSSES*, Joyce compresses all the swarming life of Dublin into a single book. In *The Gift*, as if in reply, Nabokov offers us a capital *and* a continent, Berlin and Eurasia, in a novel as crowded and rapidly changing as a city street, as massive and diverse as the largest of land masses.[1] A tender love story, a portrait of an artist as a young man, a meticulous inventory of a social milieu, a vivid travel fantasy, an exploration of fate, a passionate tribute to a whole literary heritage, an original investigation of the relation between art and life, half a shelf-ful of biographies, nostalgic, panegyric, tragic, and polemical—*The Gift* is all these and more.

Its main story covers three years (1926–1929)[2] in Fyodor Godunov-Cherdyntsev's life as a young émigré in Berlin: the rapid expansion of his literary gift, from an unnoticed volume of delicate reminiscent verse to a flamboyant and savagely outspoken biography of a revered historical figure and finally to the very idea for *The Gift* itself. As the book gradually discloses, it has also been from its first page Fyodor's tender thank you to fate for the gift of Zina Mertz, the woman he will marry.

Few novels concentrate so intently on the consciousness of their central character, but around Fyodor there rotate others who are the heroes of their own substantial stories, characters from other eras or other climes (Siberian exiles, Tibetan lamas, Russian Old Believers on the shore of Lob-Nor), a host of St. Petersburg and émigré and German figures, historically real, actual but disguised, purely fictional or doubly imaginary, secondary, subsidiary or downright peripheral, made to live in only a line or two, or allowed a hundred pages to themselves. In one chapter Fyodor recounts the life of his famous father, a naturalist who appears to have died ten years earlier on his last expedition to Central Asia. In another he presents unabridged his scandalously irreverent portrait of the nineteenth-century Russian writer Nikolay Chernyshevsky. And through his own tale Fyodor weaves the story of Yasha Chernyshevsky (no relation to the writer), another young émigré whom Fyodor has never even met and whose suicide drives his father, Fyodor's friend Alexander Chernyshevsky, quite insane.

II

With all its diversity, *The Gift* initially appears sprawling and aimless—just as *Ulysses* had seemed to its first readers. Nabokov purposely heightens the effect. The novel begins:

> One cloudy but luminous day, towards four in the afternoon on April the first, 192– (a foreign critic once remarked that while many novels, most German ones for example, begin with a date, it is only Russian authors who, in keeping with the honesty peculiar to our literature, omit the final digit) a moving van, very long and very yellow, hitched to a tractor that was also yellow, with hypertrophied rear wheels and a shamelessly exposed anatomy, pulled up in front of Number Seven Tannenberg Street, in the west part of Berlin. The van's forehead bore a star-shaped ventilator. Running along its entire side was the name of the moving company in yard-high blue letters, each of which (including a square dot) was shaded laterally with black paint: a dishonest attempt to climb into the next dimension.

That meandering first sentence prefigures the whole vast novel. The signpost of hour and date ought to announce an important event, but before we reach object or action an overladen parenthesis blocks the route. Nabokov makes the digression worth the detour. Lucid and labyrinthine, always playful and inescapably serious, Fyodor's multileveled mind enriches the world he observes so acutely. By proclaiming himself a hawker of the quack medicines of "realism," he wryly undermines his own sales pitch. Behind the irony, he proclaims his allegiance to Russian literature's standard of truth: *real* truth, not the sham potions of realism. And he can turn the commonplace of a signwriter's shading into "a dishonest attempt to climb into the next dimension"—and an implicit contrast to his own *honest* attempt to do the same. The first paragraph continues:

> On the sidewalk, before the house (in which I too shall dwell), stood two people who had obviously come out to meet their furniture (in *my* suitcase there are more manuscripts than shirts). The man, arrayed in a rough greenish-brown overcoat to which the wind imparted a ripple of life, was tall, beetle-browed and old, with the gray of his whiskers turning to russet in the area of the mouth, in which he insensitively held a cold, half-defoliated cigar butt. The woman, thickset and no longer

young, with bowlegs and a rather attractive pseudo-Chinese face, wore an astrakhan jacket; the wind, having rounded her, brought a whiff of rather good but slightly stale perfume. They both stood motionless and watched fixedly, with such attentiveness that one might think they were about to be short-changed, as three red-necked husky fellows in blue aprons wrestled with their furniture.

Some day, he thought, I must use such a scene to start a good, thick old-fashioned novel.

If this *were* a good, thick old-fashioned novel, of course, no character inside the book could stand outside it in this way; two sets of people moving into the same building on the first page would be sure to find themselves in the same story; and such meticulous description of the couple watching their furniture arrive would inevitably signal their impending prominence in the plot. In fact Fyodor never gets to meet them, and nothing ever comes of his own shifting home: the opening of the novel is an April Fool's trick on the reader.

The pointed irrelevance of the beginning anticipates the methods of the whole novel. Despite Fyodor's acute observation and his gymnastic imagination, despite marvelous surprises of every kind—verbal, pictorial, psychological, philosophical—the novel might well vex readers at first by its apparent lack of direction.

Though the whole book is a love story, for instance, Zina enters to end Fyodor's bleak loneliness only after two hundred pages have elapsed, the entire first half of the book.

How then can the *whole* book be a love story? Fyodor explains, three pages before the novel ends, when he tells Zina his plan for a new autobiographical novel in which he will show how fate has tried to unite them. Chapter 1 opens with fate's first move, to install Fyodor in the same building as Margarita Lorentz, the woman with the pseudo-Chinese face—Zina's former drawing teacher, whom she still visits. But one of the Lorentzes' closest friends irks Fyodor so much he avoids them, "so that all this cumbersome construction went to the devil, fate was left with a furniture van on her hands and the expenses were not recovered." Chapter 1 ends with a literary evening at which Charski, an incidental lawyer, solicits Fyodor to help a Russian girl translate some documents into German. Though he needs the money, Fyodor turns down the job because he finds Charski repellent—and only much later does he learn that the girl was Zina. "Then finally, after this failure, fate decided to take no chances, to install me directly in the place where you lived," which marks the division between the first two chapters, at 7 Tannenberg Street, and the last three, at 15 Agamemnon Street. (Even this ploy almost fails, for Zina is out when her objectionable stepfather shows Fyodor over the apartment, and only a blue ball dress—which turns out not even to be hers—ensures that fate can entice Fyodor to take the room.) At last, in the middle of the novel, Zina and Fyodor meet, and her zealous interest in his poetry does the rest. By the end of the novel, their love verges on fruition—and now discloses to Fyodor in fond retrospect a pattern that seems to indicate persistence on the part of fate.*

Suddenly everything that had seemed pointless at the beginning of the novel swells with meaning and sends a charge of delight through the book's and the reader's nerves. The April Fool's joke returns, but as a thrill of pleasure, now that the very irrelevance of the Lorentzes has become a key. All that had seemed aimless discloses a tender hidden purpose, and a double one at that: fate's plan, and Fyodor's homage to his love. Behind all the rankling clutter of life, the novel appears to suggest, something inexplicably benign seems to lurk.

III

Frustration suddenly replaced by joy at the generosity of life: that is the pattern of *The Gift*. For every setback in Fyodor's way, life offers him a free ride forward, provided he recognizes when to hop aboard. At the beginning of the novel he has come down from his new apartment to buy cigarettes. The shop he enters does not stock the kind he likes, "and he would have left empty-handed if it had not been for the tobacconist's speckled vest with mother-of-pearl buttons and his pumpkin-colored bald spot. Yes, all my life I shall be getting this extra little payment to compensate my regular overpayment for merchandise foisted on me."

Like others in *The Gift*, Fyodor feels acutely "the disastrous imperfection of the world in which [he] still continued to reside." But in the last chapter of the novel, where he thinks up the idea for *The Gift* itself, he muses for a moment that he should write "a practical handbook: *How to Be Happy*." In a sense *The Gift* itself is that book.

Nabokov takes the bold risk of allowing his novel to appear a loose, baggy monster almost until the end, because life itself can often seem so formless and rumpled, so decidedly *not* tailored to fit. But for all that is tiresome in Fyodor's life—exile, poverty, loneliness, the necessity of changing from room to inhospitable room, or a simple everyday irritation like not finding the cigarettes he wants—he has a dis-

* A theme drawn of course from Nabokov's life: see above, pp. 212–13. For the relationship between Nabokov and Fyodor, see below, pp. 462–65.

position for happiness. If we look at the world with a trust in all it offers—and not with the Lorentzes' fear they are about to be short-changed—it teems with unregarded treasures.

The Gift's special mixture of delay and delight conditions even the texture of the moment, the structure of the sentence. Long before this novel, Nabokov had mastered a fluid, swift style and the knack of modulating it: the elegant economy of *The Defense*, the spareness of *Camera Obscura*, the manic energy of Hermann in *Despair*. He could tell a story rapidly, but he also knew that while from the outside other people's lives might look as if they unwound with the speed of a cinema reel, our own self-awareness in the present extends outward in all directions, a densely furnished space with an almost immobile bulk and depth, in no way resembling a slender ribbon of film unwinding at speed from a spool. In *The Gift* Nabokov creates the sense of self in the present, the density and stasis of the moment, more directly than he ever has before. It takes Fyodor a packed page to cross from the tobacconist's to the corner pharmacy, and one long sentence gives way to another much longer, still more repeatedly interrupted:

As he crossed toward the pharmacy at the corner he involuntarily turned his head because of a burst of light that had ricocheted from his temple, and saw, with that quick smile with which we greet a rainbow or a rose, a blindingly white parallelogram of sky being unloaded from the van—a dresser with mirrors across which, as across a cinema screen, passed a flawlessly clear reflection of boughs sliding and swaying not arboreally, but with a human vacillation, produced by the nature of those who were carrying this sky, these boughs, this gliding façade.

He walked on toward the shop, but what he had just seen—whether because it had given him a kindred pleasure, or because it had taken him unawares and jolted him (as children in the hayloft fall into the resilient darkness)—released in him that pleasant something which for several days now had been at the murky bottom of his every thought, taking possession of him at the slightest provocation: my collection of poems has been published; and when, as now, his mind tumbled like this, that is, when he recalled the fifty-odd poems that had just come out, he would skim in an instant the entire book, so that in an instantaneous mist of its madly accelerated music one could not make any readable sense of the flicking lines—the familiar words would rush past, swirling amid violent foam (whose seething was transformed into a mighty flow-ing motion if one fixed one's eyes on it, as we used to do long ago, looking down at it from a vibrating mill bridge until the bridge turned into a ship's stern: farewell!)—and this foam, and this flickering, and a separate verse that rushed past all alone, shouting in wild ecstasy from afar, probably calling him home, all of this, together with the creamy white of the cover, was merged in a blissful feeling of exceptional purity. . . .

In *The Gift* Nabokov creates a special style for Fyodor, where almost every long sinuous sentence bulges with parentheses, like a snake rendered sluggish after swallowing too many plump, irresistible mice. Sentences stretch to accommodate their ample prey, the unruliness and the stray beauty of an inexhaustible world. Here as so often Fyodor picks out the radiance and strangeness around him—the white parallelogram of sky, the unexpectedly human vacillation of those reflected boughs—or a source of remembered delight, a burst of pride in his literary gift. But after sentence upon sentence even of his radiant reflections, his style begins to seem clogged and able to advance only with difficulty, like the story itself. We become twitchy at getting nowhere—a feeling Fyodor himself often shares. But in accord with the novel's pattern, even crueler frustrations turn into the most unexpected rewards.

After Fyodor returns from the shops, the telephone rings. His friend Alexander Chernyshevsky reads out from a rapturous newspaper review of Fyodor's first book, *Poems*, but refuses to divulge the source until Fyodor comes to their literary soirée that night. That afternoon Fyodor rereads this little book of his verse devoted to his early past: he recalls the memories behind the poems, he roams through fascinating images of childhood and St. Petersburg, he criticizes himself for not quite expressing the vision he had in mind, he imagines the sensitive reviewer's approbation. The poems themselves begin in frustration (a ball rolls under a piece of furniture, is dislodged, and rolls over the floor to settle under an impregnable sofa) and ends in a little triumph (when at the end of his childhood the furniture gets rearranged, there the ball lies revealed, still alive and incredibly dear). After Fyodor finishes savoring his book, the first lines of a new poem stir within his mind, full of his gratitude that his work has been understood—but the rhythm fizzles out. Then when he arrives at his friend's home, Chernyshevsky shows him the date on today's newspapers: April Fool! That ecstatic review was nothing but a hoax.

The chapter continues to meander. Fyodor's disappointment at that nasty prank lingers, but as an exercise in imaginative sympathy he tries to peer out from within Chernyshevsky's unbalanced mind, and imagines his friend seeing his dead son Yasha seated across the room. Fyodor recounts the suicide pact that led to Yasha's death, itself a case study in fulfillment foiled in this world. In a trio of close friends (two men, one woman) each comes to love the next and to be loved by the third, and within this circle of friendship, as Yasha's diary puts it, there forms a rigid triangle of despair. Slowly the idea of a suicide pact takes root. They will disappear, "all three together, in order that—already in a different world—an ideal and flawless circle might be restored." Yasha shoots himself, but the other two fail to follow: whatever happiness the hereafter might hold, it cannot be stormed at gunpoint.

Nabokov recounts Yasha's engrossing tragedy at speed, a whole drama in a few pages. But this swift story only emphasizes how little we have advanced in Fyodor's life: after fifty densely packed pages, we have covered no more than a few hours in an uneventful day.

Fyodor returns from the soirée, not only depressed after the review has proved a cruel deception, but also tormented by an uncompleted thought he cannot recall and dreading the imminent night of insomnia his new quarters will cause him. Then he discovers he has locked himself out of his apartment—which suddenly seems a much more desirable place than a moment ago. He paces the street, wondering what to do, until the sway of a streetlamp "nudged something off the brink of his soul where that something had been resting, and now, no longer with the former distant call but reverberating loudly and close by, rang out 'Thank you, my land, for your remotest . . .' and immediately, on a returning wave. 'most cruel mist my thanks are due. . . .' And again, flying off in search of an answer: '. . . by you unnoticed. . . .' " As the verses begin to cohere in his mind, the house door opens to let a visitor out, and he rushes in to spend his first night in his room in the blissful frenzy of completing the poem.

The poem Fyodor could not catch on a surge of buoyant fulfillment lands glistening on the beach in the wake of his frustration—which it amply recoups. And for us a day that had gone nowhere, we now recognize, has already shown us in less than a chapter more images of a writer than many a finished portrait of the artist: Fyodor's mind in action, transforming the world it observes; his professional pride, his professional disappointment; numerous samples of his first completed work, and his recollections of its sources and its shortcomings; a new work in the making, its hesitant start, its enraptured rush toward completion.

IV

With its characteristic density, *The Gift* records all aspects of a writer's life and work: tradition and the individual talent; the childhood that underlies the adult work; the slow growth of the writer's mind and art; the mature imagination active in its everyday world; all the stages of composition and publication, from the vague foreglow of a new work to the reviews the finished book receives, and even the writer's own harsh final review as his next work already dawns.

Nabokov does not present Fyodor as an image of himself—though as we shall see Fyodor's art reveals some of the secrets of his own— nor does he believe in the invented author whose genius should be taken on trust: samples must be submitted, please. Fyodor obliges with four ample samples which structure the novel's five long chapters. In chapter 1, his *Poems*, twelve-line vignettes of childhood, slight and lithe as a girl gymnast but without the strength to bear the load of the past Fyodor wants them to carry. By recording how the poems activate Fyodor's sense of what he *meant* them to mean, Nabokov has it both ways: the tiny drops of polished amber, the great northern forest of the past from which they came.

Chapter 2 shows Fyodor now settled into his Tannenberg Street room but chafing all the same at being compelled to live in a Germany he finds abhorrent and to teach foreign languages rather than devote himself wholly to his art. Eager to escape from the cramped and drab life he is forced to lead, he labors with rapture on a biography of his father, as if to pass through the constricting walls of his room and out to wherever his father might be—the wild spaces of Central Asia, or even paradise itself. Here the novel lifts and soars. Himself an avid lepidopterist, Fyodor had asked his father in 1916 to be allowed to join a further expedition to Tibet, but was refused because of the war. Now he sets off in imagination with his father (who never returned from that last voyage), traveling through territory that in sheer wonder outdoes all previous literary landscapes—eerily strange and beautiful, but observed with the trained eye of the naturalist.* Manly, heroic, adventurous in tone, Fyodor's account of his father could not be more unlike the precious miniatures in his *Poems*. But then comes the frustration: despite his desperate urge to discover what became of his father—whether he really did die on that last expedition, whether he will one day return in person, not just in Fyodor's dreams, whether he

---

* Fyodor of course, although a skilled naturalist, has never been to Central Asia himself, and like Nabokov has to rely on the works of Russian explorer-naturalists as well as the vividness of his own imagination. Nabokov has Fyodor stress the virility of his father—a quality Nabokov also valued highly in his own father—but did not know that the chief model for the explorer in Godunov Senior, the celebrated Nikolay Przhevalsky, was homosexual [see Donald Rayfield's *The Dream of Lhasa: The Life of Nikolay Przhevalsky (1839–1888), Explorer of Central Asia*].

remains somehow alive beyond the last lonely ridge of death—Fyodor comes to feel he has lost his way in conjecture and, beset by doubts that the old man would approve the book, he contemplates abandoning his project. When his landlady gives him notice, that decides the matter: he will pack his manuscript away, never to unpack it again.

Chapter 3 opens with Fyodor installed at 15 Agamemnon Street. As the morning noises reverberate through the thin wall beside his bed (the toilet flushing,* his landlord hawking up phlegm, the janitor's wife with her vacuum cleaner), Fyodor tries to compose a poem addressed to an unnamed woman who seems to share his rejection of the mundane for the loftier things of the spirit. The poem records their regular meetings under the streetlights of summer evenings, but Fyodor has to face the tedium of an afternoon of giving private language lessons before reaching the night's rendezvous. He waits for the woman, almost finishing his poem as she emerges from the dark—and a résumé of their relationship discloses that she is his landlord's stepdaughter, the sullen girl whose searing aloofness at today's midday meal seemed only to dry the air to a crackling tension.

Just as the novel refrains from the merest hint of Zina while it records the apparent aimlessness behind Fyodor's first shifting house, so within this chapter directly introducing her, her name remains suppressed until the midpoint of the chapter, the midpoint of the novel. As narrator, Fyodor wishes to intensify both the sense of thwartedness and the delicious shock of the compensatory release—for him, at the time, for us now, as we discover that the new flat has brought Zina into his life, as we witness his excitement in creating a poem for her that celebrates their walks through the free night air and enshrines the proud values of the imagination by which they both set such store.

Another strand of underpayment and delayed overpayment weaves its way in and out of this day. Fyodor has visited a Russian bookstore and noticed an article on Nikolay Chernyshevsky in a Soviet chess magazine. Thinking it might amuse his friend Alexander Chernyshevsky to read about his namesake, Fyodor tries to buy it, but the shopgirl cannot find its price and knowing he is already in debt to the store lets him have it gratis. Fyodor muses on the artistry of a good chess problem, its fresh combination of two classic themes or its utter novelty of method. As he leafs through the magazine, he discovers that the chess problems would not have been worth paying for, since the

* Hugh Kenner comments somewhere on Joyce's unprecedented portrayal of his hero (Stephen Dedalus) with *lice* in his hair. Nabokov introduces Zina, heroine of a novel of genuine romance, through the sound of her flushing the toilet.

conscientious student exercises of the young Soviet composers were not so much "problems" as "tasks": cumbrously they treated of this or that mechanical theme (some kind of "pinning" and "unpinning") without a hint of poetry; these were comic chess strips, nothing more, and the shoving and jostling pieces did their clumsy work with proletarian seriousness, reconciling themselves to the presence of double solutions in the flat variants and to the agglomeration of police pawns. . . .

Suddenly he felt a bitter pang—why had everything in Russia become so shoddy, so crabbed and gray, how could she have been so befooled and befuddled?

That night Zina tells Fyodor she regrets that he did not write his book on his father: " 'I have such a clear feeling that one day you'll really lash out. Write something huge to make everyone gasp.' 'I'll write,' said Fyodor Konstantinovich jokingly, 'a biography of Chernyshevsky.' " Unknown to Fyodor, what he thinks a mere jest has already found fertile soil and is about to germinate. Within days he glances at the excerpts from Chernyshevsky's diary in the chess magazine and recognizes the same shoddiness of thought that appalled him in the chess problems. This self-defeating quality in Chernyshevsky's mind—and in all the Soviet heirs to his thought, from chess problemists to writers and political theorists—fascinates Fyodor so much he decides he *will* write about the man. In a magazine so disappointing as to be not worth buying—although he obtained it free in any case—he has found the idea for his next book.*

V

For all the brash playfulness of his treatment of Chernyshevsky, Fyodor knows the seriousness of the issues. Since the 1860s the influence of Chernyshevsky and other "men of the sixties" had been so strong in Russian literature that their first commandment, that art should have no other gods before the cause of social reform, had established a censorship of the left no less oppressive than the censorship of the tsarist bureaucracy. This censorship persisted after

---

* The chess magazine is *8 × 8*, a transparent allusion to the Soviet chess journal *64*, where the first official publication of Nabokov's work (his commentary on the chess problem in the Russian version of *Speak, Memory*) would take place in August 1986, more than half a century after this chapter of *The Gift* was first written. Ironically, *64* censored out a sentence summarizing the very reflections on the shoddiness of Soviet chess problems that Nabokov assigns to Fyodor.

the revolution, even in the otherwise extraordinary freedom of the emigration, let alone under the tyranny of Lenin and Stalin. Fyodor's book is an exuberant challenge to censorship, tauntingly demonstrating the freedom of art—its freedom, even, to be positively perverse—in its gleeful irreverence toward Chernyshevsky. His challenge is accepted when Vasiliev, his usual publisher, refuses to touch the book—just as in real life the Socialist Revolutionaries eager to print all of Nabokov's work they could get for *Sovremennye Zapiski* omitted that one chapter from *The Gift*: "a pretty example," as Nabokov observed, "of life finding itself obliged to imitate the very art it condemns."[3]

Fyodor treats Chernyshevsky as an intellectual buffoon whose ideas do not deserve the compliment of rational opposition. He quotes enough Chernyshevsky to let his crude materialistic epistemology condemn itself; he suggests a mental and emotional muddle behind Chernyshevsky's aesthetics that invalidates any claim to their serious consideration. But Fyodor pays less attention to argument than to the way Chernyshevsky's life continually undermines his own philosophy, as if fate took revenge on him for his beliefs. Chernyshevsky is a materialist, but almost blind and deaf to the material world: shortsighted, living in abstractions and books, unable to tell beer from Madeira, Siberian flora from European, a horsefly from a wasp. A lover of mass audiences, he ends in the near-solitude of exile, where the few around him pay him no heed. A believer in common sense, he is surrounded by madmen, a neurotic wife, a psychotic son. A champion of at least a certain kind of freedom, he wins for himself only imprisonment and leaves behind a legacy of censorship. Grimmest irony of all, perhaps, he had aspired to invent a perpetual motion machine as the first step to a material solution to the problems of life, and instead in his last years becomes such a machine himself, translating "with machine-like steadiness volume after volume of Georg Weber's *Universal History*" in order to support his family, thereby turning his brain "into a forced labor factory" that represents "the greatest mockery of human thought."[4]

Within the context of *The Gift*, Chernyshevsky stands as the supreme example of someone continually and unrelentingly thwarted by life. Fyodor's mastery of this theme of futility and failure in Chernyshevsky, on the other hand, marks the first great triumph of his own art. But he does not depict life confounding all Chernyshevsky believes in merely to mock an uncongenial spirit: he thinks Chernyshevsky doomed to trip over his world at every step precisely because his philosophy faces life the wrong way round.

In his thesis "The Aesthetic Relations of Art to Reality" Chernyshevsky advanced the claim that art is only an inferior imitation of a prior reality, material and obvious and commonplace. Fyodor proposes instead to reverse priorities, to show that life follows art. He believes things cannot be understood only in material terms: those who really attend to life discover that the play of consciousness they must exercise to apprehend their world seems to correspond in some mysterious way to a force of conscious playfulness somehow concealed behind life.

Chernyshevsky loved accumulating the seemingly solid facts encyclopedias purvey. He valued the measurable, tangible parts of a world that, because it is mechanical and subject to general laws, can be confidently predicted. Fyodor too loves to accumulate, but he prefers the stray, disregarded detail to the accepted commonplace. He sees a life full of intangible beauty, splendidly overstocked, blessedly more complex than we can know, and utterly unforeseeable.

History for Fyodor will always surprise us. *In retrospect*, though, we can trace its themes—which will not be shared generalizations, but unique patterns of individuality. Life prizes the particular, allows things to develop as differently as they can, but somehow traces its patterns through the very differences between things, and leaves individual imaginations to perceive these differences and patterns in their own way. Fyodor treats Chernyshevsky's life accordingly. Anything but self-effacing as a biographer, he boldly labels what he decrees to be the themes of Chernyshevsky's life (shortsightedness, the perpetual motion machine, fate's vengeance, and forty or so more) and, like a cross between a conjuror and a sorcerer, patters freely about his power to call them up or dismiss them.

The sum of all the themes Fyodor finds in Chernyshevsky adds up to a very individual man. Because he considers his subject afresh, as a unique person and not the saintly icon of the progressives, he can detect the fatal flaw everywhere in Chernyshevsky's destiny that reduces all his hopes to nothing. Chernyshevsky's esteem for the solid world of common sense makes him ignore so much (the strangeness of human life, the particularity and unpredictability of things, the eccentricity of what merely happens to appeal to *his* imagination) that this clumsy, cloudy-headed materialist simply cannot help stumbling his way through his world. What at first seems a mocking hostility on fate's part and Fyodor's proves to be an unrelenting focus on what is unique in the man, and therefore irreplaceable, vulnerable, frail. Long before it ends, the biography elicits a sense of pity that could not have been generated without such careful attention to the themes of Chernyshevky's life and the balking of his every hope.

VI

Fyodor had abandoned his memorial to his father when he sensed that his imaginative flight into unknown Asia was only an indulgence that polluted the purity of his father's science and courage with his own mere fancies. His life of Chernyshevsky becomes a corrective to all that had troubled him in his homage to his father: now he will locate his art not in an easy escape into a paradise of the imagination but in a return to the real world where he can still discover harmony even in what he finds distasteful in life, even in a man whose attempt to establish a materialist's paradise has led to his own private hell and the hell of modern Russia. In the biography of his father, Fyodor had traveled to Siberia and found it a realm of breathtaking beauty; here he returns to the same region with Chernyshevsky, who can find nothing in the new world around him to redeem the bleakness of exile. Apart from their bravery, Chernyshevsky and Konstantin Godunov-Cherdyntsev are opposed in every way. Nothing could defy Chernyshevsky's decree that art and science should worship the general good more resolutely than Godunov's unstoppable pursuit of what happens to interest him, nothing could be more unlike Godunov's prizing of the hitherto undiscovered and his deep sense of the strangeness of life than Chernyshevsky's commitment to "what everyone knows."

As a youth Fyodor had sought to travel on his father's last expedition. Now he relinquishes his memoir of his father when he decides himself unworthy to accompany him even in imagination. Yet Fyodor is already a kind of explorer himself, an explorer of the past. He probes his own childhood in his *Poems*, conscious that their frail charms could never survive even an allusion to his father's high deeds. He studies his father's life for the abortive biography, but rejects the images that arise before him as armchair traveling that puts him at no risk. Now in the *Life of Chernyshevsky* he dares to become as bold an explorer of time as his father had been of space, traveling into the inhospitable territory of Chernyshevsky's thought and coolly exposing himself to critical ambush.

Less obviously, Fyodor has been an explorer of the beyond. In his *Poems* he has probed his own childhood, gingerly trying to discern something in the darkness beyond the dawn of his consciousness that might tell him what to expect when night falls on his life. Fascinated by the possibility that his father may return, even from death, Fyodor attempts in his next work to discover the transcendental secret the old explorer seemed to carry with him in life.

Causation in Nabokov is never a rigorously mechanical affair, a cog marked "cause" inevitably turning a cog marked "effect"—and least of all when it comes to the mysterious origins of a work of art. Fyodor tells us that he was first prompted to begin the life of his father as he resavored the perfection of Pushkin's prose style, which he comes to associate, in some private, inexplicable way, with the perfection he wants to imagine surrounding his father on his trek further into the unknown. Significantly Fyodor describes his own move from Tannenberg Street (and work on his father's life) to Agamemnon Street (and work on Chernyshevsky) as a move from Pushkin to Gogol, whose art Nabokov saw as a deliberate flattening of all that was less than fully human in our lives, to appeal, at brief moments, to something more than the human, "that secret depth of the human soul where the shadows of other worlds pass like the shadows of nameless and soundless ships."[5] When Fyodor leaves behind the lucid searchlight of Pushkin to illuminate Chernyshevsky's life with the help of Gogol's sputtering fireworks, Nabokov intends a shift in Fyodor's art to another dimension. "The prose of Pushkin is three-dimensional; that of Gogol is four-dimensional, at least."[6]

Fyodor had told Zina that by means of the sonnet enclosing the life of Chernyshevsky he hoped the biography would wriggle free of the flat, rectangular carapace of a book, "which by its finiteness is opposed to the circular nature of everything in existence," and become instead a "continuously curving, and thus infinite, sentence." Chernyshevsky dies, as we might expect, on the last page of the biography, but only then is his birth finally recorded, to be followed by the first half of the sonnet "which we here give in full"—and which therefore sends us back to the biography's first page. After the sestet that opens the *Life of Chernyshevsky* come these lines:

> A sonnet, apparently barring the way, but perhaps, on the contrary, providing a secret link which could explain everything—if only man's mind could withstand that explanation. The soul sinks into a momentary dream—and now, with the popular theatrical vividness of those risen from the dead they come out to meet us: Father Gavriil, a long staff in his hand, wearing a silk, garnet-red chasuble, with an embroidered sash across his big stomach; and with him, already illuminated by the sun, an extremely attractive little boy—pink, awkward, delicate. They draw near. Take off your hat, Nikolya.

Fyodor has implied throughout the *Life of Chernyshevsky* that some fate may be at work designing people's lives according to its own harmonies. In this bizarre opening-close-reopening of the biography, he also hints that the key to life might be that in death we can return to our past, to perceive the care with which everything has been arranged, the pity that was waiting to be elicited and that ultimately turns out to be as enriching as direct happiness within life. He anticipates what Nabokov would later write in the foreword to *The Eye*: "The forces of imagination which, in the long run, are the forces of good remain steadfastly on Smurov's side, and the very bitterness of tortured love proves to be as intoxicating and bracing as would be its most ecstatic requital."[7] When Fyodor offers six lines of verse at the beginning of the biography and calls it a sonnet, or eight lines at the end and declares the sonnet is given in full, he ushers in via a joke and a momentary twinge of frustration a vision of life in which the aesthetic relations of art and reality are completely inverted and a hidden artfulness encompasses even a life that had seemed to deny art.

VII

In *The Gift*'s fifth and final chapter, Fyodor's life opens out, his lungs expand, his frustrations fade away. The *Life of Chernyshevsky* provokes a spate of reviews, many indignant, most misconstruing Fyodor in one way or another, one (by Koncheyev, the only poet of his generation whom Fyodor holds in high regard) brilliantly receptive and admiring—and all ample compensation for the one mere April Fool's Day review of chapter 1. Throughout the novel, Fyodor has chafed in the confines of his rented rooms. Now, in the warm summer of 1929, he suns himself day after day in the Grunewald, luxuriating in its space and freedom. His relationship with Zina had reached an impasse, since she has absolutely refused to let him show her any sign of affection within the apartment, where her stepfather had once made lecherous advances to her. Now that problem has suddenly been resolved: her mother and stepfather are shifting to Copenhagen, and the Agamemnon Street flat will be left to her and Fyodor.

Most important of all, the idea for *The Gift* steals up on Fyodor. As he approaches the state of mind in which he will conceive the book, his intuition of life's mysterious artfulness begins to brighten his whole sky. He walks down a street loud with traffic, wincing and grumbling to himself, but in a moment he can muse that "all this skein of random thoughts, like everything else as well—the seams and sleaziness of the spring day, . . . the coarse, variously intercrossing threads of confused sounds—was but the reverse side of a magnificent fabric." Note the "sleaziness" here: the ostensibly repulsive has its own part to play. Just as he has learned in his writing to abandon easy idealization and to discern the pattern and pity of art even in the distasteful parts of life, so he now applies the same principle to his own existence, discovering poetry in a railway cutting, finding a paradise in the junk-bestrewn Grunewald park, descrying in the uninviting apartments where he has had to live the secret seal of fate's generosity.

At last, he has the structure for his next great work: the story of fate's efforts to place himself and Zina side by side. This structure suddenly redeems all the setbacks and shapes all the shapelessness of the beginning of the book. It also explains why *The Gift* itself contains, complete and unabridged, the most puzzling sample of Fyodor's artistry, the *Life of Chernyshevsky*. Fyodor's strategies in the Chernyshevsky book can be appreciated fully only as his corrective to his life of his father. The Chernyshevsky biography, in turn, explains the aims of *The Gift* itself, for the earlier book is "firing practice," "an exercise, a tryout" that trains Fyodor to handle the themes of fate. The *Life of Chernyshevsky* and *The Gift* operate, of course, in entirely different modes. In the Chernyshevsky excursus the themes of fate occur in condensed form, deliberately and rampantly obtruded. Fyodor rarely attempts to render the feel of life, but tugs on one thematic string after another to make a puppet Chernyshevsky jerk. In the much subtler art of *The Gift*, per contra, he preserves the texture of the passing moment, the muddle, the apparent lack of direction, and yet demonstrates that even here fate may still be at work, that all this aimlessness can be turned over to disclose one vast design.

After this, the novel's final paragraph ends with a paragraph printed as prose, but in fact following with perfect regularity the intricate stanza form of Pushkin's great verse novel, *Eugene Onegin*. Fyodor's farewell to his book—mimicking Pushkin's farewell to Onegin and the reader—invites us to look beyond the horizon of the page. There, if we peer with care, we will see that Fyodor and Zina as they reach their apartment on that first night they have it to themselves will find themselves locked out. But by the time Fyodor comes to write that radiant last paragraph of the novel, that frustration has been long forgotten in years of happiness with Zina. The formal perfection of the *Eugene Onegin* stanza stands as a celebration and an invitation to return to the beginning and to recognize the formal perfection and the tender design of everything that had at first seemed so haphazard and even malign.

VIII

Like Fyodor, Nabokov too was fascinated that fate had so nearly introduced him to his future wife several times before they finally met (see chapter 10 above). Fyodor's tribute to fate is also Nabokov's thank you for the gift of Véra Slonim.

In fact, in *The Gift* Nabokov draws on his own past more than anywhere else in his fiction. As *Speak, Memory* reveals, he saw the attempt of memory to probe the very dawn of consciousness as a counterpart to the attempt to probe what lies beyond its sunset: Fyodor's poems testing his memories of early childhood speak for Nabokov too. Vyra, the place that mattered more than anywhere to Nabokov, becomes Fyodor's Leshino in detail after detail. Nabokov's admiration for his father becomes Fyodor's for *his* father and his lepidopterological passion finds its outlet in both Fyodor's and the elder Godunov's.

The Gift concerns itself above all with the growth of Fyodor's literary talent. Once again Nabokov looks into the mirror of his own past to paint Fyodor's portrait. His first struggles in verse—the easy adjective, the mesmeric spell of Bely's metrical schemes—were handed over so faithfully to Fyodor that when Nabokov translated his memoirs back into Russian he omitted the chapter on his own early verse rather than repeat what he had already set before his Russian readers in the person of Fyodor. Like Sirin, Fyodor evolves from verse to prose, while maintaining an unusually poetic tint in his mature prose style. Nabokov passes on to his character all his essential passions—for his homeland, his family, his home, his language, his literature, his lepidoptera, his chess, his loves—and even surrounds him with the same accidentals, his émigré existence, his language teaching, his distaste for Berlin, his sunbathing in the Grunewald.[8]

And yet Nabokov had no intention of presenting us with a sheaf of snapshots of himself as a young man. To protect his privacy, he changed in Fyodor everything that his first audience was most likely to know about Vladimir Sirin. Educated at Cambridge and knowing little German, Sirin stood out in the eyes of fellow émigrés by his English air. Fyodor on the other hand knows German well, and has attended university in Berlin.* Nabokov's father was famous in Russia, and renowned for his almost chivalric courage, but he was a statesman; Fyodor's father, though also legendary for his fearlessness, is a naturalist and explorer who abjures all politics. Most of all Nabokov took care to make Fyodor's art as different from his own as he could. Over the last fifteen years, in poems, stories, plays, and novels, Sirin

---

* Nabokov further distanced himself from Fyodor by introducing in the incidental writer Vladimirov a young novelist who matched his maker in name, age, looks, dress, Anglicized education, and literary and social style: "As a conversationalist Vladimirov was singularly unattractive. One blamed him for being derisive, supercilious, cold, incapable of thawing to friendly discussions—but that was also said about Koncheyev and about Fyodor himself, and about anyone whose thoughts lived in their own private house and not in a barrack-room or a pub."

had demonstrated an endless narrative inventiveness. Fyodor, for all that Nabokov means his literary genius to be taken seriously, cannot invent but needs real lives to feed on: his own childhood, his father's travels, Chernyshevsky's woes, his own happiness and Zina's.

By having Fyodor choose real lives rather than fiction Nabokov not only differentiated his character from himself but made it possible for him to express some of his own most private concerns. The senseless death of a father he revered was the most shocking event of his life, but one he could never treat directly. By making Godunov Senior a naturalist and an explorer, he can live out his own thwarted dream of exploring Central Asia, and add an element of sheer spectacle to contrast with the cramped quotidian routine of Fyodor's Berlin, but he can also surround Fyodor's father with his own father's heroic aura, and by having the elder Godunov disappear and perhaps die in the paradise of his remote Asia, he can have Fyodor both try in imagination to probe the enigma of his father's death and hope against hope for his return.

The most unexpected, the most un-Nabokovian of all Fyodor's works of course is his *Life of Chernyshevsky*. But the very remoteness of this sample of Fyodor's work from everything else his maker had ever written should itself put us on our guard, for Nabokov never resorts to camouflage more assiduously than when he has something especially valuable to hide. Fyodor's art advances immeasurably when he rejects the easy idyll, the romance, the glamor, and the achievement of his father's life for the humiliating trials of someone as antithetical to him as Chernyshevsky. In this unexpected sense, Fyodor's switch from the paradisal to the hellish mirrors Nabokov's own switch from a positive expression of his values and his life in the early 1920s to the inversions and the negatives that from the late 1920s allowed him to test his own ideas against lives much less happy than his own. Like his creator, Fyodor finds the courage to explore spiritual deprivation before reaffirming the richness of spirit he finds in life and beyond. That marks the boldest leap in all his art, and surely it is no accident that for Fyodor this change comes after he falls in love with Zina, just as for Nabokov the shift from his lyrical positives to his dramatic negatives comes after his marriage to Véra, and his immediate exposure to her tough-mindedly critical attitude to her world.

In *The Gift* Nabokov drew not only on his private life and on the progress of his art but also on the public world around him. Never again would he re-create in such exhaustive detail a city's parks and squares, its offices and shops, its buses and streetcars, its modes and mores. Fyodor's Berlin is of course the eccentric Berlin of the emigration, and above all émigré literary Berlin: soirées, readings, rivalries, reviews, the petty politics of the Union of Emigré Writers. Joyce liked to think that if Dublin were destroyed it could be re-created from *Ulysses*. Berlin's Russian literary emigration *was* destroyed by Hitler, but *The Gift* allows us to revisit that lost world.

More than that, though. The emigration for Fyodor is a life of incessant annoyance: these cramped apartments in place of that spacious past with its built-in future prospect of exploring with his father all the wilds of Asia. Back in Russia his father could pursue his science at will, but now in the emigration Fyodor finds himself hindered every day in his art because the minute size of the émigré audience will never allow him to earn his living as a writer and will condemn him to squander his time and his energy in the drudgery of teaching foreign languages. This of course had been exactly Nabokov's situation at Fyodor's age, but for both writers all the immediate irritations of a minutely observed world make possible the very theme of ultimate plenitude and triumph that pervades *The Gift*, their finest work to date: in the apparent negatives of the world around them, they subject their own values to their most searching examination and discover the basis for their most resounding affirmations.

IX

However much he incorporated of his own past and Berlin's present into *The Gift*, Nabokov had no inclination merely to transcribe life, if such a thing were possible. From first page to last *The Gift* also pays tribute to, takes issue with, or tries to transcend other literary works.

Few things in literature excited Nabokov more than the opening of Gogol's *Dead Souls*. In that novel's first paragraph two muzhiks whom we will never see again wonder whether the wheel of a carriage rolling by would make it to Moscow, or even Kazan. As Nabokov explains in his book on Gogol,

> The *muzhiks* are not interested in the question of the precise itinerary that the *britzka* will follow; what fascinates them is solely the ideal problem of fixing the imaginary instability of a wheel in terms of imaginary distances; and this problem is raised to the level of sublime abstraction by their not knowing the exact distance from N. (an imaginary point) to Moscow, Kazan or Timbuctoo—and caring less.[9]

At the end of the novel's first paragraph, the carriage passes by a young man described in minute detail—and again never seen further. Nabokov thought this a stroke of genius:

> Another special touch is exemplified by the chance passerby—that young man portrayed with a sudden and wholly irrelevant wealth of

detail: he comes there as if he was going to stay in the book (as so many of Gogol's homunculi seem intent to do—and do not). With any other writer of his day the next paragraph would have been bound to begin: "Ivan, for that was the young man's name." . . . But no: a gust of wind interrupts his stare and he passes, never to be mentioned again.[10]

The first page of *The Gift*—the hypertrophied rear wheels of the tractor pulling the Lorentzes' moving van, the detailed picture of the Lorentzes themselves—is Nabokov's tribute to one of the great moments in Russian literature, just as the *Eugene Onegin* stanza on the last page of the novel pays homage to another. But Nabokov goes one further than Gogol. The Lorentzes not only prove to be irrelevant to the course of Fyodor's life, but Fyodor can seize on that very irrelevance as "proof" of fate's blundering eagerness to introduce him to Zina. Irrelevance becomes key evidence, inept accident the hallmark of masterly design.

The Gift was Nabokov's tribute to the whole Russian literary heritage, which he saw as oscillating between tribulation and triumph.[11] In the center, the genius of writers like Pushkin, Gogol, Tolstoy, and Chekhov, ready to speak the truth as they saw it; to their right, a government that did not want the truth spoken at all; to their left, those who, rightly opposing an autocratic government, tried to press-gang writers' free imaginations into a disciplined army of liberation. Nabokov had to tackle Chernyshevsky *and* his contemptible opponents in the tsarist secret police *and* the Pushkin whose genius remained so immeasurably beyond Chernyshevsky's clumsy grasp.

For Nabokov Fyodor's context, like any great Russian writer's, had to include not only the literature of Russia but also that of Western Europe. In *The Gift* he looks directly to the work of Proust and Joyce, in a spirit of homage and challenge. As in *A la recherche du temps perdu*, the whole story is the writer's evolution to the stage where he can compose the book before us, the structure a search through wasted time for the clues to the past's pattern, the style a leisured one that allows image to flower within meditative image—although Fyodor's mind has a more playful and less opulent turn than Marcel's. Like *Ulysses*, *The Gift* renders the dense life of a city, follows in minute detail the mental acrobatics of a young writer roaming the city streets, begins and ends with a motif of keys, traces a son's special search for his father and in fact makes of the relationship between father and son a kind of metaphysical riddle. It could even be that Joyce's implied contrast between the bustle of Dublin's streets and the mighty wanderings of Ulysses inspired Nabokov to set in opposition cramped Berlin and the vast spaces of Fyodor's father's odysseys. Whatever the case, Nabokov certainly did not copy. Nothing in literature anticipates the sure and at the same time freaky evolution of Fyodor's gift, from his early verse trinkets to the awesome wonderlands he makes his father traverse, from the scorn and sympathy of the life of Chernyshevsky, to all that looms behind his decision to write *The Gift*.

X

One of the central themes of Nabokov's work has always been that time, if we could return to it endlessly, might disclose evidence of a richness and design obscured by the crowdedness of passing mortal time. He has constructed *The Gift* accordingly, inviting us to return again and again to discover more and more unsuspected design even after we think we have already discovered far more than one set of events could ever seem to hold.

On the first day of the novel, Fyodor finds himself locked out on the street—and just then a particularly cruel day turns into a special gift for him as a new poem stirs within his mind. In the middle of the novel, Fyodor describes a second long and tiresome day two years later that ends almost in rapture as he stands in the streets of the summer night, composing a far better poem, a poem for Zina, who now steps at last as if from the poem and into the novel, right at its halfway mark. On the novel's last day, Fyodor and Zina are about to be locked out on the streets together when the splendid final poem points playfully to their imminent fate and implicitly back to the novel's beginning.

In his *Poems* Fyodor had begun with a poem on a lost ball, and ended with another: "The Found Ball." In his much more boisterous *Life of Chernyshevsky*, he rounded off the biography with the octet of a sonnet that leads back to the concluding sestet at the beginning of the *Life*, "so that the result would be not the form of a book . . . but a continuously curving, and thus infinite, sentence." Now at the end of *The Gift* itself Fyodor's art has advanced again, to a still finer poem that incorporates its playfulness and its invitation to return much more subtly than in Fyodor's previous book, and with a haunting note that will not die away:

> Good-by, my book! Like mortal eyes,
> imagined ones must close some day.
> Onegin from his knees will rise
> —but his creator strolls away.
> And yet the ear cannot right now
> part with the music and allow
> the tale to fade; the chords of fate

> itself continue to vibrate;
> and no obstruction for the sage
> exists where I have put The End:
> the shadows of my world extend
> beyond the skyline of the page,
> blue as tomorrow's morning haze
> —nor does this terminate the phrase.

Something vibrates beyond the end in his poem, as if beyond death, as if returning us to our beginning in a rush of joy, as everything that had seemed pointless and even irksome fits into one grandly munificent design.

When we return to the beginning of the novel, we see that fate, no mere prankster after all, has treated Fyodor with extraordinary generosity to allow him to incorporate all he wants of his life and his developing art into the testimony of *The Gift*. The book's first day shows him not only installed in Tannenberg Street as if to meet Zina through Frau Lorentz, but apprised by Alexander Chernyshevsky of that hoax review, which prompts him both to recall his *Poems*—the first sample of his literary art—and to reexplore his early childhood. And at the same time, Alexander Yakovlevich's call permits Fyodor to link Yasha and his father with his own loss of his father, as "a kind of mocking variation on the theme of his own hope-suffused grief." That day of monstrous frustration proves to be fate's gift to Fyodor: it hands him what he will come to realize is the perfect opening of the novel he should write in celebration of his double gift, his literary talent and his Zina.

XI

The whole of *The Gift* prepares for Fyodor's writing *The Gift*, but how does the idea for the book actually come to him?

In the summer of 1929, Fyodor sunbathes in the Grunewald every day, enjoying a well-earned rest after giving birth to Chernyshevsky. Every day he visits the spot in the park where Yasha shot himself. On June 28, around 3 P.M., he visits that hollow again. Yasha's father has died, his mother has gone to Riga, and

> already her face, the stories about her son, the literary evenings at her house, and Alexander Yakovlevich's mental illness—all this that had served its time—now rolled up of its own accord and came to an end, like a bundle of life tied up crosswise, which will long be kept but which will never again be untied by our lazy, procrastinating, ungrateful hands. He

was seized by a panicky desire not to allow it to close and get lost in a corner of his soul's lumber room, a desire to apply all this to himself, to his eternity, to his truth, so as to enable it to sprout up in a new way. There is a way—the only way.

Fyodor does not explain what that way is: presumably, the way of art. He ascends another slope and catches sight of a young man in a black suit: Koncheyev. An intense conversation develops between them, full of philosophical fire—until we find that the man in the suit is a German who merely looked for a second like Koncheyev. As he has done once before, at the end of chapter 1, Fyodor has not merely imagined a conversation with Koncheyev, but lures us as readers into believing a marvelous interchange of ideas takes place, only to exasperate us when he admits to the fabrication. Why?

Fyodor has never had much sympathy for Yasha's passionate desire for a spiritual communion with Rudolf Baumann, the other man in the three-way suicide pact that only Yasha fulfills. Suddenly, in a flash of intense yearning to share his innermost thoughts with a person he momentarily supposes to be Koncheyev, Fyodor understands Yasha's own urge.

Not only that, it gives him the first germ of a novel. What if he were to turn his own desire for some ideally intense communication with Koncheyev—a desire always thwarted in real life—into concrete form, by concocting some heady conversation with Koncheyev and then exposing its hopelessly invented status? Yasha's eagerness to share his soul with Rudolf Baumann could then serve both as a parallel to Fyodor's own unsatisfied wish for an ideal and flawless communication with another man and as a contrast to the real communication that Fyodor and Zina have established.

Back from the Grunewald that evening (his clothes are stolen, and he walks through an outraged city in his swimming trunks—a hilarious scene), Fyodor writes to his mother:

> You know, I'm black as a gypsy from the Grunewald sun. Something is beginning to take shape—I think I'll write a classical novel, with "types," love, fate, conversations.

The precise hour and date of the afternoon scene, recalling the Turgenevian touch ("towards four in the afternoon on April the first, 192–") that begins the novel; the explicit parody of the classical novel in the encounter with Koncheyev (" 'Oh, that is less interesting,' said Fyodor, *who during this tirade* [as Turgenev, Goncharov, Count Salias, Grigorovich and Boborykin used to write]"); the reference to "conversations" (otherwise scarce in *The Gift*) and to "types" (Fyodor had earlier dismissed Yasha's story as too "typical" for his taste)—all pin-point this afternoon at the Grunewald as the occasion when the first impulse for *The Gift* flashes into Fyodor's mind. As in the case of the *Life of Chernyshevsky*, Nabokov stresses that the origins of a work of art can be absurdly oblique and improbable—the more so, in all likelihood, the richer the work.

That night, after finishing his letter to his mother, Fyodor hears Zina answer the telephone. She tells him he must go to his old landlady at Tannenberg Street at once. As Fyodor leaves, "the premonition of something incredible, of some impossible superhuman surprise splashed his heart with a snowy mixture of happiness and horror." At last he reaches his old room, where he had written the account of his father. He knows *who* will enter in a moment. The door opens, his father stands there, and Fyodor knows from the sounds he makes "that this was the true resurrection, that it could not be otherwise, and also: that he was pleased—pleased with his capture, his return, his son's book about him." As he is wrapped in his father's arms, Fyodor wakes: it has all been a dream, but unbearably real.

When Fyodor wrote the letter to his mother he mentioned, before telling her he was ready to write a novel, that the other day he had suddenly forgotten the street number of his sister's Paris address:

> one writes an address heaps of times, automatically and correctly, and then all of a sudden one hesitates, one looks at it consciously, and one sees you're not sure of it, it seems unfamiliar—very queer . . . You know, like taking a simple word, say "ceiling" and seeing it as "sealing" or "sea-ling" until it becomes completely strange and feral, something like "iceling" or "inglice." I think that *some day* that will happen to the whole of life.

In his dream that night he reaches his old room at Frau Stoboy's:

> The room was exactly as if he had still been living in it: the same swans and lilies on the wallpaper, the same painted ceiling wonderfully ornamented with Tibetan butterflies (there, for example, was *Thecla bieti*).

In fact, in waking life, when Fyodor first entered that room nearly three years ago he had only thought how hard it would be "to transform the wallpaper (pale yellow, with bluish tulips) into a distant steppe," how hard to write here his life of his father. Now in the dream the ceiling depicts Tibetan butterflies his father has named. And as Fyodor knows, naturalists normally abbreviate a common genus name like *Thecla* to its first letter, making the butterfly *T. bieti*, and a virtual anagram of "Tibet." Why does this anagram link so pointedly with the anagrammatic "ceiling" in his letter to his mother?

Because above that ceiling at Frau Stoboy's live the Lorentzes, unwitting pawns in the opening gambit of Fyodor and Zina's fate.

Though the novel says nothing explicitly, Fyodor wakes up from his dream with everything his new book needs, and that night he outlines it all for Zina. His dream—the strangely significant ceiling of his Tannenberg Street room, Zina, the phone call, Frau Stoboy—has alerted him to the game of fate in his own life. It has revived in his mind the day of his arrival at Tannenberg Street, his dread that he would not be able to write his father's story there, the call from Alexander Chernyshevsky. Now he has the key to incorporating all he wants to in his new book: Alexander Chernyshevsky and Yasha; Zina and himself; and all his art, starting from his *Poems* and their nonexistent review, and including even the unfinished life of his father that he wrote at Tannenberg Street and that after this strange dream he now feels he has permission to publish.

XII

In the Grunewald on the second-to-last day of *The Gift* Fyodor thinks of Yasha and of Koncheyev, and the first idea for a new novel. Now on the novel's last day, after his hauntingly intense dream, Fyodor finds the perfect place to begin this new book: his move to Tannenberg Street, with fate's help. But because that opening will lead easily and naturally into Alexander Chernyshevsky's telephone call it puts at his disposition an even more important parallel than the one he has already thought of constructing between himself and Yasha. Alexander Chernyshevsky's half-crazed sense that he is in touch with his dead son can serve Fyodor as a parallel to his own search through his art for access to his dead father.

After his son's death Alexander Chernyshevsky passes through a phase in which he seems to see Yasha's ghost everywhere. As his sanity ebbs still further, he becomes alarmed at the infiltration of the world by all manner of spectral forces and nominates himself "Chairman of the Society for Struggle with the Other World." On his deathbed his mind has cleared, and he repudiates his recent obsession entirely: "There is nothing [after death]. It is as clear as the fact that it is raining." Except that outside the lowered blinds of the dying man's room the sun in fact is shining, the tenant upstairs has watered the flowers on her balcony, and the water trickles down with a drumming sound.

Unlike Alexander Chernyshevsky, Fyodor keeps lucidly sane, but in all his art he has tried to grope beyond death, and especially toward his dead father. His dream of his father seems to provide the key to the role of fate in his own life and to prepare the way for *The Gift* itself. And although he will not put it into so many words, he now intuits that his father has been somehow involved in the strangely generous pattern of fate in his life, and has left him a message in this dream.

That at least seems to be how Fyodor reads the dream, for in the course of *The Gift* he appears to have deliberately suggested his father's posthumous influence over his life.*

The evening after he wakes from the dream Fyodor tells Zina his plan to commemorate their fate in his book; they head back to the apartment; and the novel breaks off with a pointedly Pushkinian stanza. Certainly, that unusual closure pays tribute to Russia's greatest poet. But Fyodor also intends another much more personal tribute.

Fyodor has earlier set up an uncommonly insistent relationship between Pushkin and his own writing about his father, a man who "took little interest in poetry, making an exception only for Pushkin." Fyodor had been impelled in the first place to begin his account of his father's travels by the example of Pushkin's verbal perfection. After steeping himself in Pushkin's prose Fyodor had then "passed to his life, so that in the beginning the rhythm of Pushkin's era commingled with the rhythm of his father's life," to the degree that he could even write: "With Pushkin's voice merged the voice of my father." Fyodor associates his Tannenberg Street room from first day to last with the account of his father that he begins and ends there. As he leaves for his next flat, he notes that the distance "from the old residence to the new was about the same as, somewhere in Russia, that from Pushkin Avenue to Gogol Street."

The Pushkinian lines that end *The Gift* begin "Good-by, my book!"—but they imply that things endure beyond this farewell: "no obstruction for the sage exists where I have put The End." These closing lines pointedly echo and refute the dispirited, apparently final

---

* Nabokov too was ready to trust he would see his dead father again, ready to believe his father may have helped him even in a Cambridge examination room. In an early poem like "Easter" he could treat his faith in his father's continued existence in direct, positive form; by the time of *The Defense* he can present in a gruesomely negative form the theme of a loving father trying to influence his son from the beyond (see above, pp. 193, 194, 239, 333–39). Now in *The Gift*, in this respect as in so many others, Nabokov finds a way to incorporate the negative—the frustration theme, the Chernyshevsky theme—into the larger positives of the Godunovs. Nabokov's privately expressed confidence in his father's unseen presence and Fyodor's covert thanks for the role he supposes *his* dead father has played in his life would seem to imply that in *The Gift* Nabokov is himself paying tribute to the contribution he imagines V. D. Nabokov continues to make to his own life—and perhaps even to *The Gift* itself.

good-by Fyodor makes at the end of chapter 2 to his Tannenberg Street room:

> This already dead inventory will not be resurrected later in one's memory: the bed will not follow us, shouldering its own self; the reflection in the dresser will not rise from its coffin; only the view from the window will abide for a while, like the faded photograph, fitted into a cemetery cross, of a trim-haired, steady-eyed gentleman in a starched collar. I would like to wish you good-by, but you would not even hear my greeting. Nevertheless, good-by. I lived here exactly two years, thought here about many things, the shadows of my caravan passed over this wallpaper, lilies grew out of the cigarette ash on the carpet—but now the journey is over.

When Fyodor farewells his room here, he assumes he will never return to his draft version of his father's life—which he fears his father would disapprove of—or to the room itself: nothing will be resurrected. But his final dream takes him back to Tannenberg Street and to his father, whose words leave him with a sense "that this was the true resurrection, that it could not be otherwise."

At the end of chapter 2, suspecting a spectral veto, Fyodor abandons his work on his father. The old man's shade may or may not have prompted him, but Godunov Senior would have been right to hope the work might be deferred. Fyodor in chapter 2 tries too urgently to accompany his father to regions he cannot know, and for all its beauty his brave exercise in filial loyalty would never have succeeded as a book able to stand on its own. But now, after he has learned to master the themes of fate even in Chernyshevsky's alien life, he discovers how to detect the pattern of fate's generosity within his own past. And now, as he prepares to pay tribute to his father's role in bringing him to Zina, then in allowing him to see this as the handiwork of fate and therefore in inspiring him with the idea for *The Gift*, his failed search in chapter 2 for some sign from his father can itself become part of *The Gift*'s pattern of necessary hindrance before unimaginably generous help, part of the proof that his father has somehow kept in touch.

Now at the end of *The Gift*, convinced he has his father's imprimatur, aware that his dream of his father has handed him the key to the whole novel, Fyodor pays his tribute. He has already declared that Pushkin's voice merged with his father's; now he ends the novel with Pushkinian lines that invite us to return to the beginning. As he evokes the end of *Eugene Onegin*, Fyodor sends us back to his arrival at Tannenberg Street, fate's first push toward Zina, and describes that

scene in terms that evoke the beginning of *Dead Souls*. No lover of
Russian literature could fail to know that it was Pushkin who gave
Gogol the idea for *Dead Souls*—as Fyodor's strangely Pushkinian father seems to have prompted both Fyodor's first move toward Zina
and toward the novel that now commemorates that first prompting of
a kindly fate.

XIII

Fyodor ends the novel: "no obstruction for the sage exists where I
have put The End: the shadows of my world extend beyond the sky-
line of the page, blue as tomorrow's morning haze." In the Russian
original he refers to the shadows by way of metaphor—and what a
metaphor: "the prolonged ghost of being." When we do return to the
first lines of the book, we find the moving van with its "yard-high blue
letters . . . shaded laterally with black paint: a dishonest attempt to
climb into the next dimension." But Fyodor himself climbs into the
next dimension through images of shadow that suggest his father's
presence at pivotal moments within his life.

At this point we should remember that after Fyodor writes his *Life
of Chernyshevsky* he begins to read the work of the French sage—and
Nabokov's invention—Pierre Delalande. In his masterwork, *Discours
sur les ombres*, Delalande elegantly and repeatedly repudiates the idea
of death's finality: "I know that death in itself is in no way connected
with the topography of the hereafter, for a door is merely the exit from
the house and not a part of its surroundings, like a tree or a hill. One
has to get out somehow, 'but I refuse to see in a door more than a hole,
and a carpenter's job.' " As Fyodor tells Zina of his plans to write *The
Gift*, he also explains that first he must translate Delalande's book as
a final discipline, a final preparation for *The Gift*. When he does come
to write *The Gift*, he shows he has not forgotten those "shadows" in
Delalande's *Discours*.

One instance must suffice. Two weeks after fate at last gets Fyodor
installed in the same apartment as Zina, Zina brings him a well-
thumbed copy of his poems for him to sign. Two days later he catches
her to apologize for the quality of the poems: "It's not the real thing,
the poems are bad, I mean they're not all bad, but generally speaking.
Those I've been publishing these last two years in the *Gazeta* are much
better." Zina responds by recalling his best poem, remembered from
a public reading, and brings out from her room a pile of newspaper
clippings—his and Koncheyev's verse. Now suddenly the frustration
of that hoax review vanishes utterly in this unforeseeable extra recom-

pense: he has at last been introduced to someone who will be his ideal reader—and much more.

A few evenings later, Fyodor overhears from his room that Zina has been told to descend with the key for guests due to arrive. He invents a pretext for going out himself, and finds her by the glass door, playing with the key looped on her finger. The light goes out, as lights do in European hallways unless reactivated. A passage that stresses the keys that form such a part of Fyodor's fate now leads into a paragraph where the light from the street, the shadow, and the patterns falling over Fyodor and Zina in their first romantic encounter acquire an extraordinarily emphatic force.

> Through the glass the ashen light from the street fell on both of them and the shadow of the iron design on the door undulated over her and continued obliquely over him, like a shoulder-belt, while a prismatic rainbow lay on the wall. And, as often happened with him—though it was deeper this time than ever before—Fyodor suddenly felt—in this glassy darkness—the strangeness of life, the strangeness of its magic, as if a corner of it had been turned back for an instant and he had glimpsed its unusual lining. Close to his face there was her soft cinereous cheek cut across by a shadow, and when Zina suddenly, with mysterious bewilderment and a mercurial sparkle in her eyes, turned toward him and the shadow lay across her lips, oddly changing her, he took advantage of the absolute freedom in this world of shadows to take her by her ghostly elbows; but she slipped out of the pattern and with a quick jab of her finger restored the light.

Just whose hovering presence Fyodor intends to imply here he specifies through two verbal details: the rainbow effect (the chapter devoted to his father begins with a rainbow and Fyodor's unforgettable image: "Once in Ordos my father, climbing a hill after a storm, inadvertently entered the base of a rainbow—the rarest occurrence!—and found himself in colored air, in a play of light as if in paradise"), and his sense of "the strangeness of life," which he has never felt so strongly until this moment (although as a parent Konstantin Godunov had mysteriously transmitted to Fyodor his own appreciation of "the innate strangeness of human life").

When they rendezvous the next night Zina explains why she slipped away from his first touch the previous evening. She has only recently broken off her engagement (to a man she never loved) and in any case she will not allow the least hint of a relationship between herself and Fyodor to pass between them within the apartment building. She cannot mention the real reason: her stepfather's advances, his trying to take stealthy advantage of her sheer proximity, would contaminate any hint of intimacy between herself and Fyodor within these same walls.

Fyodor has phrased the previous night's scene by the glass door as if to imply his father's presence, as if his father expected this moment to seal his success in bringing them together. But things are not so simple: fate has not counted on Zina's squeamishness about her home—another caprice of free will that, like Fyodor's avoiding the Lorentzes because of Romanov, defers the goal fate has in mind. For all Nabokov's bold hints of fate's detailed intervention in Fyodor's life, he ensures that Fyodor and Zina react freely in ways even fate could not foresee. Zina has decreed they are not to meet as lovers within the apartment—but fate then incorporates this unexpected ban into its pattern through the poetic centerpiece around which the novel revolves.

Except as Fyodor's new landlord's mute and unnamed stepdaughter, hostile to her stepfather's overweening vulgarity, Zina does not appear in the novel, named and identified as Fyodor's beloved, until the midpoint of the middle chapter. Just as Fyodor completes a poem celebrating their nightly vigils outside—the only place she will allow them to meet—she steps out of the shadows. In its imagery and its rousing, heroic tone the poem Fyodor has been composing for her all day evokes his abandoned work on his father's travels:

> In honor of your lips when they kiss mine
> I might devise a metaphor some time:
> Tibetan mountain-snows, their glancing shine,
> and a hot spring near flowers touched with rime.
>
> . . . .
>
> Those are not clouds—but star-high mountain spurs;
> not lamplit blinds—but camplight on a tent!
> O swear to me that while the heartblood stirs,
> you will be true to what we shall invent.

Fyodor had drafted these lines in the morning, before bestirring himself from bed. The final movement comes as he waits for Zina that night:

> Within the linden's bloom the streetlight winks.
> A dark and honeyed hush envelops us.
> Across the curb one's passing shadow slinks:
> across a stump a sable ripples thus.
> The night sky melts to peach beyond that gate.
> There water gleams, there Venice vaguely shows.
> Look at that street—it runs to China straight,

and yonder star above the Volga glows
Oh, swear to me to put in dreams your trust,
and to believe in fantasy alone,
and never let your soul in prison rust,
nor stretch your arm and say: a wall of stone.

These lines too pay quiet tribute to Fyodor's father: the Volga, the street that runs to China, even Venice, which for Fyodor recalls the picture in his father's study of Marco Polo leaving Venice.* But in celebrating his and Zina's nocturnal walks and talks, Fyodor's lines also evoke and transpose from a minor to a major key the poem he began under a "ghostly circle" of light when he was locked out in chapter 1—a poem that lamented his solitude, his having only himself to talk to as he paced the night. At the same time this poem for Zina, set as prose within the novel, anticipates the end of the novel, and another poem printed as prose that looks forward to Fyodor and Zina left together out on the street.

One paragraph ends as Fyodor reaches the last line of his poem for Zina; as the next begins, she at last steps directly into the novel, coming "out of the darkness, like a shadow leaving its kindred element." The paragraph ends:

What was it about her that fascinated him most of all? Her perfect understanding, the absolute pitch of her instinct for everything that he himself loved? In talking to her one could get along without any bridges, and he would barely have time to notice some amusing feature of the night before she would point it out. And not only was Zina cleverly and elegantly made to measure for him by a very painstaking fate, but both of them, forming a single shadow, were made to the measure of something not quite comprehensible, but wonderful and benevolent and continuously surrounding them.

Fyodor trusts in the constant kindness of fate, despite all the apparent evidence that life wants to mock or thwart him. The lives of the Chernyshevskys, the famous writer and the obscure student and his half-demented father, might seem to prove even more conclusively than his own experience that any design behind human affairs could be only that of a heartless prankster. But Fyodor knows better: he recognizes that the real key to his world can be found in the hidden generosity behind the obvious frustration.

* In the untitled poem that commemorates Nabokov's first evening walks with Véra in a similarly magical world of streetlamps and shadows, they too see Venice in a Berlin canal: see above, pp. 216–17.

By its very shape, life forces frustration upon us: the solitude of the soul, the passing away of time. But Fyodor understands that these are only the steep price life exacts for its otherwise impossible gifts: our independence of spirit, the uniqueness and frailty of every moment. But through his love for Zina, he overcomes his loneliness; through his art, he makes triumphant sense of the frustrations of time. And perhaps beyond death—*there, tam, là-bas,* where his father seems in some way responsible for the fortunes of his private fate—even the high cost of life's best offerings might be redeemed by one last great gift, if the past has been preserved, if the self can be transcended.

Destitute: France, 1938–1939

Paris was becoming the center of émigré culture

and destitution.

—Look at the Harlequins!

I

FROM THE TIME Nabokov had first conceived his *Life of Cherny-shevsky* he knew it would provoke as much outrage as admiration. Now that Rudnev had refused to publish the chapter at all, the fire-work show ought to have been canceled, but in the first few months of 1938, even without Chernyshevsky, Sirin managed to spark one explosive reaction after another.

In January 1938, while he was wintering in Menton, a new install-ment of *The Gift* appeared in *Sovremennye Zapiski*. His friend George Hessen wrote from Paris to tell him:

> You're a genius. If your chess or tennis or football were remotely like your writing, you old scoundrel, you could concede Alékhine a pawn and Budge fifteen points and make Hayden a reserve goalkeeper in any professional team.[1]

In the novel's new installment, Nabokov has Fyodor read a re-view by "Christopher Mortus" of Koncheyev's latest book.[2] Every émigré at once recognized Mortus as Georgy Adamovich:

> "I do not remember who said—perhaps Rozanov said it somewhere," began Mortus stealthily; and citing first this unauthentic quotation and then some thought expressed by somebody in a Paris café after some-one's lecture, he began to narrow these artificial circles around Kon-cheyev's *Communication*. . . .
>
> It was a venomously disdainful "dressing down" without a single re-mark to the point, without a single example—and not so much the critic's words as his whole manner made a pitiful and dubious phantom out of a book which Mortus could not fail to have read with delight and from which he avoided quoting in order not to damage himself with the dis-parity between what he wrote and what he was writing about. . . . "Peo-

ple friendly to Koncheyev's talent will probably think them enchanting. We shall not quarrel—perhaps this is really so. But in our difficult times with their new responsibilities, when the very air is imbued with a subtle moral *angoisse* (an awareness of which is the infallible mark of 'genuineness' in a contemporary poet), abstract and melodious little pieces about dreamy visions are incapable of seducing anyone. And in truth it is with a kind of joyous relief that one passes from them to any kind of 'human document,' to what one can read 'between the words' in certain Soviet writers (granted even without talent), to an artless and sorrowful confession, to a private letter dictated by emotion and despair."[3]

Aldanov wrote indignantly to Nabokov that everybody in the *Poslednie Novosti* offices, even the typist, recognized Georgy Adamovich behind the mask of Mortus. Rather than seeing in that fact a tribute to Nabokov's satiric accuracy, Aldanov felt only the indecorum of it all. (Khodasevich, on the other hand, wrote to Nabokov that Mortus was wild, "—but that's useful.")[4] Nabokov replied to Aldanov that *The Gift* paints the whole complex life of a writer, and just as he had to endow Fyodor with certain literary traits akin to his own, so he had to render a whole milieu:

> I was guided not by an urge to laugh at this or that person (although there would be no crime in that—we are not in class or in church), but solely by a desire to show a certain order of literary ideas, typical at a given time—which is what the whole novel is about (its main heroine is literature). If in this case a style of criticism I feature corresponds to the style of particular figures and fops, that is natural and unavoidable. My friends need not be offended. Smile, Mark Alexandrovich! You say that *The Gift* can count on a very long life. If that's the case, then it's all the more obliging to take along for the ride, free of charge, some of my contemporaries who would otherwise have stayed at home forever.

Nabokov wrote that letter in bed, having caught a cold after a winter swim. He prayed that the Paris production of *The Event* would bring in some money: "My financial situation is utterly desperate. It's a mystery to me how I exist at all."[5] Thanks to the hubbub unleashed by *Poslednie Novosti*'s harsh reviews of the play, it would run four full performances—in émigré terms, a rampant success.

II

The Event (Sobytie)

Set in a provincial town sometime this century, *The Event* begins on a note of alarm that lasts until the play ends: the painter Alexey Troshcheikin hears the grim news that Barbashin is back in town.* Six years ago, Troshcheikin's wife, Lyubov, would have been ready to marry Barbashin, but for his volcanic temper. When she chose Troshcheikin instead, Barbashin had tried to shoot them both. As he was overpowered and disarmed, he had cried that he would return to finish off the job. Now he has been released from prison earlier than anyone expected, and over the whole play hangs the question: will he succeed in carrying out his threat?[6]

Since the day Barbashin fired at her, Lyubov's life has been a series of bitter disappointments. She has had to live with the fact that her husband is a self-obsessed coward. Her son, her one comfort since her marriage, has died at the age of two, three years before the play starts. She has since acquired a lover, Ryovshin, not from any tenderness toward him but from disgust at a marriage that has made her strident and bereft of self-respect.

In act 1, the news of Barbashin's return follows the morning row between Lyubov and her husband. Without money and too deep in debt to be able to escape the town until he puts the last touches on two commissioned portraits, Troshcheikin flies into a panic that pervades the play and sets everyone else on edge. Lyubov receives the news quite differently: forced to watch once again all her husband's worst features, she cannot help fondly recalling her love for Barbashin. Though it happens to be the fiftieth birthday of her mother—a "writer" of pretentiously clotted prose in a bloodless symbolic vein—Lyubov resolves not to let her husband's frenzy scotch the planned celebration.

Throughout act 2, that afternoon, every ring of the doorbell seems about to announce Barbashin and sudden death. Instead there enter, one after another, guests for Antonina Pavlovna's birthday or gossips eager to announce Barbashin's return. Apparently chaotic, the scene is in fact a masterpiece of comic structure in its tension between birthday and threatened death-day. As the stage fills with more and more people who seem less and less real and Antonina Pavlovna turns the guests into an audience for her latest effusion, Lyubov and Troshcheikin advance to the front of the stage, a scrim drops at their backs, and the other characters seem to freeze behind it as if into one of Troshcheikin's paintings. For the only time in the play, Lyubov and

---

* Though the characters have Russian names there is no indication of a place of action. Some readers have assumed a prerevolutionary Russian setting, others an émigré one, presumably in a town like Riga where Russian was widely spoken. When checking with a lawyer friend about the details of Barbashin's release, Nabokov asked him to keep in mind the common denominator of European codices, with a glance back at the Russian.

Troshcheikin talk tenderly to one another, anxious to escape not simply Barbashin but the whole meaningless babble of their lives. A ripple of alarm behind the screen seems to presage the entry of Barbashin. No, once again—not Barbashin, but news that his accomplice has just purchased a gun.

Act 3, that evening: Lyubov discovers that the moment of communion she fancied between herself and Troshcheikin while her mother was reading was an illusion. He remains concerned only with escape, and even suggests that she should spend two weeks in the country with her lover Ryovshin if in return Ryovshin will pay for their tickets to safety. Lyubov reviles him and daydreams that when Barbashin appears she will elope with him. Troshcheikin has hired a farcical detective to patrol the street below, but as he conducts him down the back stairs, leaving Lyubov alone, the doorbell rings, and in walks— not Barbashin, but a guest and in fact a complete stranger who mistook the time of the birthday party. The play ends as he mentions, quite by chance, that he saw a man he knows, a certain Barbashin, at the station platform, about to leave the country for good. "He asked me to say hello to our mutual friends, but you wouldn't know him, I'm sure. . . ."

There the curtain falls. But although *The Event* entirely lacks its promised event, the play swarms with movement, like a Chekhov drama played at 78 r.p.m., with all the gestures jerkier and the voices either more squeakily comic or more gratingly shrill.

For Nabokov writing for the stage was like playing chess without his queen. In fiction his prose could thrive on capturing the unpredictables of the moment (a chance visual impression, a whim of private thought) and at the same time transcending the moment by the sheer force of style. In drama he can achieve neither effect. No wonder his moves on the chessboard of the stage seem at first glance so much weaker than his normal game. But Nabokov relished the challenge, and sought other modes of attack: a breakneck speed, a sense of headlong direction quite alien to his novels.

He rapidly sketches a plausible human predicament—the Troshcheikins' discordant present, their past peril, their menacing future—and allows it to create the tense expectation that Barbashin's entry on stage will precipitate the play's climax. Then the event refuses to happen. Nabokov deeply admired Chekhov's subversion of the implicit determinism of drama, but he regretted that Chekhov did not venture far enough. Lecturing on drama at Stanford in 1941, he would make clear how much he detested the determinism that arises as a by-product of the theater's need for economy of exposition, in hoary formulas such as: " 'By the by, I met your Australian cousin yesterday. He said he would be coming to see you one of these days.' General consternation. A minute later, Australian cousin comes in."[7] *The Event* parodies the formula as Nabokov attacks determinism head on: carefully prepared causes do not lead to their supposed effects, the rifle hung on the wall in act 1 does not fire at all in act 3. Instead another quite unexpected tragedy looms behind the final curtain: that there is no stagy denouement to resolve the Troshcheikins' fortunes; that, as in Chekhov at his best, life's muddle simply continues. Even though Troshcheikin has exposed his full cowardice and Lyubov has revealed the full measure of her contempt, they must find some way for their lives to go on.

Even more than Chekhov, *The Event* evokes Gogol. As in *The Government Inspector*, a new fact in a provincial town throws the characters into a state of frenzied consternation that lasts the duration of the play, until the final disclosure. In Gogol's play the announcement at the end of the real inspector's *arrival* exposes the absurdity of the town's deceptive fawning before Khlestakov; in Nabokov's, the announcement of Barbashin's *departure* discloses the full nastiness of Troshcheikin's hysteria.

In his last, ultrareligious phase, Gogol reinterpreted his inspector as death, a Last Judgment before which no spurious appeasements will work. In *The Event*, per contra, the threat of death suddenly lifts at the end: there will be no Last Judgment, no "Vengeance is Mine, I will repay." Instead, however, we ourselves after death may be compelled to review our lives from outside our mortal sense of self. Troshcheikin often paints two portraits of the local burghers: one version to satisfy their self-image, another in which he depicts them as the grotesques they really are. But at the beginning of the play he tells Lyubov of his plan for another kind of painting: "try to imagine that this wall is missing, and instead there is a black abyss and what looks like an audience in a dim theater, rows and rows of faces, sitting and watching me. And all the faces belong to people whom I know or once knew, and who are now watching my life." At the end of the play it seems as if Troshcheikin's own self-satisfied self-portrait disintegrates, and he realizes he must join the audience that has looked on the other portrait, Troshcheikin the grotesque, exposed in all his contemptible cowardice, the "heartless, unfeeling, petty, morally vulgar" creature that Lyubov has called him.

But for all Nabokov's acknowledgment of his great predecessors in Russian drama, it is his own work that provides the real key to *The Event*. From the first moment of the play, when a child's ball rolls across the empty stage, Nabokov shows he can devise splendid theatrical effects, but he finds the best spur to his invention in inverting the special conditions he creates in his fiction. In *The Gift* he had realized his aims better than in anything else he had written to date. Fyodor, unequivocally an artist of genius, controls his own life story in studied retrospect, allowing time to unfold in leisurely fashion and at his command. He personifies art as a transcending of time and self and the terror of the void. Troshcheikin too has the imagination and intelligence of the true artist, but he inhabits a world where the maelstrom of life threatens at every moment to engulf the frail raft of his art.

In *The Gift*, Fyodor's first book of poems began with a ball rolling under an impregnable sofa: as the whole novel illustrates, he knows how to make art from all the frustrations of life. *The Event* on the other hand begins with Troshcheikin railing at his wife because the balls he needs for a picture are scattered all over the apartment. Life has disrupted art, in the most natural way: the boy whose portrait he is painting has kicked the balls around after his last sitting. And unlike Fyodor, Troshcheikin can only rant like a child at life's inconvenient little intrusions upon his art.

Life also erupted into Troshcheikin's studio six years earlier when Barbashin fired at him and his wife. Now, when it threatens him again, and could put an end not only to his art but to his very existence, he responds only with panicky cowardice. Fyodor on the other hand has always demonstrated the uncompromising courage of art. Fyodor also persistently attempted to enter the imagination of others; Troshcheikin refuses to admit any view but his own. Fyodor erected his own literary memorial to his father; Troshcheikin simply tries to forget the death of his son. Fyodor celebrated his love for Zina; Troshcheikin destroys any happiness with Lyubov through his infantile self-concern. Fyodor learned to master the sly indirections of fate; Troshcheikin quivers before a destiny he mistakenly supposes obvious. Ignoble, selfish, cravenly terrified by time and death, he stands as the antithesis of all Nabokov valued in art.

The end of act 2 sinks into unreality as "real life" degenerates into a cracked chorus of stylized characters and the fake "art" of Antonina Pavlovna offers a falsely lulling escape. Lyubov and Troshcheikin step forward out of those second-rate worlds and toward our more substantial one. The scene behind freezes into one of Troshcheikin's paintings. As if art were the true index of reality, this moment of high artifice seems to reveal the hidden truths of the Troshcheikins' lives and allow the couple a throb of deeper feeling than they have time for amid the clatter of the everyday. But the moment turns out to belong only to Lyubov, not to Troshcheikin: her sense of communion has gone quite unshared. Nabokov has remarked, "It takes a good deal of spiritual depth to produce a masterpiece."[8] Troshcheikin lacks that depth: the whole play shows him exposing his hideous self so that at the end even he must see his meanness of spirit. Lyubov on the other hand is no artist and knows little about Troshcheikin's métier, but she can envisage stepping outside time and the self and the shoddiness of her world. In that eerie moment when she approaches our "rows and rows of faces," Lyubov too exposes herself, but in a way that shows she belongs in a richer world. She may continue in a ridiculous marriage that shrivels her spirit, she may become even more shrewish and bored, but somehow she remains connected with a world beyond her life whose gaze she need not fear.

The premiere of *The Event* took place on Friday, March 4, 1938, in the Russian Theater's usual venue, the Salle des Journaux of the Bibliothèque nationale. The play's director and set designer, the painter and writer Yuri Annenkov, had inspired his cast with his zeal and inventiveness, but on the first night the tone of the audience was set by the stuffed shirts and the fulsome furs in the front row. After the first act, enthusiasm; after the second, cool bepuzzlement; after the third, icy rejection. The following day the dejected troupe decided that the second performance, on Sunday, would have to be the last. On Sunday morning, as if in confirmation, *Poslednie Novosti* printed a hostile review. But that night the audience was quite different, with George and Iosif Hessen in the front row beside a laughing and twitching Khodasevich. There were six curtain calls after each of the first two acts, and many in the audience voiced their amazement at the *Poslednie Novosti* review. On Monday the *Poslednie Novosti* staff, themselves in a state of civil war, were flooded with reports of husbands and wives in battle over the play. Nothing else in the history of émigré theater had stirred such controversy—nothing else had so boldly defied theatrical convention—and as the newspapers rushed to remark, *The Event* had become *the* event of the season.[9]

III

Under the chickfluff of the mimosas in Menton's early spring, Nabokov was still longing for a route to England or America. He approached George Vernadsky of Yale about establishing a permanent course there in Russian literature. After a negative reply, he wrote back the next month that he now expected to be taking his family to England in the autumn.[10] In the afterglow of the completed *Gift*, he composed one chess problem after another.[11] He still had no French *carte d'identité*, and only *Laughter in the Dark* for a likely income.

On April 22 *Laughter in the Dark* was published, his first work to appear in the United States. Some reviews were very favorable ("To an amazing knowledge of what makes men tick, he adds refined simplicity. . . . Mark this rising star!" "In all ages there are writers who plunge deep into those forces which motivate humanity. . . . Vladimir Nabokoff is one of those"),[12] others cynically took advantage of the book's wry synopsis in its first paragraph to read no further. But no one bought the book, and the film companies Nabokov had hoped to interest thought it too cosmopolitan and too vulnerable to censorship.[13]

When the rest of the *Laughter in the Dark* advance came through, it had been whittled down by fees and commission and tax from $300 to $182.25.[14] Nabokov wrote to the journalist Lolly Lvov of his "ghastly destitution." His cry for help was heard by Sergey Rachmaninov, who, although he had never met Nabokov, had long been a Sirin fan and promptly cabled him 2,500 francs.[15]

Actually it should be kept in mind that throughout their years in France the Nabokovs always had enough to eat and—except perhaps in Moulinet in July 1938—decent, clean accommodation. The ghastly destitution, as Nabokov could later explain, "was more of next day's threat than an actual situation."[16] With no savings as a buffer, no regular income and just enough from the latest small advance or loan to last another week or two's rent, there was every reason for steady panic. In retrospect, knowing that disaster never quite came, the Nabokovs could realize that their day-to-day living conditions—apart from their not being able to afford peace of mind—were far from the image the word "poverty" suggests. By this time the experience had even taken on a romantic tinge ("proud émigré destitution")[17] quite absent from the sense of humiliating frustration, degradation, and alarm that seemed so unrelenting at the time.

IV

In April *The Event* was published in *Russkie Zapiski*—a journal set up as a sister to *Sovremennye Zapiski* but now a monthly run by Milyukov—and rehearsals for the play were under way in Prague. By now Nabokov was roaming the hills between Menton and Roquebrune for butterflies[18] and dreaming up amid the wisteria a long new story. It took him the second half of May and all of June to compose "Istreblenie tiranov" ("Tyrants Destroyed").[19]

In a country where the ruler's portrait lines the street and his voice booms from every corner loudspeaker, someone who knew him in his youth records the parallel growth of the tyrant's power and of his own obsessive urge to assassinate the man. He has no illusions, no interest in politics, no means of breaching the security around the ruler, no way of warding off a postassassination purge, no confidence that an assassination now will protect his country from suffering unspeakable tortures in future centuries. And as he depicts the disparity between the sullen mediocrity he knew and the divinity the state has created, he realizes that far from making the ruler fearful he has only made him ridiculous. But that, he suddenly realizes, is the answer: laughter offers the one release that can destroy the solemn ruler's might and save his own imperiled sanity. As Nabokov later remarked, everything can disintegrate at the furtive tickle of the comic: "words, conventions of everyday life, systems, persons— . . . I think laughter is some chance little ape of truth astray in our world."[20]

No one would disagree with Nabokov that a free mind's freedom beats enslaved thought. He demonstrates mental liberty superbly here, in paragraph after paragraph of brilliant writing, as his character broods on politics or anything else. But this story, almost his longest, remains a disappointment. Its distended structure labors to give birth to a frail and unviable conclusion, and although Nabokov exposes with devastating accuracy the inanity of hero worship and statist planning, his portrait of the ruler as a young man—gloomy dullness and nothing else—completely fails to convince. "Tyrants Destroyed" would later expand into parts of *Bend Sinister*, where the character of Paduk, the tyrant and schoolmate of the hero, would remain the weakest thing in the novel.

V

Early in the year, Nabokov had sent off his 1930s short stories to the book-publishing branch of *Russkie Zapiski*, who recommended that the stories be published in two volumes rather than one.[21] Only one volume in fact appeared before the war. With a small advance for the stories and no new income in sight, the Nabokovs decided to quit Menton for a less popular spot. They settled on Moulinet, in the Alpes Maritimes, a village rating no stars in the Michelin guide. At the beginning of July, on the eve of their departure, Bunin paid them a visit. The last time he had called on them, in Cannes, Nabokov had embarrassed his guest by showing him an article citing Bunin on Sirin. "So you call me a monster!" he teased. Now Bunin arrived amid the chaos of packing. Somehow their meetings seemed destined for disjunction.[22]

In the second week of July the Nabokovs boarded a bus for Moulinet, thirty-five kilometers inland up a road winding through steep, tufted crags loaned from some Chinese landscape painting. The Nabokovs stopped at the Hotel de la Poste, the second and smaller and second best of Moulinet's hotels, three squat, shuttered stories on the village square. Around this charming hamlet set two and a half thousand feet higher than the coast, the flora and fauna had an unexpectedly northern aspect. Nabokov relished the marvelous hills and innumerable unfamiliar flowers. Here on July 20 and 22, on the steep slopes above the village, at an altitude of four thousand feet, he saw and captured two specimens of a butterfly that looked strikingly different from the other "blues" around. In his first American butterfly article he would bestow on it the name *Plebejus (Lysandra) cormion.* "It may not rank high enough to deserve a name," he later admitted, "but whatever it be—a new species in the making, a striking sport, a chance cross—it remains a great and delightful rarity."[23] It was the closest he had yet come to his lifelong dream of discovering a new species.

With Europe readying for war, the fields around Moulinet were studded with the tents of a military camp, and music in the square and shots from maneuvers beyond the village drowned out the cowbells. The Nabokovs ate at Moulinet's "best" hotel, until Vladimir made the mistake of entering the kitchen and mistook for a plateful of caviar what was in fact a mass of flies covering a dish of meat. After that, the landlady of their own hotel cooked for them, but then an epidemic of dysentery raged through the camp, and when they noticed maggots in their ham the Nabokovs hesitated to eat anything but jam from jars they had just unsealed. As soon as they found a Russian pension advertised in Cap d'Antibes, they wrote for rooms and took a red tour bus, braying on its horn at the blind corners, back down to the coast.[24]

They moved in to the pension in the last week of August: Villa les Cyprès, 18 Chemin de l'Ermitage, a grand house in the middle of the slender peninsula. Once the property of the Duke of Leichtenberg (a Russian despite his name), it was now the—"Russian, very Russian"—House of the Union of the St. George Cross for Disabled Veterans. The parasol pines and the blue bays encircling the cape were idyllic, but Nabokov was irked by the legend spread by "envious idiots" in Paris that his family were luxuriating on the Côte d'Azur: "We just can't go anywhere." Their situation was wretched, they had never been so poor, it all seemed a slow death, they just did not know what to do next.[25] Nabokov wrote for financial help to the Russian Literary Fund in the United States: "I can't say how much a small monthly support would help. My material situation has never been so terrible, so desperate. My literary income is not even half of a very modest budget." The fund could send only $20.[26]

At a time when Noel Coward was the best paid writer in the world, Nabokov turned to another play, not in expectation of stupendous wealth but merely in the hope of adding to the small payment from the play's periodical publication another small payment if the Russian Theater took it for the coming season. During September he wrote *Izobretenie Val'sa* (*The Waltz Invention*) and posted off the manuscript on October 3.[27]

VI
The Waltz Invention (Izobretenie Val'sa)

As Gleb Struve commented in his role as historian of émigré literature, Nabokov for all his avowed apoliticism reflected the torments of the highly politicized decade of the 1930s more than other émigré writers.[28] Though Fyodor disavowed any aims other than purely artistic ones in his *Life of Chernyshevsky*, Nabokov did not. He had written the Chernyshevsky biography in reaction to the Soviet Union's enforced implementation of socialist realism as the state aesthetic, and he declared flatly that his critique of Chernyshevsky marked "the defeat of Marxism and materialism."[29] But despite all the deaths Stalin's policies had caused in the last ten years, Hitler seemed the more immediate evil. In 1937 and 1938, as soon as he and his family had safely extricated themselves from Nazi Germany, Nabokov had begun to turn a cold eye back on the country where he had spent the last fifteen years. His first attack had been the direct assault of "Cloud, Castle, Lake." Then in chapters 2, 3, and 5 of *The Gift* he had let his detestation of German vulgarity color Fyodor's reaction to the country enough for one excerpt from these new chapters, published in *Poslednie Novos i*, to provoke a rabid attack in March 1938 from the pro-Nazi *Novoe Slovo* in Berlin.[30] Then came "Tyrants Destroyed," and in the last of the series, *The Waltz Invention*, Nabokov aimed the weapon of his art at the megalomaniac fantasies about to rend Europe.

A lightweight nightmare, a study in insanity, a succession of comic one-liners and dramatic sight gags, and a fable about the puerility of political or any other dreams, *The Waltz Invention* revolves around Salvator Waltz, who hopes to save the world by means of a device he has invented that can cause massive explosions at any distance. (The play was written, as Nabokov later reminded readers, years before

---

* In Russian the title is a deliberately misleading pun: before the audience realizes there will be a character named Waltz, they will naturally assume the title means "The Invention of the Waltz."

atomic bombs were first designed.) In act 1 the minister of war receives him and promptly dismisses him as a madman, only to have Waltz recalled after the mountain visible out the window has its top neatly blown off at the stroke of noon. In act 2 Waltz has passed the tests imposed by the minister and his generals, turning the remote spots they designate into palls of dust. They are ready to offer him millions for his machine, but he wants only to become the benevolent dictator of the world, instituting as his first decree universal disarmament. There is no choice for them but to accept. Act 3: Waltz as head of state finds himself faced with the vexations of power: inertia, civil discontent, paperwork, unpleasant decisions (in an effort to bend other countries to his will, he obliterates a city of six hundred thousand). What he now desires above all is rest from his onerous responsibilities, and a fabulous palace into which he can retreat with a fabulous harem. The girls paraded before him are not enough: he wants *one* particular girl, but the girl's father, anticipating the demand, has hidden her away and will protect her from Waltz even at the cost of his own death, his country's, his world's.

At this point Waltz's fantasy collapses: his dream whispers to him that after all he *has* no machine, and the scene suddenly reverts to Waltz's appointment with the minister of war at the beginning of the play. Now the appointment takes place in earnest, not in Waltz's imagination, and this time, when he cannot convince the minister he has the machine he claims and threatens to blow up the mountain in the distance, the minister simply has him carried away ranting.

As Nabokov comments:

> If, from the very first, the action of the play is absurd, it is because this is the way mad Waltz—*before* the play starts—imagines it is going to be, while he waits outside, in a viking-style armchair—imagines the interview he has managed to wangle through old Gump and its fabulous consequences; an interview which in reality he is granted only in the last scene of the last act. As his waiting-room dream unfolds, broken by the intermissions of oblivion between the acts of his fancy, there occurs now and then a sudden thinning of the texture, a rubbed spot in the bright fabric, allowing the nether life to glimmer through.

The texture thins for instance when Waltz thinks he sees a child's toy car and reacts with almost hysterical alarm: does he know that he is only a child, that the infantilism of his simple dream shows through? Or the ambiguous figure of Trance (*Son*, "Dream" in the Russian) jars the illusion: ostensibly a reporter, he offers to become Waltz's impresario, and serves as factotum, confidant, Mephistophelean prompter and stage manager of his dream, until at last he wakes

Waltz out of his reverie altogether. In a sense Trance seems to be the mind's sly skepticism that half-realizes this is all a dream but remains prepared, up to a point, to suppress its awareness for the sake of the fantasy.

Nabokov's comic inventiveness of language and gesture has never been better. The curtain rises on the minister of war and his faithful aide in a puzzling pose: the colonel, we discover, is trying to extract a speck from his master's eye ("Well, would you like me try with my tongue?" he asks a few lines later). In the shaky reality of Waltz's world, dialogue teeters back and forth between the casual and the stylized, allowing Nabokov's verbal imagination, for once, almost full scope even within the constraints of drama. Waltz especially can talk like a poet or a book.

Unfortunately wit and fancy without the interest of a credible situation soon begin to pall. In the first act there is at least the pleasure of waiting for Waltz's power to be vindicated. In the second act the farce of the Council of War (Generals Hump, Lump, Gump, Bump, and so on) will satisfy an audience wanting only to laugh, but the jokes soon seem to be merely stalling for time. The third act shows Waltz harassed by the imperfection of his dream, but the various sub-scenes succeed each other with no sense of direction and at an increasingly hallucinatory speed. For the fantastic succession of unrelated oneiric images to hold our attention we need some compensation for the absence of an unfolding story. Certainly Nabokov avoids the ponderous symbolism of Strindberg's *A Dream Play* and comes much closer to the lucid phantasmagoria of Joyce's Nighttown (Waltz's dream in fact seems to derive in part from Bloom's brief role there as reformer of the world). Where Joyce's witches'-brew lexicon and bubbling metamorphoses easily outweigh the absence of normal dramatic interest, Nabokov remains bound by the presence of real actors on a stage and cannot stop the dream from losing its spell.

All the same it comes as a shock when we are bumped right out of the dream and back to Waltz's initial audience with the minister of war. In the few speeches that follow, Waltz has lost all his verbal magic. He is no more than a sorry crackpot, who in his dreams had had genius.

In one sense Waltz is an image of us all, a measure of the gap between the desires that run riot in our dreams and the waking reality we know we must acknowledge. He represents the idleness of unchecked fancy, in which we begin by shedding our bumbling selves and end with the whole world at our feet.

Nabokov values the imagination in us all, the power of every mind to re-create its own world. But he also knows the difference between the ordinary dreamer and the artist and the madman. The artist who can create the special world of a work of art seems almost to overcome the mortal status of a creature bound by conditions it has not determined. Waltz imagines re-creating his world, but his fancies degenerate into the most insipid visions of omnipotence and luxury. And being a madman he cannot see the difference between the world within and the world outside that resists his fancies. He is just one step away from the dictator who insists the outer world be re-created to satisfy the banal images he harbors within. Nabokov was writing *The Waltz Invention* after Hitler had swallowed up Austria and was about to take his first bite at Czechoslovakia. In Waltz he evokes not only the tragic dreamer in us all, but also the infantile madman history so often lets loose on our world. He comes far closer here than in "Tyrants Destroyed" to suggesting a Hitler, a Lenin, a Stalin, when he shows that the lunatic, the tyrant, and the poet are of imagination all compact.

VII

While Nabokov was writing *The Waltz Invention*, Hitler's appetite for Czechoslovakia started a wave of panic buying in Paris. Calm quickly returned after the Munich Agreement and Nabokov, at last equipped with a *carte d'identité*, decided to settle in Paris.[31] Leaving Cap d'Antibes in mid-October, the family stopped several days en route at the farm of their friends Mikhail and Elizaveta Kaminka, at L'Honor de Cas, near Montauban, where they shared the peasant farmhouse with the Kaminkas, their cattle, and a dog.[32] In Paris, accommodation was in short supply, and the Nabokovs had to take what they could. A friend had secured for them an apartment in the sixteenth arrondissement, 8 rue de Saigon, between the Etoile and the Bois de Boulogne. This luxurious little studio in a fashionable part of town had been fine for the dancer there before them but was much too small for a family of three. As Nabokov recalled, it consisted of no more than

> a huge handsome room (which served as parlor, bedroom and nursery) with a small kitchen on one side and a large sunny bathroom on the other. Evening guests had to be entertained in the kitchen so as not to interfere with my future translator's sleep.[33]

Among these kitchen-table guests was Khodasevich:

> He was, physically, of a sickly aspect, with contemptuous nostrils and beetling brows, and when I conjure him up in my mind he never rises

from the hard chair on which he sits, his thin legs crossed, his eyes glittering with malevolence and wit, his long fingers screwing into a holder
the half of a *Caporal Vert* cigarette.[34]

Others Nabokov saw often in Paris included George Hessen; two
inseparable friends a generation older—"my chaps," Nabokov called
them—Ilya Fondaminsky and Vladimir Zenzinov; Mark Aldanov; the
poet Alla Golovina, sister of Nabokov's acquaintance, the poet Anatoly Steiger; and the writer Galina Kuznetsova, Bunin's former live-in
mistress.[35]

In October if not earlier Nabokov wrote the story "Poseshchenie
muzeya" ("The Visit to the Museum").[36] While living in Menton early
in the year, he had been amused by a visit to the local museum: "It has
everything from paintings by Ferdinand Back to a ramshackle collection of faded butterflies. And do you know what two statues stand at
the entrance? Pushkin and Peter the Great (saving in utterly wild fashion two people drowning—the original stood on a little square on the
embankment in St. Petersburg)."[37] It was that mixture of France and
Russia that lit Nabokov's fancy.

In "The Visit to the Museum," an émigré visiting a small French
town has been asked by another émigré—whom the first regards as all
but mad—to check in the local museum a portrait of his Russian
grandfather. He finds the picture, but by stealthy degrees, as one ex-
hibit hall leads to another, the tiny museum becomes endless and ominous. After many panicky twists and turns the narrator at last finds
himself out on the street. Snow is falling, and when he catches sight
of a shop sign he realizes he is in Russia. The émigré's dream of returning to the Russia of old has become the nightmare of finding himself in the Sovietized Russia of the present. Even worse, the nightmare remains real. Declining to describe his arrest and subsequent
ordeals, the narrator concludes: "Suffice it to say that it cost me incredible patience and effort to get back abroad, and that, ever since, I
have foresworn carrying out commissions entrusted one by the insanity of others." This wry, disconcerting tale about solitude and the
crowd, madness and sanity, time and space succeeds because Nabokov makes every step along the museum corridor so vivid and reasonable that we cannot say at what point he ushers us beyond the
real. Even at the end when we find ourselves in Leningrad and we
know something has snapped, Nabokov calmly confirms that, yes,
the impossible *has* happened, and it is part of our world.

In November Nabokov completed another story he had conceived
in the Riviera: "Lik."[38] A neurotic émigré with a bad heart, an actor on
tour in a Riviera town, Lik feels he has been shunned by life and

hopes that death may be his cue for entry into a truer reality. Perhaps if he dies on stage, he muses, he may drift off through death into the world of the play and enjoy the embraces of the heroine and even the mere company of the play's other characters, who as actors outside their roles simply ignore him. As he buys new white shoes for his last performance in the town, he encounters a former schoolmate from Russia, a bully who once regularly attached himself to Lik and now drags him to his squalid home, plies Lik with wine he should not drink, berates him for the gap between his own misery and the cushy life he thinks Lik leads. At last Lik tears himself away, his mind a blur, his heart near collapse. Just as death seems inevitable, he remembers his shoes, takes a taxi back to Koldunov's—and finds Koldunov on the floor, his face blasted by a gunshot he has fired into his mouth, his feet spread wide and shod in Lik's new shoes. Apparently assigned the central role of the hero about to die, Lik finds that even death relegates him to the periphery.[39] The story's seemingly inevitable end turns into a surprise that rounds out better than any other conclusion could have done the patterns of both Koldunov's and Lik's own lives. Fate cannot be detected in advance, however many signs it seems to plant, but in retrospect, by some inherent artistic magic, its imposed accidents seem to fulfill the unique and as if preexistent harmony of each individual life.

In December *The Waltz Invention* was to have had its premiere, until Annenkov, who was to have directed the play, became angry with the management of the Russian Theater over some trifles and withdrew from the production.[40] No replacement could be found. In compensation Nabokov himself stepped on the stage for a reading on December 2 at 5 rue Las Cases: "Lik" in the first half, "The Visit to the Museum" in the second.[41]

During December he also gathered impressions for another story. In Berlin more than a decade ago he had written a poem in honor of Nadezhda Plevitskaya, the immensely popular cabaret singer of Russian folk songs. She was now being tried in Paris for having in September 1937 aided her husband, General Skoblin, to abduct the head of the All-Russian Military Union in Paris, General Evgeny Miller (General Kutepov, the organization's previous head, had also been murdered in 1930). She was found guilty and sentenced to twenty years' hard labor. Five years later Nabokov would turn her wildly improbable past into "The Assistant Producer," the first short story he would write in English.

Already in December 1938 Nabokov had begun his first English novel, *The Real Life of Sebastian Knight.* The decision to become an English writer, though it did not yet mean ceasing to write in Russian, was one of the most difficult he had ever made. True, the first fairy tales his mother read to him were English, as were the first books he had tottered through himself. His family had all been enthusiastic Anglophiles, he had studied at Cambridge, he had been accurately described in his Sirin role as the most Western of all Russian writers. But on the other hand he had struggled against all the odds to become a great *Russian* writer. For two decades he had resolutely perfected his talent, though cut off from his native soil, from an audience large enough to support his writing, from any prospect that his work, for all the acclaim it had received within the emigration, would find its way into Russia's national literary treasury or an international literary market. Page by page he had conned the four volumes of Dahl's great dictionary, line by line he had analyzed the rhythms of Russian verse. For fifteen years he had locked himself in a Germany he disliked, because by refusing to master its language he could prevent his own being diluted. During that time he had perfected a prose style whose sinewy suppleness the Russian language had never known and discovered fictional forms, unprecedented even in the great tradition of Pushkin, Gogol, Chekhov, and Tolstoy, that allowed him to express new kinds of literary truth. Alone of his generation he had withstood the bitter air and the barren soil of exile to grow into a major writer.

In the early 1920s it had been possible for émigrés to hope that the Soviet system would collapse. Late in that decade and early in the next Sirin's own work had been welcomed as proof that the emigration, scanty and bedraggled though it may be, could produce with its freedom more than the largest nation on earth could manage with all its state sweaters and pipes for state writers. But now German dreams of conquest warned that soon there may not be even an emigration left to write for. With a son to support, Nabokov had to turn elsewhere. In England or America an academic post in Russian literature, if only he could find it, might feed both body and soul. But with English spoken around him it would be hard to preserve his Russian at full strength, even if an emigration still survived. Could he become an English writer?

He had found he could translate his own work better than an Englishman. He had even rewritten one of his novels in English, and received more for the advance than he could ever hope to make in émigré Europe. Now, with the Soviet Union riding high in Western opinion as the world's bulwark against fascism, a novel set in the emigration would be impossible. But how could he write for English readers, when he knew their milieu less well than they did themselves? He had already written autobiographical sketches of a Russian's early associations with England. Could that material, spliced perhaps with his recent impressions of literary London, provide the germ of an English novel?

The Real Life of Sebastian Knight shows that it could. For all the novel's Englishness, however, it was also the product of purely Russian factors: the real research Nabokov had carried out for Fyodor's *Life of Chernyshevsky* and the invented frustrations of Fyodor's life of his father; Nabokov's affair with Irina Guadanini and his determination to keep that an unknown part of his own biography. Most of all the novel relies on Nabokov's effort in *The Gift* to construct at length and in detail the life of a writer. Now he redeployed similar themes, but without *The Gift*'s compulsion to be compendious and with the parodic lightness he had mastered in *The Event* and *The Waltz Invention*. Never before had he packed such a complex structure into such a small space with such seeming ease. In view of the speed with which the novel sprang up, it seems likely he carefully prepared the ground during his otherwise fallow spring in Menton.

In Paris the Nabokovs' search for a two-roomed flat turned up nothing. With Dmitri playing or asleep in the one main room of their apartment, Nabokov had to retreat into the bathroom to write, using a suitcase over the bidet as a desk. When the sun went down the room quickly chilled and his fingers would grow numb from the cold and the long hours of writing.[42] The whole time he spent on the novel he was oppressed by the knowledge that his mother had fallen seriously ill and that Hitler's tightening grip on Czechoslovakia made it impossible for him to visit her.[43] And he had to compose the novel not in his special Russian but in what he felt was a second-rate brand of English. Despite the circumstances, he wrote on unflinchingly. A British literary competition for which he wanted to enter the novel required manuscripts to be received in London by the end of January 1939. On January 29 he reported to a friend that he had finished the book and despatched it.[44]

VIII
The Real Life of Sebastian Knight

The Real Life of Sebastian Knight purports to be the biography of the writer Sebastian Knight (born St. Petersburg, 1899, of an English mother and a Russian father; died 1936), researched and drafted in 1936 by his half brother V. (born 1906 to his father's second, Russian, wife).[45] After emigration in 1919, V. settles with his mother in the Russian community in Paris, while Sebastian at Cambridge cuts himself off from his native language and his past. Even in St. Petersburg, Sebastian had taken his mother's name, signing his poems—written in English—with a chess knight. Moving from Cambridge to London, Sebastian in 1924 finds the ideal mistress-muse in Clare Bishop and blossoms at once as a novelist. During his adult years, V. sees him only briefly, in 1924 and 1929; in January 1936 he receives a letter from Sebastian, written to his surprise in Russian, and shortly after, a telegram from his doctor. Sebastian's last novel had described the unearthly secret a dying man seemed about to divulge; V., who has read the book, rushes to Paris in anticipation of hearing a similar secret himself—only to find Sebastian dead. He retraces his brother's past and realizes that to understand the heartache of Sebastian's last years he must track down the unknown Russian love whom Sebastian met in 1929.

More than any other Nabokov work, *The Real Life of Sebastian Knight* bares its devices, like an X ray of a grinning conjuror. The fun of the book begins in its comically frustrated biography: first, V.'s recollections of his and Sebastian's shared homes in Russia (even there the boys lived wholly separate lives) and the ample and generous reminiscences of a close Cambridge friend, then a gradual losing sight of Sebastian, except for fleeting glimpses in passing mirrors, until the book ends in darkness, a nightmarishly slow sprint toward the dying Sebastian, the awful inaccessibility of the dead. Sebastian's one-time secretary, Mr. Goodman, an unscrupulous speculator on the literary market, encounters no such difficulties in dashing off his own biography of the man, for he merely subsumes Sebastian's life under social generalizations and glibly attributes his death to the inability of a sensitive soul to withstand the anguish of the epoch. "What epoch?" asks V., who knows that the past is compounded of particulars, and that Sebastian was above all an individual. V. parodies the assumption that there can be an open sesame to another's past, and shows us the barred doors and the *trompe-l'oeil* archways that have thwarted him. Somehow, though, he manages to render the color of Sebastian's mind, his gleeful scorn for dead ideas, his knight moves of thought, his enchantingly strange novels. As the biography of a writer, V.'s book is exemplary: the exclusion from Sebastian's life does not matter, because the art and mind are intact. V.'s self-conscious parody of the limitations of biography turns his own work into a playful meditation on the inviolability of the individual and the mystery of the past.

Although time crumbles and slips again and again to bar the way to Sebastian's private life, we arrive there eventually, even if the road still feels blocked. One of the delights of the story is the warm imaginative sympathy of Sebastian's love, Clare Bishop, herself no writer but his ideal companion, editor and audience, and touchingly doomed in her own right. Discovering that he has inherited his mother's fatal angina, Sebastian becomes restless, unable to feel that his happiness with Clare is anything but the jesting decoy of his own mortality. He leaves Clare to pursue another woman who has a disastrous effect on his morale. Although he recognizes at once she will bring him only misery, he cannot break off the chase.

As we follow V.'s quest for Sebastian's lethal last love and as we draw closer to Sebastian's death, we sense more and more sharply that Sebastian's novels somehow anticipate V.'s search or that the search somehow reenacts the novels. We seem about to resolve this crescendo of echoes as the book itself swells with the promise of an all-deciding disclosure from the dying Sebastian—and that in turn mimics the pattern of Sebastian's last novel. Listening to the sleeping patient breathe, V. experiences a profound spiritual communion that courses through his whole being. But it all turns out to be a ghastly mistake. After he had spelled out "Knight" in agitation and explained "It's an English name," the French sanatorium staff had directed him to the unlit bedside of someone named Kegan. "Oh-la-la!" the embarrassed nurse exclaims when she realizes the error, "The Russian gentleman died yesterday." Here the novel closes, with V. declaring that "those few minutes I spent listening to what I thought was his breathing" have changed his life completely, for he has learned

> that the soul is but a manner of being—not a constant state—that any soul may be yours, if you find and follow its undulations. The hereafter may be the full ability of consciously living in any chosen soul, in any number of souls, all of them unconscious of their interchangeable burden. Thus—I am Sebastian Knight. . . . I am Sebastian, or Sebastian is I, or perhaps we both are someone whom neither of us knows.

What are we to make of this dizzying ending? Has V.'s lifelong obsession with his half brother hardened into a kind of lucid madness? Perhaps—but Sebastian's last project was a fictitious biography; the parodic biography that is *The Real Life of Sebastian Knight* seems to match the tone and the innovative strategies of Sebastian's own work; they both write in English, but at the last Sebastian proves to be inescapably the Russian that V. has been all along; it is only the letter *v* that distinguishes the Russian "Sevastian" from English "Sebastian."

Or is it that Sebastian's spirit helps V. in his search, that in his hereafter he "consciously lives" in V.'s soul? V. has a dim sense of being helped in this way. Just when he appears to have reached a dead end in the search for Sebastian's lover and decides he may have to paint a deliberately incomplete portrait of Sebastian, he meets a person named Silbermann who offers to sleuth for him. Within the week this strange stranger produces from a hotel register the names of the four Russian women staying at Sebastian's hotel in 1929. Silbermann's list even leads en passant to the discovery of Sebastian's first Russian love, Natasha Rosanov, whose very existence had been unknown to V. and whose romance with Sebastian explains some of the allure of Nina Rechnoy. It is as if V.'s recognition that the portrait must remain incomplete, and even a parody of any attempt at biographical completeness, has prompted Sebastian's shade to agree to another sitting or two.

In his last year of life Sebastian becomes convinced he has unwarrantably neglected the ordinary, just as he has always neglected his rather colorless half brother. It is this that prompts him to plan the fictitious biography of a decidedly unexceptional "Mr. H.," and to write to V. just before he dies. This mysterious last letter induces in V. an ominously portentous dream of Sebastian. Later that week, as he rushes through the dark to Sebastian's bedside, he seems himself to enter the world of dream, night, the Stygian mist of Sebastian's last novel: his panic almost takes him across to that other shore where Sebastian now dwells. After this brush near death V. circles back to explore Sebastian's life. By its parodic account of the search, V.'s book follows the rhythms of Sebastian's mind, as if he were "consciously living" in Sebastian's soul—and yet the parody that proves how well he has tuned himself to Sebastian's mental undulations depends on the impossibility of the mortal quest for another's self. V.'s frustrations attest to the fact that the utter independence of souls must be the very basis of mortal existence—but the novel also suggests that even ordinary mortals in passing through death might become artists of a kind more gifted than the most talented of human imaginations and learn how to follow the contours of real, not merely invented, souls.

But if we peer closely at Silbermann, the figure who most vividly suggests that Sebastian's shade may have guided V., we see that he is not a real person nudged into V.'s path by some spectral influence but a purely magical creature, and almost an escapee from one of Sebastian's books. Rather than "I am Sebastian," we must read "Sebastian is I": Sebastian seems to have invented V. and his entire quest for Sebastian Knight. If we accept that conclusion, the whole of *The Real Life of Sebastian Knight* would mirror Sebastian's first novel, where during a murder investigation the corpse disappears, and one of the suspects unmasks himself to disclose that he is the man presumed dead.

Once we discern such parallels between Sebastian's novels on the one hand and the quest for Nina or the account of that quest on the other, they begin to multiply until we see that the novels have been designed from the start to reflect the retracing of Sebastian's life. Not only the search for Sebastian must be a fiction, but his mortal life— even those parts of it that have appeared blessedly accessible, his books—begins to dissolve. The further we press the quest for Sebastian, the less we know about him. At this stage, having reached a point where we recognize that the writer within the novel has invented every part of Sebastian that we see, we might as well concede that this author after all is Vladimir Nabokov.

Of course we knew before we picked up the book that Nabokov was its author. But in trying to remain on the level of the book, we fall through one trapdoor after another: V. as mad, V. as Sebastian, V. transmuted into Sebastian via Sebastian's shade, Sebastian inventing V., Sebastian himself totally invented. The drop from level to level has been designed from the start, and Nabokov makes us aware of the sinking in the pit of our stomach as we fall from floor to floor. He plays with our reluctance to close the covers on the book's world, to leave the level on which things seem to exist. The riddle of being, he suggests, is something we have to try to answer within life, but the solution can come, if at all, only on shutting life up.

That is one way to read the book: as a philosophical puzzle cut to Nabokov's impersonal plan. But V.'s dissolving into Sebastian and Sebastian into Nabokov can also be read in an opposite way that makes the human and the personal urgent again.

The story of Nina is the heart of the book: why does Sebastian leave the wonderful Clare Bishop and fall helplessly in love with a woman who soon tires of him and makes him wretched? This mysterious lover is pinned down only when V. discovers that a woman ostensibly talking about someone else has been talking about herself—just as V. may be none other than Sebastian talking about himself, or the "someone whom neither of us knows" may be the author talking about himself in a way that disguises his personal disclosures.

The Real Life of Sebastian Knight is a novel about the inaccessibility of the past. But Sebastian's past has been inaccessible for V. only because he respected his brother's privacy. After Sebastian's death V. visits his flat and finds two separate bundles of letters. After only a moment's hesitation, he follows Sebastian's instructions to destroy them unread. One bundle, as he guesses from the handwriting, must come from Clare Bishop; the other, as he notices just before the fire turns the paper black, from a woman writing in Russian. V. spends the next few months discovering that to understand Sebastian's last years he must find out who that Russian woman was.

In his own life Nabokov hoped that, after his request to Irina Guadanini, *his* letters to her would be destroyed, and that his private life would frustrate any future researcher as thoroughly as Sebastian's privacy would have frustrated V. had not Silbermann magically intervened. With his past apparently sunk, and with the self-contained and self-reflexive structure of *The Real Life of Sebastian Knight* appearing to exclude external referents and to argue against searching for them, Nabokov could touch on his own immediate personal themes: his change of language, his burying of his past with Irina Guadanini.

Mme Lecerf feigns not to be Russian, and it is the proof that she is that gives her real identity away. Sebastian at Cambridge and after had also pretended not to be Russian, but cannot escape his identity at the end: he is classed as "the Russian gentleman" in the sanatorium where he dies. In order to recount the life of an apparently English author who ultimately cannot cut his Russian heartstrings, V. must himself become an English writer against his will. In his first English novel, knowing he will have to set Russian fiction aside, Nabokov distances the agony of that sacrifice into art—but lets us glimpse what his forswearing his language and heritage will cost him.

When Sebastian imprudently leaves his English mistress for the Russian Nina Rechnoy, part of her allure is that she reminds Sebastian of his first love, Natasha Rosanov. Sebastian's first idyll with Natasha on the quiet waters of a Russian river* pointedly recalls Nabokov's own first love for Valentina Shulgin, to whom, back in 1915, he consecrated all his early Russian verse. Nabokov declares obliquely that while his mind tells him he ought now to remain an English writer, his heart urges him back, against all prudence, to the charms of his Russian muse.

Although Nina evokes Russia, she is also simply herself, a strangely alluring woman for whom Sebastian feels a passion that causes him to leave the splendid woman he loved. Nabokov has projected onto Sebastian a stylized alternative continuation of his own recent past: a writer leaves a woman obviously ideal for him to follow another who fatally attracts him, and finds his life destroyed as a consequence.

Wondering at Sebastian's highly oblique use of his intimate life, V. declares:

> The light of personal truth is hard to perceive in the shimmer of an imaginary nature, but what is still harder to understand is the amazing fact

* The link between Nina Rechnoy and Natasha Rosanov is marked by the fact that *rechnoy* is the Russian adjective from *reka*, "river."

that a man writing of things which he really felt at the time of writing, could have had the power to create simultaneously—and out of the very things which distressed his mind—a fictitious and faintly absurd character.

It is even harder to understand how Nabokov could generate out of the things that distressed *him* a book that blends intensely personal emotion and such detached, exhilarating intellectual delight.

Searching for an Exit: France, 1939–1940

> DR. RAY'S VOICE: They have all their papers now.
>
> They are all set to go.
>
> Good-bye, gray Paree!
>
> HUMBERT: Good-bye, gray Paree. Now, my dear,
>
> don't lose your passport.
>
> —*Lolita: A Screenplay*

I

UNCERTAIN of his English in *The Real Life of Sebastian Knight*, Nabokov in January 1939 asked his friend Lucie Léon Noel to check his manuscript for solecisms. She recalls:

> Volodia started coming over several afternoons a week, around 3 p.m. He was always on time. He was most anxious that this first novel in English should sound neither "foreign" nor read as though it had been translated into English. We both sat at the large mahogany desk and worked for several hours each time.

That mahogany table was the one at which for twelve years Paul Léon had worked with Joyce on *Finnegans Wake*: an apostolic succession for our times!

> I would read out a sentence and see how it sounded. Most of it read amazingly smoothly. Occasionally a word had to be changed, or a more suitable synonym sought. Sometimes one word was better than two. We would argue the point, and I might delete my suggestion, or he would capitulate. He would then read it out again, in his deep baritone, and I would listen. We had a little trouble with certain passages, but the author knew exactly the manner in which he wished to convey his thoughts. With most passages we had no trouble at all.
>
> I was so entranced by the sheer magic of the story that I could hardly wait to see how it would all end. Every evening I would tell my husband about it.[1]

One day in early February, while these afternoon sessions were still in progress, the Léons invited the Nabokovs to dinner with their friends James Joyce and Eugène and Maria Jolas, publishers of the avant-garde magazine *transition*. The Léons were disappointed that Nabokov did not sparkle that night before Joyce, and Mme Léon wondered whether he might have felt intimidated. Reading her memoir thirty years later Nabokov was amused to be accused for once of bashfulness rather than arrogance:

> . . . but is her impression correct? She pictures me as a timid young artist; actually I was forty, with a sufficiently lucid awareness of what I had already done for Russian letters preventing me from feeling awed in the presence of any living writer. (Had Mrs. Léon and I met more often at parties, she might have realized that I am always a disappointing guest, neither inclined nor able to shine socially.)[2]

Nabokov's own impression of the occasion was simply "a long friendly evening of talk. I do not recall one word of it but my wife remembers that Joyce asked about the exact ingredients of *myod*, the Russian 'mead,' and everybody gave him a different answer." Joyce gave Nabokov a copy of *Haveth Childers Everywhere*, one of the advance versions (1930) of part of *Finnegans Wake*. Nabokov had nothing yet published in English, alas, to hand Joyce in return.[3]

Nabokov spent a few days in bed with bronchitis in the second week of February—not very restful in the confines of 8 rue de Saigon—before he and his family moved down into the Porte de St. Cloud area, the heart of poorer Russian Paris, to the grandly named but small and shabby Hotel Royal Versailles, 31 rue Le Marois, where Avgust Kaminka and his wife also lived. Wherever they moved, Nabokov found Paris oppressive, and in later years would always recall it as the gray, gloomy city on the Seine. Sitting in the Deux Magots with George Hessen and his French translator, he ran the city down. "Parizh," he would say, in the Russian manner: "Pas riche."[4]

Even as Nabokov had rushed to complete *The Real Life of Sebastian Knight* in January he had been struck with a new idea for a book, "flashing like a hill, in my carriage window, now to the left, now to the right, and soon I'll get off and climb—I can already hear the crunching of the scree."[5] Whatever the idea, it was for a Russian work. He was still not ready to relinquish Russian, he was still part of an émigré community, he still had no immediate prospect of reaching England or America. His reputation guaranteed his work a place in the best émigré journals. *Sovremennye Zapiski* or *Russkie Zapiski* may not pay as much as a British or certainly an American publisher could afford, but what if those publishers across the waters did not buy his work at all? Nobody had taken his autobiographical sketches, and for the next two years *The Real Life of Sebastian Knight* would be rejected by one firm after another.

Apart from the practical pressures, there were the creative ones. Throughout 1939 the momentum of *The Gift* carried on almost undiminished. Nabokov had been delighted the previous October when Abram Kagan, who had run Petropolis Press in Berlin until Hitler squeezed him out, had agreed to publish *The Gift*, including the unpublished chapter 4. By December Nabokov hoped that the novel might already be at the printers. Whatever happened to the projected edition remains unclear, but Nabokov's imagination did not want to leave *The Gift* alone. At some time, apparently in 1939, he promised Aldanov a new novel, a continuation of *The Gift*, already by far his longest Russian novel.[6] In fact by late in the year that continuation had evolved into a new novel altogether, *Solus Rex*. Before the process of fission was quite complete, however, Nabokov seems to have entertained the idea of a two-volume *Gift*. What had loomed in his mind in January may have been either a first glimpse of volume two or perhaps an appendix that he certainly planned at some stage to add to volume one along with the story "The Circle," which he now saw as appendix one.

The spring of 1939 seems the likeliest time for Nabokov to have written this still unpublished "Second Appendix to *The Gift*."[7] In *The Gift* Fyodor in 1927 undertakes to write a biography of his father, but abandons it. When he comes to write *The Gift* itself, however, he relates at length in chapter 2 his attempt to compose the biography, and especially his efforts at accompanying his father in thought on his dangerous and mysterious last expedition. The "second appendix" consists of material prepared by Fyodor for the abandoned biography. He describes his frustration with the inadequate butterfly manuals of his childhood, always reluctant to tax the amateur by including subspecies and local races—which in fact is just what the eager amateur wants!—and particularly poor in regard to Russian fauna. Konstantin Godunov's *Butterflies and Moths of the Russian Empire* (four volumes out of a proposed six, 1912–1916), by contrast, supplies everything young Fyodor (or young Vladimir) could have dreamed of. Fyodor quotes "full-blooded and free-flowing" passages from his father's work that he considers the key to his own style, then summarizes at length his father's revolutionary notions about taxonomy, the species concept, evolution, and mimicry, as set out in a thirty-page résumé Konstantin Godunov composed on the eve of his fatal last journey. Especially in its opening pages, this "second appendix," despite its abstract and highly specialized nature, contains some of Nabokov's finest and most exciting writing. Nowhere else in his work do his passion for butterflies, his precision of memory, his penchant for metaphysical speculation, and his scrupulous science fuse at such heat.

II

Though still unable to resist his Russian muse, even after *The Real Life of Sebastian Knight*, Nabokov was becoming more and more determined to break into the English-speaking world. He secured a powerful letter of recommendation from Mikhail Rostovtzeff, the renowned archaeologist and ancient historian at Yale, to support his bid for a post in England, where he was headed in April on another reading-and-job-search mission.[8] He also drew up letters of recommendation for Ivan Bunin and the philosopher Nicholas Berdyaev to sign.[9] (Berdyaev he had met through their common friend Fondaminsky.) He asked Gleb Struve if, "in view of my catastrophic poverty," he would help organize a reading of his English pieces.[10] Since he could rely on Struve's English he did not draft a complete letter of recommendation for him, but confined himself to a few suggestions:

> A . . . author (embellish)
> Enjoys a wide . . . but owing to the special position of an émigré author poor!!!
> talented!! The pride of the emigration!!
> New Style!! . . .
> Grant or fellowship
> ~~Looking for a job, until~~
> He is looking for a job, and there is a possibility
> of his obtaining it, but for this he ought to stay in
> this country for a few months.

(That deleted "Looking for a job, until" is a revealing slip.) Three days later Nabokov wrote to Struve again "to express how the hope of a possibility of becoming established in England stirs me up. This is a life and death question for me. I implore you also to do all you can for a reading. I know this can't be easy for you, but if you knew how it is for me now—I'm simply perishing."[11]

That was literally true of his mother. Nabokov had left for London on April 1 before news came that his mother had been taken to hospital, to the third-class room that was all she could afford. Nabokov's own conditions in London on the other hand were a sudden step up to comfort. He stayed with the Sablins, the family of the former Russian chargé d'affaires—Konstantin Nabokov's successor—where a butler, "a perfect Jeeves," brought him breakfast in bed and looked for somewhere to dispose of the guest's unseemly hat. Nabokov checked in the British Museum's vast collections for other examples of the peculiar butterfly he had caught above Moulinet, and found nothing to match it. On April 5 he read new Russian works in the Sablins' reception room. A week later he read a chapter of *The Real Life of Sebastian Knight* at a dinner organized by Struve in the home of Struve's friend Angelica Harris (a Russian by birth) and her husband, Alan (a publisher by trade). The purpose of the evening was not just to display Nabokov on the elusive past but to amass donations and prospects for his murky future. One opportunity briefly gleamed in the Russian Department at the University of Leeds—and quickly faded.[12]

In the last week of April Nabokov returned to Paris and moved with Véra and Dmitri into a dingy apartment at 59 rue Boileau, where at least they would have two bedrooms with bath and kitchen. They had their remaining books and papers shipped from storage in Berlin.[13]

On May 2 Elena Nabokov died in Prague. Nabokov walked into a room where his high-spirited friends George Hessen and Mikhail Kaminka were devising a practical joke on him. " 'My mother died this morning' was all that he said in a simple uninflected voice, and he rubbed his forehead with his fingertips for just a moment."[14] Since his father's untimely death, the greatest tragedy of his European life had been his inability to support his mother and to spend as much time with her as he would have liked. Over the last seven years he had seen her only during one spell of a few weeks in the summer of 1937, he had not been with her during her final illness, and now he had to reconcile himself to not attending her funeral. He was also deeply concerned at what would happen to his eight-year-old nephew Rostislav, his sister Olga's son, whom his mother had raised. For all his fondness for the boy, he had to accept that he was unable to help. After the war, as the Communists closed in on Czechoslovakia, he would try to sponsor Rostislav to join him in America, but he would be too late.

In April Eugene Vinaver, brother of one of V. D. Nabokov's Constitutional Democrat colleagues and now professor of French at the University of Manchester, had written inviting Nabokov to speak. On the strength of Nabokov's French essay on Pushkin, he asked him to talk on some aspect of nineteenth-century Franco-Russian literary relations. They would pay expenses and a fee.[15] This could be the opportunity Nabokov had been waiting for.

He reached London again on May 31, staying this time with Vera Haskell (related by marriage to Aldanov) and her family. Francis Haskell remembers Nabokov, who knew the boy was interested in butterflies, coming up in the evenings to chat with him in the nursery.[16] The

Manchester talk went ahead, presumably, but that would be as close as Nabokov ever came to a position in Britain.

Then for a moment it seemed an American job might materialize just as Nabokov had hoped. The Harvard historian he had met and liked in Prague and Berlin, Mikhail Karpovich, wrote to say that his former student Philip Mosely, now on the Cornell faculty, was an enthusiastic Sirin fan and wanted him for a temporary but possibly renewable post. Nabokov cabled his acceptance at once, but this lifeline too was withdrawn, and Nabokov would be an American citizen and almost fifty before he began to teach at Cornell.[17]

III

The day Nabokov returned from London to Paris, June 14, marked the death of his friend Vladislav Khodasevich, in Nabokov's judgment "the greatest Russian poet of our time." He had last seen him a month earlier. When he had called again on May 21, Khodasevich's cancer had already become too far advanced for him to receive his friend. Nabokov attended the funeral and wrote a majestic tribute to Khodasevich for *Sovremennye Zapiski*.[18]

Nabokov had not expected to afford a holiday in the summer of 1939, but something his translators had sold (perhaps "The Potato Elf," which was published in *Esquire* later that year) suddenly made travel possible. Retaining their Paris flat, the family headed off at the end of June for the Savoy Alps. They had written ahead to the Pension Briandon in the village of Seythenex, but on inspection refused to take the rooms, and the proprietress instead found them pleasant, quiet quarters in a friend's home. Dmitri enjoyed the change of clime and fauna almost as much as his father, but not the food. After the boy's second round of stomach troubles, his parents decided to descend from the mountains. They bought tickets for Cannes, but with no definite destination in mind. On the train, French travelers warned them there would be no accommodation left in Cannes at this point of the season. Why not get off at Fréjus?

They did. Nabokov took Dmitri to the beach while Véra went looking for rooms in St. Aygulf. When she returned, Nabokov had already found a pleasant Russian pension, Pension Rodnoy. There they could have two rooms not booked up until the beginning of August, and then transfer to the ground floor of a house that their buoyant Polish-Russian proprietress had located for them nearby. Both places were close to the wide, sandy beach where the Nabokovs spent almost every day that summer.[19]

Here as at Seythenex Nabokov rethought parts of *The Waltz Invention* for the planned Russian Theater production at the end of the year.[20] At the end of July he also received the latest issue of *Sovremennye Zapiski*, in which his dignified memorial piece for Khodasevich appeared—and something else he had written that Khodasevich would have appreciated even more.

Throughout the 1930s, Khodasevich and Nabokov had each been convinced that the other was regularly denied his due by the Paris critics, and especially Adamovich, the most influential, for no better reason than envy. Over the last five years, Nabokov had written a few fine poems but had published none. It hardly seemed worthwhile: although even Adamovich had had to concede the brilliance of his prose, he still dismissed Sirin's verse outright, and other critics took up his tune. On Khodasevich's death, Nabokov wrote another poem, "Poety" ("The Poets"). To trap Adamovich, he composed it in a meter he had never used in his mature poetry, signed it "Vasily Shishkov," and sent it off to *Sovremennye Zapiski*.[21]

His hoax succeeded even better than Khodasevich's "Vasily Travnikov" fabrication of 1936. Adamovich failed to spot the clues contained in the pseudonym—which echoes and pays homage to "Vasily Travnikov" not only in sound but in sense, or rather in two senses.* On August 17 Adamovich's review of the latest *Sovremennye Zapiski* appeared in *Poslednie Novosti*, asking: "Who is Vasily Shishkov? . . . Every line, every word is talented." Adamovich cited all he could and lamented he had no space "to quote the whole of this splendid poem, but once again I must ask who is this Vasily Shishkov? Where does he come from? It is quite possible that in a year or two everyone to whom Russian poetry is dear will know his name."[22] Late in August, as the Hitler-Stalin pact was signed and the threat of war rumbled louder, Nabokov read Adamovich's review and could not resist the light relief of a playful answer to the repeated "Who is Vasily Shishkov?" He sat down at once to write the story "Vasily Shishkov," published this time over his regular pen name, Sirin.[23]

In this slight, curious piece the young poet Vasily Shishkov collars Sirin at a literary evening and asks him to read his poetry. He tests Sirin's frankness by handing him a sheaf of poor verse he has concocted that morning. Welcoming the older writer's forthright disap-

---

* In an innocent sense "Shishkov" could derive from *shishka*, pine cone, thereby matching the botanical root of *trava*, grass, in "Travnikov." But the word *travit'*, meaning to bait, to badger, seems a likelier reason for Khodasevich's choosing the name for his invented poet, and Nabokov allows for that sense of provocation too, since *shish* means a *fico*, a gesture of contempt with the fingers. Shishkov was also the maiden name of Nabokov's great-grandmother, Nina von Korff.

proval, he then brings out a thin, worn sheaf: his *real* verse, which Sirin reads with delight. Shishkov seeks his support in setting up a freakish émigré journal. When the venture fails, he asks Sirin to look after his verse should he disappear. Nothing more is heard of him: he vanishes without trace.

The story eerily reflects both the mood of the Shishkov poem "The Poets" (we poets, unable to bear more, will simply fade away—into death, into silence) and the disappearance, first into poetic silence and now into death, of Khodasevich himself. Apart from the sheer cheek of the whole thing, the story's main charms are the characterization of the half-naive, half-canny Shishkov, a sort of émigré Rimbaud, and Nabokov's comments on criticism of his own work: "As to the so-called Readers' Judgment, I feel, at that trial, not as the defendant, but, at best, as a distant relative of one of the least important witnesses."

When the story was published, Adamovich was forced to admit he had been duped. He tried to justify his enthusiasm: "In parodies and counterfeits, inspiration sometimes breaks utterly free and even forgets it began in play." Mellowly magnanimous in victory, Nabokov responded many years later—and after Adamovich had given him his belated due—"I fervently wish all critics to be as generous as he."[24]

IV

The Nabokovs returned to rue Boileau at the beginning of September.[25] On the eve of war, Paris was much quieter than it had been in the previous summer's panic: now, people calmly accepted that history had changed gear and the time had come to prepare for battle. Two days before war was declared, a blackout was imposed. Electricity department workers leaned their long ladders against the ornate streetlamps to veil the lights. Residents bought blue paper strips to cover their windows and soon grew accustomed to the daytime gloom within. Schoolchildren were evacuated from Paris by the trainload. In 1914 crowds had thronged the streets cheering "A bas le Kaiser!" Twenty-five years later, on the morning of September 3, 1939, rain fell heavily on Paris, and the glistening pavements were quiet and almost empty. When war was declared, the few shoppers and workers about on the streets clutched their gas masks in their hands and strode purposefully on.

Like many parents who feared Paris would be bombed, the Nabokovs sent their child out of town, to stay with Anna Feigin in Deauville. Nabokov looked around him at the changed city and wrote in English a brief sketch—now lost—of Paris at war. He submitted it to leading British and American magazines such as the *Spectator* and the *Atlantic*. *Esquire* thought it "poised, frequently distinguished writing—but a prose poem," and like the other journals, declined to publish.[26]

Unaware of this piece Mark Aldanov, who worked at *Poslednie Novosti*, responded to the typescript of "Vasily Shishkov" that Nabokov had sent there: "It's war! War! How can you waste your time on such trifles?" As Nabokov later commented, "Aldanov regards literature as a sort of enormous Pen Club or Masonic Lodge binding talented and *talentlos* writers alike to a smug contract of mutual good-will, consideration, assistance and favorable reviews."[27]

Aldanov's literary diplomacy may have been of no value to Nabokov, but his personal help would be a godsend. Late in the summer Professor Henry Lanz of Stanford University had asked Aldanov if he would be interested in teaching a summer course in Russian literature at Stanford in either 1940 or 1941. Since Aldanov did not at that stage plan to move to the United States he suggested Lanz approach Nabokov.[28] His friend was delighted: although it was only a short-term position, it would immediately remove much of the difficulty of obtaining an American visa. At last, after seven years, his dream might be realized.

No one in America or Britain wanted to publish *The Real Life of Sebastian Knight*, and with no other new work to sell Nabokov had no money at all. He and Aldanov were the only Russian writers in Paris who had tried to live exclusively on their literary labors. For Aldanov, that included his post at *Poslednie Novosti*. In Nabokov's case, there was no such steady prop, and from the time he returned from Fréjus his friend Savely Kyandzhuntsev, who now owned a cinema, had to support him to the extent of a thousand francs a month.[29] Welcome patronage, but not enough. Nabokov advertised in *Poslednie Novosti* for English-language pupils. Three people responded: the daughter of a Russian Jewish public figure; Roman Grynberg, a businessman with a keen interest in literature; and Maria Marinel, a musician.[30] Both Grynberg and Maria Marinel and her sisters became friends of the Nabokovs, not only in the little time left them in Paris but also through the decades they overlapped in America, where Grynberg even started up a journal that would publish some of Nabokov's few late Russian works.

Maria, Ina, and Elizaveta Marinel formed a successful harp trio (hence the stage surname formed from their first names—their original surname had been Gutman). Since Maria was not physically strong, Elizaveta accompanied her through blacked-out Paris, meekly waiting downstairs during the hour-long lessons. After two or three lessons, Nabokov found out. "How could you do such a thing? Bring her up straight away!" From that point on Elizaveta would sit in the apartment during the lesson. Once while her sister was "in class," talking English, Elizaveta noticed Nabokov turn round to the clock and suddenly switch to Russian. The hour was up: like Fyodor, Nabokov would not teach a moment beyond the contracted time.[31]

At the end of September a bout of influenza brought on an attack of intercostal neuralgia which kept Nabokov in bed for a week. There a new story came to mind:

> As far as I can recall, the initial shiver of inspiration was somehow prompted by a newspaper story about an ape in the Jardin des Plantes, who, after months of coaxing by a scientist, produced the first drawing ever charcoaled by an animal: this sketch showed bars of the poor creature's cage.[32]

Perhaps Nabokov misremembered a photograph that appeared in the newspapers that year: a chimpanzee at the London zoo with a paintbrush in its hand.[33] In any case the inspiration merged with another idea. In *The Gift* Zina's repellent stepfather confides to Fyodor that if he had time he would whip off a novel about a man who marries a woman in order to have access to her daughter, only to find the daughter cold and aloof. Plainly, he is telling his own story, and Zina's hostility toward her stepfather and her reluctance to allow Fyodor the least hint of tenderness within their apartment spring from the stepfather's clumsy advances a few years earlier. Now Nabokov returned to the situation but chose a more single-minded pervert who finds that the marriage that should provide illicit freedom of access to his stepdaughter becomes his cage, from which death is the only exit.

Nabokov spent October and November writing "Volshebnik" ("The Enchanter"), his longest short story or his shortest novella.[34]

V
"The Enchanter" ("Volshebnik")

A forty-year-old with an unfulfilled passion for young girls marries an ailing woman for the sake of her twelve-year-old daughter. When the mother dies he takes the daughter on holiday, hoping to fool her a move at a time into accepting sex as a fairy-tale game. But that first night he cannot resist fondling her sleeping body. As he dissolves in bliss, he sees her now wide-awake eyes staring at him in horror. She begins to scream uncontrollably. He rushes out to escape from her, from the staring hotel guests, from life itself—and is hit by a thundering truck.

Can we assess this long story in its own right, or only as a precursor to *Lolita*? Like Humbert, the protagonist here sees his private fancies as vastly more subtle, refined, and altogether remarkable than ordinary adult passion, but also as something to be confined to the realm of mere longing—until a particular girl and the prospect of access to her through her mother lead him further than he intends. But the wooing and death of the mother lack the special combination of suburban plausibility and fairy-tale wish fulfillment that makes healthy Charlotte Haze's proposal to Humbert and the surprise of her death so artistically satisfying.

"The Enchanter" suffers in other ways. There is no Quilty, of course, but also no Annabel Leigh, no childhood precursor, no island of entranced time to add a metaphysical shimmer to the tale. At the same time the story remains far too abstract. Paris and the Riviera are static backdrops, not playgrounds for the eye and the imagination like Humbert's America; the nameless central trio are mere outlines beside the luminous colors and subtle shading of Lolita, Charlotte, Humbert.

Because Humbert tells his own story every page of *Lolita* crackles with tension: between his free self-consciousness and his unrelenting obsession, between his guilt and his confidence that his case transcends everyday morals. In "The Enchanter" the third-person narration neither animates nor enchants. Nabokov tries to compensate for the abstraction of the story and the absence of a live storyteller by the sheer stuffing of style. Eager to reveal his character's mind but overanxious not to appear limited by its capacity or confined by its predilections, Nabokov begins with uncharacteristic and unconvincing ponderousness as the hero supposedly muses in self-justification:

> Knowing, rationally, that the Euphrates apricot is harmful only in canned form; that sin is inseparable from civic custom; that all hygienes have their hyenas; knowing, moreover, that this selfsame rationality is not averse to vulgarizing that to which it is otherwise denied access . . .

Even if *Lolita* had never been written, "The Enchanter" would still have to be judged a failure. No matter how intelligent, the story's style cannot by itself vivify its unrealized world. Nevertheless we should be grateful for this failed experiment. It reminds us that even after his bold choice of subject in *Lolita*, Nabokov still had to find the characters, psychology, plot, setting, narrative voice, and tone to suit. "The Enchanter" testifies to the sheer difficulty of the task he undertook in *Lolita*, no matter how easy, how harmonious, how perfect he made it all look on his second try.

"One blue-papered wartime night" Nabokov read the story to a group of friends: Aldanov, Fondaminsky, Zenzinov, and his doctor, Mme Kogan-Bernstein. But *Sovremennye Zapiski* did not take it. Nabokov offered it to Abram Kagan of Petropolis Press—a story in the style of Boccaccio and Aretino, he described it—but the war had halted Petropolis's program, and in any case Nabokov himself began to feel dissatisfied with his own work. It remained unpublished until almost ten years after his death.[35]

VI

By late October 1939 Nabokov had settled arrangements at Stanford with Lanz. Now ready to apply for a visa, he sought affidavits from eminent Russians in America: the artist Mstislav Dobuzhinsky, the sociologist Pitirim Sorokin, and his friend the historian Mikhail Karpovich, who appears to have put him in touch with Alexandra Tolstoy, the novelist's daughter. Head of the newly established Tolstoy Foundation, which looked after the interests of Russian émigrés in America, Alexandra Tolstoy secured an affidavit for Nabokov from Sergey Koussevitzky, the longtime conductor of the Boston Symphony Orchestra.[36]

While Nabokov struggled with bureaucratic rigmarole, he had also been grappling for months with something far more congenial, a chess problem that would be "totally new." He hoped to construct a problem whose solution an ordinary solver could find without difficulty, while an expert would be misled into suspecting a more sophisticated solution and only after the "pleasurable torments" of chasing this mirage

> the by now ultrasophisticated solver would reach the simple key move (bishop to c2) as somebody on a wild goose chase might go from Albany to New York by way of Vancouver, Eurasia and the Azores. The pleasant experience of the roundabout route (strange landscapes, gongs, tigers, exotic customs, the thrice-repeated circuit of a newly married couple around the sacred fire of an earthen brazier) would amply reward him for the misery of the deceit, and after that, his arrival at the simple key move would provide him with a synthesis of poignant artistic delight.

In *Speak, Memory*, where Nabokov equates the conception of that chess problem with the simple solution to the problem of exile (America!), he misdates the problem to mid-May 1940, immediately before his departure. In fact it was on November 19, 1939, that he at last managed to express this unprecedented chess theme, and, realizing its novelty, set down his own gloss on the problem at once.[37] But there was a good reason for his later confusion about dates: within weeks of composing his chess problem, he realized that with the affidavits that he had obtained, the real-life problem of an American visa was solved.

The visas could not be picked up without exit permits from France. With Dmitri still in Deauville, Véra Nabokov was free to traipse from office to office and *guichet* to *guichet*. At the préfecture she was told their passports had been lost. For the only time in her life she resorted to a bribe. Telling the official she absolutely had to have the passports, she was ushered into a small room where no one could overhear. When the official left in search of the passports, she placed 200 francs on the table. "What's this?" he asked on his return. "It's for you," she replied. "I want those passports." He disappeared again, leaving her wondering would he return with someone to arrest her. Instead he informed her that the passports were at the Ministry of the Interior. Since most subway stations were closed on account of the war, she had to make the long trek to the Ministry of the Interior on foot. Although the passports were not there either, this time staff were helpful and rang around to discover that they were at the Foreign Ministry. Two months after the ordeal began, Nabokov was at last called in to sign for the passports and the *visas de sortie*—while his wife worried that this might still be a trap to arrest him for the bribe.[38]

In mid-December, long before all their papers had been safely stamped, Dmitri returned from Deauville as the calm of the "phony war" lulled Paris into thinking it was safe.[39] He was an obstreperous child and rarely restrained. While his parents staged a party in their small flat, he played with a toy airplane in the same room, adding his whine and roar to the plane's. The noise was deafening, but the Nabokovs allowed it to continue. Elizaveta Marinel suggested to Dmitri: "People don't understand. Let's go to your room." She sat with him next door so that the party could go on. His parents came in every ten minutes, grateful and embarrassed that their new friend was sacrificing her time for the sake of the party.[40]

Nina Berberova remembers another incident. When she came to visit, she was surprised to see a flat almost empty, with barely any furniture. Nabokov, who had had influenza, was lying on his bed, pale and thin. As they chatted, he suddenly stood up and took his guest into the five-year-old Dmitri's room.

> On the floor lay toys, and a child of exceptional beauty and refinement crawled among them. Nabokov took a huge boxing glove and gave it to the boy, telling him to show me his art, and Mitya, having put on the

glove, began with all his child's strength to beat Nabokov about the face. I saw this was painful to Nabokov but he smiled and endured it. This was training, his and the boy's. With a feeling of relief I left the room when this was over.[41]

Nabokov wanted to prepare his son to face the world with courage and without complaint. But doting on Dmitri as he did, he was brought to the verge of panic by the thought that he might lose his son in the war, and that dread haunted his imagination powerfully enough for the image of the loss of a child to shape his fiction for another twenty years: directly in *Bend Sinister*, "Signs and Symbols," and "Lance"; in a bizarrely inverted form in *Lolita*; in the mirror-reversal of *Pale Fire*'s Hazel Shade.

Sometimes when Nabokov wrote through the night, Véra would ask a friend the next day to take Dmitri so that his father could catch up on his rest.[42] By now Nabokov's current work was his last, never-to-be-completed, Russian novel.

VII
From *The Gift* to *Solus Rex*

Here a manuscript allows us a rare glance at Nabokov's creative processes, at all the continuities, disruptions, redirections, and reappropriations normally disguised by the self-containedness and the apparent inevitability of the finished works. In a folder marked "*The Gift*, Part II," Nabokov mapped out part of a second volume of *The Gift*.[43] One chapter shows Fyodor and Zina settled in Paris in 1937, having escaped from Germany: Fyodor returns to their one-roomed flat one day eager to write, but when he sees that Zina cannot rid the place of her stepfather's nephew, an enthusiastic Nazi, he storms out in a rage.

An outline of the "last chapter" has Zina killed in a ridiculous accident. Fyodor grieves for her, both on the Riviera, where he meets a man named Falter, and back in wartime Paris, where he sees Koncheyev. The novel ends with Fyodor reading to Koncheyev his continuation of Pushkin's unfinished drama, "Rusalka" ("The Water-Nymph"). Like *The Gift* itself, this projected second volume was to end with Pushkin, but with much less radiance ahead.

In *The Gift* the last, *Eugene Onegin*–like, paragraph rounds the novel off with a flourish, but at the same time it hints at something unfinished, both in its own story (Fyodor and Zina about to return to that locked apartment) and in its allusion to the abrupt, pointedly unresolved ending of *Eugene Onegin*. In the continuation, Nabokov planned to complete an unfinished Pushkin work as a means to a second ending-that-is-not-an-ending. Since the whole novel was to have been structured around Zina's death, it is no accident that in the conclusion to "Rusalka" Nabokov has the prince lured down through a watery death to meet the immortal spirit of the girl who died for love of him. Several years later in America, when he had at last abandoned all hope of completing the novel, Nabokov published this conclusion to Pushkin's poem separately and in his own name, with no indication that it had been composed to serve quite another function.[44]

Another line of development suggested itself. After Zina's death Fyodor derives pleasure only from an internal life that has as little as possible to do with an external world he now considers quite meaningless. Nabokov has Fyodor engage a prostitute and savor with grim satisfaction the disparity between their banal trysts and the private mental shimmer with which he surrounds them. Good readers of Nabokov will sit up with a jolt on reading these encounters: Nabokov not only drops here line after line that he will pick up ten years later for Humbert's meeting with a young French prostitute ("*Je vais m'acheter des bas*," for instance, and a comment on the girl's emphatic manner of accenting the "b"), but he also lets slip the name Botkin, which he will retrieve twenty years later for *Pale Fire*.

Nabokov may have developed some of the strands of his projected continuation of *The Gift* during the creative quiet of spring and summer 1939, but references to Fréjus and the war indicate that he filled the notebook no earlier than September 1939. Perhaps he broke off the project then to follow the more urgent inspiration of "The Enchanter," and found by the end of November that the idea of a husband's reeling before the senselessness of his wife's death* had taken on too much life of its own to remain part of *The Gift*. By now it had begun to evolve into a new novel altogether: *Sclus Rex*.

What was to have been this new novel's second chapter was published in the last issue of *Sovremennye Zapiski* in April 1940, and must have therefore been completed by February. Since Nabokov would not commit part of a work to print without everything in place, he must have had the whole novel designed by the beginning of 1940, no more than a month after he completed "The Enchanter" and returned to the theme of bereavement in the new setting he now had in mind for it.

"Ultima Thule," presumably written in March and April 1940, was to have been chapter 1 of *Solus Rex*.[45] When the novel was finally abandoned, it was published as a separate story that takes the form of a

---

* Perhaps an echo of Nabokov's retrospective dread that he might have lost Véra through his affair with Irina Guadanini?

letter from the artist Sineusov to his recently dead wife. Perfectly lucid but still saturated by grief, he mocks the absurdity of addressing his dead beloved and speculates on her possible reactions if she can read what he writes.

Sineusov wants to tell his wife of Adam Falter, his former tutor in St. Petersburg, whom they had recently met on the Riviera. Falter seems to have been driven mad after stumbling by chance on the answer to the riddle of the universe (when he makes the mistake of explaining it to a psychiatrist, the psychiatrist promptly dies of heart failure). Always fascinated by metaphysics and now desperate for some glimmer of hope that his wife somehow survives, Sineusov tries to lure Falter into disclosing his secret, but Falter, although plainly something more and something less than human,* easily outmaneuvers his interlocutor—and then declares that "amid all the piffle and prate I inadvertently gave myself away—only two or three words, but in them flashed a fringe of absolute insight—luckily, though, you paid no attention." This marvelous story, one of Nabokov's best, succeeds in numerous ways: the anguish of Sineusov's bereavement, visible under his compulsive, self-defensive playfulness about death; the superb speculations his mind gives rise to; the images of Falter before "the bomb of truth . . . exploded in him"; the image of Falter *after* this event, which manages to convince us for the duration of the story to suspend disbelief in a man both unable to retain any normal attachment to the world—he cannot even switch on a light—and at the same time possessed of an all-resolving insight; and the metaphysical catch-as-catch-can between Falter and Sineusov.

Within "Ultima Thule" there are no more than a few slight hints at the story's connection with the Thulean strands of *Solus Rex*. Some Nordic poet has apparently commissioned Sineusov to illustrate a long poem of his, entitled "Ultima Thule." Though the poet disappears and seems unlikely to return, Sineusov continues to work on the project as a way of keeping the pangs of his wife's loss at bay. As he writes to her, " 'Ultima Thule,' that island born in the desolate, gray sea of my heartache for you, now attracted me as the home of my least expressible thoughts." Nabokov comments:

> In the course of evolving an imaginary country (which at first merely diverted him from his grief, but then grew into a self-contained artistic obsession), the widower becomes so engrossed in Thule that the latter starts to develop its own reality. Sineusov mentions in Chapter One that he is moving from the Riviera to his former apartment in Paris; actually,

---

* *Falter* is German for "butterfly": like a butterfly, he has been through a process of radical metamorphosis.

he moves into a bleak palace on a bleak northern island.* His art helps him to resurrect his wife in the disguise of Queen Belinda, a pathetic act which does not let him triumph over death even in the world of free fancy. In Chapter Three she was to die again, killed by a bomb meant for her husband, on the new bridge across the Egel, a few minutes after returning from the Riviera.[46]

Chapter 2 of *Solus Rex*, published separately as a story of the same name, shows us the king on the day his wife will die.[47] He recalls how he found himself on the throne exactly five years ago after discovering he was unwittingly enmeshed in an assassination plot against his cousin Prince Adulf, heir to the Thulean throne.

Much in Ultima Thule and the whole of *Solus Rex* anticipates Zembla and *Pale Fire*: a direct metaphysical probing of death; an imaginary northern land with an imaginary northern language; palace intrigues, a queen in the Riviera, the wrong person assassinated, the term *solus rex* itself and the accompanying image of a solitary king; a heady atmosphere of homosexuality and a mirror-inversion of ordinary morals. Nevertheless Zembla and Thule could not be more distinct. In Zembla all is crystalline, bathed in the serene light of Kinbote's self-satisfaction and his sense of the radiant harmony of his country and its inverted mores. Thule by contrast seems aptly summed up in its ubiquitous cobwebs or its tangled heather that, as legend reports, "entwined the stirrups and shins" of a disloyal army. Everything is webby and dangerous, a disconcertingly complex, branching array of politics, history, sociology, and psychology in which the naive, uneasy, self-reproachful King repeatedly suffers the embarrassment of finding himself snagged in a thorny world.

One of the finest things in the story is the contrast between the hesitant, asocial K., who although King seems constitutionally unable to master the rules by which his world works, and his ebullient, decadent cousin, the homosexual Prince Adulf, intuitively alert to the rules of any environment and ready to play them or break them at will. Both Adulf's assurance within the rules and his readiness to defy them seem to link him in some mysterious way with Falter (before *and* after his metamorphosis).

But what exactly are the connections between the two published fragments of *Solus Rex*? No doubt there were to be as many strange reverberations between their two disturbingly different worlds as between Shade's poem and Kinbote's commentary in *Pale Fire*, but the

---

* The name "Sineusov" already links ancient Rus and Scandinavia, for the earliest known rulers of Kievan Russia were the three Scandinavian princes Riurik, Sineus, and Truvor.

sheer magnitude of the difference both teases our curiosity and reminds us we cannot possibly guess at the whole from the magnificent parts that survive. Nabokov concludes his note on the novel: "what really makes me regret its non-completion is that it promised to differ radically, by the quality of its coloration, by the amplitude of its style, by something undefinable about its powerful underflow, from all my other works in Russian."[48]

It is worth noting the singular position of *The Gift* in its maker's oeuvre. In the five years before writing the book Nabokov composed six self-contained novels. *The Gift* itself then spanned the next five years and set up powerful reverberations in his mind that lasted for decades: the story "The Circle," in January 1934, still within Fyodor's world, like the unpublished lepidopterological "second appendix" to *The Gift*, of 1939; the protest against capital punishment in *Invitation to a Beheading*, an echo of Nikolay Chernyshevsky's protests but turning his method of social realism on its head; Nabokov's own autobiography, after Fyodor's invented one; *The Event*, rebounding from Fyodor's artist-as-hero to depict the artist as coward; the parodic biography of a writer's life in *The Real Life of Sebastian Knight*; "The Enchanter," developing into a novella Boris Shchyogolev's idea for a novel about a man who marries in the hope of securing access to his stepdaughter-to-be; and the planned second volume of *The Gift*, which then turns into *Solus Rex*, another novel conceived on a grand scale. "The Enchanter" and *Solus Rex* in turn become the original of *Lolita* on the one hand and *Bend Sinister* and *Pale Fire* on the other. Almost all of Nabokov's major artistic projects for thirty years can trace their origins back to *The Gift*.

Another strange fact. The two large-scale Russian projects Nabokov began after *The Real Life of Sebastian Knight*, "The Enchanter" and *Solus Rex*, both foundered before being salvaged and turned into eminently seaworthy English galleys, *Lolita* and *Pale Fire*. It was as if writing one novel in English unleashed something in Nabokov's personal fate or tilted something in his mind that would prevent his next Russian works from finding fulfillment until their transmutation into English.

VIII

In April 1940, after the German attack on Norway, headlines in France asked: "Whose turn next? Sweden? Holland? Romania? Yugoslavia?" No one thought to add Belgium and France. But already before the new German push toward Paris the Nabokovs were preparing to leave. By April 20 Vladimir had obtained a passport for himself and his family and was expecting to receive an American visa within the week.[49]

After France had refused him a work permit and condemned his family to near-poverty, after its officials had made America as difficult as possible to reach, Nabokov felt little loyalty to the country he found himself in. He had no desire whatsoever to be drafted into the French army and to leave behind a wife and son who as foreigners and Jews in a country vulnerable to Germany's military might would be gravely at risk. After Pearl Harbor, already feeling himself a loyal American in a country unlikely to be invaded, he would feel quite differently and would want to volunteer for service. But for now he saw his only duty as simply getting his family out.[50]

A Jewish rescue organization in New York, HIAS, had chartered a ship for a refugee crossing. The organization was directed by Yakov Frumkin, an old friend of Nabokov's father, who like many other Russian Jews was glad to be able to repay the dead man for his bold stands against the Kishinyov pogroms and the Beilis trial by now offering his son a cabin for half fare.[51]

With America appearing not far over the horizon, Nabokov had begun to fill several thin exercise books with notes for future lectures. Only skimpy fragments on Turgenev and *Anna Karenin* survive, but he could report to Karpovich that he had a full-year course on Russian literature ready and was delivering it to the walls of his room. Later he would recall having written perhaps two thousand pages of lecture notes.[52]

As departure loomed, Dmitri Nabokov recalls, the whole family worried whether the inspiration for *Solus Rex* could survive all the dislocations of the journey.[53] It would not, and Nabokov would have to pack away in his trunks and leave them there for years not only his unpublishable "The Enchanter" and his uncompletable *Solus Rex* but all his fame in the Russian emigration. Twenty years later, with "The Enchanter" now metamorphosed into *Lolita* and with *Solus Rex* reforming in his mind as *Pale Fire*, he would sail back across the Atlantic—on a liner proud to display in its library *Lolita* and the first of the Sirin novels to be translated in its wake—as a famous American writer headed for a triumphal tour of Europe and a series of grand parties to launch the French and English and Italian editions of his most famous novel.

None of this could be foreseen in the desperate spring of 1940. Before anything else, $560 had to be found for the remaining half fare, still an impossible sum for the Nabokovs to raise by themselves. A patroness of the arts, a Mrs. Marshak, organized a benefit reading for which, appropriately, Nabokov chose among other things "Cloud,

Castle, Lake." Aldanov and Frumkin took him around various wealthy Jewish families soliciting more funds. Many of the Nabokovs' old friends chipped in, too, and at last the fare was raised.[54]

In the second week of May, the Germans invaded Holland, Belgium, and Luxembourg, and killed and wounded more than a hundred in their first bombing raid over France. By May 15 they had overrun the French border at a number of points and the French commander-in-chief warned his government that he could not guarantee the security of Paris for more than a day. It was high time for Nabokov to say his farewells. He called on Kerensky, and found Bunin and the Merezhkovskys there. By now he was on tolerable speaking terms with Merezhkovsky's wife, Zinaida Gippius, and she was even prepared to recognize his talent. But she annoyed him with her questions: "You're going to America? Why are you going? Why are you going?" She began to insist that the Nabokovs travel to Calais by bus, for it was rumored that the French army had commandeered all trains for troop transport. Nabokov said goodbye to Kerensky, a perfunctory farewell to Bunin, and descended the steps with the oracular, dark-bearded Merezhkovsky and the overpainted Gippius.[55] The Russian émigré culture he had known had less than a month to live.

Nabokov left some of his books and papers in a wickerwork trunk in the large and airy basement of Ilya Fondaminsky's apartment building, along with his collection of European butterflies. When the Germans reached Paris in June, Fondaminsky's belongings were ransacked, the butterfly collection destroyed, the papers strewn in the street. Fondaminsky's niece managed to retrieve most of the papers, and after years lying in a coal cellar they reached the Nabokovs in America in 1950.[56] But Fondaminsky was taken off to a concentration camp and died there. Nabokov's brother Sergey, who had often called in to the flat on rue Boileau, was out of the city as the family made ready to leave. He too would die in a German camp.

As Nabokov and his family had left Russia in 1919, a last-minute hitch had delayed their boat until Bolshevik machine guns were strafing the harbor. Now on the eve of Nabokov's departure from France, around May 19, Dmitri was running a temperature of 104°. Dr. Kogan-Bernstein told his parents that if there were any other boat, she would advise them not to move him, but as there was none, they had no choice but to go. Nabokov was apprehensive lest signs of the boy's fever might prevent their being allowed on board.[57] They handed in the key of 59 rue Boileau—three weeks later the building was destroyed by German bombs—and left for the station.[58]

The German advance had been so rapid that the Nabokovs' boat, the *Champlain*, was now to leave not from Le Havre as first planned, and not from Cherbourg, the next choice, but from St. Nazaire, right around the spout of Brittany. Because of Dmitri's illness, they took a first-class sleeper and plied him with sulfamide tablets every four hours. They emerged from the station and walked down to the port with a healthy boy strolling between them, a parent in each hand.[59] Their worries were over.

ACKNOWLEDGMENTS

THIS HAS never been an official or authorized biography, but the book would never have been undertaken and written had not Véra Nabokov condoned my researches. She gave me access to her husband's papers in Montreux and the Library of Congress, she submitted to endless interviews, and she trusted to what I would do with my independence. In return I let her see all I wrote and took note of her painstaking comments on matters of style, fact, and interpretation in every part of my text and at several stages of its composition. Our occasionally lively, even fierce, disagreements have never impinged a jot on my freedom to write what I construe the evidence requires.

Dmitri Nabokov has repeatedly tried to square my need for information with his strong desire to defend his parents' instinct for privacy. Although publicly hostile to any negative opinions of his father based on ignorance or impercipience, he has also respected and defended my independence and my right to the sometimes severe judgments I pass on individual Nabokov works.

Nabokov's sister Elena Sikorski, now living in Geneva, has always been eager to guide me through the past she and her brother knew and to pass on all the information she has received from her extensive network of Soviet sources. Nabokov's cousin Sergey Nabokov of Brussels has given me all the information he could about the genealogy of the Nabokov family. Sergey Nabokov, Elena Sikorski, and Dmitri Nabokov have also commented in detail on the parts of my text covering the periods with which they were most familiar: family background, 1910s–1920s, and 1940s onward, respectively.

I would also like to thank the following individuals for sharing their recollections of Nabokov and/or making available correspondence and other documents. Many have been exceptionally generous.

In the United States: Meyer H. and Ruth Abrams, Ithaca, N.Y.; Robert M. Adams, Santa Fe; Vladimir Alexandrov, New Haven; the late Elizaveta Marinel-Allan, New York; Robert Alter, Berkeley; Samuel Anderson, Lawrence, Kans.; Svetlana Andrault de Langeron, St. Petersburg, Fla.; Alfred and Nina Appel, Evanston, Ill.; Marina Astman, New York; Gennady Barabtarlo, Columbia, Mo.; Natalia Barosin, New York; Nina Berberova, Princeton; Sylvia Berkman, Cambridge, Mass.; Alison Bishop, Ithaca, N.Y.; Max Black, Ithaca, N.Y.; Alexander Brailow, Keuka Park, N.Y.; Clarence Brown, Princeton; F. Martin Brown, Colorado Springs; Matthew J. Bruccoli, Columbia,

S.C.; Richard M. Buxbaum, Berkeley; Frank Carpenter, Cambridge, Mass.; Phyllis and Kenneth Christiansen, Grinnell, Ia.; Milton Cowan, Ithaca, N.Y.; Lucia Davidova, New York; Jean-Jacques Demorest, Tucson; Jason Epstein, New York; Ephim Fogel, Ithaca, N.Y.; J. Vail Foy, Moscow, Ida.; John G. Franclemont, Ithaca, N.Y.; Hannah French, Rye, N.H.; Orval and Helen French, Ithaca, N.Y.; Herbert J. Gold, San Francisco; Hannah Green, New York; Albert J. Guerard, Palo Alto; Claudio Guillén, Cambridge, Mass.; John Hagopian, Binghamton, N.Y.; Joel Hedgpeth, Santa Rosa, Calif.; T. C. Heine, Jr., Waverley, Ia.; Frederic W. Hills, New York; Glenn Horowitz, New York; Marjorie Horowitz, Montclair, N.J.; the late Archbishop Ioann, Santa Barbara; the late George Ivask, Amherst, Mass.; Augusta Jaryc, Ithaca, N.Y.; D. Barton Johnson, Santa Barbara; Alison Jolly, New York; Michael Juliar, Highland Park, N.J.; H. Peter Kahn, Ithaca, N.Y.; Simon Karlinsky, Berkeley; Sergey Karpovich, Washington, D.C.; Edward Kasinec, Berkeley; Wilma Kerby-Miller, Palo Alto; Alexander B. Klots, Putnam, Conn.; James Laughlin, Norfolk, Conn.; Irving Lazar, Beverly Hills; Harry and Elena Levin, Cambridge, Mass.; Beverly Jane Loo, New York; Peter Lubin, Cambridge, Mass.; James McConkey, Ithaca, N.Y.; Robert McGuire, New York; William and Paula McGuire, Princeton; Beatrice McLeod, Ithaca, N.Y.; John Malmstad, Cambridge, Mass.; Sidney Smith Marshall, West Chester, Pa.; William Maxwell, New York; Arthur and Rosemary Mizener, Ithaca, N.Y.; the late Nathalie Nabokov, New York; Stephen Jan and Marie-Luce Parker, Lawrence, Kan.; Katherine Reese Peebles, Boston; Ellendea and the late Carl R. Proffer, Ann Arbor, Mich.; Mark Raeff, New York; Charles Remington, New Haven; Roger Sale, Seattle; May Sarton, York, Me.; Michael Scammell, Ithaca, N.Y.; Arthur M. Schlesinger, Jr., New York; R. Lauriston and Ruth Sharp, Ithaca, N.Y.; Don Stallings, Caldwell, Kan.; Isabel Stephens, Woodstock, Vt.; Leon Stilman, St. Petersburg, Fla.; Mary and the late Gleb Struve, Berkeley; Ronald Sukenick, Boulder, Colo.; Susan Summer, New York; the late Marc Szeftel, Seattle; Frank Taylor, New York; Elizabeth Trahan, Monterey, Calif.; Aileen Ward, New York; Edward Weeks, Boston; Ross Wetzsteon, New York; the late E. B. White, North Brooklyn, Me.; Ella Keats Whiting, Bedford, Mass.; Ronald S. Wilkinson, Washington, D.C.; Bart Winer, New York.

    In France: the late Alexandre Bacherac, Paris; Evgenia and René Cannac, Paris; Vera Kliatchkine, Paris; Irina Komaroff, Paris; E. A. Lijine, Paris; the late Mary McCarthy, Paris; Tatiana Morozoff, Paris; Ivan and Claude Nabokoff, Paris; Mme Jean Paulhan, Paris; Frederic Raphael, St. Laurent-La-Vallée; Alain Robbe-Grillet, Paris; Louba Schirman, Paris; Zinaida Shakhovskaya, Paris; Maria Vereshchagina, Paris; Edmund White, Paris.

In Switzerland: Carlo Barozzi, Montreux; Jacqueline Callier, La Tour-de-Peilz; the late Louise Fürrer, Territet; Pierre Goeldlin de Tiefenau, Lausanne; the late Martin and Margaret Newstead, Fontanivent; Heinrich-Maria and Jane Ledig-Rowohlt, Vaud; Peter Ustinov, Vaud.

In England: Julian Barnes, London; Michele Field, London; Francis Haskell, Oxford; Jarmila Hickman, Oldham; W. F. Madelung, Oxford; Tamara Talbot-Rice, Fossebridge; George, Lord Weidenfeld, London.

In the Soviet Union: Anatoly Alexeev, Evgeny Belodubrovsky, Alexander Dolinin, Leningrad; Tatiana Gagen, Moscow; Evgeny Shikhovtsev, Kostroma; Natalia Styopin and Sergey Task, Moscow; Natalia Tolstoy, Leningrad; Oleg Volkov, Moscow.

In Canada: Patricia Brückmann, Toronto; John Melby, Guelph; and Elizabeth Lonsdale Webster, Toronto; in Spain: Hélène Jakovlev, Tarragona; in Germany: Dieter E. Zimmer, Hamburg; in Finland: Pekka Tammi, Helsinki; in Ireland: Jack Sweeney, Corofin; in New Zealand: Michael Gifkins.

The collections and staff of the following archives, libraries, and museums have been helpful, often invaluable:

Auckland Public Library; Bayerische Staatsbibliothek, Munich; Bibliothèque de documentation internationale contemporaine, Paris-Nanterre; Bibliothèque d'études orientales et slaves, Paris; Bibliothèque municipale, Antibes; Bibliothèque municipale, Menton; Bibliothèque nationale, Paris; British Library; Bryn Mawr College Library; Cambridge University Library; Central Historical Archive of Leningrad Province, Leningrad; Central State Archive of Literature and Art, Moscow; Central State Historical Archive, Leningrad; Columbia University Library; Cornell University Library; Deutsche Staatsbibliothek, East Berlin; Dom Plekhanova, Leningrad; Harvard University Libraries (Houghton, Lamont, Widener); Helsinki University Library; Hoover Institute; Humanities Research Center, University of Texas at Austin; Institute of Russian Literature (Pushkinskiy Dom), Leningrad; Lenin Library, Moscow; Library of Congress; Musée Cantonal de Zoologie, Lausanne; Museum of Comparative Zoology, Harvard; Preussischer Kulturbesitzunginstitut, Berlin; Princeton University Library; Rozhdestveno Local History Museum; Saltykov-Shchedrin State Public Library, Leningrad; Stanford University Library; Trinity College Library, Cambridge; Universitni knihovna (Klementinum), Prague; University of Auckland Library; University of California Library, Berkeley; University of Illinois Library, Urbana; University of Lund Library; University of Toronto Library; University of Uppsala Library; Vilis Lācis State Library, Riga; Washington University Library; Wellesley College Library; Yale University Library; Yalta Local History Museum.

In particular I would like to thank Dr. E. S. Leedham-Green of the Cambridge University Archives for suggesting much I would not have known to look for; to Eila Tervakko and the staff of the Slavonic Division, Helsinki University Library, for always being there to offer assistance but letting one explore their splendid collection so freely on one's own; to the staff of the Columbia University Library Rare Books and Manuscripts section, especially Stephen Corrsin, Susan Summer, and Ellen Scaruffi, who ensured I missed nothing in the constantly expanding Bakhmeteff Archive; to Natalia Buynyakova of the Central Historical Archive of Leningrad Province for offering such prompt and precise pointers to the most diverse materials.

I would like to express my gratitude to the New Zealand University Grants Committee for awarding me a Claude McCarthy Fellowship, without which I could not have begun this project; to the University of Auckland for further research grants and for allowing me the time to complete the task; and especially to the University of Auckland English Department, and particularly Professors Don Smith and Terry Sturm, for their continued support and forbearance.

For comments on matters of fact and style in my manuscript I would like to thank the following: Professor Simon Karlinsky, University of California, Berkeley, and Professor Gennady Barabtarlo, University of Missouri, Columbia, who both read the manuscript closely and generously volunteered many original suggestions about matters literary and historical; Gilles Barbedette, Paris, Professor D. Barton Johnson, University of California, Santa Barbara, Professor Stephen Jan Parker, University of Kansas, Dr. Pekka Tammi, University of Helsinki, and Dieter Zimmer, Hamburg, who read and commented astutely on the entire manuscript; Dr. Chris Ackerley, University of Otago, Professor John Malmstad, Harvard, Professor Michael Millgate, University of Toronto, Associate-Professor Michael Neill, University of Auckland, and Professor Charles Remington, Yale, who made helpful observations on those parts of the manuscript they saw; Frederic W. Hills, New York; my editors at Princeton, Robert Brown, Beth Gianfagna, Lois Nesbitt, and Donald Yelton; and above all, my first reader, Bronwen Nicholson. For generous help with computers, I must thank David Joel; and with typing, Bronwyn Joel and, once again, Bronwen Nicholson.

Unless otherwise indicated, all photographs are from the Vladimir Nabokov Archives, Montreux.

ALL books listed here are by Vladimir Nabokov unless otherwise noted. All unpublished material, except for interviews conducted or letters received by the author, derives from the Vladimir Nabokov Archives unless otherwise indicated. Within critical sections on individual Nabokov works, page numbers for quotations from the work in question will not be cited in the notes.

Ada	*Ada or Ardor: A Family Chronicle*. New York: McGraw-Hill, 1969.
Appel, *AnL*	Alfred Appel, Jr., ed. *The Annotated Lolita*. New York: McGraw-Hill, 1970.
Appel, *NDC*	Alfred Appel, Jr. *Nabokov's Dark Cinema*. New York: Oxford University Press, 1974.
Appel and Newman	Alfred Appel, Jr., and Charles Newman, eds., *Triquarterly* 17 (Winter 1970), Nabokov special issue; repr. as *Nabokov: Criticisms, Reminiscences, Translations and Tributes* (New York: Simon & Schuster, 1970).
BB	Brian Boyd
BS	*Bend Sinister*. 1947; repr. New York: Time, 1964.
CE	*Conclusive Evidence*. New York: Harper, 1951.
ColB	Bakhmeteff Archive, Columbia University
CornUA	Cornell University Archives
CUA	Cambridge University Archives
DB	*Drugie berega*. New York: Chekhov Publishing House, 1954.
Defense	*The Defense*, trans. Michael Scammell with VN. New York: Putnam, 1964.
DN	Dmitri Vladimirovich Nabokov (son)
DS	*Details of a Sunset and Other Stories*, trans. DN with VN. New York: McGraw-Hill, 1976.
EIN	Elena Ivanovna Nabokov (mother)

EO	Alexander Pushkin, *Eugene Onegin*, trans. and with commentary by VN. New York: Bollingen, 1964; rev. ed., Princeton: Princeton University Press, 1975.
ES	Elena Sikorski (née Nabokov) (sister)
EW	Edmund Wilson
Field, *Life*	Andrew Field. *Nabokov: His Life in Part*. New York: Viking, 1977.
Field, *VN*	Andrew Field. *VN: The Life and Work of Vladimir Nabokov*. New York: Crown, 1986.
Ferrand and Nabokov	Jacques Ferrand and SSN. *Les Nabokov*. Montreuil, France: privately printed, 1982.
Gibian and Parker	George Gibian and Stephen Jan Parker, eds. *The Achievement of Vladimir Nabokov*. Ithaca: Cornell University Center for International Studies, 1984.
Gift	*The Gift*, trans. Michael Scammell and DN with VN. New York: Putnam, 1963.
Glory	Trans. DN with VN. New York: McGraw-Hill, 1971.
GS	Gleb Struve
Hoover	Hoover Institute, Stanford University
IB	*Invitation to a Beheading*, trans. DN with VN. New York: Putnam, 1959.
KDN	Konstantin Dmitrievich Nabokov (uncle)
KQK	*King, Queen, Knave*, trans. DN with VN. New York: McGraw-Hill, 1968.
KW	Katharine White
LATH	*Look at the Harlequins!* New York: McGraw-Hill, 1974.
LC	Library of Congress
LCNA	Nabokov Archives, LC
LCS	Shakhovskoy Archives, LC (see also ZS)
Lects	*Lectures on Literature*, ed. Fredson Bowers. New York: Harcourt Brace Jovanovich/Bruccoli Clark, 1980.
LectsR	*Lectures on Russian Literature*, ed. Fredson Bowers. New York: Harcourt Brace Jovanovich/Bruccoli Clark, 1981.
Lolita	New York: Putnam, 1958.

Mary	Trans. Michael Glenny with VN. New York: McGraw-Hill, 1970.
MUSSR	*The Man from the USSR and Other Plays*, trans. DN. New York: Harcourt Brace Jovanovich, 1984.
N1	Unpublished VN notes to Andrew Field, February 20, 1973, VNA.
N2	Unpublished VN notes to Andrew Field, August 31, 1973, VNA.
ND	*Nabokov's Dozen*. Garden City, N.Y.: Doubleday, 1957.
NRS	*Novoe Russkoe Slovo*. Daily. New York.
NWL	*The Nabokov-Wilson Letters*, ed. Simon Karlinsky. New York: Harper & Row, 1979.
NYRB	*New York Review of Books*
NZ	*Novyy Zhurnal*. Journal. New York.
Perepiska	*Perepiska s sestroy*. Ann Arbor: Ardis, 1985.
PF	*Pale Fire*. New York: Putnam, 1962.
PN	*Poslednie Novosti*. Daily. Paris.
PP	*Poems and Problems*. New York: McGraw-Hill, 1971.
Quennell	Peter Quennell, ed. *Vladimir Nabokov: A Tribute*. London: Weidenfeld & Nicolson, 1979.
RB	*A Russian Beauty and Other Stories*, trans. DN and Simon Karlinsky with VN. New York: McGraw-Hill, 1972.
Rivers and Nicol	*Nabokov's Fifth Arc: Nabokov and Others on His Life's Work*, ed. J. E. Rivers and Charles Nicol. Austin: University of Texas Press, 1982.
RLSK	*The Real Life of Sebastian Knight*. Norfolk, Conn.: New Directions, 1941.
S	*Soglyadatay*. Paris: Russkie Zapiski, 1938; repr. Ann Arbor: Ardis, 1978.
SL	*Selected Letters 1940–1977*, ed. DN and Matthew J. Bruccoli. New York: Harcourt Brace Jovanovich/Bruccoli, Clark, Layman, 1989.
SM	*Speak, Memory: An Autobiography Revisited*. New York: Putnam, 1966.
SO	*Strong Opinions*. New York: McGraw-Hill, 1973.

SSN　　　　　Sergey Sergeevich Nabokov (cousin)

Stikhi　　　　Ann Arbor: Ardis, 1979.

SZ　　　　　*Sovremennye Zapiski*. Journal. Paris.

TD　　　　　*Tyrants Destroyed and Other Stories*, trans. DN with VN. New York: McGraw-Hill, 1975.

TsGALI　　　Tsentral'nyy gosudarstvennyy arkhiv literatury i iskusstva (Central State Archive for Literature and Art), Moscow.

TT　　　　　*Transparent Things*. New York: McGraw-Hill, 1972.

VC　　　　　*Vozvrashchenie Chorba*. Berlin: Slovo, 1930; repr. Ann Arbor: Ardis, 1976.

VDN　　　　Vladimir Dmitrievich Nabokov (father)

VDN,　　　　VDN, "Vremennoe Pravitel'stvo," *Arkhiv Russkoy Revolyutsii* 1
ProvGovt　　　(1922); trans. and ed. Virgil D. Medlin and Steven L. Parsons, *V. D. Nabokov and the Russian Provisional Government* (New Haven: Yale University Press, 1976).

VéN　　　　　Véra Nabokov

VF　　　　　*Vesna v Fial'te*. New York: Chekhov, 1956; rept. Ann Arbor: Ardis, 1978.

VN　　　　　Vladimir Nabokov

VNA　　　　Vladimir Nabokov Archives, Montreux.

VNRN　　　　*Vladimir Nabokov Research Newsletter*. Lawrence, Kan. 1978– . From no. 13, 1984, becomes *The Nabokovian*.

WCA　　　　Wellesley College Archives

WL　　　　　Nadine Wonlar-Larsky (née Nabokov). *The Russia That I Loved*. London: Elsie McSwinney, 1937.

Yale　　　　　Beinecke Library, Yale University

ZS　　　　　Zinaida Shakhovskoy (see also LCS)

A BIBLIOGRAPHY of materials consulted—archival, library and museum collections, periodical collections, and books and articles wholly or in part about Nabokov's life or the lives of his father and grandfather—will be included in the second volume of the biography, *Vladimir Nabokov: The American Years*.

The standard bibliography of Nabokov's works is Michael Juliar's *Vladimir Nabokov: A Descriptive Bibliography* (New York: Garland, 1986), to which additions and annual supplements are made in the journal, *The Nabokovian*. The *Nabokovian* also supplements Samuel Schuman's much less comprehensive annotated bibliography of Nabokov criticism, *Vladimir Nabokov: A Reference Guide* (Boston: G. K. Hall, 1979).

INTRODUCTION

Epigraph: George Feifer interview with VN, *Saturday Review*, November 27, 1976, 22.
1. Unpublished VN verse album, October–November 1917, VNA.
2. *SM*, 276.
3. *SO*, xi.
4. *CE*, 217.
5. *SM*, 35–36.
6. Note concerning *Gift* MS, VNA.
7. *SM*, 31–32.
8. Feifer interview, 22.
9. *SM*, 296–97.
10. Feifer interview, 22.
11. *Ada*, 97.
12. Source unretrieved: an unpublished passage in VNA in which VN was talking about his relationship to his own father.

CHAPTER 1. LIBERAL STRAINS

Epigraph to Part 1: Kurt Hoffman interview with VN, Bayerischer Rundfunk, 1972.
Epigraph: VN speech in honor of Iosif Hessen, cited in Hessen, *Gody izgnaniya* (Paris: YMCA, 1979), 96.

1. *SM*, 185.

2. *SO*, 187; *DB*, 43.

3. BB interview with SSN, September 1982; SSN to BB, October 10, 1983.

4. *DB*, 43.

5. VN to SSN, January 21, 1966, VNA; *CE*, 30.

6. Nikolay Ikonnikov, *Noblesse de Russie: Les Nabokov* (Paris, 1960); Ferrand and Nabokov, 134.

7. *SM*, 65.

8. *SM*, 179, 55.

9. In S. V. Yushkov, *Akty XIII-go-XVIII-go vekov*, cited in Ferrand and Nabokov, 120.

10. Manuscript index card, March 6, 1957, VNA.

11. VN to SSN, March 15, 1959, VNA.

12. Cf. *Obshchiy Morskoy Spisok*, St. Petersburg, 1893, 7:575–76, and Terence Armstrong letter, *TLS*, October 21, 1977, 1239.

13. Ferrand and Nabokov, 19; *SM*, 52.

14. Lecture notes, VNA.

15. See P. E. Shchegolev, ed., *Petrashevtsy v vospominaniyakh sovremennikov* (Moscow: Gosudarstvennoe Izdatel'stvo, 1926), esp. p. 72, I. I. Benediktov, "Za shestdesyat' let." The anarchist Bakunin also had grateful memories of Nabokov as commandant: see Ferrand and Nabokov, 81.

16. Joseph Frank, *Dostoevsky: The Years of Ordeal, 1850–1859* (Princeton: Princeton University Press, 1983), 15–16.

17. *SM*, 53.

18. Alexander Hertzen, in Shchegolev, *Petrashevtsy*, 98.

19. *NWL*, 195–96.

20. D. A. Milyutin, *Dnevnik D. A. Milyutina* (Moscow: Lenin Library, 1947–50), 3:123; A. A. Polovtsov, *Dnevnik gosudarstvennogo sekretarya A. A. Polovtsova* (Moscow: Nauka, 1966), 1:76. For D. N. Nabokov's subsequent career, see Jarmila Hickman, "D. N. Nabokov, Minister of Justice 1878–1885, in the Context of the Reform of 1864" (M.A. thesis, University of Manchester, 1982); A. F. Koni, *Ottsy i deti sudebnoy reformy* (Moscow: Sytin, 1914) 170–71.

21. P. A. Zaionchkovsky, *The Russian Autocracy in Crisis, 1878–1882* (1964; trans. Gary M. Hamburg, Gulf Breeze, Fla.: Academic International Press, 1979), 186–87.

22. SSN in Ferrand and Nabokov, 85.

23. Vera Dmitrievna Pikhacheff (née Nabokov), *Sem' let vo vlasti tyomnoy sily* (Belgrade: Novoe Vremya, 1929); rev. ed., *Memoirs (Seven Red Years)*, trans. Janet Crawford (Rowsley: Bibliophilia, 1935), 38.

24. Lecture notes, VNA.

25. Koni, *Ottsy i deti sudebnoy reformy*, 169.

26. A. F. Koni, *Sobranie sochineniy* (Moscow: Yuridicheskaya Literatura, 1966), 2:361; P. A. Zaionchkovsky, *The Russian Autocracy under Alexander III* (1970; trans. David A. Jones, Gulf Breeze, Fla.: Academic International Press, 1976), 45; Alexander III to D. N. Nabokov, November 4, 1885, ColB.

27. Cited in KDN, *The Ordeal of a Diplomat* (London: Duckworth, 1921), 98.

28. "On Revisiting Father's Room," Quennell, 128.

29. Simon Karlinsky, "The True Father of Bolshevism," *Saturday Review*, September 4, 1976.

30. Henrys, "Gazette du Palais," *L'Illustration* 33 (April 16, 1859): 251; *SM*, 56–57; Nicolas Nabokov, *Bagazh: Memoirs of a Russian Cosmopolitan* (New York: Atheneum, 1975), 114; BB interview with VéN, December 1986.

31. BB interview with VéN, December 1986.

32. VN reports the offer of the title, *SM*, 58. But six years later Alexander III snappishly refused to consider awarding D. N. Nabokov any honor (Polovtsov, 2:337), while Nicholas II almost immediately on becoming tsar conferred on him the St. Andrew's Cross (see below, p. 32). See also Polovtsov, 1:357. For Maria Nabokov's receptions, see Polovtsov, 1:191 (Polovtsov never forgave D. N. Nabokov for barring an early promotion).

33. *SM*, 155.

34. Pikhacheff, *Memoirs*, 9; WL, 16; BB interview with Tamara Talbot-Rice, March 1983; Nicolas Nabokov, *Bagazh*, 116.

35. *SM*, 154–55; Sergey Task MS, "V gost'yakh u Nabokova" (interviews with former Nabokov servants), VNA.

36. Pikhacheff, *Memoirs*, passim; WL, passim.

37. KDN to Anton Kardashev, April 19, 1922, ColB.

38. *SM*, 173; Pikhacheff, *Memoirs*, 18, 20-21, 25.

39. VDN, "Peterburgskaya gimnaziya sorok let tomu nazad (Stranichka vospominaniy)," *Novaya Rossiya* 1 (April 1922), 22; Pikhacheff, *Memoirs*, 8; WL, 11.

40. Richard S. Wortman, *The Development of a Russian Legal Consciousness* (Chicago: University of Chicago Press, 1976), 287; VDN, "Peterburgskaya gimnaziya," 20; *SM*, 173.

41. Allan Sinel, *The Classroom and the Chancellery: State Educational Reform in Russia under Count Dmitry Tolstoi* (Cambridge: Harvard University Press, 1973).

42. "Peterburgskaya gimnaziya," 22, 23.

43. A. A. Kizevetter, *Na rubezhe dvukh stoletii* (Prague: Orbis, 1929), 102.

44. Reported by B. L., "Sobesedovanie o russkoy intelligentsii," *Rul'*, February 9, 1922, 2.

45. R. A. Kazakevich, "Iz istorii studencheskikh volneniy v Peterburgskom universitete," *Vestnik Leningradskogo Universiteta* 13 (1958): 170.

46. N. Mogilyansky, "V. D. Nabokov (Iz vospominaniy)," *PN*, April 1, 1922, 2.

47. Zaionchkovsky, *Russian Autocracy in Crisis*, 265.

48. VN mistakenly records the date as January 1891 (*SM*, 174). According to VDN's diploma, his final examinations took place September–November 1891.

49. VDN, *ProvGovt*, 137–38.

50. "Nishchenstvo i brodyazhestvo, kak nakazuemye prostupki," read November 1894, pub. *Zhurnal Sankt Peterburgskogo Yuridicheskogo Obshchestva*, no. 3 (1895): 9–73.

51. *SM*, 174; *PN*, March 30, 1922, 2.

52. A. Makletsov, "V. D. Nabokov, kak uchyoniy kriminalist," *Rossiya i Slavyanstvo*, April 23, 1932, 2.

53. *Soderzhanie i metod nauki ugolovnogo prava: Zadachi akademicheskogo prepodavaniya* (St. Petersburg, 1896).

54. V. D. Nabokov, "Raboty po sostavleniyu sudebnykh ustavov. Obshchaya kharakeristika sudebnoy reformy," in N. V. Davydov and N. N. Polyanskiy, eds. *Sudebnaya Reforma* (Moscow: Ob'edinenie, 1915), 348, 350.

55. *Mitteilungen der Internationalen Kriminalistischen Vereinigung* 17 (1910), 327.

56. Makletsov, 2.

57. VDN, "Raboty . . . ," 352–53.

58. *SM*, 277; Richard Pipes, ed., *The Russian Intelligentsia* (New York: Columbia University Press, 1961).

59. *SO*, 288; *N1*.

60. *SM*, 66; Konstantin Vasilievich Rukavishnikov was connected by the Russian genealogist L. M. Savelov (*Biograficheskiy ukazatel' po istorii, geraldike i rodoslovoyu rossiyskogo dvoryanstvo*, 2d ed., Ostrogozhek: Azarovoy, 1897) to the Kazan Rukavishnikovs, ennobled in the late seventeenth or the eighteenth century (*Dvoryanstvo i krepostnoy stroy v Rossii*, Moscow, 1975, app. 4).

61. *CE*, 30.

62. From a lecture by P. E. Kovalevsky to the Société d'Ancienne Noblesse Russe of Brussels in the early 1970s, cited in a letter from SSN to VN, February 10, 1973, VNA.

63. *SM*, 72.

64. *DB*, 59; *SM*, 66, 72.

65. *MUSSR*, 318.

66. *DB*, 59; *SM*, 72.

67. *CE*, 118.

68. *SM*, 166.

69. *SM*, 65; *DB*, 45.

70. *SM*, 67.

71. *SM*, 40, 121; *DB*, 33.

72. N. V. Shaposhnikov, *Heraldica* (St. Petersburg, Pozharov, 1900), 1:220; *Adresnaya kniga goroda S. Petersburga na 1895 g.* (St. Petersburg, 1895), 907, 1132.

73. *DB*, 59; *WL*, 60; *MUSSR*, 318.

74. BB interview with ES, June 1982.

75. *SM*, 40; ES to BB, November 14, 1983.

76. *SM*, 143.

77. *WL*, 150–51; Ferrand and Nabokov, 70–71.

78. I. V. Hessen, *Rul'*, March 30, 1922, 1.

79. Unpublished chapter of *CE*, LCNA.

80. VN to KW, November 27, 1949, and January 28, 1950; *SL*, 95–96; and December 2, 1949, VNA.

81. *SM*, 174; *SO*, 214.

82. I. V. Hessen, "V dvukh vekakh. Zhizneniy otchyot," *Arkhiv Russkoy Revolyutsii* 22 (1937): 154

83. Hessen, "V dvukh vekakh," 205.

84. Hessen, "V dvukh vekakh," 154.

85. "Proekt ugolovnogo ulozheniya i smertnaya kazn'," *Pravo*, January 30, 1900, 257–63.

86. *Ministerstvo Yustitsii za sto let, 1802–1902* (St. Petersburg: Senatskaya Tipografiya, 1902), 168, 169.

87. M. Vinaver, *PN*, March 30, 1922, 2; A. Tyrkova, "V. D. Nabokov i Pervaya Duma," *Russkaya Mysl'* 6–7 (1922): 279–81.

88. *Daily Dispatch and Manchester Morning Chronicle*, March 31, 1922, 6.

89. *LectsR*, 142n.

90. See below, pp. 408–17.

91. *IB*, 223.

92. VéN to Frank Harper, April 28, 1960, VNA.

CHAPTER 2. A WORLD AWAKENING

Epigraphs: VN to GS, May 1931, Hoover, cited *NRS*, June 5, 1979; *RLSK*, 15–16.

1. See *DB*, 77; *SM*, 36.

2. VN to Walter Minton, April 20, 1958, VNA.

3. K., "Sobranie pamyati V. D. Nabokova," *Nash vek*, April 3, 1932, 7.

4. Cited in Appel, *AnL*, 406.

5. *SO*, 17; *SM*, 236.

6. *Teatr i zhizn'* 1–2 (September 1921), 7 (January 1922), 8 (March 1922), 9 (April 1922).

7. *SO*, 171; Field, *Life*, 86.

8. Cf. Aleksandr Blok, *Sobranie sochineniy* (Moscow and Leningrad: Khudozhestvennaya Literatura, 1963), 7: 311.

9. *Rul'*, November 29, 1921, 5.

10. *SO*, 266.

11. *DB*, 35.

12. Lecture, VNA.

13. *SM*, 237.

14. Kizevetter, *Na rubezhe dvukh stoletii*, 242.

15. *Time*, May 23, 1969, 48.

16. *SM*, 36.

17. VN to KW, March 4, 1949, VNA.

18. *WL*, 99.

19. *LATH*, 239.

20. *SM*, 21; BB interviews with VéN and ES, December 1984.

21. Hessen, *Gody izgnaniya*, 93–94

22. *SM*, 191–92.

23. KDN to Donald Nesbit, March 15, 1907, private coll.

24. *SM*, facing p. 129.

25. WL, 71.

26. *Lolita*, 314; *DB*, 76; *SM*, 86.

27. *SM*, 24.

28. Unpublished chapter of *CE*, LCNA.

29. *SM*, 103.

30. *SM*, 21–22.

31. *SM*, 21.

32. Unpublished chapter of *CE*, LCNA.

33. *SM*, 75; *DB*, 64.

34. *SM*, 40.

35. VN to EIN, ca. June 1924, VNA.

36. BB interview with ES, August 1982; *N1*.

37. *SM*, 23.

38. Unpublished chapter of *CE*, LCNA.

39. Bernard Pivot interview with VN, May 30, 1975, from TS in VNA.

40. *DB*, 68.

41. Willa Petchek interview with VN, "Nabokov since *Lolita*," *Observer Magazine*, May 30, 1976, 18.

42. Alden Whitman interview with VN, October 6, 1971, from TS in VNA.

43. David Holmes interview with VN, BBC, November 5, 1959, from TS in VNA.

44. *SM*, 86.

45. *SM*, 310.

46. Unpublished note, VNA.

47. *SM*, 24.

48. *SM*, 59.

49. *SM*, 58–59.

50. BB interview with VéN, June 1982.

51. *SM*, 302.

52. BB interviews with ES, December 1981 and June 1982.

53. *DB*, 164; *SM*, 180.

54. *DB*, 166.

55. BB interview with ES, June 1982.

56. Nabokov incorrectly records the appointment as commander-in-chief of the Russian army in the Far East (*SM*, 27); actually Kuropatkin was not appointed to this position until the autumn of 1904. Nabokov's aunt remembers much more inaccurately. She recalls herself seated in an audience in the music room of her brother's home, listening to a recital by the celebrated Wagnerian soprano Felia Litvinne, when a messenger came to inform an astonished Kuropatkin that Japan had declared war by its attack on Russian destroyers in Port Arthur (WL, 119). Kuropatkin's diary shows that he was not at the Nabokovs' that night ("Dnevnik A. N. Kuropatkina," *Krasnyy Arkhiv* 2

[1922]: 109, 111), and what lies behind "Aunt Baby's" association of Kuropatkin, the beginning of the war, and her brother's house seems irretrievable.

57. *SM*, 96; unpublished notes, VNA; *DB*, 138.

58. *SM*, 75–76.

59. Unpublished chapter of *CE*, LCNA.

60. *SM*, 25–26.

61. Henri Jaton interview with VN, October 5, 1963, for Radio Suisse Romande, from TS in VNA.

62. *SM*, 26.

63. *SM*, 87; *DB*, 77, 91.

64. *SM*, 196–97.

65. Unpublished note, VNA.

66. *SM*, 26, 27.

CHAPTER 3. FIRST REVOLUTION AND FIRST DUMA

Epigraph: *SL*, 95.

1. Hessen, "V dvukh vekakh," 154, 263.

2. Aleksandr Makletsov, "V. D. Nabokov—Uchyonyy," *Rul'*, April 8, 1922, 1–2.

3. Ibid., and Makletsov, "V. D. Nabokov, kak uchyonyy kriminalist," *Rossiya i Slavyanstvo*, April 23, 1932, 2; VDN, "Plotskie prestupleniya," *Vestnik Prava*, 32:9–10 (November–December 1902), 129–89; VDN, *Elementarnyy uchebnik oscbennoy chasti russkogo ugolovnogo prava* (St. Petersburg, 1903), chap. 6.

4. "Geroicheskoe nachalo lichnogo podviga," *Obshchee delo*, April 7, 1922, 1.

5. "Kishinyovskaya krovavaya banya," *Pravo*, April 27, 1903, 1283–85.

6. M. L. Ganfman, "V. D. Nabokov," *Rul'*, March 30, 1922, 1; Iosif Hessen, "Let sorok nazad," *Zarya* 2 (1942): 5.

7. Hessen, "V dvukh vekakh," 154; Ganfman, "V. D. Nabokov," *Rul'*, March 30, 1922, 2. Andrew Field calls this V. D. Nabokov's "formal break with the tsarist regime" (*Life*, 70). In fact Nabokov retained court title, chancellery position, and teaching post for almost another two years. Field adds that "it is not too much to say that the liberal movement in Russia grew greatly in scope and maturity as a result of that article." This is sheer bluster.

8. Richard Pipes, *Struve: Liberal on the Left, 1870–1905* (Cambridge: Harvard University Press, 1970), 369.

9. Pipes, 369–70.

10. Pipes, 329.

11. Pipes, 370.

12. *SM*, 175.

13. S. Yu. Vitte, *Vospominaniya* (Moscow, 1960), 2:373. Field (*Life*, 72) garbles several misunderstood sources to declare that "a new *Kammerjunker* uni-

form for Court functions had to be ordered for him a month before he was deprived of his Court title in January 1905"—a preposterous error made possible only through Field's ignorance of V. D. Nabokov's attitude toward the government in December 1904.

14. ES to BB, October 26, 1985; *SM*, 184.

15. Ariadna Tyrkova-Williams, *Na putyakh k svobode* (New York: Chekhov, 1952), 269; *Russkie vedomosti*, January 15/28, 1905; *Zhurnal zasedaniya gorodskoy dumy*, 1905:9.

16. Official certificate, April 27, 1905, VNA. VN implies that his father may have been dismissed because of the Kishinyov article nearly two years earlier (*SM*, 174). Field cites Tyrkova-Williams ("After the 9th of January Nabokov read a speech in the St. Petersburg Duma . . . against the firing upon workers. For this speech he was deprived of his status as a *Kammerjunker*") and proclaims: "A variant explanation which is not confirmed in any other source, but many are the tales that Clio, the goddess of history, has to tell" (*Life*, 74). Field does not cite his other sources, which seem to be only *Speak, Memory*, and he does not know enough to realize that on this occasion VN, following another SSN conjecture, was wrong.

17. *SM*, 175.

18. *DB*, 20.

19. Henri Jaton interview with VN for Radio Suisse Romande, October 5, 1963, from typescript in VNA.

20. *SM*, 28.

21. *SM*, 28–29.

22. August Lepik to VN, February 23, 1965, VNA.

23. *SM*, 35.

24. Jaton interview.

25. *SM*, 34.

26. Ann Erickson Healy, *The Russian Autocracy in Crisis, 1905–1907* (Hamden, Conn.: Anchor, 1976), 263, 28.

27. *DB*, 86.

28. Sergey Task MS, "V gost'yakh u Nabokova" (interviews with former Nabokov family servants), VNA.

29. "Sovremennoe polozhenie i takticheskoe zadachi K.D.-skoy partii," *Pravo*, 41 (October 25, 1905): 3404.

30. *DB*, 86.

31. *SM*, 102–3.

32. *DB*, 89.

33. Healy, *Russian Autocracy*, 159.

34. *Vestnik partii narodnoy svobody* (*Herald of the Party of the People's Freedom*).

35. See Kizevetter, *Na rubezhe dvukh stoletii*, 404–10, an excellent summary of the party's principles by a leading CD; also Charles E. Timberlake, ed., *Essays on Russian Liberalism* (Columbia: University of Missouri Press, 1972); Healy, *Russian Autocracy*; Stephen J. Bensman, "The Constitutional Ideas of the Russian Liberation Movement: The Struggle for Human Rights during

the Revolution of 1905" (Ph.D. diss., University of Wisconsin, Madison, 1977).

36. Nurit Eeretzky interview with VN for *Ma'ariv*, January 19, 1970, from TS in VNA.

37. A. A. Kizevetter, cited in Bensman, "Constitutional Ideas," 379.

38. *SM*, 153.

39. Cf. *NWL*, 33.

40. Cf. Bensman, "Constitutional Ideas," 378–80.

41. He wrote to an English translator: "I know nothing about 'classes,' " and had been about to continue "This obsession of [the British?]" but left it at that. VN note on letter from Michael Scammell, April 19, 1962, VNA.

42. *PN*, March 30, 1922, 2.

43. *My Russian Memoirs* (1931; repr. New York: AMS Press, 1969), 106.

44. Tyrkova-Williams, *Na putyakh . . .* , 270, 271.

45. Bernard Pares, *Russia and Reform* (London, 1907), 548.

46. Hessen "V dvukh vekakh," 155.

47. Quoted from the stenographic record of the First Duma in Healy, *Russian Autocracy*, 192.

48. A. F. Koni, *Sobranie sochineniy* (Moscow, 1966), 2:362.

49. *N2*.

50. Hessen, "V dvukh vekakh," 155.

51. Healy, *Russian Autocracy*, 204; Ariadna Tyrkova, "V. D. Nabokov i pervaya duma," *Russkaya Mysl'* 6–7 (June–July 1922): 279–81.

52. See Milyukov, *Political Memoirs*, 111; Vasily Maklakov, *The First State Duma*, trans. Mary Belkin (Bloomington: Indiana University Press, 1964), 192–93; S. S. Oldenburg, *Last Tsar*, ed. Patrick J. Rollins, trans. Leonid I. Mihalap and Patrick J. Rollins (Gulf Breeze, Fla.: Academic International Press), 2:205–10.

53. "Protsess 169 deputatov pervoy gosudarstvennoy dumy: Rech' V. D. Nabokova," *Vestnik Partii Narodnoy Svobody*, 49 (December 18, 1907), 2118.

54. VDN, "Deyatelnost' partii narodnoy svobody v gosudarstvennoy dume," *Vestnik Partii Narodnoy Svobody*, 30 (October 1, 1906), 1603.

55. Fischer, *Russian Liberalism*, 202.

56. Pares *My Russian Memoirs*, 124.

57. Cited in KDN to Donald Nesbit, August 10, 1906, private coll.

58. KDN to Donald Nesbit, August 23, 1906, private coll.

CHAPTER 4. BUTTERFLIES

Epigraph: Jacob Bronowski interview with VN, scheduled for August 1963, from TS in VNA.

1. *SM*, 120, 121, 187; *DB*, 113; Bronowski interview.

2. Bronowski interview.

3. *SM*, 192.

4. EIN to VN, December 11, 1937, VNA.

5. *SM*, 97.

6. Pivot interview.

7. *SM*, 105.

8. *DB*, 98, 105; *SM*, 113.

9. *DB*, 101.

10. VDN, *ProvGovt*, 97; *SM*, 184; unpublished note, VNA; VéN and ES to BB, October 21 and 26, 1985.

11. *SM*, 50; Natalia Teletova to ES, October 31, 1988, private coll.

12. KDN to Donald Nesbit, March 15, 1907, private coll.; VDN to A. F. Koni, November 21/December 4, 1906, Pushkinsky Dom, Fond 134, inv. 3, no. 1152.

13. *SM*, 37–39, 123; *Gift*, 34–36.

14. *SM*, 19–21; Fyodor (*Gift*, 23) makes the same effort of imagination.

15. Cf. *Gift*, 23; *RB*, 170.

16. "Net, bytiyo—ne zybkaya zagadka," written May 6, 1923, *Stikhi*, 105; Dieter Zimmer interview with VN, "Despot in meiner Welt," *Die Zeit*, November 1, 1966, from TS in VNA.

17. Strannik (Archbishop Ioann), "Nachalo Nabokoviany," *Russkaya Mysl'*, June 1, 1978, 10.

18. *DS*, 160, 161.

19. *SO*, 206, 39.

20. *SM*, 39.

21. BB interviews with ES, September 1982 and December 1984.

22. BB interview with VéN, September 1982.

23. Bronowski interview.

24. *SM*, 68.

25. *DB*, 58, 63; *SM*, 71–72, 74.

26. *DB*, 57.

27. *SM*, 149, 147.

28. *Literaturnaya gazeta*, March 1989.

29. Helga Chudacoff interview with VN, pub. *Die Welt*, September 26, 1974, from TS in VNA.

30. *Lects*, 251.

31. BB interview with VéN, November 1982.

32. Field, *Life*, 93.

33. Unpublished notes, VNA.

34. *SM*, 153–54, 169; *DB*, 161.

35. *SM*, 36, 91, 92, 157; *DB*, 28; Field, *VN*, 387.

36. Hessen, "V dvukh vekakh," 257, 259–60; O. O. Gruzenberg, "Moya pamyatka o V. D. Nabokove," *Rul'*, April 2, 1922, 1; cf. KDN to Donald Nesbit, December 26, 1907, private coll.

37. VDN, "Pis'ma V. D. Nabokova iz Krestov k zhene. 1908 g.," ed. VN, *Vozdushnye puti* 4 (1965): 265; VDN, *Tyuremnye dosugi* (St. Petersburg, 1908), 10, 12, 30–33, 37–38, 60–61.

38. "Pis'ma V. D. Nabokova . . . ," 271.

39. *SM*, 176.

40. "Pis'ma V. D. Nabokova . . . ," 268.

41. KDN to Donald Nesbit, August 26, 1908, private coll.; *SM*, 29–30; VN to VéN, August 22, 1924, VNA; WL, 134–35. Field (*Life*, 71) wrongly implies that this ploy prevented the celebrations altogether. Despite VN's repeated corrections, Field chose to ignore his subject's clear memories of the event, which are entirely corroborated by K. D. Nabokov's letter, written the next day.

42. *SM*, facing p. 160.

43. *SO*, 189; *SM*, 123.

44. Pivot interview.

45. VN to Katharine White, January 10, 1950, and VN to EIN, March 27, 1925, VNA.

46. *DB*, 51.

47. VN notes to Field, June 12, 1970, VNA.

48. Unpublished chapter of *CE*, LCNA.

49. *SM*, 149–52, 159; *DB*, 140; unpublished notes, VNA.

50. *SM*, 143–45. I am indebted to Pekka Tammi, *Problems of Nabokov's Poetics: A Narratological Analysis* (Helsinki: Academia Scientarium Fennica, 1985), 58–59, for stressing the consistency of this theme. It can be found especially in the still unpublished story "Sounds," in the stories "Torpid Smoke" and "Recruiting," and above all in *The Gift*.

51. VN to Roger Angell, January 23, 1976, VNA; *SO*, 56–57; *LectsR*, 11; *EO* 2:328.

52. David Holmes interview with VN; VN to Malcolm Muggeridge, May 5, 1954, VNA; unpublished notes, VNA; cf. Field, *Life*, 283–84.

53. VN, ' Reputations Revisited," *TLS*, January 21, 1977, 66; Bernard Safarik interview with VN for Swiss German television, 1974, from MS in VNA; *SM*, 188; *DB*, 166.

54. *DB*, 106, 149, 151; *SM*, 114, 160.

55. *SM*, 197; *CE* MS draft, LCNA.

56. *SM*, 202, 203.

57. VN to Sergey Potresov, September 28, 1921, ColB.

58. *SM*, 81, 123–24; *DB*, 60, 117–18; *SO*, 5; Roberto Tabozzi interview with VN for *Pancrama*, conducted October 16, 1969, from TS in VNA.

59. MS, "Vtoroe prilozhenie k *Daru*," LCNA.

60. Lepidoptera MSS, VNA.

61. *Lects*, 253.

62. *SM*, 139.

63. *SM*, 124–25.

64. "Vtoroe prilozhenie k *Daru*," LCNA.

65. *LectsR*, 12.

66. *SM*, 130.

67. *DB*, 85.

68. *SM*, 206, 207.

69. *SM*, 207.
70. *SM*, 199; *SO*, 178.

CHAPTER 5. SCHOOL

Epigraph: *Lolita*, 179.
1. Unpublished note, VNA.
2. Field, *Life*, 110; *SM*, 185. It was Osip Mandelstam who described the Literary Fund as "that citadel of radicalism" (*The Prose of Osip Mandelstam*, trans. Clarence Brown [Princeton: Princeton University Press, 1965], 98).
3. *SM*, 180; Field, *Life*, 114, 127; *N1*.
4. VN to Samuil Rosov, September 4, 1937, VNA; unpublished poem, "Yunost'," November 6, 1923, EIN album, VNA. Field describes Tenishev in great detail, but not the Tenishev of VN's day, and wrongly supposes he can equate Mandelstam's reminiscences of the school (see chap. 6 below) with VN's. Despite *DB*, 169 and *SM*, 257, for instance, he implies, incorrectly, that Tenishev still had a uniform when VN was there: "The school costume was of an English character" (*Life*, 115).
5. *LectsR*, 224; Field, *Life*, 115; Pivot interview; *SM*, 185; ES to BB, September 29, 1985.
6. *DB*, 170; VN to Rosov, September 4, 1937.
7. *SM*, 182–83, 186.
8. Field, *Life*, 94; BB interview with ES, December 1981; VN to Rosov, September 4, 1937, VNA; *DB*, 169.
9. *DB*, 168; VN to Rosov, September 4, 1937; cf. *BS*, 63.
10. VN to Rosov, September 4, 1937; *Defense*, 27–28; *DB*, 170.
11. "Vtoroe prilozhenie k *Daru*," LCNA.
12. *N1*; VN to Rosov, September 4, 1937.
13. Pivot interview.
14. Pivot interview; VN notes to Field, June 12, 1970, VNA.
15. Lecture notes, VNA.
16. *DB*, 169.
17. *NWL*, 311.
18. *SO*, 42–43, 46, *SM*, 177; *DB*, 176.
19. Pivot interview; *N1*.
20. *LectsR*, 110.
21. "Reputations Revisited," *TLS*, January 21, 1977, 66.
22. *RLSK*, 91.
23. *NWL*, 220.
24. Lecture notes, VNA.
25. *N1*.
26. *NWL*, 72.
27. Lecture notes, VNA.
28. Lecture notes, VNA; *NWL*, 94.
29. VN to Elizaveta Malozemov, ca. January 1938, VNA.

30. *N1*.

31. The phrase comes from Sergey Gorodetsky, who published another Acmeist manifesto in the same year as Gumilyov. Quoted in Renato Poggioli, *The Poets of Russia 1890–1930* (Cambridge: Harvard University Press, 1960), 215.

32. Quoted in Poggioli, *Poets*, 214.

33. *EO MS* rote, VNA.

34. *RLSK*, 28.

35. *SM*, 191.

36. *Gift*, 161

37. *RB*, 4; unpublished chapter of *CE*, LCNA; VN notes to Field, June 12, 1970, VNA; Field, *VN*, 383; Henri Jaton interview with VN, October 5, 1963, from TS in VNA.

38. *NWL*, 241, 246; *SM*, 208, 210.

39. *SM*, 61, 256; *Perepiska*, 56; lepidoptera MSS, VNA.

40. *SM*, 212; Don-Zhuanskiy spisok, VNA.

41. *SM*, 162–66; cf. also the story "A Bad Day," *DS*, 33–34; *DB*, 154; VN to Katharine White, January 10, 1950, VNA.

42. *Gift*, 124, 126.

43. *DB*, 173.

44. VDN, "Duel' i ugolovnyy zakon," *Pravo*, no. 50 (1909): 2729–44, and no. 51 (1909): 2833–47.

45. *Novoe Vremya*, October 16–21, 1911; *Rech'*, October 18–22, 1911; *Russkie Vedomosti*, October 19–20, 1911; *Russkoe Slovo*, October 19, 1911.

46. *DB*, 171, 173; *SM*, 188–89; "Orache," *DS*, 52.

47. *SM*, 193.

48. *NWL*, 102–3; VN to Rosov, September 4, 1937; *DB*, 119, 174; *DS* 44–46.

49. VN to Rosov, September 4, 1937; *DB*, 174; *N1*.

50. Field, *Life*, 115; *N1*.

51. VN notes to Field, June 12, 1970.

52. VN to Rosov, September 4, 1937; Rosov to VN, January 27, 1972, VNA.

53. VN to Rosov, September 4, 1937; *N1*, *N2*; Field, *Life*, 126; *DS* 44–45; Field, *VN*, 45–46.

54. VN to William Maxwell, February 16, 1963, VNA; *SM*, 183; Field, *VN*, 34; BB interview with ES, December 1986.

55. *SM*, 211.

56. *SO*, 17. *Perepiska* 56.

57. *SO*, 17. *SM*, 92, 94; *DB*, 82; VN to Katharine White, April 17, 1957, VNA.

58. VN diary, January 25–30, 1943.

59. "Moya pamyatka o V. D. Nabokove," *Rul'*, April 2, 1922, 1.

60. Field, *Life*, 93–94.

61. *Gift*, 126.

62. *SM*, 154–55. Nabokov dates the event Easter 1915. But his grandmother sold Batovo in 1913, after spending the previous winter there, and then moved to Gatchina (see n. 69 below and text). During the winter of 1914–15, moreover, V. D. Nabokov was stationed with his regiment at Vyborg. Pre-

sumably the tutor accompanying the Nabokov boys was Zelenski, not his 1914–15 replacement Sakharov ("Volgin").

63. *SM*, 74, 168 (where he is called "Noyer"); *DB*, 62 ("Noisier"); ES to BB, September 29, 1985.

64. *SM*, 126–27.

65. *SM*, 257.

66. *SM*, 257–58; *DB*, 149; Field, *VN*, 46; ES to BB, September 29, 1985. VN mistakenly writes at *SM*, 257 that Sergey "went to my father's former gimnasiya" (which was in fact the Third).

67. *SM*, 114–15.

68. *SM*, 168–69; *DB*, 160; *CE*, 120; *Perepiska*, 58, 59n.

69. KDN to Donald Nesbit, November 4, 1913 and July 14, 1914, private coll.; *WL*, 157–58.

70. *SM*, 197–99.

71. *SM*, 215.

72. *SM*, 217.

73. *SM*, 227.

74. "Dozhd' proletel" ("The rain had flown"), *PP*, 19. The poem is dated in an unpublished album, VNA.

75. VN to Sergey Potresov, September 28, 1921, ColB.

76. *SM*, 216–17.

77. *SM*, 85; *Mary*, 46; *DB*, 74; ES to BB, October 29, 1985.

78. *SM*, 217, 225.

CHAPTER 6. LOVER AND POET

Epigraphs: *Glory*, 33; *Defense*, 79–80.

1. VDN, *ProvGovt*, 106–7.

2. I. V. Hessen, "V dvukh vekakh," 326–27; *SM*, 47; Tsuyoshi Hasegawa, *The February Revolution: Petrograd, 1917* (Seattle: University of Washington Press, 1981), 4; VDN, *ProvGovt*, 107.

3. VDN, *ProvGovt*, 37; *SM*, 47; *DB*, 40.

4. Mati Laansoo interview with VN, 1973, pub. *VNRN* 10 (1983): 43; VN to Potresov, September 28, 1921; VN to Andrew Field, February 3, 1967, VNA.

5. VDN, *ProvGovt*, 37; *Perepiska*, 89 (= *SL*, 226).

6. *SO*, 125.

7. *Mary*, xii, 31–33; BB interview with VéN, January 1982.

8. VN notes to Field, June 12, 1970.

9. VéN to BB, November 25, 1985.

10. *SM*, 230; *Mary*, xii, 57–58.

11. *SM*, 231; *Mary*, 56; *Stikhi*, 189; *SM*, 232.

12. VN notes to Field, June 12, 1970; *SM*, 231; *DB*, 199.

13. *SM*, 231–33; *DB*, 200; *Mary*, 67–68.

14. VDN, *ProvGovt*, 37. Despite Trotsky's slur in calling him "a legalised deserter" (*History of the Russian Revolution*, trans. Max Eastman [London: Gol-

lancz, 1932], .:1951), VDN did not request a transfer from the front; it took him by surprise. Cf. also SSN in Ferrand and Nabokov, 74–75.

15. *SM*, 23:; *Stikhi* (Petrograd: Union, 1916), 18; Field, *VN*, 36.

16. VN notes to Field, June 12, 1970; *SM*, 234, 236, 237; *Mary*, 69–70.

17. *DB*, 20:; *SM*, 234–35; *DB*, 206.

18. *N1*; Field, *Life*, 118, 120; *DB*, 206; *SM*, 186; ES to BB, September 29, 1985.

19. *The Prose of Osip Mandelstam*, ed. Clarence Brown, 109–10, 128–31; Field, *Life*, 121; *N1*.

20. VN to Rosov, September 4, 1937; *NWL*, 77, 102; *DB*, 170, 206; *SM*, 238; VN to VéN, April 16, :932, VNA. Gippius's verse collections are: *Pesni*, 1897; (as Vl. Bestushev), *Vozvrashchenie*, 1912, and *Noch v zvyozdakh*, 1915; (as Vl. Neledinsky), *Tomlenie dukha*, 1916. Although Field calls Gippius's collections "minuscule" (*Life*, 119), the Bestushev volumes are each more than 150 pages.

21. *SM*, 186.

22. Lecture notes, VNA.

23. Aleksandr Blok, *Sobranie sochineniy*, 7:95, 478–79, 495; Rosov to VN, October 21, 1936; Field, *Life*, 120–21.

24. Field, *Life in Art*, 363; VN to Field, February 3, 1967; V. D. Nabokov, *Iz Voyuyushchey Anglii* (Petrograd: Union, 1916), 3, 19, 129.

25. Field, *VN*, 42; Field, *Life*, 116.

26. The seventh issue of *Yunaya Misl'* was rediscovered in Leningrad's Saltykov-Shchedrin Library by Evgeny Belodubrovsky. No copy of issue number 6 has been located.

27. *Perepiska*, 56, 58 (the date "1919" on p. 58 is a misprint for "1916"); National Book Award Acceptance Speech, 1975, pub. *Nabokovian* 13 (Fall 1984), 17. The poem appeared in *Vestnik Evropy*, July 1916.

28. Unpublished notes for public reading, Coll. Zenzinov, ColB.; Hessen, *Gody izgnanya*, 94; *SO*, 154. Poems dated in verse album, December 1917–June 1918, VNA.

29. *SM*, 239. The August 1916 issue of *Vestnik Evropy* records *Stikhi* as having reached the editors in July. Presumably it had gone on sale about June and the young author received an advance copy in late May, just before the move to the country.

30. *N1*; Field, *Life*, 122–23.

31. *SM*, 237–38.

32. *CE MS*, VNA.

33. *Perepiska*, 58.

34. *SM*, 199–200.

35. *SM*, 240.

36. VN to Potrescv, September 28, 1921; Field, *Life*, 118; *SM*, 238–39.

37. *SM*, 7:, 72; VéN to Mrs. F. M. Markos, April 5, 1948, VNA; album, *Bessmertna k rodine lyubov'*, Rozhdestveno Local History Museum, 1982; *N1*; Field, *VN*, 39.

38. *DB*, 59; *SM*, 240; Field, *Life*, 97. The Don Juan list records three names between Valentina Shulgin and the next leading lady; a draft letter, VN to KW, September 4, 1949, refers to "various ~~affairs~~ adventures with married

women"; VéN to BB, November 25, 1985; BB interview with ES, December 1986.

39. *SM*, 240.

40. *SM*, 36; *CE*, 183.

41. See George Katkov, *Russia 1917: The February Revolution* (London: Collins, 1969); Lionel Kochan, *Russia in Revolution, 1890–1918* (London: Paladin, 1970); William G. Rosenberg, *Liberals in the Russian Revolution: The Constitutional Democratic Party, 1917–1921* (Princeton: Princeton University Press, 1974); and Hasegawa, *February Revolution*.

42. VDN to A. F. Koni, January 20/February 2, 1917, Pushkinskiy Dom, Fond Koni, no. 134, op. 3, item 1152; Field, *Life*, 123; BB interview with VéN, January 1982; VDN, *ProvGovt*, 39; VN notes for Field, June 12, 1970; *SM*, 254; "E.L." ("Ona davno ushla"), *Gorniy put'*, 128.

43. VDN, *ProvGovt*, 39.

44. VDN, *ProvGovt*, 40.

45. VDN, *ProvGovt*, 40–41; Hasegawa, 363–65.

46. VDN, *ProvGovt*, 41–43.

47. Baron B. E. Nolde, "V.D. Nabokov v 1917 g.," *Dalekoe i blizkoe* (Paris, 1930), trans. as "V. D. Nabokov in 1917" in VDN, *ProvGovt*, 18–20; *ProvGovt*, 49–55; Leonard Schapiro, "The Political Thought of the First Provisional Government," in Richard Pipes, ed., *Revolutionary Russia* (Cambridge: Harvard University Press, 1968), 101–2.

48. VDN, *ProvGovt*, 55–56.

49. Raymond Pearson, *The Russian Moderates and the Crisis of Tsarism 1914–1917* (London: Macmillan, 1977), 171; VDN, *ProvGovt*, 58.

50. Trotsky, *History of the Russian Revolution*, 1:208; VDN, *ProvGovt*, 79.

51. I have modified Leonard Schapiro's phrase "radical revolutionaries and republicans at heart" (*The Russian Revolutions of 1917: The Origins of Modern Communism* [New York: Basic Books, 1984], 56) with the help of Raymond Pearson's "revolutionary liberals," applied to VDN and other First Duma CD leaders (Pearson, *Russian Moderates*, 36).

52. Quoted Kochan, *Russia in Revolution*, 206.

53. He had been excluded for signing the Vyborg appeal, and sought and obtained restoration under the Provisional Government's political amnesty. Album of VDN memorabilia, VNA. Cf. also I. I. Petrunkevich, "Iz zapisok obshchestvennogo deyatelya," *Arkhiv Russkoy Revolyutsii* 21 (1934): 452.

54. VDN, *ProvGovt*, 34–35, 87; Nolde, in *ProvGovt*, 22; I. V. Tseretelli, *Vospominanie o Fevralskoy Revolyutsii* (Paris: Mouton, 1963), 1:156; Rosenberg, *Liberals*, 102–15.

55. Simon Karlinsky, in *NWL*, 12.

56. VN to Rosov, September 4, 1937; *SO*, 299; Field, *Life*, 118, 121; *N1*.

57. Russian lecture on Gogol, VNA.

58. VN to Rosov, September 4, 1937.

59. VéN to BB, October 21, 1985; *SM*, 121; VN to Rosov, January 3, 1976, VNA.

60. The poems in *Dva puti* can be approximately dated by their sequence in VN's typescript album of 1916–17, VNA.

61. Rosov to VN, June 6, 1960; *SM*, 241; *Mary*, 75. To judge by VN's reference to the burning peat ("It can be proved, I think, by published records that Alexander Blok was even then noting in his diary the very peat smoke I saw," *SM*, 241) this scene could be dated August 3/16. Blok also records an evening tinted by burning peat on June 30/July 13, but at *CE*, 176, VN places the meeting with "Tamara" after Kerensky's appointment as prime minister.

62. V. T[atarinov], "Sobranie natsional'nogo soyuza v Berline," *Rul'*, July 12, 1921, 5.

63. Tseretelli, *Vospominanie*, 2: 263; Rosenberg, *Liberals*, 157, 170–75.

64. Hesser, "V dvukh vekakh," 369–70; "Sobranie pamyati V. D. Nabokova," *Nash vek*, April 3, 1932, 7; Field, *Life*, 77

65. VDN, *ProvGovt*, 79–80; Rosenberg, *Liberals*, 183–85.

66. Typescript album of 1916–17, VNA; addressee figures from verse album of December 1917–June 1918, VNA.

67. In VNA.

68. Also in VNA, *Stikhotvoreniya 1917* was written between September 23/October 6 and November 15/28, according to MS album of December 1917–June 1918.

69. VDN, *ProvGovt*, 153–54, 97; Rosenberg, *Liberals*, 241–52; VDN, "Vremennoe Pravitels'vo," *Arkhiv Russkoy Revolyutsii* 1 (1922): 36; cf. VDN, *ProvGovt*, 78.

70. VDN, *ProvGovt*, 158.

71. VDN, *ProvGovt*, 162; Schapiro, *Russian Revolutions*, 135–36; VN album, *Stikhotvoreniya 1917*, 19.

72. Sergey Melgunov, *The Bolshevik Seizure of Power*, trans. James S. Beaver, ed. Sergey Pushkarev (Santa Barbara: ABC–Clio, 1972), 127; *DB*, 165; *SM*, 181–82.

73. *DB*, 210; Field, *Life*, 137.

74. VDN, *ProvGovt*, 135–36.

75. VDN, *ProvGovt*, 166.

76. *SM*, 242.

77. VN album *Stikhotvoreniya 1917*, 24, VNA; *SM*, 242.

78. *DB*, 210; *SM*, 242; lecture notes on Kafka, VNA.

79. *SM*, 242–43.

80. *SM*, 243–44.

CHAPTER 7. FORETASTE OF EXILE

Epigraph: SM, 244.

1. *SM*, 242.

2. VN album, *Stikhotvoreniya 1917*, 28, 34, VNA.

3. *SO*, 178, 200; *SM*, 66; *DB*, 210.

4. *SM*, 244.

5. "A Few Notes on Crimean Lepidoptera," *Entomologist* 53 (February 1920): 29–33.

6. *PP*, 15.

7. *SM*, 288–92.

8. BB interview with SSN, September 1982; Nicolas Nabokov, *Bagazh*, 110, 111; *SM*, 245.

9. Ariadna Tyrkova-Williams, *From Liberty to Brest-Litovsk* (London: Macmillan, 1919), 334–35.

10. Schapiro, *Russian Revolutions*, 147; Rosenberg, *Liberals*, 271.

11. VDN, *ProvGovt*, 173–77; Hessen, "V dvukh vekakh," 381–82.

12. VDN, *ProvGovt*, 177; Schapiro, *Russian Revolution*, 147; *SM*, 177.

13. VDN, *ProvGovt*, 177; VN verse album, "Tsvetnye Kameshki" (December 1917–June 1918), VNA, pub. *PP*, 21, *Stikhi*, 8.

14. Rosenberg, *Liberals*, 358–59; N. Krishevskiy, "V Krymu (1916–1918 g.)," *Arkhiv Russkoy Revolyutsii* 13 (1924): 107.

15. VN notes to Field, June 12, 1970.

16. VDN diary, in album of VDN memorabilia, VNA.

17. VDN diary.

18. *SM*, 245; BB interview with ES, December 1986; VDN diary.

19. VDN diary; VN album, "Tsvetnye Kameshki."

20. VN album, "Tsvetnye Kameshki."

21. *SM*, 244, 245–46, 251; VDN diary; BB interview with VéN, December 1984; *Mary*, 89. VN and ES both remembered the surprise guest as Tsyganov, the second chauffeur, but VDN was writing on the very day Osip arrived, and Osip's daughter, Ekaterina Shchetinin, also remembers her father leaving to join VDN some months after the Revolution (Ekaterina Shchetinin to ES, April 2, 1989, private coll.).

22. "A Few Notes on Crimean Lepidoptera," 30–31; *SM*, 130–31; *DB*, 121; "Vladimir Nabokov—A Profile," *The Last Word* (Wellesley College), April 1943, 19.

23. VDN diary; Field, *Life*, 130; *N1*; *SM*, 245.

24. VDN diary; V. A. Obolensky, "Krym v 1917–1920 g.g.," *Na Chuzhoy Storone* 5 (1924): 23.

25. VDN diary.

26. D. S. Pasmanik, *Revolyutsionnye Gody v Krymu* (Paris: privately printed, 1926), 94; VDN diary.

27. VN notes to Field, June 12, 1970.

28. Zinaida Shakhovskaya, "V. I. Pol' i 'Angel'skie Stikhi' Vl. Nabokova," *Russkiy Almanakh* (Paris, 1981), 233.

29. VN album, "Tsvetnye Kameshki"; "A Few Notes on Crimean Lepidoptera," 30, 32; VDN diary.

30. VDN diary.

31. *N1*; BB interview with SSN, September 1982 (it was S. D. Nabokov's home in Yalta that fielded the calls); Shakhovksoy, "V. I. Pol' . . . ," 233.

32. Pasmanik, *Revolyutsionnye Gody*, 110.

33. Lepidoptera MSS, VNA; *SM*, 247.

34. "A Few Notes on Crimean Lepidoptera," 31–32; *DB*, 215.

35. *SM*, 249, 251; *Mary*, 91; draft letter, VN to Valentina Shulgin, LCNA.

36. SSN to BB, December 18, 1985, January 27, 1986; *DB*, 217; *SM*, 250–51.

37. VN to Walter Minton, September 9, 1966, VNA; *SM*, 249; *Glory* 18. VN once invited Andrew Field to mine *Glory* for biographical details about the Crimea, but later withdrew the invitation (*Life*, 129).

38. *SM*, 248.

39. *CE*, 182.

40. *SM*, 248; letter to Natalia Dmitrievna ———, n.d. (ca. October 1918), LCNA; unpublished chapter of *CE*, LCNA.

41. Lecture, VNA; *DB*, 213.

42. *DB*, 213.

43. "Krym," *Zhar-Ptitsa* 1 (August 1921): 36, repr. *Gorniy put'*, 109; *EO* 3:286–87; *Yaltinskiy Golos*, September 15 and 8, 1918; Pasmanik, 77; *DB*, 214; Obolensky, 21.

44. *Pnin*, 178–80; Field, *Life*, 131.

45. VN to EIN, September 10, 1932, VNA; *EO* 3:534; Voloshin, *Stikhotvoreniya* (Paris: YMCA, 1982), 1:230. Nabokov remembered the effect but not quite the right word: in 1942 he recalled it as "i neosushchestvimaya" ("and unrealizable" rather than "unrealized") (*NWL*, 73); by the 1950s the recollection had decayed further to "i nepreodolimaya" ("and insurmountable") (*EO* 3:534).

46. *EO* 3:534; *N1*; VN to EIN, September 10, 1932.

47. *SO*, 57; *NWL*, 78.

48. VN verse album, "Stikhi 1918" (September 1918–January 1919), p. 17, VNA; BB interviews with ES, December 1981 and June 1982.

49. BB interview with ES, December 1981; draft letter, VN to Valentina Shulgin, LCNA; draft letter, VN to Natalia Dmitrievna ———, n.d. (ca. October 1918), LCNA; note in workbook "Stikhi i Skhemy," LCNA; *N1*.

50. *LectsR*, 110; *Gorniy put'*, 91. The notebooks are in VNA.

51. ES to VN, May 26, 1950, VNA; *Perepiska*, 62; BB interviews with ES, December 1981 and June 1982.

52. *Gift*, 163.

53. *Gorniy put'*, 33.

54. Field, *Life*, 270; BB interview with Charles Remington, February 1987.

55. VN to Vladislav Khodasevich, April 26, 1934, Yale.

56. "Stikhi i Skhemy," LCNA; *DB*, 27; *SM*, 34; "Zvezda," in album "Stikhi 1918," 26.

57. Sergey Makovsky, *Na Parnase Serebryanogo Veka* (Munich: Tsentral'noe Ob'edinenie Politicheskikh Emigrantov iz SSSR, 1962), 356n.; "Angely" TS, VNA; *Gorniy put'*, 98–106. For VN's religion, see Shakhovskoy, "V. I. Pol' . . . ," and Field, *Life*, 88–89; for VN's denials, *PP*, 13–14; *N1*.

58. Shakhovskoy, "V.I. Pol' . . . , " 233.

59. VDN diary.

60. *Glory*, 11.

61. "Stikhi i Skhemy" album, LCNA.

62. Rosenberg, *Liberals*, 372. Despite the evidence, Andrew Field declared that V. D. Nabokov's post "was in some respects a nominal . . . one" (*Life*, 130)!

63. Pasmanik, *Revolyutsionnye Gody*, 128; *SM*, 177; Rosenberg, *Liberals*, 372.

64. *History of the Russian Revolution*, 2:30, 3:232; VDN, *ProvGovt*, 146, 160; Pasmanik, *Revolyutsionnye Gody*, 93, 122; *Lolita*, 317.

65. VN album, "Stikhi 1918," 110–13; *PP*, 19; Nicolas Nabokov, *Bagazh*, 111.

66. *SO*, 97.

67. VN verse album, "Stikhi 1918," 125–37.

68. *Gorniy put'*, 52; VN to Cecile Miauton, June 1919, VNA; Field, *Life*, 134.

69. VN verse album, January–June 1919, 26, 34; VN to Cecile Miauton, June 1919, VNA; *SM*, 200.

70. N. N. Bogdanov, "Krymskoe kraevoe pravitel'stvo," MS, Crimean Provisional Government Archive, Hoover, 14; Pasmanik, *Revolyutsionnye Gody*, 145–46, 149–51.

71. Rosenberg, *Liberals*, 375; Bogdanov, "Krymskoe kraevoe pravitel'stvo," 19.

72. *Perepiska*, 65; *PP*, 25; "Zhurnal Zasedaniya Soveta Ministrov Krymskogo Kraevogo Pravitel'stva," *Arkhiv Russkoy Revolyutsii* 2 (1921): 139; Nicolas Nabokov, *Bagazh*, 96.

73. "Zhurnal . . . ," 141.

74. VN to Cecile Miauton, June 1919; *SM*, 251; "Zhurnal . . . ," 141.

CHAPTER 8. BECOMING SIRIN

Epigraph to Part 2: Herr Schroeder-Jahn interview with VN, 1966, from TS, VNA.

Epigraph: *SM*, 269.

1. VN to Cecile Miauton, June 1919; VN verse album, January–June 1919, 60; BB interview with SSN, September 1982; *Mary*, 101; *Glory*, 27.

2. VN to Cecile Miauton, June 1919; VN notes to Field, June 12, 1970; BB interview with ES, December 1981; BB interview with SSN, September 1982; SSN to BB, December 31, 1984.

3. VN to Cecile Miauton, June 1919; VN verse album, "Stikhi 1919," p. 61, VNA; ES to VN, April 4, 1958, VNA.

4. "Akropol'," *Stikhi*, 23; BB interviews with SSN, September 1982 and December 1984.

5. *N1*; VN notes to Field, June 12, 1970; Field, *Life*, 135.

6. VN to Cecile Miauton, June 1919; *SM*, 253; *NWL*, 156.

7. VN to Cecile Miauton, June 1919; *Glory*, 40; *SM*, 253; "Familial Matters" Folder, VNA; *Perepiska*, 65; VéN to BB, February 1986.

8. *SM*, 60; KDN, *Ordeal of a Diplomat* (London: Duckworth, 1921).

9. VN to Cecile Miauton, June 1919; *SM*, 253; "Vladimir Nabokov—A Profile," *The Last Word* (Wellesley College), April 1943, 21.

10. *SO*, 171; verse album, January–June 1919, 81; *SM*, 254; VN to EIN, October 16, 1920, VNA.

11. *SM*, 258; Gleb Struve, "Dnevnik chitatelya: Pamyati V. V. Nabokova," *NRS*, July 17, 1977, 5; BB interview with Struve, May 1983.

12. VN to Rosov, September 4, 1937.

13. VN verse album, "Stikhi 1919," 4, VNA; "Familial Matters" Folder, VNA; album January–June 1919, VNA.

14. Admissions Logbook, Trinity College Library; *SM*, 253; G. M. Trevelyan, *Trinity College: An Historical Sketch* (Cambridge: Trinity College, 1943, 1983), 90 (R. Robson in the latest edition, 90n., doubts Byron's bear was housed in Great Court); VN, "Universitetskaya poema," *SZ*, 33 (1927), stanza 10; *DB*, 221.

15. Harrison obituary, *Times*, March 30, 1943; J. A. Venn, *Alumni Cantabrigiensis* (Cambridge: Cambridge University Press, 1947); *Glory*, 58; *SM*, 259; *N1*; VN notes to Field, June 12, 1970; Field, *Life*, 139; VN to EIN, ca. February 1920 and June 7, 1921, VNA.

16. *SM*, 259; *DB*, 220–21; *NWL*, 181.

17. *DB*, 221; "Kembridzh," *Ru!*, October 28, 1921, 2; *Glory*, 54; VN to EIN, November 6, 1920, VNA; admissions Logbook, Trinity College; BB interview with VéN, December 1984.

18. *N1*; *SM*, 260–64, 267; *DB*, 221–25; *Glory*, 57; *RLSK* 44, 46; "Kembridzh." The "desert sands" citation remains unidentified: *SM? SO?*

19. Field, *VN*, 67; *N1*; *DB*, 223; Magpie and Stump Debating Society Minutes, Trinity College Library (its text has a slip of the pen: "He derived immediate help from England": perhaps the club secretary intended to write "derided," then deciding not to complete the sentence and let posterity glimpse this example of Nabokovian scorn, mentally switched to another sentence, with the word "advised" in mind); *SM*, 179.

20. *LectsR*, frontispiece.

21. *RLSK* 46; *SM*, 260; "Kembridzh"; *Glory*, 61; *N1*.

22. VN notes to Field, June 12, 1970; *N1*; *Cambridge University Reporter*, January 14, 1920, 511.

23. BB interview with VéN, February 1983.

24. *Entomologist*, 53:681 (February 1920): 29–33.

25. *SM*, 268, 261.

26. *SM*, 265; *DB*, 226.

27. VéN to Reuben Abel, January 31, 1968, VNA; "Remembrance," *English Review*, no. 144 (November 1920): 392; *DB*, 226; *NWL*, 79; questionnaire, 1938, VNA; *SM*, 266.

28. VN verse album, October 1919–March 1920, VNA, 42; Field, *Life*, 139.

29. Hugh Mulligan interview with VN, November 1976, from TS in VNA; VN notes to Field, June 12, 1970; album, October 1919–March 1920, 31; VDN to A. S. Yashchenko, January 21, 1921, Hoover. After his 1970 comment about a "penultimate" plane ride, VN in fact flew several times in Europe in his last few years.

30. Council Minute Book 1918–19, CUA; Spalding's *Cambridge Directory* 1919–20, 198–99; Minutes of the Lodgings Houses Syndicate, CUA; *DB*, 221; *SM*, 259; *Glory*, 56.

31. BB interview with VéN, January 1982; *TLS*, September 30, 1920, 638, reviews Lutyens's *Poems and Verses*; VN to EIN, October 16, 1920, VNA; *SM*, 268; *DB*, 227; Don-Zhuanskiy Spisok; *N1*; Field, *Life*, 141; Field, *VN*, 66.

32. VN to EW, June 8, 1944, Yale; Field, *Life*, 140; Field, *VN*, 62; *Granta*, February 27, 1920.

33. Robert Hughes interview with VN, January 3, 1966, from TS in VNA; Robert Robinson interview with VN, *Listener*, March 24, 1977, 367; *SM*, 267; *DB*, 227; Field, *Life*, 140. Other evidence for Nabokov's studying zoology in general and continuing it into his second term includes the fellow boxer in his zoology class, fought with during the Lent term; Struve, "Dnevnik chitatelya: Pamyati V. V. Nabokova"; VN to VDN, June 10, 1920, VNA, which suggests VN's zeal in reading French literature in the Easter term may be a catch-up exercise and a compensation for his having slacked in his previous course; VN to Véra Slonim, January 8, 1924, VNA; VéN to L. Mazza, Mondadori publishers, December 26, 1961, VNA.

34. VDN to Ivan Petrunkevich, April 30, 1920, ColB, and to VN, March 12, 1920 and April 20, 1920, VNA.

35. Lucie Léon Noel, "Playback," *Triquarterly* 17 (Winter 1970): 212; Field, *VN*, 66; BB interview with Harry and Elena Levin, February 1987; Don-Zhuanskiy Spisok.

36. VN to VDN, June 10, 1920, VNA; *Student's Handbook to the University and Colleges of Cambridge*, 1919–1920, 460. The principal French teachers were E.G.W. Braunholtz (for medieval and early Renaissance literature), Professor O. H. Prior and Dr. H. F. Stewart. *Cambridge University Reporter*, June 18, 1921, 1178.

37. Field, *Life*, 140; verse album, "Nostalgia," April 1920–July 1921, VNA.

38. VN to EIN, April 26, 1920, VNA.

39. *SM*, 258.

40. *Glory*, 70–71.

41. VN to EIN, November 6, 1920, and VN to EIN and VDN, June 10, 1920, VNA.

42. VN to EIN and VDN, June 10, 1920.

43. VN to EIN, dated (perhaps incorrectly) by VN in 1960s "Feb. 1920"; VDN to Ivan Petrunkevich, June 29, 1920, ColB, and to VN, July 14, 1920, VNA.

44. Andrey Levinson, *Rul'*, May 28, 1921, 2; *N1*.

45. WL, 204; BB interview with ES, June 1982; VDN to Petrunkevich, June 29, 1920.

46. BB interview with Marina Astmann, March 1983.

47. VDN to Paul Milyukov, September 6 and 19, 1920, ColB; George Hessen to VN and VéN, April 29, 1945, VNA.

48. VDN to A. Tyrkova-Williams, October 3, 1920, ColB.

49. VN to EIN, October 16, 1920, VNA.

50. VN to EIN, October 15, 1920, VNA; Hessen, *Gody izgnaniya*, 103; VDN to VN, November 1, 1920, VNA.

51. VN to EIN, November 6, 1920, VNA; Field, *VN*, 64; *SO*, 292.

52. Collected in book form as *Russia in the Shadows* (London: Hodder & Stoughton, n.d.).

53. VN to EIN, November 8, 1920, VNA.

54. *NWL*, 181; *DB*, 221.

55. VN to EIN, November 18, 1920, VNA; *SM*, 268.

56. VDN to VN, November 1, 1920, VNA; Hessen, *Gody izgnaniya*, 121.

57. "Painted Wood," *Carrousel* 2 (1923): 9.

58. VN to EIN, February 23, 1921; passport, LCNA; VN to EIN, January 25 and May 27, 1921, VNA; *DB*, 227.

59. VN to EIN and VDN, February 5 and 19, 1921, VNA; verse album, "Nostalgia," 80; Don-Zhuanskiy Spisok; Field, *VN*, 66.

60. VN to EIN and VDN, February 5, and to EIN, February 23, 1921, VNA.

61. BB interview with VéN, August 1982 and VéN to BB, June 13, 1988; Don-Zhuanskiy Spisok.

62. VN to EIN, April 27 and 24, 1921, VNA; verse album, "Nostalgia," 89.

63. VN to EIN, April 27, 1921, VNA; Examination Lists and Medieval and Modern Languages Tripos, CUA; VN to VDN and EIN, April 29, 1921, VNA; "V. Sh.," *Stikhi*, 72.

64. VN to VDN and EIN, May 11, 1921, VNA; "Rupert Bruk," *Grani* 1 (1922): 216, 231.

65. See poems "V. Sh."; "Khudozhnik-nishchiy"; "Bezhenets"; "Oblaka"; "Pir"; "Koni"; "P'yanyy rytsar' "; "Ya dumayu o ney"; "Pero"; VN to EIN, May 23 and 27, 1921, VNA; *Cambridge University Reporter*, May 17 and June 18, 1921, 996, 1178.

66. VN to EIN, June 7, 1921, VNA; Svetlana Andrault de Langeron (née Siewert) to BB, January 31, 1984; BB interview with ES, December 1981.

67. Svetlana Siewert album, private coll.; "Glaza," *Grozd'* (Berlin: Gamayun, 1923), 37; *Stikhi*, 50 and cf. 294; poem, cited in letter from ES to Svetlana Andrault de Langeron, October 25, 1949, private coll.

68. Svetlana Andrault de Langeron to BB, December 15, 1983 and November 8, 1984; VN verse album, "Stikhi," July 1921–January 1923, 32, VNA.

69. BB interview with ES, December 1981.

70. *Rul'*, September 6 and November 15, 1921, 5; EIN album of VN's verse, VNA; BB interview with ES, September 1982; *N1*; VDN to Isaac Shklovsky (Dioneo), May 14, 1921, TsGALI, Fond 1390, opis' 1, no. 49, cited in Evgeny Belodubrovsky and Evgeny Shikhovtsev, "Iz Materialov o Nabokove v Sovetskikh Arkivakh," unpublished MSS, VNA.

71. V. E. Tatarinov, *Golos emigranta*, 12 (April 1922), 8; Nicolas Nabokov, *Bagazh*, 102, 106, 108; BB interviews with VéN, August 1982, and ES, September 1982.

72. *Bagazh*, 102, 108–9, 110–11.

73. "Zhar-Ptitsa," *PN*, September 1, 1921, 3.

74. *Rul'*, August 14, September 3 and 11, 1921; *Vremya*, September 26, 1921.

75. "Familial Matters" Folder, VNA; VN to EIN, June 3, VDN to VN, October, and VN to EIN and VDN, October 24, 1921, VNA.

76. VN to Svetlana Siewert, November 1921, and VDN to VN, November 19, 1921, VNA.

77. D. S. Mirsky, *A History of Russian Literature* (1926, 1927; New York: Knopf, 1973), 406.

78. VN, "Pamyati A. M. Chornogo," *PN*, August 13, 1932; Endi, "Pamyati A. Chornogo i M. Voloshina," *Nash vek*, September 25, 1932, 5; *Russkaya kniga*, no. 9 (1921), 47.

79. VDN to VN, October 20, 1921, and VN to VDN and EIN, October 24, 1921, VNA.

80. "Skital'tsy," *Grani* 2 (1923): 69–99.

81. VN to EIN, November 25, 1921; the poem was published without title, *Grozd'*, 11.

82. VN to EIN, October 20, 1921, VNA; VN to ES, late 1947, *Perepiska*, 52 (incorrectly dated winter 1948); *NWL*, 106; VN to de Calry, April 12, 1961, VNA; BB interview with Alfred Appel, Jr., April 1983.

83. *SM*, 116.

84. Svetlana Andrault de Langeron to BB, January 31, 1984.

85. P. Sh., "Grani," *Rul'*, January 8, 1922, 6; VN to EIN, December 1, 1921, and VDN to VN, January 29, 1922, VNA.

86. Passport stamp, LCNA; *N1*; VN to EIN, January 27, 1922, VNA.

87. Passport stamp, LCNA; Hessen, *Gody izgnaniya*, 103.

88. *Rul'*, March 2 and 29, 1922.

89. Hessen, *Gody izgnaniya*, 123, 134; "V. D. Nabokov," lecture by Nikolay Astrov, March 28, 1932, ColB.

90. For details of the event see *Rul'* and *PN*, March 29/mid–April 1922, and *Rul'*, July 13–15, 1922 (the trial).

91. EIN transcript of VN diary, VNA.

92. *Rul'*, March 31–April 9, 1922.

93. *Stikhi*, 66; passport stamp, LCNA; Council Minute Book, CUA.

94. VN to EIN, May 27, 1922, VNA.

95. VN to EIN, May 27 and 22, 1922; *SO*, 102–3; *SM*, 272; *N1*.

96. *Cambridge University Reporter*, May 16 and June 17, 1922, 947–48 and 1141–42; VN to EIN, June 2 and May 22, 1922, VNA; *DB*, 230; *N1*; degree diploma and passport stamp, LCNA.

97. VN to EIN, June 2, 1922.

CHAPTER 9. REGROUPING

Epigraph: LATH, 3.

1. *DB*, 42; unpublished chapter of *CE*, LCNA; Hessen, *Gody izgnaniya*, 136–37.

2. Svetlana Andrault de Langeron to BB, January 31 and November 1, 1984; BB interview with ES, December 1984.

3. Field, *Life*, 147; VN to EIN, July 24, 1922; Svetlana Andrault de Langeron to BB, December 15, 1983.

4. Nabokov remembered translating Carroll "one summer" (VéN to S. J. Parker, September 18, 1973, VNA). Although he also added offhandedly that he translated Rolland and Carroll more or less simultaneously, both the moderately advanced inflation and the fact that he never once mentioned *Alice* in letters from Cambridge, while referring a dozen times to *Colas Breugnon*, seem to limit the *Alice* translation to the summer of 1922.

5. *SM*, 283; Robert Hughes interview with VN, January 1966, from TS in VNA.

6. VéN to Parker, September 18, 1973; Warren Weaver, *Alice in Many Tongues: The Translations of "Alice in Wonderland"* (Madison: University of Wisconsin Press, 1964), 90–91.

7. See Robert C. Williams, *Culture in Exile: Russian Emigrés in Germany, 1881–1941* (Ithaca: Cornell University Press, 1972); L. Fleishman, R. Hughes, O. Raevsky-Hughes, *Russkiy Berlin 1921–1923* (Paris: YMCA Press, 1983); Hessen, *Gody izgnaniya*; Mark Raeff, TS, "Russian Culture in Emigration."

8. *Marina Tsvetaeva: The Woman, Her World and Her Poetry* (Cambridge: Cambridge University Press, 1986), 115.

9. *SO*, 85–86. Nabokov erred in classifying Bely as frankly pro-Soviet at this time.

10. VN to Pavel Mikhailovich (surname unknown), December 27, 1934, VNA.

11. Fleishman et al., *Russkiy Berlin*, 84–85.

12. *Rul'*, October 22, 1922, 9, and November 12, 1922, 9; *Veretyonysh'* 3 (1922): 6; *Novaya Russkaya Kniga* 10 (1922): 44; *Nakanune*, November 26, 1922, 8; Fleishman et al., *Russkiy Berlin*, 86–87.

13. Z. Arbatov, "Nollendorfplatzkafe," *Grani* (Frankfurt) 41 (1959): 111.

14. GS, "Iz moikh vospominaniy ob odnom russkom literaturnom kruzhke v Berline," in Leonid Rzhevsky, ed., *Tri yubileya Andreya Sedykh* (New York: Literaturnyy Fond, 1982), 189–94; GS, *NRS*, July 17, 1977, 8, and August 7, 1977, 5; minutes of Bratstvo, November 29, 1922, Struve archive, Hoover; Alexander Brailow to BB, October 20, 1983.

15. *TD*, 142; VN to EIN, ca. July 1924, VNA; BB interview with VéN, December 1981; and see poems "Podruga boksyora" (written November 16, 1922), *Nash Mir*, May 11, 1924, 1–2, and "Geksametry: Ivanu Lukashu" (written June 5, 1923), EIN album, VNA.

16. BB, "Nabokov Bibliography: Aspects of the Emigré Period," *VNRN* 11 (Fall 1983): 21–24; *Dni*, March 25, 1923.

17. Nina Berberova, *Kursiv moy* (New York: Russica, 1983), 1:369.

18. *Rul'*, January 28, 1923.

19. VN verse albums, 1918–1923, VNA.

20. Gerald S. Smith, "Nabokov and Russian Verse Forms," *Russian Literature Triquarterly* 24 (1990).

21. Alfred Appel, Jr., "Remembering Nabokov," in Quennell, 19–20; VéN to Appel, October 2, 1970.

22. Svetlana Andrault de Langeron to BB, December 1983–November 1984.

23. VN, *Nikolai Gogol* (Norfolk, Conn.: New Directions, 1944), 106.

24. VN verse album, January–November 1923, VNA.

25. EIN album, VNA.

26. VN to EIN, April 4, 1928, VNA.

27. EIN album, VNA.

28. *Rul'*, May 20 and 24, 1923.

29. BB interview with VéN, December 1981; *N1*; Field, *Life*, 201.

30. Field, *Life*, 159; Field, *VN*, 112.

31. See Janet K. Gezari, "Roman et problème chez Nabokov," *Poétique* 5 (1974): 99–100, for an excellent analysis of the problem.

32. *Gody izgnaniya*, 97.

33. *SM*, 281; "Pamyati I. V. Gessena," *NRS*, March 31, 1943, 2. The 1943 obituary became the basis for the Hessen tribute in *SM*, which improves what it includes but omits certain details. I have therefore conflated the two passages: before the first and after the second ellipsis, the text follows the obituary, while between the ellipses it derives from the autobiography.

34. *Gody izgnaniya*, 94–96; "Pamyati I. V. Gessena."

35. *Rul'*, April 1, 1923.

36. *Gody izgnaniya*, 96; Field, *VN*, 97; BB interview with VéN, December 1986; Alexander Brailow to BB, December 29, 1983.

37. The poem (pub. *Rul'*, June 24, 1923; repr. *Stikhi*, 106–7) is dated June 1, 1923, EIN album, VNA. VéN would prefer to be kept out of the biography altogether, and therefore takes issue with this account of her first meeting with VN, even to the extent of denying that she first met him at a charity ball, as VN clearly states ("I met my wife, Véra Slonim, at one of the émigré charity balls in Berlin," *SO*, 127). In the 1960s and 1970s Nabokov regularly reminded himself in his diaries to commemorate their first meeting. On the space for May 8 in his 1963 diary, he wrote: "40 years since Véra and I met." In his 1969 diary on May 8 he simply records "*profil volchiy*" ("wolf's profile"), a phrase from the poem "The Encounter" that evidently suffices to sum up their first meeting.

38. VN to Svetlana Siewert, May 25, 1923, from transcript in LCS.

39. *Glory*, 163–64; VN to Svetlana Siewert, May 25, 1923.

40. Field, *Life*, 202.

41. *Glory*, 163–64; *N1*; Field, *Life*, 202; BB interview with VéN, December 1981; VéN to BB, July 7, 1986.

42. VN to EIN, June 19, 1923; *SL*, 3–4; VN to Svetlana Siewert, May 25, 1923.

43. Pub. *Rul'*, October 14, 1923; trans. DN, *MUSSR*, 289–307; BB interview with VéN, May 1989.

44. Pub. *Rul'*, August 14 and 16, 1924; trans. DN, *MUSSR*, 269–83. The translation that follows is my own.

45. Alden Whitman interview with VN, October 6, 1971; see above, chap. 2, n. 42.

46. VN to Véra Slonim, July 1923, VNA.

47. VN to Véra Slonim, July 1923; passport, LCNA; VN verse album, January–November 1923; VéN to BB, May 2, 1986.

CHAPTER 10. ENTER THE MUSE

Epigraph: Gift, 338.

1. BB interviews with VéN, December 1981, June and August 1982, December 1984, and May 1989.

2. Field, *Life*, 178; N1.

3. *LATH*, 3.

4. VN to Heinrich Maria Ledig–Rowohlt, May 2, 1975, VNA.

5. BB interview with VéN, May 1989; Field, *Life*, 177; VéN to BB, May 2, 1986.

6. VéN to Field, March 10, 1973, VNA.

7. BB interviews with VéN, February, June, and August 1982 and May 1989; VéN to BB, May 2, 1986; VéN to A. A. Goldenweiser, June 8, 1957.

8. VéN to Field, March 10, 1973; BB interviews with VéN, June 1982 and December 1984; Field. *Life*, 178.

9. BB interviews with VéN, December 1981, September 1982, and December 1984; VéN to Goldenweiser, June 8, 1957 and March 6, 1967, ColB.

10. Field, *Life*, 180.

11. BB interview with VéN, January 1980, June 1982, December 1986.

12. ES to VN and VéN, August 28, 1956, VNA; VéN to BB, May 2, 1986.

13. Pub. *Stikhi*, 115–16, dated September 25, 1923.

14. EIN album, VNA.

15. *Rul'*, September 21 and 25, December 2, 1923.

16. *SM*, 278–79; *DB*, 238–39.

17. "Udar kryla," *Russkoe Ekho* 21 (January 1924); "Bogi," EIN album, VNA.

18. EIN album, VNA; Field, *VN*, 126; Arbatov, "Nollendorfplatzkafe," 111.

19. *Dni*, December 25, 1923.

20. Hessen, *Gody izgnaniya*, 112.

21. VN to Katharine White, March 4, 1949, VNA; BB interview with ES, December 24, 1981; ES to BB, May 29, 1986; *Rul'*, January 8, 1924, 5; VN to Véra Slonim, December 30, 1923; for the Czech grants, see also Karlinsky, *Marina Tsvetaeva*, 125–26. While the rest of the Nabokov family moved to Prague, Sergey remained in Berlin.

22. VN to Véra Slonim, January 8, 1924, VNA.

23. VN to Véra Slonim, January 14, 16, 17, and 24, 1924, VNA.

24. VN to Véra Slonim, January 24, 1924; *DB*, 242–43; VéN to Simon Karlinsky, September 24, 1984, VNA; "Posvyashchenie k 'Tragedii Gospodina Morna,' " dated January 26, 1924, EIN album, VNA.

25. VN to EIN, January 31, 1924, VNA.

26. *RLSK*, 84.

27. BB interviews with VéN, December 1981, December 1984, January 1985; VN to EIN, January 31, 1924; Field, *Life*, 161.

28. VN to EIN, January 31, 1924.

29. Russian émigré periodicals abound in descriptions of the Bluebird; in English, see Alex de Jonge, *The Weimar Chronicle* (New York: Paddington Press, 1978), 161.

30. VN to Véra Slonim, January 24, 1924, and to EIN, January 31, 1924.

31. VN to EIN, January 31, 1924; Field, *Life*, 163; EIN album, VNA.

32. Hessen, *Gody izgnaniya*, 142; Grigory Landau, *Vozrozhdenie*, December 1, 1931.

33. VN to EIN, January 31 and March 6, 1924, VNA; *Rul'*, March 16, 1924, 8.

34. GS, *NRS*, July 17, 1977, 8; BB interview with GS, May 1983; *Rul'*, March 23 and 28, 1924.

35. "Port" pub. *Rul'*, May 24, 1924; "Blagost' " dated in EIN album, VNA, pub. *Rul'*, April 27, 1924, 6–7; repr. *VC*. "Grace" is VN's translation of "Blagost' ": VéN to S. J. Parker, November 27, 1972, VNA.

36. *Russkoe Ekho*, April 20, 1924, 6–8.

37. VN to EIN, April–May 1924, VNA.

38. VN to EIN, April–May 1924; *N1*; Field, *VN*, 68.

39. Dated in EIN album, VNA; pub. *Russkoe Ekho*, June 8, 15, 22, 29, and July 6, 1924; repr. *VC*; trans. DN with VN, *RB*.

40. *RB*, 220.

41. VN to EIN, April–May 1924.

42. *Rul'*, April 16, 25, and 30, May 21 and 25, and June 18, 1924; *Dni*, April 16 and May 11, 1924; EIN album, VNA; *Nash Mir*, June 5, 1924.

43. VN to EIN, early June 1924.

44. BB interview with VéN, December 1981.

45. VN, cited in Appel, *NDC*, 155.

46. VN to EIN, June 14, 1924, VNA; the story was duly published, *Russkoe Ekho*, April 12, 1925, 88.

47. Dated *TD*, 142; *Segodnya*, June 22, 1924; trans. DN with VN, *TD*.

48. Dated, VN to EIN, June 14, 1924; pub. *Segodnya*, July 13, 1924; repr. *VC*; trans. DN with VN, *DS*.

49. VN to EIN, June 14, 1924.

50. VN to EIN, ca. July 6, 1924, VNA. VN means stories already sold to newspapers.

51. VN to EIN, July–August 1924, VNA; *Rul'*, August 8, 1924.

52. VN to EIN, ca. July 6, July–August, and August 30, 1924, VNA.

53. VN to EIN, ca. July 6, 1924; VN to Véra Slonim, July 13, 1924, VNA.

54. VN to Véra Slonim, July 17, 1924, VNA.

55. Dated July 22–25, 1924 in first pub., *Segodnya*, September 28, 1924; repr. *VC*; trans. DN with VN, *DS*.

56. VN to EIN, July–August 1924.

57. VN to Véra Slonim, August 19 and 24, 1924.

58. Dated August 25–26, 1924, MS, LCNA.

59. BB interviews with VéN, September 1982 and December 1984; VN to EIN, August 30, 1924 and ca. September 28, 1924, VNA.

60. Alan Levy interview with VN, April 1971, from TS in VNA.

61. Dated on MS sent to EIN, September 6, 1924; pub. *Rul'*, September 16, 1924; repr. and trans. *PP*, 28–29.

62. EIN album, VNA.

63. Dated *TD*, 170; pub. *Rul'*, November 2 and 4, 1924; repr. *VC*; trans. DN with VN, *TD*.

64. EIN album, VNA.

65. VN to EIN, December 13, 1924, VNA.

66. Dated VN to EIN, December 13, 1924; pub. *Rul'*, January 6 and 8, 1925; repr. *VC*; trans. DN with VN, *DS*. See also above, 71–72.

67. VN to EIN, December 18 and ca. 22, 1924, January 13 and 23, 1925, VNA.

68. *Rul'*, January 29, 1925; repr. *VC*; trans. DN with VN, *DS*.

69. *DS*, 82.

70. *Rul'*, February 18 and 27, 1925.

71. VN to EIN, March 13, 1925; *Rul'*, March 17, 1925.

72. VN to EIN, March 27, 1925.

73. Field, *Life*, 180–81; cf. *Defense*, 177.

74. BB interview with ES, November 1982.

75. VNA.

76. VN to Véra Slonim, January 13, 1924.

CHAPTER 11. SCENES FROM ÉMIGRÉ LIFE

1. BB interviews with VéN, December 1981, September and November 1982, December 1984; VéN to BB, August 27, 1986.

2. *LATH*, 51.

3. *DS*, 82; *Mary*, xi ("started . . . soon after my marriage"); *SO*, 191 ("married . . . in the midst of my writing my first Russian novel"); *Mashen'ka* MS, LCNA.

4. *Rul'*, April 19, 1925; *SM*, 283; VN to GS, February 3, 1931, Hoover; Simon Karlinsky to BB, September 10, 1987. The first occurrence of "krestoslovitsa" I can find in the émigré press is in *Rul'* 's weekly supplement, *Nash Mir*—to which VN contributed—in February 1925, almost six months before it occurs in any other émigré paper.

5. VN to EIN, May 27, June 30, October 13, 1925, VNA; VN to GS, February 20, 1926, Hoover; Field, *Life*, 153; Field, *VN*, 393.

6. *N1*; VN to EIN, May 27, 1925; BB interview with VéN, September 1982.

7. *Rul'*, June 1 and 10, 1925; poem pub. *Rul'*, June 4, 1925.

8. VN to GS, ca. August 1, 1925, Hoover.

9. VN to EIN, June 30, 1925; pub. *Rul'*, September 26, 1925; trans. DN, *New Yorker*, February 18, 1985.

10. *SM*, 298.

11. BB interview with VéN, December 1981.

12. VN to GS, July 22 and ca. August 1, 1925, Hoover; BB interviews with VéN, December 1981, September 1982, December 1984.

13. "Lyublyu ya goru" ("I Like That Mountain"), pub. *Rul'*, September 19, 1925, repr. and trans. *PP*, 34–35; "Ten' " ("The Shadow"), pub. *Rul'*, September 13, 1925, repr. *Stikhi*, 173–74; VN to VéN, August 27, 29, 31 and September 2, 1925, and to EIN, September 4 and 6, 1925, VNA; VN Schwarzwald notebook, VNA; VéN to BB, August 27, 1986.

14. VN to EIN, September 6 and 28 and October 13, 1925, VNA; BB interviews with VéN, December 1981, September 1982, January 1985.

15. VN to EIN, September 28, 1925.

16. VN to EIN, September 28 and October 31, 1925, VNA; *SO*, 118.

17. VN to EIN, October 13, 1925.

18. VN to EIN, October 31, 1925; *Mashen'ka* MS, LCNA.

19. *Mary*, xi.

20. *NWL*, 147.

21. VN to Michael Glenny, February 3, 1970, quoted Jane Grayson, *Nabokov Translated* (Oxford: Oxford University Press, 1977), 126.

22. VN to EIN, October 31, 1925; pub. *Rul'*, November 12 and 13, 1925; repr. *VC*; trans. DN with VN, *DS*.

23. Pub. *Rul'*, December 24, 1925; repr. *VC*; trans. DN with VN, *DS*.

24. *Ada*, 470; cf. BB, *Nabokov's "Ada": The Place of Consciousness* (Ann Arbor: Ardis, 1985), 13–16.

25. See *Vladimir Nabokov: The American Years*, chap. 26.

26. VN to EIN, October 13 and 31, 1925; VéN to BB, August 27, 1986; Field, *Life*, 182; MS, LCNA.

27. "Lyzhnyy pryzhok" ("The Ski Jump"), pub. *Rul'*, January 24, 1926; repr. *Stikhi*, 179–80.

28. BB interview with VéN, December 1981 and December 1984.

29. VN to EIN, January 7, 1926, VNA; *Rul'*, December 25 and 30, 1925.

30. VN to EIN, January 7, 1926; Hessen, *Gody izgnaniya*, 146–48.

31. VN to EIN, May 18, 1931, VNA.

32. Unpublished memoir, Elena Jakovlev (née Kaminka); VN notes, VNA; Field, *Life*, 200.

33. G. Hessen to VN, April 29, 1945, VNA; BB interview with Nathalie Barosin, April 1983; G. Hessen to VN, May 20, 1953, VNA.

34. BB interviews with VéN, November 1982 and January 1985.

35. See obituaries and memorials in émigré press from December 17, 1928, esp. G. Landau, *Rul'*, December 23, 1928, and S. Frank, *Rul'*, December 17, 1929; A. Bakhrakh, *Po pamyati, po zapisyam* (Paris: Presse Libre, 1980), 85–88; Z. Arbatov, "Nollendorfplatzkafe," *Grani* 41 (1959): 113.

36. BB interview with VéN, December 1981; GS, *NRS*, July 17, 1977; Evgenia Cannac, *Russkaya Mysl'*, December 29, 1977.

37. *Nash vek*, January 1, 1932 and April 23, 1933; Yu. Ofrosimov, *NZ* 84 (1966): 83; Alex Brailow to BB, December 29, 1983.

38. BB interviews with VéN, September 1982, December 1984, January 1985; MSS of Tatarinova-Aykhenvald circle talks, VNA.

39. "Igra" MS, VNA; *BoxSport* (Berlin), November 27 and December 4, 1925.

40. VN to EIN, January 24, 1926, VNA; Cannac, *Russkaya Mysl'*, December 29, 1977.

41. VN to GS, January 3, 1926 and February 20, 1926, Hoover; "Britva" MS, LCNA; pub. *Rul'*, February 19, 1926.

42. *Rul'*, February 17, 1926.

43. Agreement, VNA; *Rul'*, March 21, 1926; VN to EIN, April 6, 1926, VNA.

44. By Aykhenvald in *Rul'* and GS in *Vozrozhdenie*.

45. VN to EIN, April 1, 6, and 23, 1926, VNA; Field, *Life*, 155; VéN to Alfred Appel, Jr., November 9, 1977, VNA; BB interview with VéN, September 1982; "Ivan Vernykh" MS, VNA.

46. *TD*, 40; pub. *Rul'*, June 27 and 29, 1926.; repr. *VC*; trans. DN with VN, *TD*, 41-58.

47. VN to EIN, July 10, 1926, VNA; BB interview with VéN, December 1984; VN to VéN, June 6, 1926, VNA; MS, "Neskol'ko slov . . . ," VNA.

48. BB interviews with VéN, June 1982, December 1984, January 1985.

49. For Lukash, see Arbatov, "Nollendorfplatzkafe," 119; for Tsvetaeva, cf. VéN to Ekaterina Elenev, December 1, 1952, VNA, and Karlinsky, *Marina Tsvetaeva*, 222-23, 249-50.

50. BB interview with VéN, January 1985.

51. Untitled MS, VNA.

52. *Rul'*, July 18, 1926; VN to EIN, July 10, 1926.

53. BB interview with VéN, December 1981.

54. *Sovremennye Zapiski* 30 (January 1927); repr. *VC*; trans. DN with VN, *TD*.

55. VN to EIN, July 15, 1926, VNA; BB interview with VéN, December 1981, September 1982, January 1985; *NWL*, 69.

56. BB interview with VéN, December 1981, November 1982, December 1984.

57. VN to GS, February 19, 1927, Hoover; BB interviews with VéN, September 1982, December 1984, January 1985; Field, *VN*, 106.

58. VN to EIN, October 26, 1926, VNA. Only act 1 was published in *Rul'*, January 1, 1927.

59. My translation differs slightly from DN's, *MUSSR*, 85-86.

60. DN discusses the "elsewhere" theme, *MUSSR*, 7.

61. VN to EIN, October 26, 1926.

62. Field, *VN*, 104, 101-2.

63. *SM*, 283; BB interview with VéN, January 1985.

64. VN to GS, February 19, 1927, Hoover. Pub. *Sovremennye Zapiski* 33 (November 1927).

65. In other words, using vowels for feminine rhymes and consonants for masculine, Pushkin's ababeecciddiff becomes Sirin's aabeebiiccodod.

66. See Alexander Pushkin, *Eugene Onegin*, trans. and with commentary by VN (New York: Bollingen, 1964), esp. 1:15–59.

67. VN to GS, March 31, 1928, Hoover.

CHAPTER 12. IDEAS AWAY

1. Pivot interview, May 1975, from TS in VNA.

2. *Rul'*, January 25, 1927; *N1*.

3. Dated on MS, LCNA; pub. *Rul'*, March 6, 1927; repr. *VC*; trans. DN with VN, *DS*.

4. *DS*, 72.

5. *Ru1'*, January 1 and April 5, 1927; VN to EIN, March 18, 1927, VNA.

6. Pub. *Rul'*, May 22, 1927; repr. *VC*; trans. DN with VN, *DS*.

7. Pub. *Rul'*, June 26, 1927; repr. *Stikhi*, 201; *Pravda*, July 15, 1927; Slava Paperno and John Hagopian, in Gibian and Parker, 100–2.

8. *Rul'*, May 22 and June 1, 1927. Field (*VN*, 129) absurdly supposes VN's participation in this revue to be decisive proof that Evreinov was a major influence on his work.

9. *N1*; VN to EIN, September 22, 1927; BB interview with VéN, January 1985.

10. VN to Aykhenvald, July 29, 1927, in S. V. Shumikhin, "Pis'mo Very i Vladimira Nabokovykh Yu. I. Aykhenvaldu," *Nashe nasledie* (1988): 2, 113, TsGALI, Fond 1175, inv. 2, no. 133.

11. *SO*, 309–10.

12. *Rul'*, August 23, 1927.

13. MS, LCNA; pub. *VC*; trans. DN with VN, *RB*, 83–115.

14. Cf. VN to GS, February 1929, Hoover.

15. VN to EIN, September 22, 1927, VNA; "Shakhmatnyy kon' " MS, LCNA; pub. *Rul'*, October 23, 1927; review, *Rul'*, November 16, 1927.

16. Khodasevich review, *Rul'*, December 14, 1927; VN to EIN, October 30, 1927, VNA; Cannac, *Russkaya Mysl'*, December 29, 1977, and *Russkiy Almanakh*, 363; Field, *Life*, 153.

17. *Rul'*, October 30, November 18, 19, 24, December 10, 11, 1927, and January 25, 1928; "Chelovek i veshchi" MS, VNA.

18. Field, *VN*, 119.

19. VN to EIN, January 25, February 13 and 18, 1928, VNA.

20. VN to EIN, June 7, 1927, and March 29 and 31, 1928, VNA; agreement, VNA.

21. VN to EIN, April 4, 1928; Cannac, *Russkaya Mysl'*, December 29, 1977.

22. BB interview with VéN, January 1983.

23. Cannac, *Russkaya Mysl'*, December 29, 1977.

24. VN to EIN, April 4, 1928, VNA; *Korol', Dama, Valet* (Berlin: Slovo, 1928), 260.

25. *KQK*, viii.

26. *SM*, 298; *PF*, 234

27. See Ellen Pifer's chapter on *KQK* in her excellent *Nabokov and the Novel* (Cambridge: Harvard University Press, 1980).

28. Here as elsewhere I generally follow the Russian version; the English version reworks the ending.

29. BB interview with VéN, December 1981.

30. BB interviews with VéN, December 1981; VéN to A. A. Goldenweiser, June 8 and 14. 1957, ColB.

31. For pub. date, *Rul'*, September 23, 1928; Aykhenvald review, *Rul'*, October 3, 1928; public debate at 6 Martin-Luther-Strasse, November 4, 1928, from TS notice, VNA.

32. Agreement, VNA.

33. VN to "Dear poets," November 30, 1928, VNA; *N1*; BB interview with VéN, January 1985; Field, *Life*, 222–23.

34. Pub. *Rul'*, December 25, 1928.

35. *N1*; VN to EIN, December 17, 1928; VN, "Pamyati Yu. I. Aykhenval'da," *Rul'*, December 23, 1928; *Rul'*, December 18, 1928; Field, *Life*, 169; *Segodnya*, December 24, 1928.

36. BB interviews with VéN, December 1981 and September 1982.

37. VéN to BB, August 27, 1986; GS, *NRS*, July 17, 1977; "Notes on the Lepidoptera of the Pyrénées Orientales and the Ariège," *Entomologist* 64 (1931): 255.

38. "Notes . . . ," 255; VN to GS, February 1929, Hoover; BB interview with VéN, January 1985.

39. "Notes . . . ," 255–56; BB interviews with VéN, September 1982 and January 1985; *EO*, 3:433; *SM*, facing p. 256.

40. Untitled MS, VNA; see "A Matter of Chance" above, p. 231.

41. BB interview with VéN, February 1983; VéN notes, 1986, VNA. Field (*VN*, 132) completely muddles the idea: "Nabokov also told me that he had intended to impart a sexual aspect to Luzhin, who would see a black beard on his wife, but that he abandoned that element of the novel."

42. *Defense*, 7.

43. *SM*, facing p. 256.

44. "Notes . . . ," 268; BB interview with VéN, January 1985.

45. *SM*, 131; "Notes . . . ," 270; BB interviews with VéN, September 1982 and January 1985.

46. *Rul'*, May 22, 1929.

47. "Notes . . . ," 270; VN to GS, ca. late February 1930, Hoover.

48. VN to EIN, July 26, 1929; BB interview with VéN, December 1981; Field, *VN*, 155.

49. BB interviews with VéN, December 1981, September 1982, January 1985.

50. VN to EIN, ca. end of June and August 8, 1929, VNA; VN to GS, January 25, 1929, Hoover; BB interview with VéN, December 1986.

51. VN to EIN, August 15, 1929; VéN to EIN, July 26, 1929, VNA.

CHAPTER 13. NABOKOV THE WRITER

Epigraph: MS, LCNA.

1. *RB*, 111.
2. "Sadom shyol Khristos s uchenikami " ("Na godovshchinu smerti Dostoevskogo"), pub. *Rul'*, November 11, 1921; repr. *Grozd'*, 19.
3. *RLSK*, 68.
4. See esp. "The Art of Literature and Commonsense," first pub. 1942 as "The Creative Writer," now in *Lects*, 371–80.
5. *BS*, 168.
6. Gerald Clarke interview with VN, *Esquire*, July 1975, 69.
7. *SM*, 218.
8. *SO*, 43.
9. See Part 4 of *Ada*, Van's "Texture of Time." Nabokov acknowledges that Van's treatise has been influenced by Bergson (*SO*, 290) and accepts its basic conclusions (*SO*, 185–87).
10. *SM*, 275.
11. *SM*, 301.
12. *Nabokov's "Ada,"* chaps. 4–5. For a more detailed discussion of the relationship between VN's philosophy and his style and strategies than is possible here, see *Nabokov's "Ada,"* chaps. 1–3.
13. *KQK*, 1.
14. *KQK*, 2.
15. *SM*, 69.
16. "Pouchkine, ou le vrai et le vraisemblable," *Nouvelle Revue française* 48: 282 (March 1937): 377; trans. DN, *NYRB*, March 31, 1988.
17. *Gift*, 145.
18. "Vtoroe dobavlenie k *Daru*," MS, LCNA.
19. *Ada*, 434.
20. *BS*, 39.
21. *KQK*, 33.
22. *RLSK*, 67.
23. *Ada*, 437.
24. *MUSSR*, 341; published text here corrected according to MS, VNA.
25. *PF*, 63.
26. For the best study of this subject—comprehensive, sensitive, astute, albeit ponderously scholastic—see Pekka Tammi, *Problems of Nabokov's Poetics: A Narratological Analysis*.
27. *TT*, 94.
28. *SM*, 20.
29. *Ada*, 220–21.
30. *SM*, 151–52.
31. *BS*, 155–56.
32. *TT*, 82.
33. VéN to Charles Timmer, December 20, 1949, VNA.

CHAPTER 14. THE DEFENSE

1. Written February–August 1929; pub. *SZ*, 40–42 (October 1929–April 1930); in book form, Berlin: Slovo, 1930; trans. Michael Scammell with VN, New York: Putnam, 1964.

2. *Looking at Pictures* (London: John Murray, 1960), 107.

3. *Ada*, 221.

4. "'The Problem of Pattern: Nabokov's *Defense*," *Modern Fiction Studies* 33, no. 4 (Winter 1987): 575–604.

5. Ibid., 600.

6. Ibid., 585.

CHAPTER 15. NEGATIVE AND POSITIVE

1. VN to EIN, August 15, 1929, VNA.

2. Field, *VN*, 155.

3. *Glory*, x. Cf. also *The Eye*, 7.

4. For an account of the journal, see Mark Vishnyak, *Sovremennye Zapiski: Vospominaniya redaktora* (Bloomington: Indiana University Slavic and East European Series, 1957).

5. *Vozrozhdenie*, May 5, 1932.

6. Kirill Zaitsev, *Rossiya i Slavyanstvo*, November 9, 1929; Georgy Adamovich, *Illyustrirovannaya Rossiya*, December 7, 1929; Khodasevich, *Vozrozhdenie*, May 5, 1932.

7. Nina Berberova, *The Italics Are Mine*, trans. Philippe Radley (New York: Harcourt Brace Jovanovich, 1969), 318.

8. *Nouvelles littéraires*, February 15, 1930.

9. Zaitsev, *Rossiya Slavyanstvo*; VN to GS, ca. February 1930, Hoover.

10. Quoted Lev Lyubimov, *Novy Mir* 3 (March 1957).

11. See above, p. 121.

12. Berberova, *The Italics are Mine*, 248.

13. Nikolay Andreev, in Niklay Poltoratzky, ed., *Russkaya literatura v emigratsii* (Pittsburgh: University of Pittsburgh Slavic Department, 1972), 33.

14. VN to EIN, October 18, 1929, VNA.

15. *SO*, 68, 29; *LATH*, 80; VN interview with Andrey Sedykh, *Segodnya*, November 4, 1932; Hessen, *Gody izgnaniya*, 101.

16. VN interview with Bernard Pivot, May 30, 1975, from TS in VNA; VN to EIN, January 19, 1930, VNA.

17. Pub. *SZ*, 44 ([October] 1930); in book form, Paris: Russkie Zapiski, 1938; trans. DN with VN. *The Eye* (New York: Phaedra, 1965).

18. From the English version, which though substantially the same has improved here on the Russian.

19. *Rul'*, March 4, 1930.

20. *Rul'*, March 5, 1930; Evgenia Cannac, *Russkaya Mysl'*, December 29, 1977; VéN album, VNA.

21. *Chisla* 1 (March 1930): 233–36.

22. Anton Krayniy (Zinaida Gippius), *Chisla* 2–3 (August 1930): 148–49.

23. VéN to Simon Karlinsky, July 18, 1979, VNA; VN to GS, June 3, 1959, Hoover; *Rul'*, January 30, 1929; *SO*, 39.

24. Levinson, *Nouvelles littéraires*, February 15, 1939; Andrey Luganov, *Za svobodu*, March 1930, and S. Nalyanch, *Za svobodu*, April–May? 1930 (from clippings, VNA); Adamovich, *PN*, May 15, 1930, and Gr. A.D., *Russkiy Invalid*, February 22, 1932. Among reviewers who rated VN a triumph of Russian literature, see GS, *Rossiya i Slavyanstvo*, May 17, 1930, and A. Savelev, *Rul'*, October 1, 1930.

25. MS, LCNA; pub. *SZ*, 43 ([July] 1930); trans. *ND*.

26. *Gift*, 329.

27. *Gift*, 330.

28. *Rul'*, May 1, 1930, May 6, 1931, April 26, 1932; BB interview with VéN, January 1985.

29. *Gift*, 328; BB interview with VéN, November 1982.

30. Pub. *Rul'*, May 4, 1930; repr. *Stikhi*.

31. VN to GS, October 26, 1930, Hoover; *Glory*, x; BB interview with VéN, June 1979.

32. *Glory*, x.

33. VN to VéN, May 12, 1930, VNA.

34. Cf. Robert Hughes interview with VN, TS dated January 3, 1966, VNA.

35. VN to VéN, May 12, 17, and ca. 21, 1930, VNA.

36. VN to VéN, May 12, ca. 16, and 17, 1930, VNA.

37. Nikolay Raevsky to ES, April 25, 1986, private coll.; Raevsky, "Vospominaniya o Vladimire Nabokove," *Prostor* 2 (February 1989): 112–17.

38. VN to VéN, May 17, 20, 21, and 22, 1930; *Nedelya*, May 28, 1930.

39. VéN to A. A. Goldenweiser, May 22, 1958, and March 6, 1967; Goldenweiser to VéN, July 29, 1938, ColB; VN to VéN, ca. May 21, 1930; BB interviews with VéN, December 1981 and February 1983.

40. *Rossiya i Slavyanstvo*, May 3, 1930.

41. Vishnyak, *Sovremennye Zapiski*, 28, 89, 99, 292, 320; Vishnyak, *Gody emigratsii 1919–1969* (Stanford: Hoover Institute, 1970), 48–49. Fondaminsky paid some of the advance money with the income his wife derived from her family's tea plantations in Ceylon.

42. *SM*, 286–87.

43. G. P. Fedotov, *Novyy Zhurnal* 18 (1948): 317; V. N. Bunin, in I. A. and V. N. Bunin, *Ustami Buninykh*, ed. M. Grin (Frankfurt: Possev, 1981), 2:236.

44. *Glory*, x. Field, *Life*, 214, ruins the story, implying that Fondaminsky was recruiting Nabokov for the first time for *SZ*, and even—despite all the din earlier in 1930 caused by the installments of *The Defense* that had just appeared in *SZ*—has Nabokov hand Fondaminsky the manuscript of *The Defense* to publish!

45. VN to VéN, May 17, 1930.

46. *Rul'*, September 26, 1930; *Podvig* MS, LCNA.

47. *Podvig*, pub. *SZ*, 45–48 (February 1931–January 1932); in book form, Paris: Sovremennye Zapiski, 1932; trans. DN with VN, *Glory*, (New York: McGraw-Hill, 1972).

48. *Gift*, 189.

49. *RB*, 179.

50. *LATH*, 16.

CHAPTER 16. BRIGHT DESK, DARK WORLD

1. *Rul'*, October 19 and November 23, 1930; *Le Mois* 6 (June–July 1931), 143.

2. MS, VNA.

3. VN to EIN, February 25, 1931, VNA.

4. VN's answer to Bobbs-Merrill questionnaire, 1937–38 ,VNA.

5. *SO*, 163–64; Appel, *NDC*, 137, 310–11; Hessen, *Gody izgnaniya*, 105.

6. Bobbs-Merrill questionnaire

7. *Rul'*, March 24, 1931.

8. TS, EIN album, 1931–32, VNA; pub. *Novaya gazeta*, 1 (May 1, 1931).

9. *RLSK*, 91.

10. GS, *NRS*, June 5, 1979.

11. "Les écrivains et l'époque," *Le Mois* 6 (June–July 1931).

12. VN to GS, May 8, 1931, Hoover.

13. VN to EIN, May 18 and 26, 1931, VNA; pub. *SZ*, 49–52 ([May] 1932–[May] 1933), as *Camera Obscura*; book form, as *Kamera obskura* (Paris: Sovremennye Zapiski, 1933); trans. W. Roy as *Camera Obscura* (London: John Long, 1936); trans. and rev. VN, as *Laughter in the Dark* (Indianapolis: Bobbs-Merrill, 1938).

14. VN to Walter Minton, November 4, 1958, VNA.

15. VN to EIN, May 26, 1931, VNA.

16. Alexander Brailow to BB, October 20, 1983.

17. Dated MS, LCNA; pub. *PN*, July 12, 1931; repr. *S*; trans. DN with VN, *DS*.

18. Cf. *CE*, 116.

19. *PN*, November 19, 1931.

20. VN to GS, January 19, 1931, Hoover.

21. VN to GS, June 7 and July 3 and 17, 1931, Hoover.

22. "Iz Kalmbrudovoy poemy 'Nochnoe puteshestvie,' " MS, VNA; pub. *Rul'*, July 5, 1931; repr. *Stikhi*.

23. Grigoriy Aronson, *NRS*, December 8, 1963.

24. *DS*, 164; pub. *PN*, October 20, 1931; repr. *S*; trans. DN with VN, *DS*.

25. *PF*, 52.

26. *Rul'*, October 11, 1931.

27. Pub. *PN*, November 22, 1931; repr. *S*; trans. DN with VN, *RB*. Dated only by the fact that a gap of two to four weeks was normal between composition and *PN* publication.

28. *PN*, November 2, 1931.
29. *PN*, November 18, 1931.
30. TS, EIN album, 1931–32, VNA; pub. *VF*; trans. DN with VN, *RB*.
31. *RB*, 46; cf. *N1*.
32. *PN*, March 22, 1935.
33. See review by Khodasevich, *Vozrozhdenie*, March 10, 1939.
34. *Nash vek*, January 1, 1932; *PN*, January 3, 1932; GS, *Russkaya Literatura v Izgnanii*, 281.
35. *Nash vek*, December 6, 1931; *PN*, January 18, 1932.
36. *SO*, 97–98; lecture notes, VNA; Field, *Life*, 157; BB interview with VéN, November 1982.
37. Pub. *PN*, January 1, 1932; repr. *S*; trans. DN with VN, *DS*.
38. *Nash vek*, December 20, 1931.
39. Field, *Life*, 160.
40. VN to Bertenson, ca. December 1932, VNA.
41. TS, EIN album, 1931–32; pub. *PN*, January 31, 1932; repr. *S*; trans. DN with VN, *DS*.
42. *Vozrozhdenie*, November 3, 1931; *Nash vek*, November 8 and December 13, 1931, January 10 and February 21, 1932; VN to Samuel Rosov, September 4, 1937; Field, *Life*, 154; *N1*; BB interview with VéN, February 1983.
43. VN to Rosov, September 4, 1937.
44. VN to GS, January 24, 1932, Hoover; BB interviews with VéN, September 1982 and January 1985; VN to VéN, April 18, 1932.
45. *Vozrozhdenie*, April 8, 1932.
46. Printed invitation, VéN album, VNA; *Vozrozhdenie*, March 4, 1932.
47. Pub. *PN*, March 27, 1932; repr. *S*; trans. DN with VN, *TD*.
48. VN to VéN, April 8 and 11, 1932, VNA.
49. VN to VéN, April 8–19, 1932, VNA.
50. VN to VéN, April 16, 1932, VNA.
51. VN to VéN, April 16 and 18, 1932.
52. VN to VéN, April 16 and 18, 1932.
53. VN to VéN, April 19, 1932; "Khvat" dated in first pub., *Segodnya*, October 2 and 4, 1932; repr. *S*; trans. DN with VN, *RB*.
54. *Nash vek*, May 15, 1932.
55. Dated *TD*, 186; pub. *PN*, July 3, 1932; repr. *S*; trans DN with VN, *TD*.
56. Pub. *PN*, July 31, 1932; repr. and trans. *PP*.

CHAPTER 17. DISTANT PROSPECTS

1. Alexander Brailow to BB, October 20, 1983.
2. *TD*, 158; VN to Khodasevich, July 24, 1934, Yale; VN to GS, August 11, 1932, and August 1932, Hoover; *N2*; BB interview with Elizaveta Marinel-Allan, March 1983; DN, "Close Calls and Fulfilled Dreams: Selected Entries from a Private Journal," *Antaeus* 61 (Autumn 1988): 299.

3. MS, LCNA.

4. Pub. *SZ*, 54–56, January–October 1934; in book form, Berlin: Petropolis, 1936; trans. VN, *Despair*, London: John Long, 1937; rev. ed. New York: Putnam, 1966.

5. MS, LCNA.

6. *Lolita*, 316–17.

7. *SO*, 193.

8. BB interview with VéN, December 1981.

9. VN to VéN, October 17, 1932.

10. Ibid.

11. VN to VéN, October 31 and 22, 1932, VNA.

12. VN to VéN, October 24, 1932, VNA.

13. VN to VéN, October 25 and 28, 1932, VNA.

14. VN to VéN, November 14, 1932, VNA.

15. VN to VéN, October 22–November 24, 1932, VNA.

16. VN to VéN, October 24, 1932.

17. Berberova, *Kursiv moy* (New York: Russica, 1983), 1:369.

18. VN to VéN, November 2, 1932.

19. VN to VéN, October 24, 1932.

20. VN to VéN, October 31 and November 3, 1932.

21. VN to VéN, October 25–November 8, 1932.

22. Thompson correspondence, VNA; Field, *Life*, 232; VN to VéN, October 25, 1932.

23. VN to VéN, November 2, 1932.

24. VN to VéN, November 5, 8, and 10, 1932.

25. VN to VéN, November 5, 1932.

26. VN to VéN, November 14 and 18, 1932; VN in *Pamyati Amalii Osipovny Fondaminskoy* (Paris: privately printed, 1937), 71.

27. VN to VéN, November 21, 1932.

28. VN to VéN, November 16, 1932; *PN* and *Vozrozhdenie*, November 17, 1932.

29. VN to VéN, November 16, 18, and 21, 1932.

30. VN to VéN, October 24–November 22, 1932.

31. VN to Alexander Koulischer, November 19, and to Princess Shakhovskaya, November 22, 1932, LCS; *PN*, November 22, 1932.

32. VN to Sergey Bertenson, ca. December 1932, VNA.

33. In Poltoratsky, *Russkaya literatura v emigratsii*, 8.

34. For dates see VN to Vadim Rudnev, November 11, 1933, University of Illinois, Urbana.

35. *NWL*, 148; diary, December 3, 1969, VNA.

36. VN to GS, August 23, 1933, Hoover.

37. BB interviews with VéN, February 1983 and January 1985; VN to VéN, January 18 1936; Field, *VN*, 28.

38. *PN*, March 16, 1933; BB interview with VéN, September 19, 1982; VéN to A. A. Goldenweiser, June 3, 1957 and March 6, 1967, ColB.

39. *N2*; cf. Field, *Life*, 200, and *VN*, 158, where Field places this after the Kristallnacht, which occurred late in 1938, nearly two years after the Nabokovs had left Germany forever.

40. Field, *Life*, 199.

41. VN to GS, April 29, 1933, Hoover.

42. Ibid.

43. GS, *Russkaya Literatura v Izgnanii*, 239.

44. BB interview with VéN, December 1982.

45. Dated May 23, 1933, in first pub., *PN*, June 4–5, 1933; repr. *VF*; trans. DN with VN, *TD*.

46. VN to ZS, July 1933, LCS; I. I. Fondaminsky to VN, May 19, 1933, LCNA.

47. Dated *RB*, 10; pub. *PN*, July 23–24, 1933; repr. *VF*; trans. *RB*.

48. VN to GS, ca. August and August 23, 1933, Hoover.

49. VN to GS, August 23, 1933.

50. VéN to A. A. Goldenweiser, May 22, 1958.

51. VéN to Andrew Field, May 10, 1973; cf. Field, *Life*, 199–200.

52. *American Mercury*, July 1933, 318; cf. Parry, *NRS*, July 9, 1978.

53. Hessen, *Gody izgnaniy*, 70.

54. *Segodnya*, January 3, 1934; *Vozrozhdenie*, January 11, 1934.

55. Alfred Appel, "Nabokov: A Portrait," in Rivers and Nicol, 19.

56. Yakovlev to VN, January 18, 1934, VNA.

57. Dated, VN to EIN, February 14, 1934, VNA; pub. *PN*, March 11–12, 1934; repr. *VF*; trans. DN with VN, *RB*.

58. Note, VNA.

59. *RB*, 254.

60. VN to EIN, February 12, 1934, VNA.

61. Aldanov, in *NZ* 80 (1965): 285; VN to EIN, February 28, 1934, VNA.

62. Pub. *PN*, April 8, 1934; repr. *S*; trans. DN with VN, *RB*.

63. Dated, VN to EIN, April 3, 1934; pub. *Illyustrirovannaya Zhizn'*, September 27, 1934; repr. *VF*; trans. DN with VN, *TD*.

64. VéN to ZS, April 10, 1934, LCS.

65. VN to Khodasevich, April 26, 1934, Yale.

66. VN to Khodasevich, May 15, 1934, Yale; *N1*; EIN to VN and VéN, ca. May 12, 1934, VNA; Field, *Life*, 199.

67. *SM*, 295–96.

68. VN to EIN, May 16 and 17, 1934, VNA.

69. VN to EIN, May 16, 1934; agreements files, VNA.

CHAPTER 18. TRANSLATION AND TRANSFORMATION

1. *SO*, 68; dated in MS, LCNA. In 1985 Nikita Struve absurdly attributed to VN the novel *Roman s kokainom* (*Novel with Cocaine*), first published in part in mid-1934 and written by a virtual unknown, "M. Ageev" (Mark Levy). Not only is the novel set in Moscow (where VN had never been) and plainly the

work of an ex-addict (VN despised drugs) who had talent but not VN's style, it was written when VN was engrossed in compiling his *Life of Chernyshevsky* and then in composing *Invitation to a Beheading*. When the journal *Chisla* published the first part of *Roman s kokainom*, VN in his next letter to Khodasevich (July 24, 1934, Yale) compared the style of the journal as a whole to the most philistine marketing campaign in the Russian émigré press: advertisements for Tokalon beauty cream, claimed by its makers to remove blackheads (for two of the advertisements, see my letter, *TLS*, March 6, 1987). By 1934, VN and Khodasevich were close enough to let each other in on the hoaxes they staged against their literary opponents in the emigration, who included the *Chisla* crowd. Even if VN had written *Roman s kokainom* and for some strange reason sought to keep the fact hidden from his wife and from Khodasevich, his pride would never have let him—no matter how desperately he might want to mask his authorship—apply the greasepaint of Tokalon cream.

2. VN to GS, July 30, 1934, Hoover.

3. Pub. *PN*, August 18, 1934; repr. *S*; trans. Simon Karlinsky with VN, *RB*.

4. VN to Khodasevich, July 24, 1934, Yale.

5. VN to Vadim Rudnev, June 11, 1934, Urbana; VN to EIN, August 13 and 24, 1934, VNA; VN to ZS, September 15, 1934, LCS.

6. VN to EIN, September 14, and to Rudnev, December 27, 1934, VNA; VN to Rudnev, November 25, 1934, Urbana.

7. VN to Rudnev, December 27, 1934.

8. Pub. *SZ*, 58–60 (June 1935–February 1936); in book form, Paris: Dom Knigi, 1938; trans. DN with VN, New York: Putnam, 1959.

9. "*Invitation to a Beheading*: Nabokov and the Art of Politics," *Triquarterly* 17 (1970): 46. For a very different approach to the novel, see D. Barton Johnson's fine *Worlds in Regression: Some Novels of Vladimir Nabokov* (Ann Arbor: Ardis, 1985), sections 1 and 5.

10. *NG*, 68; *NWL*, 33; *Triquarterly* 17 (1970): 56.

11. *SO*, 184.

12. *SO*, 189.

13. *IB*, 6.

14. VéN to Andrew Field, December 11, 1965, VNA. Margaret Byrd Boegeman tries to show that *Invitation to a Beheading* was influenced by Kafka, but provides no concrete evidence. She points out, as if in proof that Nabokov *must* have known Kafka's work well, that in a 1936 book the émigré critic Vladimir Weidle published "some incisive criticism of Kafka"—but disregards the fact that *Invitation to a Beheading* had been written two years earlier ("*Invitation to a Beheading* and the Many Shades of Kafka," Rivers and Nicol, 105–24).

15. VN to GS, December 2, 1932, Hoover.

16. *Gift*, 215.

17. VN to Berlin City Hall, April 10, 1935, LCNA.

18. VN to Denis Roche, February 10, 1935, and to Doussia Ergaz, October 30, 1951, VNA.

19. Pub. *PN*, March 3, 1935; repr. *VF*; trans. DN with VN, *Triquarterly* 27 (1973), repr. *RB*.

20. *Vozrozhdenie*, April 4, 1935; Anatoly Steiger to ZS, July 5, 1935, in ZS, *Otrazheniya* (Paris: YMCA, 1975), 88; Hessen, *Gody izgnaniya*, 94–96, 104–5.

21. VN to EIN, March 9 and April 23, and to Kirill Nabokov, ca. April 1935, VNA.

22. VN to Hutchinson & Co., May 22, 1935; *SL*, 13.

23. VN to Hutchinson & Co., June 14, 1935, VNA.

24. Field, *Life*, 206; BB interview with VéN, June 1982; VN to Hutchinson, June 27, 1935, VNA.

25. Field, *VN*, 175; BB interviews with Irina Komaroff, March 1983, and with VéN, December 1981; VN to EIN, July 23, 1935, VNA.

26. Pub. *PN*, August 18, 1935; repr. *VF*; trans. DN with VN, *TD*.

27. VN to Ellen Rydelius, November 5, 1935, to VéN, February 2, 1936, and C. Huntington to VN, March 17, 1937, VNA.

28. VN to EIN, September 8, 1935, VNA; *NYTBR*, August 18, 1935; VN to GS, August 13, 1935, Hoover.

29. Pub. *PN*, September 22, 1935; repr. *S*; trans. DN with VN, *DS*.

30. VN to EIN, September 8, 1935, VNA; *Despair*, 7.

31. VN and VéN to EIN, October 3, 1935, VNA; VN to ZS, ca. October 1935, LCS.

32. VN to EIN, December 29, 1935, VNA; *Despair*, 7.

33. VN to EIN, December 29, 1935, VNA, and to ZS, December 29, 1935, and ca. March 1936, LCS.

34. VN to ZS, January 9 and February 2, 1936, LCS; VN to VéN, January 20, and to EIN, March 23, 1936, VNA; *SO*, 174–75.

35. VN to ZS, ca. October 1935, LCS, and to VéN, January 20 and 27, 1936, VNA.

36. VN to VéN, January 27 and 30, 1936, VNA.

37. VN to VéN, January 30, 1936, VNA; VN to ZS, February 2, 1936, LCS.

38. *NZ*, 155 (1984), 132; *SM*, 286; VN to Roman Grynberg, December 16, 1944, ColB.

39. *SM*, 286–87.

40. VN to VéN, February 1, 1936; cf. Field, *Life*, 193.

41. John Malmstad, intro. to Khodasevich, *Derzhavin* (Munich: Wilhelm Fink, 1975), v.

42. Field, *Life*, 193; VN to EIN, March 23, 1936, VNA; M., *Vozrozhdenie*, February 13, 1936.

43. Berberova, *NZ*, 57 (1959), 114–15; Berberova, *Triquarterly* 17(1970): 225; Field, *Life*, 193–94. Cf. Alexander Bakhrakh, *Po pamyati, po zapisyam* (Paris: La Presse libre, 1980), 101.

44. Vishnyak, *Sovremennye Zapiski*, 213; VN to VéN, January 30–February 27, 1936; Field, *Life*, 209.

45. VN to VéN, February 24, 1936, VNA.

46. *Vozrozhdenie*, February 13, 1936; VN to EIN, March 23, 1936, and VéN to Field, December 11, 1965, VNA.

47. Robert Hughes interview with VN, September 1965, from TS, VNA.

Field, *Life*, 195, manages to construe the Charleroi adventure as part of a trip from Germany to Belgium.

48. Invitation, VNA; VN to VéN. February 27, 1936.

49. VN to GS, March 15, 1936, and to Nina Berberova, n.d., Hoover; VN to Altagracia de Jannelli, March 2, 1936, LCNA.

50. VN to GS, March 15, 1936, Hoover.

51. Dated in VN to ZS, April 30, 1936, LCS; first pub. *SZ*, 61 (July 1936); repr. *VF*; trans. *Harper's Bazaar*, May 1947, repr. *ND*.

52. VN to EIN, February 26, 1935, VNA; VN to ZS, April 12, 1935, LCS; VéN to A. A. Goldenweiser, May 22, 1958, June 3, 1957, March 6, 1967, ColB.

53. Robert Williams. *Culture in Exile*, 348.

54. VN to Karpovich, May 24, 1936, ColB.

55. *N1*.

56. *SM*, 299; *N1*; VN to VéN, January 20, 1936, VNA.

57. *SM*, 300; VN to EIN, April 26 and June 1, 1936, VNA; DN, "Close Calls and Fulfilled Dreams,'' 300.

58. He had announced to his mother at the end of 1935 his plan to rewrite his English reminiscences (VN to EIN, December 29, 1935, VNA), but "Mademoiselle O," his trip, his work on *The Gift* and "Spring in Fialta" would appear to have delayed the rewriting until now.

59. *SM*, 10–11.

60. *N1*; Familial Matters Folder, VNA; VN to EIN, April 26, 1936, VNA; Field, *Life*, 200; VN to ZS, July 6, August 7 and 8, 1936, LCS; BB interviews with VéN, January 1985 and December 1986; *SM* MS, VNA.

61. MS, LCNA; VN to Mikhail Karpovich, October 2, 1936, ColB.

62. VN to Hutchinson & Co., August 28, 1936, SL, 16.

63. VN to GS, ca. April–May 1936, Hoover; GS, *NRS*, July 17, 1977; VN to Molly Carpenter-Lee, October 7, 1936, VNA; Molly Carpenter-Lee note, n.d., Hoover.

64. VN to Hutchinson, November 28, 1936, SL, 17. Agent Otto Klement took the remaining £35 of the advance for each book: VN to John Long, February 12, and John Long to VN, March 18, 1947, VNA.

65. *PN*, September 11, 1936; Kaun to VN, November 24, 1936, LCNA; VN to Molly Carpenter-Lee, November 1, 1936, VNA.

66. VN to Rostovtzeff, December 9, 1936, ColB.

67. VN to Pares, November 16, 1936, VNA.

68. VN to ZS, November 17 and December 1, 1936, LCS; "Pouchkine, ou le vrai et le vraisemblable."

69. For departure date, see VN to ZS, January 16, 1937, LCS.

CHAPTER 19. ON THE MOVE

1. VN to ZS, January 16, 1937, LCS; BB interview with SSN, September 1982; *PN*, January 21, 1937.

2. VéN notes, 1986.

3. Hessen, *Gody izgnaniya*, 256.

4. VéN to Andrew Field, March 10, 1973, VNA.

5. *Vozrozhdenie*, January 30 and February 13, 1937.

6. *PN*, January 28, 1937.

7. *Ustami Buninykh*, 3:23; Berberova, *The Italics Are Mine*, 262; VN to Irina Guadanini, June 21, 1937, private coll.

8. VN to Vera Kokoshkin and Guadanini, August 28, 1936, private coll.; BB interview with VéN, December 1986; Vera Kokoshkin diary, private coll.

9. BB interview with Tatiana Morozoff, March 1983; Kokoshkin diary.

10. See memoir by Irina Guadanini's stepfather, Vladimir Kokoshkin, "F. F. Kokoshkin," ed. Vera Kokoshkin and Irina Guadanini, *NZ* 74 (1963): 207–8.

11. VN to VéN, May 15, 1937, *SL*, 26.

12. BB interview with VéN, December 1986; VN to VéN, February 20, 1937, *SL*, 12.

13. *SO*, 86; unpublished chapter of *CE*, LCNA; VN interview with Claude Jannoud, *Le Figaro littéraire*, January 13, 1973.

14. *Russkiy v Anglii*, January 31 and March 3, 1937.

15. *SO*, 162, and Appel, *NDC*, 137; VN to John Long, February 25, 1937, VNA; BB interview with GS, May 1983.

16. Katharine Ridley to GS, February 16, 1937, Struve Coll., Hoover; GS to VN, November 16, 1973, and C. Huntington to VN, March 17, 1937, VNA.

17. *SM*, 271; VN to Samuil Rosov, September 4, 1937, VNA.

18. *SM*, 271–72. For VN's identification of Nesbit as R. A. Butler (who hardly seems to fit the bill), see chap. 8 above.

19. *SM*, 273.

20. Sablin Coll., ColB.

21. VN to GS (early March 1937), Hoover; VN to VéN, March 30, 1937, *SL*, 21.

22. VN to GS, ca. mid–March 1937, Hoover; Office Central des Réfugiés Russes to VN, March 15, 1937, LCNA; VN to VéN, February 20, 1937 (*SL*, 18–19) and April 16, 1937, VNA; VéN to A. A. Goldenweiser, July 4, 1957, ColB; BB interview with VéN, February 1987.

23. VN to VéN, April 15 and February 20, 1937, *SL*, 22–23, 19; VN to ZS, April 10, 1937, LCS.

24. Gisèle Freund and V. B. Carleton, *James Joyce in Paris: His Final Years* (London: Cassell, 1966), 44–45. See also Noel Riley Fitch, *Sylvia Beach and the Lost Generation* (New York: Norton, 1983), 217, for an interior photograph taken the same day.

25. VN to VéN, April 15 and May 15, 1937, *SL*, 23, 26.

26. VN to VéN, May 15, 1937, *SL*, 25.

27. *N1*; Field, *Life*, 226.

28. VN to VéN, May 15, 1937, *SL*, 25; Guadanini diary, private coll.; BB interview with VéN, December 1981; VN to Vera Kokoshkin and Irina Guadanini, June 1, 1937, private coll.

29. *SM*, 306; VN to Kokoshkin and Guadanini, June 1, 1937; BB interview with VéN, September 1982.

30. VN to Irina Guadanini, June 14, 21, and 22, 1937, private coll.

31. VN to Irina Guadanini, June 22 and 23, 1937, private coll.; VéN notes, 1986.

32. Date and location in MS, LCNA; pub. *Russkie Zapiski* 2 (November 1937); repr. *VF*; trans. VN and Peter Pertzov, *Atlantic*, June 1941; repr. *ND*.

33. *ND*, 123.

34. Exposition card, LCNA; VéN to BB, June 5, 1987; VN to ZS, August 22, 1937, LCS.

35. Gallimard agreement, July 5, 1937, VNA; VN to Guadanini, June 19, 1937, private coll.; Guadanini diary.

36. VN to Guadanini, July 21, 1937, private coll.

37. VN to Guadanini, July 15, 1937, private coll; BB interview with VéN, December 1986.

38. VN to Guadanini, July 15, 1937.

39. VN to Guadanini, July 21 and 28 and August 2, 1937, private coll.

40. VN to Guadanini, August 2, 1937.

41. VN to Guadanini, July 28, 1937; VN to ZS, August 22, 1937, LCS.

42. Rudnev to VN, August 4, 1937, LCNA; VN to Rudnev, August 6, 1937, VNA.

43. VN to Guadanini, August 7, 1937, private coll.

44. Kokoshkin and Guadanini diaries.

45. Rudnev to VN, August 10–13, 1937, LCNA.

46. VN to Rudnev, August 16, 1937, LCNA.

47. Rudnev to VN, September 2, 1937, LCNA, and September 6, 1937, VNA.

48. VéN notes, 1986; BB interview with Tatiana Morozoff, March 1983; Aletrus [Irina Guadanini], "Tunnel'," *Sovremennik* 3 (1961):7–8.

49. *EO*, 3:235–36.

50. *Triquarterly* 17 (1970): 251.

51. *SO*, 119.

52. Kokoshkin diary; BB interview with Morozoff, March 1983.

53. *N1*, *N2*: Bobbs-Merrill agreement, September 27, 1937, VNA; VN to Fritz Korner, November 5, 1937, LCNA.

54. *Camera Obscura* endpapers, VNA.

55. VN to Raisa Tatarinov, November 12, 1937, LCNA; VéN to Magda Nachman-Acharia, December 16, 1937, VNA; BB interview with VéN, December 1981 and 1984; VéN to BB, April 16, 1982.

56. VN to Raisa Tatarinov, November 12, 1937; *SM*, facing p. 257.

57. VN to Raisa Tatarinov, November 12, 1937; Hessen, *Gody izgnaniya*, 256; VéN to Magda Nachman-Acharia, December 16, 1937.

CHAPTER 20. **THE GIFT**

1. Written 1933–early 1938, pub., except chap. 4, *SZ*, 63–67 (April 1937–October 1938); in book form, complete, New York: Chekhov Publishing House, 1952; trans. Michael Scammell and DN with VN, New York: Putnam,

1963. For the English version as for the French (*Le Don*, trans. Raymond Girard [Paris: Gallimard, 1967]), VN himself translated all verse and word-play.

2. Ronald E. Peterson, "Time in *The Gift*," *VNRN* 9 (Fall 1982), 36–40, dates the book's events 1925–1928. His chronology is internally consistent, but out by one year.

3. *Gift*, 9.

4. David Rampton (*Vladimir Nabokov*, Cambridge University Press, 1984), attempts to prove VN's distortion of Chernyshevsky, but his selectivity, emphasis, and strategy reveal he would rather appear the successful prosecutor than seek to understand VN's aims. Alexander Dolinin (VN, *Izbrannoe*, Moscow: Raduga, 1990) demonstrates conclusively VN's fidelity to the documentary evidence.

5. *NG*, 149.

6. *NG*, 145.

7. *Eye*, intro.

8. For VN's use of his recent past in *The Gift*, see chaps. 12–19.

9. *NG*, 76.

10. *NG*, 76–77. VN first singled out these features of the opening of *Dead Souls* for special praise in an unpublished 1927 lecture for the Tatarinov-Aykhenvald circle.

11. See *Vladimir Nabokov: The American Years*, chaps. 1–10.

CHAPTER 21. DESTITUTE

Epigraph: LATH, 51.

1. George Hessen to VN, January 13, 1938, LCNA.

2. In his poem "From Vivian Calmbrood's 'The Night Journey,' " VN had mocked at Adamovich via the phrase *Adamova golova* ("skull") (see above, p. 370. As John Malmstad points out, the death's-head moth, with its skull-like markings, was also known in Russian as "Adamova golova," and defined in Dahl's dictionary as "Sphinx Caput *mortuum*" (*Minuvshee* 3[1987]:286): hence the name Mortus.

3. *The Gift*, 179–80.

4. Aldanov to VN, January 29, 1938, Khodasevich to VN, January 25, 1938, LCNA.

5. VN to Aldanov, February 3, 1938, VNA.

6. Pub. *Russkie Zapiski*, April 1938; trans. DN, *MUSSR*.

7. Lecture notes, VNA; cf. *MUSSR*, 335.

8. Source untraced.

9. *PN*, March 4–19, 1938; *Vozrozhdenie*, March 11, 1938; George Hessen to VN, March 7, 1938, Zenzinov to VN, March 7, 1938, Iosif Hessen to VN, March 8, 1938, LCNA.

10. VN to Vernadsky, February 1 and March 21, 1938, ColB.

11. Chess MSS, VNA.

12. *Call*, San Francisco, May 14, 1938; *Hartford* (Conn.) *Times*, May 7, 1938.

13. F. Dearstyne to Altagracia de Jannelli, July 7, 1938, LCNA.

14. Angus Cameron to Altagracia de Jannelli, April 23, 1938, LCNA.

15. Rachmaninov to VN, May 28, 1938, LCNA.

16. *N1*.

17. *SM*, 234.

18. "Butterflies of Europe" MS, VNA.

19. For dates of composition, cf. VN to Mark Vishnyak, May 13 and 27, June 13, 1938, Hoover; pub. *Russkie Zapiski*, August–September 1938; repr. *VF*; trans. DN with VN, *TD*.

20. *RB*, 154.

21. Mikhail Pavlovsky to VN, May 3, 1938, LCNA.

22. VN to ZS, ca. July 1938 and September 12, 1937, LCS; BB interview with VéN, March 1982.

23. *Journal of the New York Entomological Society*, September 1941, 266; *SM*, facing p. 288; VéN to ZS, ca. July 1938.

24. VéN to ZS, ca. July 1938; BB interviews with VéN, December 1981, April 1982, and June 1989, and with VéN and DN, December 1984.

25. VN to ZS, September 1938, LCS; BB interview with VéN, April 1982.

26. VN to Vernadsky, ca. September 1938, Mark Villchur to Vernadsky, October 5, 1938, ColB.

27. Dated in foreword to *The Waltz Invention* (New York: Phaedra, 1966), and VN to Mark Vishnyak, October 3, 1938, Hoover; pub. *Russkie Zapiski*, November 1938; trans. DN with VN, *The Waltz Invention*.

28. *Russkaya Literatura v Izgnanii*, 243.

29. VN to Jannelli, July 14, 1938, VNA.

30. *Novoe Slovo*, March 20, 1938.

31. Ministère de l'Intérieur to Maklakov, August 5, 1938, LCNA.

32. VN to ZS, October 15, 1938, LCS; BB interview with VéN, December 1981, September 1982.

33. *SO*, 89; *N1*; BB interview with VéN, December 1981.

34. *SM*, 285.

35. BB interview with VéN, January 1983.

36. Pub. *SZ* 68 (March 1939); repr. *VF*; trans. DN with VN, *Esquire*, March 1963; repr. *NQ*, *RB*.

37. VN to Aldanov, February 3, 1938, VNA.

38. Dated in first pub., *Russkie Zapiski*, 14 (February 1939); repr. *VF*; trans. DN with VN, *New Yorker*, October 10, 1964; repr. *TD*.

39. Lik's very name contains the same double implication. In Russian *lik* means "visage" or "a face on a sacred icon," suggesting Lik will be the person in focus. But the word is impossible as a Russian surname and must be a transliteration from some other European language ("Leek"? "Licque"?). His name preserves the fact that he is not of Russian origin: even as an émigré he is an outsider.

40. *PN*, November 8, 1938; VéN to ZS, November 29, 1938, LCS.

41. *PN*, November 24, 1938; VéN to ZS, December 2, 1938, LCS.

42. VN to Nina Berberova, January 29, 1939, Hoover; VN to ZS, December 1938, LCS; VN to Aldanov, October 20, 1941, ColB.

43. BB interview with VéN, December 1981.

44. VN to Janelli, January 25, 1939, VNA; VN to ZS, [January 29, 1939], LCS.

45. Pub. Norfolk, Conn.: New Directions, 1941.

CHAPTER 22. SEARCHING FOR AN EXIT

Epigraph: Lolita: A Screenplay (New York: McGraw-Hill, 1976), 10–11.

1. Triquarterly 17 (Winter 1970): 215.

2. Triquarterly 17 (Winter 1970): 219; SO, 292.

3. SO, 86; Appel, AnL, 404.

4. VN to Vishnyak, February 10, 1939, Hoover; BB interview with VéN, December 1981; BB interview with Irina Komaroff, March 1983; George Hessen to VN, November 30, 1951, VNA.

5. VN to ZS, [January 29, 1939], LCS.

6. VN to Kagan, October 6 and December 19, 1938, and Aldanov to VN, April 14, 1941, ColB.

7. MS, LCNA.

8. Rostovtzeff, March 14, 1939, LCNA.

9. Draft letter by VN in Berdyaev's name, April 2, 1939, and in Bunin's name, April 1, 1939, SL, 30, and Bunin to VN, April 3, 1939, VNA.

10. VN to GS, March 14, 1939, Hoover.

11. VN to GS, March 17, 1939, Hoover.

12. E. Hofeld to VN, March 31, 1939, April 12, 1939, and VN to VéN, April 3, 1939, VNA; Journal of the New York Entomological Society, September 1941, 266; PN, March 26, 1939; GS to VN, April 2, 1946, June 20, 1947, VNA; L. P. Hartley to GS, April 20, 1939, Hoover; B. Mouat Jones to VN, May 1, 1939, LCNA.

13. SM, 258; BB interview with VéN, December 1981.

14. SM, 66; Field, Life, 86.

15. Vinaver to VN, April 22, 1939, VNA.

16. VN to GS, May 30, 1939, Hoover; BB interview with Francis Haskell, March 1983.

17. Karpovich to VN, June 3, 1939, VNA; VN to Karpovich, June 15, 1939, ColB.

18. "O Khodaseviche," SZ 69 (1939); trans. VN in Simon Karlinsky and Alfred Appel, eds. Triquarterly 27 (Spring 1973), repr. as The Bitter Air of Exile (Evanston, Ill: Northwestern University Press, 1973) and in SO; John Malmstad, "Iz perepiski V. F. Khodasevicha," Minuvshee 3 (1987): 279. In his account of Khodasevich's funeral Field pictures VN lunging at Nikolay Otsup, a foe of both VN and Khodasevich, and being pulled off by shocked mourners (VN, 186). In PN, however, Otsup was not recorded as being present at the funeral at all, although many mourners much less well known were listed.

19. SM, 306; VN to Berberova, June 1939, Yale; BB interviews with VéN, December 1981 and April 1982.

20. *WI* foreword.

21. Gerald Smith points out the metrical camouflage, "Nabokov and Russian Verse Form," *Russian Literature Triquarterly* 24 (1990).

22. Adamovich, *PN*, August 17, 1939. For VN's account of the background, see *TD*, 204–6, *PP*, 95, and unpublished chapter of *CE*, LCNA.

23. Pub. *PN*, September 12, 1939; repr. *VF*; trans. DN with VN, *TD*.

24. *PN*, September 22, 1939; *TD*, 206.

25. BB interview with VéN, December 1981 and January 1985.

26. BB interview with VéN, December 1981; *Atlantic* and *Esquire* correspondence, October and November 1939, LCNA; H. Wilson Harris, *Spectator*, to Mrs. Hessell Tiltman, October 12, 1939, VNA.

27. *N1*; cf. Field, *Life*, 218; *NWL*, 126.

28. Aldanov to A. A. Goldenweiser, August 1, 1940, ColB; *SO*, 127.

29. Elizaveta Kyandzhuntsev to Irina Komaroff, December 18, 1939, LCS.

30. BB interview with Elizaveta Marinel-Allan, March 1983.

31. Marinel-Allan interview.

32. VN to Mark Vishnyak, September 30, 1939, Hoover; *SO*, 15; VN diary, December 3, 1969; *Lolita*, 313.

33. *Libération*, August 31, 1986, 27.

34. MS, VNA. Pub. in French, trans. Gilles Barbedette from English trans. by DN, Paris: Rivages, 1986, and subsequently in English, trans. DN, New York: Putnam, 1986.

35. *Lolita*, 314; Russian *Lolita*, 290; Marinel-Allan interview; Abram Kagan to VN, n.d., LCNA.

36. VN to Dobuzhinsky, October 31, 1939, ColB; to Alexandra Tolstoy, and to Koussevitzky, November 10, 1939, Koussevitzky Coll., Music Division, LC; and to Karpovich, October 10, 1939, ColB; Sorokin testimonial, November 16, 1939, LCNA.

37. Chess MSS, VNA; *SM*, 291–92.

38. BB interviews with VéN, June 1982 and January 1985; *N1*.

39. Elizaveta Kyandzhuntsev to Irina Komaroff, December 16, 1938; BB interview with VéN, January 1985.

40. Marinel-Allan interview.

41. Berberova, *The Italics Are Mine*, 324.

42. Marinel-Allan interview.

43. MS, LCNA.

44. "Rusalka," *NZ* 2 (1942).

45. Pub. *NZ* 1 (1942); repr. *VF*; trans. DN with VN, *New Yorker*, April 7, 1973, repr. *RB*.

46. *RB*, 147.

47. Pub. *SZ* 70 ([April] 1940); trans. DN with VN, *Triquarterly* 27 (Spring 1973), repr. *RB*.

48. *RB*, 148.

49. VN to Karpovich, April 20, 1940, ColB.

50. Cf. Field, *VN*, 197; VN to Marinels, April 26, 1942, private coll.

51. *N1*; VéN to A. A. Goldenweiser, July 4, 1957, ColB.

52. *SO*, 5; Robert Hughes interview with VN, September 1965, TS, VNA; lecture notes, VNA; VN to Karpovich, April 20, 1940.

53. BB interview with DN, December 1981.

54. National Refugee Service to Sergey Koussevitzky, April 24, 1940, Koussevitzky Coll., Music Division LC; *N1*; Marinel-Allan interview; Field, *VN*, 195; BB interview with VéN, December 1986.

55. Nikolay All interview with VN, *NRS*, June 23, 1940; Field, *Life*, 227–28; *N1*.

56. VN to Nathalie Simon, September 25, 1946, VNA; BB interview with VéN, February 1982.

57. BB interviews with Elizaveta Marinel-Allan, March 1983, and with VéN, January 1985.

58. Nikolay All interview with VN, *NRS*, June 23, 1940; DN, *Enchanter*, 103.

59. *SM*, 309–10; BB interviews with VéN, December 1981 and January 1985; VéN to A. A. Goldenweiser, December 28, 1957, ColB.

THROUGHOUT the index, "N" stands for Vladimir Vladimirovich Nabokov and "VDN" for his father, Vladimir Dmitrievich Nabokov. All Nabokov works are listed under "Nabokov, Vladimir Vladimirovich: Works."

Abbazia, 51, 57
Acmeism, 94
Acropolis, 163–64
Ada (character). *See* N: Works—*Ada*
Adamovich, Georgy, 4, 198, 350, 374, 415, 424, 425, 479–80, 509–10, 578n.2; alters attack on N, 369–70; belatedly admits N's talent, 510; feud with Khodasevich, 371; hostility toward N, 343–44; as Mortus, 351; N attacks in "The Night Journey," 370–71; reaction to *The Defense*, 343–44
Adèle (maid), 220
Ageev, M. *See* Levy, Mark
agents, N's, 417, 426. *See also* Ergaz, Doussia; Janelli, Altagracia de; Klement, Otto
Aida (Verdi), 164
Ai Petri, 140, 144, 145
Akhmatova, Anna, 94, 108
Aksakov, Sergey, 30
A la recherche du temps perdu (Proust), 149
Albinus (character). *See* N: Works—*Laughter in the Dark*
Aldanov, Mark, 198, 221, 228, 256, 342, 391, 423–25, 430, 433, 434, 437, 480, 493, 505, 507, 511, 514, 522; N's relationship with, 392–93; passes on to N job offer at Stanford, 511
Alékhine, Alexander, 259, 275–76, 479
Aleksandrov, 229
Alexander I, 40
Alexander II, 19–21, 29, 49n
Alexander III, 21, 25, 32, 535n.32
Alexandra (tsaritsa), 122
Alice in Wonderland (Carroll), 197, 414, 557n.4
All Quiet on the Western Front (Milestone film), 376

Alter, Robert, 410–11
"America" (peat bog near Vyra), 81
American Mercury, 403
Amfiteatrov-Kadashev, Vladimir, 199, 200, 206
Anna Karenin (Tolstoy), 79, 306, 521
Annenkov, Yuri, 485, 494
Annensky, Innokenty, 93
Antwerp, 397, 422–23
Aretino, Pietro, 514
Arzamas (Berlin writers' group), 238
Athens, 163–64
Atlantic Monthly, 511
Aucassin and Nicolette, 174
Audiberti, Jacques, 437
Austen, Jane: *Emma*, 106
Avksentiev, Nikolay, 442
Aykhenvald Circle, 256–57, 276, 350, 373; naming of, 288
Aykhenvald, Yuli [pseud. B. Kamenetsky], 4, 200, 201, 201n, 228, 229, 230, 238, 261, 274, 286; as critic, 256–57; death of, 287–88
Azef, Evno, 390n

"Baby, Aunt." *See* Wonlar-Lyarsky, Nadezhda
Bach, Johann Sebastian, 339
Bad Kissingen, 84
Bad Rotherfelde, 197
Bakhchisaray, 148
Bakst, Leon, 39
Bakunin, Mikhail, 534n.15
Balashov, Andrey, 131
Balmont, Konstantin, 93
Balzac, Honoré de, 297
Baratynsky, Evgeny, 150

Barbashin (character). *See* N: Works—*The Event*

Bardeleben, General von, 341, 377

Baring, Maurice, 178n

Batovo, 25, 45, 46, 77, 80, 105, 107

Beach, Sylvia, 437

Beaulieu, 51

Beckett, Samuel, 304

Bednyy, Demian, 273

Beethoven, Ludwig van, 397

Beilis, Mendel, 104, 521

Bellotto, Bernardo, 103

Bely, Andrey, 93, 115, 150, 180n, 198, 200, 220, 463; *Petersburg*, 149, 151–52; *Symbolism*, 149

Benckendorff, Count, 435

Benediktov, Vladimir, 150

Benois, Alexander, 39, 391

Berberova, Nina, 342, 391, 392, 424, 425, 426, 515–16; identifies N and Khodasevich encounters with Fyodor-Koncheev exchanges (*The Gift*), 392; reaction to *The Defense*, 343

Berdyaev, Nicholas, 506

Berezin, 100, 101

Bergson, Henri, 109n, 280, 566n.9; influence on N, 294–95

Berlin, 84–85, 176–431 passim; economic depression in, 372–73; N leaves, 431; N's addresses in, 176–84, 226–44, 260, 263–88, 341–431, 437; N's reasons for remaining in, 234–35, 382, 495

—Russian emigration in: early phases of, 176–77; effect of inflation on, 217; émigré/Soviet boundary temporarily blurred in, 198; exodus from, 220; meagerness of historical records in, 270–71; N family's centrality in, 184–85; in early 1930s, 349, 373; numbers swell in, 180; publishing in, 185–86, 220; reasons for boom in (1921–24), 197–99

Bertenson, Sergey, 230n, 376, 397

"Bertrand, Véronique," 215. *See also* Nabokov, Véra Evseevna

Bezborodko, Prince, 3, 72

Bezpalov family, 205

Biarritz, 73–75, 78–79, 97

Binz, 262, 274, 278

Bishop, Morris, 4

Biskupsky, General, 427, 430

Blok, Alexander, 38, 91, 93–95, 117, 180n, 186, 191, 290, 363, 549n.61; "Incognita," 207; N talk on, 257; "The Twelve," 156–57, 186

Blokh, Raisa, 277

Bloody Sunday, 56–57, 70

Bluebird (Russian cabaret, Berlin), 560n.29; N's sketches for, 227, 231, 233, 234, 254

Bobbs-Merrill (American publisher), 445

Bobrovsky, 154

Boccaccio, Giovanni, 229, 514

Borges, Jorge Luis, 373

Boris Godunov (Musorgsky), 192

Bosch, Hieronymus, 306

Bosporus, 163

Boucher, François, 49n

Box (dachshund), 220, 243

Boys' Own Paper, 80, 91

Brailow, Alexander, 382

Bratstvo kruglogo stola. *See* Brotherhood of the Round Table

Brave New World (Huxley), 374

Breitensträter, Hans, 257

British Museum, 507

Brockhaus, 96

Bromberg family, 262, 440

Bronze Horseman (Pushkin), 37

Brooke, Rupert, 171, 182

Brotherhood of the Round Table, 200, 277–78

Browning, Robert, 91

Brussels, 397, 422, 425–26, 432

Bryusov, Valery, 93, 150, 180n, 256

Buchinskaya, Nadezhda. *See* Teffi

Budberg, Baroness, 435

Bukharin, Nikolay, 411

Bulgarin, Tadeusy, 287

Bulla, Karl, 74

Bunin, Ivan, 4, 180, 193, 291, 342, 401, 403–4, 425, 434, 487, 493, 506, 522; envy of N, 433; N sends *Mary* to, 257n; N's preference for verse rather than prose of, 94, 290; N's relations with, 423–25; N's tribute to, 369; praises "A University Poem," 269; reaction to *The Defense*, 343; *Selected Poems*, N review of, 290

Burness, Mr. (tutor), 77

Burov, Alexander, 374

Butler, R. A. ("Rab"): as possible prototype of "Nesbit" (q.v.), 168, 576n.18

Butler, Samuel: *Erewhon*, 416

butterflies. *See* N: Life—lepidoptera

Byron, George Gordon, Lord, 167, 202, 204, 230

cabarets, Berlin, 227–28. See also Bluebird; Karussel
Cage, John, 95
Calry, Count Robert Louis Magawly-Cerati de, 168, 186, 188, 189, 194, 219
Cambridge, 88, 137, 166–93 passim; in *Death*, 204; in *Glory*, 356–61; in *The Real Life of Sebastian Knight*, 497; in "A University Poem," 267–69. See also N: Life—at Cambridge
Canaletto, Antonio, 103
Cannac, Evgenia, 277, 278, 287
Cannes, 440–45
Capablanca, José Raoul, 275–76
Cap d'Antibes, 488–92
capital punishment. See death penalty
Carpenter-Lee, Molly, 430
Carroll, Lewis, 415; *Alice in Wonderland*, 197, 414, 557n.4
Carrousel (émigré journal, Berlin), 218
Cartier, 164
Catherine the Great, 3, 40, 72
CD. See Constitutional Democratic (CD) party
censorship, Russian: eased, 1905, 59; of *The Gift*'s *Life of Chernyshevsky*, 441–43, 457; of the left, 456–57; lifted, after February 1917, 126; N on, 466; reinstated, after November 1917, 139
Cervantes, Miguel de, 38
Chagall, Marc, 39, 246
Chaikovsky, Peter, 40
Chaliapin, Fyodor, 39, 40
Champlain (ship), 522
Chaplin, Charlie, 363, 397
Chatsky, Leonid, 199, 200
Chatterbox, 422
Chavchavadze, Nina (née Romanov), 174
Chekhov, Anton, 23, 38, 91, 96, 98, 101, 116, 136, 184, 350n, 358, 390n, 466, 495; *The Cherry Orchard*, 264; influence on N, 482–83; N's affinity with, 92; *The Three Sisters*, 264
"Chenston." 370
Cherkasskaya, Marina, 164
Chernyshevsky, Nikolay, 22–23, 35, 36, 38, 93, 296, 311, 398–400, 401, 408, 409, 416, 428, 442, 447, 455–62, 466, 473, 489, 520; N on, 406–7; role in Russian literature

and history, 398–99; *What Is to Be Done?*, 398, 403
Cherry Orchard, The (Chekhov), 264
Chesterton, G. K., 79
Chisla (émigré journal, Paris), 350, 374
Chocolate (Tarasov-Rodionov), 375, 411
Chorny, Sasha (Alexander Glikberg), 186–99, 229
Chrétien de Troyes, 174
Christ, Jesus, 156, 233, 292
Christopher (valet), 74
Chuang Tzu, 373
Chufutkale, 148
Chukokkala (Chukovsky), 117
Chukovsky, Korney, 117, 121, 186
Chums, 80
Church, Henry, 437
Cincinnatus. See N: Works—*Invitation to a Beheading*
Cingria, Charles-Albert, 437
Cinizelli's (circus, St. Petersburg), 89, 90
Clair, René, 363
Clark, Kenneth, 325
Cohn, 377
Colas Breugnon (Rolland), 176, 177, 181, 197
"Colette." See Deprès, Claude
Conan Doyle, Sir Arthur, 79
Conrad, Joseph, 79, 211; N talk on, 257
Constance, 244
Constantinople, 159, 163
Constituent Assembly, 126, 131, 139, 141; elections for, 133–34
Constitutional Democratic (CD) party, 33, 59, 60, 70, 86, 111, 125–26, 127, 130, 132, 136, 145, 154, 184, 394, 430, 433, 437, 507; "new tactic" and schism, 189–90; political philosophy of, 61–63
Coppée, François, 69
Corneille, Pierre, 69
Cornell University, 3, 32, 270, 508
Corot, Jean Baptiste Camille, 358
Council of the Russian Republic, 155; VDN as member of, 132–33
"Covetous Knight, The" (Pushkin), 370
Coward, Noel, 489
Craig, Edward Gordon, 103
Crime and Punishment (Dostoevsky), 91, 150
Crimea: establishment of Crimean regional government, 154–55; evacuation of, 159–60; first Bolshevik takeover of, 140; German entry into, 143

Crimean provisional regional government, 154–60, 205
Crimean War, 19
Crooked Mirror (cabaret, St. Petersburg), 103
Cummings, Mr. (drawing master), 75, 102–3
Curie, Marie, 123

Dahl, Vladimir, 171, 176, 289, 345, 495
Dallwitz, von (landlord), 263, 291, 341
Danechka (girlfriend), 206
D'Annunzio, Gabriele, 76
Dante Alighieri, 76
Darwin, Charles, 280–81
Davydov, 32
Dead Souls (Gogol), 194, 465–66, 474, 578n.10
death penalty, 65, 131, 219, 416, 520; struggle against, as N family theme, 18–19, 33–36
Decembrists, 18, 18n, 19, 128
Deich, Lev, 22
de la Mare, Walter, 171
Demidov, Igor, 391
Denikin, General, 154, 155, 159, 168
Deprès, Claude ("Colette"), 79, 97, 305
Derzhavin, Gavril, 424
Derzhavin (Khodasevich), 399
Diaghilev, Sergey, 39, 42, 174
Dickens, Charles, 34, 38, 107, 183, 355; *Great Expectations*, 96
Dietrich, 219
Dmitrievichi (family of Dmitri Dmitrievich Nabokov, q.v.), 138, 159, 164
Dobřichovice, 234–35
Dobuzhinsky, Mstislav, 39, 103, 258–59, 514
Domaine Beaulieu, Solliès-Pont, 205, 207, 208–11
Dom Iskusstv, 199–200
Dorzenik, Osip, 142, 143, 550n.21
Dostoevsky, Andrey, 19
Dostoevsky, Fyodor, 22, 23, 34, 35, 36, 76, 184, 363, 374, 379, 392, 396, 398, 416; *Crime and Punishment*, 91, 150; mock-execution of, 19; N to translate, 212; *Notes from Underground*, 383; as prisoner of General Ivan Nabokov, 18–19
Dostoevsky, Mikhail, 19
Dostokiyan, 425
Dresden, 379

Dreyer, Carl: *La Passion de Jeanne d'Arc*, 363
Dreyfus, Alfred, 104
Drozdov, Aleksandr, 199, 203, 278
Druzhnosel'e, 369
duels, 81n, 182, 275, 287, 350, 374; VDN near-duel with Mikhail Suvorin, 98–99; N calls out Aleksandr Drozdov, 203; N's interest in, 150; Evsey Slonim and, 215; Spiresco affair, 272
Dumas, First, 34, 41, 59, 61, 63, 75, 84, 86, 136; Second, 63, 70; Fourth, 123–25
Duse, Eleonora, 39
Dymant, Dora, 202
Dzerzhinski, 436

Edelweiss, Martin (character). *See* N: Works—*Glory*
Efron, Sergey, 261
Ehrenburg, Ilya, 198
Eilukhin, Aleksandr, 228, 233, 238
Ekaterina I (childhood girlfriend), 97
Ekaterina II (childhood girlfriend), 97
Elijah, 233
Eliot, T. S., 196
Ellis, Havelock, 400
emigration, Russian, 197–99; espionage in, 260–61, 494; N as chronicler of, 245–47, 263–66, 268, 279, 347, 464–65; N on, 161
England: as potential refuge for Nabokovs, 376, 421, 430, 432, 485, 495, 505, 507–8
English Review, 171
Entomologist, 82, 354
Erewhon (Butler), 415–16
Ergaz, Doussia, 393
Esquire, 508, 511
Eugene Onegin (Pushkin), 79–80, 156–57, 443–44, 462, 516
Eveline (Cambridge girlfriend), 173
Evreinov, Nikolay, 103, 564n.8; N meets, 391–92; N plays part of, 273
Evsey (Vasily Rukavishnikov's gardener), 113
Evtushenko, Evgeny, 117
"Exegi monumentum" (Pushkin), 41
Ezhov, Nikolay, 436

Fabergé, 37, 42
"Fancyname, Margaret" (Cambridge girlfriend), 173
Fassbinder, Rainer Werner, 422n
Faulkner, William, 304, 305

Faust, 204
Fayard (French publisher), 344, 393
Feigin, Anna, 241, 262, 290–91, 377, 400, 407, 409, 420, 429, 437, 439, 445, 510; character of, 382; types *Mary*, 254
Felzen, Yuri, 392
Fet, Afanasy, 54, 398
Field, Andrew, 4, 115, 428 539n.7, 539–40n.13, 540n.16, 543n.42, 544n.4, 547n.20, 562n.8, 565n.41, 568n.44, 572n.39, 575n.47, 580n.18
Finnegans Wake (Joyce), 425, 503, 504
Firens, Paul, 422
Fiume (Rijeka, Yugoslavia), 51
Flaubert, Gustave, 29, 38, 91, 156; *Madame Bovary*, 92, 378; preparation and transition in, 225
Florence, 32, 191
Földes, Jolán: *La Rue du chat qui pêche*, 434
Fondaminsky, Amalia, 390, 394–95, 423
Fondaminsky, Ilya, 63, 271, 370, 390–91, 392, 393, 394–95, 396, 423–24, 432, 433, 437, 440, 445, 446, 493, 506, 514, 568n.41; as chief prop of *Sovremennye zapiski*, 355–56; death of, 522
Food of the Gods (Wells), 428
France, Anatole, 76
Franzensbad, 438–39
Franz Ferdinand, Archduke, 110
Fredericks, Count, 65
Fréjus, 508–10, 511, 517
Freud, Sigmund, 91, 109n, 260, 306, 363, 364, 391, 403; N talk on, 257
Freund, Gisèle, 437
Friedman, 128
Friends of Russian Culture (émigré group, Berlin), 228, 230
Front Page (Milestone film), 376
Frost, Robert, 4
Frumkin, Yakov, 521, 522
Futurism, Russian, 94–95
Fyodor. *See* N: Works—*The Gift*

Gagarin, Princess, 37
Gallimard (French publisher), 440
Gamayun (émigré publisher, Berlin), 197
Ganin (character). *See* N: Works—*Mary*
Gapon, Father, 56
Gardiner, Stanley, 170
Gaspra, 134, 136–49
Gaydarov, Vladimir, 181–82

Gazdanov, Gayto, 342
Germany: N's antipathy toward, 489
Gerzenshtein, 66, 67
Ghika (childhood girlfriend), 51
Gibson, J. J., 306
Gippius, Vladimir, 114–16, 120–21, 547n.20; and pressure for social responsibility, 115–16, 128
Gippius, Zinaida, 115, 121, 342, 344, 350, 391, 425; belatedly admits N's talent, 522
Gladkov, Fyodor, 260
Glenny, Michael, 246
Glikberg, Aleksandr. *See* Chorny, Sasha
Gnedov, Vasilisk, 95
Godunov-Cherdyntsev, Fyodor and Konstantin (characters). *See* N: Works—*The Gift*
Goebbels, Joseph, 411, 431
Goethe, Johann Wolfgang von, 38, 368, 415
Gogol, Nikolay, 91–92, 185, 287, 355, 363, 374, 460, 495; *Dead Souls*, 194, 465–66, 474, 578n.10; *The Government Inspector*, 103, 483; N talk on, 257; N schoolboy essay on, 128–29
Gold Rush, The (Chaplin), 397
Golovina, Alla, 493
Golubtsov, Vladimir, 15
Goremykin, Ivan, 65
Gorky, Maxim, 117, 136, 155–56, 197, 198, 256, 374
Gorlin, Mikhail, 276, 354; founds Poets' Club, 277
Gorny, Sergey, 199, 200, 206, 242
Gorodetsky, Sergey, 31n, 545
Goudy, Alexander, 174
Government Inspector, The (Gogol), 103, 483
Goya, Francisco José de, 391
GPU (Soviet secret police), 220, 220n, 241, 260
Graf Zeppelin, 341
Grani (almanac), 186, 187, 188–89
Grantchester, 182–83
Grasset (French publisher), 393
Graun, Heinrich, 16, 428
Graun family: inheritance from, 429
Great Expectations (Dickens), 96
Greenwood, Miss (girls' governess), 111
Grinberg, Lyudmila (family librarian), 80, 118
Grinberg, Savely, 435
Group Theater (émigré theater, Berlin), 258, 263, 273

Gruber, 85
Grum-Grzhimaylo, Grigory, 137, 400
Gruzenberg, O. O., 104
Gryazno River, 32, 46
Grynberg, Roman, 511
Grzhebin (émigré publisher, Berlin), 197–98
Guadanini, Irina, 433–34, 437, 438–39, 440,
    441, 443–44, 517n; and *The Real Life of Se-
    bastian Knight*, 496, 501–2
Guillén, Jorge, 4
Gumilyov, Nikolay, 94, 363
Gutman. *See* Marinel entries
Gzovskaya, Olga, 182, 184

Hamlet (Shakespeare), 225, 325, 362, 416
Hamsun, Knut, 76
Hands of Orlac, 363
Hannibal, 289
Hardy, Oliver, 363
Hardy, Thomas, 232
Harris, Alan and Angelica, 507
Harrison, Ernest ("Spy"), 167, 170, 178, 436
Hartley, L. P., 435
Harvard University, 180n, 270, 393, 428
Haskell, Francis and Vera, 507
Headless Horseman, The (Mayne Reid): N's
    translation of, 81
Hegel, Georg Wilhelm Friedrich: dialectic
    triad modified by N, 294–95
Heine, Heinrich, 145
Hellens, Franz: *Oeil-de-dieu*, 422
Henry VIII, 169
Hermann (character). *See* N: Works—*De-
    spair*
Hessen, Georgy, 255, 267, 356, 363, 400,
    407, 479, 485, 493, 504, 507
Hessen, Iosif, 54, 59, 118, 130, 177, 189,
    191–93, 228, 254, 256, 267, 363, 378, 403–
    4, 405, 418, 485; as colleague of VDN, 33;
    encourages N's early work, 205–6
Hessen, Sergey, 117–18, 378
HIAS (Jewish refugee organization), 521
Hindenburg, Paul von, 378, 382
Hitler, Adolf, 3, 5, 6, 27, 34, 67, 156, 256,
    270, 342, 378, 400, 402, 411, 427, 439, 465,
    489, 492, 496, 505, 509; appointed chancel-
    lor, 382
Hlebnikov. *See* Khlebnikov, Viktor
Hodasevich. *See* Khodasevich, Vladislav
Hofeld, Evgenia (girls' governess), 111–12,
    141, 142, 164, 220, 242, 419

Hoffmann, E.T.A., 259
Hofmann, 77, 82
Hogarth Press, 401
Hokusai, 297
Hollywood, 230n, 376, 445
Home, Rachel (governess), 44
Homer, 215
Horace, 29
Housman, A. E., 171
Hugo, Victor, 34, 69, 76
Humbert, Humbert (character). *See* N:
    Works—*Lolita*
Hume, David, 169
Hunt, Miss (governess), 52
Hutchinson (English publisher), 407, 429–30
Huxley, Aldous: *Brave New World*, 374

Ibsen, Henrik: *Peer Gynt*, 222
Imatra, 119, 123
Imperial School of Jurisprudence, 23, 26, 28,
    43, 54, 57
inflation, German (1922–23), 217
intelligentsia: Russian sense of term, 29, 148
Ioann, Archbishop (Dmitri Shakhovskoy),
    71
Ionesco, Eugène, 256
Iretsky, Viktor, 353
Ivan (name of two N valets, St. Petersburg),
    74
Ivanov, Georgy, 198, 351, 354, 370–71, 374,
    425; attacks N in *Chisla*, 350; N attacks,
    "The Night Journey," 371, 371n; *Raspad
    atoma*, 350n
Ivanov, Vsevolod, 260
Ivanov, Vyacheslav, 93
Iz Voyuyushchey Anglii (VDN), 118

Jaloux, Edmond, 425
James, Henry, 91, 304
James, William, 90–91, 306
Jannelli, Altagracia de, 403, 432, 445
Joan of Arc, 235
Johnson, Samuel, 167
Jolas, Eugène and Maria, 504
Joyce, James, 103, 167, 178, 304, 344, 437; at-
    tends N reading, 4, 434; *Finnegans Wake*,
    425, 503, 504; influence on N, 491; N in-
    vited to meet, 425; N meets, 504; *A Por-
    trait of the Artist as a Young Man*, 455n;
    Ulysses, 149, 166n, 194, 301, 312, 364, 379,
    397, 447, 448, 464–65, 466

Joyce, Lucia, 178
Juliar, Michael, 533

Kachurin (character). See N: Works—"To Prince S. M. Kachurin"
Kafka, Franz: and *Invitation to a Beheading*, 415, 425, 573n.14; *Metamorphosis*, 149; N "remembers" seeing, 202
Kagan, Abram, 505, 514
Kalashnikov, Mikhail, 167–68, 171, 172, 174, 175, 178–79, 181, 182, 183–84, 186, 188
Kamenetsky, B. See Aykhenvald, Yuli
Kamenka (Sayn-Wittgerstein estate), 96
Kamensky, Anatoly, 350, 350n
Kaminka, Avgust, 177, 190, 192–93, 258; subsidizes Elena Nabokov, 255; subsidizes *Rul'*, 254–55
Kaminka, Elizaveta, 285, 291, 425, 492
Kaminka, Mikhail, 255, 271–72, 286, 291, 425, 492, 507
Kaplan, Sergey, 242, 244, 254, 259, 267
Karamzin, Nikolay, 95
Kardakov, Nikolay, 259, 291
Karlinsky, Simon, 23, 198, 233n, 344n, 377–78
Karpovich, Mikhail, 428, 430, 508, 514, 521; aids N's entry into US, 378
Karussel (émigré cabaret, Berlin), 218
Kasatkin-Rostovsky, Prince, 350
Kaun, Alexander, 393, 430
Keaton, Buster, 363
Keats, John, 91
Kennedy, John Fitzgerald, 22
Kenner, Hugh, 455n
Kerensky, Alexander, 126, 131, 132–33, 143, 390–91, 425, 434, 437, 522
Khlebnikov, Viktor, 92, 95
Khodasevich, Vladislav, 4, 107, 198, 200, 220, 342, 344, 344n, 391, 393, 406–7, 408–9, 416, 423, 425, 432, 480, 485, 492–93, 573n.13; death of, 508; *Derzhavin*, 399; feud with Adamovich, 371, 509; joint reading with N, 424–25; N pays tribute to, 508, 509–10; N reviews, 276; N visits, 392
Kinbote, Charles (character). See N: Works—*Pale Fire*
King Lear, 6, 365
Kipling, Rudyard, 79, 94, 182
Kishinyov pogrom, 55, 179, 521, 540n.16
Kleist, von, 184

Klement, Otto, 407, 409, 575n.64
Klub pisateley (writers' group, Berlin), 200
Klyatchkin, Roma (girlfriend, Berlin), 206
Knipper, Olga, 184
Kogan-Bernstein, Dr. Elizaveta, 437, 514, 522
Kokoshkin, Fyodor, 139, 141, 433
Kokoshkin, Vera and Vladimir, 433
Kolberg, 290–91, 341
Kolbsheim, 390, 397
Kolchak, Admiral, 168, 220
Kolomeytsev, Admiral Nikolay, 98–99, 124
Kolomeytsev, Nina, 124
Konoplin, Ivan, 219–20
Konstantin Konstantinovich, Grand Duke, 273
Konstantin Nikolaevich, Grand Duke, 19
Korff, Maria von. See Nabokov, Maria
Korff, Nina von, 24
Kornilov rebellion, 132
Korostovets, Vladimir, 227, 230
Kortner, Fritz, 435
Korvin-Piotrovsky, Vladimir, 199, 200; as member of Poets' Club, 277–78
Koussevitsky, Sergey, 40, 514
Kozhevnikov, Vladimir, 278
Kozlov, Nikolay, 31
Kozlov, Olga Nikolaevna. See Rukavishnikov, Olga Nikolaevna
Kozlov, Praskovia Nikolaevna. See Tarnovsky, Praskovia
Kramař, Karel, 220, 221
Krechetov, Sergey, 200, 206, 239
Kresty prison, 76
"Kreutzer Sonata" (Tolstoy), 261
Krug, Adam (character). See N: Works—*Bend Sinister*
Krummhübel, 254
Krym, Solomon, 154, 155, 158, 205, 208
Kuindzhi, Arkhip, 39
Kuprin, Alexander, 193, 342, 392
Kuropatkin, General, 50, 538n.56
Kutepov, General, 494
Kuzmin-Karavaev, Elizaveta. See Maria, Mother
Kuznetsov, 146
Kuznetsova, Galina, 493
Kyandzhuntsev, Savely, 101, 116, 212, 394, 395, 425; subsidizes N, 511

Ladinsky, Antonin, 391, 425
Lakshin, Mme, 228
Lamb, Charles, 202
Landau, Grigory, 254, 255
Landor, Walter Savage, 166
Lanz, Henry, 511, 514
Laplace, 280
Larivière, Mlle (character). *See* N: Works—
Ada
Lasker, 185
Laughlin, James, 4
Laurel, Stan, 363
Lazarevsky, Boris, 350, 350n
Le Boulou, 288–90, 396
Leeds, 507
Leichtenberg, Duke of, 488
Leigh, Annabel (character). *See* N: Works—
Lolita
Leiris, Paul, 173
Lenin, Vladimir, 23, 58, 117, 126–27, 134,
139, 156, 168, 197, 398, 433, 435, 457, 492
Lensky. *See* Zelenski, Filip
Léon, Paul, 425, 434, 503–4
Léon Noel, Lucie, 174, 178, 425, 434; checks
The Real Life of Sebastian Knight, 503–4
Leonov, Leonid, 260
Lepel, Frau von (landlady), 244, 341
Lermontov, Mikhail, 97, 287, 393
Lettres philosophiques (Voltaire), 182
Letuchaya mysh' (Moscow cabaret), 227
Levin, Harry, 4
Levinson, André, 351, 392, 400; review of
The Defense, 343
Levitan, Isaak, 39
Levy, Mark: *Roman s kokainom*, 573n.13
liberalism: as N family trait, 18, 23–24
Liberation, Union of, 56
Liberation movement, Russia, 55–56
Library of Congress, 32, 226
Lichterfelde, 183–84, 202
Liebelei (Schnitzler), 148
Lieven, Prince, 37
Life, 74
Linderovski. *See* Okolokulak, Boris
Literary Club (émigré group, Berlin), 229
Literary Fund, Russian, 38, 86, 121, 139,
148; in America, 488
Litvinne, Félia, 538n.56
Livadia, 149–59
Lloyd, Harold, 363
"Locomotions." *See* Bluebird (cabaret): N's
sketches for

Lody. *See* N: Life—nicknames
Loewenfeld, Rafael, 176
Lomonosov, Mikhaylo, 150
London, Jack, 211
London, 165–66, 172, 173–74, 176; N's ad-
dresses in, 165–76, N's trips to, 435–36,
506, 507–8; Russian emigration in, 435
Long, John (British publisher), 417, 430, 435
Loris-Melikov, Count, 49
Loustalot, 50
Lubrzynska, Eva, 123, 130, 142, 168, 172,
173, 183; character of, 165
Lubrzynski, Mikhail, 168
Lucette (character). *See* N: Works—*Ada*
Luga, 289
Lukash, Ivan, 4, 199, 200–201, 205, 206, 218,
220, 227, 228, 229, 230–31, 233, 238, 242,
254, 261, 391; departure from Berlin, 255
Lütke, Count, 17
Lutyens, Eva. *See* Lubrzynska, Eva
Lutyens, Sir Edwin and Robert, 173
Luzhin, Aleksandr Ivanovich (character).
See N: Works—*The Defense*
Lvov, Lolly, 230, 486
Lvov, Prince, 126
Lyarsky. *See* Wonlar-Lyarsky entries
Lyaskovsky, 375

McCarthy, Desmond, 435
McCarthy, Mary, 4
Madame Bovary (Flaubert), 92, 378
"Mademoiselle O" (character). *See* Miauton,
Cécile
Main Thing, The (Evreinov), 273
Makarov, 257
Maklakov, Vasily, 394, 437
Malevsky-Malevich, Sviatoslav, 422, 432, 445
Maltsev, 102
Manasein, N. A., 27
Manchester, 507–8
Mandelstam, Osip, 94, 115, 544nn. 2 and 4
Mansfield, Katherine: N on, 402
Marcel, Gabriel, 393, 426, 434
Margot (character). *See* N: Works—*Laughter
in the Dark*
Maria (childhood girlfriend), 97
Maria, Mother (Elizaveta Kuzmin-Kara-
vaev), 392
Marianna (childhood girlfriend), 97
Marienbad, 439–40
Marinel, Elizaveta, 511–12, 515
Marinel, Ina, 511

Marinel, Maria, 511–12
Marseilles, 164, 210–11, 229
Marshak, Mrs., 521
Martin (character). *See* N: Works—*Glory*
Marx, Karl, 23, 260, 350, 363
Marx brothers, 363
Matusevich, Iosif, 353
Maurois, André, 399
Max. *See* Okolokulak, Boris
Mayakovsky, Vladimir, 95, 198
Measure for Measure (Shakespeare), 225
Mechnikov, Ilya, 154, 154n
Melville, Herman, 211
Menton, 445–46, 479–87, 493, 496
Merezhkovsky, Dmitri, 193, 342, 391, 425, 522
Merlin, Mister, 90
Mertz, Zina (character). *See* N: Works—*The Gift*
Mesures (journal, Paris), 426, 437
Metamorphosis (Kafka), 149
Meyerhold, Vsevolod, 39
Miauton, Cécile, 60–61, 69–70, 75, 80, 106–7, 188, 422; as model for Mlle Larivière (*Ada*), 69
Michaux, Henri, 437
Mikhail Alexandrovich, Grand Duke, 124–25
Miklukho-Maklay, Nikolay, 400
Milan, 51
Milestone, Lewis, 230n, 397; suggests N come to Hollywood, 376
Miller, General Evgeny, 494
Miller, Henry, 350n
Milyukov, Paul, 66, 110, 111, 122–23, 124–27, 132, 143, 145, 177, 184, 391, 486; and death of VDN, 188–93
Milyutin, Dmitri, 20
Miriam (girlfriend, Cambridge), 173
Mir iskusstva (journal, St. Petersburg), 39
Misdroy, 262, 286
Mois, Le (journal, Paris), 364
Moltrecht, 259
Monnier, Adrienne, 437
Montauban, 492
Montreux, 270; Montreux Palace Hotel, 4, 290
"The Monument" (Pushkin), 41
Morskaya Street (St. Petersburg), 33, 39, 142, 212; described, 37–38, 49–50, 103; taken by Red Guard Staff, 144; Zemstvo Congress at, 55–56

Mortus, Christopher, 578n.2. *See also* Adamovich, Georgy
Moscow Art Theater, 39, 40, 103, 182, 184, 376
Mosely, Philip, 508
Moulinet, 486, 487–88, 507
Moynahan, Julian, 444
Mozzhuhin, Ivan, 145, 145n
Mrosovsky, Peter, 168, 194
Murnau, F. W.: *The Last Laugh*, 363
Muromtsev, Sergey, 41, 84
Musorgksy, Modest: *Boris Godunov*, 192
Musset, Alfred de, 118, 119, 202
Myasoedov, 402

N——, Vadim Vadimych (character). *See* N: Works—*Look at the Harlequins!*
Nabok Murza (legendary ancestor), 15, 16
Nabokov, Alexander Ivanovich (great-great-grandfather), 17
Nabokov, Anna Alexandrovna (great-grand-mother), 19
Nabokov, Avdokim (probable ancestor), 16
Nabokov, Dmitri Dmitrievich (uncle), 32, 138
Nabokov, Dmitri Nikolaevich (grandfather), 19–26, 32, 34, 36, 49, 534n.20, 535n.32; anti-Semitism, opposition to, 27; liberalism of, as influence on N, 23–24
Nabokov, Dmitri Vladimirovich (son), 22, 305, 409, 420, 422, 427, 429, 436–37, 438, 440, 443, 445, 496, 507, 508, 510, 515, 521, 522–23; birth of, 407; character of, as child, 515–16; as mountaineer, 17; as racing-car driver, 428; as singer, 16; as translator of N's work, 6
Nabokov, Elena Ivanovna (née Rukavish-nikov) (mother), 33, 38, 39, 43, 45, 46, 47–48, 49, 50, 54, 57, 60, 67, 68, 74, 75, 76, 96, 98, 102, 111, 124, 134, 142, 177, 184, 187, 189, 194, 195, 230, 232, 243, 277, 291, 305, 341, 362, 377, 409, 419, 434; appearance of, 32; burning of correspondence with N, 271; character of, 32, 185; death of, 506–7; family background of, 30–32; jewels of, 41–42, 138, 164, 165; moves to Prague, 220–21; N's last visit to, 438–39; nervous disposition of, 43, 233; in old age, 405, 496; pride in husband's politics, 65; reaction to husband's death, 191–93, 196; and religion, 72, 354; transcribes N's

works, 38, 186; visits Berlin from Prague, 242, 254
—influence on N: anti-materialism, 294; kindness to animals, 74; passion for collecting, 69; poetry, 38, 92; religious unconventionality, 153; training in memory and in visual imagination, 41–42, 44, 45
Nabokov, Elena Vladimirovna (sister). *See* Sikorski, Elena Vladimirovna
Nabokov, Filat (probable ancestor), 16
Nabokov, General Ivan Alexandrovich (great-granduncle), 17–19, 534n.15
Nabokov, Ivan (son of cousin Nicolas), 445
Nabokov, Kirill Vladimirovich (brother), 50, 96, 220–21, 378; N criticizes poetry of, 354, 362; N's solicitude for, 419, 422, 432
Nabokov, Konstantin Dmitrievich (uncle), 26, 43, 67, 72, 165, 174, 233, 506
Nabokov, Luka (probable ancestor), 16
Nabokov, Maria Ferdinandovna (née von Korff) (paternal grandmother), 24–25, 26, 46, 77, 105, 107, 176, 185, 535n.34, 545–46n.62
Nabokov, Nathalie (wife of cousin Nicolas), 390, 394, 397, 445
Nabokov, Nicolas (cousin), 16, 40n, 156, 185, 390, 445
Nabokov, Nikolay Alexandrovich (great-grandfather), 17, 19
Nabokov, Olga Vladimirovna (sister). *See* Petkevich, Olga Vladimirovna
Nabokov, Sergey Dmitrievich (uncle), 138, 141
Nabokov, Sergey Sergeevich (cousin), 15, 428, 432
Nabokov, Sergey Vladimirovich (brother), 43, 44, 48, 50, 51, 57, 60–61, 77, 84, 86, 90, 105, 107, 118, 121, 134–35, 136, 142, 149, 159, 165, 166, 172, 173, 175, 183, 185, 194, 196, 391, 546n.66, 559n.21; as actor, 135; appearance of, 174; death of, 70, 522; diffidence of, 43, 70; homosexuality of, 106, 396; late improvement in N's relations with, 396–97; music, interest in, 106; N's remoteness from in childhood, 52, 70; stutter of, 43
Nabokov, Sophia (Onya) (cousin), 49, 52, 176
Nabokov, Véra Evseevna (née Slonim) (wife), 202, 211, 221, 241, 243, 244, 254, 255, 260, 261, 291, 305, 341, 350, 354, 356,

363, 377, 378, 379, 389, 394, 396, 400, 401, 419–21, 422, 425, 429, 432, 434, 436–37, 438–39, 440, 443, 445, 507, 508, 517n; and bribe for passports, 515; character of, 215; as contributor to *Rul'*, 210; on *The Defense*, 291; early life of, 213–15; initiation into Poets' Club, 278; learns to catch butterflies, 289; memory of, 215; possible influence on N's art (theme of absurdity of inability to revisit past), 253–54, 283; and privacy, 215, 407, 558n.37
—jobs: compiler of German-French dictionary, 267; French stenographer, 403; German stenographer, 286; guide and interpreter, 403; language tutor, 355; secretary to engineering firm, 427; secretary to law firm, 355
—relationship with N: early meetings with, 216–17; engagement to, 233; first meeting with, 206–8, 213, 558n.37; marriage to, 239–40; near-meetings with in past, 212
Nabokov, Vladimir Dmitrievich (father), 24, 39, 42, 43, 45, 46, 50, 85, 86, 96, 108, 110, 113–14, 117, 122, 134–35, 136, 138, 141, 163, 169, 194, 204, 206, 255, 305, 431, 433, 539n.7, 539–40n.13, 540n.16, 545–46n.62, 546–47n.14, 548n.53
—character and life: appearance, 32; assurance, 33, 64; capacity for work, 76; childhood and youth, 25–27; compassion, 104; court title, deprived of, 3; death of, 6, 7–8, 190–93, 403–4, 428, 440, death of, prefigured, 7–12, 67, 99–100, as disciplinarian, 105; dislike of snobbishness, 15; duelling, 98–99; fatalism of, 131, 140; humor of, 172; lepidoptera, passion for, 68; library of, 80; manliness of, 97–98; manner of, 185; military service of, 111; and move to Berlin, 176; optimism of, 76; as president of Literary Fund, 38, 86, 139; pride in N, 391; public roles of, in Berlin, 184; and religion, 72, 153; seeks reinstatement in Assembly of Noblemen, 127; selflessness of, 59, 148n; theater, interest in, 39–40, 103
—influence on N: Blok, interest in, 186; boxing and chess, 144, 172; and discipline, 105–6; fate, sense of, 100, 100n; internationalism, 29; kindness to animals, 74; lepidoptera, 68, 76, 144; liberalism, 84; literature, 38, 69–70, 90–91; moral values,

61; politics, and N's indifference to, 61, 115–16; *poshlost'*, loathing of, 156; Pushkin, love of, 95; responsibility, individual, 28–29, 103; social class, attitude to, 63

—journalism: as editor of *Rech'*, 66–67, 70; as founder and editor of *Rul'*, 173–74, 177; joins *Pravo*, 32–33

—law: as criminologist, 27–28; and 1917 legal reforms, 126, 130; on sexual matters, 54; as teacher in Imperial School of Jurisprudence, 28, 43, 54, 57

—in N's work: "Evening on a Vacant Lot," 381; *The Gift*, 68, 98, 381, 397–98; *Speak, Memory*, 7

—politics: anti-Semitism, opposition to, 27, 55, 104, 521; Bloody Sunday, protest against, 57; as chancellor of first Provisional Government, 3, 125–26; and Constituent Assembly elections, 139; cultural motivation of his politics, 156; death penalty, opposition to, 33–34; drafts Grand Duke Mikhail's abdication manifesto, 125; in February Revolution, 123–26; imprisonments, 76–77, 139; Kerensky invites to become minister of justice, 131; launches opposition career, 32–33; liberalism of, 26; loss of political rights, 66, 70; as minister of justice, Crimea, 154–60; in 1905 revolution and First Duma, 54–67; opposition to Milyukov's "new tactic," 189–90; parliamentary style of, 64; in Petrograd after October Revolution, 138–40; as president of Editorial Commission for Constituent Assembly elections, 134; as shadow minister of justice, 66; signs Vyborg Manifesto, 66

—role in N's career: as critic of N's work, 187; selects poems for *Gorniy put'*, 186; suggests translation of *Colas Breugnon*, 176–78

—works: *Iz Voyuyushchey Anglii*, 118; *Provisional Government*, 143, 155

NABOKOV, VLADIMIR VLADIMIROVICH (entries are arranged within the categories: Art and Thought; Life and Character; Works)

Art and Thought:
—afterlife: 7, 71, 153–54, 333–39, and father's death, 194, 239 (*see also* N: Art—the

beyond); —art: and the beyond, 11, and generosity of life, 293, as image of limits of consciousness transcended, 9, 11–12, inherent artfulness of life, 10–11, 458, inversion of, 365–66, 384–89, and science, 182; —artfulness behind life, 12, 92, 296, 298, 318, 319; —artistic inspiration, mystery of, 460, 469–74; —artists: criminals and the insane as, 308, 384–89, false claimants to title of, 11–12, responsibilities of, 409

—the beyond: 6, 11, 182, 319, 349, 361, early attempts to render, 234 (*see also* N: Art—afterlife); —biography: 428–29, 497–500, hostility to, 147, N on, 399, Pushkin's as exception, 147

—causation, 460; —censorship, 466; —chess, 203, 236, 275–76, 289–90, 321–40; —chess problems, 138, 455–56; —coincidence, 372; —colored hearing, 58, 144, 152; —the commonplace, rejection of, 35, 238; —"common sense," rejection of, 292–93; —consciousness: 42, 45, 300–319, 321, behind life, 296, and childhood illness, 71, decay of, into automatism, 281–83, 285, early attempts to transgress limits of, 218, emotion as aspect of, 305, freedom of, and N's style, 301–3, 312, limits of, 9–10, 11, 247, 294, N's attempt to transcend, 309–19, power of, 247, primacy of, 279, 293–94, 296, as prison, 5, 307–8, senses as aspect of, 305–6, thought as aspect of, 304–5; —courage, 98; —curiosity, 82, 297, 315–19

—death: 6, 34–36, 310–11, as possible transcending of prison of self, 283, as possible transcending of prison of time, 283, 319, as transcendence, parody of, 389; —death penalty, opposition to, 34–36, 416; —death scenes, 232, 314; —design: 9, 83, 319, 323, 331, 339, 467–68, in nature, 297–98; —detail, 12, 250–51, 297; —determinism: opposition to, 92, 224, 482–83, and plot, 357–58; —dialogue, 304; —discovery: 12, 83, 320, 352, and N's strategies, 315–19; —drama: 482–83, as not N's natural mode, 223–24, 263

—emigration, Russian, as subject, 245–47, 263–66, 268, 279, 347, 464–65; —epistemology, 82–83, 314–19; —epoch, rejection of notion of, 353, 364, 393, 409, 497; —eth-

N: Art (*continued*)

ics, and blindness of self, 307–8; —evidence for character's talents, 248; —evolution, in nature: 82, 294, 505, of butterfly wing markings, 295, creativity of, 280; —evolution of literature, 93; —exile: 85, 245–46, as exile from past, 147–48

—false continuation, device of, 232, 298–99; —fate: 5, 34, 67, 99–100, 142, 299–300, 372, 457, 477, 494, characters usurp role of, 299, 366, persistence of, 212–13, 449–50, 462–63; —freedom, 224, 247; —future: denial of, 298–99, openness of, 280

—generalizations, hostility to, 4, 84, 129, 257, 293, 353, 458; —generosity of life, 225, 293, 450, 477–78; —ghosts, 310, 312; —gravity, overcoming, 254; —groups, hostility to, 84, 119

—happiness, 292–93, 450–51; —harmony of individual life, 148, 225, 307, 361, 458, 494

—independence: 4, 8, as converse of pattern, 9, 293, 331, 339; —individuality, 28–29, 458; —internationalism, 29; —inversion of own positives into negatives, 279, 283–84, 289, 336–37, 346–47, 353–54, 407, 472n

—knowledge, obstacles to, and N's style, 314–19

—laughter, 487; —lepidoptera: in "The Aurelian," 351–52, in "Christmas," 71–72, 236, in *The Gift*, 352, 398, 463, 505–6, and metamorphosis and metaphysics, 71, in "Ultima Thule," 518, 518n; —liberalism, and family background, 23–24; —literary influences on: Bely 149–52, Bergson, 294–95, Brooke, 171, Chekhov, 482–83, de la Mare, 171, Housman, 171, Joyce, 491, Pushkin, 204, 222, Shakespeare, 222, 224, Symbolism, 294, Voloshin, 149; —logic, limitations of, 169; —loss, 5, 10, 305, 308, 406; —love, and transcendence of self, 310 (*see also* N: Art—married love)

—magic, 90; —married love, 283–85, 365, 443–44; —Marxism, critique of, 489; —materialism, critique of, 489; —as maximalist, 304, 306; —memory: 45, 293–94, 311, as consolation, 5, and perception, 329, prefigures death's transcendence of time, 283; —metaphysics, 83; —meter, interest in, 149–51; —mimicry, natural, 9, 82, 83, 293, 298, 318, 505; —mind, freedom of, 8; —miraculous in life, 236; —as moralist, 385

—narrative point of view, 311, 348, 379, 386–88, 421; —narrative preparation and transition, 225; —nostalgia, 51; —"not text but texture," 308, 333

—obsession, 296

—pain, 11, 12; —parody, 91, 224, 363–64, 384, 497–99; —particularity, 8, 35, 82, 84, 458; —past: disappointed repetition of, as theme, 119–20, inaccessibility of, 137, 249, 252–54, 283, 294, 311–12, 497–500, pattern in, 299–300; —pattern: 9, 151, 299–300, 323, 329, 332, 336, 337–39, 458, as converse of independence, 9, 293, 331, 339, in N's work, 298; —pessimism, rejection of, 292; —politics, 62, 116–17; —*poshlost'*: 367, 402, 411–15, as antithesis of art, 365–66, loathing of, 156, as reduction of consciousness, 281; —precision, 69, 151, 297, 305; —privacy, 271; —psychology: 275, and harmony of individual life, 306–7, and rejection of false concentration of mind, 191, 302–3

—racism, opposition to, 317; —reader, role required of, 12, 314–19, 331–32; —reality: 82, betrayal of, by *poshlost'*, 410–11, deceptiveness of, 151, 224, 296, 314, inexhaustibleness of, 297, 412–15; —reason, critical, 5, 186; —reasoned argument, distrust of, 5, 169; —recurrence, 300; —religion, 295, 354; —religious imagery, 251–53, 320; —responsibility, 11, 12, 225–26; —rhyme, 94; —romanticism, 95; —Russia, 20

—self: inaccessibility of another's, 497–500; as prison, 10, 283–84, 293; and struggle to escape prison of, 310–11; transcendence of, 478; transcendence of, in death, 498; transcendence of, through art, 384–89

—shift from verse to prose, 354, 363; —social class, 5, 63; —space: 320, and independence of objects and details, 297, and pattern in natural world, 297–98; —spiral, dialectic, 294–95, 336, 339; —stepping-into-picture motif, 48; —"struggle for existence," rejection of, 292–93; —style, N's, evolution and implications of, 6–12, 250–53, 278–79, 292–320

—taxonomy, 82–83; —theater, attitude to, 40

—time: 45, 248, 252–53, 298–300, 320; and design, 9, 83, 467–68; and freedom of N's prose style, 301–3, 312; pattern in, 299–300 (see also N: Art—fate; —future; —past); as prison, 9, 10, 311–14, 329; transcendence of, 9

—tragedy, N's objections to, 224

—unsportaneousness, predisposition toward, 9, 37–38

—wonder, 11, 12, 250, 292; —written language, N exploits conditions of, 311, 312–14, 319

Life and Character:

—as actor: 232–33, 239, in role of Evreinov, 273, in role of Pozdnyshev, 261, in Schnitzler's *Liebelei*, 148; —aloofness from epoch, 3; —ambidextrousness, 72–73; —ancestry, 15–36, 423; —animals, tenderness to, 74, 390; —anti-Semitism: directed at N, 400, 403–4, opposition to, 27, 80, 179, 400; —appearance, 174, 176, 200, 391; —assurance, 4, 64, 103–4, 346

—birth of, 37; —as boycotter, 52, —butterflies (see N: Life—lepidoptera)

—at Cambridge: 166–95, nostalgia for Russia at, 174–75, Russianness at, 167–68, studies at, 170, 554nn.33 and 36; —capacity for work, 76; —charity appeal, 375–76; —chess, 141, 160, 244, 259; —chess problems: composing, 137, 152, 166, 485, 514–15, and N's art, 317, 331–32, retrograde analysis in, 205; —childhood: discipline in, 43, 105, and emulation of Yuri Rausch in, 52–53, 81, exceptional role of, 44, 47, happiness in, 13, as mathematical prodigy in, 71, security of, 78, 336, spoilt in, 43; —childhood innocence, regard for, 73; —children, love of, 407; —christening, 42; —cinema: interest in, 363, 376, 397, writing for, 230, 231, 368, 376, 425, 445; —clairvoyance, episode of, 71; —clothes, shortage of, 267, 277, 395, 421; —"colored hearing," 44, 58, 306; —composition: 221, 274, 276, 290, N's habits of, 345, 399, 405, 409; —conjuring: 89–90, and N's art, 317–18; —consciousness, dread of losing, 129; —conservatism, and rebelliousness, 61; —courage: 516, games of, 81,

120; —Crimea, exile in, 134–60; —crossword puzzles, 228, 241, 561n.4; —cruelty, abhorrence of, 22; —culture, attitudes to, 29

—as dancer, 164, 165; —as debater, 168–69; —dental problems, 44, 84, 144, 437; —dreams, 171, 171n, 288; —and duelling, 203, 272, 287, 350

—employment: bank clerk, 196, boxing coach, 267, compilation of Russian grammar, 267, farm laborer, 208–9, film extra, 205, 239, freelance translator, 267, 276, reviewer, 267, tennis coach, 267, tutor, 196, 219, 234–35, 241–42, 274, 276, 355, 511–12; —"Englishness" in Berlin, 229, 463; —escape from Berlin, dreams of, 232, 378, 394, 396, 403, 406; —exile, prefigurations of, 114

—fate: playing up to N, 5–6, 137, 147–48, N's prefigured by father's, 66–67; —father (VDN): death of, 191–94, 196, 472n; influence of, 70, 398, N's reverence for, 32, 61, 397–98; —as a father, 407, 420, 421, 422, 428, 515–16; —feelings, concentration of, 4, 8; —fidelity, attitude to, 4, 434, 443–44; —foppishness as youth, 80, 111

—general knowledge, range of, 185; —gratitude, 394; —groups, reluctance to join, 352

—happiness, predisposition for, 10, 88; —hoaxes, literary: 424, "The Night Journey," 371, "Vasily Shishkov," 509–10, "The Wanderers," 187; —homosexuality, attitudes to, 73

—illnesses: appendicitis, 129, bronchitis, 504, and "brushing through death," 71, neuralgia intercostalis, 399–400, 401, 512, pneumonia, 70–71, 123, psoriasis, 434, 437, typhus, 112; —imagination, deliberate exercise of, 79; —income (1930s), 417–18; —individuality: 4, 79, 87–88, parents' tolerance of, 84; —inherits Rozhdestveno, 121; —insomnia, 166; —interviews, conditions on, 312

—jealousy, 120

—languages: English, in childhood, 44, 47, 57, 87, transition to writing in, 6, 407, 419–22, 428–29, 432, 445, 446, 494–96, 501, 503–4, 520; French, 61, 432, writings in, 364, 431; German, 87, 274, 415;

N: Life (*continued*)

Latin, 150; Russian, 6, 171, 495, 501, 504–5

—lepidoptera: 4, 507; in Berlin, 244, and Berlin-Dahlem, 259, 345; breeding, 135; Central Asia, planned expedition into, 137, 398; childhood passion for, 68–84; collections left behind, 159, 522; in Côte d'Azur, 440–41, 486; in Crimea, 136–37, 142, 144, 145–46; in Finland, 119; in Greece, 164; in London (British Museum), 507; method of killing, 289; mimicry, 82; in Misdroy, 262; in Moulinet, 488; and N's art, 317; in N's fiction, 71–72, 236, 351–52, 398, 463, 505–6, 518, 518n; N's scientific discoveries in, 83; as obsession, 105–6; in Prague, 354, 378; in Pyrénées, 288–90; in southern France (Var), 208–9; and species concept, 505; species named after, 17; and taxonomy, 82, 505; as trademark, 74; tropical expedition, dreams of, 354

—love: adolescent sexuality, 81, 85, 97, 109; Claude Deprès, 78–79; "Don Juan list," 97; early love of women, 51–52; Ghika, 51; Irina Guadanini, 433–44; Roma Klyatchkin, 206; Eva Lubrzynska, 123–32, 165–73; Véra Nabokov (*see* N: Life—Véra; and Nabokov, Véra Evseevna); Miss Norcott, 52; Novotvortseva, 164; Polenka, 96; Marianna Shreiber, 174, 181; Valentina Shulgin, 112–20; Svetlana Siewert, 183–202; Lidia Tokmakov, 147; youthful affairs, 122, 146–47, 173, 547–48n.38; Zina, 73–74

—manuscript albums of verse: 131–32, 135, 142, *Nostalgia*, 174, *Stikhi i skhemy*, 152, *Tsvetnye kameshki*, 140; —manuscripts, dating of, 408; —matreshki, love of, 50n; —memory: 45, of own works, 418, visual, 103, 278; —military service, attitude to, 5, 521; —mother, support for, 242, 377, 405, 409, 507; —music, unresponsiveness to, 5, 40

—name, 3n, 166; —namedays, family, 78; —Nansen passport, 437–38n, 438; —nicknames, 76–77, 172, 173; —normality, 4; —nostalgia, 3, 45, 51, 85, 177

—observation, gift of, 101; —optimism, 76, 343, 347

—painting and drawing, 39, 75, 102–3;

—paucity of biographical data (late 1920s–early 1930s), 270–71; —pity, 22, 74; —politics: indifference to, 115–16, responsiveness to in 1930s, 489; —poverty, 267, 377, 409, 421, 428, 430–31, 480, 486, 488–89, 506, 511, 515; —privacy, passion for, 106; —pseudonyms: Vivian Calmbrood, 187, 370–71, Cantab., 180, 181, V. Cantaboff, 180, 181, 218, Valentin Nabokov, 118, Vasily Shalfeev, 261, Vasily Shishkov, 509–10, Vladimir Sirin, 43, 43n, 180–81, 187, Dorian Vivalcomb, 181; —public readings: 206, 228–29, 230, 257, 267, 276, 277, 355, 373, 377, 379, 395–96, 397, 418, 422–23, 424, 426, 432–33, 434, 439, 494, 521–22, reading style of, 395

—reading: adolescent, 90–95, childhood, 47, 79–80; —religion: abandons, 72, indifferent to, 152–53, moderates dismissal of, 354; —responsibility, 103, 271; —restraint, 8; —reviews, alleged indifference to, 121

—school, 133–86; —Scrabble, 137–38; —servants, attitude to, 105; —smoking, 117, 181, 182, 289, 395; —sleep, 241; —social class, attitude to, 541n.41; —solitariness: 4, 271, 352, 463n, own sense of, 276, 504; —Soviet Union: invitation to return to, 375, N's "rehabilitation" in, 456n; —speech, distaste for own, 312; —sports: boxing, 75, 100, 168, 173, 257, 267, 272, 356, 515–16, savate, 100, skiing, 254, soccer (goalkeeping), 88–89, 101, 168, 173, 177, 189, 359, 376–77, tennis, 75, 165, 168, 177, 183, 259, 267, 291, 440; —sunbathing, 369

—teasing, 185; —theater, exposure to, 40, 103; —trains, love of, 48–49, 53, 57, 79; —translations: of own works, by himself, 421, by others, N's supervision of, 246, 409, 419–20; —tutors, 75–113 passim

—underestimation of early work, 272

—Véra Nabokov: early meetings with, 216–17, engagement to, 233, first meeting with, 206–8, 213, marriage to, 239–40, 283–84, near-meetings with in past, 212, relationship to, 438, 444 (*see also* Nabokov, Véra Evseevna); —visas, identity cards and passports, difficulties with, 379, 425–26, 432, 436, 437–38, 485, 492, 511, 514–15, 520–21

—writing: in childhood, 57, 81, 96, 96n, early reviews of, 117–18, 185–86, literary criticism by, 185–86, 189, 267, youthful verse, 107–9, 111, 113–14, 131–32, 151, 166

Works:

—*Ada*: 11, 17, 29, 48, 49n, 67, 69, 73, 82, 102, 104–5, 120, 152, 178n, 248, 250, 298, 299, 300, 302, 304, 305, 306, 307, 308, 310, 311, 313, 314, 357, 359, 386, 410, composition of, 276, 399, sources of, 16, 78, "The Texture of Time," 304; —"Admiralteyskaya igla" (*see* "The Admiralty Spire"); —"The Admiralty Spire," 401–2; —"Aerial Island," 395; —"An Affair of Honor," 274–75; —"Agasfer" (*see* "Ahasuerus"); —"Ahasuerus," 218, 228; —"And all that was, and all that will be," 202–3; —"Angels," 149, 152–53; —*Anya v strane chudes* (trans. of *Alice in Wonderland*): 197, reception of, 201; —"The Assistant Producer," source of, 294; —"The Aurelian": 351–52, public readings of, 355, 423; —"Autumn," 117–18

—"Bachmann": 235–36, 308, German serialization of, 291; —"A Bad Day," 369, 376, 437; —*Bend Sinister*: 8, 58, 88, 212, 224, 248, 284, 296, 298, 299, 303, 304, 305, 308, 310, 314, 315–17, 407, 411, 439, 487, sources of, 516, 520; —"Bilet" (*see* "The Ticket"); —"Biology," 182; —*Bird of Paradise*, 362; —"Blagost' " (*see* "Grace"); —"Bogi" (*see* "Gods"); —"Bolshaya medveditsa" (*see* "The Great Bear"); —"La Bonne Lorraine," 235; —"Breaking the News": 405–6, 417, public reading of, 424; —"Britva" (*see* "The Razor"); —"A Busy Man," 371–72, 373

—*Camera Obscura*: 363, 364–68, 378, 391, 417, 451, composition of, 362–64, Czech translation of, 417, English translation of, 407, 409, 419, 430, film adaptation of, 376, 435, French translation of, 393, 396, 417, public reading of, 373, 377, research for, 361–62, as written for cinema, 368 (see also *Laughter in the Dark*); —"Cavalier of the Moonlight" (with Lukash), 228, 238–39; —*Chelovek iz SSSR* (see *The Man from the USSR*); —"The Chess Knight," 275, 289; —"Childhood," 189;

—"The Chinese Screens," 233, 234, 254; —"Christmas," 71–72, 236, 272; —"A Christmas Story," 287; —"Chto vsyakiy dolzhen znat' " (*see* "What Everyone Should Know"); —"The Circle": 404–5, 417, 520, as Appendix 1 of *The Gift*, 505; —"Cloud, Castle, Lake": 439, 489, public reading of, 521–22; —*The Cluster*: 184, 194, 202, 220, reviews of, 201; —"Colette," 79; —*Conclusive Evidence*: 15, 32–33, 407, composition of, 420–21, 422, genesis of, 428–29, 520, revision of, 16 (see also *Speak, Memory*); —"Crimea," 185

—*Dar* (see *The Gift*); —"A Dashing Fellow," 379; —*Death*, 34, 204, 225; —*Dedushka* (see *The Granddad*); —*The Defense*: 69, 70, 214, 235, 284, 289–90, 292, 296, 305, 307, 308, 318, 320, 321–40, 346, 351, 357, 363, 410, 451, 472n, composition of, 276, 289–91, French translation of, 355, 393, 396, 400–401, 405, genesis of, 275–76, 289–90, 565n.41, German translation of, 355, reception of, 341–45, reviews of, 568n.24, sources, 78, 275–76, 276n, 289–90, Swedish translation of, 417; —*Despair*: 4, 11, 29, 296, 304, 308, 310, 382–89, 395, 406, 417, 420, 451, composition of, 389, 397, English translation of, 407, 409, 419–22, 429–30, 432, 435, 436, 446, film adaptation of, 376, 397, 422n, French translation of, 440, public reading of, 396, sources, 288–89, 341, 363; —"Details of a Sunset," 232; —"Detstvo" (*see* "Childhood"); —"The Doorbell," 273; —"Dostoevsky without Dostoevskyitis," 363; —"Dozhd' proletel" (*see* "The rain has flown"); —"The Dragon," 236, 281; —"Draka" (*see* "The Fight"); —"Drakon" (*see* "The Dragon"); —*Drugie berega*, 152, 456n (see also *Speak, Memory*); —*Dva puti* (see *Two Paths*; —"Dvoe" (*see* "The Two")

—"Easter," 193, 472n; —"Easter Rain," 231; —*The Empyrean Path*: 189, 220, reviews of, 201; —*The Enchanter*, 512–14, 517, 520, 521; —"The Encounter," 207–8, 210, 558n.37; —English autobiography, 1936 (unpublished), 428–29, 432, 435, 446, 495, 505, 520, 575n.58; —"Esli veter sud'by radi shutki" (*see* "If the wind of fate . . . "); —*Eugene Onegin* (translation and commentaries), 18, 22, 81, 149, 276;

N: Works (*continued*)
—"Evening on a Vacant Lot," 380–81;
—*The Event*, 255, 273, 446, 480–85, 486,
496, 520; —"Exile," 242; —*The Eye*: 8, 28,
310, 346–50, 357, 389, 461, composition
of, 345, family reading of, 354, French
translation of, 418, public reading of,
349–50, 355; —*The Eye*, (collection), 487
—"A Few Notes on Crimean Lepidoptera," 170; —"A Few Words on the
Wretchedness of Soviet Literature," 260;
—"The Fight," 242–43, 273; —"Finis,"
202; —"First Love," 79, 395; —"The Fountain of Bakhchisaray (in memory of
Pushkin)," 148
—*The Gift*: 8, 10, 34–35, 68, 98, 105, 137,
146, 212, 248, 250, 255, 285, 299, 305, 308,
309, 310, 311, 357, 360, 398, 410, 416, 417,
418, 419, 420, 427, 428–29, 431, 444, 447–
78, 479–80, 485, 543n.50, composition of,
276, 401, 403, 405, 406–7, 408–9, 416, 422,
426, 429, 431, 441–43, 444, 446, continuations of, 505–6, 516–17, 520 (see also N:
Works—*Solus Rex*), genesis of, 397–400,
Life of Chernyshevsky, 22, 296, 304, 409,
416, 418, 441–43, 457, 479, 489, 578n.4,
N's differentiation of Fyodor from himself, 397–99, 463–64, publication of, 441–
43, 505, public reading of, 432–33; Second
Appendix to, 520, as source of other N
works, 496, 512, 520, sources of, 78, 95,
219, 258, 351, 352–53, 355, 363, 369, 373,
375, 376, 377n, 381, 392, 397–400, 462–63,
464–65, and Symbolism, 93; —*Glory*, 48,
142, 153, 175, 188, 210, 214, 310, 353–61,
362, 365, 370, 418, 551n.37, 568n.44;
—"Gods," 219; —*Gorniy put'* (see *The Empyrean Path*); —"Govoryat po-russki" (*see*
"Russian Spoken Here"); —"Grace," 229,
232, 292; —*The Granddad*, 34, 209, 225;
—"The Grand Piano," 258; —"The Great
Bear," 151; —"Groza" (*see* "The Thunder-
storm"); —*Grozd'* (see *The Cluster*);
—"Guardian Angel," 153; —"A Guide to
Berlin," 250–53, 292, 294, 297
—*Happiness*, 237, 241, 245, 292;
—Heine, translations of, 145; —"Home,"
179
—"I dreamed of you so often," 183;
—"If the wind of fate . . . ," 182; —"In a
Castilian alley," 203; —"In Memory of L.

I. Shigaev," 406; —"In Radiant Autumn," 144, 146; —"Inspiration, rosy
sky," 395; —"In Spring," 141–42; —*Invitation to a Beheading*: 34–35, 204, 250, 281,
308, 310, 314, 402, 410–17, 419, 425, 439,
520, composition of, 408–10, public reading of, 422–23, sources of, 219; —"I remember in a plush frame," 216–17;
—"Istreblenie tiranov" (*see* "Tyrants Destroyed"); —"It is Me," 420–21, 428 (*see
also* N: Works—*Conclusive Evidence*;
—English autobiography; —*Speak,
Memory*); —"Ivan Vernykh," 259;
—"Izgnan'e" (*see* "Exile"); —*Izobretenie
Val'sa* (see *The Waltz Invention*)
—*Kamera obskura* (see *Camera Obscura*);
—"Kartofelnyy El'f" (*see* "The Potato
Elf"); —"Katastrofa" ("The Catastrophe")
(*see* "Details of a Sunset"); —"Kavaler lun-
nogo sveta" (*see* "Cavalier of the Moonlight"); —"Khvat" (*see* "A Dashing Fellow"); —*King, Queen, Knave*: 278–86, 288,
295, 296, 321, 336, 346, 350, 357, 386, 434,
composition of, 277–78, genesis of, 274,
275, 278–79, German translation of, 286–
87, reviews of, 286, sources of, 254, 274;
—"Kitayskie shirmy" (*see* "The Chinese
Screens"); —*Korol', dama, valet* (see *King,
Queen, Knave*); —"Korolyok" (*see* "The
Leonardo"); —"Krasavitsa" (*see* "A Russian Beauty"); —"Krug" (*see* "The Circle"); —"Krym" (*see* "Crimea"); —"K
svobode" (*see* "To Liberty")
—"Lance": 299, source of, 516; —"Lastochki" (*see* "Swallows"); —"Laughter
and Dreams," 218; —*Laughter in the Dark*:
8, 11, 29, 284, 299, 308, 363, 446, film adaptation of, 486, provisional titles for,
445, publication of, 485–86, reviews of,
486, revision of *Camera Obscura*, 365n, 445
(see also *Camera Obscura*); —"Lebeda" (*see*
"Orache"); —"The Leonardo," 402; —"A
Letter that Never Reached Russia," 237–
38; —"Lik," 493–94, 579n.39; —"Lips to
Lips," 373–74, 422; —"Little Angel," 395;
—"The Living Water" (with Lukash),
227; —*Lolita*: 3, 4, 6, 8, 11, 15, 29, 54, 73,
74, 78, 109n, 120, 248, 249, 261, 270, 284,
297, 299, 300, 301, 302–3, 305, 306, 307–8,
309, 310, 311, 351, 385, 386, 407, 410, 521,
compared to *The Enchanter*, 512–14, com-

position of, 276, sources of, 516, 517;
—*Look at the Harlequins!*, 212–13, 241, 253,
285, 308, 345, 361, 407; —'Love of a
Dwarf," 230, 232, 234; —"Lyubov' karlika" (*see* "Love of a Dwarf")

—"Mademoiselle O": 428–29, 432, composition of, 390, 422, public reading of,
425–26; —*The Man from the USSR*: 263–67,
279, composition of, 258, performance of,
272–73; —*Mary*: 78, 112, 114, 120, 130,
146, 146n, 152, 205, 245–49, 250, 252, 254,
263, 265, 272, 276, 277, 278–79, 280–81,
283–84, 285, 286–87, 293–94, 299, 320,
321, 357, composition of, 237, 241, 244–
45, German translation of, 277, public
reading of, 257, reviews of, 246–47, 258,
sources of, 233, 245; —"A Matter of
Chance": 231–32, 233, first version, 289;
—"Mest' " (*see* "Revenge"); —"Music,"
377–78, 395; —"Muzyka" (*see* "Music")

—"Nabor" (*see* "Recruiting"); —"Natasha," 234; —"Nezhit' " (*see* "The
Sprite");

—"The Night Journey," 370–71; —*Nikolka
Persik* (translation of Rolland, *Colas
Breugnon*). 176, 177, 181, 189, 197, 201;
—"La Nuit de décembre" (translation),
118; —"A Nursery Tale," 259–60, 272

—"Obida" (*see* "A Bad Day");
—"Oblako, ozero, bashnya" (*see* "Cloud,
Castle, Lake"); —"On Generalities," 353;
—"Opovoshchenie" (*see* "Breaking the
News"); —"Orache," 99, 376; —"Osen' "
(*see* "Autumn"); —*Otchayanie* (see *De-
spair*); —"The Outburst," 261–62

—"Painted Wood," 218; —*Pale Fire*: 4,
8, 28–29, 54, 171, 203, 224, 248, 249, 250,
285, 296, 299, 303, 305, 307, 308, 309, 310–
11, 314, 333, 372, 407, 410, 420, 521, composition of, 276, 399, genesis of, 17,
sources of, 516, 517, 519, 520; —"Pamyati
L. I. Shigaeva" (*see* "In Memory of L. I.
Shigaev"); —"Paskhal'nyy dozhd' " (*see*
"Easter Rain"); — 'The Passenger," 272;
—"Perfection," 379–80; —"Pilgram" (*see*
"The Aurelian"); —"Pis'mo v Rossiyu"
(*see* "A Letter that Never Reached Russia"); —*Pnin*, 248, 308, 407; —"Podlets"
("The Scoundrel") (*see* "An Affair of
Honor"); —*Podvig* (see *Glory*); —*Poems*
(1916), 118–21, 547n.29; —*Poems and Prob-

lems*, 152; —"The Poets," 509–10;
—"Poety" (*see* "The Poets"); —*The Pole*,
209–10, 225, 235; —*Polyus* (see *The Pole*);
—"The Port," 210–11, 229; —"Poryv" (*see*
"The Outburst"); —"Poseshchenie
muzeya" (*see* "The Visit to the Museum"); —"The Potato Elf": 229–30, 232,
English translation of, 508, film adaptation of, 376; —"Pouchkine, ou le vrai et le
vraisemblable," 431, 432, 434, 507;
—*Priglashenie na kazn'* (see *Invitation to a
Beheading*); —"Putevoditel' po Berlinu"
(*see* "A Guide to Berlin")

—"The rain has flown," 108–9, 129–30,
156; —*Rayskaya ptitsa* (see *Bird of Paradise*);
—"The Razor," 257–58; —*The Real Life of
Sebastian Knight*: 95, 121, 188, 203, 212,
226–27, 299, 308, 310, 311–12, 496–502,
503–4, 520; composition of, 494–96, publication of, 505, 511, public reading of, 507,
sources of, 425, 436; —"Recruiting," 420,
543n.50; —"The Return of Chorb": 249–
50, 283, 284, 294, English translation of,
401; —*The Return of Chorb* (collection),
291, 345, 351; —"The Reunion," 375;
—"Revenge," 229; —"Royal' " (*see* "The
Grand Piano"); —"Rozhdestvenskiy
rasskaz" (*see* "A Christmas Story");
—"Rozhdestvo" (*see* "Christmas");
—"Rupert Brooke," 182; —"Rusalka" (*see*
"The Water-Nymph"); —"A Russian
Beauty," 408, 417, 424; —*A Russian's
Early Association with England* (see *N:
Works*—English autobiography, 1936);
—"The Russian Song," 218; —"Russian
Spoken Here," 219–20

—*Schastie* (see *Happiness*); —"Seraphim," 153; —"Shakhmatnyy kon' " (*see*
"The Chess Knight"); —"Signs and Symbols": 297, 308, source of, 516; —"Siriniana," 187–88; —"Skazka" (*see* "A Nursery Tale"); —*Skital'tsy* (see *The Wanderers*);

—"A Slice of Life," 421; —"Slovo" (*see*
"The Word"); —"Sluchay iz zhizni" (*see*
"A Slice of Life"); —"Sluchaynost' " (*see*
"A Matter of Chance"); —*Smert'* (see
Death); —*Sobytie* (see *The Event*); —*So-
glyadatay* (see *The Eye*); —"Solnechnyy
son" (*see* "The Sun Dream"); —*Solus Rex*
(novel): 224, 505, 516–20, composition of,

N: Works (*continued*)
521; —"Solus Rex" (story), 518–19; —"Sounds," 217–18, 219, 238, 292, 310, 543n.50; —"Sovershenstvo" (*see* "Perfection"); —*Speak, Memory*: 7–12, 16, 33, 45, 47, 48, 56, 69, 75, 79, 80, 81, 97, 99–100, 107, 108–9, 119–20, 138, 144, 146, 146n, 152, 158, 168, 243, 253, 301, 305, 306, 309, 313–14, 356, 369, 407, 410, 423, 428, 429, 456n, 514–15, sources of, 376, 428–29, 435; "themes" in, 42, 44, 49, 51, 69, 97, 109; —"Spring in Fialta": 426–27, French translation of, 438, source of, 354; —"The Sprite," 180, 203; —*Stikhi* (1916) (see *Poems* [1916]); —"A Stroke of the Wing," 219, 226, 236; —"The Sun Dream," 203–4, 218; —"Svetloy osen'yu" (*see* "In Radiant Autumn"); —"Swallows," 175 —"Terra Incognita": 296, 373, public reading of, 424; —"Terror," 261–62, 342; —"The Thunderstorm," 233–34; —"The Ticket," 273; —"Time and Ebb," 299; —"To an Unborn Reader," 395; —"To Liberty," 140; —"To Prince S. M. Kachurin," 255; —"Torpid Smoke," 418, 419, 543n.50; —"Torzhestvo dobrodeteli" (*see* "The Triumph of Virtue"); —"To the Muse," 395; —*The Tragedy of Mr. Morn*, 220–26, 227, 228, 229, 263; —translations: from *Hamlet*, 362, from Landor, 166, from Seamus O'Sullivan, 166 (see also N: Works:—*Anya v strane chudes*; —*Nikolka Persik*; —"La Nuit de décembre"); —*Transparent Things*, 250, 284, 289, 298, 301, 308, 310, 311, 312, 314, 318–19; —"The Triumph of Virtue," 350; —"The Two," 156–57; —*Two Paths*, 131; —"Tyazholyy dym" (*see* "Torpid Smoke"); —"Tyrants Destroyed": 58, 486–87, 489, 492, sources of, 400 —"Udar kryla" (*see* "A Stroke of the Wing"); —"Uldaborg," 353; —"Ultima Thule," 203, 255, 284, 305, 308, 310, 361, 517–19; —unfinished and untitled works: novel (1932), 378; short story (1926), 261; —"A University Poem": 267–69, 271, 273, 275, 279, 342, 355, 433, 563n.65, public reading of, 277–78; —"Usta k ustam" (*see* "Lips to Lips"); —"Uzhas" (*see* "Terror") —"The Vane Sisters," 372, 372n; —"Vasily Shishkov," 509–10, 511; —"Vecher na pustyre" (*see* "Evening on a Vacant Lot"); —"The Venetian Woman," 235; —"Vengeance," 232; —"Vesna v Fial'te" (*see* "Spring in Fialta"); —"Vesnoy" (*see* "In Spring"); —"The Visit to the Museum," 493, 494; —"Voda zhivaya" (*see* "The Living Water"); —*Volshebnik* (see *The Enchanter*); —"Vozvrashchenie Chorba" (*see* "The Return of Chorb"); —"Vstrecha" (poem) (*see* "The Encounter"); —"Vstrecha" (story) (*see* "The Reunion")

—*The Waltz Invention*: 489–92, 496, production of, cancelled, 494, 509; —*The Wanderers*, 187; —"The Water-Nymph," 516–17; —"What Everyone Should Know," 363; —"The Window," 395; —"The Word," 203, 218

—"Yalta Pier," 148

—"Zanyatoy chelovek" (*see* "A Busy Man"); —*Zashchita Luzhina* (see *The Defense*); —"Zvonok" (*see* "The Doorbell"); —"Zvuki" (*see* "Sounds")

Nabokov, Vlass (probable ancestor), 16
Nabokovian, 533
Nabokov River, 17
Na Cherdake (émigré literary group, Berlin), 276
Nachman-Achariya, Magda, 400
Nadezhda (ship), 159–60, 163
Nakanune (pro-Soviet newspaper, Berlin), 199, 200, 203, 278
Nansen, Fridtjof, 437–38n
Nansen passport, 437–38n, 446
Napoleon, 18, 185, 197
Nash mir (émigré weekly, Berlin; supplement to *Rul'*), 228, 561n.4
Nash vek (émigré weekly, Berlin; successor to *Rul'*), 373
Nausée, La (Sartre), 262n
Nekrasov, Nikolay, 127, 363
Nellis, 101
Nemirovich-Danchenko, Vasily, 117
Nemirovich-Danchenko, Vladimir, 39
"Nesbit," 168, 435–36, 576n.18. *See also* Butler, R. A.
Neva River, 18, 30, 31, 37, 51
New Economic Policy (NEP), 197–98
Newman, Alice (landlady), 172, 181
New Russia (newspaper, London), 172, 179

Newton, Sir Isaac, 167, 280
New York Times Book Review, 421
Nice, 49, 211
Nicholas I, 40
Nicholas II, 32, 42, 59, 75, 110, 122–23, 124–25, 535n.32
Nietzsche, Friedrich, 76, 150
Nijinsky, Vaslav, 39
Nikolay Mikhailovich, Grand Duke, 400
Nikolay Platonych (schoolteacher), 129
Nimzowitsch, 259
1984 (Orwell), 374
Nobel Prize, 403
Noel, Lucie Léon. *See* Léon Noel, Lucie
Noir, Jacques, 242
Nolde, Baron, 125
"Norcott, Miss" (governess), 49, 50–52
Notes from Underground (Dostoevsky), 382
Nouvelle revue française (Paris), 344, 393, 422, 434
Nouvelles littéraires (Paris), 344, 400
Nova Zembla, 17
Novoe slovo (émigré newspaper, Berlin), 489
Novoe vremya (newspaper, St. Petersburg), 98–99, 215
Novotvortseva (lover, Greece), 164, 395
Nussbaum (tutor), 105, 546n.63

"O, Mademoiselle." *See* Miauton, Cécile
October Manifesto, 59, 64
Octobrists, 64
Odessa, 214
Odoevtseva, Irina, 350, 425
Oeil-de-Dieu (Hellens), 422
Ofrosimov, Yuri, 239, 258, 261, 263, 273, 276, 373
Okolokulak, Boris (tutor), 79
Olga (childhood girlfriend), 97
O'Neill, Eugene, 211
Orbis (émigré publisher, Berlin), 212, 214–15
Orczy, Baroness: *Scarlet Pimpernel*, 91
Ordyntsev (Ordo, tutor), 75
Oredezh River, 25, 30, 31, 46, 102
Orlando (Woolf), 402
Orwell, George, *1984*, 374
Osorgin, Mikhail, 392
Ostrovsky, Alexander, 258
O'Sullivan, Seamus. *See* Starkey, James
Osvobozhdenie (pre-revolutionary émigré newspaper, Stuttgart), 55
Oswald, Lee Harvey, 22

Otechestvennye zapiski (nineteenth-century Russian journal), 441
Othello, 224
Otsup, Nikolay, 350, 374, 580n.18
Ovid, 147
Oxford, 165

Pahlen, Count, 20
Pan, Alexis (character). *See* N: Works—*The Real Life of Sebastian Knight*
Panin, Countess Sofia, 134, 136, 139, 141, 433
Pannonia (ship), 164, 165
Pares, Sir Bernard, 64, 431
Paris, 51, 164, 211, 271, 288; N's addresses in, 390–97, 423–26, 432–38, 440, 492–522; N's desire to move to, 394, 396, 400, 432; N's dislike of, 504; N's reasons for avoiding, in 1920s, 235; N's trips to, 390–97, 423–26; N's wartime sketch of, 510–11; Russian emigration in, 217, 341–44, 391–96, 432
Parker, Stephen Jan, 357n
Paromonov, N. E., 403
Parry, Albert, 403
Party of the People's Freedom. *See* Constitutional Democratic (CD) party
Pasmanik, Daniil, 156
Passionate Friends (Wells), 91
Pasternak, Leonid, 198
Pau, 396
Paulhan, Jean, 393, 422, 426, 437
Pavlova, Anna, 39, 165, 246
Pedenko (tutor), 75
Peer Gynt (Ibsen), 222
Pelageya (childhood girlfriend), 97
Peltenburg, 214
Pepys, Samuel, 349
Perpigna (Rukavishnikov chateau), 43, 396
Person, Hugh (character). *See* N: Works—*Transparent Things*
Perun, 233n
Peter, Saint, 233
Peter the Great, 37, 40, 493
Petersburg (Bely), 149, 151–52
Peterson, Natalia de, 51
Petkevich, Olga Vladimirovna (née Nabokov) (sister), 44, 88, 111, 121, 149, 184, 185, 255, 378, 507; burns N letters to mother, 271
Petkevich, Rostislav, 378, 507

Petlyura, Simon, 214
Peto's (St. Petersburg toyshop), 89
Petrarch, Francesco, 112
Petrashevtsy, 19
Petrograd, 111. *See also* St. Petersburg
Petrograd Duma: VDN as member of, 130
Petrograd Soviet, 123–27, 131, 134
Petropolis Press (Berlin), 505, 514
Petrunkevich, Ivan, 136, 138
Peucker family (cousins), 141
Peucker, Lydia von (aunt), 138
Peucker, Nicholas von (uncle), 138
Phaleron, 163
Pilnyak, Boris, 198, 260
Pinter, Harold, 263
Piombo, Sebastiano del, 235
Piotrovsky, Nina, 278
Piraeus, 163
Pirandello, Luigi, 235
Pirogov (chauffeur), 102
Plehve, Count von, 54
Plevitskaya, Nadezhda: as Soviet agent, 261; trial of, 494
Pobedonostsev, Konstantin, 21
Poe, Edgar Allan, 91, 203, 316; "Silence," 210
Poets' Club, 277–78, 287, 371
Pohl, Vladimir, 138, 143–44, 152, 153, 156
"Poindexter, Louise," 81; name bestowed on American dancing girl in Berlin, 84–85
Polenka (girlfirend), 96, 97n, 102, 305
Polevitskaya, Elena, 184, 228
Polo, Marco, 477
Ponizovski, Alexander, 178, 425
Popov, 100–101
Popper, Sir Karl, 169
poshlost', 156, 281, 365–66, 367, 402, 411–15
Poslednie novosti (émigré newspaper, Paris), 177, 190, 373, 374, 375, 391, 402, 417, 418, 424, 442, 480, 485, 489, 509, 511; N's shift to, 369
Prague, 196, 232, 271; N's dislike of, 235, 378; N's family moves to, 220–21; N's trips to, 220–26, 233, 243, 353, 378–79, 438–39; Russian emigration in, 217, 220; Russian Historical Archive in, 354
Pravda, 59, 273
Pravo (journal, St. Petersburg), 33, 39, 55, 56, 59, 76, 206
Press Ball Gazette (émigré broadsheet, Berlin), 258
Princess Obolensky School, 213–14

Protocols of the Elders of Zion, 179
Proust, Marcel 73, 293, 354, 363, 397, 425, 445; *A la recherche du temps perdu*, 149, 466
Provisional Government, First, 123–27, 130
Provisional Government (VDN), 143, 155
Przhevalsky, Nikolay, 398, 400, 454n
Punch, 80
Pushchin, Ivan, 18
Pushkin, Alexander, 29, 36, 38, 81n, 82, 91, 92, 93, 95, 97, 115, 116, 148, 150, 175, 178, 184, 185, 215, 230, 238, 287, 363, 393, 399, 424, 431, 434, 460, 472–74, 493, 495, 507; N family as associates of, 18; N parodies biographers of, 147; N talk on, 257; and Russian Culture Day, 242; as symbol of spiritual liberty to N, 18, 22, 41
—works: *Bronze Horseman*, 37; "The Covetous Knight," 370–71; *Eugene Onegin*, 79–80, 156–57, 201, 268–69, 443–44, 462, 466, 516; "The Monument," 41; *Rusalka*, 516–17; verse dramas of, as influence on N, 204, 222
Pykhachev family, 78

Quarenghi, Giacomo, 72
Quatsch (theatrical revue), 273
Quennell, Peter, 435
Quilty, Clare (character). *See* N: Works—*Lolita*

Rabelais, François, 176
Rachmaninov, Sergey, 3, 486
Racine, Jean, 69
Radočovice, 243
Raduga, 187
Raevsky, Nikolay, 354, 378
Ransom, John Crowe, 4
Raspad atoma (Georgy Ivanov), 350n
Rasputin, Grigory, 122
Rathaus, Daniil, 350, 354
Rausch von Traubenberg (Paris), 394
Rausch von Traubenberg, Baron Yuri, 15, 122, 146; death of, 157–58; N's emulation of and rivalry with, 52–53, 80–81, 96, 107, 120
Rausch von Traubenberg family, 78
Razin, Stenka, 416
Rech' (newspaper, St. Petersburg), 39, 61, 98, 104, 110, 130, 135, 136, 139, 177, 179, 206, 254, 256; VDN as editor of, 70
Reid, Mayne, 81
Reinhardt, Max, 103

Remizov, Alexey, 198, 200, 342, 391; *Zvezda nadzvezdnaya*, reviewed by N, 287
Revolutions, Russian: "first revolution" (1905), 54–60; February 1917, 123–26; October 1917, 3, 132–33
Rex, Axel. *See* N: Works—*Laughter in the Dark*
Ridel, Mme, 426
Ridley, Katharine, 435
Rimbaud, Arthur, 91, 510
Robinson, Miss (governess), 61
Roche, Denis, 393, 418, 434, 438
Rölke, Frau (landlady), 243
Rolland, Romain: *Colas Breugnon*, 176, 177, 181, 197, 557n.4
Roman s kokainom (Ageev), 573n.13
Romanov, Nina. *See* Chavchavadze, Nina
Romanov, Prince Nikita, 178, 186, 445; as original of Vadim (*Glory*), 175
Ronsard, Pierre de, 210, 394
Rosenberg, William, 154–55
Rosov, Samuil, 101, 129, 130, 166
Rostovtzeff, Mikhail, 430–31, 506
Rousseau, Jean-Jacques, 80, 327
Roy, Winifred, 445
Rozhdestveno (village and manor, province of St. Petersburg), 31, 46, 72, 73, 77, 97, 112, 119, 120, 257, 289; N's inheritance of manor, 3
Rudnev, Vadim, 63, 391, 395, 409, 441, 479; refuses to publish N's *Life of Chernyshevsky*, 441–43
Rue du chat qui pêche, La (Földes), 434
"Ruka," 233
Rukavishnikov, Elena Ivanovna (mother). *See* Nabokov, Elena Ivanovna
Rukavishnikov family name: etymology of, 30
Rukavishnikov, Ivan Vasilievich (grandfather), 30–32, 43, 46, 91
Rukavishnikov, Olga Nikolaevna (grandmother), 31, 43
Rukavishnikov, Vasily (great-grandfather), 30
Rukavishnikov, Vasily Ivanovich (uncle), 30, 31, 32, 43, 46, 74, 78, 111, 113, 120, 133, 144, 297, 396; death of, 121; fondness for N, 73, 121; homosexuality of, 73
Rukavishnikov, Vladimir Ivanovich (uncle), 31
Rul' (émigré newspaper, Berlin), 186, 190, 193, 195, 200, 205, 206, 210, 217, 230, 231,

254–56, 258, 273, 274, 363; begins publication, 179–80; collapse of, 373; decline of, 228, 355, 369; early success of, 198; establishment of, 177; N as contributor to, 180; N reviews for, 267, 276, 278; offices attacked, 373
Rulik (Nabokov family "newspaper"), 184
Russia, 15–160 passim; N's departure from, 160; N's nostalgia for, 174–75; N's sense of revisiting its flora and fauna, 244
Russian Culture Day, 242
Russian Literary Club, Berlin, 229, 230
Russian Literary-Artistic Circle, Berlin, 230, 239
Russian Nationalist Students' Union, Berlin, 206
Russian Sports Club, Berlin, 376–77
Russian Theater, Paris, 446, 485, 489, 494, 508
Russkaya mysl' (pre-revolutionary journal, St. Petersburg), 129
Russkie zapiski (émigré journal, Paris), 486, 487, 504
Russkoe ekho (émigré newspaper, Berlin), 230, 231
Russo-Japanese War, 50, 52, 58, 98, 538n.56
Ruths-Speicher, 427
Ryleev, Kondraty, 46n
Ryndina, Lydia, 239
Ryovshin (character), 255. *See also* N: Works—*The Event*

Sablin, Evgeny 436, 506–7
St. Moritz, 188
St. Nazaire, 523
St. Nicholas Magazine, 80
St. Petersburg, 3, 15–139 passim; N's attitude to, 40
St. Petersburg Duma, 57
Sak, Alexander, 242–43, 243–44, 259, 267
Sakharov, Nikolay (tutor), 75, 107, 112, 113, 545–46n.62
Salieri, Antonio, 351
Sarajevo, 110
Sarton, May, 4
Sartre, Jean-Paul: *La Nausée*, possible influence of N on, 262n
Saurat, 290, 396
Saveliev, A. A. *See* Sherman, Savely
Sayn-Wittgenstein, Elizaveta, 96
Sayn-Wittgenstein family, 78, 369
Scarlet Pimpernel (Orczy), 91

Schmidt, I. F., 228
Schnitzler, Arthur (*Liebelei*), 148
Schubert, Franz, 145
Schuman, Samuel, 533
Schumann, Robert, 145
Schurmann, Georg, 16
Schwarzwald, 244
Scott, Captain Robert Falcon, 209–10
Scott, Sir Walter, 183
Sebastopol, 140, 158, 159–60
Sebastopol Sketches (Tolstoy), 424–25
Segerfeld, Tatiana (lover), 122
Segodnya (émigré newspaper, Riga), 231
Seitz, 82
Sergeevichi (family of Sergey Dmitrievich Nabokov, q.v.), 138, 159, 163, 164
Serov, Valentin, 39
Severyanin, Igor, 92
Seyfulina, Lydia, 260
Seythenex, 508
Shabelsky-Bork, Peter, 190–91
Shade, John and Sybil (characters). *See* N: Works—*Pale Fire*
Shakespeare, William, 29, 37n, 38, 91, 304, 416; as influence on *The Tragedy of Mr. Morn*, 222, 224; *Hamlet*, 225, 325, 362, 416; *King Lear*, 6, 365; *Measure for Measure*, 225; *Othello*, 224; *The Tempest*, 225, 416; *Titus Andronicus*, 365; Tolstoy's critique of, 6
Shakhovskaya, Princess, 397
Shakhovskaya, Zinaida, 397, 421, 422, 432, 445
Shcheglovitov, E. G., 104
Sheldon, Victoria (governess), 47–48
Sherman, Savely [pseud. A. A. Saveliev], 255–56, 373
Shimkevich, 31
Shingarev, Andrey, 139, 140, 433
Shklovsky, Viktor, 198
Shmelev, Ivan, 342
Shreiber, Marianna (girlfriend, Cambridge), 174, 181
Shtein, 192
Shulgin, Vadim, 112
Shulgin, Valentina (girlfriend), 97, 109, 112–14, 118, 119–20, 122, 123, 130, 142, 145, 146, 147, 152, 160, 182, 183, 237, 245, 250, 279, 305
Shustov, Nikolay, 100, 105–6
Siewert, Kirill, 197

Siewert, Klavdia, 196
Siewert, Roman, 202
Siewert, Svetlana (fiancée, Berlin), 183–84, 186, 188–89, 192, 198, 203, 204, 208, 209; engagement to broken off, 201–2; N proposes to, 196
Siewert, Tatiana, 183–84, 188, 196–97, 198
Sikorski, Elena Vladimirovna (née Nabokov) (sister), 61, 88, 108, 111, 149, 159, 184, 220, 255, 354, 378; as N's favorite sibling, 150–51
"Silence" (Poe), 210
Silhouettes of Russian Writers (Aykhenvald), 256
Simferopol, 136
Sineusov (character). *See* N: Works—"Ultima Thule"
Sinyaya ptitsa. *See* Bluebird
Sirin, Vladimir. *See* N: Life—pseudonyms
Skit Poetov (Prague writers' group), 354
Skoblin, General, 261, 494
Skoropadsky, Paul, 214
Slonim, Evsey (father-in-law), 212, 241, 244; death of, 286; life and career of, 213–15
Slonim, Slava, 213, 241; death of, 286
Slonim, Véra Evseevna. *See* Nabokov, Véra Evseevna
Slovo (émigré publisher, Berlin), 177, 189, 198, 206, 256, 258, 286–87, 291
Smena Vekh, 199
Smoke (Turgenev), 182
Smolensky, Vladimir, 392, 425
Smurov (character). *See* N: Works—*The Eye*
Snessarev, 98–99
Social Democratic (SD) party, 63, 64
Socialist Revolutionary (SR) party, 58, 62–63, 64, 140, 189, 342, 389, 425–26, 442, 457
Sokolov, Sergey, 200n
Solliès-Pont, 208–11, 441
Solomon, 168
Solzhenitsyn, Alexander, 171n
Somov, Konstantin, 39
Song of Igor's Campaign, 174
Sorin, Savely, 146, 146n
Sorokin, Pitirim, 514
Soviet literature: N's attacks on, 260, 350
Sovremennik (nineteenth-century Russian journal), 441
Sovremennye zapiski (émigré journal, Paris), 185–86, 257, 261–62, 350, 362, 369, 390, 400, 409, 417, 441–44, 445, 457, 479, 486,

504, 508, 509, 514, 517, 567n.4; accepts *Glory* before completion, 355–56; role of, in emigration, 340–42

Spectator, 511

Spengler, Oswald, 353, 363

Spiresco, Kosta, 271–72

Spolokhi (émigré journal, Berlin), 199, 200

Stalin, Joseph, 21n, 117, 412, 435, 457, 489, 492

Stanford University, 482, 511, 514

Stanislavsky, Konstantin, 39, 103, 184

Starkey, James [pseud. Seamus O'Sullivan], 166

Steen, Jan, 235

Steiger, Anatoly, 493

Stein, Gertrude, 344

Stepun, Fyodor, 403

Stevens, Wallace, 196

Stinnes, Hugo, 214

Stolypin, Peter, 70, 75

Stowe, Harriet Beecher: *Uncle Tom's Cabin*, 107

Strachey, Lytton, 399

Strakhovsky, Leonid, 199n. *See also* Chatsky, Leonid

Stravinsky, Igor, 246

Stresa, 77

Strindberg, August, 431

Struve, Gleb, 199, 200, 206, 212, 228, 242, 288, 344n, 364, 370, 408, 421, 430, 435, 489, 506, 507; as chronicler of émigré literature, 165; introduces N to English audience, 401

Struve, Peter, 26, 55, 100n, 165

Sulkevich, Suleiman, 154

Sunday Express, 178

Supervielle, Jules, 393, 437

Suvorin, Alexey, 98

Suvorin, Mikhail, 98–99, 215

Svyatopolk-Mirsky, Prince Dmitri, 54–55

Swinburne, Algernon, 400

Symbolism: as influence on N's metaphysics, 294; N on, 204; N's reading of Symbolist poets, 92–95; and synesthesia, 58

Symbolism (Bely), 149

Taboritsky, Sergey, 190–91, 427–28

Tagantsev, 28

"Tamara." *See* Shulgin, Valentina

Tarasov-Rodionov, Alexander: invites N to Soviet Union, 375; *Shokolad*, 375, 411

Tarnovsky, Praskovia Nikolaevna (great-aunt), 31

Tarr, Raisa. *See* Tatarinov, Raisa

Tartakover, S.: N review of, 276n

Tatar nationalists, 140

Tatarinov (Tarr), Raisa, 228, 256–57, 258, 260, 286, 288, 425, 434

Tatarinov, Vladimir, 199, 200, 228, 254, 256, 258, 261

Tatarinov-Aykhenvald circle. *See* Aykhenvald Circle

Tate, Allen, 4

Technische Hochschule, Berlin, 214

Teffi (Nadezhda Buchinskaya), 173, 425

Tegel cemetery, Berlin: VDN's grave at, 193, 239

Tempest, The (Shakespeare), 225, 416

Tenishev, Prince Vyacheslav, 86

Tenishev School, 86–133 passim, 166, 212, 376, 378, 394, 435, 544n.4

Tennyson, Alfred, Lord, 202

Terapiano, Yuri, 392

Thompson, C. Bertrand, 393–94

Thompson, Lisbet, 393–94

Thomson, Sir J. J. ("Atom"), 167

Three Sisters, The (Chekhov), 264

Time, 74

Times (London), 227

Titus Andronicus (Shakespeare), 365

Tokmakov, Lidia, 147

Tokmakov family, 146

Tolstoy, Aleksey, 117, 184, 278, 374–75; "defection" from emigration of, 198–99

Tolstoy, Alexandra, 514

Tolstoy, Dmitri, 26

Tolstoy, Leo, 36, 38, 74, 76, 81, 91, 94, 136, 176, 184, 275, 294, 301, 351, 363, 374, 398, 407, 466, 495; *Anna Karenin*, 79, 306, 521; critique of Shakespeare, 6; *Haji Murad*, 145; "How Much Land Does a Man Need?," 259–60; "Kreutzer Sonata," 261; meeting with N, 4, 34; N's affinity with, 92; *Sebastopol Sketches*, 424–25; *War and Peace*, 85, 425

Tolstoy Foundation, 514

Toulon, 208, 210

transition, 504

Trapezund (ship), 159

"Travnikov, Vasily," 424, 509. *See also* Khodasevich, Vladislav

Trial, The (Kafka), 415

Trinity College, Cambridge, 166–68; Magpie and Stump Debating Society, 168–69; Wren Library, 179, 186. *See also* Cambridge

Trinity Magazine, 179

Trotsky, Leon, 125, 143, 155, 433, 546–47n.14

Trudoviki (Labour) party, 61

Tsenzor, Dmitri, 350

Tsetlin, Mark, 185–86, 435

Tsetlin, Tatiana, 435

Tsvetaeva, Marina, 198, 220, 221, 256, 261, 342, 344n, 410n, 425

Tsyganov (chauffeur), 550n.21

Turgenev, Ivan, 34, 81, 176, 257, 407, 521; *Smoke*, 182

Tyutchev, Fyodor, 93, 290, 398

Ullstein (German publisher), 177, 198, 254, 277, 288, 341; buys German rights to *King, Queen, Knave*, 286

Ulysses (Joyce), 149, 194, 301, 312, 364, 379, 447, 448, 465

Uncle Tom's Cabin (Stowe), 107

Union of Russian Theater Workers, Berlin, 230

Union of Russian Writers and Journalists, Berlin, 186, 206, 219–220, 258, 261, 273, 276, 350, 356, 363, 403, 464; infiltrated by GPU, 260–61; N on committee of, 353; Press Balls, 258, 276, 373; as source for *The Gift*, 353

United States: N mentioned in, 403, 421, 486; as potential refuge, 376, 393, 428, 430, 432, 485, 495, 508, 511

Uritski, Moisey, 436

Ustin (janitor, St. Petersburg), 68, 114

Uzcudun, Paolino, 257

V. (character). *See* N: Works—*The Real Life of Sebastian Knight*

VIR (anti-Bolshevik society), 260–61

Vadim Vadimych (character). *See* N: Works—*Look at the Harlequins!*

Van (character). *See* N: Works—*Ada*

Van Eyck, Jan, 297

Varlamov, 32

Veber, Georgy, 102

Veen, Ada, Lucette, and Van (characters). *See* N: Works—*Ada*

Vengerov, Zinaida, 178n

Venice, 216, 476–77

Vereteno (émigré almanac, Berlin), 199

Vereteno (émigré writers' group, Berlin), 199–200, 203

Verlaine, Paul, 91

Vermeer, Jan, 325

Vernadsky, George, 437, 485

Verne, Jules, 79

Vestnik Evropy (pre-revolutionary journal, St. Petersburg), 118

Vinaver, Eugene, 507

Vinaver, Mme, 391

Vinaver, Maxim, 63–64, 154, 155, 507

Vinberg, Colonel, 190

Vishnyak, Mark, 261, 343, 391, 393, 442

Vladimirovichi (children of Vladimir Dmitrievich Nabokov, q.v.)

Vogue, 74

Volgin. *See* Sakharov, Nikolay

Voloshin, Maximilian, 148–49, 221, 551n.45

Voltaire, François Marie Arouet de: *Lettres philosophiques*, 182

Volya Rossii (émigré journal, Prague), 362

Vossische Zeitung (newspaper, Berlin), 286, 291, 417; serializes *Mary*, 277

Vozrozhdenie (émigré newspaper, Paris), 408, 424

Vronskaya, 118

Vrubel, Mikhail, 39

Vyborg Manifesto, 66, 70, 75–76, 104

Vyra (N estate and manor, province of St. Petersburg), 31, 42, 46, 47, 51, 57, 58, 68, 72–73, 77–78, 80, 91, 96, 97, 105, 107, 110, 112, 129–30, 131, 134, 142, 146, 175, 182, 212, 217, 289, 305, 369, 429, 463; absence of electricity in, 102; later fate of, 257; N's devotion to, 45; and N's feeling of childhood security, 78; N's nostalgia for, 3, 78, 177; winter at, 60

Wagner, Richard, 197, 538n.56

War and Peace (Tolstoy), 85, 425

Weidle, Vladimir, 392, 398, 424

Weil, Ganz and Dieckmann, 355, 400

Wellesley College, 270

Wells, George, 178–79

Wells, Herbert George, 91, 178, 179, 419; *The Food of the Gods*, 428; N's admiration for, 178n; *The Passionate Friends*, 91; visit to Ns in St. Petersburg, 178n; *The War of the Worlds*, 178n

Westinghouse, 98
Westminster Gazette, 227
What Is to Be Done? (Chernyshevsky), 398, 403
White, Elwyn Brooks ("Andy"), 4
White, Katharine, 4
Wiesbaden, 52
Wilbur, Richard: "Walking to Sleep," 380–81
Wilde, Oscar, 76, 79
William the Conqueror, 197
Wilson, Edmund, 4, 20, 148n, 246
Witte, Count Sergey, 56
Wonlar-Lyarsky, Nadezhda, 42, 43–44, 538n.56; as "Aunt Baby," 76–77
Wonlar-Lyarsky family, 78
Woolf, Leonard, 435
Woolf, Virginia, 304; *Orlando*, N on, 402
Wordsworth, William, 218, 327, 370
World War I, 107–8, 110–11, 116
Wrangel, General, 180, 189

Yagoda, Genrikh, 436
Yakobson, V. F., 218, 220, 228, 230
Yakovlev, Elena, 255, 260
Yakovlev, Nikolay, 192, 200, 260; supplies names of extinct noble lineages, 255, 404
Yalta, 15, 136, 140, 141, 143, 149, 160, 214, 426
Yaltinskiy Golos (newspaper, Yalta), 148

Yan-Ruban, Anna, 138, 145
Yaremich, 103
Yunaya mysl' (Tenishev school magazine), 117–18
Yuzhny, Yakov, 227, 230

Zaitsev, Boris, 198, 342, 391, 393
Zaitsev, Kirill: reviews *The Defense*, 343, 347
Zalkind, Evgenia. *See* Cannac, Evgenia
Zamyatin, Evgeny, 415; on N, 374
Zaretsky, 287
Zasulich, Vera, 20
Zelenski, Filip (tutor), 80, 84–85, 97, 105, 106, 107, 545–46n.62
Zemstvo Congress, 55–56
Zenzinov, Vladimir, 63, 390, 390n, 395, 423, 424, 425–26, 433, 493, 514
Zharov, 257
Zhar-ptitsa (émigré journal, Berlin), 185, 187
Zhernosekov, Vasily Martinovich, 57–58, 69, 105
Zhukovsky, Vasily, 35, 150, 215, 416
Zina (character). *See* N: Works—*The Gift*
Zina (childhood girlfriend), 73–74, 97
Znosko-Borovsky, E. A., 275–76
Zola, Emile, 76
Zoorland: in *Glory*, 357; in "Uldaborg," 353
Zoppot, 243
Zoshchenko, Mikhail, 260, 375
Zweig, Stefan, 364